Previous *Washington Post* Books
Published by Scribner

Trump Revealed

The Mueller Report

The Mueller Report Illustrated:
The Obstruction Investigation

Donald Trump and His Assault on Truth

Previous Books by
Kevin Sullivan and Mary Jordan

Hope: A Memoir of Survival in Cleveland

The Prison Angel

Previous Books by Mary Jordan

The Art of Her Deal: The Untold Story of Melania Trump

TRUMP ON TRIAL

THE INVESTIGATION,
IMPEACHMENT, ACQUITTAL
AND AFTERMATH

KEVIN SULLIVAN and MARY JORDAN

STEVE LUXENBERG, Editor

The Washington Post

SCRIBNER

New York London Toronto Sydney New Delhi

Scribner
An Imprint of Simon & Schuster, Inc.
1230 Avenue of the Americas
New York, NY 10020

First Scribner hardcover edition August 2020

Manufactured in the United States of America

1 3 5 7 9 10 8 6 4 2

Library of Congress Cataloging-in-Publication Data has been applied for.

ISBN 978-1-9821-5299-4
ISBN 978-1-9821-5301-4 (ebook)

Insert Photograph Credits

1. Carlos Barria/Reuters; 2. House Judiciary Committee via Associated Press; 3. U.S. Embassy, Kyiv; 4. Volodymyr Hontar, UNIAN; 5. Saul Loeb/AFP/Getty Images; 6. Sheleah Craighead/White House, via Associated Press; 7. Tom Williams/CQ-Roll Call/Getty Images; 8. Bonnie Jo Mount/*The Washington Post*; 9. Matt McClain/*The Washington Post*; 10. Matt McClain/*The Washington Post*; 11. Jahi Chikwendiu/*The Washington Post*; 12. Bonnie Jo Mount/*The Washington Post*; 13. Bill O'Leary/*The Washington Post*; 14. Carlos Osorio/Associated Press; 15. Brittany Greeson for *The Washington Post*; 16. Jim Lo Scalzo/EPA-EFE/Rex/Shutterstock; 17. Melina Mara/*The Washington Post*; 18. Senate Television via Associated Press; 19. Melina Mara/*The Washington Post*; 20. Mandel Ngan/AFP via Getty Images

For journalists everywhere

Contents

Note to Readers xi
Prologue xiii
List of Principal Figures xxiii

Part One: Threats

1: Watch Your Back 3
2: "Ready to Rumble" 15
3: Walking the Fine Line 25
4: "Courage Is Contagious" 30
5: High Fives 41
6: The I-Word 46
7: "They Tried to Take Me Down!" 53
8: "I Think Your Boss Doesn't Like Ukraine" 62
9: "Who Put You in Charge?" 69
10: "Where Exactly Is the Line for You?" 74
11: Flyover 82
12: "Drug Deal" 85
13. "Stray Voltage" 91

Part Two: Risk

14: "Do Us a Favor" 103
15: The "Big Stuff" 118
16: Plan B 127
17: Ukraine in a Box 135

18: "Credible Urgent Concern" 142
19: "Dig Very Hard, and Very Fast" 154
20: Nadler's Audition 160
21: "Not Waving You Off" 167
22: The Women Who Kill 172
23: "You Don't Really Want to Do This" 181

Part Three: Impeachment

24: "Isn't It a Perfect Call?" 191
25: "That's Close to a Spy" 207
26: Welcome to the SCIF 220
27: The Disrupter 229
28: Pointing a Finger 234
29: "Get Over It" 241
30: Remember Francis Rooney 246
31: "Take the Gloves Off" 251
32: "Lock Him Up!" 260
33: "KA BOOM!" 263
34: Live, from Washington 267
35: "It's Very Intimidating" 281
36: "I Will Be Fine for Telling the Truth" 293
37: Smiles All Around 302
38: "These Fictions Are Harmful" 314
39: "Potomac River Fever" 327
40: "I Don't Hate Anybody" 334
41: The Weight of History 338
42: "Please Let Her Speak" 344
43: "I Am Not an Impartial Juror" 352
44: "The President Is Impeached" 361

Part Four: Trump on Trial

45: "Trust Me to Run This" 379
46: "We Need to Get This Thing Going" 386
47: "Today, We Will Make History" 394
48: "Do You Solemnly Swear?" 399
49: Virus 403
50: "Will Senators Rise to the Occasion?" 407
51: "Your Head Will Be on a Pike" 414
52: A Small Earthquake 421
53: "Every President Believes That" 428
54: "Let the People Decide" 435
55: "This Country Is Our Masterpiece" 446
56: Never Over 453
Epilogue: One Nation, Divisible? 459

Acknowledgments 473
Notes 476
Index 521

Note to Readers

The reporting and research for this book came from the combined efforts of more than 50 *Washington Post* journalists. As a starting point, we relied on their published stories, which were informed by hundreds of interviews conducted as the Trump impeachment and trial unfolded. In a few instances, we chose to incorporate parts of those stories into the narrative, as we found them to be the best account of the events described.

We and other *Washington Post* journalists also did extensive original reporting, including dozens of interviews with central figures in the impeachment proceedings, as well as with staff members, colleagues and friends of those involved, in the United States and in Ukraine. Most of the interviews were on the record. But some sources requested anonymity to speak more freely and candidly about such divisive events. In those cases, we confirmed their accounts with others with knowledge of the same events.

We also mined the extensive public record of witness interviews, depositions, testimony and floor speeches from the House of Representatives and the Senate. The archive of C-SPAN deserves a special mention. Not only does C-SPAN have video of every House and Senate session, it has recordings and transcriptions of countless press conferences and events outside the Capitol, allowing us to watch them again and again, as if we were present.

Seeking to write a comprehensive and deep account of the third impeachment and trial in American history (President Richard M. Nixon resigned in 1974 before he could be impeached), we wanted to understand the participants' feelings and motivations as they made their choices.

Our ambition for this book was to provide a narrative account of not only what happened, but how and why. To that end: When we report or describe someone's thoughts or feelings, or say that someone "knows" something, we are drawing on interviews with that person, with someone directly familiar with that person's thinking and knowledge, or from that individual's testimony in the impeachment inquiry. If the information comes from testimony, we have provided the details (date, page number) in the notes section at the end of the book. In some cases, we benefited from notes taken during meetings or discussion and shared with us.

We sought an interview with President Trump, but our request did not yield one. As he has said, his thoughts and views can be found in the voluminous public record that he creates daily—including his tweets, his television interviews and his encounters with the media during the year of events covered by this book.

—Kevin Sullivan and Mary Jordan

Prologue

March 6, 2019, Washington, DC, and Kyiv, Ukraine

Nancy Pelosi strode into her majestic office suite in the U.S. Capitol, her forehead marked with a prominent black smudge. It was Ash Wednesday, and the speaker of the U.S. House of Representatives had received her ashes that morning from Father Patrick Conroy, the House chaplain.

"Father just came at me with a vengeance," she joked to her waiting guest, *Washington Post* reporter Joe Heim, with a big laugh. "People have gotten their ashes off of my forehead today because it was just, like, dripping."

It was a cold and gusty morning in Washington, which Heim could see through the speaker's windows, with their stunning view of the National Mall. In her private office, the yellow walls covered with historic and family photographs gave the space a feel both commanding and comfortable. Four upholstered yellow wingback chairs flanked a fireplace. Her desk had no computer. The highest-ranking elected woman in American history still preferred face-to-face talks and phone calls to email. On display was a favorite gift—pink boxing gloves, monogrammed for the five-foot-two-inch fighter.

Heim was there to interview Pelosi for a Q&A to be published in *The Washington Post Magazine*. He didn't cover Congress. He had never met Pelosi. But he had immersed himself in her biography, a mixture of privilege, promise and prowess: Her political lineage a mini-dynasty, her father winning five terms in the U.S. House, her father and brother each serving as Baltimore's mayor. Her family's towering influence on that city, wielding its power from a red-brick house in Little Italy with portraits of FDR and Harry Truman on the wall. Her early real-life lessons as the youngest of six children, and the only girl. Her formal education at an all-girls Catholic school and then at all-women Trinity, a small Catholic college in Washington, just three miles north of the Capitol, where she watched

President John F. Kennedy, the country's first Catholic president, give his inaugural address on that frigid January day in 1961.

Then, coming into her own: Her move to San Francisco, where she raised five children. Her immersion in community issues while her husband built the family's wealth through real estate and other investments. Her volunteer work for local Democrats, gradually establishing her own political base. Her 17 terms in Congress and her rise to the top of her party's ranks. Her election as speaker of the House in 2007, the first woman ever in the powerful post. Her strategic finesse in beating back a challenge to her leadership after the Democrats recaptured the House in the 2018 midterm elections. Her second stint in the job, a resurrection of sorts. Her current difficulties in controlling her rowdy and diverse caucus.

Pelosi had also done her homework on Heim. She had learned he was a fellow Catholic who had spent five childhood years in Kenya, where his father had worked for Catholic Relief Services and his mother had been a State Department nurse. Heim was surprised by Pelosi's preparation and attention to detail. "Tell me about growing up in Kenya!" she said, and then told him of taking her children to Kenya when they were young, going on a safari and a dig with famous anthropologist Dr. Louis Leakey.

"I feel close to Kenya," she said. "I found an ancient tooth there on an excavation." She paused, adding dryly, "Not mine."

Preliminaries done, rapport established, Heim eased into the interview. It started with a no-fireworks discussion about the country's political divisions, standard fare. Pelosi was waiting. She had a message to convey, something she wanted to say explicitly, more explicitly and forcefully than she had ever said it before. She didn't need to force an opening. She knew Heim would ask the question. He had to. Members of her own caucus were asking it, too. She couldn't avoid it, so she might as well confront it, contain it, control it.

The Q&A format was perfect. She could guarantee the way her answers came out, without a media filter. She had a good phrase, she thought, a phrase that would stick, a phrase that CNN, Fox, MSNBC, all the other networks could reduce to one of their crawls at the bottom of the TV screen.

The moment came, more as a statement than a question, as she was making light of her combative relationship with Donald Trump. Heim said, "There have been increasing calls, including from some of your members, for impeachment of the president."

Impeachment.

She pounced. Leaning forward in her chair, she said deliberately, so deliberately that Heim could tell it was planned: "I'm going to give you some news right now because I haven't said this to any press person before. But since you asked, and I've been thinking about this: Impeachment is so divisive to the country that unless there's something so compelling and overwhelming and bipartisan, I don't think we should go down that path, because it divides the country."

She pointed her index finger at Heim and, with an actor's timing, slowed her delivery even more, making each word its own weighted sentence: "And. He's. Just. Not. Worth. It."

The day before, in Kyiv, the capital of Ukraine, nearly 5,000 miles away, U.S. ambassador Marie "Masha" Yovanovitch had given a strikingly direct speech about the country's pernicious and persistent corruption, a subject that had become her specialty during more than 30 years in the State Department.

Danger isn't always a part of a career diplomat's biography, but it was central to Yovanovitch's. She had been caught in crossfire during a violent showdown between Russia's president and parliament, worked in an embassy in Uzbekistan sprayed with gunfire, served amid civil war in Somalia and heard the thud of falling artillery shells on the front lines of Ukraine's war with Russia. She had managed to reach the age of 60 without getting hurt and without a blemish to her reputation.

The diplomat's life suited Yovanovitch. She was good at it. That's what her colleagues and her awards told her. Her name wasn't well known in Washington, but in the circles where she traveled, in the outposts where she had learned her craft, she had a reputation for being tough, fair and direct. Two U.S. presidents, first a Republican, then a Democrat, had shown their confidence in her. George W. Bush had picked her for two ambassadorships, first Kyrgyzstan, then Armenia. Barack Obama, in his final year, had chosen her for the embassy in Kyiv, a hot spot of a different sort, its independence threatened by Russia's designs on its territory.

She had been calling out the stench of bad governance and corruption in Ukraine since her arrival in August of 2016. After Donald Trump's election a few months later, she had kept up her campaign. She had ruffled feathers at the very top of Ukraine's government and in the country's darker corners, but that was a risk she had to take. Otherwise, nothing would change, she felt.

In her speech at the Ukraine Crisis Media Center on March 5, Yovanovitch upped the ante once more. She called for the removal of Ukraine's special corruption prosecutor, who had been caught on tape allegedly coaching a suspect on how to avoid prosecution. She said he couldn't be trusted.

Yuri Lutsenko, the country's chief prosecutor, was monitoring the speech. He didn't like what Yovanovitch was saying. He didn't like what she was doing. He wanted her out. Hours later, he sent an irritated WhatsApp text message to Lev Parnas, a close associate and cigar-smoking buddy of Rudy Giuliani, one of President Trump's personal lawyers and closest confidants. The ambassador's openly calling for the firing of one of my associates, Lutsenko wrote. This would not do.

Lutsenko wrote his text in Russian, a language the two of them shared. But Parnas understood that the message was meant as much for Giuliani's ears as his own. To reach Giuliani, who spoke only English, Lutsenko needed a translator and intermediary. He needed Parnas, a Ukrainian-American who had introduced the two of them.

For months, Giuliani had been pursuing Trump's goals in Ukraine. Along with Parnas and his associate Igor Fruman, Giuliani wanted prosecutors to investigate an unsupported narrative: that Ukrainian government officials had undertaken an organized effort to collude with the Democrats on Hillary Clinton's behalf in the 2016 U.S. election. In this stew of a story they were serving up, Ukrainians were hiding the evidence, a computer server stashed somewhere in the country, and Trump was the victim of foreign efforts to interfere in the American election, not a beneficiary.

None other than Vladimir Putin, the Russian president, was a promoter of this narrative. As long ago as February 2017, while speaking to reporters in Budapest, Putin had pushed the idea that Hillary Clinton and her campaign had benefited from the support of "Ukrainian authorities." It was a classic Putin sleight-of-hand. Not our fault, Putin said. Blame Ukraine.

Since then, the narrative had been making its way around the Internet, fueled by conspiracy theorists in the echo chambers populated by some of President Trump's most fervent supporters. Giuliani liked the narrative for another reason: He needed ammunition to counter the impending report on Russian interference from Special Counsel Robert Mueller's investigative team, which had tied Washington in knots for nearly two years. Giuliani did not believe that Trump had colluded with Russia. He and Trump had been railing against the Mueller probe for months. It was a joke, a "witch hunt," "illegal," "rigged," "a disgrace."

More recently, Giuliani and his team had picked up a new scent. They had heard something enticing about former Vice President Joe Biden, one of Trump's chief political rivals. Biden's son Hunter had secured a high-paid seat on the board of Burisma, a Ukrainian gas company, while his father was serving as Obama's second-in-command. A probe of the Bidens would be a win. It could damage the candidate seen in the Trump camp as the biggest threat in the 2020 race. The Trump campaign had seen how devastating the FBI investigation into Hillary Clinton's private email server had been in 2016.

Giuliani's emerging role as a back channel on Ukraine reflected Trump's deep distrust of the "deep state," his derisive label for the people who form the backbone of the U.S. government. They are the military, diplomatic, intelligence, security, financial and public health professionals who provide expertise, analysis and advice to the occupant of the White House. The president sets policy, and this standing corps of experts helps execute it.

Trump had turned that world on its head. He viewed the deep state as an enemy to be neutralized. These men and women weren't his allies. They were weapons aimed at him, especially those career diplomats who had also worked in the Obama administration. Trump and his allies in conservative media called them "unelected bureaucrats," a term they meant as a slur. Viewed through that lens, Marie Yovanovitch wasn't a decorated diplomat who had represented her nation with dignity and bipartisan professionalism. She was a deep stater, she wasn't on their team, and she was standing in Giuliani's way. She had to go.

On Ash Wednesday, as Nancy Pelosi was explaining to Heim why she was opposed to impeaching Trump, the texting between Lutsenko and Parnas escalated, with Lutsenko complaining again about Yovanovitch: "Now the Ambassador points to bad selection of judges."

Nancy Pelosi had heard the whispers in Capitol corridors—that she wasn't up to the job, that maybe it was time to turn the speaker's gavel over to someone younger. There was a moment when she might have listened. If Hillary Clinton had won the presidency in 2016, Pelosi had thought she might retire. The Affordable Care Act would be safe, the country would be in hands she trusted. But that changed when Trump won. Now, at the age of 78, a time when others were slowing down, she had no interest in taking a break. She wasn't going anywhere. Not with Donald Trump in the White House.

Power was something she understood, something she relished. She prided herself on knowing her caucus, knowing their motivations. What made them say yes to something, and what kept them from saying no. She chalked it up to longevity. If you lead for long enough, if you learn how to persuade enough people to follow you on the hard issues, you know how to speed them up or slow them down.

She had been resisting calls to impeach Trump since taking over as speaker in January 2019. Emboldened by winning back the House in the midterms, those on the party's newly energized left wing wanted, in the now famous words of freshman representative Rashida Tlaib of Michigan, to "impeach the motherfucker." Pelosi knew how unhelpful that phrase would be in her party's appeal to the political center, which had carried the Democrats to their triumphant midterm success.

Her feelings about Trump could not be summed up in a few choice words. He infuriated her so much that she was grinding her teeth at night, prompting her dentist to make her a bite guard for sleeping. But in her calculation, she had not seen anything that merited impeachment. Pelosi feared that appearing obsessed with impeachment instead of "kitchen table" economic issues might undermine the wave of centrist freshmen who had just won in districts that had gone for Trump in 2016. She feared it could cost the party its House majority in 2020.

Since Trump's election, a small group of the House chamber's most fiery progressives had submitted legislation five times, trying to start impeachment proceedings. It was a noisy minority view that presented a headache for Pelosi. Republicans were already saying impeachment talk amounted to a coup attempt by Democrats unable to accept the valid 2016 election result.

Trump's misdeeds, as cited by Democrats, made for a long and troubling list. But each time, Pelosi held the line. In her mind, none rose to the high standard of an impeachable offense, at least none that would resonate with the American public, let alone with a clear majority of the House, and certainly none that would sway a GOP-controlled Senate run by Majority Leader Mitch McConnell.

Firing then–FBI director James Comey? Indefensible, she had said, but "until you have the facts that you can present . . . so the American people are moving with you at the same time, I don't think that our democracy is well served."

Claiming after white nationalist violence in Charlottesville, Virginia, that there had been an "egregious display of hatred, bigotry and violence on many sides"? Proof, she had said, that the president "doesn't know right from wrong, true from false, American patriotism from white nationalism." But by itself, not grounds for impeachment.

Siding with Putin over U.S. intelligence officials' determination that Russia had meddled in the 2016 election? "An embarrassment and a grave threat to our democracy," she had said. His proposed ban on immigrants from Muslim countries? "Not only unconstitutional but immoral." Shutting down the government over funding for his border wall? "Petulance and obstinance." The $130,000 in hush money to adult film star Stormy Daniels and, before that, the "Access Hollywood" tape, where he was heard boasting he could grab women "by the pussy" because he was "a star"? "Disgusting behavior."

A sorry litany, but as far as Pelosi could see, not an iron-clad, public-unifying impeachable offense among them.

Her caucus was unified on one score: Trump's behavior appalled nearly all of them. But by Pelosi's count, only a tiny fraction thought impeachment was the way to go. Her centrists counseled caution, moderates pleading for moderation. Pelosi understood. She was a famously impatient person who, even in four-inch heels, took the stairs rather than lose a minute waiting for the slow Capitol elevator. But on this, she saw patience as the only option. The Mueller investigation would be over soon. Maybe that would be a game changer. But for now, impeachment was a road that led nowhere, or at least nowhere good. The Senate belonged to the Republicans, and the Republicans belonged to Trump.

Pelosi knew that any Republicans who voted for impeachment would have to explain rejecting Trump and the narrative about his presidency so successfully pushed by Fox News and other media on the right: The soaring stock market. The massive tax cuts. The revolutionary rollback of regulations. Filling the federal judiciary with enough conservative judges, including two Supreme Court justices, to shift the courts to the right for generations, and maybe someday reverse *Roe v. Wade* and make abortion a crime. The wall to keep out all those dangerous immigrants. Trump's refreshingly blunt language that didn't talk down to ordinary Americans.

A lot of Republicans might be uncomfortable with some of Trump's policies, his crudeness, his government-by-tweet, his war on the media. But to his base, Trump was a bracing antidote to decades of elitist Democrats and wishy-washy establishment Republicans. Trump was saving America. Trump knew this calculation and had taken advantage of it on the campaign trail. "If you really like Donald Trump, that's great, but if you don't, you have to vote for me anyway. You know why? Supreme Court judges, Supreme Court judges," Trump had said at a 2016 rally in Cedar Rapids, Iowa. "Have no choice, sorry, sorry, sorry. You have no choice."

Pelosi was horrified by his policies, his cavalier disregard for facts, his apparent glee at sowing discord, his willingness to traffic in racism and misogyny while firing up his base. But as speaker, Pelosi knew that arguing policy differences in an impeachment vote was like trying to solve a math problem by quoting philosophers. She might be able to marshal her House majority, but flipping 20 Republican senators to reach the necessary 67 votes to remove him from office? Nearly impossible. It meant building a case as compelling and as damning as the one that forced Richard Nixon to resign his presidency in 1974, just two years after winning a second term by a landslide. Without a clear and powerful case—something the average American would easily grasp, something that would stir bipartisan outrage—initiating an impeachment inquiry could be perilous for the nation.

Would a failed impeachment effort damage the balance of power between the executive and legislative branches? Would impeachment become so common that it would lose the gravity the framers of the Constitution intended? Was a bipartisan impeachment with "impartial jurors" in the Senate even possible, especially in the ferocious modern media landscape where facts and reality depended on which channel you watched? Could removing Trump from office rip open enough wounds to stoke violence?

If the House were to impeach Trump, but then the Senate acquitted him, was that as good as handing him a talking point that he could repeat at every campaign rally? Would it invigorate him rather than stain him? After all, Trump was famous for counterpunching—hitting back ten times harder than he had been hit. Pelosi was all too aware that Trump was in his first term, unlike Nixon and Bill Clinton, who was impeached by the House in 1998 but acquitted in the Senate. Voters would have their say on Trump in November 2020. Was that a better remedy for his transgressions than impeachment?

As the speaker, as the one making the decision, Pelosi had to keep calibrating the risks. There was a risk to doing something, and a risk to doing nothing. She didn't want to tolerate presidential misconduct. But she also didn't want the House, or her party, to be seen as taking away the voters' power to decide Trump's fate. An impeachment couldn't be personal, or about policy differences. It had to be careful, fair and easy to understand to avoid a severe backlash in an already deeply divided nation.

So in her office on this Ash Wednesday, she fixed Heim with a look of granite-hard conviction as she jabbed her finger: "He's. Just. Not. Worth. It."

She had no idea that at the very moment she was speaking, the seeds of impeachment were being sown overseas, in a country most Americans had never visited, by a man once celebrated as "America's Mayor," on behalf of a president bent on imposing his mercurial will on everyone in his path.

List of Principal Figures

THE WHITE HOUSE

Donald Trump, president of the United States
Mike Pence, vice president of the United States
Mick Mulvaney, acting chief of staff, 2019–2020
Pat Cipollone, White House counsel

THE CABINET

Mike Pompeo, secretary of state
Mark Esper, secretary of defense
William Barr, attorney general
Rick Perry, secretary of energy, 2017–2019

THE HOUSE OF REPRESENTATIVES

Democrats (majority party)

Nancy Pelosi of California, speaker
Steny Hoyer of Maryland, majority leader
James Clyburn of South Carolina, majority whip

Republicans (minority party)

Kevin McCarthy of California, minority leader
Steve Scalise of Louisiana, minority whip

House Intelligence Committee

Adam Schiff of California, chairman
Daniel Goldman, Democratic counsel for the impeachment inquiry
Devin Nunes of California, ranking minority member
Stephen Castor, Republican counsel for the impeachment inquiry
Democrats: Val Demings of Florida; Jim Himes of Connecticut; Eric Swalwell of California
Republicans: Will Hurd of Texas; John Ratcliffe of Texas; Elise Stefanik of New York

House Judiciary Committee

Jerrold Nadler of New York, chairman
Doug Collins of Georgia, ranking minority member
Democrats: David Cicilline of Rhode Island; Swalwell; Demings
Republicans: Jim Jordan of Ohio; Matt Gaetz of Florida; Louie Gohmert of Texas

National Security freshmen Democrats

Elissa Slotkin of Michigan; Abigail Spanberger of Virginia; Elaine Luria of Virginia; Gil Cisneros of California; Jason Crow of Colorado; Chrissy Houlahan of Pennsylvania; Mikie Sherrill of New Jersey

THE SENATE

Republicans

Mitch McConnell, majority leader, Republican of Kentucky; Lamar Alexander of Tennessee; Ted Cruz of Texas; Susan Collins of Maine; Lindsey Graham of South Carolina; Ron Johnson of Wisconsin; Lisa Murkowski of Alaska; Mitt Romney of Utah

Democrats

Chuck Schumer, minority leader, Democrat of New York

THE STATE DEPARTMENT

Ulrich Brechbuhl, counselor to Secretary Pompeo
David Hale, undersecretary of state for political affairs
Philip Reeker, acting assistant secretary of state, Bureau of European and Eurasian Affairs
George Kent, deputy assistant secretary of state, Bureau of European and Eurasian Affairs
Gordon Sondland, ambassador to the European Union, 2018–2020
Kurt Volker, special envoy for Ukraine, 2017–2019

U.S. Embassy in Ukraine

Marie Yovanovitch, ambassador, August 2016–May 2019
William Taylor, chargé d'affaires (acting ambassador), June 2019–January 2020
David Holmes, counselor for political affairs

NATIONAL SECURITY COUNCIL

John Bolton, national security adviser, 2018–2019
John Eisenberg, NSC legal adviser and deputy White House counsel
Fiona Hill, senior director for European and Russian Affairs, 2017–2019
Lt. Col. Alexander Vindman, director of European affairs, 2018–2020

THE DEPARTMENT OF DEFENSE

Elaine McCusker, acting comptroller

THE OFFICE OF MANAGEMENT AND BUDGET

Michael Duffey, associate director for national security programs
Mark Sandy, deputy associate director for national security programs

THE INTELLIGENCE COMMUNITY

Joseph Maguire, acting director of national intelligence, 2019–2020
Michael Atkinson, inspector general, 2018–2020
The Whistleblower

THE GOVERNMENT OF UKRAINE

Volodymyr Zelensky, president of Ukraine
Andriy Yermak, top aide to President Zelensky, 2019–2020; chief of staff, February 2020
Andriy Bohdan, chief of staff, 2019–2020
Oleksandr Danyliuk, secretary of the National Security and Defense Council, 2019
Vadym Prystaiko, foreign policy adviser; appointed minister of foreign affairs, August 2019
Yuri Lutsenko, prosecutor general, 2016–2019

THE IRREGULAR CHANNEL

Rudolph Giuliani, Trump's personal attorney; former mayor of New York
Lev Parnas, Giuliani's associate; Ukrainian-American businessman
Igor Fruman, Giuliani's associate; Belarus-born American businessman

THE BIDENS

Joe Biden, 2020 presidential candidate; vice president of the United States, 2009–2017
Hunter Biden, son of Joe Biden; Burisma board member, 2014–2019

Part One

THREATS

CHAPTER ONE

Watch Your Back

March 19 to 29, 2019, Kyiv and Washington

On Tuesday, March 19, a Ukrainian official named Gizo Uglava contacted the U.S. Embassy in Kyiv with a disturbing story. Uglava needed to alert somebody. Nasty allegations were coming Ambassador Yovanovitch's way.

Uglava was the deputy head of Ukraine's National Anti-Corruption Bureau, known as NABU. He said he had spent the previous evening with a drunk and angry Yuri Lutsenko, the country's prosecutor general. The anti-corruption bureau and Lutsenko weren't the best of friends. Lutsenko regarded the bureau as a threat to his authority; the bureau saw Lutsenko as a product of Ukraine's corruption and not part of the solution.

Lutsenko had railed on about the ambassador, making one claim after another. How she had "destroyed" him. How she and the entire embassy were working for the Democratic Party. How the embassy had interfered in a Ukrainian investigation of Burisma and Hunter Biden. How she was an "enemy" of President Trump and the Republicans. Lutsenko had said much of this to an American journalist who had interviewed him two weeks earlier. Soon, he told Uglava, Yovanovitch "would face serious problems" in the United States.

Uglava's wasn't the first such alarm.

Earlier in the year, Yovanovitch and George Kent, the State Department official in Washington overseeing Ukraine policy, had each found themselves in unsettling conversations with Arsen Avakov, Ukraine's interior minister. Avakov warned that Lutsenko was collecting Ukrainian "mud" to throw at Yovanovitch, and had met with Giuliani and his associates. You need to watch your back, Avakov had told the ambassador.

• • •

Yovanovitch had expected blowback after her anti-corruption speech two weeks earlier. But suggesting she was corrupt and a political hack, working against her own president? She couldn't believe anyone could think that about her. She had spent her career in service to her country, no matter who occupied the White House. She knew that Lutsenko had made an alliance with Rudy Giuliani, Lev Parnas and Igor Fruman, and they were waging a campaign against her. But why?

Yovanovitch thought the foreign service was her destiny. She was an immigrant and a child of immigrants, born in 1958 in Canada. Her father was a Russian from Siberia. He had been a German prisoner during World War II, ending up in postwar Paris, where he worked as a carpenter and handyman. Her mother had grown up stateless in Nazi Germany after her family had fled the Bolshevik revolution. Separately, her parents had migrated to Canada, where they met and married. They called their daughter Masha, a reminder of their Russian roots.

Masha Yovanovitch was proud of her parents' story. They had been scarred in ways few people could understand. When she was three, they had moved to rural northwestern Connecticut, where her parents became high school teachers and had a son, Andre. The children grew up speaking Russian at home. Masha attended the Kent School, an elite private academy where her parents taught.

Her parents considered living in America a gift. She grew up believing it was her duty to repay it. She went to Princeton as a scholarship student. When she joined the State Department in 1986, she quickly felt at home. History and politics were her love, and her idols were George Kennan, the foreign service officer who designed the strategy that contained Soviet Communism through the Cold War, and George Marshall, whose peace plan for the reconstruction of postwar Europe had turned former enemies into American partners. She dedicated herself to following in those diplomatic footsteps.

In many ways, Yovanovitch was an attractive target for Ukrainian officials who had rarely been held accountable. She was a visible American presence in Kyiv, outspoken about her anti-corruption demands. Videos of her speeches and receptions were regularly posted on the embassy website. She was shaking things up, following official U.S. policy.

Now she was under attack from a man she considered corrupt, who was accusing her of corruption. There was no evidence, but the mere suggestion that she was misusing her office could be devastating to her and her career.

After Uglava left, the embassy immediately sent an email to Kent, reporting the conversation and asking for advice on handling this assault from Lutsenko, and the serious problems he said were coming.

If Yuri Lutsenko had learned anything from his years in Ukraine politics, it was that he needed to protect himself. He was a survivor, someone who had come back from the dead once. He didn't want to go there again. He was close to Ukraine's president, Petro Poroshenko, who was faltering in his bid for reelection. Lutsenko's worry was that Poroshenko's successor might want to investigate officials of the previous government for alleged corruption or other crimes.

That had happened before. It had happened to Lutsenko. In 2005, at age 40, he had taken the reins of Ukraine's Ministry of Internal Affairs, a powerful post with police oversight. After serving five years, he was accused of abusing his office soon after a new administration took power. Lutsenko denied the allegations, saying they were politically motivated, a result of his opposition to the incoming government. No use. He spent more than a year in jail awaiting trial, then another year after his conviction. In 2013, he was pardoned by the same administration that had prosecuted him.

By early 2016, Lutsenko had climbed his way back into the government, rising to the equivalent of attorney general despite possessing no law degree. By early 2019, with the election approaching and Poroshenko looking vulnerable, Lutsenko could see his future looking cloudy. Currying favor with Trump and the Americans, Ukraine's ally, might help his standing with a new government. When the opportunity came up for a meeting with Giuliani, the president's personal lawyer, Lutsenko decided, sure, why not?

He and Giuliani had one thing in common: They shared a dislike of Yovanovitch. Lutsenko knew the ambassador viewed him as part of Ukraine's corruption problem. Giuliani thought the ambassador was anti-Trump. Bashing Yovanovitch was in their mutual interest.

The barrage began early the next morning, March 20. Shortly after 9 a.m., a taped interview with Lutsenko aired on Hill.TV, a one-year-old digital channel of *The Hill*, a news site focused on coverage of Congress and the federal government. The interviewer was John Solomon, Hill.TV's top executive and a veteran reporter.

Lutsenko appeared on camera from Kyiv, with an interpreter providing a voice-over. He let loose a version of the allegations against Yovanovitch reported to the embassy the day before, and added a new, incendiary one: In August 2016, he said, Yovanovitch had given him a "do-not-prosecute" list of prominent Ukrainians. If true, that would amount to improper interference in Ukraine's internal affairs.

The ripples from Lutsenko's video soon became a wave. By 11 a.m., *The Hill*'s website had posted two articles, each linked to a three-minute clip from the Lutsenko interview, each featuring a different explosive allegation. A couple of hours later came a tweet from Fox's Sean Hannity, among the biggest names in the conservative media world. At 3 p.m., Hannity led his daily Web-based radio show with the news of Solomon's interview, adding that "I just happen to have a little birdie telling me in my ear that, well, Joe Biden may have an issue here that is bigger than anything ever alleged about Donald Trump."

Hill.TV counted its daily viewers in the tens of thousands. Hannity's radio show claimed 14 million listeners a week.

By mid-afternoon, Lev Parnas had spent a busy couple of hours on his phone, texting links of the Lutsenko interview clips to Republican friends, doing his part to rev up the conservative media echo chamber.

The previous night, he had messaged Thomas Hicks Jr., a Trump family friend and co-chair of the Republican National Committee. "Tomorrow's the big day," Parnas had written. Next on his list was Joseph Ahearn at the pro-Trump super PAC called America First Action. "Wait Tomorrow good stuff," he told Ahearn.

Parnas was pleased. The campaign to discredit Yovanovitch, months in the making, was working out. In January, after making several trips to Ukraine to cultivate connections for various business deals, Parnas and Fruman had arranged for Lutsenko to meet Giuliani in New York. Lutsenko wanted their help in pursuing his agenda. They wanted his help in pursuing theirs. The group latched on to Solomon as someone who might be interested in what they had to say.

Solomon had been a logical choice as a possible megaphone for Lutsenko's allegations. His work was admired in pro-Trump circles. He was a well-known reporter whose career had taken him from mainstream outlets, including a stint at *The Washington Post*, into the conservative media orbit, first as executive editor of the *Washington Times*. He joined *The Hill* in 2017, partly to create and develop its video operation, partly to do investigative stories. After colleagues complained of bias in his articles, *The Hill* decided to put "opinion contributor" on his work. As a TV commentator, he had become a favorite of Sean Hannity, appearing dozens of times in 2017 and 2018 to discuss his *Hill* articles.

In the days leading up to the story's March 20 debut, Parnas had been in frequent touch with Solomon by phone and email, playing the role of intermediary. "Just got word from Lev that the prosecutor general has agreed to do an interview tomorrow," Solomon wrote in one email, with a copy to Parnas. When the interview date was set, Solomon invited Parnas to be there, in case his translation services were needed. That wasn't necessary, but Parnas had watched the taping anyway from the control room at *The Hill*'s offices on K Street in Washington.

Now Parnas was trying his best to accelerate the allegations, sending WhatsApp messages to contacts. In one, he suggested to Ahearn, "Have jr. retweet it," referring to Ahearn's friend Donald Trump Jr. On another, he told Hicks at the Republican National Committee, "You should retweet it."

Half an hour later, Hicks replied, "I should probably keep my hands clean on that!"

At 7:30 p.m., *The Hill* published a third and more extensive story under Solomon's byline, a full roundup of the Lutsenko accusations. The headline: "As Russia collusion fades, Ukrainian plot to help Clinton emerges." The earlier stories were already ricocheting online. The State Department issued a statement disputing Lutsenko and calling the "do-not-prosecute" list "an outright fabrication."

Solomon quoted the State Department's protest in his story, and then added: "My reporting, however, indicates that Lutsenko isn't the only one complaining about Yovanovitch." He had obtained a letter, nearly a year old, from Pete Sessions, a Republican congressman from Texas, to Secretary of State Mike Pompeo. The letter was vague. It said only that Sessions had learned from "individuals" that Yovanovitch "has spoken privately and repeatedly about her disdain for the current Administration." That had been enough for Sessions. He asked that the ambassador be fired.

Less than 15 minutes after the third Solomon story was posted online,

Parnas copied the link into WhatsApp messages for Hicks and Ahearn. Ninety minutes later, he sent them another round.

"Watch Hannity," he told them.

At 9 p.m., Hannity seized on Solomon's reports for his prime-time TV show, a Fox powerhouse that averaged more than 3 million viewers a night. President Trump was a fan of the show as well as an occasional guest, and off the air, he sometimes called on Hannity for informal advice.

Hannity got right to it. "Breaking tonight, according to *The Hill*'s John Solomon," he said, there is "real evidence" of "collusion" to undermine Trump's presidential campaign in 2016. At the side of the screen, the chyron quoted the headline from Solomon's story: "As Russia Collusion Fades, Ukrainian Plot to Help Clinton Emerges."

"Where's the Mueller investigation into this damning new story which we now get to tonight from John Solomon?" Hannity said as he opened the show.

Hannity had three guests to talk about this "damning new story" and Lutsenko's allegations: John Solomon, Victoria Toensing and Joe diGenova. Toensing and diGenova were a Washington power couple who ran their own law firm and frequently appeared on Fox as commentators. No one mentioned that the two legal experts were Solomon's lawyers and had a hand in the arrangements that led to the story. DiGenova did say that "we also now know that the current United States ambassador Marie Yovanovitch has bad-mouthed the president of the United States to Ukrainian officials and has told them not to listen or worry about Trump policy because he's going to be impeached."

Extending his point, diGenova said: "This woman needs to be called home to the United States—"

Hannity interjected, "Oh, immediately."

DiGenova kept talking "—for consultation to answer a slew of questions about her conduct and her assault on the president of the United States."

Just after the show, at 10:40 p.m., Trump tweeted *The Hill* headline about a "Ukrainian plot to help Clinton." The retweets then began, amplifying what the president had tweeted, into the wider networks of the conservative media universe.

Fox prime-time host Laura Ingraham joined in, commenting to her three million Twitter followers: "Sounds like our Ambassador to Ukraine has some splaining to do. #UkrainianMeddling."

The next day, Trump told national security adviser John Bolton that Yovanovitch had been "bad mouthing us like crazy," and "she is saying bad shit about me and about you." Trump told Bolton he wanted her fired "today." Later that afternoon, Bolton conveyed Trump's order to Deputy Secretary of State John Sullivan.

Trump had been hearing grumbles about Yovanovitch for nearly a year. At an April 30, 2018, dinner with political donors at his Trump International Hotel near the White House, Trump was seated with Parnas and Fruman, who were discussing their plans in Ukraine. They were hoping to snag a piece of the country's lucrative gas industry.

"The biggest problem there, I think where we need to start, is we gotta get rid of the ambassador. She's still left over from the Clinton administration," Parnas told the president, without mentioning Yovanovitch's name. "She's basically walking around telling everybody, 'Wait, he's gonna get impeached, just wait.' "

Fruman was recording the conversation, capturing Trump's reply. The president turned to Johnny DeStefano, a White House aide, and ordered him to "Get rid of her! Get her out tomorrow. I don't care. Get her out tomorrow. Take her out. OK? Do it."

Ten days later, Parnas pressed the case against Yovanovitch with Pete Sessions, the Texas congressman. Sessions took immediate action, writing to Pompeo, asking him to fire Yovanovitch for disparaging the administration, citing "concrete evidence from close companions."

Over the next few months, Parnas and Fruman engineered a series of political donations, totaling half a million dollars by year's end. The first $325,000 went to America First Action, the pro-Trump super PAC. It was made in the name of a newly formed company with no assets, Global Energy Producers. Another $5,400 went to Pete Session's reelection campaign.

But nothing happened after Trump's order. The year ended with Yovanovitch still in place, still making waves about Ukrainian corruption. If they wanted her out, they had to do something different.

Yovanovitch and the embassy staff watched the unfolding events with astonishment. The Solomon stories had set off a chain reaction so rapid that it seemed inconceivable to Yovanovitch they had not been orchestrated. It was relentless, and it showed no sign of letting up.

On her popular Fox show Friday night, Laura Ingraham called Yovanovitch an "Obama holdover" who had "reportedly demonstrated clear anti-Trump bias." She interviewed diGenova, still not disclosing his complicated relationship to the stories. DiGenova said he had a bit of news. "Laura, you mentioned that Ambassador Marie Yovanovitch, contrary to what a lot of people thought, was still in her job," diGenova told Ingraham. "I learned this evening that the president has ordered her dismissal from her post as the United States ambassador to Ukraine as a result of her activities there."

Giuliani had weighed in the same day, tweeting a reference to Dan Bongino, a radio host and former Secret Service agent with 1.5 million Twitter followers. Giuliani said to "pay attention" to Bongino for "an analysis of some real collusion between Hillary, Kerry and Biden people colluding with Ukrainian operatives to make money and affect 2016 election."

On Saturday, March 23, Bongino told his Twitter fans that he'd be discussing Solomon's work on his radio show on Monday. He called the story "the most important piece you can read today." Links to the Solomon stories proliferated online. They spilled onto a thread on 4chan, the anonymous forum where trolls frequently succeed in pushing dark conspiracies onto Twitter, Facebook and other mainstream platforms. The links were shared by believers in the fringe QAnon conspiracy theory, which holds that Trump is engaged in an apocalyptic showdown with deep state saboteurs.

Some of Yovanovitch's supporters used social media to defend her. Melinda Haring, editor of UkraineAlert, a blog published by the Atlantic Council, tweeted: "The fact that @thehill printed this nonsense . . . tells you just how little editors and journalists in the US know about Ukraine." Haring's following was modest, though, compared to the more interconnected conservative media machine.

The intense reaction highlighted some of the differences between the liberal and conservative media. On the left side, talk show hosts like MSNBC's Rachel Maddow and Lawrence O'Donnell also boasted large and devoted audiences. "Saturday Night Live" and late-night comedians criticized Trump and the right with abandon and glee. Online, the progressive social media universe had developed into a noisy, unruly place where Trump was despised. But the diversity itself often made it hard for a specific message to gain traction. The conservative media tended to be more interconnected, and its messaging more disciplined and unified. If Hannity or Ingraham or Rush Limbaugh or "Fox & Friends" focused on an issue, it often showed up as a talking point across the spectrum.

That was happening now with Yovanovitch and Ukraine. On Sunday, *The Daily Wire*, an influential website in conservative circles, ran a story under the headline: "Calls Grow To Remove Obama's U.S. Ambassador To Ukraine." It was a greatest hits album replaying the week's Solomon news.

The only original reporting it contained was this: "A source close to the White House who is familiar with the matter told *The Daily Wire*: 'President Trump has been trying to remove this Obama holdover from her role in Ukraine for over a year now. . . . So the question is, who in his Administration has flaunted his requests and why are they protecting an anti-Trump, Obama flunkey?' "

The president's eldest son, Donald Trump Jr., shared the *Daily Wire* story about Yovanovitch with his Twitter followers. He said the United States needs "less of these jokers as ambassadors."

In Kyiv, Marie Yovanovitch saw Donald Trump Jr.'s tweet. It hit her like a punch in the face. It was suddenly clear to her that she had not paid enough attention. For too long, she had thought she just needed to weather the attacks, that they came with the territory. Inevitably, if you're trying to make change, you make enemies. She had tried to tune out the noise and stay focused on U.S. policy priorities: fighting corruption, supporting the rule of law and managing the American aid that supported Ukraine's ongoing war against Russia. She had never badmouthed Trump and was grateful to him for approving what she thought was badly needed equipment for the Ukrainian military, including Javelin anti-tank weapons that Obama had denied.

She had been naive. If the president's son was going to call her a joker, how could she continue to be a credible ambassador? She had seen the tweet right away, but it was now Sunday evening in Kyiv. No matter. She had to act. She emailed David Hale, the undersecretary of state for political affairs and her senior boss. Just three weeks earlier, Hale had asked her to extend her tour for another year. Now she told him the department needed to "come out strong" in support of her against these crazy smears. She said Pompeo himself needed to issue a statement saying he had full confidence in her, that the allegations were baseless, that she represented and spoke for the department, the president and the United States.

In Washington, Hale had just returned from an overseas trip when he saw her email. He called her immediately. She repeated, with some urgency, her request for a statement from Pompeo. Hale said he would speak to the secretary. He told her to send him a classified email, explaining in writing what was happening.

In Washington, as Yovanovitch was writing her email, U.S. attorney general William Barr was releasing a "summary" of the still-unpublished Mueller report. He said it had concluded there was no collusion between the Trump campaign and Russia, and that Mueller had found no conclusive evidence of a Trump effort to obstruct justice in the investigation.

At 7:15 Monday morning, March 25, Pompeo held his regular senior staff meeting with Hale, John Sullivan and Ulrich Brechbuhl, the secretary's counselor and de facto chief of staff. Hale reported that Yovanovitch wanted a Pompeo statement supporting her. The department's European Bureau had strongly requested that Pompeo back her up. Hale told Pompeo that he agreed.

Was there any evidence, Pompeo asked, to support the allegations against her? None, Hale said. Many of the things Lutsenko alleged—including the shutdown of the Burisma investigation—had happened before she arrived as ambassador. There was no reason to doubt that the ambassador, one of the department's finest and most experienced diplomats, was faithfully carrying out Trump administration policy, Hale said.

Pompeo told Brechbuhl to get in touch with those circulating the allegations on social media and within the White House and report back to him. A statement was on hold until Pompeo heard the results. After the meeting, Hale emailed Yovanovitch to update her. His assistant messaged "no statement" to the department's press office, which was awaiting a sign-off on a draft of support.

Later in the day, Trump called Bolton into his private dining room, where he was meeting with Giuliani and another of his personal lawyers, Jay Sekulow. It was the first time that Bolton realized that Giuliani was the source of Trump's ill feelings toward Yovanovitch. Trump again told Bolton he wanted her fired. Bolton relayed the message to Pompeo, who said there were no facts supporting Giuliani's claims. Pompeo said he would tell that to Trump and Giuliani.

Amid the controversy, Yovanovitch called Gordon Sondland, the U.S. ambassador to the European Union. He was a major Republican donor, a Pacific Northwest businessman, a political appointee. His government experience paled next to hers. But he knew Trump. He had recently visited Ukraine and was familiar with the issues there. She had spoken to him in the past and found him helpful.

Sondland told her she needed to "go big or go home." He said she should put out a statement, by video or tweet, declaring her full support for Trump and his policies, and saying the allegations against her were lies.

She thanked him, but she didn't take his advice. She didn't see how a foreign service officer, a diplomat, could create a public fight with people in the United States who were criticizing her—especially when those people included the president's son and the president's personal lawyer. Defend herself rather than be defended by the secretary of state? Bad idea. So she stayed silent.

Her supporters in Washington chose to speak out. On Tuesday afternoon, March 26, *The Washington Post* published an op-ed by Haring of the UkraineAlert newsletter. Haring expressed astonishment at the speed and progress of the attack on Yovanovitch. "Lutsenko used Solomon to get to Hannity to get to Trump, whose Twitter feed set thousands chattering about nonexistent collusion," she wrote. "If a bunch of obscure foreigners few Americans have ever heard of can play Trump so easily, and so obviously, what's to stop others from doing the same?"

Elsewhere in Washington, John Solomon asked the State Department for a comment on another article he was preparing. A department official told him: "Ambassador Yovanovitch represents the President of the United States in Ukraine, and America stands behind her and her statements."

But Pompeo held off on issuing the formal statement of confidence, under his name, that Yovanovitch had sought.

Rudy Giuliani wanted to tell Mike Pompeo directly what he thought of his ambassador to Ukraine, Marie Yovanovitch. He had a packet of documents for him. On March 27, seven days after Solomon's first stories appeared, Giuliani's assistant, Jo Ann Zafonte, sent an email to Madeleine Westerhout, a gatekeeper and personal aide to President Trump. The subject line: "Secretary Pompeo."

"Hate to bother you," Zafonte wrote, "but might you be able to send me a good number for above, I've been trying and getting nowhere through regular channels."

Twenty-four minutes after receiving the note, Westerhout forwarded it to a Pompeo aide. "This is Rudy Giuliani's assistant," she wrote. "What number can I give her for S?" she asked, referring to the secretary of state.

That evening, Pompeo aide Lisa Kenna emailed a State Department employee who was coordinating with Giuliani's office. "Pls have Mr. G bring the documents." The next day, the packet arrived at the State Department, addressed to "Secretary Pompeo" in scrolling calligraphy. The return address said simply "The White House." Inside was a folder embossed with the Trump Hotels logo. Giuliani's presentation was hardly subtle: He was working for the president.

The folder contained an assortment of documents Giuliani had compiled during months of work on Trump's behalf, with help from Parnas and Fruman. Some were about Yovanovitch, some weren't. There were copies of Solomon's stories. A timeline. Notes from Giuliani's talks with Lutsenko and another former Ukrainian prosecutor, Viktor Shokin, who blamed former vice president Joe Biden for his ouster in disgrace in 2016.

Together, the documents reflected Giuliani's view that he was doing exactly what a good lawyer should do: Find information favorable to his client, pursue it, see where it leads. Others might say he was out of line, but that wasn't his concern. If pushing the Ukrainians for an investigation, or sending Pompeo a file, was in his client's interest, then so be it.

Giuliani's sleuthing had started with the Mueller investigation. Trump had enlisted Giuliani's help in fending it off. As a former federal prosecutor, Giuliani was well versed in the rhythms of such an investigation. He believed that Mueller's investigation was a ridiculous waste of time and money. He had said, over and over, that Trump had done nothing wrong. But as a defense lawyer, he had to be prepared for the possibility that Mueller's final report would be damaging to his client in some way.

Giuliani had a strategy. If Mueller were to conclude that Trump had conspired with Russia, Giuliani planned to declare that Mueller had nabbed the wrong guy. After a former colleague had passed along some information in November 2018 about Ukrainian election collusion and an alleged Biden connection, Giuliani had thought to himself: Hallelujah. I now have what a defense lawyer always wants: I can go prove someone else committed his crime. The someone else? The Democrats and Ukraine. With Lutsenko's help, he could blame Ukraine for colluding with Hillary Clinton's campaign.

It wasn't Russia that had interfered, he was telling Trump and Pompeo and anyone who would listen. It was Ukraine.

Yovanovitch was a small piece of a much larger story.

CHAPTER TWO

"Ready to Rumble"

April 18 to 21, Washington and Kyiv

On the morning of Thursday, April 18, Trump tweeted a photo of himself, back to the camera, walking toward a mist evocative of "Game of Thrones," the wildly popular HBO series. It crowed "NO COLLUSION. NO OBSTRUCTION" and proclaimed: "FOR THE HATERS AND THE RADICAL LEFT DEMOCRATS – GAME OVER," in the show's distinctive, gothic-style typeface.

It was Trump's teaser for the Justice Department's 11 a.m. release of the Mueller report, as if he were promoting the finale of the ratings-busting juggernaut and its brutal, unforgiving political battles. For 22 months, investigators led by special counsel Robert S. Mueller III, the former U.S. Marine and ex–FBI director, had been methodically working their way through documents and witnesses. It was a gigantic Rubik's Cube, trying to determine how Russia had meddled in the 2016 U.S. presidential election, and whether Russia had coordinated those efforts with anyone in the Trump campaign.

When Trump heard in May 2017 that a special counsel would be appointed, he had slumped in his chair and said, "This is the end of my presidency. I'm fucked." Since then, "No collusion, no obstruction" had become a Trump mantra, created early and repeated often, a defiant denial and a rallying cry rolled into one sound bite.

Mueller's team had pursued its mission in relative secrecy, revealing its progress only through the occasional set of indictments. The mystery and guardedness had sharpened the expectations on both sides of the political divide. For Democrats, the probe was the warm, happy place that would send the contemptible Trump crashing from office in disgrace. For Republicans, it was the angry, indignant place where they could channel their fury at those loser lefties who would seize on any crazy excuse to bring down Trump, reversing the legitimate results of the 2016 election and thumbing their noses at the Republicans' half of the electorate, the 63 million voters who chose Trump.

As required, Mueller had filed his final report with the Justice Department. It was Justice's responsibility to send his findings to the House and Senate Judiciary committees. Barr said he would redact the classified bits and send the full report as soon as he could. But like a movie reviewer eager to analyze the climactic scene, Barr had made his claim that the report cleared Trump of wrongdoing.

Congressional Democrats called Barr's spoiler an outrageous mischaracterization of the report. They demanded to read Mueller's findings for themselves. On April 12, Congress adjourned for its two-week spring recess, and Barr still had not released the report.

Today was the day of the big reveal. Trump's Twitter account sent out a couple of early-morning flares. In keeping with the Hollywood vibe of the morning, one tweet included a 54-second video, featuring multiple clips with him saying "No collusion" over the past two years, as soaring martial music played in the background. Then the final frames, with him declaring: "This was an illegal takedown that failed. And hopefully somebody's gonna look at the other side."

Trump loved Twitter's immediacy. He could think of something, type it into his phone and soon people were talking about it. He bragged that his tens of millions of followers meant he had a bigger platform than most print and TV outlets. He wasn't the first president to take advantage of social media—the Obama White House had done so effectively and increasingly during his two terms—but he was first to embrace Twitter as his primary means of communication. He called it "modern day presidential."

He would post official White House statements, especially after his press secretary stopped holding daily briefings. But mostly, Twitter was another way for the president to punch back. He vented, unloaded, settled scores and YELLED AT PEOPLE IN ALL CAPS. He butchered spelling and grammar. But whatever he did, he tweeted to be retweeted, to spread his message. He would occasionally say "Watch this" to people around him, then "bing, bing, bing" as his tweet instantly went viral. He liked to calculate the time it took for an especially hot tweet to make it onto TV.

White House press aides would help prepare video clips and photos for Trump to share, like the "Game of Thrones" montage. Twitter also was a way to sidestep the mainstream media—"the enemy of the people," he often called them.

Not everyone saw his tweets. Only about one-fifth of the country were regular Twitter users, and they were more likely to be Democrats than Republicans, according to surveys. But Trump knew that the major outlets, despite objections from some critics, would report on many of his tweets. He would often make news in them, and *The Washington Post* and others had a long history of monitoring everything a president said. Many began assigning reporters to the Trump beat as early as 5 a.m., when he often picked up his phone and started typing into his @realDonaldTrump Twitter account. His early-morning tweets were often his most unvarnished of the day.

Saying something outrageous, saying it first, saying it loud—that drew attention and retweets. Twitter ran on adrenaline. Trump understood that. Some of his fans, including his wife Melania, said they wished he would tone it down. But when his critics took him to task for tweets they regarded as unpresidential or worse—when he said, for example, a TV host was "dumb as a rock"—Trump didn't back down. Twitter helped me win the election, he would say. Twitter lets me speak directly to my supporters.

He was speaking to his supporters now, with the Mueller report a few hours from public release. He told them: "The Greatest Political Hoax of all time! Crimes were committed by Crooked, Dirty Cops and DNC/The Democrats."

In a sign of Trump's relationship with his fervent following, he didn't need to spell out that "Crooked" was his nickname for Hillary Clinton.

Rudy Giuliani had been preparing for the Mueller moment for months. The president's personal lawyer had a "counter report" cued up for distribution to the press, and a full slate of media appearances planned—Fox first, CNN and Fox again in prime time. At 5:16 a.m., he texted Jacqueline Alemany, who was writing a scene-setter for Power Up, *The Washington Post*'s early-morning political newsletter.

The night before, Alemany had messaged him to "see how things are going before the big day tomorrow."

"Ready to rumble," he told her.

• • •

The Democrats were ready, too, but with Congress still in recess, most of them weren't in Washington. Nancy Pelosi was leading a congressional delegation to Germany, Britain and Ireland. The House Judiciary Committee chairman, Democrat Jerrold Nadler, was at home in New York City. The Senate chairman, Republican Lindsey Graham, was traveling in Africa. The Capitol was a near ghost town, its corridors largely empty. There would still be a burst of Democratic comment, but Barr's timing ensured that the reaction would be a scattershot roar.

Jerry Nadler was furious at Barr's highly choreographed rollout. The attorney general had scheduled a 9:30 a.m. press conference, a second shot at telling the public what to think about the yet-to-be-seen findings. After news broke of Barr's plan the previous afternoon, Nadler had tweeted: "I'm deeply troubled by reports that the WH is being briefed on the Mueller report AHEAD of its release. . . . This is wrong. #ReleaseTheReport."

Undeterred, Barr stepped to a podium at the Justice Department almost right on schedule. Flanked by his two deputies, he echoed Trump's morning mantra—"No collusion"—and dismissed a reporter's question about "spinning" the report in advance, curtly saying "No, No." He quoted the report's conclusion that "the Russian government" had illegally interfered in the 2016 election and he acknowledged that Mueller's team had listed "ten episodes" involving Trump actions that may have impeded the investigation. But, he said, the evidence was "not sufficient" to support an obstruction-of-justice charge.

As Barr was leaving the briefing room, Nadler was already tweeting. He posted a letter to Mueller, asking him to testify before the committee. "Congress and the American people must hear from Special Counsel Robert Mueller," Nadler wrote at 10:03 a.m.

An hour after Barr's press conference, the report went public on digitized disks delivered to the Judiciary committees. The media began sifting through the 448 pages, the results of an investigation based on 2,800 subpoenas, 500 search warrants and 500 witness interviews, producing 34 indictments, including people close to Trump.

Two conclusions dominated the early press accounts.

One: The Russian government wanted Trump to win and worked to make that happen. But, to the delight of Republicans: "The investigation did not establish that members of the Trump Campaign conspired or coordinated with the Russian government."

Two: Trump had potentially obstructed Mueller's probe at least ten times, as Barr had said in his preview. Influenced by Justice Department guidance that a sitting president can't be prosecuted, Mueller's team had left any further action to Congress. And to the delight of Democrats: "If we had confidence after a thorough investigation of the facts that the President clearly did not commit obstruction of justice, we would so state. Based on the facts and the applicable legal standards, we are unable to reach that judgment." And then for emphasis: "Accordingly, while this report does not conclude that the President committed a crime, it also does not exonerate him."

It didn't take long for Democrats and many in the media to convert those convoluted sentences into plainer English: The Mueller report did not clear the president of wrongdoing, as Barr had been insisting. The report was saying it was Congress's responsibility to hold the president accountable, governed by the impeachment clause of the Constitution.

Within an hour, the president's legal team declared "total victory" in a statement that questioned the investigation's legitimacy. "This vindication of the President is an important step forward for the country and a strong reminder that this type of abuse must never be permitted to occur again," said the statement from Giuliani and the three outside lawyers, Jay Sekulow, Jane Serene Raskin and Martin Raskin, hired to represent Trump during the probe.

At the White House, during an event in the East Room honoring wounded veterans, Trump told the gathering that he was "having a good day" and echoed his legal team's statement. "This should never happen to another president again, this hoax," he said.

By 11:30 a.m., Rudy Giuliani was on Fox, saying from a remote studio in Washington that "we're very, very happy." Giuliani was leaping from one topic to another, enjoying his chance to take the offensive. Anchor Bill Hemmer was finding it hard to corral the former New York mayor. At one point, Giuliani detoured into the Ukraine allegations.

"You want Russian collusion? Go look at the article in the Ukrainian papers a week and a half ago about how they've opened an investigation of their own officials for colluding with—"

Hemmer tried to steer the conversation back to the Mueller report, but Giuliani kept going, leaning forward, eyebrows raised, eyes flaring.

"—colluding with Hillary Clinton."

At that moment, Hemmer wasn't interested in Ukraine or Hillary Clinton, or why Giuliani had brought them up. Instead he asked, "Up until 60 minutes ago, how much of this report had you seen?"

Giuliani was candid. He and the legal team had seen the entire report, in advance, in a secure room at the Justice Department, starting Tuesday night. "I read every page of it," he said, pausing to let that idea sink in. "The four of us, myself, Jay, Jane, Marty . . . we were originally going to divide it up, but we decided we had to read it all and share our thoughts. It took two days."

The interview lasted 24 minutes, with no other guest to share the spotlight.

Across the ocean, Nancy Pelosi was watching. Herding 234 House Democrats from the speaker's office was hard enough. Managing them from Northern Ireland, where she had spent the day on the border with the Republic of Ireland before going to Belfast, was more challenging. But Pelosi was traveling with staff who were constantly briefing her; she was also in touch with D.C. by phone and text.

She and Senator Chuck Schumer, the New Yorker who led the Senate Democrats, had put together a joint statement, which went out before Barr's morning press conference. They criticized the attorney general for his "regrettably partisan handling" of Mueller's report and, like Nadler, called for the special counsel to testify. That was the only way to "restore public trust" in the report.

Before the Mueller report, Pelosi had held the line against impeachment. Now the report was out with a muddled message. That made matters harder. There was a pent-up frustration among some in the caucus. Pelosi needed time to assess where they stood, to assess the new risks.

Nadler was a wild card. He didn't share Pelosi's wariness about an impeachment inquiry. But as one of her committee chairmen, he had tried to stay close to her line. Now he looked at Mueller's language and saw a door swinging open. At a mid-afternoon news conference in New York, he said the special counsel's report offered "disturbing evidence that President Trump had engaged in obstruction of justice and other misconduct."

The reporters heard the door opening, too. "Congressman, when you say that it is Congress's responsibility to hold the president accountable," the first questioner asked, "does that mean impeachment?"

Nadler said: "That is one possibility." Let's see where the evidence leads, he said.

An hour later, Pelosi's more cautious, calming view could be heard in the words of her number two, House majority leader Steny Hoyer of Maryland. They had been working hand in glove to keep the pro-impeachment faction in check. Hoyer stuck to that position now. "Based on what we have seen to date, going forward on impeachment is not worthwhile at this point," Hoyer told CNN's Dana Bash. "Very frankly, there is an election in 18 months and the American people will make a judgment."

Late in the afternoon, one of the party's most progressive and best-known freshman members, Alexandria Ocasio-Cortez of New York, took to Twitter to call for the very conversation that Hoyer was trying to mute. "Many know that I take no pleasure in discussions of impeachment," Ocasio-Cortez tweeted to her 4 million followers, nearly ten times as many as Pelosi. "But the report puts this squarely on our doorstep."

Ocasio-Cortez was another wild card. She had gained a formidable reputation after just a few months in office. She was a phenomenon, no question. After winning her seat in the 2018 midterms, Ocasio-Cortez had dubbed herself and three other newly elected women of color as "the Squad," giving themselves status as a progressive voice. The nickname had caught on.

Now, Ocasio-Cortez said she would support her fellow Squad member, Rashida Tlaib of Michigan, who had filed an impeachment resolution. The "I" word was back. The word that Nancy Pelosi was trying so hard to avoid. The long Mueller probe was over, but the reverberations were just beginning.

For Trump, it was a day to savor. Shortly after 4 p.m., he and First Lady Melania Trump emerged from the White House holding hands. The president waved but did not stop to answer the reporters' shouted questions, not his usual habit.

The first couple boarded Marine One for the short hop to Joint Base Andrews in suburban Maryland, and then on to his Mar-a-Lago compound in Palm Beach, where it was 71 degrees, with clear blue skies and sunshine, a fine start to the Easter weekend.

That evening, as the Trump family relaxed in Florida, Nancy Pelosi emailed a "Dear Colleague" letter to House Democrats, citing "several alarming findings" in the Mueller report. She announced a caucus-wide conference call for Monday night, a virtual town hall from wherever they might be, "to discuss this grave matter."

The next morning in Belfast, five hours ahead of East Coast time and while most of Washington was still asleep, Pelosi was holding an early press conference, her first since the Mueller report had gone public. Asked about impeachment, she went into her best duck-and-dodge mode. "I would just say this: On any trip . . . I go on with my colleagues, we do not leave the country to criticize the president of the United States."

Two days later, with the Mueller report still convulsing political Washington, Ukrainians were electing a new president. Actor and comedian Volodymyr Zelensky won a landslide victory as millions of voters weary of war and economic hardship rebuked the ruling elites.

It was a thunderous triumph for Zelensky. His only credential for office was playing a fictional Ukrainian president on a popular TV sitcom called "Servant of the People." In a runoff against President Petro Poroshenko, who had been campaigning for a second five-year term, Zelensky had won nearly 75 percent of the vote.

When the boyish-looking Zelensky realized his election was assured, he jumped up and down like an excited kid, kissed his wife and hugged supporters. He walked onstage to the theme song from his TV show and said: "I can say as a Ukrainian citizen to all the countries of the former Soviet Union: Look at us. Everything is possible."

He had been heavily favored to win, surging to the top of a crowded field of candidates in the first round. His election was the latest in a global trend of political outsiders harnessing TV and social media to reach voters and bypass an unpopular establishment. He wasn't Trump, who also had a TV star turn as the tough-talking boss on the reality show "The Apprentice." But his victory had echoes of Trump's.

His election had come at a critical moment for his country and its 40 million people. Ukraine was pivotal to Putin's effort to maintain a sphere of influence in Eastern Europe. With guns and bombs in 2014, Putin's Russia had "annexed" Ukraine's Crimean Peninsula and had backed separatists in eastern Ukraine. Putin feared that a successful democracy in Ukraine, which shares deep historical, linguistic and cultural ties with Russia, could energize opposition within Russia and challenge his autocratic rule.

Zelensky's most powerful advantage may have been simply that he was not Poroshenko. Many voters blamed the incumbent for failing to end the war in eastern Ukraine, with its death toll of 13,000, and for allowing corruption to fester at the government's highest levels.

On his sitcom, Zelensky played a morally upright schoolteacher whose rant about corruption is caught on camera and goes viral. In his campaign, he took on Ukraine's entrenched elites and said he would not be bought. "I'm not a politician," Zelensky said during one campaign debate, channeling his character on the show. "I'm just a simple person who came to break the system."

Just before 4:30 p.m. on the U.S. East Coast, half an hour before midnight in Kyiv, Trump called Zelensky to congratulate him on his "incredible election." The U.S. president made the call from Air Force One, flying back to Washington after three days at Mar-a-Lago.

Zelensky thanked him, saying: "We had you as a great example."

"I guess, in a way, I did something similar," Trump said. "We're making tremendous progress in the U.S.—we have the most tremendous economy ever. I just wanted to congratulate you. I have no doubt you will be a fantastic president."

In Washington, U.S. Army Lt. Col. Alexander Vindman, a 43-year-old National Security Council staffer, had hurried to the Situation Room in the White House sub-basement to listen in. As the NSC's director of European affairs, Vindman shared the optimism he heard coming out of Ukraine about Zelensky and his promises of reform. But Vindman was worried about this first phone call between the two leaders. Like others at the White House, he had come to understand that unpredictability was a signature trait of the Trump era. That applied not just to the president's views on Russia and the region, but also to the way he talked about U.S. policy priorities in public and private settings.

Along with his boss, John Bolton, and others in the White House, Vindman had been eager for the call to happen. It would send the right signal to Putin. Anticipating Zelensky's victory, Bolton had paved the way in advance, urging Trump to make the call right away, on election night. At Bolton's direction, Vindman had prepared talking points and had helped with a draft news release that the White House press office would put out after the call.

The talking points called for Trump to congratulate Zelensky, and to remind the new leader of the enduring U.S. interest in an independent Ukraine as an important bulwark against Russia. If Trump followed the script, he would also reiterate the importance of reducing corruption in Ukraine—echoing what U.S. ambassador Marie Yovanovitch had been saying for several years—and offer U.S. support for Ukraine's economic development, particularly in the energy sector.

Bolton had wanted Trump to make the call before leaving Mar-a-Lago. It hadn't happened. When the heads-up came, Vindman leapt into his car and raced to the White House from his home in suburban Virginia, arriving in the Situation Room just in time.

Vindman heard Zelensky invite Trump to his inauguration, and then Trump respond that he would "look into it" and, at least, send a "great representative." Zelensky talked up Ukraine, its people and its food as an enticement for a Trump visit.

"Well, I agree with you about your country and I look forward to it," Trump said. "When I owned Miss Universe, they always had great people. Ukraine was always very well represented. When you're settled in and ready, I'd like to invite you to the White House. We'll have a lot of things to talk about, but we're with you all the way."

Trump wasn't paying attention to Vindman's talking points, but that was no surprise. Everyone at the NSC was used to the president's ad-libbed performances. Who knew Miss Universe would come up? The conversation seemed a bit rushed, but friendly and even jovial. Lot of laughter from both sides. Then, the payoff Vindman hadn't expected: *"When you're settled in and ready, I'd like to invite you to the White House. . . . We're with you all the way."*

Given all the noise from Giuliani and company about the ambassador and Ukraine, this was a very promising start, Vindman thought.

When the call ended, Vindman stood and high-fived some of his NSC colleagues. Maybe his fears about Giuliani, and his influence with Trump, would prove groundless after all.

CHAPTER THREE

Walking the Fine Line

April 22 and 23, Washington and Hoosick Falls, New York

By Easter Monday, some members of Pelosi's Democratic caucus had worked themselves into a righteous froth over the Mueller report. Many others wanted to call it a misfire and move on.

For months, Democrats had been impatiently awaiting Mueller like some sort of super-sheriff on a white horse. "It's Mueller Time!" said T-shirts worn by hopeful partisans. Now "Mueller Time" had come, and it wasn't anything like what the Democrats had hoped. Caucus members were divided about what to do next.

Pelosi still wasn't sensing any surge toward impeachment, though. It was still a small group, maybe two dozen. But as usual, she wasn't taking anything for granted. It was time once again to walk the twisty line between and among the various factions, to honor their disparate views, to sound the right alarms, to keep the pressure on Trump. Before the scheduled 5 p.m. all-caucus conference call, she sent another "Dear Colleague" letter. This one was more explicit and sharper in its language.

She did not avoid the impeachment question. She had to acknowledge that option. "While our views range from proceeding to investigate the findings of the Mueller report or proceeding directly to impeachment, we all firmly agree that we should proceed down a path of finding the truth," she wrote. She welcomed the relevant committees to keep investigating, especially on the obstruction issue. We can hold a president accountable, she argued, without a formal impeachment inquiry.

"Whether currently indictable or not," she told them, "it is clear that the President has, at a minimum, engaged in highly unethical and unscrupulous behavior." She urged her colleagues to remember that "we are proceeding free from passion or prejudice, strictly on the presentation of fact."

Her caution was evident: Let's make our next moves methodical and dedicated to gathering evidence. Less evident was whether this would work. Was she trailing rather than leading?

At 5 p.m., House members from all over the country punched in the conference call code. No press, no cameras. But also, no pretense of privacy. With more than 170 people listening, with varying agendas and sharply divergent views, the media would have no trouble getting filled in.

"This isn't about Democrats or Republicans," Pelosi told them. "It's about saving our democracy." The way to do that, she stressed, was to keep investigating and see where the inquiries lead. She invited the six committee chairmen to lay out their plans. As if to underscore Pelosi's strategy of continued investigations, Nadler told the members that, just a few minutes before the conference call, his Judiciary Committee had issued a subpoena for former White House counsel Donald McGahn, who was a central witness in Mueller's probe. The committee also was pressing ahead with plans for both Mueller and Barr to testify.

That wasn't good enough for some members. Val Demings of Florida, one of twenty-four Democrats on Nadler's committee, said she was now endorsing an impeachment inquiry. As a 27-year veteran of the Orlando police force, and that department's first female chief, Demings was a consistent liberal voice who commanded respect among her colleagues. "While I understand we need to see the full report and all supporting documents, I believe we have enough evidence now," she said.

After hearing a couple of moderate members explain their reasons for opposing impeachment or going slowly, Jared Huffman of California spoke up. We can't just talk about the political risks of impeachment, he said. There's also a political implication for not acting, for failing to go forward.

Jim Himes of Connecticut, a leader of the centrist New Democrat Coalition, listened from his home in Greenwich, the wealthy coastal enclave just north of New York City. He wasn't inclined to take the microphone in these large full-caucus settings. But today he made a passionate plea.

Stand down, he said. Proceeding with any impeachment, at least on the evidence now available, would undermine Democrats, he argued. It was also futile. The Republican-led Senate would never vote to remove Trump. The best way, the only way, to get Trump out of office was to vote him out in 2020, Himes said. Impeachment would be neutral, at best, for the Democrats, Himes felt. At worst, deeply damaging at election time, enough to hand Trump a second term.

Himes spoke for four minutes. Pelosi jumped on him in a way that Himes had not expected. "This is not about politics," she said. "This is about public sentiment. This is about the Constitution." Himes had a good relationship with Pelosi. He was on her side. But in this moment, she was shutting him down completely. Himes found it a little scary to be on the receiving end of Pelosi's cool fury.

She hadn't yelled at him. She never did that. It was a more graceful, but firm, smack-down. Pelosi wasn't just powerful because she could hand out plum committee assignments, Himes had learned. Her power was rooted in her support in the caucus and the party, her skill at managing opposing views and her formidable fundraising ability. She had also shown a rare talent for standing up to a president who liked to bully people. Himes knew that lots of people had doubted Pelosi's leadership after the 2016 election. He didn't know any Democrats who doubted her now.

Pelosi came away from the call with her strategy intact: Keep investigating. Keep conducting oversight. Keep impeachment in reserve, for now. She had an overwhelming majority backing her, but she wanted her pro-impeachment members to know she agreed with their assessment of Trump's actions, just not their solution. She had used her "Dear Colleague" letter to say so. Instead of giving the president their blessings, she wrote, "the GOP should be ashamed of what the Mueller report has revealed."

Republicans dismissed any talk of impeachment or further investigation as ridiculous. "Well, look, I think it's time to move on," said Mitch McConnell, after an event in Owensboro, Kentucky. "This investigation was about collusion, there's no collusion, no charges brought against the president on anything else and I think the American people have had quite enough of it."

White House press secretary Sarah Huckabee Sanders, appearing on "Fox & Friends," mocked the Democrats and declared game over. "If they have to get a conference call together to figure out where they're going from here, they shouldn't be in office in the first place," she said. "I think it's quite sad that they've got to have a conference call with all of their members to figure out what they're going to do with themselves now that the Mueller report is out and proven that there was no collusion and no obstruction."

• • •

In the early evening, *Washington Post* senior congressional reporter Paul Kane was talking to voters in Hoosick Falls, New York, a village of 3,500 people northeast of Albany, where Upstate New York, Vermont and Massachusetts converge.

Kane wanted to hear what they were thinking about the issues churning in Washington. He was especially interested in the swing districts that had voted for Trump in 2016, only to go Democratic in the 2018 midterms. New York's 19th fit that profile, so Kane had arranged to travel with Antonio Delgado on Easter Monday as the freshman House member crisscrossed his sprawling district.

Now Delgado stood before 75 people in a Hoosick Falls high school auditorium, discussing the news cycle's top item: the Mueller report. For seven minutes, he briefed them on the investigation, Trump and Russia.

No one raised a hand. No one clapped or booed or groaned.

Nothing.

He moved on to his legislative agenda, saying he had introduced seven bills. Claps of approval.

He talked about pushing several bipartisan measures to address problems at veterans hospitals. Applause.

He spoke about his support for electoral reform legislation to clean up Washington. Bigger applause.

He told them he was leading an effort to expand Medicare and control health-care costs.

The loudest ovation yet.

Now it was the audience's turn. Questions came on climate change, a measles outbreak, on jobs. Finally, someone asked about Mueller—a gentle inquiry, wondering if the full, unredacted report might ever be released.

It had been like this all day, as Delgado drove more than 200 miles over 11 hours through the 8,000-square-mile district, encompassing all or part of 11 counties, an area larger than Connecticut and Rhode Island combined. It included the Baseball Hall of Fame in Cooperstown, the site of the Woodstock music festival and parts of the Hudson Valley, from wealthy summer homes to job-starved river towns.

In Tannersville, 50 miles south of Albany, high school students had quizzed him about the opioid and mental-health crises. Over lunch in Leeds, a hamlet near the Hudson River, local business leaders had pleaded for a rural broadband program and more job training. They said their area was running out of plumbers. After lunch, organic farmers told the 6-foot-4-inch former high school basketball star how they protected crops from violent hailstorms.

Delgado was trying hard to stay connected to the district, not to get sucked into the Washington drama. His roots in the region helped. He was 42, African American and had grown up in nearby Schenectady. His wife, documentary filmmaker Lacey Schwartz, was a local. He went to college at Colgate University, in the neighboring congressional district. After a Rhodes Scholarship and Harvard Law School, he had a brief stint as a hip-hop artist in Los Angeles and then had worked as a lawyer in Manhattan.

He returned home to run for Congress in 2018, on a slate of economic development and "kitchen table" issues. He knew those were critical to voters in a region that was once home to major IBM and General Electric plants but now was struggling to replace those jobs. The district had voted for Obama in 2012 by more than six percentage points. Four years later, it had backed Trump by almost seven. Delgado reminded himself constantly of that math. It told him that his district's voters were not afraid of change—and could change again.

Now, after hearing and watching Delgado talk with voters on this Easter Monday in 2019, one thing stood out to Paul Kane as he wrote his story about the day: Not one voter all day had mentioned impeachment.

The next day at the White House, April 23, Bolton was called to the Oval Office. He found Trump and acting chief of staff Mick Mulvaney on the phone with Giuliani, who was urging Trump to fire Yovanovitch. Bolton could tell that Giuliani was winding the president up with all kinds of allegations against the ambassador, Hillary Clinton and Hunter Biden that Bolton regarded as third-hand or fourth-hand hearsay. Trump was amazed that Yovanovitch hadn't been dumped yet. He wanted it done, now. He told Bolton to call Zelensky and say the ambassador didn't speak for the administration.

Bolton didn't make the call. He had no idea what Yovanovitch had said to Zelensky, so he didn't know what to tell him to ignore. He called Pompeo, who groaned when he heard that Trump was volcanic. Pompeo said he had already moved up Yovanovitch's end date to June 1. He thought that would be good enough. Clearly, it wasn't. Pompeo told Bolton he would order her back to Washington immediately.

CHAPTER FOUR

"Courage Is Contagious"

April 24 to May 17, Kyiv and Washington

On Wednesday evening, April 24, Marie Yovanovitch hosted an embassy tribute to Kateryna Handziuk, a 33-year-old Ukrainian civil rights and anti-corruption activist who had died the previous year after an attacker doused her with sulfuric acid outside her home.

This was the ambassador's opportunity to celebrate Handziuk's courage and speak out once more about the brutal attack. It was the kind of event she was proud to organize. It said the right things about the United States. It was important, she thought, to show that the U.S. government's leaders understood that human rights threats were real in Ukraine. Lives were at risk.

Handziuk had died after three months of suffering and nearly a dozen surgeries. In March, at a ceremony honoring the ten 2019 recipients of the State Department's International Women of Courage award, Pompeo had recognized Handziuk's bravery. "She refused to be silenced," the secretary had said, as First Lady Melania Trump listened. "From her hospital bed, she demanded justice, setting a powerful example for her fellow citizens."

Now in Kyiv, Yovanovitch added her praise. Kateryna had "paid the ultimate price for her fearlessness in fighting against corruption and for her determined efforts to build a democratic Ukraine," Yovanovitch told her guests, which included Handziuk's family. After presenting a special "Ukrainian Woman of Courage" framed citation to Handziuk's father, Victor, she said: "I want to thank everybody, and I want to just remind you that courage is contagious."

It was the end of an unsettling month for Yovanovitch. By early April, it was clear Pompeo would not be making a personal statement of support for her. No one in Washington could tell her why. Some said Pompeo feared that President Trump might contradict him with an embarrassing tweet. Giuliani and his allies had Trump's ear for reasons she still didn't understand, and she knew they were saying awful things about her.

It was confusing to say the least. Philip Reeker, the acting head of the State Department's European and Eurasian Bureau, had told her he was enthusiastic about her staying an extra year in Ukraine. Now he was telling her that was impossible.

Yovanovitch thought that meant going back to her original timetable, leaving after the July 4 holiday and the embassy's Independence Day gala, the Kyiv mission's premier annual event. Three full years in Kyiv was fine; she would come home with her head held high, unbowed by her enemies' campaign to oust her.

The daily tweets and TV show attacks had eased somewhat, and her direct bosses continued to say she was in good standing with them. She had started to breathe a little easier. She still enjoyed Kyiv, an experience she shared with her mother, Nadia, now 90 and widowed. They had come together to Kyiv, not the typical ambassadorial pairing. There was a large residence for the ambassador, domestic help and lots to keep her mother busy. Nadia needed to use a walker, but she was far from immobile. She had plunged into life in the Ukrainian capital, joining a group of women who made *pysanka*, the intricately painted Easter eggs the country was known for. Outspoken and spry, she had become a well-known figure on the Kyiv diplomatic circuit.

Yovanovitch tried to ignore the toxic Washington politics and focus on her work. It wasn't easy. On the night of Zelensky's big election win, when Trump made his congratulatory call, Yovanovitch had been cut out of the process. She had not been invited to participate, or given a readout afterward. She had heard it went well. She figured that was the best she could hope for under the circumstances.

As Yovanovitch was mingling with her guests at the reception honoring Handziuk, an assistant interrupted. She had an urgent call from Washington. It was 9:45 p.m. in Kyiv, 2:45 p.m. in D.C.

Excusing herself, Yovanovitch went to her office. On the phone was Carol Perez, the State Department official in charge of human resources for the Foreign Service. Perez, a fellow career officer and a friend, said she was calling with a "heads-up." Things were going wrong for Yovanovitch in Washington. There was a lot of nervous talk about her on the "seventh floor," shorthand for Pompeo's office, and "up the street," department lingo for the White House.

Yovanovitch asked what it was about. Lutsenko? Giuliani? Something else? Perez said she wasn't sure, promising to find out more. Three hours later, at 1 a.m. Kyiv time, Perez called again. Her tone and message had escalated from anxious to alarming. There's "a lot of concern" about your security, Perez said. You need to be on the next plane to Washington.

"You mean my physical security?" Yovanovitch asked, incredulous, pressing Perez for more. What did that mean? What was the threat? How could they ask her to come home immediately, without any explanation? If she was being permanently recalled, why couldn't she stay for another week to pack up and leave properly? Perez couldn't, or wouldn't, say.

Yovanovitch hastily messaged her senior aides, asking them to assemble first thing in the morning at her official residence not far from the Dnieper River. At 8 a.m., the shocked gathering listened as she explained what she knew. She asked an assistant to book an immediate flight, but learned that the next available one wasn't until the following morning.

Perez hadn't told her if she would be allowed to come back to Kyiv. She assumed she could. She couldn't pack everything up in 24 hours, and she refused to drag her mother to Washington under such uncertain circumstances. Nadia was better off staying put until it was clear what was going on.

While Yovanovitch was making her arrangements in Kyiv, the phone rang at William B. Taylor Jr.'s modest bungalow in Arlington, the Virginia suburb just outside Washington. It was George Kent, his former State Department colleague, now the deputy at the European and Eurasian Bureau. Kent was calling to ask if Taylor might "hypothetically" be interested in returning to government service as the interim ambassador in Kyiv—the job he held during the George W. Bush administration.

Taylor knew that his good friend, Marie Yovanovitch, was under attack in Ukraine and, strangely, from Giuliani, the president's personal lawyer. Taylor had seen her on a recent visit to Kyiv, and she had filled him in. She felt under pressure, but she was holding steady. He had no idea that she might be on the verge of being fired. If true, it meant that the rift between the White House and its diplomatic corps was even worse than Taylor thought.

"Why are you asking me this, George?" Taylor pressed.

Kent didn't want to go into specifics. Taylor was a private citizen, not privy to the government's internal discussions, so discretion was required. "This is just hypothetical," Kent repeated.

Taylor wasn't sure what to say. "Hypothetical" meant he didn't need to say anything. He hung up thinking, if that was a feeler, it was an odd one. Everything about this episode was dismaying. Why weren't Pompeo and the State Department speaking out on Yovanovitch's behalf? In early April, Taylor had joined five other former ambassadors to Ukraine on a strong letter of support for Yovanovitch. They sent it to David Hale at the State Department. They did not send it to the media. They weren't looking for publicity. They were looking to spur the department into defending her, forcefully and publicly. The allegations in Solomon's stories were uncorroborated hearsay, they wrote, and "simply wrong." Allowing these attacks to "stand without strong rebuttal from senior officials" undermined U.S. ambassadors everywhere.

The letter didn't seem to change anything, and now there was Kent's call, suggesting the battle was lost.

At the State Department, Deputy Secretary John Sullivan gathered David Hale, Ulrich Brechbuhl and Carol Perez for a tense meeting. Sullivan told them: President Trump has "lost confidence" in Yovanovitch. She had to go. No reason was given. Sullivan simply said they needed to come up with a plan that "brought this matter to a conclusion."

Later that day, Taylor was still puzzling over his conversation with Kent when the phone rang again.

"It's no longer hypothetical," Kent told him. Yovanovitch was out, Kent said, although it wasn't public yet and wouldn't be for a while. Kent was trying to get ahead of the curve. The department needed someone steady and seasoned to calm the rattled embassy staff in Kyiv, he said. They also needed a strong U.S. hand to support Zelensky, the newly elected Ukrainian president, as he battled corruption, reformed the government and learned how to deal with the Trump administration. Taylor would serve as acting ambassador—officially, the chargé d'affaires—until a permanent replacement could be confirmed by the Senate.

Taylor wasn't eager to jump back into his old job. He was 71 and happy at the U.S. Institute for Peace, a prestigious Washington organization created by Congress with the mission to reduce violent conflicts around the world. He had a top-level position, and he cared about the work. He felt it mattered. He needed to think this through, he told Kent. He wanted to seek advice, find out more about what was happening in Ukraine.

The offer posed a unique dilemma for Taylor. For the first time in his half-century career of public service, he was unsure what his duty to his country entailed. It had always been clear during his years at West Point in the late 1960s, then as an infantry officer in Vietnam, then at various government jobs and at the State Department, his professional home for more than two decades. He had never shied away from difficult assignments. He had volunteered for diplomatic posts in Afghanistan and Iraq, where he had tried and—like everyone before him—largely failed to repair those countries' confounding reconstruction programs. He had served without a moment of regret. He considered those tough tasks on behalf of his country to be part of that "duty."

During Taylor's first tour as the Kyiv ambassador, during the last three years of the George W. Bush administration, he had fallen in love with the country. He saw Ukraine as the central front in America's continuing struggle to keep Russia and Vladimir Putin at bay. But beyond the geopolitics, Taylor had come to admire the Ukrainian people. Through a series of uprisings, many had shown themselves to be idealists determined to shed the centuries-long shadow of Russian dominance.

Zelensky's overwhelming election victory—and his earnest if sometimes naive-sounding pledges to fight the oligarchs who had looted billions from the former Soviet state—was the latest expression of that character. Taylor saw Ukraine's "spirit of youth" and the "charm represented by this new president" as evidence of a rare opportunity. With staunch support from the United States and the West, he believed, Ukraine now had a real chance to build a successful democracy and take care of its people.

But he wondered how to square his "duty" with working for Trump, who seemed to reject many of the values that had always guided Taylor. Trump was like no president he had ever served, from either party. He seemed to harbor an unshakable contempt for the so-called deep state. Maybe more importantly, Trump seemed to have an inexplicable and steadfast animosity toward Ukraine.

Taylor kept thinking: How was this a good fit?

After a long flight and a weekend in Washington that seemed to last forever, Marie Yovanovitch was sitting in Phil Reeker's State Department office at 1 p.m., Monday, April 29, waiting to learn her fate.

She had asked to meet with Brechbuhl, Pompeo's top aide. That wasn't going to happen. Reeker told her that Sullivan would be delivering the bad news. She would need to vacate her post in Kyiv as soon as possible. Pompeo had tried to protect her from the "concerted campaign" against her, Reeker said, but couldn't. Trump had wanted to get rid of her for almost a year.

She was angry, unsure what to believe. The whole thing was beyond comprehension. She and Reeker had spoken a lot about the dishonest smear campaign against her. Now she unloaded on him. Better to shout at him than Sullivan.

At her meeting with Sullivan at 4 p.m., he told her right off: You've done nothing wrong. But at this point, he said, it was better for her to just leave the job quickly and quietly, lest the president himself start tweeting against her.

All U.S. ambassadors knew they served "at the pleasure of the president." But Yovanovitch was dumbfounded that Trump—whom she had never met or spoken to—could have made such a decision against the advice of his own State Department, based on untruths spread by Giuliani and others with their own agendas. Her firing would be taken as a signal in Ukraine that the administration's anti-corruption policy wasn't serious, and as a message to American diplomats around the world that their government didn't have their backs.

That afternoon, Bill Taylor was texting with Kurt Volker, the Trump administration's special envoy to Ukraine for the negotiations to resolve its military conflict with Russia. Taylor wanted Volker's take.

"George has asked me to go to Kyiv for a while," he wrote to Volker at 5:14 p.m.

"Ah . . . good!!!" Volker responded two minutes later. "You should!"

Taylor tapped out his concern. "George described two snake pits, one in Kyiv and one in Washington."

Volker kept it light, replying with a smiley face and a sardonic "so what's new?"

Taylor stayed serious. "Yes, but he described much more than I knew. Very ugly."

He soon heard that Trump's ax had fallen on Yovanovitch, but he still wasn't ready to make up his mind.

• • •

Yovanovitch decided she would take some time off from the State Department. If possible, she would spend at least a year at Georgetown University's Institute for the Study of Diplomacy, something of a refuge for senior diplomats between assignments or ending their government careers.

Her dismissal wasn't yet public. The press statement was still under review. She decided she might as well stay in Washington for a couple of weeks. She had been planning to come in early May anyway for a special event: The National Defense University, where the military trains those tapped for leadership and where she had earned a graduate degree years earlier, was inducting her into its National Hall of Fame on May 9.

On Monday, May 6, word of her early departure began to circulate in Kyiv. The State Department hastily put out the press statement. Yovanovitch was "concluding her three-year diplomatic assignment in Kyiv," the statement said, "as planned."

The community of Ukraine watchers at think tanks and universities, along with several reporters, jumped on the statement as a sham. "I'm totally aghast by reports that US ambassador in #Ukraine is being removed in the wake of intense scandal-mongering by Trump fake news machine," tweeted Andrew Weiss of the Carnegie Endowment for International Peace, calling Yovanovitch "a fine career diplomat who's been subjected to a stream of insane accusations for the past year."

At the State Department, David Hale wasn't happy with the press statement. When he saw the draft, he had objected to the words "as planned." Delete those, he had recommended. It hadn't happened.

Several press accounts the next day made clear that Yovanovitch wasn't ending her tour "as planned." She was being "recalled" after "political attacks by conservative media outlets and Donald Trump Jr.," wrote Josh Rogin of *The Washington Post.* As Rogin's story was posted online, two top House Democrats made public an April 12 letter they had sent privately to Pompeo, asking him to defend her. Now the authors of that letter, Majority Leader Steny Hoyer and Foreign Affairs chairman Eliot Engel, called on Pompeo to reverse the "White House's outrageous decision to recall her," labeling it a "political hit job."

It felt like a case of too little, much too late. Two days later, Yovanovitch went to the National Defense University for her Hall of Fame induction. She listened to the speakers applaud her integrity, accomplishments and experience. The next day, she flew back to Kyiv to pack up.

• • •

The ouster of Yovanovitch had been a major victory for Giuliani and his circle, but Zelensky's victory had complicated their plans. Their connections were to Poroshenko. Now they would need similar cooperation from Zelensky's team to generate investigations into Ukrainian meddling in the 2016 election and the Bidens.

Giuliani already had a planned trip to Kyiv for a paid speech about the Middle East. Why not a meeting with president-elect Zelensky at the same time? Giuliani discussed the idea at a meeting in the Oval Office with Trump, Mulvaney, White House counsel Pat Cipollone and Bolton. He said he would press Zelensky for investigations into Hillary Clinton and the 2016 election, or Hunter Biden, or both. Bolton saw the two matters as confused conspiracy theories. He could hardly keep them straight. Trump told Bolton to call Zelensky and urge him to have the meeting. Bolton didn't do it.

Giuliani made his intentions public, telling the *New York Times* explicitly of his goals. The article ran May 9, causing a stir in Washington and Kyiv. It was an unsubtle bit of pressure, but maybe it would get results.

In Kyiv, Zelensky and his aides were in a quandary. They didn't want to be dragged into a domestic political fight in the United States and risk jeopardizing Ukraine's bipartisan support in Congress. "This is definitely not our war," a Zelensky confidant told *Washington Post* reporter Anton Troianovski, who was following up on the *Times* report. "We have to stay away from this as much as possible." But they needed Trump's support, especially in their war with Russia, and it was increasingly clear that persuading Trump meant making Giuliani happy.

As Zelensky and his team struggled with what to tell Giuliani about a meeting, he abruptly canceled his trip. On May 10, he told Fox News host Shannon Bream that he was scrapping the trip because he would be walking into a group of people around Zelensky who "are enemies of the president and in some cases enemies of the United States."

Alarm bells went off in Kyiv. Zelensky hadn't been inaugurated yet, and Trump's personal lawyer was trashing him publicly. The United States had given Ukraine about half a billion dollars a year on average, in political and military aid, since 2015. The International Monetary Fund, with major funding from Washington, was critical to keeping Ukraine's economy afloat. Zelensky needed Trump. So Zelensky needed Giuliani, or so he thought.

As Zelensky was trying to understand Giuliani's aims, Giuliani was frustrated that Zelensky hadn't jumped at the chance to meet him. He wasn't going to let that stop him, he told *Washington Post* reporter Josh Dawsey. "What I'm pushing for—don't let the crooks bury the case for the second time," he fumed to Dawsey. "It's all part of a corrupt arrangement between United States political officials of the Democratic Party and Ukrainian officials to dig up dirt on Republicans." Giuliani was adamant. "I'm going to make sure that nothing scuttles the investigation that I want," he told Dawsey.

On May 12, Parnas met with Zelensky aide Sergey Shaffer in Kyiv. Parnas conveyed a message from Giuliani: Zelensky needed to announce investigations into the Bidens or the U.S.-Ukraine relationship "would be sour." Without an announcement of investigations, Parnas said, the Trump administration wouldn't be sending Vice President Mike Pence to the inauguration.

Later, Parnas messaged Shaffer on WhatsApp. Any updates? Would Zelensky announce the investigations? At that point, Shaffer blocked his messages on WhatsApp. Parnas took that as a no. He called Giuliani to pass along the news.

Parnas found Giuliani's reply memorable.

"OK, they'll see," Giuliani said.

On Monday, May 13, Bill Taylor rushed to the White House for an afternoon meeting with Vindman and Fiona Hill, his boss at the NSC. Taylor was leaning against taking the ambassador post, but he hadn't closed the door yet. The meeting would give him a chance to get a sense of the White House team he'd be working with, and a better feel for the conflicts over the administration's policy toward Ukraine.

When Taylor arrived at the Old Executive Office Building, Vindman was waiting for him. Hill arrived about 15 minutes late, distraught over the readout she had received from Trump's Oval Office meeting earlier in the day with Viktor Orban, Hungary's far-right nationalist leader.

Orban, largely a pariah among other European Union leaders for his hard-line policies on immigration, freedom of speech and other basic rights, had spent a significant portion of the meeting parroting the Putin line on Ukraine. Ukraine wasn't "a real country," Orban told Trump. It was irredeemably corrupt, he insisted. Never mind Zelensky's election.

Hill had opposed inviting Orban to the White House, concerned about the signal it would send to the rest of the world. She also feared the ideas the Hungarian leader would plant in Trump's head. Now her worst fears were coming true. It seemed that Trump was buying all of it, she told Taylor and Vindman.

They spent much of their meeting brainstorming ways to counter Orban's propaganda. Could they get the Polish president, who had a good relationship with Trump and a deep suspicion of the Russians, to counter the Orban-Putin line? "Maybe President Trump will listen" to him, Taylor suggested.

Taylor found Trump's chummy relationship with Orban troubling. He also was bothered by something else Hill and Vindman told him. The State Department and NSC staff had wanted Trump to sign a congratulatory letter to Zelensky, to be hand-delivered by the official delegation to Zelensky's inauguration on May 20. Such missives were standard stuff. Vindman had drafted the letter, which had been approved by Hill and national security adviser John Bolton. Trump had refused to sign it.

After nearly five years away from government service, Taylor found it invigorating to be back in the White House, but he emerged from the meeting thinking that he couldn't do it. He couldn't serve a president who had such contempt for Ukraine and the Ukrainians. Trump seemed more inclined to support Putin than Ukraine, a key U.S. ally. Their views didn't have to align, Taylor thought, but they had to intersect somewhere.

At home, Taylor turned to his wife, Deborah, for advice. She leaned liberal, while he had worked for both parties but tended to vote Republican. She also was more cynical about Washington's ways. "What makes you think they won't do to you what they did to Masha?" she asked him, referring to Yovanovitch by her nickname.

Deborah Taylor worried about what a stint in Ukraine, even a temporary one, might do to her husband. He had a profound respect for the regular diplomatic channels and an instinct for compromise. Both were potentially lethal traits inside the Trump administration, she thought. She urged him to turn down the job.

Taylor had been working his contacts, and he didn't like what he was hearing. People—not only Deborah—were advising him to stay clear. He reached out to Stephen Hadley, who had served as George W. Bush's national security adviser. Hadley was one of the few Republican foreign policy stalwarts who had tried to maintain a working relationship with Trump and his foreign policy inner circle. He would understand Taylor's misgivings.

Taylor rattled off the risks—political, reputational and personal. His biggest worry, he told Hadley, was that his service to Trump might end up doing more harm than good. Could he serve a president whose values and worldview ran counter to his? Hadley's counsel was sobering and to the point. "If your country asked you to do something, you should do it, but only if you can be effective," he said. "And the only way you'll know you can be effective is if you have the support of Pompeo."

A good idea, Taylor thought, but he was reluctant to ask for a meeting with the secretary of state. It seemed presumptuous. On the other hand, it would be a good test. He would need Pompeo's backing to succeed in this politically fraught assignment. If the secretary declined to meet, Taylor would know that he probably couldn't count on Pompeo if push came to shove. Taylor put in the request.

The more he thought about it, though, the more he became convinced that he should not take the job. He had an idea who should: Kurt Volker.

Taylor called Volker and urged him to consider it. Volker already knew some of the terrain, he had relationships in Ukraine, he had a firsthand view of the Russian conflict as Trump's special envoy. He could step right in, without a steep learning curve.

But Volker wasn't looking for a full-time, all-consuming government post. He was serving as the special envoy as a volunteer, without pay, so that he could continue to work his paid job as the executive director of the McCain Institute for International Leadership, set up by the Arizona senator in 2012. Volker also had a side gig as senior adviser at the BGR Group, a lobbying firm. He had kids in college and was about to get remarried. He couldn't afford the pay cut, he told Taylor.

As they texted back and forth, it was clear both had reservations about Trump's Washington.

"I'm still trying to navigate this new world," Volker wrote.

"I'm not sure that's a world I want to set foot in," Taylor replied.

He couldn't hesitate for much longer. He needed to pass or commit fully. Otherwise, he would never survive or accomplish anything.

In or out? He still wasn't sure. He hoped to hear from Pompeo soon.

CHAPTER FIVE

High Fives

May 20, Kyiv

Volodymyr Zelensky high-fived cheering fans outside the Ukrainian parliament building as he made his way to his swearing-in as president. The slender 41-year-old, in a dark blue suit and matching tie, bounced among his supporters like a teenager, gleefully jumping up to kiss an older man on his bald head.

He posed for selfies. Hundreds of upraised phones snapped his picture. Then he bounded up the wide steps covered in a red carpet. Guards swung open the massive double doors to the main parliament chamber.

Lawmakers at their desks applauded vigorously as Zelensky walked briskly to the front. There, he placed his right hand on a copy of the Ukrainian constitution and the Peresopnytsia Gospel, a thick and tattered gold-colored religious text from the 16th century, and took the oath of office.

In his first act as head of state, he smiled broadly and announced that he was disbanding parliament. He ordered new elections in two months and demanded that lawmakers strip themselves of their long-standing right to immunity from prosecution. He called on them to remove the head of the security services, the defense minister and the prosecutor general from their posts. If the startled members of the suddenly lame-duck parliament had been wondering whether Zelensky was serious about shaking up the government, they had their answer.

"I really do not want my pictures in your offices. No portraits! A president is not an icon, an idol, or a portrait," Zelensky said. "Put photographs of your children there instead. And before making any decision, look them in the eyes."

The U.S. delegation, led by energy secretary Rick Perry, sat in a reserved section of the chamber, listening through earpieces to the translation of the young president's bold rhetoric. This was not the usual speech. This was a breath of badly needed fresh air in a country rife with corruption. There was even a line that seemed tailored just for them. Quoting "one American actor" who became "a cool American president," Zelensky embraced one of Ronald Reagan's signature statements: "Government is not the solution to our problem; government is the problem."

Zelensky's message was clear. Corruption was his nemesis, the government itself was his target. Marie Yovanovitch had been making much the same arguments in her anti-corruption speeches. She was in Kyiv, packing up to leave with her mother later in the day, but she was not invited. The embassy's number two, Joseph Pennington, was taking her place at the inaugural festivities. In one of her last official acts, she recorded a farewell video for the embassy's social media accounts, pledging that U.S. support would continue for the new Zelensky administration. She made no mention of the circumstances that had led to her ouster.

Yovanovitch's ouster left the U.S. Embassy with no ambassador at this critical moment of transition in the Ukrainian government. Similarly, the delegation list for the inauguration had been in flux for weeks. At first, Vice President Pence was going. Then he wasn't. No one at the NSC or the embassy, working together on the list, was quite sure why.

The date for the inauguration had not been set until four days before, complicating planning efforts. Pence's schedule was tight, as usual, but not even Pence's adviser on Europe, Jennifer Williams, knew whether that was the reason. A White House aide had called a week before the inauguration, informing her that Trump had told Pence not to go. No explanation offered.

Pence's absence bothered Zelensky's team. They had hoped the vice president would be there as a show of Trump's support, in part because Vice President Biden had led the U.S. delegation to Poroshenko's inauguration in 2014. They tried to find out, but no one was saying much beyond the usual reasons—schedules, timing. First, Trump had fired the ambassador. Now this. The relationship wasn't off to a good start. How much had Trump soured on Ukraine? It was worrisome.

David Holmes, a senior adviser at the embassy, had a theory about Pence's pullout. It could be summed up in two words: Rudy Giuliani. Since Zelensky's election in April, Giuliani had been all over the media, making his usual noise about Ukraine, calling on the new president to investigate Joe Biden's son and to find out about any Ukrainian interference in the 2016 U.S. election. Then there was Giuliani's "enemies of the president" comment about the people around Zelensky. That sort of harsh rhetoric made it easy for Trump to tell Pence not to go.

Giuliani had no official U.S. job, but he occupied a dual role that was creating plenty of confusion. His designation in 2017 as a cybersecurity adviser to Trump had been useful for him as he sought and landed consulting gigs abroad, including a contract to help the Ukrainian city of Kharkiv improve emergency services. Then in 2018, his appointment as Trump's personal lawyer had put him in the public eye on a nearly daily basis. Now, when he talked about Ukraine, was he speaking for the president? Himself? Both? Neither the embassy nor the NSC staff could figure it out. In their view, it was maddening, disruptive and a threat to U.S. policy.

Without Pence, without an ambassador, the U.S. delegation to the inauguration was a patchwork arrangement. The final list, whittled down to five, had firepower. But it was less senior than Holmes and others had hoped. Rick Perry took Pence's place. Joining him was Kurt Volker. From the NSC came the council's top Ukraine expert, U.S. Army Lt. Col. Alexander Vindman. Accompanying them, but technically not a delegation member, was Senator Ron Johnson, a Wisconsin Republican and a longtime defender of Ukraine's interests.

Also on the list: Gordon Sondland, the U.S. ambassador to the European Union, a choice that surprised some at the NSC and the embassy. Ukraine wasn't an E.U. member, which meant Sondland had no obvious role. When Sondland's name showed up on the early drafts of the delegation list, the list makers removed him. Sondland made a few phone calls, to State, to Mulvaney's office at the White House. The White House put him back on.

Sondland, Volker and Perry didn't know each other well, but their views on Ukraine aligned, for the most part. They felt the new president needed the Trump administration's strong support to check neighboring Russia. That support required continuing U.S. aid. Anything less would send the wrong signal to Russia.

Volker was hoping they could put a Trump-Zelensky meeting on track. Trump had already suggested one in his April 21 phone call after Zelensky's election. A high-profile visit to the White House, with a coveted sit-down in the Oval Office, would send the right message to Putin.

Before leaving for Kyiv, Vindman had drafted a congratulatory letter from Trump. The idea was for the delegation to deliver it to Zelensky as a show of good relations between the two nations. The draft went up the line for the president's signature, but it never came back. Vindman didn't know what happened, but he suspected it had to do with the anti-Zelensky narrative being pushed by Giuliani.

On Inauguration Day, a brilliantly sunny Monday, the delegation met with U.S. Embassy officials for an 8 a.m. briefing. Giuliani's bashing of Ukraine on TV and social media came up. What was Giuliani's agenda? David Holmes, from the embassy, found Sondland's reaction memorable. "Dammit. Rudy," Sondland said. "Every time Rudy gets involved, he goes and fucks everything up."

At the parliament building, the delegation arrived to find crowds, camaraderie and a collection of foreign dignitaries. Putin was not among them. The Russian president, who saw Zelensky as a new and more vocal opponent in the regional power struggle, gave no sign that he was ready to compromise. Putin's spokesman pointedly asserted that Crimea, which Russia had seized by military force in 2014, was "a region of Russia."

Now, in his inaugural address, Zelensky said that ending the war in eastern Ukraine was his top priority. He would "make the fire stop." But he would not cede territory to Russia to do so. Those lands belonged to Ukraine, and they must be returned to Ukraine, he said. He promised to find a way. "I am ready to lose my popularity, my ratings and—if need be—I am ready to lose this post in order to bring peace."

The parliament came to its feet, cheering, applauding. The parliament he had just fired. It was a surreal moment. Zelensky closed by trying to lift Ukraine's spirits. "All my life I tried to do all I could so that Ukrainians laughed. That was my mission," he said. "Now I will do all I can so that Ukrainians, at least, do not cry anymore."

The U.S. delegation was caught up in the bright, shiny Zelensky moment. "The United States will stand with the people of Ukraine," Perry said at a press conference after the ceremony. "America is here to send a clear message. The president of the United States has asked us to come, to share with the people of Ukraine, that they can count on the United States, count on working with this president."

Outside the parliament building, the U.S. officials gathered with Zelensky and his wife for an official photo. They stood on a red carpet, in the glare of the sunlight. Zelensky, eager for U.S. support, held a private session with the delegation. Perry came with a list of people he trusted in the energy industry. He encouraged Zelensky to consult with them.

Vindman offered Zelensky two bits of advice. Both were warnings. Beware of Russia, he said. Be even more alert than you already are. Also, stay out of U.S. domestic politics. Beware of "nongovernmental actors" asking you to investigate anything. He did not mention any names.

The U.S. delegation members came away impressed. Vindman saw the new president as a willing partner who would root out corruption, lock in reforms and allow Ukraine to prosper. Volker agreed. He thought Zelensky was genuinely interested in taking Ukraine in a new direction. Sondland found him articulate, funny, charming, smart and energetic. An outsider unafraid of entrenched government power. The kind of guy who would have good chemistry with Trump.

They planned to tell the president just that when they returned to Washington.

CHAPTER SIX

The I-Word

May 22, Washington

Nancy Pelosi called a caucus meeting for 9 a.m. on Wednesday, May 22. Impeachment was gaining ground. She had to put up a stop sign.

On Monday night, at the weekly strategy session with her senior leadership team, four members of Jerry Nadler's Judiciary Committee had come at her with a full-court press, arguing that the committee should open a formal impeachment inquiry. She had resisted. A few hours later, Nadler himself had buttonholed her, making his case, lobbying hard.

Give us the green light, Nadler said. Trump is impeding our efforts to follow up on the Mueller report. The committee could go to court, asking for help in enforcing its subpoenas, but that could take months. Opening a formal impeachment inquiry, invoking the House's constitutional powers, could be the best way to obtain the documents and get testimony that Trump was blocking.

Pelosi said no. Too soon, she said. Too risky. Too far ahead of the public. The other committees were making progress in their investigations, and that was the way to go. Earlier in the day, a federal judge had ruled against Trump in a lawsuit, upholding a subpoena issued by the House Committee for Oversight and Reform, which was looking into the president's financial dealings. Keep investigating, Pelosi told Nadler. Let the court battles play out.

Nadler had retreated, grumbling. So had the others. They were a minority, still small, no more than three dozen, if that. But Pelosi needed to prick the balloon before it grew any larger.

Now, facing the full caucus in the windowless meeting room known simply as HC5, she turned to her trusted senior leaders to make the case. Five were particularly key: Steny Hoyer and Elijah Cummings of Maryland, James Clyburn of South Carolina, Eliot Engel of New York and John Lewis of Georgia. Arrayed before them, on simple mesh-backed chairs with no armrests, sat close to 200 people with varying loyalties and agendas.

Empty, the room seemed spacious, row after row of 20 seats across, divided by a narrow aisle. Full, it felt cramped. Outside, it was lovely May weather, clear skies, temperatures heading toward 73 degrees. But HC5 was underground, and there was a restless current running through the room as the senior leaders repeated Pelosi's message: Keep investigating. Keep accumulating evidence. Until we know more, until we can show more, talk of impeachment is premature.

These five had a special kind of cred to make that argument. They had been here before, 20 years ago. The five had stood, with dozens of other Democrats, behind President Bill Clinton on the White House lawn on that December day in 1998 when the Republican-controlled House had voted to impeach him. They knew how it felt—the despair, the irrevocable rift. "It tore the country apart" was how House member Anna G. Eshoo of California remembered it.

Eshoo was a Pelosi loyalist to the core. They were close in age, Eshoo just two years younger, and closer as friends. The two usually agreed on matters of policy and politics. Together, they had watched and learned from Clinton's impeachment.

In 1998, the public clearly understood the case against Clinton revolved around an extramarital affair and lying under oath to cover it up. A crime, perhaps, but the Democrats had argued it wasn't a high crime, certainly not the kind that merited impeachment and removal. Clinton was acquitted by the Republican-controlled Senate, with a handful of GOP senators defecting to the Democrats on one of the two impeachment articles. Now House Democrats were trying to piece together a case from the Mueller report, which wasn't conclusive in many of its findings. Building public support would take time, if it could be built at all. Pelosi was right, Eshoo felt. They needed to tap the brakes. It's very difficult to un-ring a bell, she thought.

Pelosi's stance was shaped by the voter backlash that greeted Republicans in 1998. Weeks after opening their formal impeachment inquiry of Clinton, the Republicans had fared badly in the midterm elections. The Democrats had gained five House seats, hardly a windfall, but the opposite of the historical pattern: An incumbent president's party, in a second term, generally loses seats—often, quite a lot of them.

At the caucus meeting, Pelosi hammered home the point that the public had to be with you for impeachment to work. She believed that the public would never support a strictly partisan impeachment, or one over a policy disagreement. That's a key reason she had opposed calls from antiwar liberals to impeach Republican president George W. Bush for his handling of the Iraq War.

Pelosi knew these arguments were unlikely to sway the caucus's most progressive members, including Alexandria Ocasio-Cortez of the Bronx. AOC, as she was known to her legion of fans on social media, had already ensured a place for herself in congressional history. At 29, she had become the youngest woman ever elected to the House. Not only that, she got there by knocking off a powerful House leader in her 2018 primary. She had defeated Joe Crowley, the Democratic caucus chair, a ten-termer widely regarded as a possible speaker.

Since arriving in Washington, Ocasio-Cortez had been treating other party elders with the same deference she had shown Crowley—speaking her mind, demanding change, pushing, pushing, pushing from the left. But she wasn't a gadfly. She had not joined the small movement advocating for someone other than Pelosi in the speaker's chair, saying in a November 21 tweet that included a clever qualifier: "All the challenges to Leader Pelosi are coming from her right, in an apparent effort to make the party even more conservative and bent toward corporate interests. Hard pass. As long as Leader Pelosi remains the most progressive candidate for Speaker, she can count on my support."

On the day of the Mueller report's release in April, Ocasio-Cortez put herself firmly on the record as pro-impeachment. The day before the caucus meeting, after Trump had blocked former White House counsel Don McGahn from testifying before the House Judiciary Committee, she retweeted another progressive House member's call for impeachment and added: "It is just as politicized a maneuver to not impeach in the face of overwhelming evidence as it is to impeach w/o cause. Congress swore an oath to uphold the Constitution. That includes impeachment."

Now, as Pelosi and her leadership team took questions, Ocasio-Cortez spoke up. The "only thing" that gave her pause, she said, was the Senate. She knew impeachment would die there. But that wasn't a reason for the House to shy away from doing what was necessary and right.

Pelosi's cautious counsel also wasn't swaying David Cicilline of Rhode Island, a junior member of her leadership team. Cicilline wasn't a newcomer to politics. He had served eight years as mayor of Providence and was now in his fifth congressional term. He wanted an impeachment inquiry. Listening to the debate at the meeting helped clarify his thinking. "We need to vindicate the rule of law in this country and demonstrate that you cannot just trash the Constitution," he said afterward, "and expect the Congress of the United States to accept that."

The agitation from her left was a concern for Pelosi, but for the moment, it was no threat to her leadership. After the brief challenge to her candidacy for speaker had fizzled, she had managed to unify and solidify her grip on the caucus. Republicans had helped by painting her as the enemy, a liberal bogeyman. And whatever doubts remained about her leadership abilities, most had been washed away in January, when she had outplayed Trump over a lengthy government shutdown.

So when Pelosi argued to the caucus that the court battles were moving in the Democrats' direction, that it was time to be patient, she had a clear majority on her side. No impeachment. Not yet anyway. Trump was still not worth it.

After the meeting, NBC's Kasie Hunt grabbed Ocasio-Cortez for a brief interview, curious about the pro-impeachment faction's reaction.

"Are you satisfied with what leadership had to say?" Hunt asked.

"You know, I think," Ocasio-Cortez said, "I was satisfied with the openness of the conversation and the discourse that we're having as a caucus."

Pelosi stepped to the microphones, staying on message. "It was a very positive meeting, a respectful sharing of ideas and a very impressive presentation by our chairs. We do believe it's important to follow the facts, we believe that no one is above the law, including the president of the United States."

Then she dropped a verbal hand grenade. The recent victories for the Democrats in court, she said, demonstrated something damning about the president. "We believe that the president of the United States is engaged in a cover-up—in a cover-up."

The statement was intentional, not improvised. She was making a point. Her caucus was under control, but many were angry. She was venting that anger for them, in arresting language that she hadn't used before.

An hour later, Pelosi and Chuck Schumer arrived at the White House for talks with Trump about infrastructure. Despite the bad blood over the Mueller report, the leaders on both sides were looking for a deal that would put massive new investment in the nation's crumbling roads, bridges and airports. It was necessary, it was important, it had public support.

Today's agenda was to discuss how to pay the huge tab, or the "pay fors" in legislative shorthand. Pelosi and Schumer suspected that Trump didn't have his "pay fors" lined up, and that they wouldn't be making much progress. They were seated at the Cabinet Room's long conference table when Trump walked in, a few minutes late. He didn't bother to sit down. He was on a tear, steamed up over Pelosi's "cover-up" remark.

He stood at the end of the table, making no move toward his regular seat in the middle. "I want to do infrastructure. I want to do it more than you want to do it. I'd be really good at that, that's what I do," he said. "But you know what? You can't do it under these circumstances. So get these phony investigations over with."

He then walked out, without giving anyone else a chance to speak. Pelosi thought to herself: This was a waste of time. Back on Capitol Hill, she told reporters that Trump had a "temper tantrum" and then said: "I pray for the president of the United States, and I pray for the United States of America."

Still fuming, the president bounded into an impromptu press conference in the Rose Garden. "Instead of walking in happily into a meeting, I walk in to look at people that have just said that I was doing a cover-up," he said. "I don't do cover-ups."

He threw in some choice remarks about Pelosi's morning meeting with her caucus. "All of a sudden I hear last night they're going to have a meeting right before this meeting to talk about the 'I-word.' The 'I-word.' Can you imagine?"

His anger flowed into his Twitter account. At 1 p.m. came a four-part series of tweets. "So sad that Nancy Pelosi and Chuck Schumer will never be able to see or understand the great promise of our Country. They can continue the Witch Hunt which has already cost $40M and been a tremendous waste of time and energy for everyone in America. . . . You can't investigate and legislate simultaneously—it just doesn't work that way."

The last of the thread was aimed directly at Pelosi. "Democrat leadership is tearing the United States apart, but I will continue to set records for the American People—and Nancy, thank you so much for your prayers, I know you truly mean it!"

• • •

After Trump's dramatic exit, Pelosi was the headline speaker at an afternoon event hosted by the Center for American Progress, a progressive think tank.

The center's director, Neera Tanden, was acting as moderator, but Pelosi didn't need much prompting. She called her meeting with Trump "very, very, very strange," which got the progressive crowd laughing. She described the various court challenges, the battle over the president's financial records at Deutsche Bank and his continued refusal to turn over his tax returns. She said he was ignoring subpoenas from Congress, which had been one of the articles of impeachment against Nixon in 1974. "In plain sight, in the public domain, this president is obstructing justice and is engaged in a cover-up," she said. "And that could be an impeachable offense."

The crowd applauded loudly. But reporters at the event were confused: Now Pelosi is dropping the I-word, the word she was trying to tamp down? Is she holding the caucus back, or pushing it ahead? What's going on here?

The day's rhetorical fireworks lit up the political echo chambers. Trump's retort to Pelosi—"I don't do cover-ups"—became the basis for a mini-meme, generating a flood of references to the $130,000 in hush money paid to adult-film star Stormy Daniels. A popular version included an image of one $35,000 Trump check to his former lawyer, Michael Cohen, who acted as middleman for the Daniels transaction.

On the conservative side, it was Pelosi's dropping of the I-word and her repeated use of "cover-up" that dominated talk shows and Twitter. On Fox News, Republican representative Andy Biggs of Arizona said Pelosi "threw gas on the fire" with her language. Biggs said she was "trying to incite and mollify, quite frankly, her base and those in her caucus who want an impeachment hearing."

Lou Dobbs, one of Trump's most passionate defenders on Fox, teed off on the Democrats during his evening show. "Nancy Pelosi, Chuck Schumer, Adam Schiff, Jerry Nadler and the rest of the radical Dimms leading the Democratic Party into the abyss with their coarse, vapid and vile politics . . . The Dimms are no longer borderline evil. They've crossed that line. And with Nancy Pelosi's senseless baseless claims today, among which that the president is involved in a cover-up, she's consigned her party to futility and failure in 2020."

A few hours later, just before 10:30 p.m., Trump tweeted his last Pelosi volley of the evening. "In a letter to her House colleagues, Nancy Pelosi said: 'President Trump had a temper tantrum for us all to see.' This is not true. I was purposely very polite and calm, much as I was minutes later with the press in the Rose Garden. Can be easily proven. It is all such a lie!"

CHAPTER SEVEN

"They Tried to Take Me Down!"

May 23, Washington

Drew Harwell, a *Washington Post* reporter specializing in coverage of the digital world, was at home in Silver Spring, Maryland, early on Thursday morning, May 23, sifting through his overnight emails. One caught his still-sleepy eyes.

A tipster had written from the West Coast, saying he had come across something odd. It was a video of Nancy Pelosi posted online. She was giving a talk, and she seemed drunk. The tipster suspected the clip was a fake. Googling for reporters with a track record for writing about doctored videos, he had found Harwell's name.

Take a look, he urged Harwell.

Harwell clicked.

The video was of Pelosi's appearance the day before at the Center for American Progress. A moderator was asking her questions. Many reporters were there, listening as she said Donald Trump's refusal to cooperate with House investigators amounted to a "cover-up" that "could be an impeachable offense."

Harwell listened now, too. She did sound drunk, just as the tipster had said. She was slurring phrases, "the United Schtates of Uh-merica." But it was so blatant that Harwell thought it couldn't possibly be authentic. Wouldn't somebody in the press have noticed if the Speaker of the House had shown up in such a dreadful state? Especially while accusing the president of a cover-up? Everything pointed to a fake.

Politics wasn't Harwell's beat. But he had been reading the recent news stories about Pelosi and her impeachment balancing act. Was the video a political dirty trick, an attempt to undermine her credibility when she needed to be at the top of her game?

Still in his sweatpants, Harwell began thinking through his next steps. First and most important: Was the video already circulating widely? That was his baseline criterion for investigating doctored videos. Why give oxygen to something no one had seen?

Harwell had been down these digital pathways before. In November 2018, White House press secretary Sarah Huckabee Sanders had shared a video online of CNN White House reporter Jim Acosta at that day's briefing. Acosta was pressing for an answer to his questions, using a handheld microphone, and a young White House aide had come over to take it away. Their arms collided as Acosta fended off her reach for the mic. Working with experts at *The Post* and elsewhere, Harwell discovered that the version had been altered by someone—slowed down, and a few frames copied and added—to make Acosta seem more aggressive.

That story had put Harwell on the radar of tipsters who wanted to alert him to other fakes. The Pelosi video merited more scrutiny. As with the Acosta video, it would be easy enough to find C-SPAN's recording for comparison.

It wasn't yet 7:30 a.m. when Harwell started his digital dive. Checking Facebook, he saw the questionable video on multiple pages. On one, run by a conservative site called Politics WatchDog, the video already had nearly a million views. Enough to keep going, Harwell thought.

He watched the C-SPAN version. Pelosi sounded normal. He adjusted the playback speed to 75 percent, an option while using YouTube. Bingo. Pelosi sounded like she had in the other video. Harwell forwarded the link to several forensic experts he knew from earlier stories. He sent queries to YouTube, Facebook, Twitter and Google, seeking comment. Around the same time, one of the experts got back to him. No doubt. The video had been deliberately doctored.

Harwell messaged Elyse Samuels, a colleague on *The Washington Post* video team. Samuels was a whiz at analyzing video. She determined that, as Harwell had suspected, the speed had been slowed to about 75 percent. But that wasn't all, she told him. To correct for how the speed change would deepen the tone of Pelosi's voice, the video had been altered to modify her pitch. It was simple to do. No high-tech wizardry required.

One key question remained: Was it a political smear? Maybe it was just somebody trying to be funny. But if politics wasn't part of the agenda, why choose Pelosi to mock? Logically, it seemed safe to say that the person wasn't a Pelosi fan. And that "somebody" was placing the fake video on message boards and regional news sites. The original tipster had emailed back, saying he had seen it on the *Oregonian* newspaper's site, in the comments section of all places.

Whatever the motive, Harwell thought, the episode showed how even simple, crude manipulations could move quickly through the digital ecosystem. Soon, people who hadn't even seen the video would be saying: Did you hear about Nancy Pelosi? How she was drunk at a speech?

As his editor had said when Harwell alerted him, this was turning out to be a good story.

While Harwell was chasing down the origins of the doctored video, Pelosi was back on the public stage, holding her weekly news conference on Capitol Hill.

After taking the "I" word for a test drive at her Center for American Progress talk, after Trump's storming out of their meeting on infrastructure, Pelosi was expecting a larger-than-usual crowd of reporters with tougher-than-usual questions. A C-SPAN camera crew was there, of course.

She primed the pump, using the word "cover-up" again, just as she had the day before. She brought up Trump's walkout, calling it a "temper tantrum" and a "stunt," part of his "bag of tricks" to divert attention from his many problems.

Cover-up. That word again, echoes of the Nixon Watergate scandal. Was this Pelosi's not-so-subtle way of indicating a shift from no, he's not worth it, to hold on, I might be changing my mind? Or was this that favorite Washington gambit, a trial balloon, to see how the public might react? Or was this just more of the same, another Pelosi attempt to appease those in her caucus who were demanding that she push the "I" button?

The reporters were keen to ask. But before they had their chance, Pelosi said, "The House Democratic Caucus is not on a path to impeachment." Then, in the same breath, she offered a new and provocative explanation for her resistance. Impeachment was what Trump wanted, she claimed. Impeachment was part of his reelection strategy. Impeachment would allow him to play the victim, knowing the Senate would never vote to convict him. By not taking the bait, Pelosi was thwarting his plan.

"That's where he wants us to be," she said.

When the time came for questions, the reporters aimed directly at her subtle shifts in position. "Yesterday you said that the president may have engaged in impeachable offenses," one said. "Yet today, you're saying you're not on a path to impeachment. Can you explain why you're opposed to launching an impeachment inquiry that many of your members want to do?"

Pelosi maneuvered around the question, circling it, addressing both sides. "Let me be really, very clear. The president's behavior in terms of his obstruction of justice, the things that he is doing, it's very clear, it's in plain sight, it cannot be denied. Ignoring subpoenas, obstruction of justice. Yes, these could be impeachable offenses."

But investigation was the best route for now, she said. "Impeachment is a very divisive place to go in our country. And what—we can get the facts to the American people through our investigation, it may take us to a place that is unavoidable in terms of impeachment, or not. But we're not at that place."

Pelosi had a plan. She had told her aides: She wanted to deliberately wind Trump up. Let him reveal himself as erratic and volatile. At the end of her prepared remarks, she said: "Again, I pray for the president of the United States. I wish that his family or his administration or his staff would have an intervention for the good of the country." Calling for an "intervention" would get a rise out of him, no doubt.

It didn't take long. A few hours later, Trump turned a White House event on federal aid to farmers into a fuming gripe session about Nancy Pelosi. He said her family intervention remark was "a nasty-type statement." He said she had "lost it" mentally. He suggested that a new North American trade deal under negotiation was too complicated for her to understand. He denied that he wanted to be impeached.

Trump loved insulting schoolyard nicknames, like "Cryin' Chuck" Schumer and "Crooked Hillary." But he hadn't come up with a keeper for Pelosi. He made a stab with "Crazy Nancy," but then immediately told the reporters, "I don't want to say that, because then you'll say it's a copy of 'Crazy Bernie,' " his moniker for Democratic presidential candidate Bernie Sanders of Vermont.

He said he was certain about one thing, though. Pelosi had changed. "I've been watching her for a long period of time. She's not the same person."

Something about Pelosi seemed to bug him. Perhaps he was frustrated that his verbal blows seemed to land on her like so many downy feathers. Perhaps he found her harder to deal with because she was a woman. Whatever it was, she needed to use it to her advantage.

For the moment, she had Trump red in the face and her caucus under control. Not a bad place to be. For the moment.

As Pelosi was talking to reporters at the Capitol, four men sat in the Oval Office, talking to Trump about their trip to Ukraine for the Zelensky inauguration three days earlier. It wasn't going well.

Gordon Sondland was settled in one armchair. Next to him, getting more uncomfortable by the minute, were Rick Perry, Volker and Senator Ron Johnson. Sondland could hear White House aides coming and going behind him, but he wasn't registering who was there. He was too focused on the problem right in front of him: a very unhappy-looking president of the United States.

Sondland and the others had arranged the meeting. They had wanted to give Trump a report on the inauguration trip and promote Ukraine's new president as a corruption-buster worthy of Trump's support. But they had barely sat down when Trump interrupted. He wasn't buying it. He wasn't interested. The Ukrainians were not on his list of favorite people.

"They were out to get me," he said. "They tried to take me down."

Trump railed on, complaining about Ukrainian deceit and treachery. "Horrible, corrupt people," he said. Sondland was alarmed. So was Volker. Their goal of arranging a Trump-Zelensky meeting was in trouble. Trump doesn't want anything to do with Ukraine, Sondland thought. His hostility is deep and intense.

The problem was quickly apparent to him and Volker. They were too late. Others had the president's attention on Ukraine, including Rudy Giuliani, who was peddling an ominous, darker story: that Ukraine's new president was one more bad guy, with bad people around him, bent on doing bad things.

"Talk to Rudy," Trump told them. "Rudy knows."

Rudy. Rudy. Rudy. Everything seemed to come back to Giuliani.

Now, with Trump saying, "Rudy knows," Sondland was realizing that Giuliani wasn't some rogue actor. He was Trump's eyes and ears. If the "Three Amigos"—as Sondland had jokingly referred to himself, Perry and Volker—had any hope of changing the Ukraine narrative, they would have to talk to Rudy, Sondland thought.

But first, they needed to emerge from the meeting with something they could use to repair the damage Giuliani was doing. Sondland could see that it wasn't going to be easy. Trump was repeating himself, like a needle stuck on an old-fashioned record album. "They tried to take me down," he was saying. "Terrible people."

Volker saw an opening. Instead of arguing, he told Trump: You're right. Ukraine has long been a terrible place. Corruption is endemic. Zelensky agrees with you. He ran on a campaign to clean it up, and that's why he won. It won't be easy. He'll meet with fierce and powerful resistance. That's why he needs your support. He can't do it alone.

For two years, Volker had been serving as Trump's special envoy to Ukraine, with a mission to help the country in its hostile standoff with Russia. He had the most Ukraine experience in the room, and he leaned on that credibility now. He described Zelensky as Ukraine's best chance in 20 years to break the grip of corruption that had held the country back since winning its independence from Russia.

Volker had only met Trump in person once before. It wasn't a positive experience. In September 2017, Trump was scheduled for a talk with then–Ukrainian president Petro Poroshenko at the U.N. General Assembly in New York. Before the meeting, Volker wanted to persuade Trump that Ukraine was worthy of U.S. support. For months, Trump had been making clear that he wanted a better rapport with Russia. Volker feared that Trump's overtures toward Putin might mean sacrificing good relations with Ukraine.

Just before Trump's arrival then secretary of state Rex Tillerson told Volker that he should expect about 45 seconds to grab the president's interest. Volker had been hoping for 15 minutes. He rushed through his pitch. Trump's impatient reply sounded, to Volker, like talking points from Putin's script.

Trump argued that Ukraine was really part of Russia, that most Ukrainians wanted to have a close relationship with Moscow, that the country was "totally corrupt," more a kleptocracy than a democracy. Volker knew enough not to contradict the president. "You're making some good points, sir," he told Trump, and then tried to steer the conversation in a more pro-Ukraine direction.

Now, in the Oval Office, Volker could see that the president's skepticism of Ukraine had only hardened. To Volker, Trump's antagonistic stance made no sense. The administration's strong support of Ukraine, which had bipartisan backing, had been a foreign policy success story for Trump. The election of Zelensky, a charismatic, pro-Western leader, suggested that even better days lay ahead.

"This is a new crowd," Volker told Trump. "This guy is different."

"That's not what I hear," Trump said. "I hear he's got some terrible people around him."

The amigos tried different tacks, taking turns. Sondland told Trump he was excited about Zelensky, about his team. Perry and Volker stressed Ukraine's strategic importance in the region. But nothing was working. "Talk to Rudy," Trump said. Sondland felt himself getting pissed off.

Senator Johnson felt he was in the strongest position to push back on Trump's views. He was the only person in the delegation who did not work for the president. He stressed that no one was asking the president to support corrupt oligarchs and politicians. He told Trump: Look, you and Zelensky have a lot in common. Like you, Zelensky is a political newcomer facing strong resistance from entrenched interests, both outside and inside government. A reference to the deep state never hurt with Trump.

Looking for a way forward, Johnson asked Trump if he could keep his reservations about Ukraine private until he met with Zelensky. Trump agreed, but said he wanted Zelensky to know exactly how he felt about corruption in his country before arranging any sort of visit. As they got up to leave after about 20 minutes, Sondland didn't know where they stood. Maybe Trump would make a phone call to Zelensky. Maybe not. Maybe he would be willing to meet with Zelensky at some point. Maybe not.

There was only one clear directive. "Talk to Rudy," Trump said. Rudy would set them straight.

Sondland didn't like the idea of involving Giuliani. He thought the State Department should be carrying out Trump's policy in Ukraine. He didn't understand why the president's personal lawyer should be involved at all. But Trump didn't trust his own diplomats and analysts, just like he didn't trust much of the FBI or the Department of Justice. Sondland resigned himself to the idea that serving the interests of the United States, and a president he admired, meant talking to Rudy.

The meeting was most jarring for Volker, who knew Ukraine so well and U.S. foreign policy in the region. Perry was a former governor of

Texas. Sondland was a wealthy hotelier who got his job because he was a Trump megadonor. Johnson had a keen interest in Ukraine, but his background was running a business in Wisconsin before being elected to Congress. Volker had worked as a CIA analyst, had spent years in Europe as a diplomat and had served as U.S. ambassador to NATO.

Volker had two options, he told himself. He could ignore the problem, at the expense of U.S. policy and Ukraine. Or he could try to fix it. Not much of a choice, he felt. He would talk to Giuliani. People at the State Department and the NSC would be furious. They would tell him, no, that's crazy, it can't work, the Ukrainians won't understand what's going on, we don't need Giuliani and his irregular channel.

But Volker had convinced himself that it was the only way to go. Yes, it was risky. Yes, it was unorthodox. What else could they do?

He didn't share with Bill Taylor any details from the Oval Office meeting. That would have ended any possibility of Taylor taking the Kyiv job. Better to wait for Taylor to talk with Pompeo. A conversation with the secretary wouldn't satisfy all of Taylor's concerns, but it might get him to yes. Volker hoped Taylor could be turned around. If they were going to contain Giuliani, it would be important to have a like-minded ally at the embassy.

Even as Harwell was preparing his story about the "drunk" Pelosi video, word about it was spreading. Rudy Giuliani had tweeted a link to it, asking: "What is wrong with Nancy Pelosi? Her speech pattern is bizarre." Giuliani eventually deleted the tweet, but his original message was clear evidence that the video was being seen in conservative circles.

Later on Thursday, President Trump tweeted a different video taken from the Fox Business Network, a selectively edited clip focused on Pelosi's pauses and verbal stumbles. The two videos fed into what Pelosi's defenders have called sexist and conspiratorial portrayals of the health of America's highest-ranking elected woman. They also resembled political videos that posed similar questions about Hillary Clinton's fitness in 2016.

Just before 3 p.m., not quite eight hours after Harwell had first seen the tip, his story went online, along with side-to-side clips of the original video and the doctored one. His queries to officials at YouTube, Twitter and Facebook had produced widely different responses. YouTube immediately removed the videos because they violated "clear policies that outline what content is not acceptable to post." Twitter did not take the video down. The company declined to comment, but its published policies permitted "inaccurate statements about an elected official" as long as they didn't include efforts at election manipulation.

Facebook declined to remove the video, even after its own independent fact-checking groups, Lead Stories and PolitiFact, had deemed the video to be fake. "We don't have a policy that stipulates that the information you post on Facebook must be true," Facebook said in a statement. The company said it would "heavily reduce" the video's appearances in people's news feeds and append an informational box with links to the fact-check sites.

Pelosi herself didn't raise much of a fuss about the fakes. She was used to online assaults. There was probably not much use in fighting them anyway. After Facebook decided not to pull the fake video, Facebook groups kept promoting it. The Politics WatchDog page hosted a user poll with the question: "Should Pelosi video be taken down?" When a majority voted no, the page's administrator wrote, "The people have spoken. Video stays."

That was posted alongside an emoji of a wineglass.

CHAPTER EIGHT

"I Think Your Boss Doesn't Like Ukraine"

May 28 to June 4, Washington and Brussels

On May 28, Bill Taylor drove the five miles from his home in Arlington to State Department headquarters in Foggy Bottom, not far from the Lincoln Memorial. It was a drive he had made hundreds, if not thousands, of times before. This trip was particularly important. Secretary Pompeo had agreed to see him to discuss the ambassador's job in Kyiv. As Taylor navigated Washington traffic, the reservations he had been hashing over for weeks were buzzing in his head. Soon, he would have to decide: in or out?

Taylor arrived alone, took the elevator to the seventh floor and was escorted into a conference room next to the secretary's office. Soon he was joined by Kurt Volker, Pompeo adviser Ulrich Brechbuhl and finally by Pompeo. Suspecting he wouldn't have much time with them, Taylor wasted none of it. He laid out his worries, including his fear that Trump was going to abandon the administration's strong support of Kyiv in pursuit of a deal with Putin.

"I think your boss doesn't like Ukraine," Taylor told Pompeo.

The secretary acted as though he had been expecting that. In public, Pompeo could come across as hotheaded and defensive. Privately with Taylor, he was calm and confident.

"Bill, you're right," the secretary said. "And it's my job to turn him around."

Taylor liked the sound of that. He hadn't known what to expect, but he had hoped Pompeo might listen. They were both West Point alums, 17 years apart. Both had excelled in engineering; the younger Pompeo had ranked first in his class and Taylor had finished fifth.

Pompeo used a physics equation, their common language, to explain his strategy for handling Trump on Ukraine: "Force equals pressure over a period of time." In other words, he would continue to make the case, and eventually, he would bring Trump around.

Sitting across from the secretary, Taylor knew that the equation was "force equals pressure times area," but he kept his mouth shut. He understood what Pompeo was telling him. He asked about the congratulatory letter to Zelensky that Trump had refused to sign, saying he was told the president had torn it up.

"I hadn't heard about that," Pompeo told Taylor. He turned to Brechbuhl. "Find out about this," Pompeo said, then promised he would do his best to get a letter signed as soon as possible.

Taylor was encouraged. Coming into the meeting, he had been skeptical of Pompeo, who had remained largely silent when Giuliani and his crowd had been bashing Marie Yovanovitch. Taylor could hear his wife Deborah's words still ringing in his ears: "What makes you think they won't do to you what they did to Masha?"

But this face-to-face discussion was giving Taylor a more nuanced impression of the secretary. The more they talked, the more he was convinced that they agreed on the fundamentals, that the best way to counter Russia was to maintain strong support for Zelensky.

Pompeo was saying what Taylor needed to hear, but he also heard caveats. He sensed that Pompeo needed to protect his relationship with Trump, who could be mercurial and vindictive. The secretary didn't have a free hand. Taylor felt Pompeo would be limited in what he could say and do publicly on Taylor's behalf if Giuliani and others turned against him. If Trump were to abandon Ukraine in favor of a rapprochement with Putin and Russia, Taylor told Pompeo, he would have to quit. They shook hands. Pompeo didn't demand an answer on the spot. As Taylor drove home across the Potomac River, he found himself leaning toward taking the job—and taking the risks.

A day or so later, Taylor learned that Pompeo had prevailed on Trump to sign a new congratulatory letter for Zelensky, promising a White House meeting at some undetermined date. The May 29 letter was a good start, Taylor hoped, in a new chapter in Trump's relations with Zelensky and Ukraine.

It was also a lesson for Taylor in how Trump's Washington worked. Pompeo hadn't worked through John Bolton and the usual National Security Council channels. Trump's signature on that letter was the result of a process that Taylor still didn't quite understand. But now it was the world he was walking into, with eyes wide open.

A few days later, Taylor returned to the State Department and picked up Trump's letter to Zelensky, tucked into a manila envelope. The Ukrainians had already received an electronic copy, but Taylor wanted one he could deliver when he arrived in Kyiv in a few weeks. By then, he hoped, a date for the White House meeting would be set.

It would be a good start to his return to the ambassador's role.

Late in May, Diana Pilipenko, an investigator for the Democratic staff of the House Intelligence Committee, was working with her colleagues on a memo for their boss, chairman Adam Schiff. For weeks, she had been scouring Ukrainian and Russian news sites, YouTube channels, social media, any news sources that mentioned Rudy Giuliani and Ukraine. The committee was trying to figure out Giuliani's agenda, go deeper. He was the president's lawyer for the Mueller investigation. That was over. Now what was he up to?

Pilipenko had been hired by the committee because of her Russian language fluency and expertise in tracking illicit international financing. But she happened to have been born in Ukraine, and her ability to speak and read Ukrainian was a fortuitous break. For months, she and other committee investigators had been largely focused on Trump's business activity related to Moscow, including discussions about a proposed Trump Tower that was never built.

They had been aware that Giuliani was making noise about Ukraine, but a May 9 article in the *New York Times* by Kenneth P. Vogel really caught their attention. It was headlined, "Rudy Giuliani Plans Ukraine Trip to Push for Inquiries That Could Help Trump." It said Trump's personal lawyer "is encouraging Ukraine to wade further into sensitive political issues in the United States, seeking to push the incoming government in Kiev to press ahead with investigations that he hopes will benefit Mr. Trump." The article also said Giuliani planned to travel to Kyiv "to meet with the nation's president-elect to urge him to pursue inquiries" about "two matters of intense interest to Mr. Trump."

Giuliani's agenda sounded crazy. The president's lawyer was to meet a foreign leader and press him to meddle in U.S. politics for Trump's benefit? Hard to believe, but this was straight from Giuliani's own mouth. According to the article, Giuliani was looking into whether Ukrainians had secretly worked to help Hillary Clinton's 2016 campaign, as well as Hunter Biden's role with the Burisma gas company, for which he was paid $50,000 or more a month.

"There's nothing illegal about it," Giuliani said of his planned trip. "Somebody could say it's improper. And this isn't foreign policy—I'm asking them to do an investigation that they're doing already, and that other people are telling them to stop. And I'm going to give them reasons why they shouldn't stop it because that information will be very, very helpful to my client, and may turn out to be helpful to my government."

The article was raising all kinds of questions and red flags for the committee staff. Pilipenko was well suited to look for the answers. Before joining Schiff's team, she had worked on money-laundering and anti-corruption cases at Deloitte, the huge accounting firm, and the Center for American Progress, a progressive D.C. think tank. Her master's degree from Harvard had focused on Russia, Eastern Europe and Central Asia.

The Giuliani connection wasn't new to Pilipenko and her colleagues. They had seen the John Solomon stories in *The Hill* that first aired Lutsenko's allegations, and they had noticed that Giuliani had been appearing on Fox News and elsewhere to unload on Ukraine, the Bidens, the Clintons, Marie Yovanovitch and the Mueller probe. On May 1 in the *Times*, Vogel had published an in-depth story about Hunter Biden and Burisma, noting Giuliani's role in pushing the media to write about it.

The staff's memo on Giuliani's Ukraine activity kept getting longer. The idea was to help Schiff understand Ukraine's complicated political landscape and how Giuliani might be working it. Pilipenko found and translated articles in the Ukrainian press that mentioned Giuliani. The staff knew that in memos for the boss, the more detail the better. This was his method, his way of absorbing information.

Schiff, who was about to turn 59, had made a career of untangling complex plots. After law school at Harvard and a clerkship for a federal judge in Los Angeles, he had served as an assistant U.S. attorney for six years. He led the prosecution of Richard W. Miller, the first FBI agent ever to be indicted on a charge of espionage, who was eventually convicted of trading classified documents to the Soviet Union for gold and cash.

That sort of case—intricate, complicated, challenging—appealed to Schiff. He liked working on these puzzles better than running for office. As the chairman of the Intelligence Committee, he could marshal the resources to conduct an investigation of consequence. He wasn't yet sure whether Ukraine qualified, but the completed memo intrigued him. He read it again, then set it aside, then read it again.

Schiff told his people, already working seven days a week, to keep digging.

Volodymyr Zelensky's first foreign trip as Ukraine's president was not to America, as he had hoped, but it sure looked like it. On June 4, he joined a gala Fourth of July celebration, hosted by E.U. ambassador Gordon Sondland in Brussels. It was a lavish Yankee Doodle Dandy affair with European Union flourishes.

That this Independence Day–themed party was being held a month early didn't seem to matter. Hundreds of guests milled around Autoworld, a cavernous Brussels museum filled with antique cars. The food stations featured all-American fare: pizza, hamburgers and fries and Jelly Belly dispensers filled with lime, cherry and tutti-frutti flavors. Servers in red-white-and-blue bow ties offered Veuve Clicquot French champagne and Stella Artois Belgian beer, displaying America's affection for their allies' alcohol.

On a stage flanked by the U.S. and E.U. flags, Sondland introduced Jay Leno, and the former late-night TV star delivered an American stand-up routine. The SHAPE International Band, made up of musicians from the 29 NATO nations, played classic American tunes. The event was underwritten by 36 major corporations, including several from Sondland's home region in the Pacific Northwest: Microsoft, Starbucks, Nike, Expedia and Boeing.

Zelensky and his wife, Olena, were welcomed as honored guests. Since the discouraging May 23 Oval Office session with Trump, Sondland had seen some evidence of a thaw in the president's ice-cold attitude toward Ukraine and the country's new president. He had written Zelensky and promised him a White House meeting. Sondland wasn't quite sure why. But at least he did it.

Now Zelensky was in Brussels, working the crowd. So was Trump son-in-law Jared Kushner, an emissary straight from the White House inner circle. Surely that was a good sign, the Ukrainians thought. Zelensky mingled with the U.S. officials who were key to his country's security and prosperity. He was meeting with European officials, too, assuring them of his anti-corruption, pro-West policies.

But nothing was of higher priority for Zelensky and his team than creating good relations with Trump—and proving that he was not, as Rudy Giuliani had so publicly alleged, surrounded by "enemies" of Trump and America. So he schmoozed with the Americans beneath a massive U.S. flag and gave a thumbs-up sign as he posed for a photo with Leno—two comedians, one the Ukrainian president and the other an American icon.

Performing a diplomatic warm-up act for "my old friend Jay Leno," Sondland joked that he knew the party was "a little early, but what's a month among friends?" He saluted U.S.-Europe relations, cheerfully glossing over the ongoing friction between the Trump administration and America's traditional European allies: "In spite of our relatively minor, though headline-grabbing, differences this is a relationship that delivers results for ourselves and others. Everyone in this room is part of that story."

Sondland, too, was part of that story. A year earlier, he was a wealthy hotelier and generous Republican Party donor. Now, he was an ambassador demonstrating his diplomatic showmanship to the European Union community. For Sondland, at 61, the ambassador's job was like a basketball star giving baseball a try.

He had never held a position in government before. He was the son of immigrants who had fled Nazi Germany and made their way to Seattle, where they later established a dry-cleaning business. He amassed a fortune by acquiring and managing luxury hotels. He and his wife established themselves as prominent philanthropists, making major donations to the Seattle and Portland art museums. They were proud of their personal art collection, which Sondland had put in the "$5 million to $25 million" category when he filled out his federal financial disclosure form.

He portrayed himself as close to Trump, but he hadn't started out that way. He was a longtime supporter of establishment Republicans, supporting Jeb Bush in the 2016 campaign. When Bush dropped out, Sondland switched his allegiance to Trump, becoming one of his co-chairmen for Oregon and Washington State.

It wasn't a comfortable fit. Upset with Trump's anti-immigrant comments, Sondland removed himself as a sponsor of a Seattle fundraiser for the candidate. He issued a statement, through a company spokesman, explaining his change of heart. Trump's "constantly evolving positions" were at odds with his "personal beliefs and values," he said, and he could no longer support Trump's candidacy. Sondland didn't stay away for long, though. After Trump was elected, he routed $1 million to the president-elect's inaugural fund, using a collection of companies that obscured his involvement.

In Brussels, Sondland quickly developed a reputation for being amiable, stubborn and fond of the trappings of the ambassador's job. He carried a wireless buzzer into meetings at the U.S. Mission that enabled him to silently summon staff to refill his teacup. He ordered up expensive renovations at the U.S. ambassador's baronial residence. Sondland thought the property needed updating, but one U.S. senior official described the various expenditures—$25,000 to an American rug company, thousands more for new furniture and custom woodworking—as "18th century Jefferson-in-Paris behavior."

Sondland sometimes chafed at the constraints of his assignment. He traveled for meetings to Israel, Romania and other countries with little or no coordination with other officials. He acquired a reputation for being careless about security and was chastised for using his personal phone for government business. He shuttled frequently back to Washington, often seeking face time with Trump on his visits. When he couldn't gain entry to the Oval Office, he would meet with Mulvaney. Some at the NSC thought Sondland exaggerated how much time Trump and Mulvaney gave him.

Now, at his early Fourth of July extravaganza, Sondland was in his element: America's host and toastmaster, introducing Leno to a gathering of European leaders and conveying the best wishes of President Trump.

Immediately afterward, Sondland presided over a private dinner for 24 at the U.S. Mission's building in central Brussels. Sondland sat at the center of the long table, directly across from Kushner. Guests included the president of Poland, the prime ministers of Romania and Georgia and a collection of other European and NATO dignitaries. Energy secretary Rick Perry sat next to Leno. Ulrich Brechbuhl and Phil Reeker were there, representing the State Department. The U.S. ambassador to Poland, prominent Republican activist Georgette Mosbacher, stood out in the sea of blue suits with her flame-red hair, bright red pantsuit and stars-and-stripes scarf.

Zelensky was on Kushner's immediate right, not quite the Oval Office meeting that Zelensky wanted so badly, but a step in the right direction. Why would the president's son-in-law sit with a man who, as Giuliani had claimed, had people around him consorting with enemies of Trump and America?

CHAPTER NINE

"Who Put You in Charge?"

June 18, Washington

On June 18, Fiona Hill, the top White House specialist on Europe and Russia, convened an impromptu meeting in her third-floor quarters of the Old Executive Office Building, next to the White House. The ornate structure, a landmark dating to the 19th century, was home to the National Security Council and its hundreds of employees. It was a vital nerve center, the place where Hill and other national security experts coordinated U.S. policy toward every corner of the globe.

Hill had pulled together the group to talk European projects and issues, in part because Gordon Sondland was in town again. Some of the NSC staff had taken to joking that Sondland spent more time wandering the West Wing's corridors than the hallways of the U.S. Mission to the E.U. in Brussels.

In a more traditional White House, Hill and Sondland would have been in close contact. Her NSC responsibilities included coordinating the administration's policy for all of Europe. That intersected with Sondland's role as ambassador to the European Union and its 28 members. But as Hill now understood, Trump's White House operated with its own rules.

Sondland's official role was limited to enlisting European support for resolving Ukraine's conflict with Russia. But Sondland wasn't content to stay in his designated lane. Hill and NSC colleagues were confused about why Sondland was inserting himself into Ukrainian matters so often. Ukraine wasn't a member of the European Union, and Sondland's background didn't suggest any special knowledge or experience with the country's complex issues and characters. He doesn't know what he's doing, Hill thought. He's driving off-road, in unfamiliar territory, without guardrails or GPS.

From Hill's perspective, there were now two distinct fronts in the U.S.

relationship with Ukraine: a formal diplomatic channel driven by the usual policy considerations, and a separate, shadow effort pursuing a less-than-transparent agenda on the president's behalf.

Hill had watched the irregular channel emerge with a sense of bewilderment and alarm. The ouster of Yovanovitch, whom Hill had known for years, had set senior NSC and State Department officials on edge. Giuliani's frequent appearances on cable television, in which he talked openly about exposing supposed Ukrainian conspiracies against the president, which Hill knew to be false, added to their unease.

Nothing had "officially" changed for Hill and her Ukraine team. There were no NSC memos circulating with new policy prescriptions for Kyiv, no White House directives. That was part of Hill's concern. She felt most comfortable working within well-understood procedures, but on Ukraine, she felt off balance, marginalized. She was seeing only pieces of a larger puzzle. She was struggling to understand the roles of these unexpected players, outside and inside the government, particularly Sondland.

The E.U. ambassador was genial, funny, charming, she thought. A savvy guy, and well meaning. But his freewheeling style troubled her. Several of the U.S. ambassadors in Europe complained that he had shown up in their countries without any forewarning. He didn't seem to think he needed to coordinate with anyone else. Maybe that worked fine when he was running his hotel business, but in foreign affairs there were so many differing agendas and personalities. When the U.S. government said something, it was better if its emissaries spoke with one voice, from the same general script.

Hill had asked her boss, John Bolton, how to handle Giuliani, standard bearer of the emerging irregular channel. He told her: Steer clear.

But Sondland was different, Hill felt. He wasn't some rogue actor outside the government. He was part of the European team. She needed to work with him—or, at least, keep him in check.

Sondland arrived for the meeting with Hill in the company of other State Department officials. Several NSC officials joined the group, including Lt. Col. Alexander Vindman, who worked under Hill as the top adviser on Ukraine. Hill's office was spacious, with a large desk and separate seating area around a coffee table. The view wasn't much—massive heating and air-conditioning units dominating an inner courtyard. But it was still prime real estate in Washington's power circles.

As Sondland laid out his latest initiatives, talking fast, Hill found herself interrupting—"whoa, go back"—to slow him down. She asked him to explain several diplomatic efforts that she was, inexplicably, hearing about for the first time. Hill felt herself growing impatient.

They had such different styles and backgrounds. Hill came at a problem with a scholar's eye. Having served as the top U.S. intelligence officer on Russia during George W. Bush's administration and then for one year of Obama's presidency, she respected the rigor of the policy-making process, the need for gathering facts and debating their meaning. She believed that Sondland disdained such things. He seemed to regard the meeting as not fully deserving of his time.

At one point, as Sondland talked about what he was doing with Ukraine, Hill thought she needed to put the brakes on: "Gordon, you're in over your head. I don't think you know who these people are."

Sondland kept talking. When he announced that he had been "put in charge" of Ukraine policy, the meeting stopped cold.

Hill bristled. "You're not," she said, her surprise and irritation showing. "Who has put you in charge?" she demanded.

Sondland seemed perplexed by Hill's indignation. He leaned back against his seat for a second, then pressed forward.

"The president," he said.

Hill was stunned. Well, that shuts me up, she thought to herself.

Aware of the mystified faces around him, Sondland tried to soften the impact of what he had just said. He said he was "fully coordinating" his Ukraine endeavors with the State Department and White House officials, which Hill understood to mean Mulvaney.

There it was. Hill had just run directly into the irregular channel. She hadn't fully appreciated how powerful it was. And Sondland? He was seizing the role of liaison. He was telling them there was no point in trying to undercut him. He was the president's inside guy.

Hill had known that there would be such moments of humiliation in working for Trump.

She had taken the NSC job, normally a career-capping achievement, against the advice of many of her peers in the foreign policy establishment who were appalled by Trump's rhetoric, behavior and lack of interest in issues.

Her friends had warned her about reputational damage. She was among Washington's most respected experts on Russia, the coauthor of an acclaimed book on Putin. Russia had just waged election warfare against the United States with fake social media posts that appeared to come from Americans disparaging Hillary Clinton and promoting Trump. Hill would be going to work for the prime beneficiary of that attack, someone who was praising Putin with inexplicable consistency. One of her longtime associates stopped speaking with her after she decided to say yes.

Hill saw things differently. She regarded working in the White House as her duty. It was a chance to use her expertise to help shape the administration's Russia policy. She saw a danger to the country if its best and brightest refused to accept important roles in government because of Trump.

Within days of her arrival at the White House, it became clear to Hill that she would have little if any regular interaction with the president. The distrust he exhibited in public toward policy experts matched his approach inside the West Wing. He barely tolerated briefings. He appeared to see most issues through the prism of his own personal stake in them. He seemed to listen to few voices other than those he called in off-hours from the White House residence.

Her early encounters with the president were demoralizing. She had joined an Oval Office meeting with then national security adviser H. R. McMaster to help Trump prepare for a call with Putin on Syria. Trump appeared to mistake her for clerical staff, handing her a marked-up memo and instructing her to rewrite it. Hill froze, clutching the document and hesitating on whether to inform the president that she was his top Russia adviser. Trump interpreted her stunned look as insubordination.

"What's the problem with this one?" he shouted, railing at McMaster to take her away. McMaster escorted Hill out of the room and scolded her for upsetting the president. For a while, they thought it best for her to stay away.

That was difficult, but nothing compared to what she soon encountered online and at home. Somehow, her name began turning up in the far-right-wing corners of the Internet. At work, she arrived on many days to find obscene voice-mail messages on her White House phone. She came under sustained attack by the conspiracy theorists behind the website InfoWars. Roger Stone, Trump's longtime political confidant, appeared on one webcast to declare that Hill was in league with liberal philanthropist George Soros to secretly undermine the Trump agenda from within. Afterward, NSC security teams logged hundreds of external threats against Hill and her NSC colleagues.

One woman left repeated menacing messages on Hill's home phone. Hill found her middle-school-age daughter replaying one of the messages over and over, transfixed and traumatized by the viciousness in the woman's voice. Hill's daughter wondered where the woman was. Could she be nearby? Were they in danger?

She comforted her daughter and resolved to keep her head down, keep doing her job. She was nearing the end anyway. In a month, after more than two years at the NSC, she would be going back to scholarly pursuits. Sondland, Giuliani, the question of whether and when Trump would meet with Zelensky—all that would soon become her successor's concern.

She had a reputation as a master notetaker, but she would be leaving those notes behind in a collection of well-labeled boxes, destined for the presidential records office and eventual archiving. She had no reason to think they would be needed anytime soon.

CHAPTER TEN

"Where Exactly Is the Line for You?"

June 19 to June 26, Washington

A waiter at the St. Regis Hotel in Washington brought eggs and home fries for Nancy Pelosi at 8 a.m., but she waved the plate away. She'd eaten breakfast two hours earlier. Now it was time to get down to business: a conversation with 30 journalists at an event hosted by the *Christian Science Monitor*.

This was familiar turf for Pelosi. The June 19 event was her 13th appearance at this newsmakers' breakfast, a venerable custom in Washington since the 1960s. She knew the drill. No shouted questions. No scrum among the reporters. This was a chance for the press to go deeper, to ask about issues sometimes shoved aside by the daily news scramble.

Pelosi was relaxed. She laughed when her aide slipped her a note during her opening statement, correcting her on a date. She talked expansively, looking around the table, making eye contact, as she touched on health care, clean water, pending bills and other subjects. But she knew the one topic on everyone's mind: impeachment. Was she still a no, or had anything she had seen from the committees investigating Trump been enough to propel her closer to yes?

She didn't wait for the question.

"Why don't we hear what you want to hear about?" she told the group. She had her script prepared. "We are in a mode of legislate, investigate, litigate," she said. "We do believe the president is undermining" the Constitution's checks and balances and "that is a serious threat."

This was Pelosi's latest impeachment dance. Not quite opening the door. Not quite closing it. In the last few weeks, "legislate, investigate, litigate" had become one of her mantras. It was her way of saying: I'm keeping all options alive.

It didn't hurt that most House Democrats regarded her with a certain amount of fear. She knew it. She used it. She had just reined in Nadler, who had threatened to go rogue. When House majority whip James Clyburn, a close ally, had suggested that an impeachment inquiry was inevitable during an early June interview with CNN's Jake Tapper, Pelosi had deployed her staff like a Special Forces unit. Clyburn walked back his comment.

But she also knew this: Rebelliousness would continue to flare. The latest poll numbers made that inevitable. Earlier in the week, a new NBC News–*Wall Street Journal* national survey showed impeachment gaining ground among Democratic voters. Forty-eight percent now favored the start of formal hearings, up from 30 percent in May's poll. Still, an overwhelming majority of Republicans and independents remained sharply opposed. The stark divide was worrying. In Pelosi's continuing risk assessment, it wasn't good enough for the needle to move on only one side of the aisle. Impeachment could not work without bipartisan support, she kept saying, emphatically and publicly.

About 60 Democrats were now backing calls for an impeachment inquiry, according to a recent *Washington Post* story, nearly a quarter of her caucus. She had acknowledged the frustrations of her pro-impeachment members, deploying her own strong language, even saying Trump should be "in prison." That bought her some goodwill on her left, at least for now.

Gerry Connolly of Virginia saw the precariousness of Pelosi's position. She was "holding it together," he told *Washington Post* reporter Rachael Bade, "but it's fragile because we're kind of one event, one piece of explosive testimony, one action by Trump away from that dam collapsing."

–

At the *Monitor* breakfast, the rising tide toward impeachment was on Jerry Zremski's mind. A reporter for the *Buffalo News*, he was tracking the evolving views of Brian Higgins, a Democrat from western New York. Just the day before, Higgins had joined those calling for an impeachment inquiry, citing Trump's uncooperative stance. Higgins said the House had "a legitimate legislative purpose" in seeking documents and testimony.

"What do you think of Congressman Higgins's argument?" Zremski asked Pelosi.

Caution, that's what she thought. "I don't think you should have an inquiry unless you are ready to impeach," she said. Support for impeachment had to "run deep." She pushed both fists sharply downward at her side to convey just how deep. "It can't be the Democrats impeach in the House," she said, "and the Republicans exonerate in the Senate."

The next impeachment question came through a side door: Would undertaking an impeachment inquiry get in the way of a deal with the White House on infrastructure?

Her answer ended with a pivot to Trump's resistance to the House investigators. He was giving Congress more reasons to believe he was obstructing justice, she said, "and that's what has affected members. They're like, 'It's self-evident that he is obstructing justice. He's ignoring subpoenas.'"

She reminded the roomful of journalists that one of the proposed articles of impeachment against Nixon, the only president ever to resign the office, had accused him of obstructing Congress. Her inference was clear. Was she hinting that Trump's refusal to cooperate might soon make him "worth it"? Was she changing her mind?

That's what Tal Kopan of the *San Francisco Chronicle* wanted to know. She quoted Pelosi's earlier words back to her. "Circling back to the impeachment conversation, you said it's about patriotism and upholding the Constitution, not politics," Kopan said. "You've also said pretty clearly you believe the president is engaging in a criminal cover-up. You believe there is obstruction of justice. Where exactly is the line for you?"

Pelosi pressed the tips of her fingers together and rested her hands on the table. "When we stop finding even more information." She paused for emphasis and added, "Every day, we see more—so why would we stop with a less strong case?"

"If you're going to go down this path," she said, pausing, reformulating, choosing her words carefully. "You have to make sure that the public has an understanding of why."

The breakfast was full of reporters well versed in the politics of impeachment, including A. B. Stoddard of RealClearPolitics. Stoddard had been interviewing first-term moderates who had won seats in Trump territory in 2018, sweeping Democrats back into control of the House. Pelosi was keen to protect them from any blowback from impeachment. If this group couldn't win reelection, the Democrats would likely lose the House.

Stoddard was hearing something different, something new. "I was surprised in conversations with some of your members in Trump districts that they are not as afraid as the media describes them to be of impeachment," she told Pelosi. "For posterity's sake, for history's sake, they think it might be important."

Stoddard didn't name them, but she described them. "They did not spend their lives in politics. They spent it in national security and in the law." She was talking about newcomers like Elissa Slotkin of Michigan, Abigail Spanberger and Elaine Luria of Virginia, Mikie Sherrill of New Jersey. All had military or intelligence backgrounds.

"They don't think this is a radioactive topic," Stoddard went on.

That got Pelosi's attention. She listened intently as Stoddard asked her question.

"Some have proposed censure," Stoddard said. If it seemed obvious that the Republican-controlled Senate would never vote to remove Trump, she asked, could the House "for history's sake, pass a censure resolution that would force the Republicans in the Senate to say something about the president's conduct?"

Pelosi shot that down without hesitation. She thought censure was a meaningless and weak measure.

"No, I think censure is just a way out," she said. "If you're going to go, you ought to go. In other words, if the goods are there, you must impeach." Censure would be letting him off too lightly if the evidence showed he had violated his oath of office. "That's a day at the beach for the president," Pelosi said, eliciting a few laughs. "Or at his golf club, or wherever he goes to get that complexion."

Pelosi reached back in history to quote Thomas Paine, the philosopher whose writings helped inspire the American Revolution in 1776: "The times have found us."

"The times have found us now, and all of you as well." She stressed the word "us," glancing around the table. "Not that we place ourselves in a category of greatness of our founders," she said, not wanting to sound grandiose. In an appeal to the media, she said: "This is an important time for our country, and I count on all of you to be messengers of truth." She didn't directly mention Trump, but warned of "authoritarians" attacking the press, "to silence or chill."

"So, don't chill!" she said, to loud laughter from the reporters. "The times have found us. It's not time for any of us to chill!"

• • •

That afternoon, the conservative-leaning *Washington Examiner* published a short story, about 540 words, on its website. The headline: "Pentagon to send $250M in weapons to Ukraine." It was not big news, but it was of interest to those who followed Ukraine and kept tabs on U.S. foreign military aid. The aid would bring total U.S. security assistance to Ukraine to $1.5 billion since 2014.

There was no apparent controversy about the package or the policy. The story quoted Rick Berger, a former Senate Budget Committee staffer, now at the American Enterprise Institute, as saying there was broad bipartisan support in Congress for helping Ukraine fend off Russia. "These aid packages are very well tailored to the things that, by and large, the Ukrainian military actually needs," Berger said.

Kurt Volker had gone to Capitol Hill the day before to testify about the administration's policy. The special envoy told the Senate Foreign Relations Committee that "security assistance to Ukraine is vitally important. I think it has had an impact both psychologically as well as militarily on the professionalization and the capacity of the Ukrainian forces. I think it's also important that Ukraine reciprocate with foreign military purchases from us as well, and I know that they intend to do so."

The Russ Read story in the *Examiner* made some noise at the White House. Within hours of the article's publication, President Trump told aides he had questions about the aid. Trump's interest caught officials in the Pentagon and the Office of Management and Budget by surprise. It was the first they'd heard of any presidential reservations about the package, which had already been approved by all the appropriate agencies.

It was head-scratching. Someone must have shown the article to Trump, and someone must have known the reaction it would provoke. But why?

A phone call from Mick Mulvaney's office to OMB's acting head, Russell Vought, triggered a chain reaction down the line. At 6:32 p.m., Michael Duffey, OMB's associate director for national security programs, emailed Vought a link to the *Examiner* story. "Russ—here is a story from the Washington Examiner. . . . Looking into options and will follow up."

It was late in the day, but Duffey got right to work. Five minutes later, he emailed Elaine McCusker, a career civil servant about to become the Defense Department's acting comptroller. "Elaine—The President has asked about this funding release, and I have been tasked to follow-up with someone over there to get more detail. Do you have insight on this funding?" Duffey's email included a link to the *Examiner* story.

At 8 p.m., McCusker replied, "Copy, will get you a paper in the morning."

A week later, on Wednesday night, June 26, ten Democratic presidential hopefuls took the stage at the Adrienne Arsht Center for the Performing Arts in Miami for the first of a series of debates. Ten more candidates would appear on the same stage the next night to face questioning from NBC News moderators.

The candidates had drawn lots to decide which night they would appear. Senator Elizabeth Warren of Massachusetts had the prized center spot on Night One, because she had the highest poll ratings in her group. The rest of the biggest fish in the field had all drawn spots on Night Two. That meant Joe Biden, Senator Bernie Sanders of Vermont, Senator Kamala Harris of California and mayor Pete Buttigieg of South Bend, Indiana, would be battling each other for airtime and space the next night.

Looming over it all was Trump, who claimed he would not be watching as he flew to Japan for a two-day Group of 20 meeting, where he would discuss trade disagreements, escalating tensions in the Middle East and the stalled nuclear negotiations with North Korea. The night before, House Democrats had announced that Robert Mueller would testify in mid-July, infuriating Trump. "Does it ever end?" he wrote on Twitter.

Now, two hours before the Night One debate's scheduled 9 p.m. start time, Trump tweeted that his fans should follow his surrogates for real-time analysis of the debate while he was in the air: "Sorry, I'm on Air Force One, off to save the Free World!"

The Democratic contenders started off with a weighty discussion of health care and economic policy. The moderate-progressive divide was on full display in exchanges over health insurance, free college tuition, giant corporations and taxes on the wealthiest Americans.

About 35 minutes into the debate, a Trump tweet came flying in from a refueling stop in Anchorage, Alaska: "BORING!" Halfway through, an audio glitch forced NBC to cut away to an unplanned commercial break. Trump, former star of his own TV show, tweeted his critique from somewhere over the Pacific: "@NBCNews and @MSNBC should be ashamed of themselves for having such a horrible technical breakdown in the middle of the debate."

He didn't bother attacking any of the Night One candidates by name.

Instead, he targeted the man who would be center stage on Night Two: Joe Biden, the front-runner in the polls.

Trump tweeted: "Ever since the passage of the Super Predator Crime Bill, pushed hard by @JoeBiden, together with Bill and Crooked Hillary Clinton, which inflicted great pain on many, but especially the African American Community, Democrats have tried and failed to pass Criminal Justice Reform."

The two hours of talk ended with barely a mention of impeachment. In Washington, Nancy Pelosi was working hard to keep her caucus from splintering on the issue.

In late June, Volker huddled with Pompeo at the secretary's Foggy Bottom office. Volker was heading to Toronto soon for an international conference. Zelensky would be there, and Volker had scheduled a sit-down with him. Before leaving Washington, he wanted to update Pompeo on the administration's Ukraine strategy and his concerns about Giuliani.

As the special envoy to Ukraine, Volker didn't get a lot of face time with the secretary, who spent most of his time focused on Iran and North Korea. In the lingo of the State Department, Ukraine was a "sixth floor" country—important enough to draw real interest from Congress, but not a top priority for Pompeo and his leadership team, who had their offices on the seventh floor.

Volker saw that as a plus. He wasn't laboring on some backwater issue, but he also didn't have the secretary's office constantly dictating policy to him. There was some freedom to maneuver, a chance to show some creativity. It was that mindset Volker wanted to bring to the problem posed by Giuliani's involvement in Ukraine. He was reluctant to put his concerns in writing, so he laid it out for the secretary in person.

"We have a Rudy problem," Volker told Pompeo.

A month had passed since the dismal Oval Office session with Trump. There was still no date for Zelensky's Oval Office meeting with Trump. The Ukrainians were getting antsy. Volker wanted to break the logjam. "Talk to Rudy," the president had said. But talking to Rudy wasn't a plan, and Volker needed a plan.

Volker prided himself of being a Washington operator and problem solver. He was 54 years old, wore neatly tailored suits, expensive loafers and rimless glasses. His upcoming wedding, scheduled for October, was set to take place at Washington's National Cathedral, the site of the most elite Washington weddings and funerals—including those of presidents. In 2016, when members of the Republican foreign policy establishment were putting together an open letter saying he would be "the most reckless president in American history," Volker had been a rare voice of caution. "Please don't publish this letter," he pleaded with Eliot A. Cohen and Eric Edelman, two former Bush administration officials organizing the effort.

Not that Volker disagreed with their opinion of Trump. But he argued that Trump might win the election, so it was essential for the party's foreign policy experts to maintain good relations with him. The inexperienced president would need their counsel.

Volker had no idea then that Trump's aversion to the established order would run so deep, or that he would be caught in the middle of the battle between the new and old power centers, as he was now. But he knew that Pompeo was too busy with other crises to deal with the Rudy problem, so he had worked up a strategy. It required going outside of the regular diplomatic channels. He wanted Pompeo's blessing, but Volker would carry it out.

He told Pompeo that he wanted to connect Zelenksy's top advisers directly with Giuliani. The idea was to convince Giuliani that Zelensky was no threat to Trump, and that Zelensky was serious about stamping out corruption in Ukraine. Once Giuliani could see for himself that Zelensky and his team were allies and eager to work out any issues, he would stop running him down to Trump.

"Good idea," Pompeo told Volker.

Volker had his green light. Would it be worth the risk?

CHAPTER ELEVEN

Flyover

July 4, Washington

It was hot, humid and drizzly on Independence Day, and the Washington air felt wet as a big dog's breath. Still, people streamed to the National Mall by the tens of thousands, some from all over the country, to celebrate the nation's 243rd birthday.

They came for the Salute to America, an extravagant display of patriotic pride and military hardware that was imagined and largely choreographed by Trump himself. They stood, shoulder to shoulder along the Reflecting Pool, for hours, tolerating persistent sprinkles and occasional downpours to wait for the president's early-evening entrance. Some wore "Make America Great Again" hats.

Nearby were people whose handmade signs made clear they were there to celebrate America's independence, but not its current leader. A 20-foot inflatable Baby Trump balloon sat on its diaper nearby, banned by federal officials from flying, but making its tantrum-throwing point anyway. Smaller Baby Trump balloons were harder to ban.

Trump emerged just before 6:45 p.m., below the stone feet of the man who wrote the Gettysburg Address, near the spot where Dr. Martin Luther King Jr. once spoke of his dream for a better world. Holding hands with his wife Melania, Trump strolled toward the podium to the strains of "Hail to the Chief," smiling broadly and waving to a VIP-filled grandstand festooned with red-white-and-blue bunting.

"Hello America, hello!" he said to delirious cheers and a flyover by Air Force One.

For this grand occasion, the president's speechwriters had prepared a grand speech, which he delivered from the teleprompters he so disliked. The rhetoric was lofty and largely nonpartisan. Trump invoked great names and moments from U.S. history: Jefferson, Washington, Hamilton, Lewis and Clark, Edison, Alexander Graham Bell, the Wright brothers. He addressed legendary NASA flight director Gene Kranz, who was there watching: "Gene, I want you to know that we are going to be back on the moon very soon," Trump said. "And someday soon, we will plant the American flag on Mars."

The planes zoomed across the gray sky, a majestic airborne parade. There were Coast Guard and Marine helicopters, F-22 Raptors, B-2 Stealth bombers and F-18 fighter jets. For the finale, the Navy's famous Blue Angels streaked overhead to a rousing version of "The Battle Hymn of the Republic."

"God bless you. God bless the military. And God bless America. Happy Fourth of July," Trump said.

An hour later, as thousands waited on the Mall for the annual fireworks display, the party's host was back at the White House, back to Twitter. As soon as he had finished speaking, his Twitter account was posting compliments about the show. "Epic," read the first. "The #SalutetoAmerica was awesome." said the second.

For the next three hours, the good reviews kept flowing. He also retweeted attacks on former NFL quarterback Colin Kaepernick, Kamala Harris, the media and Joe Biden. He highlighted a *Washington Examiner* story that cited a poll showing "plummeting" support for Biden, under the headline: "Biden faces his Waterloo in Iowa as campaign momentum stalls."

Fox's Sean Hannity, on his Fourth of July show at 9 p.m., praised the country and its leadership and then warned darkly of a plot against Trump. "That's why frankly, we have been spending so much time and sounding the alarm about the corrupt, high-ranking, not rank-and-file bureaucrats in the deep state, in the intel community, in the FBI, Department of Justice and elsewhere—those that tried to subvert the will of 'We the people' . . . to take down a duly elected President Donald Trump. Pack of lies."

In Sioux City, Iowa, Democratic presidential candidate and Afghanistan war veteran Pete Buttigieg found the Salute to America display of weaponry disheartening. "Reducing our nation to tanks and shows of muscle just makes us look like the loudmouth guy at the bar instead of the extremely diverse and energetic nation that we are," he said. "Unfortunately, we have one more moment of division at the very date when we are supposed to be celebrating what unifies us."

As Trump was speaking at the Lincoln Memorial, Nancy Pelosi was with her family at their Napa Valley home, north of San Francisco, eating Mexican food and rereading the Mueller report.

Trump critic Justin Amash, the congressman from Michigan, celebrated the Fourth of July in his own style, announcing in a *Washington Post* op-ed that he was quitting the Republican Party and becoming an independent.

Amash wrote that he was a lifelong Republican who had grown disenchanted with party politics. He did not mention Trump by name in his essay, but he had earlier said that the Mueller report "describes a consistent effort by the president to use his office to obstruct or otherwise corruptly impede the Russian election interference investigation." Trump's actions amounted to "impeachable conduct," Amash had said.

Trump responded to Amash's decision with scorn. "Great news for the Republican Party as one of the dumbest & most disloyal men in Congress is 'quitting' the Party," he tweeted. "Knew he couldn't get the nomination to run again in the Great State of Michigan. Already being challenged for his seat. A total loser!"

CHAPTER TWELVE

"Drug Deal"

July 10, Washington and Kyiv

On a glorious summer Wednesday in Washington, two top Zelensky advisers arrived at the White House for talks. The Ukrainian president had been in office for less than two months, waiting for a promised meeting with Trump that hadn't happened. This July 10 visit was a big step forward.

Andriy Yermak and Oleksandr Danyliuk, the Zelensky emissaries, were already well known to some of Trump's Ukraine team. They had dressed in dark suits, but John Bolton greeted them in his West Wing office looking like an ad for summer, wearing a cheerful suit in a pale color that almost matched his famous bushy eyebrows and mustache. This was their first chance to meet Bolton, and they were hoping to make a good impression and convey a sense of urgency about their mission: to show the world, and especially Putin, that Trump supported Zelensky.

The U.S.-Ukraine relationship had been pushed into the doubtful category by Giuliani's harsh comments about Zelensky and his advisers, the failure of either Trump or Pence to attend Zelensky's inauguration and the unnerving saga of Marie Yovanovitch's firing. Yermak and Danyliuk wanted to leave with those doubts reduced. They hoped to nail down a time and place for a Trump-Zelensky one-on-one.

They were sure, as were Volker and others on the American side, that the two leaders would hit it off if only they spent some time together. At the very least, Yermak and Danyliuk wanted to set up a phone call, preferably ahead of Ukraine's parliamentary elections on July 21. Zelensky needed a win to strengthen his mandate. Showing that Trump stood with him could help.

Now the two aides sat in Bolton's office, just steps from the Oval Office, with the people who they believed could make that happen: Bolton and his chief Ukraine lieutenants, Fiona Hill and Alexander Vindman, as well as the trio who had led the delegation to Zelensky's inauguration—Rick Perry, Gordon Sondland and Volker. The U.S. side was also eager for Bolton to get a sense of Zelensky's team, especially Danyliuk, his national security counterpart.

Winning over Bolton was never easy. His assessments of people and policies could be blunt and lacerating. In a political career that started when he was a high school student volunteering for uber-hawkish 1964 GOP presidential candidate Barry Goldwater, Bolton had earned a reputation for his hard-line conservative views and abrasive treatment of perceived fools. The son of a Baltimore firefighter, he preferred decision to debate. He had argued that military strikes in Iran and North Korea would be more effective than trying to negotiate with the leaders of those governments.

The man Danyliuk needed to impress was known for his penetrating knowledge of foreign affairs and his grasp of how to steer the policy-making process. Now 70, Bolton had traveled a path from Yale Law to jobs in three Republican administrations. In 1986, he worked on the Supreme Court confirmation of conservative icon Antonin Scalia, and in 1987, on the failed confirmation of Robert Bork, a battle in the partisan wars that had come to define modern Washington politics. In 2000, Bolton had helped George W. Bush's team in the decisive Florida recount, where he earned a reputation for being aggressive—and for winning. As president, Bush had made Bolton his U.N. ambassador in 2005, over bipartisan objections, by skirting the Senate with a recess appointment.

Trump admired Bolton's fists-flying tough talk in TV appearances and had hired him as his national security adviser in April 2018, to the dismay of Democrats, and a not insignificant number of Republicans. On his watch, the Trump administration had pulled out of major deals with Russia and Iran. Danyliuk was meeting with a wily grizzly bear.

Bolton opened the discussion by urging that Zelensky keep his inaugural promises to end his country's endemic corruption. Bolton and Perry then talked about the importance of reforming Ukraine's energy sector. Zelensky and his team wanted to take a hard look at Ukraine's approach to national security matters, and Hill was hoping that Bolton might have some advice for them.

The meeting seemed to be going well, although Volker worried that the Ukrainians were too deep into the weeds in describing their bureaucratic restructuring proposals. They need to speak more about big-picture issues, Volker thought.

Then the dynamic suddenly changed. Danyliuk had been coached by Sondland to press Bolton on a date for the presidential meeting. But when Danyliuk raised the question, Bolton deflected. Known for his combative personal style, Bolton was also a by-the-books guy. He wasn't going to pull out his calendar and pencil in a date on the spot. There was a protocol to follow. The first step: Discuss the parameters. What would be the agenda? The venue? How would this further U.S. interests?

Bolton was all too aware that some foreign leaders simply wanted a grip-and-grin photo with the U.S. president for their office wall and the news media. Bolton was also worried about the big unknown: What was the president's attitude these days toward Ukraine? Would he be guided by Rudy Giuliani, or would he follow the advice of his professional staff? Bolton wasn't sure, and not being sure, he wasn't about to throw out dates for a meeting that Trump might reject with a wave of his hand.

For months, Bolton had been annoyed and agitated by Giuliani's anti-Ukraine campaign. He had told Hill, "Giuliani's a hand grenade that is going to blow everybody up." Hill had watched Bolton turn up the volume on his TV whenever he saw Giuliani on Fox News. It was one way that Bolton could keep tabs on what the president's personal lawyer was up to.

For now, Bolton was set on being friendly and noncommittal, promising to get back to the Ukrainians later. Then Sondland spoke up. "Well," Sondland said, "we have an agreement with the chief of staff for a meeting if these investigations in the energy sector start."

Whoa.

Hill could see Bolton stiffen in his chair. Sondland had just blindsided her boss, a big no-no in the NSC world. The E.U. ambassador was suggesting that, without the input of Bolton and his staff, Mulvaney had already signed off on a meeting, provided the Ukrainians start "investigations."

Bolton, Hill and Vindman knew what that meant: Burisma and the Bidens. A supposed Ukrainian role in helping the Democrats in the 2016 election. In other words, what Giuliani and his crowd had been saying on TV and everywhere else. The NSC team had warned Volker to stay away from Giuliani. What they were seeing now, it seemed to them, was Giuliani's campaign making its way into the national security adviser's office, in the West Wing, practically at the door of the Oval Office.

Hill could feel Bolton's anger. Sondland didn't seem to notice. He also didn't see his statement as a cannon shot. He was stating the reality as he understood it.

Bolton, with a glance at the clock, announced that he had other appointments. The meeting was over. He told the Ukrainians that he looked forward to working with them. He led them out of the office.

Sondland, Volker, Yermak, Danyliuk, Perry and Bolton walked outside and posed for a photo, under bright sunshine, puffy clouds and the American flag waving over the White House. Sondland thought everything had gone pretty well, all things considered.

Bolton was done, but Sondland wasn't. He invited Yermak and Danyliuk to follow him to the Ward Room, a basement room with dark wood paneling, near the Situation Room, often used for meetings by national security officials. He said he wanted to talk about "next steps." Vindman was there, too.

As Hill was leaving the meeting, Bolton pulled her aside. Go with them, he told her, and report back.

In the Ward Room, Vindman became alarmed when Sondland emphasized the importance of Ukraine announcing investigations into the 2016 election, the Bidens and Burisma. He told Sondland that the conversation was not appropriate. He said the NSC would not support any politically motivated investigations, which he believed could undermine U.S. national security interests.

Sondland then explained his view and said Mulvaney backed him. The investigations were a "deliverable" required for a Trump-Zelensky meeting.

As Hill arrived, she picked up the tension in the room. She told Sondland: "We can't make any commitments at this particular juncture because a lot of things will have to be worked through in terms of the timing and the substance."

Sondland cut her short. "We have an agreement that they'll have a meeting," he replied. He didn't view the exchange as heated, just a disagreement over details.

Hill said that she didn't want to continue the discussion in front of the Ukrainians. Sondland asked them to step out of the room. While they waited in the hallway, near the door to the Situation Room, Hill told Sondland: Stop. We can't make any commitments. Bolton had been very clear, she said. Any White House meeting between Trump and Zelensky had to be scheduled through the proper procedures.

Sondland persisted. He talked about his discussions with Mulvaney and mentioned Giuliani. That was enough for Hill. Anything involving Giuliani was the opposite of proper procedure. Sondland seemed annoyed. He told Hill he had other meetings, and the gathering broke up.

As Vindman was getting ready to escort the Ukrainians out, he and Hill had a quick conversation, sharing their discomfort. Hill said: We need to let the NSC lawyers know what just happened.

Hill went directly to Bolton's office, and told him what she had witnessed. Bolton was furious. He thought what was happening was bad policy, questionable legally and unacceptable as presidential behavior. He directed her to go immediately to John Eisenberg, the National Security Council's senior lawyer, and report the entire sequence of events. She was struck by his memorable parting words: "You go and tell Eisenberg that I am not part of whatever drug deal Sondland and Mulvaney are cooking up," he said.

That afternoon, Hill and Vindman had separate meetings with Eisenberg. The lawyer listened impassively but attentively, taking detailed notes on a yellow legal pad.

Vindman had seen the Giuliani irregular channel at work for months. But only now was he understanding the finer details, the explicit tradeoff. It seemed clear to him that Trump was using a White House meeting as leverage to pressure Zelensky to investigate his political rivals.

That evening Perry tweeted the group photo, and then Bolton retweeted it, saying: "Great discussion today with Oleksandr Danylyuk, Secretary of Ukraine's National Security and Defense Council, on U.S. support for Ukrainian reforms and the peaceful restoration of Ukrainian territory."

Yermak and Danyliuk left the White House without a meeting date and with an unsettling story to tell their president.

In Kyiv that day, acting ambassador Bill Taylor had met with Zelensky's chief of staff Andriy Bohdan and foreign policy adviser Vadym Prystaiko. They told Taylor they were alarmed and disappointed. It was Giuliani again. He had sent them a message through Yuri Lutsenko saying a call between the two presidents was unlikely.

Taylor thought Giuliani, who was growing frustrated with a perceived lack of cooperation from Kyiv, was playing hardball. And once again, Giuliani's back channel was Lutsenko, the prosecutor general who had stirred up so much trouble in his interviews with *The Hill*'s John Solomon.

Everyone involved was starting to clearly see the dynamics at work in the Trump administration's Ukraine policy. There would no meeting without Giuliani's nod. From Taylor's point of view, it was crazy.

Just before 8 a.m. Washington time, 3 p.m. in Kyiv, before the White House meeting, Taylor and Kurt Volker had exchanged text messages. Taylor said he had just met with the two Zelensky aides. They were "very concerned about what Lutsenko told them." According to Giuliani, they said, a presidential meeting "will not happen."

"Advice?" Taylor wrote.

Volker replied immediately. "Good grief. Please tell [Zelensky's foreign policy adviser] to let the official USG representatives speak for the U.S." Lutsenko "has his own self-interest here."

Taylor: "Exactly what I told them. And I said that [Giuliani] is a private citizen."

This kind of interference was what Kent had warned him about, what he had worried about in taking the job. He briefed Pompeo's chief aide at the State Department, and he waited to hear the outcome of the White House meeting involving Bolton and Zelensky's aides.

A few hours later, he texted Volker, saying he was eager to hear if the meeting had "resulted in a decision on a call."

No reply.

At 10:26 p.m. in Washington, 5:26 a.m. in Kyiv, Taylor tried again: "How did the meeting go?"

Volker responded three minutes later: "Not good—let's talk."

CHAPTER THIRTEEN

"Stray Voltage"

July 18 to 24, Kyiv and Washington

On July 18, Ambassador Bill Taylor sat in a conference room at the American Embassy in Kyiv and booted up the teleconferencing system for a routine meeting with colleagues working on Ukraine policy in Washington. After his first month in Ukraine, he was cautiously optimistic. Zelensky had made good on his inauguration promises, appointing reform-minded ministers and quickly opening the country's High Anti-Corruption Court, which the previous administration had stalled. Perhaps this time, Taylor hoped, Ukraine would finally make a true break from Russian influence and its own history of corruption.

Taylor was more concerned about what the Americans were up to. Before accepting the post in late May, he had met with an emotional Masha Yovanovitch, just returned from Ukraine. She still didn't understand all the machinations that had led to her recall, or why Trump had listened to her few opponents instead of her many supporters in his own government. As his wife had pointed out, Taylor couldn't be sure the same thing wouldn't happen to him. He was glad to have arrived in Kyiv with Trump's letter inviting Zelensky to the White House, but since then, he could see no progress on scheduling the meeting.

Sondland's role was a continuing mystery to Taylor. In late June, Sondland had said over the phone that Zelensky must not stand in the way of "investigations." Taylor wasn't sure what Sondland was talking about, but his language was odd enough that Taylor wrote it down in his notebook. Then, before a scheduled June 28 phone call with Zelensky on a range of pending issues, Sondland had cut out most of the usual government participants. He told everyone on the call—the Three Amigos plus Taylor—that he didn't want it transcribed.

It seemed like Sondland was trying to keep the usual policy players out of the loop. But the call itself had stayed on the talking points: energy policy, reopening a bridge that had been blown up in eastern Ukraine during fighting with the Russians in 2015 and the tentative plans for the White House meeting.

Taylor understood that the Three Amigos represented the "irregular channel" of American policy making and he was the "regular channel." But he had come to believe that all of them were aligned in pursuit of a strong U.S.-Ukraine relationship.

Sondland hadn't been invited to join today's video conference call. On the screen, Taylor could see colleagues from the alphabet soup of government agencies responsible for handling American policy toward Ukraine, including the NSC, DOD and OMB. Vindman chaired the meeting from a room in the Old Executive Office Building. George Kent, who oversaw policy toward Ukraine and a few other former Soviet countries, and Ukraine specialist Catherine Croft represented the State Department. This was a regular meeting of the group known as the Sub-Policy Coordinating Committee, the lowest level for discussing Ukrainian issues.

In Kyiv, Taylor was joined by his colleague David Holmes and other embassy staffers. Among the agenda items: a program intended to help the Ukrainian energy sector defend against cyberattacks. It was a small program, only a million dollars, but there was concern at some agencies that the Department of Energy wasn't running it well. This was the sort of granular work that, bit by bit, extended the influence of U.S. foreign policy around the world.

Toward the end of the nearly two-hour meeting, someone in Washington spoke up. On his screen, Taylor couldn't see who it was, but he heard a woman say that she was representing the OMB, and that she had a message from her boss: OMB was blocking further spending of the nearly $400 million in security aid Congress had allocated for Ukraine.

Taylor was astonished. A critical pillar of American support for Ukraine was under threat, and he had no idea why. Nor did anyone else on the call, including the OMB representative. As representatives of every agency pressed for some explanation, she could only apologize and explain that she didn't normally deal with these issues. It was the middle of the summer and people were on vacation; she was filling in for a colleague. All she knew was that Mick Mulvaney had ordered a hold on the aid at the direction of the president—that was the message she had been told to deliver.

Taylor, Holmes and their colleagues sat in shock. What did this mean? Taylor knew the regular channel wasn't likely to provide him with the answer. He texted Sondland and Volker. "OMB . . . just now said that all security assistance to Ukraine is frozen, per a conversation with Mulvaney and POTUS," he wrote. "Over to you."

Sondland replied: "All over it."

In Washington, Vindman left the meeting concerned. The group had reached an absolute consensus. Freezing the aid was a mistake and it needed to be released, and fast. Now the bureaucracy had to respond, to provide the information to get the money back on track. Vindman started to get ready for the meeting at the next level, the Policy Coordinating Committee itself, one step closer to the cabinet and Trump administration decision makers.

The next day, Taylor called Vindman and Fiona Hill. It was her last day at the NSC. Taylor asked if there had been a change in U.S. policy toward Ukraine. No, they assured him. They confirmed that Mulvaney had ordered the freeze, but said they thought it was temporary, a hiccup until the White House's questions were answered. Yes, Mulvaney was skeptical of Ukraine. But no, he couldn't single-handedly alter American foreign policy, they said.

That same day, July 19, Volker met with Giuliani for breakfast at the Trump Hotel in Washington. Volker was on his guard, but he also needed to be on his game. It was time to put in motion the plan he had cleared with Pompeo a few weeks earlier, to connect Giuliani with Zelensky's team and change the dynamic that was threatening to destroy an important alliance.

Giuliani was late, but the maître d'hotel directed Volker to the former mayor's regular table. Volker was expecting to talk with Giuliani one-on-one. He was surprised when Giuliani showed up with several associates, who grabbed seats at a nearby table. Giuliani came over with Lev Parnas in tow. Volker was already wary. He saw Giuliani and his freelance diplomacy as a problem, and here was the problem in tandem. They sat, sipping coffee, as Volker prepared to make his pitch.

Volker, ever the diplomat, didn't want to confront Giuliani or put him on the defensive. He wanted to make Giuliani think they were on the same team. A few minutes into their chat, a woman rushed up to get

Giuliani's autograph—an exchange that took about ten minutes. The meeting was scheduled for an hour. Volker was worried he was running short on time. So he got directly to business.

"I know you're talking to people in Ukraine and I want to make sure you're talking to the right people," Volker told Giuliani. His message was that Lutsenko wasn't trustworthy, and Giuliani shouldn't be dealing with him. "If you would like to get in touch with the real Ukrainian government, they've said they'd like to be in touch with you and I think it is a good idea," Volker said.

"Good idea," Giuliani agreed, nodding to Parnas. "We came to the same conclusion."

Volker, pleased, gave Zelensky his endorsement. "I'm pretty convinced he's the real deal," he said. As a newcomer to politics, he might not know how to get the job done yet. But he was honest and working hard to learn. He deserved the Trump administration's support, Volker said.

That wasn't good enough for Giuliani. He said Zelensky had to prove he was trustworthy by investigating Ukrainian interference in the 2016 election and opening a probe of the Bidens and Burisma.

Volker was dismayed. This was exactly what he was trying to avoid. He decided to take a stand. He bluntly told Giuliani that Biden would never have used his position as vice president to help his son or enrich himself. He had known Biden for decades. He was a man of integrity, Volker said. It was simply not credible to think Biden would be influenced in his duties.

Giuliani didn't say anything. Volker thought he was trying not to argue the point. Encouraged, Volker turned to Giuliani's other claim, that Ukrainians had interfered in the U.S. election and might be hiding the DNC's server somewhere in Ukraine. Volker had no information to offer, but he decided not to dismiss the allegation entirely. It was plausible, he said, that some Ukrainians might have sought to meddle in the election or tried to "buy influence."

They discussed next steps. Giuliani said he would be happy to meet Yermak, a top aide to Zelensky. Volker quickly promised to make the introductions. The plan was now in motion.

Sondland was working another track, still trying to help Zelensky get his meeting with Trump—in exchange for investigations.

He composed an email with an urgent tone. Ukraine was holding parliamentary elections in two days, offering an opportunity. "I talked to Zelensky just now. He is prepared to receive POTUS's call. Will assure him that he intends to run a fully transparent investigation and will 'turn over every stone.' He would greatly appreciate a call prior to Sunday so that he can put out some media about a 'friendly and productive call' (no details) prior to Ukraine election."

From his ambassador's perch in Brussels, Sondland sent the message to Pompeo, Perry, Mulvaney and other senior officials. Mulvaney got back to him quickly, saying he had asked the NSC to set up a call.

In a three-way WhatsApp text conversation with Volker and Taylor, Sondland let them know that a Trump-Zelensky phone call was imminent. He was typing fast, and his message began with a misspelling. "I spike directly to Zelensky and gave him a full briefing. He got it."

Volker had news of his own to report. "Had breakfast with Rudy this morning – teeing up a call w Yermak." Then he added, without elaboration, "Most impt is for Zelensky to say that he will help investigation." Taylor chose not to comment on that part of the conversation.

The irregular channel was working overtime.

Four days later, on July 23, Taylor dialed in to a secure video teleconference. After talking with Vindman and Hill, he felt more confident that the aid freeze was a bureaucratic snafu. Frustrating, but the kind of thing that would be resolved through meetings, emails and persistent pressure on the powers back in Washington. The conference Taylor now joined had been convened as the necessary next step in a bureaucratic chain, leading to the principals—the heads of each agency. The goal was to create a paper trail to show them that everyone supported releasing the aid.

Tim Morrison, Fiona Hill's replacement on the NSC, chaired the meeting. One by one, attendees presented their case that the aid was critical to Ukrainian security and to the U.S-Ukraine relationship. Taylor was particularly glad to hear Laura Cooper, representing the Department of Defense, explain why her agency believed the money was well spent.

Since 2014, the United States had sent $1.5 billion in security assistance to Ukraine, mostly used to purchase equipment like counter-artillery radar, drones, sniper rifles, grenade launchers, communications systems, night vision goggles and medical supplies, as well as training for the soldiers on the front lines in eastern Ukraine. To most Americans, the main goal behind spending the money—containing Russian aggression—seemed abstractly geopolitical, if they knew about the faraway conflict at all.

But for Taylor, who had watched in horror as Russia invaded in 2014, the money meant saving Ukrainian lives. So far, more than 13,000 Ukrainians had died in the conflict. Every day, the Ministry of Defense held a half-hour ceremony at their headquarters to honor soldiers who had been killed on that date each year since the fighting began. As soldiers in camouflage uniforms held bouquets of roses to honor fallen comrades, a large bell was struck once for each soldier who had died. Sometimes visiting foreign dignitaries attended the ceremony, and the ministry issued a press release to mark the occasion, concluding with the line, "Glory to the Heroes who laid down their life defending free and independent Ukraine!"

Mostly, though, the somber ceremony was unnoticed by all but the families who attended to mourn their loved ones—more every year. By bolstering Ukrainian military defenses, Taylor believed American money lessened the death toll. If it could make the Ukrainian military strong enough to persuade the Russians to give up the fight, the money might even hasten the arrival of peace. So he was relieved to hear all but two representatives from OMB agree that the aid should be released.

Beyond concerns that the aid freeze would set back the Ukrainian military and the bilateral relationship, the officials on the call questioned if it was even legal. Congress had already allocated the money, and the Department of Defense had certified that Ukraine had made sufficient progress on rooting out corruption to receive the funds. By law, the money had to be spent by the end of the fiscal year on September 30—in two months. If it wasn't, the Trump administration could be in violation of the Impoundment Control Act, passed in 1974 by Congress in response to President Nixon's efforts to withhold funding for programs he didn't like.

The call ended with no answer to the biggest question: Why was the aid being held up? Another meeting one level up was planned. In the meantime, Taylor was relieved to hear that the departments of both State and Defense would keep preparing to spend the aid money as they waited.

As far as Taylor knew, none of the Ukrainians knew about the freeze, and he hoped they would never need to.

• • •

On a lovely Wednesday morning, July 24, political Washington braced for a much-anticipated spectacle. Mueller was testifying before Congress. He would answer questions before two separate panels, Jerry Nadler's House Judiciary Committee and Adam Schiff's House Intelligence Committee.

July had been hotter than usual, with a string of days stuck in the 90s, but the humid weather had just broken. It was comfortable and cool as Mueller walked into the Capitol for what promised to be a newsworthy day.

Impeachment-inclined Democrats had high hopes that this would be a turning point. Television cameras were ready, covering it live. Americans were watching on television or catching snippets online. This was a chance to rev the engine, to build the public support that Pelosi kept saying was so crucial, to bring Donald Trump's misdeeds into a clear context that everyone could understand.

As the day wore on, it became crushingly apparent to many Democrats that they had expected too much. Mueller, who was 74, had a stellar reputation for his work in law enforcement. But during seven televised hours, he seemed old and tired and flustered. He came across as imprecise rather than razor-sharp.

His words on the page had been strong: Russia had interfered in the election; the Trump campaign had welcomed that interference, even if there was no evidence of direct cooperation. On obstruction of justice, Mueller wrote that he was leaving that question to Congress, but he also made it clear that his investigation did not clear the president of the charge.

His words in person, however, seemed to deaden his 448-page report rather than bring it to life. By the time he had left the witness chair, it seemed to many Democrats that impeachment had reached the end of the line, too.

Schiff, interviewed afterward on CNN, was already looking ahead. He focused on the 2020 election as one way to hold Trump accountable. "We do need to be realistic, and that is, the only way he's leaving office, at least at this point, is by being voted out, and I think our efforts need to be made in every respect to make sure we turn out our people."

As the media dissected Mueller's performance, and the bad reviews mounted, the president began tweeting favorites. "Impeachment's over!" he wrote, attaching an ABC TV clip of five analysts talking about the dashed expectations. He tweeted a rotating series of slides showing the cost and size of the Mueller probe ("$30+ Million Spent," "675 Days," "500+ Witnesses") that ended with two zeroes—"0 Collusion" and "0 Obstruction." The video was a popular one, with more than 6 million views. That was followed by a clip of Trump on camera, telling reporters, "The Democrats lost so *big* today. Their party is in a shambles right now."

Several Republican members of Congress, speaking before banks of microphones, declared that the day had showed, once and for all, that Mueller's investigation had cleared the president. Trump retweeted clips of each one and wrote the same grateful message. "Thank you, @GOPLeader McCarthy!" "Thank you, @RepDougCollins!" "Thank you, @Jim_Jordan!" "Thank you, @DevinNunes!"

Sean Hannity opened his nightly show with a declaration. "Fox News Alert. The Witch Hunt is dead, gone, it is buried. The real Russia investigation is only beginning." Using his voice and hands dramatically for emphasis, he said the Mueller hearing capped off "one of the single biggest, most epic embarrassments in history. What happened today should shock the conscience of every American." The screen chyron said: "Mueller Delivers Disaster for Democrats."

Hannity's guests were Giuliani and Sekulow, the president's lawyers. The trio tore apart Mueller's investigation. Hannity congratulated his guests on their hard work. "You had the entire media industrial complex spreading lies and conspiracies. You had to counter that. You had Democrats spreading lies and conspiracies. You had more misinformation than I think I've ever seen in my life."

Vindman was on edge. The Trump-Zelensky phone call was finally happening, much to the relief of the Ukrainians. It was set for the next morning, Thursday, July 25. As the NSC's lead on Ukraine, he had again drafted the president's talking points and a tentative press release, which had gone up the chain of command to Bolton in the usual way.

The talking points had almost written themselves. There was broad U.S. government consensus that U.S. policy should focus on shared national security interests, including support for Ukraine in its fight to hold off Russia and help for Zelensky in his battle against corruption and his opening up of opportunities in the energy industry.

But Vindman was still worried about the direction the call might take. There was always a risk of a detour, especially since Trump liked to ad lib. And then there was Gordon Sondland's bald declaration with the

Ukrainians at the July 10 meeting—"investigations in the energy sector." Nothing of that sort would appear in Vindman's talking points, if he could help it. The NSC lingo for items that didn't belong in the conversation: "stray voltage."

He and Hill and Bolton had agreed: Let's try to keep the president on track.

No stray voltage.

Part Two

RISK

CHAPTER FOURTEEN

"Do Us a Favor"

July 25, Kyiv and Washington

Oleksandr Danyliuk stood. He preferred to be on his feet. He and a handful of other aides were prepping President Zelensky for his second phone call with President Trump.

The first, on the night of Zelensky's election three months earlier, had been a breeze, almost chummy, with Trump's tantalizing offer: "When you're settled in and ready, I'd like to invite you to the White House." A good first step, but now Danyliuk wanted concrete results. A White House meeting, preferably in the Oval Office, would be the signal of solidarity that Zelensky needed, the signal to Putin that the United States was standing firmly by its ally.

The phone call with Trump was 30 minutes away. Zelensky was sitting in a small room near his office on the fourth floor of the massive presidential administration building in central Kyiv. The room was only big enough for a table and a couple of small couches, but it had a lovely view of Saint Sophia's Cathedral, shimmering on a gorgeous summer day. The Ukrainians were on edge. The Trump call had been scheduled for a few days earlier, but the U.S. side postponed at the last minute. Now they were half expecting another delay.

Danyliuk, who advised Zelensky on foreign policy and defense, paced while other aides sat at the table. He thought he had a good understanding of the Americans. He had earned an MBA at Indiana University and worked for several years at McKinsey & Company, the American consulting firm. He spoke English, along with French and Spanish. But his studies had not fully prepared him for Trump.

Earlier in the morning, Kurt Volker had texted Zelensky aide Andriy Yermak, who was also in the room prepping the president. "Heard from White House," Volker had written, and "assuming President Z convinces trump he will investigate /'get to the bottom of what happened' in 2016, we will nail down date for visit to Washington. Good luck!"

Danyliuk had told Bill Taylor a few days earlier that Zelensky was sensitive about being treated as some sort of pawn in Trump's reelection fight. Now Danyliuk was urging Zelensky to be careful. He advised him to talk about U.S. investment in Ukraine, especially in the energy sector. Use the phrase "the swamp" when telling Trump he shared his desire to shake up entrenched bureaucracies—Trump would like that. The idea of suggesting a Trump Tower in Kyiv was raised, but quickly shot down.

The top priority, Danyliuk argued, was to push for a specific date for the face-to-face meeting. Danyliuk was acutely aware that both Zelensky and Trump were the type to veer off in unexpected directions. Waiting for the White House operator to call, he worried that the conversation between the presidents could end without any substantial agreement on how to move forward.

In Washington, Vindman waited apprehensively in the White House Situation Room with a handful of other aides. His anxiety about the call, and what direction it might take, was shared by some of his colleagues. Bolton had talked of his fear that the conversation might turn out to be a "disaster" because Trump might press for political investigations.

For Vindman, this part of his portfolio was also personal. Ukraine was in his genes. Born in Kyiv, he was three years old when his family emigrated to the United States in the late 1970s, settling in Brooklyn. Growing up, he learned the story of his family's flight from the anti-Semitism they had encountered when Ukraine was still part of the Soviet Union.

The Vindmans embraced the United States with patriotic zeal. In 1985, a documentary called "Statue of Liberty" featured Vindman and his identical twin brother, Yevgeny. They were nine years old when filmmaker Ken Burns, himself a Brooklyn native, had come to their neighborhood, known as "Little Odessa," after the Ukrainian port city on the Black Sea. Burns was in search of material to tell the story of New York harbor's famous beacon of freedom and welcome for immigrants.

The Vindman boys, fluent in Russian and Ukrainian as well as English, both chose careers in the U.S. military. Alexander enlisted in the Army and served in South Korea, Germany and Iraq, where he was wounded by an improvised explosive device and was awarded the Purple Heart.

Later, he earned a master's degree at Harvard in Russian, Eastern Europe and Central Asian studies. That led to Defense Department postings at the Kyiv and Moscow embassies. Yevgeny took a different path, but it led to a brotherly reunion. He became an Army lawyer, and now also worked on the NSC staff.

In the Sit Room, the mood tilted toward somber. There were nods and brief hellos, but little chatter. Vindman was joined by his new boss, Tim Morrison, Fiona Hill's replacement as the NSC's top specialist on Russia and Europe. Also in the room were two aides from Vice President Pence's office: U.S. Army Lt. Gen. Keith Kellogg, his national security adviser, and Jennifer Williams, his adviser on European and Russian affairs. Several notetakers stood ready. The practice of routinely recording calls had ceased in the 1970s, after Nixon's Oval Office tapes became central evidence in the investigations that ended his presidency.

Others were listening from elsewhere in the White House, including Robert Blair, top aide to Mulvaney, and deputy national security adviser Charles Kupperman.

At about 9 a.m. in Washington—4 p.m. in Kyiv—a White House operator made the call. Trump, in his private residence on the second floor, got on the line at 9:03 a.m. Vindman's talking points called for the president to start by congratulating Zelensky on his party's recent parliamentary victory.

In the Sit Room, everyone was quiet. Some scribbled notes.

"Congratulations on a great victory," Trump began, opening the conversation as the talking points had suggested. *"We all watched from the United States and you did a terrific job. The way you came from behind, somebody who wasn't given much of a chance, and you ended up winning easily. It's a fantastic achievement. Congratulations."*

An interpreter relayed Trump's remarks. Zelensky had Post-it notes in front of him, written by his advisers. He started with flattery, as they had suggested.

"You are absolutely right Mr. President. We did win big and we worked hard for this. We worked a lot, but I would like to confess to you that I had an opportunity to learn from you. We used quite a few of your skills and knowledge and were able to use it as an example for our elections."

He joked, *"I think I should run more often so you can call me more often and we can talk over the phone more often."*

Trump's interpreter repeated what Zelensky had said. Trump laughed and said that was a good idea.

Zelensky laid the flattery on thicker. "*Well yes, to tell you the truth, we are trying to work hard because we wanted to drain the swamp here in our country. We brought in many, many new people. Not the old politicians, not the typical politicians, because we want to have a new format and a new type of government. You are a great teacher for us and in that.*"

"Drain the swamp." "Great teacher." Zelensky was hitting his marks perfectly. Trump accepted the compliment.

"*Well it is very nice of you to say that,*" he said. Then he pivoted sharply to terrain that wasn't among the talking points.

"*I will say that we do a lot for Ukraine. We spend a lot of effort and a lot of time. Much more than the European countries are doing and they should be helping you more than they are. Germany does almost nothing for you. All they do is talk and I think it's something that you should really ask them about. When I was speaking to Angela Merkel, she talks Ukraine, but she doesn't do anything. A lot of the European countries are the same way so I think it's something you want to look at. But the United States has been very, very good to Ukraine. I wouldn't say that it's reciprocal necessarily because things are happening that are not good, but the United States has been very, very good to Ukraine.*"

It was a classic Trump talking point, a gripe about burden-sharing and payback. It was a little whiff of the Trump who railed against Ukraine when Sondland, Volker and Rick Perry had met with him in the Oval Office after Zelensky's inauguration. "They tried to take me down," he said then. Now, he was confronting the new president directly, suggesting that Ukraine wasn't "necessarily" good to the United States.

Zelensky didn't object. He agreed that Europe's leaders—particularly Merkel in Germany and French president Emmanuel Macron—were not doing enough, especially in enforcing existing sanctions on Russia. Zelensky wrapped his reply in more flattery. "*Yes, you are absolutely right. Not only 100 percent, but actually 1,000 percent. And I can tell you the following: I did talk to Angela Merkel and I did meet with her. I also met and talked with Macron and I told them that they are not doing quite as much as they need to be doing on the issues with the sanctions. They are not enforcing the sanctions. They are not working as much as they should work for Ukraine. It turns out that even though logically, the European Union should be our biggest partner, but technically the United States is a much bigger partner than the European Union. And I'm very grateful to you for that because the United States is doing quite a lot for Ukraine. Much more than the European Union, especially when we are talking about sanctions against the Russian Federation. I would also like to thank you for your great support in the area of defense. We are ready to continue to cooperate for the next steps, specifically we are almost ready to buy more Javelins from the United States for defense purposes."*

Zelensky had executed a quick pivot of his own, telling Trump he was primed to buy the Javelin anti-tank missiles that the Obama administration had refused to provide, but that the Trump administration was willing to make available.

Trump didn't react. Instead, he switched gears to the laundry list of grievances that Giuliani had brought him, beginning with CrowdStrike, the company hired by the Democratic National Committee to investigate a breach of its computers in 2016. CrowdStrike determined that the DNC network had been hacked by Russian operatives. In the narrative offered by Giuliani and others, CrowdStrike had somehow taken the DNC's server to Ukraine and hidden it there. This stew of a theory also alleged that CrowdStrike was owned by a wealthy Ukrainian, even though it was actually a California company whose co-founder was a U.S. citizen born in Russia.

Trump said, *"I would like you to do us a favor though because our country has been through a lot and Ukraine knows a lot about it. I would like you to find out what happened with this whole situation with Ukraine, they say CrowdStrike . . . I guess you have one of your wealthy people . . . The server, they say Ukraine has it. There are a lot of things that went on, the whole situation. I think you're surrounding yourself with some of the same people. I would like to have the attorney general call you or your people and I would like you to get to the bottom of it. As you saw yesterday, that whole nonsense ended with a very poor performance by a man named Robert Mueller, an incompetent performance, but they say a lot of it started with Ukraine. Whatever you can do, it's very important that you do it if that's possible."*

In the Sit Room, Vindman was jolted to hear the president repeating a theory that had been thoroughly debunked. In Kyiv, some of the aides around Zelensky quietly Googled "CrowdStrike," which they had never heard of.

Trump's words were a tangle, a challenge for the interpreter. Zelensky didn't ask what "this whole situation with Ukraine" meant, but he let Trump know that he wasn't about to argue. His goal was to "work hard" on "getting our two nations" closer.

"Yes, it is very important for me and everything that you just mentioned earlier. For me as a president, it is very important and we are open for any future cooperation. We are ready to open a new page on cooperation in relations between the United States and Ukraine. For that purpose, I just recalled our ambassador from United States and he will be replaced by a very competent and very experienced ambassador who will work hard on making sure that our two nations are getting closer. I would also like and hope to see him having your trust and your confidence and have personal relations with you so we can cooperate even more so. I will personally tell you that one of my assistants spoke with Mr. Giuliani just recently and we are hoping very much that Mr. Giuliani will be able to travel to Ukraine and we will meet once he comes to Ukraine. I just wanted to assure you once again that you have nobody but friends around us. I will make sure that I surround myself with the best and most experienced people. I also wanted to tell you that we are friends. We are great friends and you Mr. President have friends in our country so we can continue our strategic partnership. I also plan to surround myself with great people and in addition to that investigation, I guarantee as the president of Ukraine that all the investigations will be done openly and candidly. That I can assure you."

Zelensky had brought up Giuliani, unprompted, embracing the man who had said that Zelensky had people around him who were "enemies of Trump and, in some cases, enemies of the United States." He had assured Trump "once again that you have nobody but friends around us." For some of those listening in, there was no clearer sign that the Ukrainian was working overtime to get himself in Trump's good graces.

Hearing Zelensky's near apology and reassurances, Trump did not change the subject as he had done after the Javelins. He stayed on his grievances, mentioning former ambassador Marie Yovanovitch, and saying what he wanted Zelensky to do, offering Attorney General William Barr as a liaison.

"Good because I heard you had a prosecutor who was very good and he was shut down and that's really unfair. A lot of people are talking about that, the way they shut your very good prosecutor down and you had some very bad people involved. Mr. Giuliani is a highly respected man. He was the mayor of New York City, a great mayor, and I would like him to call

you. I will ask him to call you along with the attorney general. Rudy very much knows what's happening and he is a very capable guy. If you could speak to him that would be great. The former ambassador from the United States, the woman, was bad news and the people she was dealing with in the Ukraine were bad news, so I just want to let you know that. The other thing, there's a lot of talk about Biden's son, that Biden stopped the prosecution and a lot of people want to find out about that so whatever you can do with the attorney general would be great. Biden went around bragging that he stopped the prosecution so if you can look into it. . . . It sounds horrible to me."

Yovanovitch, "bad news." The Bidens, "if you can look into it. . . . It sounds horrible to me." Vindman felt the call was getting worse and worse. Now Trump was pressing his own domestic political agenda. Vindman lifted his head and looked at Morrison. Their eyes met. Vindman was sure he saw concern in Morrison's eyes, too, but neither said anything. They returned to their note-taking.

Zelensky kept peddling hard, trying to reassure Trump on his gripes.

"I wanted to tell you about the prosecutor. First of all, I understand and I'm knowledgeable about the situation. Since we have won the absolute majority in our parliament, the next prosecutor general will be 100 percent my person, my candidate, who will be approved, by the parliament and will start as a new prosecutor in September. He or she will look into the situation, specifically to the company that you mentioned in this issue. The issue of the investigation of the case is actually the issue of making sure to restore the honesty so we will take care of that and will work on the investigation of the case. On top of that, I would kindly ask you if you have any additional information that you can provide to us, it would be very helpful for the investigation to make sure that we administer justice in our country with regard to the ambassador to the United States from Ukraine as far as I recall her name was Ivanovich. It was great that you were the first one who told me that she was a bad ambassador because I agree with you 100 percent. Her attitude towards me was far from the best as she admired the previous president and she was on his side. She would not accept me as a new president well enough."

Zelensky misstated Yovanovitch's name, and he didn't specify what she had done to oppose him. Vindman and his NSC colleagues knew the opposite to be true. Yovanovitch had agreed with the assessment of the Ukraine experts at the State Department and NSC, seeing Zelensky as a promising partner and serious about rooting out his country's deep-seated corruption.

Trump picked up the Yovanovitch thread, ominously.

"Well, she's going to go through some things. I will have Mr. Giuliani give you a call and I am also going to have Attorney General Barr call and we will get to the bottom of it. I'm sure you will figure it out. I heard the prosecutor was treated very badly and he was a very fair prosecutor so good luck with everything. Your economy is going to get better and better I predict. You have a lot of assets. It's a great country. I have many Ukrainian friends, they're incredible people."

In Kyiv, Danyliuk was concerned that the conversation might end without the two men agreeing on a personal meeting. He slipped Zelensky a note, reminding him to steer Trump in that direction.

"I would like to tell you that I also have quite a few Ukrainian friends that live in the United States. Actually, last time I traveled to the United States, I stayed in New York near Central Park and I stayed at the Trump Tower. I will talk to them and I hope to see them again in the future. I also wanted to thank you for your invitation to visit the United States, specifically Washington, D.C. On the other hand, I also want to ensure you that we will be very serious about the case and will work on the investigation. As to the economy, there is much potential for our two countries and one of the issues that is very important for Ukraine is energy independence. I believe we can be very successful and cooperating on energy independence with United States. We are already working on cooperation. We are buying American oil but I am very hopeful for a future meeting. We will have more time and more opportunities to discuss these opportunities and get to know each other better. I would like to thank you very much for your support."

Seeds planted.

"Good. Well, thank you very much and I appreciate that. I will tell Rudy and Attorney General Barr to call. Thank you. Whenever you would like to come to the White House, feel free to call. Give us a date and we'll work that out. I look forward to seeing you."

There was no specific date, but Trump was inviting him, again, to the White House. Zelensky said he was pleased.

"Thank you very much. I would be very happy to come and would be happy to meet with you personally and get to know you better. I am looking forward to our meeting and I also would like to invite you to visit Ukraine

and come to the city of Kyiv which is a beautiful city. We have a beautiful country which would welcome you. On the other hand, I believe that on September 1 we will be in Poland and we can meet in Poland hopefully. After that, it might be a very good idea for you to travel to Ukraine. We can either take my plane and go to Ukraine or we can take your plane, which is probably much better than mine."

Trump: *"Okay, we can work that out. I look forward to seeing you in Washington and maybe in Poland because I think we are going to be there at that time."*

Zelensky: *"Thank you very much, Mr. President."*

Trump: *"Congratulations on a fantastic job you've done. The whole world was watching. I'm not sure it was so much of an upset but congratulations."*

Zelensky: *"Thank you, Mr. President. Bye-bye."*

The call ended at 9:33 a.m. It had lasted half an hour.

In Kyiv, as the call ended, several aides flashed a quick thumbs-up. Chocolate and vanilla ice cream was brought in for the men on the warm afternoon, and they dissected the call as they ate. Parts of the call had confused the Ukrainian side; they were still trying to figure out "CrowdStrike." What was that all about?

One Zelensky aide was happy that what he called the "elephant in the room"—Giuliani, Burisma, the Bidens, the 2016 investigation—was brought out into the open. He thought Zelensky had done well to hear Trump out, without committing to anything. The aide didn't sense that Trump was demanding anything in return for a meeting. Others in the room worried that it wouldn't matter, and that Trump would find a way to claim that Ukraine would be investigating the Bidens and the 2016 election.

But another aide worried that it wouldn't matter, that Trump would find a way to send out a tweet, claiming that Ukraine would be investigating Biden and the 2016 election.

Danyliuk was not thrilled. He was happy with the progress toward building a relationship between the two presidents, but he had wanted a specific date for a White House meeting. He couldn't get a clear read about what Zelensky thought. The president didn't show much emotion. He just seemed relieved that the call had finally taken place.

As they finished their bowls of ice cream, the initial euphoria wore off.

There was a general feeling that the two leaders had not discussed much of substance—and that for all the flattery, they still hadn't accomplished any of the goals they had set going into the call. Now what?

In Washington, as Vindman replayed the call in his mind, his distress kept rising. From early in the call, he had sensed that Trump was projecting a different tone from the April 21 conversation. That one had been positive, even funny. This time, Trump's voice had an edge. It seemed heavier, even dour.

Worse, to Vindman's ear, Trump was clearly demanding that a foreign government investigate a political rival and U.S. citizen. He thought that was wrong. When Trump said, "Do us a favor," Vindman tried to put himself in Zelensky's shoes. There was such a vast power disparity between the president of the United States and the president of Ukraine. When the U.S. president asked for "a favor," Vindman believed, Zelensky could only interpret it as a demand, one that he could not realistically refuse. For a White House meeting to happen, Vindman thought, Zelensky understood that he needed to do as Trump had asked.

Every president sets his own foreign policy, and Trump was under no obligation to follow staff-prepared talking points. That wasn't what bothered Vindman. In his view, the call had undermined U.S. national security interests. The big picture was Russia; Ukraine was just a key supporting player. Vindman was astonished that Trump would endanger that bedrock U.S. foreign policy goal for personal political reasons. If Zelensky were seen to be running a politically motivated investigation for Trump, it could endanger Ukraine's broad bipartisan support in Washington. Democrats might withdraw their support for Ukraine, jeopardizing hundreds of millions of dollars in aid now and into the future. Vindman thought it put Ukraine in an impossible bind.

Tim Morrison had a different take on the call. Unlike Vindman, Morrison did not hear anything that struck him as illegal. The call was merely proof of what he had heard from Fiona Hill during hours of briefings before she left. There was a separate track of Trump foreign policy, with Giuliani at the heart of it, and Sondland straddling the line, a foot in both. Stay away from all of it, she had said, especially any conversations with Giuliani. Morrison had decided to follow her advice.

Now, when he heard Trump raise the issue of the DNC server, he realized that Hill had been absolutely right. But mainly, Morrison was concerned about the way Zelensky had been talking to Trump. He was flattering Trump instead of making the full-throated endorsement of the anti-corruption reform agenda that Morrison had hoped to hear. He found Zelensky obsequious and the conversation disappointing.

Morrison also thought Trump had his own priorities for Ukraine. He had heard Trump's message about the country's corruption problem and getting Europe to contribute more for Ukraine's security. Morrison knew the White House had recently put a hold on the U.S. aid that Congress had authorized. But Morrison wasn't too concerned. He was confident that Pompeo, Bolton, Secretary of Defense Mark Esper and CIA director Gina Haspel would persuade Trump that Zelensky was a corruption-fighter who deserved the money.

Jennifer Williams, from Pence's staff, was too busy taking notes during the call to see how others in the Sit Room were reacting. She found the conversation highly irregular. She had never heard the word "CrowdStrike" before and she wasn't aware of the efforts to generate investigations of the Bidens and the 2016 election. She had been on many calls with other world leaders, and it caught her by surprise when Trump talked about issues that were so clearly related to a political agenda, and not to U.S. foreign policy. Inappropriate, she thought.

Morrison knew that a MEMCON, government-speak for a "memorandum of the conversation," would be generated by the notetakers. If that memo leaked, there could be all kinds of consequences. Supporters would see Trump being Trump, transactional and freewheeling. Opponents might see Trump abusing his power. Morrison also worried about how such a leak might play in Ukraine. Would the conversation, with all its unusual flourishes, cause Zelensky problems?

Immediately after the call, Vindman and Morrison turned to the press release that needed to go out. The draft that Vindman had done was useless. Now, in the Sit Room, they crossed out sentence after sentence. In the end, the statement said the two leaders had "discussed ways to strengthen the relationship between the United States and Ukraine, including energy and economic cooperation. Both leaders also expressed that they look forward to the opportunity to meet."

No one reading that statement could know how little it reflected the call. They handed the rewrite to an NSC press officer for distribution to the media.

• • •

Vindman, still upset, went to see his brother, an NSC lawyer, in his office in the Old Executive Office Building adjacent to the White House. He closed the door. He expressed concern and alarm about the call, about the future of U.S.-Ukraine relations, even about the possibility that Trump might have broken the law.

The brothers talked in lowered voices for a few minutes about what to do. They decided that Vindman should report what had happened to John Eisenberg, the top NSC lawyer. After the July 10 White House meeting with Sondland and the Ukrainians, he had gone to Eisenberg to report his misgivings. Eisenberg had invited him to come back if he had any other concerns, he remembered.

Vindman knew that Trump had a jaundiced view of career government officials, and he did not know why. As an Army officer, his oath required him to protect the Constitution. It was his duty, he felt, to tell someone what he had witnessed.

The brothers went together to Eisenberg's office. Once again, as he had two weeks earlier, Eisenberg listened closely, taking notes on a yellow legal pad, page after page. For 20 minutes, Alexander Vindman narrated the call. Yevgeny Vindman stood by, a silent witness.

When Vindman finished, Eisenberg said, "We will take a look at this." It was curt, but Vindman believed Eisenberg understood the seriousness of what had happened.

Eisenberg, a former Justice Department official, had served as the NSC's top legal adviser since the start of the administration. His tenure included several legal crises, including the Mueller investigation. He was known to his colleagues as conscientious and cautious, an honest broker. But they also saw in him an expansive view of the power of the presidency.

As the brothers were getting ready to leave, Eisenberg's deputy, Michael Ellis, entered. He was there to discuss the possibility of putting the rough transcript of the Trump-Zelensky call on a classified computer server, which would strictly limit access to the document. Vindman was uncomfortable. Why would the transcript need to be handled that way? Was someone seeking to hide it?

Morrison also went to see Eisenberg and Ellis. He didn't share Vindman's level of concern about the call, but he thought the lawyers needed to know about it, and the problems that could follow if it leaked out.

A call that was supposed to solve problems had ended up creating new ones. It was less than perfect, virtually everyone agreed.

As Trump's call with Zelensky was ending, an OMB official named Mark Sandy was sending an email to his OMB supervisor, Michael Duffey: "Mike, here's the OGC [Office of General Counsel]-approved, revised footnote."

Sandy knew his "footnote," while destined for a routine budget document, was no minor matter. It spelled out that OMB had the power to hold up security aid for Ukraine until August 5, "to allow for an interagency process to determine the best use of these funds."

The carefully worded paragraph was the product of a week's worth of work by Sandy. A former Marshall Scholar who earned a degree in politics and economics at Oxford, Sandy had spent years at the OMB, across administrations of both parties. He had even served, briefly, as the agency's acting director for the first month of the Trump administration. Now he was back in his position as deputy associate director for national security, working with the Defense Department and a few other agencies.

A week earlier, Sandy had returned to work after a ten-day leave. Duffey had pulled him aside after a meeting at the Old Executive Office Building with some surprising news: The president wanted the military aid for Ukraine frozen. The Pentagon portion amounted to $250 million of the $400 million Congress had approved.

Why? Sandy asked. Duffey said he didn't know. How long would the freeze last? Duffey didn't know that either. Their mission was to figure out a way to do it. Congress had already ordered the money spent. What were the options?

Puzzled, Sandy went back to his office in the New Executive Office Building, across Pennsylvania Avenue. Before his leave, he had seen Duffey's emails to the Pentagon, saying the president had raised questions about the Ukraine aid. But as far as Sandy knew, those questions hadn't led to any policy change. What had happened since then?

Later that day, Duffey proposed a novel solution, something Sandy had never seen done before: How about a footnote attached to the "apportionment," the legal document laying out how an agency is spending congressionally approved funds?

Sandy had worked on thousands of budget documents in his twelve years at OMB. He had never seen a hold placed on money after Congress had been told it would be spent. He warned Duffey that freezing the Ukrainian aid could violate the Impoundment Control Act, which bars the president from refusing to spend money appropriated by Congress. They needed to consult the department's lawyers.

He also checked in with Elaine McCusker, the Pentagon's acting comptroller, who had fielded Duffey's earlier emails in June. McCusker shared Sandy's misgivings. The money had to be spent before the end of the fiscal year on September 30, she said.

Sandy made sure the footnote reflected her concerns, stating that the Pentagon could "continue its planning" during the pause in aid. That would ensure that when the freeze was lifted, as everyone expected, there would be no delay in spending the money—and no violation of the law.

On the morning of July 25, Sandy sent the lawyer-approved footnote to Duffey, who forwarded it to the Pentagon with a note that signaled that the freeze could cause controversy if it became public: "Given the sensitive nature of the request, I appreciate your keeping that information closely held to those who need to know."

One of the recipients was McCusker. Like Sandy, she was a career civil servant, used to dotting i's and crossing t's on the spending of American tax dollars. She wanted to make sure 100 percent that the law was followed. She sent Sandy a short message two minutes later: Had the Defense Department's top lawyer cleared the footnote?

That afternoon, top lawyers at the two agencies conferred. "I think we are good," McCusker wrote to Sandy. The money for Ukraine was officially frozen.

While Pentagon and OMB lawyers were still discussing the legalities, a Ukrainian embassy official emailed a Pentagon contact. What's going on with the security assistance? Not yet aware of the freeze, the Pentagon staffer sent back a reassuring reply: No holdup.

State Department officials also received emails from the Ukrainian embassy. Catherine Croft, a special adviser on Ukraine, was impressed at the Ukrainians' "diplomatic tradecraft," as she called it, finding out so quickly that a freeze was afoot.

The emails were evidence of what Bill Taylor had been so eager to avoid. That an official freeze, even a temporary one, would set off tremors on both sides of the Atlantic.

• • •

After work that evening, the Vindman brothers drove home together, as they did almost every day. They lived on the same street, four houses apart, in the Virginia suburbs of Washington. Their wives, both redheads, were close friends. So were their children. They were still dazed.

Over dinner that night at a nearby Latin American restaurant, Vindman's wife listened to his brief, circumspect account of the day's events. He was leaving out details, but not his reaction. What he had heard, he told her, had profoundly disturbed him. They were both silent for a minute. Then he said: "If what happened today gets out, the president will be impeached."

CHAPTER FIFTEEN

The "Big Stuff"

July 26, Kyiv and Washington

Gordon Sondland was in a good mood. It was early Friday afternoon in Kyiv, sunny and warm, and he had just finished a series of successful meetings with top Ukrainian officials, including an hour with President Zelensky, fresh from his phone call with President Trump.

The E.U. ambassador would by flying back to Brussels later in the afternoon, but he had time for a celebratory lunch and a fine bottle of wine, now that the Trump-Zelensky call had finally taken place. He had invited two aides and David Holmes, the embassy's top political officer, to be his guests at SHO, a restaurant with rustic wooden tables, an open kitchen and a bright, modern feel.

The timing of their Zelensky session was a happy coincidence. It had been scheduled before the Trump call. Kurt Volker was also in town, so he had joined Sondland and Bill Taylor. Holmes was there, taking notes.

Zelensky seemed mostly positive about the Trump call. "Three times" Trump had raised "some very sensitive issues," Zelensky said. He planned to follow up on those issues when he met Trump "in person." Holmes wasn't sure what Zelensky was talking about. He hadn't seen an official readout of the call yet—no one in the embassy had—so he didn't know what these "sensitive issues" might be.

Holmes was curious about something that had happened after the Zelensky meeting that morning. At the last minute, Holmes was told to follow Sondland to take notes on his chat with Zelensky adviser Andriy Yermak. But when Holmes arrived at Yermak's office, an aide stopped him. The two men had decided to meet alone, she said, no note-taking. Holmes didn't know why. He waited outside.

Now Sondland and the embassy trio were sipping wine on SHO's lovely outdoor terrace, looking over the menu, which offered several kinds of caviar, veal cheeks and lamb tongue. Volker and Taylor hadn't been able to come. They were headed to the military front lines in eastern Ukraine for a firsthand look at the forces battling Russian-backed forces.

To Holmes, the lunch felt mostly social, with Sondland talking about marketing strategies in his hotel business. Holmes wanted to ask Sondland about his meeting with Yermak, why it needed to be private. But it didn't feel like the time or place.

The appetizers arrived, and Sondland told the group that he was going to call the president to update him. It was not yet 7 a.m. in Washington. Sondland tapped his cellphone. It was remarkable, the others thought, that Sondland could just pick up his unsecured phone and call the president.

More than once, they heard him say: Gordon Sondland, I'm holding for the president. Holmes thought Sondland seemed a little impatient. Suddenly, Sondland's demeanor changed. The call wasn't on speaker, but Holmes could hear Trump's unmistakable voice booming from the cellphone, so loud that Sondland held the phone away from his ear.

Sondland said he was calling from Kyiv, that he had met with Zelensky. Sondland was bantering, like two friends chatting. He told Trump that Zelensky "loves your ass." The saltiness seemed to be Sondland's way of conveying Zelensky's willingness to work with the United States.

"So, he's gonna do the investigation?" Trump said.

"He's gonna do it," Sondland replied.

Sondland was emphatic. Zelensky would do "anything you ask him to," he told Trump. Holmes was struck by the words, so he started typing a few notes in his phone as the conversation continued. It shifted to another matter of importance to the president: efforts to free the American rapper A$AP Rocky from a Swedish jail, at the request of reality television star Kim Kardashian. Sweden was a European Union member, so as the E.U. ambassador, Sondland had been making inquiries.

The rapper was being held for his alleged role in a street brawl, and Trump had come to his defense several times on Twitter, at one point saying a video showed A$AP Rocky had been harassed by troublemakers. "Give A$AP Rocky his FREEDOM," Trump had tweeted the day before, hours after talking to Zelensky. "We do so much for Sweden but it doesn't seem to work the other way around. Sweden should focus on its real crime problem! #FreeRocky."

Now Sondland was telling Trump that the rapper was "kind of fucked there" and "should have pled guilty." He recommended that Trump "let him get sentenced, play the racism card, give him a ticker-tape when he comes home." He said Sweden "should have released him on your word," but that, at least, "you can tell the Kardashians you tried."

When Sondland hung up, he told his tablemates that Trump had been in a bad mood, as he often is early in the morning, a broad hint that this wasn't the first such chat. The call had been so open, the opposite of private, that Holmes decided to ask Sondland for his candid assessment of Trump's views on Ukraine.

"Is it true that the president doesn't give a shit about Ukraine?" Holmes asked.

It's true, Sondland said.

Holmes said: Why not?

He only cares about the "big stuff," Sondland said.

He told Sondland: There's plenty of big stuff happening in Ukraine. For starters, a war with Russia.

Sondland said he meant "big stuff" that benefited Trump. Like the "Biden investigation."

As Sondland was chatting up Trump, Nancy Pelosi started her morning trying to stamp out a little fire smoldering in her caucus by meeting with Alexandria Ocasio-Cortez.

Tension had been mounting with the Squad since late June, when Ocasio-Cortez and her three colleagues criticized fellow House Democrats for supporting an emergency funding bill for operations on the U.S. southern border. It had originated in the Senate. "A vote for Mitch McConnell's border bill," tweeted Squad member Ilhan Omar of Minnesota, "is a vote to keep kids in cages." Rashida Tlaib of Michigan had declared: "If you see the Senate bill as an option, then you don't believe in basic human rights."

Their criticism did not sit well with Pelosi, who had agreed to move the bill through the House. She was doing a slow burn. A few days later, in an interview with *New York Times* columnist Maureen Dowd, she let loose. The border bill was the strongest she could get. The Squad might be popular online, but that did not translate to clout in Congress. "All these people have their public whatever and their Twitter world," she told Dowd. But in the House, "they're four people, and that's how many votes they got."

Ocasio-Cortez shot back—on Twitter. "That public 'whatever' is called public sentiment," she wrote after Dowd's column appeared. "And wielding the power to shift it is how we actually achieve meaningful change in this country."

The feuding escalated a few days later. Meeting with the full caucus behind closed doors on July 10, Pelosi pointedly said: "You got a complaint? You come and talk to me about it. But do not tweet about our members and expect us to think that that is just okay." She didn't name anyone. She didn't need to.

The goodwill that Ocasio-Cortez had generated in her first few weeks, when she had supported Pelosi's bid to return as speaker, was in danger of disappearing. Fifty years apart in age but equally resolute, the two women had not had a one-on-one meeting in five months.

Ocasio-Cortez thought the speaker had gone too far in dismissing the Squad members. Yes, they were at odds about impeachment, but this latest spat had crossed a line for Ocasio-Cortez. She said so during an interview with *The Washington Post*'s Rachael Bade after the caucus meeting. "When these comments first started, I kind of thought that she was keeping the progressive flank at more of an arm's distance in order to protect more moderate members, which I understood." But "the singling out of newly elected women of color" had become "just outright disrespectful."

Now Pelosi was attempting to change the tone by inviting Ocasio-Cortez to her office. Congress was about to recess for its summer six-week break, and it seemed like a good time to hash out their differences. When they emerged, neither woman would discuss specifics of their chat, but Pelosi tweeted out a smiling photo of the two of them, arm-in-arm, and wrote: "Today, Congresswoman @RepAOC and I sat down to discuss working together to meet the needs of our districts and our country, fairness in our economy and diversity in our country."

Within an hour of that tweet, Pelosi met with reporters at her weekly news conference. She was asked whether she and Ocasio-Cortez had been able to "bury the hatchet."

"I don't think there ever was any hatchet," Pelosi said.

"She called you downright disrespectful," a reporter reminded her.

Pelosi did not bite. "We're in a political arena," she said. "We have our differences. . . . It's like you're in a family. In a family you have your differences, but you're still family."

She looked at the reporter who asked the question, and said: "Does your family always agree on everything?"

• • •

At the White House that morning, Vindman was finding it hard to concentrate. He was still reeling from the Trump-Zelensky phone call. He was missing Fiona Hill, his favorite sounding board. She had left the White House a week earlier, and was traveling, off the grid.

As was standard practice, it fell to him to review the call's rough transcript for accuracy. He made a couple of corrections. He noticed that the transcript did not note that Zelensky had explicitly mentioned Burisma. Vindman fixed it, then turned to another looming problem. In five days, he was to help lead a committee on the Ukraine that would include top officials from the State and Defense departments and from the intelligence community. How should he handle what he had heard on the call? He phoned George Kent. As the deputy assistant secretary of state for European and Eurasian affairs, Kent was on the interagency committee. Vindman trusted him.

Vindman told Kent about the president's call, and he said he was planning to raise his concerns with the committee for guidance. Kent told Vindman that was a good idea, that the committee members needed to understand what was happening.

After his call with Kent, a familiar face stopped by Vindman's office to say hello. He was a CIA analyst, an expert on Ukraine who would likely be representing the agency at the committee meeting. Vindman didn't know him well, but he had security clearance. Vindman could tell him of the call confidentially. Vindman motioned him inside his office. The CIA analyst seemed disturbed by what he was hearing. He clearly shared Vindman's concerns.

Vindman felt he had done all he could do. He had reported his concerns confidentially to the appropriate people. He would also raise them at the committee meeting in a few days.

After his talk with Vindman, the CIA analyst went back to the agency's headquarters in Langley and jotted down notes. He wanted to chronicle Vindman's words while they were still fresh in his mind: crazy . . . *frightening . . . completely lacking in substance related to national security.*

The CIA analyst had served a stint at the NSC earlier in the Trump administration and had been in meetings with the president. He believed Trump was entirely capable of what Vindman had described. He also felt a calming sense of duty. He needed to report what he had heard.

Someone needed to investigate, to find out whether the commander-in-chief had abused his office for his own political gain. But whom should he tell?

He approached a CIA lawyer he knew well, saying he wanted to share something in confidence, as an anonymous report. As he told the story, the lawyer's eyes grew wide. Let's go back over a few points, he said, then I'll take the information to Courtney Simmons Elwood, the CIA's general counsel.

The lawyer promised not to share the analyst's identity with Elwood.

At the Capitol, Pelosi's weekly news conference was still going strong. CNN congressional reporter Manu Raju asked about impeachment: "Some of your Democratic colleagues believe you're simply trying to run out the clock. . . . Are you?"

It wasn't an idle question. There was grumbling from House members who favored impeachment. Some suspected Pelosi wasn't just being cautious. Her strategy, they thought, was to keep them at bay until 2020 arrived. Then, with the presidential primaries about to begin, Pelosi could argue that it made more sense to let voters decide Trump's fate.

"No, I'm not trying to run out the clock," Pelosi said, irritation in her voice. "Let's get sophisticated about this, okay?" she said, holding her hands out wide. She let out an annoyed little laugh and repeated: "Okay?" On impeachment, she said, "we will proceed when we have what we need to proceed, not one day sooner."

Before Mueller's testimony, the pro-impeachment faction had been growing. By the time of Pelosi's news conference, a *Washington Post* count put the number at 101. The faction was as determined as ever, but Pelosi was repeating her mantra: Legislate. Investigate. Litigate. Wait.

"Everybody has the liberty and the luxury to . . . criticize me for trying to go down the path in the most determined, positive way," she said. "I'm willing to take whatever heat there is there to say a decision will be made in a timely fashion . . . when we have the best, strongest possible case."

Pelosi had barely finished speaking when Jerry Nadler stood before reporters and announced a much more aggressive posture. The Judiciary Committee, which he chaired, would ask a federal judge to enforce congressional subpoenas seeking grand jury information related to the Mueller investigation.

His position aligned with two-thirds of Pelosi's mantra—investigate and litigate—and he said Pelosi had signed off on the move. But the back-to-back press conferences, with their strikingly different tones, showed Pelosi's difficult balancing act in keeping her caucus together. Privately, lawmakers and senior staff members were telling *Washington Post* reporters that the relationship between Pelosi's office and Nadler's committee had soured.

She was counseling caution. Nadler was blunt, pedal to the floor: "We are considering the malfeasances of the president, we're considering what remedies we can do, including the possibility of articles of impeachment."

Nadler considered the Mueller report a damning indictment of Trump, especially its conclusions about obstruction of Congress. Mueller had left the door open for Congress to investigate, and now Nadler was trying to push his way through. In public statements and in court filings, he was using the I-word like a chef using salt—liberally and often. "Because Department of Justice policies will not allow prosecution of a sitting president, the United States House of Representatives is the only institution of the Federal Government that can now hold President Trump accountable for these actions," Nadler's committee wrote in its petition to the court. "To do so, the House must have access to all the relevant facts and consider whether to exercise its full Article I powers, including a constitutional power of the utmost gravity—approval of articles of impeachment."

Nadler said Mueller's appearance before Congress two days earlier did nothing to change the conclusions of his report. "Some have argued that because he was reluctant and seemed older than some remembered him, his work is somehow diminished," Nadler said. He disagreed. He thought the Mueller report was a call to action.

So did others. "If you showed up expecting a Broadway show, sure, you may have been disappointed," said Eric Swalwell of California, who spoke to the reporters with Nadler. But, he said, Mueller's recitation of the facts had prompted six more Democrats to publicly endorse an impeachment inquiry.

Doug Collins of Georgia, the top Republican on Nadler's Judiciary committee, called the chairman's legal maneuver partisan and baseless. "Democrats want to convince their base they're still wedded to impeachment even after this week's hearing," he said. It's "a sham."

• • •

At OMB, Michael Duffey was preparing himself for that day's Deputies Small Group meeting, the next level up on the policy ladder. He was anticipating a grilling on the aid freeze.

Duffey was still learning the OMB ropes after serving as executive director of the Wisconsin Republican Party. He had worked at the Pentagon during the George W. Bush administration, but he didn't have much experience with budget issues, certainly not at Mark Sandy's level.

To steel Duffey for the expected questions, Sandy had drawn up a list: What was the reason for the hold? How long would it last? How much of the $400 million was involved? And, if it came to this, how would they explain the freeze to Congress and the Ukrainians? But by the time Duffey arrived for the meeting, he and his staff still didn't have the answers to those questions.

This high-level group almost never gathered to discuss Ukraine alone. But the aid freeze had become a serious concern. The deputy national security adviser, Charles Kupperman, was chairing the meeting. He asked each agency's representative to weigh in. From David Hale, the undersecretary of state for political affairs, came a strong plea for releasing the hold. The Pentagon's undersecretary for policy, John Rood, agreed. So did Lt. Gen. Keith Kellogg, national security adviser to Vice President Pence.

Vindman was there as a backbencher, supporting the NSC higher-ups. He listened as participants argued that the stakes were high and the timing urgent. If the freeze became public, they said, the Russians would be emboldened to act more aggressively in Ukraine. After yesterday's troubling phone call, it was a relief to hear experts from across the government affirm their support for the basic pillars of U.S. policy in Ukraine.

Once again, OMB was an outlier. Duffey's stance was seconded only by Robert Blair, senior adviser to Mick Mulvaney, speaking for Trump's acting chief of staff. The president had directed the freeze, they said, driven by his concern about corruption. He wanted to make sure Ukraine was managing the issue.

That brought a chorus of objections from the others. They weren't challenging the president's authority, they insisted. They were questioning his rationale. A few days before, Zelensky's party had triumphed in parliamentary elections. His government had real potential to turn things around. Corruption was always an issue in Ukraine. But why punish this new and promising leader for the past and threaten his progress by withholding military aid that the U.S. government had pledged?

The meeting ended with the same consensus as the first two: The aid should be released. Dislodging the money would require one more round: a Principals Committee meeting, the very top of the administration. The deputies' group agreed that Pompeo, Bolton and Secretary of Defense Mike Esper should go directly to President Trump and urge him to lift the freeze.

After the session, Tim Morrison at the NSC began trying to find a time when all the principals could be together to deliver the message. To get the aid flowing, it needed to be done quickly.

In Kyiv, Holmes couldn't get the Sondland-Trump call out of his head. How could Trump not "give a shit" about Ukraine? How could he think the "big stuff" was the Bidens? Wow. Holmes returned to the embassy, typed up his notes from the day. He wrote an email to the U.S. embassy in Sweden to brief them on the A$AP Rocky part of the call.

Everyone in the embassy understood the value of Trump and Zelensky having a personal meeting. It would be good for both leaders, both nations. But, especially after overhearing Sondland's conversation with Trump, Holmes realized there was a disconnect. The embassy staff needed to work harder to come up with ways to explain Ukraine's importance to Trump, in terms the president would find compelling.

Holmes went to see his supervisor, Kristina Kvien, the deputy chief of mission, the second-ranking officer in the embassy. He walked her though Sondland's call to Trump. Later, he told several other colleagues. He couldn't stop talking about what he had heard. The call was so unusual. He wondered if it would turn out at some point to be important.

CHAPTER SIXTEEN

Plan B

July 27 to August 28, Washington and Kyiv

Throughout the weekend, the CIA lawyer and the CIA general counsel wrestled with how to handle the serious allegations brought to them by one of their analysts.

Courtney Simmons Elwood, the general counsel, was hearing that others had raised concerns about the president's call, suggesting the analyst's account was generally accurate. The matter was obviously a delicate one. It involved the president. They needed to tell someone. But who? And how? There was no road map for this sort of allegation.

Normally, if there was a reasonable basis to suspect a crime had been committed, Elwood would feel duty bound to make a criminal referral to the Justice Department. But it was too early to make that determination. She had a lot more work to do. For now, she and the agency lawyer debated whether and how to convey the analyst's allegation that the president had crossed a red line by asking a foreign government to investigate a political rival.

They didn't see how they could avoid alerting the White House counsel's office. On Monday, July 29, Elwood contacted John Eisenberg. As the NSC's chief lawyer, he was the one most familiar with intelligence matters. He and Elwood often spoke. She told Eisenberg that the analyst, whose identity she did not know, was not the only one worried about the call. Eisenberg did not sound very surprised, indicating he knew there were rumblings.

At Langley, the analyst got an update from the CIA lawyer, who said Elwood had told the White House. That was normal and appropriate, the lawyer assured him. But Eisenberg's muted reaction left him with a funny feeling, the lawyer said. It wasn't at all clear what would happen next.

The CIA analyst started thinking about a Plan B.

• • •

Inside the White House, Vindman was feeling the repercussions. Eisenberg had pulled him aside to ask if he had talked to anyone about the July 25 call. Eisenberg said the CIA had informed him that people there had heard about the call and were concerned. Vindman replied that he had told two people: George Kent, at State, and a CIA analyst. Eisenberg told Vindman not to talk to anybody else about the call.

Vindman wondered: Had his CIA colleague discussed their conversation with anyone? He followed Eisenberg's instructions and did not discuss the call further with anyone outside the White House.

By midweek at the CIA, the analyst wanted advice. He was thinking hard about someone he could ask. It was a highly sensitive and partially classified matter. That narrowed the universe of people in whom he could confide. He thought of one person—a lawyer who worked for the Democratic leadership of the House Intelligence Committee staff. That lawyer's ultimate boss was Schiff. The analyst did not consider it a partisan issue; he was seeking advice, in confidence, from a friend, as a friend, not in his role as a committee lawyer.

He arranged a meeting. The lawyer listened as the analyst explained what had happened so far. The analyst was worried, he told his friend, that the White House might not do anything about this serious matter. They agreed that he needed legal guidance, someone with expertise in the national security field. The friend offered a suggestion, another lawyer. The second contact eventually led to a third: Andrew Bakaj, a lawyer specializing in whistleblower protection. On Saturday, August 3, the CIA analyst was at home in Washington and Bakaj was making German pancakes for his family. They spoke over an encrypted phone app for security.

The analyst spooled out the general nature of his concerns about the Trump-Zelenksy call, being careful not to reveal anything that could be arguably classified. He told Bakaj he wanted the matter properly investigated. "The only way that happens is to go to Congress," Bakaj told him. "And that means you have to go to the inspector general."

Bakaj explained that whistleblowers in the intelligence community could take an urgent concern to the inspector general for the intelligence community, Michael Atkinson. If Atkinson were to confirm that the matter was both urgent and credible, he would be legally obligated to send the complaint to Congress, Bakaj told him.

The CIA analyst was elated. He finally had a clear plan. Over the phone, he agreed to hire Bakaj, a man he had never met in person.

The CIA analyst set to work writing his complaint, usually after work, late into the evening. In frequent phone calls, Bakaj provided procedural advice only, describing the format and requirements of a complaint. To prevent any taint, the analyst needed to write it himself. He could not disclose classified information to Bakaj or anyone outside the intelligence community. Neither man wanted to put the analyst in legal jeopardy.

Bakaj thought it was likely that the complaint would be transmitted confidentially to Congress and the White House would claim executive privilege, asserting the president's right to confidentiality on certain private conversations. That would be the end of it. No one would ever learn what the president had said.

On Monday, August 12, the CIA analyst and Bakaj finally met in person at the lawyer's office in downtown Washington. The analyst said he had submitted his complaint to Atkinson's office. He did not show a copy to Bakaj.

The two men talked about what might happen next. As their meeting ended, the analyst asked Bakaj about his last name. "It's Ukrainian," Bakaj said.

"Great," the analyst said, rolling his eyes at the irony.

At the NSC, Vindman was working hard on the aid freeze.

Returning from vacation on August 12, he had been dismayed to learn that the Ukrainian money was still blocked. He was told that Bolton would be meeting with the president in the next few days. It was now Vindman's job to provide Bolton with ammunition: a presidential decision memo, justifying the aid. In the regular channel, this document was an important one, an opportunity to fuse all the arguments into one concise recommendation for action.

Vindman had never met with Trump. This memo was his most direct means of communication to the president. He drafted a background section, explaining why the United States had for years helped the Ukrainian military in its fight against Russia. He made clear that every agency in the national security world, not just the NSC, believed the money was well spent. He finished the memo on August 15. After that it was in Bolton's hands, and all Vindman could do was wait.

At the Pentagon, acting comptroller Elaine McCusker was waiting, too. It was now August 16, and President Trump was scheduled to meet with his national security team at his golf club in Bedminster, New Jersey, one of his homes away from home.

As McCusker understood it, the aid freeze was on the agenda. The principals—Pompeo, Bolton, and McCusker's boss, Secretary of Defense Mark Esper—all agreed the aid should be released. Bedminster offered an opportunity to present a united front and persuade the president to let the money go. Or, failing that, maybe getting clear guidance that the aid freeze was permanent, so Congress could be notified in compliance with the law.

The original hold had expired on August 5. OMB had extended it with a second footnote, claiming there was still plenty of time to send the aid by September 30, the legal deadline. But as McCusker well knew, lifting the freeze was not like flipping a light switch. Moving the money was a multi-step process. It could be done efficiently, but not speedily. They had to follow the rules.

A focus on such details had helped McCusker reach her top position as the Pentagon's acting comptroller. In 2016, she had won the Department of Defense's Distinguished Civilian Service Award—the highest honor the department can give. When Trump nominated her to the deputy comptroller position in 2017, she used her Senate confirmation hearing to thank others. "Amazing teammates have allowed me to leverage my skills in the service of the country that I love," she had said.

But now she was working with people who did not seem to grasp the careful process that she and her Pentagon colleagues were required to follow. She had been trying to explain that to Michael Duffey at OMB. Earlier in August, while reviewing the wording for the new footnote, she objected to saying flatly that a longer freeze would not interfere with "the timely execution" of the funds. That was no longer true, she told Duffey in an email. It might interfere, she said.

After the Bedminster meeting, McCusker heard nothing. There were press reports saying Trump's national security advisers had met with him in a secure conference room at the golf club, where they had briefed him on negotiations with the Taliban in Afghanistan and progress toward a peace settlement. No mention of the aid freeze, which still wasn't public. Eager for an update, McCusker emailed Duffey the next morning. Her subject line: "Any news?"

"No," he replied a few hours later. "Still trying to get a readout." By afternoon, he was more definitive. "Sounds like Ukraine was not discussed."

At the White House, Vindman also was trying to find out how the meeting had gone. Had his decision memo been presented? How had the president reacted? His efforts turned up contradictory accounts: The aid freeze hadn't come up, the meeting was all about Afghanistan. No, the freeze had come up, but Trump hadn't decided.

One fact was not in doubt. The freeze was still in place.

On the morning of Tuesday, August 20, Bolton decided to take Trump's temperature on the aid freeze. The only way to get the money going was to separate the aid from whatever Giuliani was telling him. When they met, Trump was adamant. He wasn't in favor of sending any aid until the Ukrainians turned over the results of their investigations into Hillary Clinton and the Bidens. Bolton suggested a meeting with Esper and Pompeo to discuss the issue. Three days later, after Bolton had left for a G7 meeting in France, Trump told Pompeo and Esper he needed a couple of days to think about it.

Time was running out, and Trump was in no hurry.

Congress had gotten wind that the aid was on hold. McCusker and her Defense Department colleagues were fielding questions from the Senate Armed Services Committee and the House Appropriations Committee. The Senate committee specifically asked if OMB had directed the hold. McCusker sent that one on to Duffey. Not her place to answer for OMB.

In the last week of August, the inquiries mounted. OMB received email queries from the offices of Senator Rob Portman of Ohio, Senator Jim Inhofe of Oklahoma, and Representative Mac Thornberry of Texas. Representative Paul Cook of California sent a personal letter to Mulvaney. They were all Republicans, and they all wanted to know why the money was on hold.

Word of the freeze was now seeping outside the government, too. On August 26, a vice president at defense contractor L3Harris Technologies emailed a Pentagon contact. "The impact of holding this case and allowing the funding to expire is extremely serious for us as the communications devices have been built and are ready to ship," the defense contractor wrote.

These inquiries exposed a risk. The longer the freeze, the more likely that it would leak to the press. Then Ukrainians would have to deal with the embarrassment of its most important ally putting a hold on vital military aid. Putin and the Russians would love that. Vindman, Taylor and others wanted to get the aid flowing again before the freeze went public.

On August 27, John Bolton arrived in Kyiv with news for the Ukrainians. In four days, Trump would be traveling to Warsaw for an 80th anniversary commemoration of the outbreak of World War II. Trump was reserving time to meet with President Zelensky. The meeting, Bolton told Zelensky's chief of staff, "would be crucial to cementing their relationship."

Holmes from the embassy was there with Bolton, taking notes. The Ukrainians were still pushing for an Oval Office visit, but they agreed that the Warsaw gathering would be a good chance for the two men to spend time together.

Morrison from the NSC had joined Bolton on the trip from Washington. After the meeting, Holmes listened as Bolton complained to Morrison and Taylor about the irregular channel. Giuliani still had the president's ear, Bolton was saying, and there was nothing he could do about it. As for Sondland, he was way outside his mandate, meddling in a country that wasn't even an E.U. member, Bolton told them. He wanted to put Sondland back in his place.

Then Bolton brought up the aid freeze. Taylor and Holmes were all ears. Bolton said a release of the money hinged on the Warsaw meeting. Zelensky needed to "favorably impress President Trump." This was news to everyone at the embassy. They didn't know the aid was contingent on anything like that.

Taylor was pretty sure Zelensky and his inner circle were still unaware of the hold, and he wanted to keep it that way. Bolton and Zelensky had a meeting the next day, and the freeze certainly was not on Bolton's agenda. Neither was Trump's request to "do us a favor" with investigations of the Bidens and the 2016 election. Instead, Bolton pressed Zelensky to block the sale to China of Motor Sich, an obscure Ukrainian defense company. During its years as a Soviet republic, Ukraine had been a central part of the Soviet defense industry. Bolton, a China hawk, was worried that Beijing might be able to use Motor Sich to enhance their fighter jets.

After the Zelenksy meeting, Taylor pulled aside one of Bolton's staff members and asked "Can I get five minutes with him?"

That night, Taylor headed over to Bolton's suite at the Sheraton, which included a meeting room and a separate space set up for secure phone calls. Taylor had only one goal: making sure that Bolton and others in Washington thoroughly understood how vital the security aid was for Ukraine, and the terrible signal sent by withholding it. Taylor had thought the aid suspension was a bureaucratic snafu that would be resolved quickly. Now he was realizing that wasn't true.

"I can't understand why this is happening," he told Bolton. Every agency except OMB was pushing for the aid to be released, yet nothing was happening. "I'm very concerned," he told Bolton.

To Taylor, the aid was a red line. Months ago, when he met with Pompeo to discuss the job, Taylor had been clear: He would quit if Trump abandoned Ukraine. Now that moment was approaching. He didn't tell Bolton, but if the aid didn't start flowing before the end of September, he would quit in protest.

Taylor didn't know Bolton well, and they didn't agree on much. Taylor thought that Bolton's "maximum pressure" campaign directed toward Iran, along with his manic push to pull out of the Obama-era Iran nuclear deal, was "dead wrong." But Taylor still respected Bolton. They were from the same Washington tribe. They revered foreign policy expertise, and they placed a high value on the process that had guided U.S. foreign policy since the end of World War II. Bolton was consistent and principled, and by Taylor's logic, even bad principles were better than no principles at all. "He's got a framework," Taylor thought. "It may be a flawed framework, but he lives by it."

The meeting didn't last long. Bolton mostly listened, and then urged Taylor to write a "first-person" cable to Pompeo, making the case for the aid as essential to supporting Ukraine and checking Russian aggression. Whenever the issue was discussed with Trump, they would need all the ammunition they could muster. "It'll get noticed," Bolton promised.

Taylor had never written a first-person cable during his 20-plus years at the State Department. He was a traditionalist, more comfortable with the standard, time-tested diplomatic format—the observational report of facts and analysis, reviewed by the embassy's experts, a solid dispatch that its readers in Washington could rely on for accurate information. Writing a first-person cable was like sending up a personal flare.

He would take a shot, first thing in the morning.

As Taylor was preparing to meet with Bolton in Kyiv, it was noon in Washington, where *Politico* reporter Caitlin Emma was finishing an email to the communications director at OMB. Her colleagues had heard that Ukraine's security aid was on hold, and that OMB was responsible. "Can you shed any light on what's going on here?" Emma wrote. "With sources accumulating, it's possible that we will write something today."

The aid freeze was about to become public, just the scenario that Taylor and Vindman had sought for weeks to avoid. *Politico*'s story went online at 6:11 p.m.

"Trump Holds Up Ukraine Military Aid Meant to Confront Russia," the headline read. OMB had no comment, but a "senior administration official" told Emma and colleague Connor O'Brien that Trump had ordered a review of the aid because he wanted to make sure other countries were "paying their fair share."

In Kyiv, it was now past 1 a.m. Bill Taylor was asleep, unaware that his worst-case scenario on the aid freeze had arrived.

CHAPTER SEVENTEEN

Ukraine in a Box

August 29 to September 9, Kyiv, Washington and Warsaw

The *Politico* story landed in Kyiv that morning like a stun grenade. At 9:27 a.m., Zelensky adviser Andriy Yermak texted Volker: "Need to talk to you." At 10:06 a.m., Yermak texted Volker again. No message this time. Just a link to the *Politico* story.

As Taylor was writing his first-person cable, Ukrainian officials were calling about the aid freeze. They were more than unhappy. Taylor thought they sounded desperate, giving him even more impetus to finish his cable.

He shared the draft with his deputy and Holmes. They offered suggestions and edits, and when it was done, they classified the cable as "Secret-NoDis," meaning it should not be distributed beyond Pompeo's office, and hit transmit. As a first-person cable, it did not include the usual statement that the document represented the consensus of the embassy's experts. This was Taylor's personal conviction, delivered directly to the secretary through the operations center at the State Department.

In the cable's last line, Taylor made plain that if the hold wasn't lifted, he would resign. This was also a first. In almost 50 years of government service, he had never made such a threat in writing. Not long after he sent the cable, he emailed his wife back in Arlington. She was planning a December visit to Kyiv. "Buy a refundable ticket," he cryptically told her. "I might be coming home."

His cable completed, Taylor picked up his cellphone for a quick text to Volker and Sondland. He wanted to let them know that Zelensky and Trump were now set to talk in Warsaw.

"Meeting on for 2:40 Sunday afternoon," he wrote.

"Outstanding!!" Volker replied a minute later.

"Fantastic News Bill," Sondland chimed in.

Taylor had a question, though. He knew the Ukrainians still wanted an Oval Office visit.

"Does this mean no Washington meeting?" Taylor asked.

"Just the opposite," Volker answered, "should open the door."

"Hope you are right," Taylor replied.

In Washington, the *Politico* story was reverberating. "President Trump should stop worrying about disappointing Vladimir Putin and stand up for U.S. national security priorities," Senator Bob Menendez said in a statement. Michael McFaul, the former U.S. ambassador to Moscow, tweeted the story with the comment, "Ugh. What a terrible signal to the newly elected president and parliament."

Julia Davis, the Russia media analyst and *Daily Beast* columnist, reported that Putin's state media was thrilled. "Sensational!" declared one television host. Another addressed Ukraine: "Terrible news for your independence."

Officials at OMB were scrambling to respond to the story. Throughout the day, they debated and revised talking points to explain the freeze. The last talking point read, "No action has been taken by OMB that would preclude the obligation of these funds before the end of the fiscal year."

When McCusker saw the talking points, she blanched. How could OMB say that? It was as if OMB were ignoring everything she had said over the last month about the Pentagon's position.

She let Duffey know she wasn't on board. "I don't agree to the revised TPs," she wrote, using the shorthand for talking points. "The last one is just not accurate . . . something we have been consistently conveying for a few weeks."

At the White House, Trump announced that he was canceling his trip to Warsaw. He needed to deal with Hurricane Dorian, which was ripping through the Virgin Islands and Puerto Rico, heading toward Florida. Vice President Pence would go instead.

Volker knew Trump's cancelation would hit the Ukrainians hard. He immediately texted Zelensky's diplomatic adviser, Vadym Prystaiko. "Trump not going to Warsaw now pence going . . . I'm so sorry," he wrote.

Volker's instincts were on target. The Ukrainians felt trapped and uncertain. No meeting with Trump. Pressure for investigations. Now the imminent loss of the security aid.

Danyliuk and Taylor were exchanging messages about the aid. Danyliuk floated an idea: release the money gradually, a portion after each new meeting, starting with Pence in Warsaw. Not possible, Taylor wrote. This was an all-or-nothing proposition. If the White House did not lift the hold before September 30, the funds would expire and Ukraine would receive none of the aid.

The Ukrainians headed into the September 1 meeting with Pence determined to find out where they stood. Zelensky opened with a question: What about the aid freeze? Pence said he didn't know the reasons behind it, but he promised to speak with Trump. The Ukrainian officials were incredulous. The freeze had been publicly reported and the vice president was saying he had no information.

Zelensky had come to the meeting with a squadron of facts about the aid, and an appeal that he thought the Trump administration would appreciate. He told Pence that Ukraine devoted more than 5 percent of its GDP to defense, a greater proportion than many European nations. He said the U.S. military aid wasn't about the money, but rather the symbolism of U.S. power backing Ukraine, which would mean something to Russia. Another Ukrainian official interjected that the money was important as well.

Pence was listening. Zelensky was giving him the full pitch. He told Pence that Ukraine had lost a large swath of its territory to Russia's invading forces, with devastating effects on the nation's economy. For the Ukrainians, U.S. backing was the difference between being able to stand up to Putin or not.

"You are the only country providing military assistance," one of Zelensky's advisers told Pence. By withholding the aid, "you are punishing us."

Pence was taking notes the entire time. He thanked Zelensky for his explanation and promised to take his arguments back to Trump.

The following day, Pence and Polish president Andrzej Duda took questions from the press at the presidential palace in Warsaw. Pence was asked about his Zelensky meeting and the status of the aid.

"Specifically, number one, did you discuss Joe Biden at all during that meeting yesterday with the Ukrainian president?" a reporter asked. "And number two, can you assure Ukraine that the holdup of that money has absolutely nothing to do with efforts, including by Rudy Giuliani, to try to dig up dirt on the Biden family?"

Biden did not come up in the discussions, Pence said. The aid question was talked about "in great detail." He said the United States would "stand strong" with Ukraine in the face of Russian aggression. "But as President Trump had me make clear, we have great concerns about issues of corruption" in Ukraine, Pence said. "I mean, to invest additional taxpayer money in Ukraine, the president wants to be assured that those resources are truly making their way to the kind of investments that will contribute to security and stability in Ukraine."

Pence called on "our European partners to step forward and make additional investments." But he also pledged to "carry back to President Trump the progress" that Zelensky and his administration in Ukraine "are making on dealing with corruption in their country."

The Ukrainians were deflated. A demand for more European aid and a dropped hint that Trump might withhold "additional taxpayer money" was not what they were hoping to hear. A meeting with Trump looked farther away than ever, and the aid freeze was firmly in place, at least for now.

Zelensky and his team left Warsaw more dejected than when they arrived.

Taylor had stayed behind in Kyiv, waiting for a readout from Warsaw. After sending his cable, he had allowed himself to think that the freeze might be lifted once Pence and Zelensky had talked. But a phone call from Morrison, in Warsaw, was beyond disappointing. Pence had said nothing to assuage the Ukrainians' anxiety.

Morrison told Taylor something else disturbing. After the Pence-Zelensky meeting ended, Morrison had watched from across the room as Sondland approached Yermak. The two men spoke briefly. Then Sondland strode over to Morrison, volunteering a briefing. Sondland said he had told Yermak that he had an idea that could help get the aid moving: The Ukrainian prosecutor general should announce that he was investigating Burisma.

Morrison was startled. He had been working for weeks to marshal a compelling case, backed by every agency, to persuade President Trump to lift the freeze. In his many conversations, no one had ever suggested that any investigations were a condition for releasing the aid. Morrison was realizing he hadn't understood the battle he was fighting. He started making a mental list of the people who needed to know about this. Taylor was at the top of his list.

Taylor shared Morrison's dismay. Tying a White House visit to some cooked-up statement about investigations was bad enough. But the millions of dollars in aid was different. It was a tangible asset that the United States had pledged to deliver and was legally required to provide. Now it appeared that the aid was being sacrificed to the president's personal political agenda.

Taylor texted Sondland and Volker right away.

"Are we now saying that security assistance and WH meeting are conditioned on investigations?" Taylor asked.

Sondland responded in less than an hour: "Call me."

The call to Sondland confirmed Taylor's fears, and then some. Yes, Sondland said, there had to be a public announcement of investigations into Burisma and alleged Ukrainian meddling in the 2016 election. And the announcement couldn't come from the prosecutor general. Zelensky had to be the one to make it. Trump wanted him in a box, he told Taylor.

Taylor was appalled. He felt he had to offer a defense of diplomatic protocol and basic decency. Trump should have more respect for Zelensky, he told Sondland, and these investigations were not in anyone's interest, no matter what Trump thought. He asked Sondland to talk to Trump. Please, *please* get him to drop these demands.

Sondland pledged to try.

Taylor spent the next few days trying to reassure various Ukrainian officials about the jeopardized aid. He had nothing good to tell them, and he wasn't going to share his deep concern about what Sondland had said.

On September 5, he hosted two senators, Ron Johnson, the Wisconsin Republican, and Democrat Chris Murphy of Connecticut. They had come to town for the opening of Zelensky's revived High Anti-Corruption Court and meetings with Ukrainian officials. After meeting with the defense minister, they attended the daily ceremony for fallen soldiers. In the Donbass that day, some 500 miles from Kyiv, shelling had killed a Ukrainian soldier. There would be one more family at next year's ceremony.

Later in the day, Taylor accompanied the senators to meet Zelensky. The Ukrainian president requested to dispense with the usual diplomatic opening. He asked: Did they know anything about the status of the security aid?

Johnson, who had called Trump to talk about the aid a few days earlier, took the lead. He reiterated the usual explanation: The president was concerned about corruption, and angry that European countries were not doing enough to support Ukraine. He downplayed the significance of what Taylor had told Danyliuk—sure, the fiscal year was about to end, but Ukraine had such strong bipartisan support in Congress that a new round of funding would be no trouble at all.

Murphy interjected. Johnson was right about Ukraine's bipartisan support, he said, but launching investigations that would benefit one American politician at the expense of another would undermine that support. Johnson didn't respond.

As the meeting ended, Johnson praised Zelensky's excellent English. He should use it as much as possible when he met with President Trump, he suggested. Zelensky, still the comedian, replied, "But Senator Johnson, you don't realize how beautiful my Ukrainian is."

On September 8, Taylor and Sondland spoke on the phone again. Taylor was eager to know: Had Sondland succeeded in lobbying Trump to drop his demands for an investigation?

Not exactly. Sondland had called Trump the day before. The president had been in a bad mood. What do you want from Ukraine? Sondland had asked him. "Nothing," Trump told him. "No quid pro quo. No quid pro quo."

The president had repeated it like an incantation. No quid pro quo, but if Zelensky did not clear things up with an announcement of investigations, they would be at a stalemate. Sondland added that he had already passed the word to Zelensky, who had agreed to make a public statement about the investigations in an interview with CNN.

Sondland didn't seem troubled by the situation. Trump was a businessman, he told Taylor. "When a businessman is about to sign a check to someone who owes him something, the businessman asks that person to pay up before signing the check," Sondland said. Taylor argued that that made no sense: Ukraine didn't owe Trump anything, and certainly didn't owe him groundless investigations into a political rival and conspiracy theories about the 2016 election.

After they hung up, Taylor texted Sondland and Volker about Ukraine's predicament: "The nightmare is that they give the interview and don't get the security assistance. The Russians love it. (And I quit.)"

The next morning, September 9, Taylor put his frustration into another round of texts. "The message to the Ukrainians (and Russians) we send with the decision on security assistance is key. With the hold, we have already shaken their faith in us. Thus my nightmare scenario." A few minutes later, he added: "Counting on you to be right about this interview, Gordon."

Sondland responded testily. "Bill, I never said I was 'right.' I said we are where we are and believe we have identified the best pathway forward. Let's hope it works."

Taylor: "As I said on the phone, I think it's crazy to withhold security assistance for help with a political campaign."

A few hours went by, then Sondland was back, invoking the president's words in his next text. "Bill, I believe you are incorrect about President Trump's intentions. The president has been crystal clear: no quid pro quo's of any kind. The President is trying to evaluate whether Ukraine is truly going to adopt the transparency and reforms that President Zelensky promised during his campaign."

Sondland gave Taylor a broad hint that he had nothing more to say. "I suggest we stop the back and forth by text. If you still have concerns, I recommend you give Lisa Kenna or S a call to discuss them directly. Thanks."

Being told to talk to "S"—shorthand for Secretary Pompeo—wasn't helpful. Pompeo already had Taylor's first-person cable. The time was drawing near when Taylor would have to decide whether to make good on his threats to quit. He didn't see how he could do his job if the aid didn't flow soon.

CHAPTER EIGHTEEN

"Credible Urgent Concern"

September 9 to 13, Washington, Kyiv and Houston

On Monday, September 9, members of the House of Representatives were rolling back into town after their six-week summer recess. While the members of Congress had been in their home districts, investigators on Adam Schiff's Intelligence Committee had kept working on their various investigations into Trump. They were seeing what they thought was a pattern—in the shape of Rudy Giuliani.

Since June, when Schiff had read the staff's six-page memo on Giuliani's Ukraine activities and told his investigators to keep digging, they had been documenting what they were now calling an "ecosystem" of Giuliani disinformation.

Just in the past few weeks, three press accounts had intensified the committee's interest in the Giuliani-Trump-Ukraine nexus. On August 21, a *New York Times* story had put Giuliani at a meeting in Madrid with Andriy Yermak. Giuliani was quoted as saying he had "strongly urged" Yermak to "just investigate the darn things" and was "pretty confident" it would happen. The headline said, "Giuliani Renews Push for Ukraine to Investigate Trump's Political Opponents."

The *Politico* story about Trump holding up Ukraine's military aid was a week later, and on September 5, a *Washington Post* editorial made one of the most explicit and troubling assertions yet. Under the online headline "Trump tries to force Ukraine to meddle in the 2020 election," the editorial connected the disparate dots. Trump had "refused to grant the Ukrainian leader a White House visit" and had "suspended the delivery of $250 million in U.S. military aid" as part of a "venal agenda" to force Zelensky into launching the Biden investigation. "Mr. Trump is not just soliciting Ukraine's help with his presidential campaign," the editorial asserted, "he is using U.S. military aid the country desperately needs in an attempt to extort it."

The editorial said the newspaper had been "reliably told" of this scheme. That meant someone on the inside, someone believed to be knowledgeable about Trump's intentions, someone upset enough to take action. Editorials at *The Post* represent the newspaper's view, so they carry no byline. The author was no secret, though. The editorial had been written by Jackson Diehl, the deputy editorial page editor. He was one of the newspaper's most senior journalists, a former foreign correspondent and foreign editor who maintained a wide set of contacts in Washington and abroad.

Beyond what they were seeing in the news, Schiff's investigators also got a "read-out" of a July 25 phone call between Trump and Zelensky, a summary released by Zelensky's office. Trump was quoted as saying that the U.S.-Ukraine relationship had been "inhibited" by Ukraine's failure to complete "investigation of corruption cases."

The investigators were not sure what it all meant. But they were sure it was worth a full and formal investigation. Schiff agreed. On Monday morning, even before Pelosi had gaveled the House back into session, the committee released a statement announcing yet another Trump inquiry. Schiff, along with the chairmen of two other House committees, would be examining whether Trump and Giuliani had sought to manipulate the Ukrainian government into helping Trump's 2020 reelection campaign.

Simultaneously, the committees sent letters to White House counsel Pat Cipollone and Pompeo at the State Department, suggesting that Trump had promoted a plan to "coerce the Ukrainian government into pursuing two politically motivated investigations under the guise of anti-corruption activity." The committees said they wanted to find out if Trump was withholding the military aid to force Ukraine's cooperation.

"If the President is trying to pressure Ukraine into choosing between defending itself from Russian aggression without U.S. assistance or leveraging its judicial system to serve the ends of the Trump campaign, this would represent a staggering abuse of power, a boon to Moscow, and a betrayal of the public trust," said the letters, signed by Schiff, Foreign Affairs Committee chairman Eliot Engel of New York and Oversight Committee chairman Elijah Cummings of Maryland.

It wasn't even noon on the House's first day back.

• • •

Less than three hours later, Schiff's committee received a curious letter from Michael Atkinson, the inspector general for the nation's various intelligence agencies. He was an independent watchdog, with the authority to look into questions of improprieties.

The letter, also sent to the Senate Intelligence Committee, said Atkinson's office had received a complaint on August 12 from an individual, a whistleblower, reporting a "flagrant problem, abuse, (or) violation of the law." Atkinson did not provide any details but said he had determined it to be a "credible urgent concern." As the law required, he said, he had forwarded the complaint on August 26 to Joseph Maguire, the acting director of national intelligence, the highest-ranking intelligence official in the government.

Normally, Maguire would have seven days to transmit a "credible urgent concern" to Congress for review. But, Atkinson said, Maguire had determined that the complaint did not rise to the level of an "urgent concern" so he was not required to share it with Congress. Atkinson said he believed Maguire was acting "in good faith," but he was alerting Congress to the situation. He also copied Devin Nunes, the ranking Republican on the House Intelligence Committee.

Schiff's staffers were intrigued. It was extremely unusual for a whistleblower complaint to be found both credible and an urgent concern. In the 16 months Atkinson had been in the job, this was the first time. Even in cases where the complaint was not considered urgent and credible, the usual practice was for the director of national intelligence to forward it to Congress anyway. But he hadn't. What was going on?

Later in the afternoon, Will Hurd's ears perked up at a "hot spots" meeting of the House Intelligence Committee, a standard briefing for the committee's members when Congress returned from recess. Schiff was alluding to new information the committee had learned, something that could affect intelligence operations and the executive branch. The chairman wasn't being specific, and that made Hurd all the more curious.

Hurd, a Republican from Texas serving his third term, had taken Mike Pompeo's seat on the committee two years earlier after Trump chose Pompeo as his first CIA director. The Intel Committee was a choice assignment, but one that came with conditions. Its members were privy to classified information, knowledge they had to keep to themselves in their public comments about national security issues.

At the "hot spots" briefing, Schiff said he might call a committee meeting in the next couple of days, which was unusual. Meetings were normally scheduled at least a week in advance. Hurd sensed the meeting could be important, but he had no opportunity to ask the chairman questions. Hurd was well versed in the issues faced daily by the committee. Before running for Congress, he had spent nine years in the CIA, from 2000 to 2009, including a tour in Afghanistan and Pakistan. He had also worked for a private cybersecurity contractor.

He was returning to Washington after an eventful and tragic summer recess at home in Texas. First, he had wrestled with whether he wanted to run for a fourth term. He felt sure he could prevail again in his sprawling district, larger than all but 21 states, stretching 550 miles from San Antonio's western suburbs to the outskirts of El Paso.

The only African American among House Republicans, Hurd had won three close elections since 2014. He had compiled a reliably conservative voting record while frequently criticizing Trump's more egregious words and actions. He had called on Trump to quit the presidential race in 2016 after the "Access Hollywood" tape showed him boasting about sexually assaulting women. He was also the leading GOP critic of Trump's border wall plan. His district included more than 40 percent of the U.S.-Mexico border, giving him a frontline perspective on the immigration debate.

As a moderate voice in the increasingly pro-Trump caucus, he had attracted media attention. That had boosted his profile. But he wasn't sure that another congressional term was how he wanted to spend his time. He had just turned 42, and he was politically ambitious. He had made visits earlier in the year to Iowa, New Hampshire, and South Carolina, three states that would play a critical role in the 2024 Republican presidential primary season. He was assessing his future in the post-Trump GOP.

His thinking had gelled on the Fourth of July weekend. On August 1, he told *Washington Post* contributor Robert Moore, the former longtime editor of the *El Paso Times*, that he was bowing out. No race in 2020. Moore's story on Hurd's decision had stunned people in political Washington. Texas senator Ted Cruz, who had narrowly survived an unexpectedly difficult reelection campaign in 2018, used Hurd's announcement to warn that Trump could not take the state for granted in 2020.

Two days after Hurd's announcement, on August 3, a man with an AK-47 assault rifle opened fire in an El Paso Walmart, killing 22 people and injuring 24 more. Police said the shooter told them he had come to the border city to "kill Mexicans." He had also posted an online manifesto complaining of a "Hispanic invasion of Texas." Trump and his supporters sometimes used that word, "invasion," to frame the immigration debate.

Hurd was one of the few Republicans to criticize such language. "This is a party that is shrinking. The party is not growing in some of the largest parts of our country," Hurd had told a June gathering in D.C. sponsored by Log Cabin Republicans, an LGBT group. "Why is that? I'll tell you. It's real simple. Don't be an asshole. Don't be a racist. Don't be a misogynist, right? Don't be a homophobe. These are real basic things that we all should learn when we were in kindergarten."

He had spent a couple of weeks in El Paso helping in the aftermath. Later that same month, on August 31, a gunman killed 7 and wounded 22 in the Midland-Odessa area, just outside Hurd's district. August and its violent bookends were still fresh in Hurd's mind as he returned to the capital just after Labor Day.

With the demands of a reelection campaign off his plate, Hurd was planning to focus his remaining 16 months in the House on what he called "honey-do's," local matters that weren't on the national radar but were important to his district. Now he was wondering about what Schiff had said. What was up?

Just before noon the next day, Tuesday, September 10, Trump upended his national security team. He announced in a terse tweet that he was firing John Bolton, the third national security adviser in a row he had sacked. "I disagreed strongly with many of his suggestions, as did others in the administration," Trump wrote.

During 17 turbulent months, Trump and Bolton had clashed on a variety of issues, especially Iran. The president had admired the outspoken contrarian he had seen on Fox News and had asked him to join the White House, but once there, Bolton had never truly become a Trump insider. He had run-ins with Pompeo, treasury secretary Steven Mnuchin, Mulvaney, Pence—even the first lady. His rivals had accused him of promoting his hawkish policies over Trump's positions, leaking to the news media and lobbying allies in Congress to pressure the president. Bolton denied that.

Bolton also had been vocal about his dislike of Giuliani's unconventional role in Ukraine. Now, just as House Democrats were demanding answers about what Trump and Giuliani were up to in Kyiv, Bolton was suddenly out. He and Trump couldn't even agree on the details of his departure. Trump insisted he had fired Bolton; Bolton insisted he had resigned. Trump said he would name a replacement the following week.

In the afternoon, Atkinson came to Schiff's office. The two men, each with a couple of staff members, sat in a small conference room. Atkinson had had a long, respected history at the Justice Department before taking the inspector general job in the Trump administration's second year. He was known as a Joe Friday—the "Just the facts, ma'am" detective from the old "Dragnet" TV series. He had helped build the case that led to the 2009 conviction of congressman William Jefferson, a Democrat from Louisiana, on corruption charges. He later worked in the new national security division created after 9/11.

Atkinson stressed that he could not go beyond what he said in his letter, because he had not been authorized to disclose the substance of the complaint by his leadership. His boss was Maguire. And Maguire's boss was the president.

Speaking slowly and deliberately, Atkinson said he had followed the whistleblower protection statute exactly. He had determined the complaint was credible, that it met the definition of "urgent concern" and that it was being withheld by Maguire. The meeting lasted nearly an hour.

Schiff and his staff now understood they needed to speak with Maguire directly. They knew Maguire to be a straight shooter; they suspected that it was the White House holding up the complaint. Maybe, if asked, Maguire would shed some light. Schiff sent a letter to Maguire demanding the complaint. The letter gave Maguire a choice in the form of an ultimatum: comply immediately or face investigation, including being summoned to testify.

On the Senate side of the Capitol, on the Republican side of the aisle, Senator Rob Portman of Ohio was also frustrated with the White House. Portman, co-chair of the Senate Ukraine Caucus, could not understand why President Trump was holding up Ukraine's military aid.

Portman had no doubt about the aid's importance. He had introduced annual amendments to increase the amount. His state was home to a large Ukrainian-American population, and he had been hearing from Ohioans upset about the freeze. This was the rare issue that combined a vital foreign policy principle and constituent service. Portman had signed on to a letter to Mulvaney urging the release of the funds. When nothing changed, he asked his staff for a list of people to call.

Portman tried Secretary of Defense Mike Esper, thinking that he might make a difference. Esper said there was nothing he could do—and that time was running out. It was now September 10. If the money wasn't freed up in the next few days, the department wouldn't be able to send the Javelin missiles that Ukraine had been promised. The decision was Trump's to make.

Later in the afternoon, Portman tried the vice president. Same story. Portman needed to talk to Trump. The following day, sometime after 6 p.m. on September 11, Portman reached the president. He asked: Can we get the aid moving? What's going on?

Trump complained that the rest of the world wasn't doing enough to help Ukraine. This was the first time Portman had heard that rationale, and the argument wasn't difficult to rebut. "Well, sure, I don't necessarily disagree, and I'm happy to look into that," he told Trump. "But at the same time, we can't hold Ukraine accountable for a lack of cooperation from our allies." It was important to get the money to Ukraine quickly for national security reasons. Trump seemed receptive.

When the call ended, Portman felt optimistic that the impasse might be ending.

About an hour later, Elaine McCusker received an unexpected email from Michael Duffey at OMB. Trump had changed his mind on the Ukraine aid, Duffey said, and OMB was rushing to get the funds spent.

McCusker was relieved. Only two days earlier, in a September 9 email, she had shared with Duffey her estimate of how much of the Pentagon's $250 million share of the aid was at risk of being left on the table even if the freeze ended that day: about $120 million.

Duffey usually answered McCusker's updates with a polite "thank you." Not this time. When he responded the next day, he made it clear that he was not going to accept any responsibility for money left unspent, and he copied his reply to the legal counsels of both departments. OMB had drafted its footnote with a clause specifically allowing the Defense Department to keep up its preparations to disburse the money, he wrote. If the president lifted the hold and Defense couldn't spend it all, that was on them.

McCusker had been shocked. She had been warning him for weeks that spending the money wasn't as simple as turning on a faucet. "You can't be serious," she replied. "I am speechless."

That was less than 24 hours ago. Now, out of the blue, after nearly two months of wrangling and worry and warnings, Duffey was telling her the money could move. His email had arrived at 7:30 p.m., too late to do anything more than alert her colleagues. But first thing in the morning, they would get the paperwork going.

She considered how to reply. With Duffey no longer trying to protect himself from the questions of hypothetical congressional investigators, it was as if they were on the same team again, sharing a sense of relief that their mutual problem had resolved itself.

"Copy," she said in her 9:30 p.m. email. "What happened?"

"Not exactly clear but president made the decision to go," he answered. "Will fill you in when I get details. . . . Glad to have this behind us."

"Agree!" McCusker wrote back.

In Washington and Kyiv the next day, September 12, word trickled out that the freeze had been lifted. At the NSC, Vindman learned only the most basic information: Trump had decided to let the money go. Mark Sandy at OMB got an email from Duffey. Kurt Volker texted Sondland and Taylor: "Hi—got an email overnight" from a congressional contact. "Says hold is lifted. Let's verify."

Taylor quickly replied: "Got the same message. Checking with NSC."

There was no explanation given for Trump's sudden reversal. The facts on the ground had not changed. The European countries were not spending more on security assistance for Ukraine. There had been no overnight breakthrough in Zelensky's efforts to combat corruption. It was puzzling to those who had been working to get the aid released.

Rob Portman's office put out a statement praising Trump and acknowledging the concerns that the president had raised during their phone call. "I strongly support the president's position that NATO allies and especially our European countries in the region can and must do more to support Ukraine," he said. The statement attributed the delay to a review by the Departments of State and Defense, even though Portman had heard straight from Esper that Defense was carefully watching the clock as the risk grew that the money couldn't flow in time.

Members of the Senate Appropriations Committee, from both parties, thought Trump was reacting to pressure from Congress. Dick Durbin, Democrat of Illinois, had an amendment ready that would withhold $5 billion from the Pentagon's budget for 2020 if the Trump administration failed to deliver the aid in the next fiscal year. Durbin's amendment was on the committee's agenda for the day. "It's beyond a coincidence that they released it the night before our vote in the committee," Durbin told a *Politico* reporter.

When the committee convened that morning, one Republican member was sure Durbin's threat had forced the administration's hand. "So why was it released?" Senator Lindsey Graham said. "Because of your amendment, that's why it was released. Because I was going to vote for it, so I think they got the message." Graham was eager to declare the problem solved, case closed. "If you're listening in the Ukraine on C-SPAN," he said, "you're going to get the money."

The Ukrainian embassy in Washington joined the chorus with a statement that looked ahead rather than back. No point in casting blame or raising new questions now that the money was about to flow. "The U.S. security and military assistance to Ukraine is crucial in combating Russian aggression," the embassy posted on its Facebook page. "It's a very important decision that truly reflects the strategic partnership of our two countries."

In Kyiv, a relieved Taylor personally conveyed the welcome news to Zelensky and his newly named foreign minister, Vadym Prystaiko. Maybe this meant the irregular channel was fading. Maybe now Taylor could focus on doing his job without worrying about the snake pits.

That afternoon, Schiff and his top investigator, Daniel Goldman, had a phone call with Maguire and his general counsel, Jason Klitenic, to press for release of the whistleblower's complaint.

Schiff told Maguire that the committee was considering a subpoena to compel him to testify about why he was withholding the whistleblower complaint. It was a drastic suggestion. A subpoena for such a high-ranking official was rare. But the law was clear and explicit, Schiff said: The director of national intelligence shall transmit such complaints to Congress.

Trying to find more about the complaint, Schiff asked Maguire: Does this have to do with anything of interest to the committee, or that the committee is investigating?

Maguire put the phone on mute. When he came back on the line, he was vague. He was saying nothing that might hint at the complaint's contents.

Schiff and Goldman were reading between the lines. Maguire was saying, essentially, it's not up to us. Schiff and Goldman were growing even more certain: The White House is calling the shots, maybe even the president himself.

In the past year, Schiff and Goldman had become a close team. They had met in June 2018, while waiting to appear as guests on Brian Williams's MSNBC show, "The 11th Hour." The two former federal prosecutors were there to talk about the day's news: Trump's suggestion that he had the power to pardon himself. Five months later, Schiff asked him to join the Intelligence Committee's Russia investigation.

Now Goldman, who used to prosecute mob cases in New York, was in the middle of something he never expected, a whistleblower complaint that might reach the White House itself.

That night, in Houston, the Democratic Party held its third presidential debate. The questions ranged widely, but not on the list: Ukraine, the aid freeze, the Schiff investigation of Trump and Giuliani.

Not one of the ten candidates mentioned impeachment. The only person talking about it was Trump himself, who gave a speech to House Republicans in Baltimore as the Democrats were trashing him in Texas. Even though Pelosi wasn't threatening impeachment, he taunted her anyway: "I told Nancy . . . 'You have to do something other than try and impeach somebody that didn't do anything wrong. You have to.' "

Trump's audience laughed its approval. Trump said: "The Mueller report is out. There's no collusion, after two and a half years. Think of it. How ridiculous: I collude with Russia. In fact, Russia said, 'You know, if we really did pick him, we made a real bad choice.' "

The next day in Kyiv, Taylor had a series of discussions with Zelensky and his aides. Taylor was feeling more optimism than he had for weeks. He had even told the Ukrainian press that he expected a Trump-Zelensky meeting would take place in New York during the U.N. General Assembly's opening session later in the month, and that staff were working to coordinate the two leaders' schedules.

But one detail from a phone call with Sondland still worried him: Sondland had said Zelensky had agreed to a CNN interview and was planning to make a statement about investigations. Could that possibly be true? Was that why the aid freeze had been lifted?

Taylor checked with Danyliuk. No interview, Danyliuk said.

The Ukrainians had long been uncomfortable with the idea of doing the investigations, so that made sense. But just in case, Taylor decided to reinforce the point. Sitting in Zelensky's formal office, Taylor told the Ukrainian president that bipartisan American support was his most valuable strategic asset. "Don't jeopardize it," he urged. "And don't interfere in our elections, and we won't interfere in your elections."

As Taylor was leaving, he ran into Yermak. He knew Yermak and Sondland had been in close touch about what Trump was demanding. He decided to give Yermak the same advice he had just given Zelensky and then asked: Were the plans for the CNN interview definitely off? Taylor thought Yermak looked uncomfortable. It made Taylor nervous. He went back to Danyliuk and asked again. Danyliuk assured him for a second time: no interview.

A few hours after the meeting, Zelensky posted a group photo on Twitter. He and three of his aides sat with Taylor around a polished wooden table in high-backed dark green leather chairs. Each was smiling slightly at the camera. "Grateful to the USA for unlocking military assistance to Ukraine & for the continued support of our sovereignty & territorial integrity," the tweet said in English. "The U.S. remains our strategic partner. We're committed to our further collaboration."

At the end of Zelensky's tweet came a string of tags: @USEmbassyKyiv @WhiteHouse @Congressdotgov and, listed first, @realDonaldTrump.

In Washington that morning, Schiff's office received a letter from Jason Klitenic, general counsel in DNI Maguire's office. The letter masterfully attempted to thread the needle, offering a legal rationale for withholding the whistleblower complaint. It asserted that because the complaint did not allege misconduct by anyone within the intelligence community, the law didn't require Maguire to forward the complaint.

One sentence jumped off the page for Schiff's staff: "Furthermore, because the complaint involves confidential and potentially privileged communications by persons outside the Intelligence Community, the DNI lacks unilateral authority to transmit such materials to the intelligence committees."

"Privileged." That word generally applied to only the president.

It was time to send that subpoena to Maguire. Schiff's staff needed to consult the other House committee chairmen and get Pelosi's backing. Schiff's lawyers drafted a letter to Maguire that said he was being subpoenaed, and that: "The Committee can only conclude that the serious misconduct at issue involves the President of the United States and/or other senior White House or Administration officials."

At about 7:30 p.m. Friday, at the end of a long week, Schiff sent the letter and Patrick Boland, the committee's communications director, put out a press release. The committee's negotiations with Maguire had led nowhere, and the complaint was still mostly a mystery. Why not see what the press might turn up?

It was time, one Schiff staffer joked, to "unleash the hounds."

CHAPTER NINETEEN

"Dig Very Hard, and Very Fast"

September 13 to 16, Washington

At 7:36 p.m. that Friday, September 13, emails carrying the Schiff press release went out simultaneously to the lengthy list of reporters following the activities of the House Intelligence Committee.

The hounds had been alerted.

Ellen Nakashima was at home with her family, trying to unwind after another busy week in the *Washington Post* newsroom. So was Greg Miller, her *Post* colleague on the national security beat. Shane Harris, a third member of their team, was celebrating his mother-in-law's birthday in New Jersey.

Ding. That sound of email arriving. What now? The pace on this beat never seemed to let up. Emails and notifications of all sorts—some important, many hardly worth more than a glance—kept the trio tethered to their phones. It was an occupational hazard, a running joke. But the heading on this one caused their news radars to blink: "Chairman Schiff Issues Subpoena for Whistleblower Complaint Being Unlawfully Withheld by Acting DNI from Intelligence Committee."

Wait. Adam Schiff had subpoenaed Joe Maguire, the government's highest-ranking intelligence official? Accusing the former vice admiral and Navy SEAL of "unlawfully" withholding information from Congress? A whistleblower? Blowing a whistle about what? And sending out an alert at dinnertime on a Friday? What was that about?

The trio had years of experience on the national security beat. They knew this was intended to draw attention. At the same time, they didn't know how seriously to take it. Since winning back the House, the Democrats had been investigating Trump constantly. Schiff's committee had taken a leading role, but it wasn't in the habit of sending out a stream of press releases. The last one had been weeks ago, in July, and it was just a copy of Schiff's opening remarks before Mueller's public testimony on his report.

The reporters found the press release, as well as Schiff's four-page letter to Maguire, was vague to the point of frustration. The committee was saying it didn't know much, so it couldn't say much. Maguire wouldn't turn over the whistleblower's complaint, as required by law, so the committee said it was going public to rachet up the pressure. The dispute itself was clear enough, but the heart of the matter was a mystery.

No details on the anonymous whistleblower, of course. But also, no information about the underlying allegation, except for a single, stunning sentence that Schiff's staff had highlighted with bold type: "The Committee can only conclude . . . that the serious misconduct at issue involves the President of the United States and/or senior White House or Administration officials." Hard for Maguire or the reporters to miss that signal, with or without the bold letters.

In New Jersey, Harris saw the remarkable line about the president and thought to himself, Okay, now you've got my interest. He decided to work the story hard in the morning. Miller and Nakashima, working independently and without communicating with each other, put out feelers to their sources right away. Do you know anything about this? Is this something serious?

Miller wanted to hear something concrete before deciding what to do.

About 90 minutes after Schiff's statement was released, Nadler appeared on CNN with host Chris Cuomo. The day before, Nadler's committee had voted to continue its "investigation to determine whether to recommend articles of impeachment with regard to President Donald J. Trump." No one seemed to know exactly what charges the committee was considering, but it was clear where Nadler wanted to end up.

Now he was on prime-time TV, the first top Democrat to be asked about the curious Schiff statement, which most viewers were hearing about for the first time.

"We have breaking news right now," Cuomo said, opening his show. "The House Intel chair has just issued a subpoena, and he's also making a very serious accusation against the acting director of national intelligence. This is big, and it's happening right now."

Then Cuomo introduced his guest with great gusto: "Impeachment, or not? Does it matter, or not? We have the one person who would know. Boy, did we get lucky on a Friday the 13th? We have the House Judiciary Committee chair, Jerry Nadler, here to help us make sense of that."

The lucky timing turned out to be a bit of a letdown. Cuomo informed viewers that Nadler had said, off camera, that he didn't know the specifics of Schiff's new allegation. But Nadler was ready with his opinion: "This fits into the pattern of the administration behavior in withholding information, in conducting complete cover-ups, and being contemptuous of the law."

Cuomo asked: Could Nadler clarify whether his committee was conducting an impeachment inquiry? "That's a made-up term without legal significance. It is, however, what we are doing," Nadler said, offering more confusion than clarity. "I'm frankly not interested in—in a nomenclature." The congressman added, for emphasis: "There are any number of possible grounds for impeachment" against Trump that could be "well beyond" the findings of the Mueller report. But it was too soon, he said, to say what might happen.

This was Nadler's posture whenever the "I" word came up: He went into verbal contortions. Cuomo showed his impatience with Nadler's bob-and-weave, interjecting at one point: "I don't care what you call it either, as long as you call it one thing."

But Nadler's primary concern wasn't the TV audience. He wanted to be careful not to get ahead of Nancy Pelosi.

It was getting late in Washington, and Nakashima and Miller weren't having much luck in their pursuit of the whistleblower complaint. One source told Nakashima he could talk the next day. Miller reached a contact, who didn't know anything specific and warned him that Schiff could be overly aggressive.

Then, at 10:40 p.m., Miller heard via message from a former intelligence officer, someone close to people on the inside. This was serious, the source said. Keep going.

Before going to bed, Miller typed out an email to Nakashima and Harris, his first to his colleagues. "Guys, I got very strong push tonight to pursue this," he wrote. "Speculation on Twitter that Maguire is refusing to turn over a whistleblower claim that came in to the IG [inspector general] because it has to do with Trump.

"Let's touch base in a.m.," Miller said.

It was 12:12 a.m. when he hit the send button.

On Saturday morning, Harris could see that the people who make up the "nat-sec" world—the community of analysts, academics and researchers who spend their working lives immersed in security and intelligence issues—were already whipped into a froth. On Twitter, some of them were dissecting Schiff's Friday night surprise, treating it as a big deal, speculating about what it meant. What was Maguire hiding? What wrongdoing had the whistleblower witnessed? How was Trump involved? *Lawfare*, a blog dedicated to covering all things nat-sec, published a brief article, summarizing the Schiff letter and linking to the documents, no new information.

Harris set up his laptop in his mother-in-law's guest room and started calling contacts developed over two decades. A former U.S. intelligence official who still had good connections in the government told him: "I don't know exactly what this is about. But I can tell you this—it's big. Dig very hard, and very fast."

Nakashima's first couple of calls were "dry holes." But a third source, a current government official, said the issue was significant. The official didn't feel comfortable providing details but made oblique references to the Supreme Court's 1974 landmark ruling that executive privilege did not allow Richard Nixon to keep tapes of his Oval Office conversations from Congress. Whoa. The source was making a Watergate reference? And bringing up executive privilege? That set off Nakashima's alarms.

At 9:39 a.m., Miller wrote to his colleagues that he had spoken to someone close to Maguire. That person didn't know the specifics but said, yes, the whistleblower complaint related directly to the president. Maguire was being told not to turn it over. Miller's source said Maguire had "no respect for POTUS," but was "in a legitimate jam," caught in a power struggle between Schiff and the White House. Maguire was "trying to do the right thing" in a "politically perilous" situation with the highest possible stakes.

The more calls the reporters made, the more it was becoming clear: Maguire was agonizing over his decision. He hadn't wanted to be the director of national intelligence in the first place, and certainly not under Trump. He was a man steeped in military reverence for rules, but he was torn by what the law required of him. Did executive privilege override the legal requirement to turn over the complaint? Was withholding it a legally defensible act, or was the White House pressuring him to break the law?

His stellar reputation was on the line. Schiff wasn't going to back off. Maguire had to deliver the complaint by Tuesday or, as Schiff's letter put it, come before the committee to "account for" his decision.

On Sunday morning, Schiff went on CBS's "Face the Nation." He wouldn't discuss specifics but said the whistleblower complaint was about "serious or flagrant wrongdoing" that "involves either the president or people around him or both." It mirrored the language in his letter to Maguire, but now he was saying it on national TV.

His remarkable statement did not ignite the kind of political firestorm that it might have in earlier administrations. The national security reporters at the major news outlets were on the case, but much of the media's attention that weekend was focused elsewhere. There was a new book, by two *New York Times* reporters, adding a new allegation of sexual misconduct by Supreme Court Justice Brett Kavanaugh during his undergraduate years at Yale. Schiff's "Face the Nation" statement seemed to get lost in the hubbub.

As Schiff was being interviewed, Nakashima was talking to another trusted contact. The contact knew the whistleblower, and they had spoken in August. The source was an expert in national security law, and the whistleblower had wanted his advice. The contact told Nakashima he was only willing to describe his conversations with the whistleblower in a general way.

He said the two men had met in a D.C. coffee shop, and the whistleblower had provided the broad outlines of his concerns without getting into details. As they spoke, the source said, he quickly concluded that the whistleblower needed a lawyer with expertise in whistleblowing cases. The source had been concerned for the whistleblower because of the significance—and ramifications—of the complaint he wanted to file. Despite the stakes involved, the source said, the whistleblower seemed calm. "It wasn't like the person was outraged or scared," he told Nakashima. "It was a person who felt they now had a duty and was trying to exercise that duty."

The next day, Nakashima wrote *The Post*'s first story about Schiff's subpoena to Maguire, adding new detail about the "unprecedented standoff" and Maguire's refusal to turn over the whistleblower's complaint. It went online Monday evening. But the *Post* trio still had not cracked the central mystery of what the complaint was about. The *New York Times* took the same cautious approach in its first account on Tuesday.

The *Post* reporters felt extraordinary competitive pressure to solve the puzzle. They got their first real break when Miller learned that the complaint involved Trump's communications with "a foreign leader" and some kind of "promise."

That was a major story, but to publish it, they needed a second source to confirm. Maybe the second source could tell them: A promise to do what? For whom?

CHAPTER TWENTY

Nadler's Audition

September 17, Washington

Tuesday arrived with morning clouds and a forecast for brilliant afternoon sun, the sort of late-summer weather that bathes Washington in its best light. While the *Post* reporters were still trying to figure out the story behind the whistleblower's complaint, Jerry Nadler convened a high-profile House Judiciary Committee hearing in the Capitol.

The witness: Corey Lewandowski, the famously aggressive political operative who had served as Trump's campaign manager in the 2016 election. Nadler wanted to know more about Trump's effort to enlist Lewandowski as a back-channel messenger, with the mission of telling then attorney general Jeff Sessions to interfere in the Mueller probe.

The day before, in a radio interview, Nadler had made his most pointed comments yet on what he thought should happen to Trump. "Personally, I think the president ought to be impeached," he told WNYC's Brian Lehrer. "We have to show that this kind of behavior—trashing the Constitution, trashing all the norms which guarantee democratic government, aggrandizing power to the presidency and destroying the separation of powers and thereby leading the president to become more and more of a tyrant—cannot be tolerated."

Nadler's blunt words had raised the stakes for the Lewandowski hearing even higher. This was the first time that House Democrats had called a key witness in the Mueller investigation to testify in public. Even for Washington, capital of the 24/7 news cycle, Lewandowski's testimony qualified as a major spectacle. CNN, Fox News and MSNBC were all interrupting their regular programming to cover it live. CBS and CNN heightened the drama by calling it an "impeachment hearing"—it wasn't, officially—in their bulletins on the hearing's opening moments.

For Nadler's purposes, Lewandowski wasn't a perfect witness. He had never delivered Trump's message to Sessions. He had asked an intermediary to do it, and the intermediary "was uncomfortable with the task and didn't follow through," according to Mueller's report. But that wasn't the point. Recruiting a courier from outside the White House to interfere with Mueller's investigation? That was worth exploring. It could help build a case for obstruction of justice.

Nadler was itching to change Pelosi's mind on impeachment. She was still resisting, still saying that public support wasn't there. But in keeping with her "legislate, investigate, and litigate" strategy, she was allowing probes of the president's behavior to continue in several committees. None was more important than Nadler's pursuit through Judiciary. If Pelosi were to reverse direction, Judiciary was the committee that traditionally handled impeachment inquiries. That would put Nadler exactly where he liked to be: holding Trump accountable.

He and Trump had a long history going back decades. The feud between the two New Yorkers, both now in their 70s, began in 1985 when Trump was an up-and-coming developer and Nadler was a New York state assemblyman. Trump's company had purchased a dilapidated railyard in Nadler's district on Manhattan's West Side, proposing to turn it into a mega-community: 7,600 apartments in six 75-story towers surrounded by television stations, a shopping mall, and the world's tallest building, a 150-story skyscraper. Trump planned to call it "Television City."

Trump boasted that it would be "the greatest piece of land in urban America." Nadler stood in opposition, supporting community activists who feared the project would cause massive congestion in the densely populated area. Nadler suggested an alternative: The city should buy the land and upgrade the rail system, an investment that would provide and preserve middle-class transportation jobs.

The two men shared New York accents, but not much else. Trump, nearly a foot taller than the five-foot-four Nadler, was born into wealth. Nadler was the son of a New Jersey chicken farmer who had moved the family to New York City after the farm had gone out of business. In politics, Nadler built a career defending the working class with a style that was more scholarly than flashy. Fighting the loud and showy developer from Queens burnished that reputation.

Seeking to bring Nadler into the "Television City" fold, Trump invited him to see models of the project. He talked of living in the penthouse, so high in the sky that he would have to call the concierge to find out the weather in the city below. Nadler told associates it was "grotesque," and he worked to kill the project.

Trump eventually offered a compromise that scaled back the project. But he wanted something in return: federal funding to move a highway so that the new residents would have unobstructed waterfront views. Nadler was unmoved, and when he won election to Congress in 1992, he vowed to block any federal money for the project. He called it "Trump pork."

Trump called Nadler "dumb" and "stupid," tagged him as "Fat Jerry" and offered some fitness advice. "If Nadler spent more time in a gymnasium losing weight, he would do the voters a bigger service," Trump said. "He needs to lose about 200 pounds." Nadler had weight-loss surgery in 2002, part of a decades-long effort to keep his size in check.

Trump never got the highway moved, but the project went forward with a less grandiose, but still substantial, design. In 2005, with parts of the complex remaining under construction after years of delays and skirmishing, Trump's company sold the property for $1.8 billion. But the name, "Trump Place," remained, displayed in two-foot-high gold letters. After Trump was elected in 2016, residents voted to have it removed.

Trump's insulting nickname for Nadler, however, survived. At the meeting with House Republicans in April, Trump recounted the story of the railyard project, dropping "Fat Jerry" into his tirade. It didn't go over well with some in the crowd. They told a *Washington Post* reporter of their discomfort, and suddenly the Trump-Nadler feud was back in the news.

When Nadler gaveled the Judiciary Committee to order that morning, he wasn't just facing a potentially uncooperative witness. He was also trying to dispel doubts in his own caucus. He knew what some of his fellow Democrats were saying: that he didn't have the gravitas, the political agility or the speaking skills to run something as huge as an impeachment inquiry, a historic process that would be televised live on national TV.

Nadler's critics in the caucus had been telling Pelosi that if impeachment ever were to happen, Schiff and his Intelligence Committee would be a better choice to run the inquiry. They regarded Schiff as a more reliable, persuasive and telegenic leader. Schiff was also a Pelosi favorite, while she and Nadler had never quite clicked in the same way.

The Lewandowski hearing was Nadler's chance to prove his critics wrong. Prove that he could handle the committee's folksy but acerbic ranking Republican, Doug Collins of Georgia. Prove that he could fend off Matt Gaetz, who would be swarming and stinging like an angry hornet as he sought to protect a Trump stalwart. Prove that he could lead a months-long impeachment inquiry, with dignity and efficiency, no matter what the Republicans might throw at him.

From the start, Nadler signaled that he was ready for battle. He summarized the Mueller report's finding: On June 19, 2017, Trump had summoned Lewandowski to the Oval Office and dictated a message for Sessions. Tell the attorney general to announce that the Mueller probe was "unfair" to him, Trump said, and order Mueller to focus only on future elections, effectively ending the probe of the 2016 campaign. Lewandowski promised Trump that he would do as asked. A month later, in a second meeting, he assured Trump that he would do it "soon." He never did. Nadler offered his view of Lewandowski's reluctance: "Mr. Lewandowski was nervous about this demand from his former boss—as he should have been. It raised serious questions about criminal conduct."

Nadler then announced that the White House had sent a letter the day before, limiting Lewandowski's testimony. Citing executive privilege, White House lawyers had instructed Lewandowski not to answer any questions about his interactions with the president or other presidential staff.

Nadler called that a bogus argument. Lewandowski had been a private citizen, not a presidential aide, when Trump had told him to talk to Sessions. "The White House is advancing a new and dangerous theory, the crony privilege," Nadler said. "This is a cover-up, plain and simple."

It was a strong opening from the bookish and occasionally tongue-tied Nadler. On the Republican side, Collins pounced with a bucket of downhome sarcasm. He dismissed the hearing as an attempt to revive settled issues from the Mueller report. Calling it "rerun season," Collins said: "They can't sell the product so they just keep packaging it differently. . . . Popcorn still tastes good."

Lewandowski straightened his shoulders and eyed the committee with cool disdain. He looked like a high school football coach with his buzz cut and athletic build. He was sworn in, then used his opening statement to fire back at the Democratic lawmakers who had subpoenaed him. "We as a nation would be better served if elected officials like you concentrated your efforts to combat the true crises facing our country as opposed to going down rabbit holes like this hearing," Lewandowski told them. "Instead of focusing on petty and personal politics, if the committee focuses on solving the challenges of this generation, imagine how many people we could help or how many lives we could save."

Without taking Lewandowski's bait, Nadler went right to his opening questions. He had five minutes, the established time limit for each side. In the flat tone of a courtroom lawyer, he asked: "Mr. Lewandowski, is it correct that as reported in the Mueller report that on June 19, 2017, you met alone in the Oval Office with the president?"

Lewandowski flipped the papers in front of him. "Is there a book and page number you can reference me to?"

Nadler could see what was coming. Lewandowski was going to stall. Nadler wasn't going to let that happen.

"Volume 2, page 90," he said. "But I simply asked you, is it correct that as reported in the Mueller report that on June 19, 2017, you met alone in the Oval Office with the president?"

"Could you please read the exact language of the report, sir? I don't have it available to me," Lewandowski said.

Nadler looked exasperated. "I don't think I need to do that, and I have limited time," he said, rolling his eyes. "Did you meet alone with the president on that date?"

"Congressman, I'd like you to refresh my memory by providing a copy of the report so I can follow along."

"You don't have a copy with you?" Nadler said.

"I don't have a copy of the report, Congressman."

Nadler turned to an aide, looking slightly flummoxed. He knew Lewandowski was playing him, taunting him, testing him. But to avoid any hint of unfairness, Nadler needed to give him a copy of the Mueller report. Lewandowski had won the moment. The cameras were running.

David Cicilline of Rhode Island, one of the more fiery Democrats, stepped in to help. This was getting out of hand. "Mr. Chairman, I request that the clock is stopped while this charade is sorted out."

A committee aide placed the thick copy of the Mueller report before Lewandowski.

"I'm sorry, Congressman, what page was it?"

"Page 90, volume 2."

"Okay, and which paragraph, sir?"

"I don't have it in front of me."

"I'd like a reference, sir, so I can follow along with what you're asking."

Nadler rolled his eyes again.

"Well, you have it in front of you. I gave you the page number."

"Where on page 90 is it, sir?"

Collins interjected. Enough, he told Nadler. Time's up. He wanted Nadler to move on, call on the next member.

Nadler was annoyed. He said no, Lewandowski was "filibustering." Collins argued back. Nadler smacked his gavel. Cicilline said Lewandowski should answer the question. Collins asked again about the clock.

Lewandowski feigned bewilderment, like a cat trying to look innocent with a wisp of a feather sticking out of his mouth.

The hearing was slipping away from Nadler before it had really started.

Nadler told the staff to set the clock ticking again. He abandoned his questions about the 2017 Oval Office meeting, asking instead whether it was correct that the White House had instructed Lewandowski to limit his answers to what was in the Mueller report. Lewandowski ignored the question, and offered to read from the White House letter. Nadler rolled his eyes again. Lewandowski, undeterred, started reading from the letter. Nadler interrupted him repeatedly. Lewandowski kept going. He finished with a statement of his own. "The White House has directed that I not disclose the substance of any discussion with the president or his advisers to protect executive branch confidentiality," he said. "I recognize this is not my privilege, but I am respecting the White House's decision."

Collins interjected again. Nadler's five minutes had expired, he said.

Nadler said he would give himself more time.

The Republicans objected, forcing a vote on the issue. Collins demanded a roll call, which required the clerk to call the name of each of the 30-plus committee members. More tedium, more momentum lost.

Democrats, with their greater numbers, won the vote. Collins accused Nadler of not following proper procedure. He demanded another roll call vote on a motion to adjourn the hearing. That, too, failed.

By now, almost 40 minutes into the hearing, nothing had been accomplished, except that Lewandowski had proven that he was a loyal soldier. Trump tweeted while Lewandowski was still testifying: "Such a beautiful Opening Statement by Corey Lewandowski! Thank you Corey!"

For five hours, Lewandowski kept his Democratic questioners at bay with Trump-style banter and slights. He called Eric Swalwell of California, a failed presidential candidate, "President Swalwell." He accused Sheila Jackson Lee of Texas of going on a "rant." She told him: "This is the House Judiciary Committee! Not a house party!" When Lewandowski talked over the usually even-tempered Pramila Jayapal of Washington, she rebuked him: "You are a witness before the Judiciary Committee. Please act like it!"

The hearing had turned into a circus without a ringmaster. Republicans used their time to praise the president and sympathize with Lewandowski. "Mr. Lewandowski, do you have a thought as to why we continue to engage in a charade that is overwhelmingly opposed by the American people?" Matt Gaetz asked.

"I think they hate this president more than they love their country," Lewandowski replied.

On the network and cable shows, a good review was hard to find, from either side of the political spectrum. Late-night comedians took gleeful aim at Lewandowski and his stonewalling performance. But Nadler and the Democrats were the focus of the most criticism.

MSNBC's Lawrence O'Donnell said, "There was a lot of bad questioning, ineffective questioning, lost points, not holding to a consistent line of inquiry." Rachel Maddow, an unabashed Trump foe, had outright scorn for Nadler's format. "I mean, hello, congressional committees, unsolicited advice here," she said, but the committee's staff lawyers "are better [at] asking questions in 30-minute uninterrupted blocks than you are in 5-minute increments."

At Fox, on Sean Hannity's show, legal analyst Gregg Jarrett's assessment was withering: "This was Nadler's maiden voyage on impeachment. And it sank before it even got out of the harbor."

For many in the Democratic caucus, Nadler's performance only confirmed their instincts. Schiff was the better choice.

CHAPTER TWENTY-ONE

"Not Waving You Off"

September 18 to 20, Washington

Early on Wednesday morning, September 18, Trump announced on Twitter that he was naming Robert O'Brien as his new national security adviser, replacing Bolton. It was a big story, and at *The Washington Post*, Shane Harris was assigned to write it. He was frustrated that the announcement story was keeping him from putting all his energy into reporting on the whistleblower complaint—the "great white," as Harris was calling it, a reference to *Moby-Dick*. Things started falling into place in the afternoon. Nakashima found a second source to confirm Miller's information about Trump's conversation with the "foreign leader" involving a "promise." Harris secured a third confirmation.

Around 6 p.m., the trio worked up an email laying out the basic facts of the story and sent it to the White House press office for comment. No response. Three hours later, *The Post* published their story online.

> The whistleblower complaint that has triggered a tense showdown between the U.S. intelligence community and Congress involves President Trump's communications with a foreign leader, according to two former U.S. officials familiar with the matter.
>
> Trump's interaction with the foreign leader included a "promise" that was regarded as so troubling that it prompted an official in the U.S. intelligence community to file a formal whistleblower complaint with the inspector general for the intelligence community, said the former officials, speaking on the condition of anonymity because they were not authorized to discuss the matter publicly.

They still didn't know which foreign leader or which country. They left for the night, but they still had calls and emails out, hoping for a break.

• • •

The *Post*'s story was read closely by investigators in Schiff's office. They were intrigued by the new details. Often, they knew more than the press about stories involving their part of the intelligence world, but not in this case. They still did not have a full understanding of what the whistleblower's complaint was about, but a "promise" to a foreign leader sounded like a potential problem. Their decision to "unleash the hounds" seemed to be working.

The next morning, Thursday, September 19, Harris was in demand. Four days earlier, Schiff's appearance on "Face the Nation" had created few waves. Now the television networks were jumping on the story. Harris was asked to appear on "The View," the popular ABC daytime talk show. He was flabbergasted by the invitation. As he sat in the *Post* studio, preparing for the interview via remote hookup, he was thinking: I write about the CIA. What am I doing on a pop-culture juggernaut like "The View"? For Harris, it was a sign that the whistleblower story was going to be a big deal.

"D.C. is buzzing," host Joy Behar said, introducing Harris, who answered questions about the story for nine minutes.

While Harris was busy with his TV appearances, Nakashima and Miller were pursuing the two major questions that still loomed large: Who was the leader Trump had talked to? What was the "promise"?

They sought the help of *Washington Pos*t researcher Julie Tate, one of the most respected journalists in the business, whose work had figured in at least nine Pulitzer Prizes. They reviewed Trump's known calls with world leaders and cross-checked them against the rough dates their sources were providing. They saw that Trump had spoken with Putin, with North Korean leader Kim Jong Un and, on July 25, with Ukrainian president Volodymyr Zelensky.

More calls, more emails. Zelensky looked like the likeliest candidate. The July 25 call was already under scrutiny by the three congressional committees as part of their inquiry into Trump, Giuliani and Ukraine.

The reporters hadn't thought to connect the whistleblower's complaint with the Ukraine investigation, announced only 10 days earlier by Schiff and the other committees. But now, they were putting the puzzle pieces into place.

Nakashima sent a message to one of her most knowledgeable sources.

The Post was preparing a story, she told him, saying that the whistleblower complaint "centers on the subject of Ukraine." She asked: Was it on target? She was certain her source would warn her if anything was incorrect.

"Not waving you off," he wrote back.

"Would you wave off that the leader is Zelensky?" she asked.

"No."

"And so basically what we have is that there was a call (July 25) and Trump promised Z he'd give him the aid if Z would launch B (Biden) probe. Any red flags there?"

"Nope."

Nakashima asked whether the complaint might also have to do with a phone call with Putin.

"Let me just leave it at this: I don't recall ever hearing specifically about a Putin call in this context."

"We were told to focus on Ukraine," she wrote.

"Not waving you off, no ma'am."

This was how the national security reporters often had to work. A piece here, a fact there, go back to sources, ask again. It was risky for people in the intelligence community to talk, especially if a story involved classified information.

A second source confirmed: It was Ukraine and Zelensky. At 8:04 p.m., *The Post* reported the Ukraine connection, in a story by Nakashima, Harris, Miller and Carol D. Leonnig. One minute later, the *New York Times* posted its account, with the same information.

The next day, Friday, September 20, the *Wall Street Journal* added to the emerging mosaic, reporting that Trump had pressured Zelensky to work with Giuliani on an investigation of Hunter Biden and his lucrative position on the Burisma board.

In Schiff's office, the spate of stories was clarifying. The whistleblower complaint was about Ukraine. Suddenly, just as the Mueller investigation into Russia's election meddling was starting to fade, it looked to the committee's investigators like Trump was seeking a dirty deal with the country right next door. Now they were even more determined to pry the whistleblower's complaint loose from Maguire's office.

It was a head-snapping turn of events, one that Trump quickly dismissed. Answering questions from reporters during an official visit with Australia's prime minister, he took a broad swipe at the press coverage.

"It's another media disaster," he said. "The media has lost so much credibility in this country."

A reporter asked, "Did you discuss Joe Biden, his son, or family with the leader of Ukraine?"

Trump replied, sharply, "It doesn't matter what I discuss." He then counterpunched, advising the reporters to look closely at Joe Biden's involvement with Ukraine. "You wouldn't, because he's a Democrat. And the Fake News doesn't look into things like that. It's a disgrace."

Asked if he had seen the whistleblower's complaint, he said no, but others at the White House had. "I just tell you, it is—everybody has read it, they laughed at it."

He then offered a scornful assessment of the stories coming out on Ukraine. "I think this is one of the worst weeks in the history of the fake news media. You have been wrong on so many things and this one will be—I wouldn't say it will top the list, because I think you can't do worse than some of the stories you missed over the last week or two, but the media of our country is laughed at all over the world now. You're a joke."

On Capitol Hill, Pelosi was taking careful note of the surge of stories on the whistleblower complaint. For months, she had been walking the impeachment tightrope, waiting to see what the committees turned up in their investigations.

Now with the Ukraine stories breaking, she had to recalibrate. To once again assess the risk of doing something versus the risk of doing nothing. She had no doubts about Trump's willingness to use the power of his office for personal and political gain. The details contained in the news articles were pushing her closer toward impeachment.

Late in the afternoon, on the campaign trail in Iowa, Biden was mobbed by reporters who wanted his reaction to Trump's criticism of his actions in Ukraine and his son's business dealings there.

"Wait a second, wait a second, wait a second," Biden said, raising his hands. He was wearing a blue, button-down shirt and his signature Ray-Ban aviator sunglasses. "Not one single credible outlet has given any credibility to these assertions," he said, finally quieting the group. "Not one single one. And so I have no comment, except the president should start to, uh, be president."

As vice president, Biden had been Obama's point person on Ukraine, helping then-president Poroshenko to stamp out corruption in close coordination with European allies. A particularly sore point was Viktor Shokin, then Ukraine's prosecutor general. By 2015, U.S. officials viewed Shokin as part of the problem and were openly calling for his removal. In Ukraine in December 2015, Biden told Poroshenko that the Obama administration would withhold a $1 billion loan guarantee unless Shokin was fired. "I looked at them and said: 'I'm leaving in six hours. If the prosecutor is not fired, you're not getting the money,'" Biden said during a 2018 speech before the Council on Foreign Relations. "Well, son of a bitch. He got fired. And they put in place someone who was solid at the time."

Biden was carrying out U.S. policy on Shokin. But the Hunter issue was personal and sensitive for him. As young boys, Hunter and his brother, Beau, had survived a 1972 car crash that had killed Biden's first wife and their young daughter. Beau had died of brain cancer in May 2015. Aides found it uncomfortable to raise issues involving Biden's family. There had been no evidence that Hunter had broken any law by accepting his lucrative position on the Burisma board. But many Democrats acknowledged it created at least the perception that Hunter Biden was trading on the vice-presidential name. His father's decision not to intervene was also widely seen as a mistake—a political one, not a legal one.

A couple of hours after Biden spoke to the reporters, his campaign issued a statement responding to Trump, citing media reports that he had pressured the Ukrainian president for political purposes. "If these reports are true, then there is truly no bottom to President Trump's willingness to abuse his power and abase our country," the statement said.

The Ukraine story was dominating the airwaves and the Internet. There was talk of the coming months being consumed by a formal impeachment inquiry. On the weekend, Harris finally found a moment to record his impressions in his private journal. He asked himself: Could this snowball into impeachment, and possibly lead to the end of Trump's presidency? Harris couldn't see that happening.

"Already we see him deploying the same defenses as with the Russia story," he wrote. "But there is something about this one. It's cleaner. It's easier to understand. It doesn't involve as many players. And it concerns conduct while he was in office. This is different."

CHAPTER TWENTY-TWO

"The Women Who Kill"

September 21 to 23, Washington, West Columbia, South Carolina, and New York

The first weekend of fall was one of operatic emotions for Pelosi. On Saturday, September 21, she joined hundreds of other mourners for the funeral of longtime NPR journalist Cokie Roberts, a Washington institution who was practically family to Pelosi. Their fathers had served in the House together. They were women who had made it to the top of their professions, and they shared a keen understanding of politics—its potential and practice, its pitfalls.

In her eulogy, Pelosi quoted Roberts's mother, Lindy Claiborne Boggs, who had served in the House after her husband's death. "Years ago, Lindy said to me: 'Darlin', know your power and use it.' What Lindy wants, Lindy gets." Pelosi paused. "So, here I am."

The crowd in the packed St. Matthew's Cathedral in Northwest Washington, where the funeral for John F. Kennedy had been held, laughed heartily. The church was filled with politicians and journalists, and the eulogies moved easily between the personal and the political. Representative Debbie Dingell of Michigan sat with Pelosi in her pew. She could see that Pelosi was trying to respect the solemnity of the moment. Now was not the time to talk politics. But after the service, Dingell watched as people kept coming up to her and saying, "We gotta move forward" on impeachment.

After the funeral, Pelosi called Drew Hammill, her deputy chief of staff. He was sitting in the Opart Thai restaurant in Chicago having lunch with a college friend. "We need to start thinking about an announcement as soon as Monday," she told him. She didn't use the word "impeachment," but he knew exactly what she meant. Here we go, he thought. They would have to decide on a time and place for an announcement, along with the drafting of a speech.

Of course, he thought, this was happening when he was on a rare, long-planned weekend off. But he would be back in D.C. in the morning to prepare for this new path and what it would bring.

The next morning, Sunday, Pelosi flew to South Carolina for the funeral of Emily Clyburn, a prolific Democratic fundraiser and the much-loved wife of House majority whip Jim Clyburn, the third-ranking Democrat in the House and one of Pelosi's closest political allies.

Stories in *The Washington Post*, the *New York Times*, the *Wall Street Journal* and others were offering mounting revelations about Trump's conduct on the Zelensky call. Reports that Trump had specifically asked Zelensky to investigate Joe Biden, with whom she had worked in Congress for decades, and his son Hunter were especially galling to Pelosi.

Trump was not being shy about his efforts to have Ukraine go after Biden. On the White House lawn that Sunday morning, as he prepared to leave on a trip to Ohio and Texas, he brushed aside any criticism of the call. "The conversation I had was largely congratulatory," he said, speaking loudly to be heard over the whirring blades of Marine One, the presidential helicopter. "It was largely corruption—all of the corruption taking place. It was largely the fact that we don't want our people, like Vice President Biden and his son, creating to the corruption already in the Ukraine." Trump's words were a bit jumbled, but his message was clear: I did nothing wrong. Joe Biden is the bad guy.

Pelosi and Adam Schiff had been in touch throughout the weekend, coordinating strategy and messaging. Schiff was interviewed on CNN's "Sunday Morning" show, not long after Trump's departure on Marine One. To Pelosi watchers, he sounded like he was channeling her thoughts. "I have been very reluctant to go down the path of impeachment. But if the president is essentially withholding military aid at the same time he is trying to browbeat a foreign leader into doing something illicit, providing dirt on his opponent during a presidential campaign, then that may be the only remedy that is coequal to the evil that that conduct represents."

That afternoon, Pelosi sent a "Dear Colleague" letter to the entire House, both Republicans and Democrats. She echoed Schiff's call for Maguire, the acting DNI, to turn over the whistleblower complaint. She said if Trump and his administration continued to block release of the complaint, "they will be entering a grave new chapter of lawlessness which will take us into a whole new stage of investigation."

At 3:14 p.m., before Clyburn's 5 p.m. funeral began, *The Washington Post*'s Rachael Bade and Josh Dawsey published a story online with a blunt opening sentence: "Democrats' frustration with Speaker Nancy Pelosi's unwillingness to impeach President Trump is reaching a fever pitch." It said many House Democrats felt they had endured an "embarrassing week" and had been outmaneuvered by Trump. Democratic rank-and-file members wanted to enforce the subpoenas that Trump was blocking. Some were in favor of holding people in contempt, even jailing or fining them. That power hadn't been used in nearly a century. Representative Steve Cohen of Tennessee was quoted as saying: "Our side says it's 'legally questionable,' 'it hasn't been used in forever,' and 'blah, blah, blah.' I say do it. . . . We back off of everything! We've been very weak."

Pelosi's flight had arrived early, and she found herself with an unexpected hour before the funeral. She started making calls to her committee chairmen. Her message: It's time to start thinking about our next moves.

The Republicans were moving quickly to undercut the whistleblower and the still-classified complaint. In a flurry of appearances on the weekend TV interview shows, the message was: Why should this person be believed? What's the motive?

House minority leader Kevin McCarthy of California, on Fox's "Justice with Jeanine Pirro," said: "No one has seen the complaint. No one knows who the whistleblower is. . . . Is this a person who is upset they've been fired?" On the same show, House member Mark Meadows of North Carolina took a different tack. "I've been working on this since back in May," he said. "This is a Ukrainian hoax, and it's not even by a legitimate whistleblower."

The "deep state" figured prominently in some of the Republican messaging. Tom Fitton, president of Judicial Watch, a conservative advocacy group, told Pirro: "You have someone in the government illegally spying on, monitoring the president or passing along rumors they're hearing as a result of their work, and then abusing the law, the Whistleblower statute" to report it. As far as Fitton was concerned, "This is just the next phase of the coup" to remove Trump from office.

On Martha MacCallum's Fox show, former Trump acting attorney general Matthew Whitaker said: "I think this is a clear example of someone that's part of the deep state, someone part of the deep state in the intelligence community, taking advantage of this whistleblower procedure." On "Fox News at Night," Brad Blakeman, a former adviser in the George W. Bush administration, dismissed the whistleblower as an "unnamed faceless bureaucrat."

Their comments soon showed up on social media, magnifying the message. At the White House, where Trump was getting ready for a three-day trip to New York for the annual opening session of the U.N. General Assembly, he thought the assertion that he was being spied on was worth a tweet. He picked up the assertion from an op-ed by Fox commentator Gregg Jarrett, who wrote: "It appears that an American spy in one of our intelligence agencies may have been spying on our own president. . . . Was this person officially asked to listen to the conversation or was he or she secretly listening in?"

The Republicans were after the whistleblower's identity and motive. The Democrats were after the whistleblower's complaint. The press was working the story hard. Something had to give.

At 11:36 a.m., Monday, September 23, Connor Joseph, press secretary for Representative Abigail Spanberger of Virginia, emailed Michael Duffy, the *Washington Post* opinions editor at large.

"Would you have any availability today to talk about a potential op-ed?" he asked.

Duffy helped review the constant flow of opinion pieces that politicians, government officials, world leaders, academics and countless others submitted for consideration. *The Post* published many more pieces online than the few that appear on the op-ed pages of the daily print edition. But most submissions were still rejected. Only the most interesting, newsworthy and urgent pieces made it. Duffy saw Spanberger as a fresh, new voice in Congress. He was curious about what she wanted to say. No harm in taking a look.

He sent an encouraging reply: "Great. Looking forward. Topic?"

Duffy knew Washington inside and out. He had spent 33 years at *Time* magazine. After joining *The Post* a year earlier, he had gone to the Hill to introduce himself to the chiefs of staffs of some of the newest members. It was seed-planting: Say hello, explain that *The Post* was open to a wide range of opinions, leave his contacts. He made a special effort to visit the offices of Spanberger and Elaine Luria. Both were from Virginia, which made them local for *The Post*. He knew from experience that all seeds don't sprout, but some do. He wouldn't know about this seed until he and Spanberger's press secretary could talk.

They spoke by phone at around 3:30 p.m. Duffy was intrigued. Joseph explained that seven "national security Democrats," freshmen with military or intelligence experience who had won in Trump-leaning districts, wanted to take a public stand in favor of an impeachment inquiry.

Duffy understood the pivotal importance of such a piece. Nancy Pelosi's resistance to impeachment was in part because of these vulnerable freshmen from swing districts. A rash inquiry could damage their chances of winning reelection, and maybe even jeopardize the party's House majority and her speakership. Now these seven were saying: No need to protect us.

Listening to Joseph, Duffy sensed that the seven were looking for more signatures. He wanted to get the process going. "Send me the piece as soon as possible," he said. Joseph promised delivery by 4:30 p.m.

Politics wasn't the first career for any of the op-ed writers. Spanberger and Elissa Slotkin of Michigan were former CIA officers. Luria and Gil Cisneros of California were former senior Navy commanders. Mikie Sherrill of New Jersey had been a Navy helicopter pilot. Jason Crow of Colorado was a former officer in the Army Rangers. Chrissy Houlahan of Pennsylvania was a former Air Force officer.

They had history together. All had been involved in efforts to get more military vets and others with national security experience elected to federal office. They had campaigned together, and once in Washington, they met each other's families. They chatted over the encrypted messaging app Signal, trading notes on tough votes and weekend plans. They dubbed their clique the G9, for the original number of members, and they set their Signal messages to disappear automatically—a bit of tradecraft from their previous careers.

Mostly, they understood each other. Each was walking a political tightrope in their home district. Like Pelosi, they had tried to steer their caucus away from impeachment's risky path and toward the issues they had campaigned on: health care, infrastructure, strengthening the economy.

The torrent of news stories about Trump and Ukraine had changed their conversation. "Is anyone starting to think differently about impeachment?" Slotkin had asked in a group message.

The Signal replies flooded in fast: They were all starting to think differently. The potential abuse of power could not be ignored. It spat in the face of everything they had sworn an oath to protect. Supporting an impeachment inquiry had always been a gamble, but now it felt like a gamble they were duty bound to take.

Jason Crow began to draft an op-ed. He dropped it into a Google document; others logged in and made edits.

For Slotkin, every comma counted. She represented Michigan's Eighth District, a 75-mile stretch of farm country and suburbia, from Lansing to Rochester, north of Detroit. Held tightly by Republicans for two decades, it had gone for Trump in 2016 by more than six percentage points. Two years later, a surge of suburban Democratic votes propelled her to victory by nearly four.

Slotkin had spent her early years in the district, on her family's farm. On 9/11, when she was in New York City attending grad school at Columbia, the attacks inspired her to enter government service, and she joined the CIA. After three tours in Iraq and stints delivering Oval Office briefings to George W. Bush and Obama, she moved home to Michigan just as Trump was sweeping into office, where he was soon denouncing the world she had just left as the deep state.

Her run for Congress had been a long shot. The race was one of the nastiest and most expensive in Michigan history. Opponents accused her of being a carpetbagging outsider. They said she was unqualified. They bizarrely claimed she had funded terrorism. On election night, the race was finally called at 1:30 a.m., with Slotkin the winner, prompting her brother Keith to observe: "Don't get in a knife fight with Elissa."

When Pelosi sought reelection as speaker, Slotkin was among the few Democrats who opposed her. It was a promise she had made to her constituents, and it was in line with her vow to be an independent, Midwestern voice in a party increasingly dominated by its liberal coastal base. Pelosi wasn't seriously challenged, but Slotkin had established herself as someone whose vote couldn't be taken for granted.

The calls for impeachment after the Mueller report hadn't swayed Slotkin. Sure, the conclusions were troubling. But impeachment was such a drastic step. The voters deserved to have their say on Trump in 2020, she thought. The whistleblower's complaint, however, struck her as altogether different. Suddenly, it wasn't about Trump's behavior in past elections. This was about the fairness of the *next* election. The president had used the power of his office for political gain, not for the nation's security interests, she thought.

Had Slotkin made a list of things she wanted to accomplish as a first-term member of Congress, helping to impeach the president would probably have ranked last, if at all. She knew it could cost her reelection. But she said she felt in her bones that the issue was "bigger than politics." The group had texted throughout the weekend, trading views on impeachment and its consequences. On Sunday night, they convened a conference call that lasted more than an hour. They debated the op-ed, its language, its likely impact. Two of the nine declined to sign—Jared Golden of Maine and Max Rose of New York. They had promised their constituents that they weren't going to Washington to take out Trump. But the other seven were in. They agreed that Connor Joseph would contact Michael Duffy at *The Post* the next day.

"The Women Who Kill." That was the half-joking nickname some in the caucus had coined for the five women—Slotkin, Spanberger, Sherrill, Luria and Houlahan—who came to Congress with military or intelligence experience. The label was meant to be funny, but it also reflected a new reality: In their first year, the five women had acquired respect and considerable clout, highly unusual in the House, where seniority has ruled since the days of parchment.

The 2018 midterms, with their large influx of new and diverse members, had played havoc with House tradition. Alexandria Ocasio-Cortez and the rest of the Squad had been the subject of media fascination since the start. They were fresh faces, all women of color, all progressives, unflinching and unpredictable. Older Democratic caucus members resented the attention they were getting from the media, and even from Pelosi.

The Women Who Kill were better positioned to gain caucus approval. There were grumblings that they were almost comically overconfident. But as moderates and veterans, they did not encounter as much resentment as the Squad members with their vast Twitter followings and well-honed media skills.

Over the years, Pelosi had developed a leadership style that had served her well trying to lead such a varied group. She was steady, not mercurial.

She tolerated long meetings and long-winded members. She handed out her committee assignments and other chits with precision and purpose. She kept score and everyone knew it. She wasn't one of The Women Who Kill. But few in the caucus messed with her. Even the freshmen knew the rule: Don't blindside the speaker.

Late on Monday afternoon, Crow, Spanberger and Houlahan huddled in Houlahan's office to make last-minute edits. The piece was short, less than 500 words, but the length didn't matter.

"These allegations are stunning, both in the national security threat they pose and the potential corruption they represent," they had written. If Trump had used his office "to pressure a foreign country into investigating a political opponent," if he had used the military aid "as leverage," if he continued to block the whistleblower complaint from going to Congress, then he had demonstrated a "flagrant disregard" for the law. "If these allegations are true, we believe these actions represent an impeachable offense."

The op-ed concluded: "We must preserve the checks and balances envisioned by the Founders and restore the trust of the American people in our government. And that is what we intend to do."

Duffy had a quick conference call with staffers of the writers to check a few details, but the piece didn't need much more than a little tidying up and a headline. As copy editors reviewed the piece, Duffy popped into the office of his boss, editorial page editor Fred Hiatt.

"We've got a good one coming," he said.

Duffy was being careful not to oversell the piece. He wanted to let Hiatt read it first, see how it landed. But Duffy knew.

It was going to land hard.

As Joseph was getting ready to send the piece to Duffy, the op-ed writers had one more important call to make. They needed to let Pelosi know what was coming, before she saw it online. No surprises.

Pelosi was in New York for the U.N. General Assembly meeting. At 5 p.m., she got on her phone in a holding room at the St. Regis Hotel, where she was attending a VIP event. Several of the seven were gathered in Slotkin's office. Others had joined the conference call from elsewhere.

They had discussed in advance what they planned to tell the speaker, and they thought it might be transformative—"a moment of inflection," in Slotkin's words. All seven were saying they were ready to go ahead; the time was right. They had the credentials—tours in battle, national service under presidents of both parties—to back up their argument that Trump's behavior had crossed a bright line.

Pelosi listened more than she spoke. One by one, they made their case. All that was left was for Pelosi to weigh in. From the speaker's tone of voice, it was evident that she grasped what they were trying to do. "Thank you," she told them simply, "for leading on this issue."

Pelosi had been ready to go. She had told Hammill so. Now the public endorsement of an impeachment inquiry by the freshmen was the last piece of the puzzle. She thought they had been courageous to take their stand. Doing it as a unified group was critical.

Debbie Dingell talked to Pelosi soon after the call with the freshmen. They had known each other for decades. Pelosi understood the freshmen weren't asking permission, Dingell thought. They were essentially granting it. They were telling Pelosi: Don't worry about us. We can take the heat. Even if this hurts us, we must go forward with this. You must go forward with this.

At 9 p.m., the *Washington Post* op-ed was published online under the headline "Seven freshman Democrats: These allegations are a threat to all we have sworn to protect." Pelosi read it on the flight back to Washington. When she finished, she pulled out a piece of loose-leaf paper and worked on the speech that she would give the next day. She wrote: "The President must be held accountable. No one is above the law."

CHAPTER TWENTY-THREE

"You Don't Really Want to Do This"

September 24, Washington and New York

Just after 8 a.m. on Tuesday, Pelosi was in her Georgetown apartment, getting ready for the day that was going to be like no other. This was the day she would formally, officially, finally announce that the House was opening the impeachment inquiry that she had resisted for so long. Breakfast over, she put on a vivid blue dress with an American flag pin.

The phone rang. It was her assistant. The White House was calling. Trump wanted to speak to her. He would be patched through to her cellphone. Hold for the president. At 8:16 a.m., Trump came on the line.

He was phoning from his Trump Tower penthouse in New York. In two hours, he would address the U.N. General Assembly and then meet separately with several world leaders. But foreign policy wasn't the reason for his call. He told Pelosi he wanted to talk about guns.

He said he had been making tremendous progress on gun safety issues with Democrats. Pelosi had no idea what he was talking about. She knew of no such progress, or any such conversations.

Done with gun legislation, he quickly turned to the allegations in the whistleblower complaint.

"Mr. President, you have come into my wheelhouse," she said, citing her extensive background in intelligence matters and her role in working on whistleblower legislation over the years.

He came out with it.

"Are you really going to impeach me?" he said. "The Senate will never convict. You don't really want to do this." He said the Zelensky call was "so perfect" and there had been "no pressure at all. . . . Literally, you would be impressed by my lack of pressure. . . . Why would I say something bad? . . . It was 100 percent perfect. I didn't ask him for anything."

He was about to release the transcript. She would see. Perfect.

She told him she was going ahead with the impeachment inquiry.

Trump switched gears. He wanted her to know: He was not the one blocking Maguire from sharing the whistleblower complaint with Congress. "I don't have anything to do with that," he said.

"Well, then undo it," she said. "Because you are asking the DNI to break the law. I mean, it's just outrageous. Mr. President, we have a problem here."

She repeatedly urged him to give Maguire the go-ahead. "Mr. President, release the complaint," she said.

"I have to go give a speech," he said. He hung up at 8:38. They had talked for more than 20 minutes.

Pelosi was left shaking her head. Either the president of the United States didn't know right from wrong, she thought, or he didn't care. Whichever it was, she felt Trump was taking the country down a dangerous path that violated the Constitution's spirit and letter. She was ready for her crosstown trip to the Capitol.

Inside the domed building, in the hallways and offices and elevators, among the aides and reporters and camera crews, there was a definite buzz in the air. Everyone on the planet seemed to have read the op-ed from the seven freshmen. It was as if a stuck valve had opened. Pelosi's vote-counters were telling her that all but 5 of the 232 sitting Democratic House members now favored an impeachment inquiry. The handful of undecideds were leaning in the same direction.

Shortly before noon, as Pelosi was walking quickly toward the House chamber, she passed Elissa Slotkin hurrying in the other direction. Neither woman slowed down. But Pelosi turned back and over her shoulder, she flashed the rookie lawmaker a thumbs-up, saying "Congratulations!"

"Thank you," Slotkin responded sheepishly, not quite sure what else to say. It didn't feel like that sort of moment.

At noon, Pelosi called the House to order for its regular session. She stayed for only a few minutes before handing off the gavel. While she was gone, John Lewis of Georgia rose to speak. He walked slowly to the well of the House, where two lecterns stood, one for each party. He had a sheaf of notes in his right hand. This was not the moment for an off-the-cuff speech.

Lewis, a House icon, was now 79 years old. He and Pelosi had arrived the same year, 1987, and had served 17 terms since. In his long and storied career as a civil rights activist, Lewis had witnessed many historic moments. He had been at Dr. Martin Luther King Jr.'s side during the 1963 March on Washington. He had been a Freedom Rider. He led the 1965 march across the Edmund Pettus Bridge in Selma, where Alabama state troopers had fractured his skull.

For months, in deference to Pelosi, he had not voiced his view of impeachment. He was voicing it now. "People approach me everywhere I go," Lewis said. "They believe, they truly believe, that our country is descending into darkness." He looked up from his notes as he turned the page. "I share their concerns for the future of our country. It keeps me up at night. We took an oath to protect this Nation against all domestic enemies and foreign enemies. Sometimes I am afraid to go to sleep for fear that I will wake up and our democracy will be gone, will be gone, and never return."

His voice was now rising, more insistent. "There comes a time when you have to be moved by the spirit of history to take action to protect and preserve the integrity of our Nation. I believe, I truly believe, the time to begin impeachment proceedings against this president has come."

Pelosi stepped away shortly after 2 p.m. for a scheduled appearance at the Atlantic Festival, an annual gathering of leaders in politics, business, tech and other fields organized by the *Atlantic* magazine. Festivals like this one need headliners, and the magazine had scored the top headliner of the moment. Pelosi was interviewed onstage by editor in chief Jeffrey Goldberg. He wasted no time in asking the question on everyone's mind.

"Is that an impeachable offense?"

"I'll be making an announcement at 5 p.m. today. Not here, not now," Pelosi said. She had the microphone and the platform, so she used them to lay the groundwork for her announcement. "We have to have the facts," she told Goldberg. "Now we have the facts. We're ready . . . for later today." She said Trump was "making lawlessness a virtue in our country." She said Trump's call for a foreign country to interfere in a U.S. election would be easier for most Americans to grasp than the complex Mueller report. "This one is the most understandable by the public," she said.

She knew that Democrats had a lot of work to persuade a solid majority of Americans—let alone 67 senators, including at least 20 Republicans—that Trump should be removed from office. She quoted Abraham Lincoln to Goldberg: "Public sentiment is everything. With it, you can accomplish practically anything. Without it, practically nothing."

While Pelosi was taking Goldberg's questions, Donald Trump was making news of his own in New York, via Twitter. Between a luncheon hosted by the U.N. secretary general and his next set of diplomatic meetings, a tweet went out announcing that he would "fully declassify" and release an "unredacted transcript" of his July 25 phone conversation with Zelensky.

The timing was pure Trump. So was the decision to go public. Trump had overruled his communications staff and several cabinet officers, including Pompeo and treasury secretary Steven Mnuchin, who had been arguing for days that releasing details of a call between world leaders would set a perilous precedent. He also was warned that releasing a transcript would fuel the calls for impeachment.

In the end, he had listened to White House counsel Pat Cipollone and Bill Barr, who said disclosure would slow or bring an end to the nonstop drip of negative stories about what had been said during the call. The transcript would be news for a week or two, Cipollone said, but then the press would move on.

A big gamble. But maybe, a big payoff. It would disarm the Democrats, keep them off balance. It might even derail the move toward impeachment. Trump decided to go ahead.

"You will see it was a very friendly and totally appropriate call," said his tweet, sent at 2:12 p.m. "No pressure and, unlike Joe Biden and his son, NO quid pro quo! This is nothing more than a continuation of the Greatest and most Destructive Witch Hunt of all time!"

Pelosi called a meeting of the Democratic caucus for 4 p.m. in HC5. The windowless room was unusually packed. Aides had set up extra chairs to accommodate everyone.

Pelosi strode in and confirmed what everyone had expected: She wanted an impeachment inquiry. She laid out the argument. Trump had asked Ukraine's president to investigate the Bidens and the debunked 2016 Ukraine election meddling theory. It was a betrayal of U.S. national security and the integrity of U.S. elections. A betrayal of the Constitution. The public could easily understand it. "We have to strike while the iron is hot," she told them. "This is a national security issue and we cannot let him think that this is a casual thing, so that's where I'm at."

She previewed the Democratic message: The president admits to this. He doesn't even see anything wrong with asking a foreign government for help in damaging a political rival. He has betrayed his oath of office. She said she wanted the impeachment hearings done "expeditiously." She warned that impeachment needed to be solemn. There would be no cheering, no applause. She asked Emanuel Cleaver of Missouri, a United Methodist pastor and a former chairman of the Congressional Black Caucus, to lead a prayer calling for a somber approach to the process ahead.

Pelosi was pleased with the tone of the meeting. But she had been in Congress far too long to let words, no matter how strong or eloquent, substitute for action. She wanted to nail things down. She had sent John Lewis on a special arm-twisting mission. Lewis approached Rashida Tlaib with a request. No smiling, no show of exuberance, he told her. No MF'ing.

Tlaib listened and complied. Later, she joked to House majority leader Steny Hoyer, "How do I say 'Impeach the Motherfucker' in sign language?" But showing that there are limits even to the persuasive powers of John Lewis, Tlaib's reelection campaign started selling $29 "Impeach the MF" T-shirts two days later. "It made Nancy go nuts," said one of Pelosi's close allies. Tlaib appeared at a rally with the T-shirts and said of Trump: "He is a dangerous person to our country, and it's about time that my colleagues realize it."

After Pelosi left the caucus meeting to make her public announcement, a rift quickly emerged. Eliot Engel and Jerry Nadler, who had been pressing Pelosi for months to start an impeachment inquiry, spoke about broadening the investigation beyond Ukraine. As committee chairmen, they had the power to make it happen, if Pelosi didn't rein them in.

The more Engel and Nadler spoke, the more uncomfortable Slotkin, Spanberger and other moderates became. Unlike Engel and Nadler, they faced tough reelection races in their districts. They would need to defend their decision. They wanted a surgical strike. Impeach Trump over Ukraine. It was clean. It was understandable. It was, to their mind, outrageous. Trump had abused his office and the Constitution. Why make it harder than it had to be?

Slotkin listened and listened. Finally, she boiled over. She stood to address her colleagues and the leadership. Stay focused on Ukraine, she urged. Get your act together. How can you announce an impeachment inquiry without knowing what that inquiry would look like? What's the plan? What's the strategy?

At the CIA and the Pentagon, her training grounds, planning was ingrained in the culture. In politics, it was often necessary to improvise as you go. But on this? Bad idea. This was too important to make up as you go along. They needed, as best they could, to map it out. How they were going to build their case, step by step. "If you are asking us to stay on message, give us a goddamn message to stay on!" she demanded. She looked around at her colleagues. Dozens could lose their seats because of impeachment, she among them. The whole country is watching. The whole world is watching, Slotkin thought.

The moderates had another goal: They wanted to limit Nadler's role. Impeachment was, generally, the turf of his Judiciary Committee. But Nadler's handling of the Lewandowski hearing had been a wake-up call. The moderates were hoping for a focused, efficient impeachment process. Their choice to lead the probe was still the calmer, unflappable Schiff.

Spanberger was waiting her turn to speak when Slotkin looked at her phone. There was her quote—"give us a goddamn message to stay on"—instantly turning up on *Politico* reporter Heather Caygle's Twitter feed. Slotkin couldn't believe it. The closed-door meeting was still in session, and the leaks were already happening. It was unbelievable.

Slotkin showed Spanberger the screen. Spanberger could not restrain herself. Holding up her phone, pointing at it, she said: "Damn it, who the hell is leaking?"

The leak was a betrayal, in Spanberger's view. It went against everything the leadership was trying to accomplish. It was the opposite of coming together, of staying on message, of respect for the process. "I've spent the last nine months answering for all the things that everybody else in this room says," she told the packed room. "Mine is a Trump district. What we did in my district"—meaning, win—"was a really difficult balance." Impeachment was such a risk, she was saying. "Please do not muck it up. Just be—be thoughtful about that."

• • •

Schiff left the room and walked into a boisterous group of about 25 reporters, shouting questions: Who will be the first witness? Will you subpoena the president? Why are you handling this and not the Judiciary Committee? Schiff offered a few vague answers. This was not the moment for specifics. He and his aides made their way through the crowd, taking more than a minute to cross the short distance to the elevator.

Finally, safely inside, Schiff leaned against the back wall as the doors slid shut. He let out a long breath: "Ooooff. I'm going to have to get used to that."

At 5 p.m., Pelosi stood in the Capitol, an array of six American flags behind her, and faced a bank of TV cameras.

"The actions of the Trump presidency have revealed the dishonorable fact of the president's betrayal of his oath of office, betrayal of our national security and betrayal of the integrity of our elections. Therefore, today, I am announcing the House of Representatives is moving forward with an official impeachment inquiry."

Reflecting the historic nature of the moment, she reprised a line she had used at the *Christian Science Monitor* breakfast back in June. "Getting back to our founders, in the darkest days of the American Revolution, Thomas Paine wrote 'The times have found us.' The times found them to fight for and establish our democracy. The times have found us today."

She had come a long way from early March, from saying "he's just not worth it." The risk of doing nothing, she had decided, was now greater than the risk of doing something. She was ready for the coming fight.

Congressional Republicans responded with a shrug of their collective shoulders. Their counter message: Impeachment was a politically motivated "sham" that would only motivate GOP voters. House minority leader Kevin McCarthy repeated the Republican mantra, born in the early days of the Mueller investigation, saying Democrats "have been trying to reverse the results of the 2016 election since President Trump took office. For them, this is all about politics. Not about facts."

In the Senate, Majority Leader Mitch McConnell of Kentucky was reading from the same page: "Speaker Pelosi's much-publicized efforts to restrain her far-left conference have finally crumbled. House Democrats cannot help themselves. Instead of working together across party lines on legislation to help American families and strengthen our nation, they will descend even deeper into their obsession with re-litigating 2016."

Trump took to Twitter with a series of messages that went out just as Pelosi was finishing her speech.

"So bad for our Country!"

"They never even saw the transcript of the call. A total Witch Hunt!"

"PRESIDENTIAL HARASSMENT!"

He was planning to make sure everyone could read the transcript soon. Then they would see. Perfect.

Part Three

IMPEACHMENT

CHAPTER TWENTY-FOUR

"Isn't It a Perfect Call?"

September 25, New York and Washington

Trump woke up in his Trump Tower penthouse, high above Fifth Avenue in Manhattan. He had another busy day ahead at the U.N. General Assembly meeting. On his schedule were talks with three different foreign leaders, including his long-promised, first-ever sit down with Ukraine's Zelensky.

But first things first for this Wednesday morning. He was still steaming at Pelosi's decision to start impeachment proceedings. His Twitter account sent an early-morning shot across Pelosi's bow: "There has been no President in the history of our Country who has been treated so badly as I have. The Democrats are frozen with hatred and fear. They get nothing done. This should never be allowed to happen to another President. Witch Hunt!"

In Washington, White House aides were preparing to welcome a dozen or so Republican lawmakers for an unusual 8:30 a.m. reading session. They had been invited to preview the document that all official Washington was waiting to see: a transcript of Trump's July 25 phone call with Zelensky. If all went according to the White House plan, the lawmakers would get a set of talking points to review, so they would be primed for media interviews when the transcript went public an hour or so later.

The group that filed into the White House included some of Trump's strongest defenders: McCarthy; House minority whip Steve Scalise of Louisiana; House members Jim Jordan of Ohio and Mark Meadows; Senator Shelley Moore Capito of West Virginia and a half-dozen others. Lawyers for the White House counsel's office handed out copies of the five-page transcript, and the reading began.

Along with the talking points, they received a pep talk from Trump, on speakerphone from New York: "Isn't it a perfect call?" He hoped they could now see that for themselves.

Trump sounded like he was in a good mood. He clearly thought he had done nothing wrong. But some in the room sensed that he was a little worried about releasing the transcript, or at least some of the details it contained. They tried to lighten the mood. One joked with the president that "this was one of his better" calls with foreign leaders, referring to embarrassing leaks early in the administration from Trump's awkward conversations with the leaders of Mexico and Australia.

Trump made a round of phone calls to other Republican allies in Congress, including Peter King, a House member from New York. King described Trump's mindset to *Washington Post* reporter Josh Dawsey. "He feels it's going to help him on balance. Rather than have it out there week after week, saying he is demanding a quid pro quo, he just gets it out here," King said.

The reading session was scheduled to be over at 9 a.m., but it was running long. In the White House press room, Dawsey and others waited for the transcript's release. Finally, White House aides distributed copies and the reporters were scanning the pages, skimming fast. Editors wanted this one online as soon as possible.

Everyone quickly saw that the document came with a disclaimer about the contents. This was a "memorandum" of the call, "not a verbatim transcript." The document "records the notes and recollections of Situation Room Duty Officers and NSC policy staff assigned to listen and memorialize the conversation in written form as the conversation takes place." It cautioned that several factors might affect accuracy, including a poor phone connection and accents. Some in the media simply called it a transcript. Others, striving for a more accurate and precise description, opted for "partial transcript" or "rough transcript."

White House officials were spinning hard, telling Dawsey and others, "This proves the president did nothing wrong. It proves all the reporting is erroneous and inaccurate." The more Dawsey read, the more he wondered, Why the hell would you give us this transcript? He could see that throughout the White House press corps, many reporters were asking themselves the same question.

The conversation seemed so transactional, so undisguised. "Do us a favor," Trump had said. And: "there's a lot of talk about Biden's son, that Biden stopped the prosecution." And: "so if you can look into it . . . it sounds horrible to me." And: "Whatever you can do, it's very important that you do it if that's possible." And: "The former ambassador from the United States, the woman, was bad news." And: "Well, she's going to go through some things." And: "I will have Mr. Giuliani give you a call and I am also going to have Attorney General Barr call and we will get to the bottom of it."

On Zelensky's side, he seemed so eager to please. Assuring Trump that "you have nobody but friends around us." And: "in addition to that investigation, I guarantee as President of Ukraine that all investigations will be done openly and candidly." And: "she was a bad ambassador because I agree with you 100 percent." And: "I stayed at the Trump Tower."

Did the transcript show that Trump had done something impeachable? That was for Congress to decide. But for many of the reporters, it raised a lot of questions, and it sure didn't look perfect.

Dawsey called Devlin Barrett and Matt Zapotosky, the *Post* reporters covering the Justice Department. They were at DOJ headquarters, getting the official interpretation of the transcript's significance. They were as surprised as the other reporters by what it showed.

DOJ officials, in the days before the transcript release, had been downplaying the exchange, telling Barrett and Zapotosky that the call was "not that bad." They said the transcript would show that Trump had not explicitly tied aid to Ukraine to the investigations he wanted. The Justice officials thought Trump was right to rip off the Band-Aid and get it all out in the open.

Other Justice Department sources had been telling Barrett that they did not agree with the president's "perfect call" assessment. They thought it would be a public and diplomatic embarrassment. It would look terrible for the president. But at the same time, they didn't see anything that added up to a crime. Bribery and campaign finance laws weren't written to encompass something like a president suggesting a White House meeting or aid in return for political investigations. Justice officials told Barrett that the exchange simply was not explicit enough to meet the legal standards for a public corruption charge.

Reading the document, Zapotosky thought that the DOJ officials were seriously underestimating the political damage it was going to cause. Perhaps Trump had not tied Ukraine's aid directly to investigations. But he was dangling a White House visit if Zelensky would do as he wanted.

What, Zapotosky wondered, could possibly be more compelling than the president's own words?

After the document's release, Nancy Pelosi convened a meeting of her leadership team. Until now, the various investigations seemed too complicated, too hard to explain. Imagine trying to sell the word "emoluments" to a divided nation. Ukraine was clear. Powerful. But was it enough?

As Pelosi and her lieutenants read the transcript, it seemed like enough. This was so egregious and so simple. They couldn't believe Trump had released this chest of pure gold for his opponents. Pelosi was amazed that Trump seemed to believe the transcript was good for him.

Pelosi favored a major shift in strategy. She would not rule out including Trump's other actions in any articles of impeachment. But for the moment, their united message would be: Ukraine, Ukraine, Ukraine. Focusing on that issue also might keep the inquiry out of the courts, avoiding the delays that had bogged down several of the other investigations, she said.

In the leadership meeting, Debbie Dingell was among those who agreed. The Democrats needed to focus on what they viewed as a clear threat to U.S. national security and the Constitution, she thought. That was something they would have no trouble making the public understand.

Capitol Hill was going bonkers over the release. It seemed that there weren't enough cameras and microphones for everyone who wanted to weigh in. At about 10:15 a.m., as the Democrats were still meeting in caucus, Pelosi sent two members, Hakeem Jeffries of New York and Katherine Clark of Massachusetts, to brief reporters.

Jeffries said the transcript was plain: Trump had pressured Zelensky to investigate the Bidens, helping his 2020 reelection campaign. "That is textbook abuse of power and the transcripts have become Exhibit A in that regard." He highlighted Trump's suggestion that Zelensky should talk to Rudy Giuliani. "What role does Rudolph Giuliani have in this government? Is he in the Department of Justice? Is he the Secretary of State? Is he an ambassador to Ukraine or the European Union?"

Answering his own questions, Jeffries said: "Rudolph Giuliani was the president's political hit man." He said Trump "directed the Ukrainian president to have a follow-up conversation with Giuliani as part of the effort to dig up dirt on Joe Biden. Period. Full stop. That is lawless. That undermines our national security. That is an abuse of power. That is unpatriotic. That undermines the electoral process in our democracy and the American people will not stand for it."

On message, Jeffries signaled that Ukraine was now the Democrats' primary target. "There is a lot of chaos, crisis, confusion, corruption and criminality to sort out with respect to the Trump administration. But, before us, at the moment, is an almost unspeakable abuse of power that the president has committed with respect to bullying the Ukrainian government to launch an investigation into the Biden family to secure political dirt."

In a different part of the Capitol, House Republican leaders were holding a news conference. They had their own message: Pelosi's newly announced impeachment inquiry was a travesty—proof that Pelosi, not the president, was abusing power.

They took turns. McCarthy said this was "a dark day for America" and that "the speaker owes an apology to this nation, and I think it's even a question whether she should stay in her job." Doug Collins, the top Republican on the House Judiciary Committee, described Pelosi as "a speaker who's lost control of the facts . . . who no longer can honestly stand before the American people and honestly be a voice for her party or for reason." Scalise dismissed Pelosi's impeachment announcement as a "wild and irresponsible accusation," capping years of anti-Trump rhetoric. "Unfortunately, we've seen this drumbeat towards impeachment," he said, "since the day Donald Trump got elected. They made it clear first with the Resist Movement, that they didn't want to acknowledge he was elected."

Earlier, at the Republican caucus meeting, Scalise had tried to make light of the day's flurry of news developments. He had passed out a "Mad Libs impeachment" form, based on the word game invented in the 1950s. Players fill in the blanks to make funny sentences. Scalise's version was based on a satirical article of impeachment: "Resolved, that Donald J. Trump, President of the United States, is impeached for _______ (made-up crime) because the Democrat Majority in the House of Representatives still refuses to accept the results of the 2016 election and since the Democrat Majority's previous impeachment attempts through _______ (sham hearing), _______ (dud report), and _________ (political stunt) failed."

Republicans were closing ranks around the president. House member Liz Cheney of Wyoming said: "Ever since President Trump was elected, the House Democrats have been careening from impeachment theory to impeachment theory." Senator Lindsey Graham, among the fiercest of Trump supporters, tweeted: "Wow. Impeachment over this? What a nothing (non-quid pro quo) burger."

Schiff and his team gathered at the Intelligence Committee's office for a group reading of the transcript.

"Holy shit," Schiff said.

He had assumed, when he heard Trump was making the transcript public, that the call wasn't as bad as they had been led to believe. Or there was something exculpatory. Or maybe the White House would release a sanitized account.

"Wait till you get to page two," one staffer said.

They had worried that the transcript would be filled with Trump-speak, the odd syntax and incomplete thoughts. But they thought the transcript was damning, and crystal clear.

"Oh my God, wait till you get to page three," said another aide.

They had expected they would need a court ruling to get the transcript, that Trump would fight them every step of the way. But now here it was, voluntarily released. They took turns reading passages out loud. "Do us a favor . . . CrowdStrike . . . Biden . . ."

They tried to understand Trump's strategy and thinking. Maybe he and his advisers honestly believed there was nothing wrong on the call. Maybe it was just the way he operated, transactional, everything was a deal. Maybe he thought that if he just kept describing it as a perfect call it would become a perfect call, at least in the eyes of his followers.

But for Schiff and everyone else in the room, the transcript read like a road map to impeachment.

Republican Will Hurd of Texas read the transcript carefully. He thought it was bumbling foreign policy. As a former CIA officer steeped in meticulous preparation, it was not how he would have handled the advance work for the call. But this was Trump, and the president did things his own way. It was sloppy, it was hard to defend, but Hurd simply didn't see any violations of law. He didn't see anything that would lead him to say at a town hall in his Texas district, This statement right here, this is impeachable.

Hurd had a bedrock belief: Impeachment required a broken law. He had come to that conclusion during his unsuccessful run for Congress in 2010. Republican primary voters regularly told him that Barack Obama should be impeached. But Hurd knew they meant that Barack *Hussein* Obama should be impeached. He recognized that bigotry for what it was, and he resolved to never support an impeachment based on anything but a crime.

Ukraine, the country at the center of this drama, was of special interest to Hurd. He had visited twice in 2017 and had become an advocate for providing military aid to the Ukrainians in their fight against the Russians. He had been outraged by Trump's July 2018 press conference with Putin in Helsinki. Trump had stood by silently while Putin tried to seem sympathetic to Ukraine and evaded responsibility for Russia's state-supported interference in the 2016 U.S. election. Hurd had been upset enough to write a blistering op-ed for the *New York Times*. "Over the course of my career as an undercover officer in the C.I.A.," he wrote, "I saw Russian intelligence manipulate many people. I never thought I would see the day when an American president would be one of them."

If his words were startling, so was his chosen forum for saying them. The *New York Times* was one of Trump's frequent "fake news" targets. Hurd was going all in. "The president's failure to defend the United States intelligence community's unanimous conclusions of Russian meddling in the 2016 election," he wrote, "and his standing idle on the world stage while a Russian dictator spouted lies confused many but should concern all Americans. By playing into Vladimir Putin's hands, the leader of the free world actively participated in a Russian disinformation campaign that legitimized Russian denial and weakened the credibility of the United States to both our friends and foes abroad."

That sort of strong talk put Hurd in a category that sometimes numbered just one. Few Republicans in Congress were willing to criticize the president so openly and candidly. If the Trump-Zelensky transcript didn't persuade the independent-minded Hurd, what chance did the

Democrats have of convincing others in the Republican party? From what Hurd had seen so far, it looked as if Pelosi's move was aimed mainly at soothing her party's left wing and minimizing the risk of incumbents facing primary challenges. The Democrats certainly didn't have enough evidence to merit impeachment, he thought. Not by a long shot.

At noon, Schiff went before the cameras. He said he was shocked at what the transcript said, and shocked that Trump thought releasing it would help his case. "What those notes reflect is a classic mafia-like shakedown of a foreign leader," Schiff said.

Keep in mind, he told the reporters, that Zelensky was desperate for U.S. support to defend his country from Russian aggression. He then provided his interpretation of what Trump was doing. "The president communicates to his Ukrainian counterpart that the United States has done a lot for Ukraine. We've done an awful lot for Ukraine, more than the Europeans or anyone has done for Ukraine," he said. "This is how a mafia boss talks. 'What have you done for us? We've done so much for you. But there's not much reciprocity. I have a favor I want to ask you.'

"What is that favor? Of course, the favor is to investigate his political rival, to investigate the Bidens. And it's clear that the Ukraine president understands exactly what is expected of him and is making every effort to mollify the president."

Around the same time that Schiff was speaking in Washington, Fiona Hill was arriving at Newark Liberty Airport in New Jersey after the long transatlantic flight from Manchester, England.

Hill had left the White House on July 19 with a plan to return to her old job at the Brookings Institution on October 15. She had spent most of September in her native England with her 85-year-old mother. Hill had tried unsuccessfully to arrange physiotherapy for her mother in the U.K., so she was bringing her to the States for treatment.

Now, as they landed at Newark and Hill turned her phone back on, it lit up with bazillions of texts and emails from journalists. The weak WiFi at her mother's house had made it hard to keep up with detailed news from Washington. But two days earlier she had managed to trade text messages with an NSC colleague, Joe Wang. He had given her a heads-up that there was something going on involving a phone call and a whistle-blower complaint. She had a sense of foreboding that it was related to

Giuliani, Sondland and the "irregular channel" she had seen emerge on Ukraine.

The day before, the Senate had passed a resolution calling on the White House to deliver the whistleblower complaint to Congress, and Trump administration officials were saying that the complaint would be released soon. Reporters were texting Hill, hoping to find out something.

As she flipped through her messages, waiting for their connecting flight to D.C., Hill turned to her mother.

"Mom, I think I'm going to get snarled up in some stuff from the NSC again."

"But you've left," her mother said.

"Yes," she said, "But some things never leave you."

As Hill was reading her texts, a few cracks in the GOP's united front on Trump's "perfect call" appeared. Senator Mitt Romney of Utah, the Republican presidential nominee in 2012, told a group of reporters that he was bothered by the contents of the transcript. "It remains troubling in the extreme," he said. "It's deeply troubling."

Washington Post political reporter Robert Costa had been working the phones with his Republican contacts, and was already hearing reservations. Some told Costa they questioned the White House's judgment in releasing the transcript. One Senate Republican told Costa it was a "huge mistake" that the party now had to confront and defend. The senator did not want to be named. The quote was worth using, even anonymously, because it showed some Republicans were worried enough to speak up but still feared Trump's anger if they spoke out publicly. Senate Republicans coming out of a private lunch at the Capitol said they were fully behind Trump and his release of the transcript.

"It's unprecedented that he's released it and there are some ramifications for the office, but people were clamoring for all the information, and he's giving it," said Senator Capito of West Virginia.

"It's a decision for the White House," Senator Rick Scott of Florida said, calling out Democrats for "hating" Trump.

"I've looked at the transcript," said Senator Joni Ernst of Iowa. "I don't see anything there."

On the House side, Peter King told Josh Dawsey that the transcript didn't amount to much. "There are a number of Republicans in the House who are definitely anti-Trump who came up to me today and said, this shows nothing," King said. "They just say, 'Is this the best they have?' "

Shortly after 2 p.m., C-SPAN was replaying the Republican press conference from earlier in the day. Steve Scalise was in mid-sentence when C-SPAN abruptly cut away to New York. There, on the sidelines of the U.N. meeting, Donald Trump and Volodymyr Zelensky—the stars of the phone call that was shaking Washington—were finally meeting face-to-face. It was neither casual nor intimate. The two men sat in black leather armchairs in a conference room at the InterContinental Hotel. Behind them, a backdrop of U.S. and Ukraine flags. Between them, a bouquet of green and white flowers. In front of them, a huge array of cameras and reporters.

Trump wore a blue suit and a trademark red tie. Zelensky wore a black suit and black tie. Trump was flanked by Pompeo, Mnuchin, Perry, Mulvaney, Kushner, Commerce Secretary Wilbur Ross and his new national security adviser, Robert O'Brien. Zelensky also had an entourage of his top advisers, less well known than Trump's, and less accustomed to the spectacle-like atmosphere.

Trump started things off with a joke, speaking as if he were a talk show host welcoming a guest. "Well, thank you very much, everybody. We're with the president of Ukraine, and he's made me more famous, and I've made him more famous," he said, to hearty laughter from the assembled aides.

Just a few months before, Giuliani had accused Zelensky of surrounding himself with "enemies of Trump." Now Trump leaned forward, met Zelensky's eyes and showered him with praise.

"He's very, very strongly looking into all sorts of corruption and some of the problems they've had over the years. I think it's one of the primary reasons he got elected. His reputation is absolutely sterling. And it's an honor to be with you," he said, reaching out to shake Zelensky's hand.

Then, another joke, this one about their past phone conversations: "And we spoke a couple of times, as you probably remember."

Zelensky, speaking in English, thanked Trump and offered a little quip of his own, gesturing toward the cameras: "It's a great pleasure to me to be here, and it's better to be on TV than by phone, I think." The aides laughed, on cue.

Keeping it light, Zelensky mentioned that this was not his first trip to New York, but that Trump had never been to Ukraine. He appealed to Trump's well-known desire to outdo President Obama, noting that Obama had never come to Ukraine during his two terms. More chuckling from the aides.

"So, can you give me a word that you will come to our great country?" Zelensky asked.

"Well, I'm going to try," Trump said. More laughter, and Zelensky smiled, clapping his hands together at Trump's dodge. Then Trump segued to his days of owning the Miss Universe pageant, and how "we had a winner from Ukraine." A Ukrainian contestant had come close in 2011, first runner-up, but no winners yet. "It's a country, I think, with tremendous potential," Trump said.

"Yes, I know it, because I'm from this country," Zelensky replied. A little laughter.

Shifting to the prize that he and his advisers had been pursuing since April, Zelensky took a swing at getting Trump to commit to a White House meeting. "I want to thank you for the invitation to Washington," Zelensky said.

"Right," Trump said.

"You invited me. But I think—I'm sorry, but I think you forgot to tell me the date."

That got the biggest laugh of the day. Trump smiled and nodded. Then he gestured toward the media, saying, "They'll tell you the date."

When reporters had a chance to question the two leaders, the tenor changed. "President Zelensky, have you felt any pressure from President Trump to investigate Joe Biden and Hunter Biden?" asked Jeff Mason of Reuters.

"I think you read everything. So I think you read text. I'm sorry, but I don't want to be involved to democratic, open elections—elections of USA," Zelensky said. "No, you heard that we had, I think, good phone call. It was normal. We spoke about many things. And I—so I think, and you read it, that nobody . . . pushed me."

Trump, leaning forward, acted as interpreter for the assembled journalists: "In other words, no pressure."

Then a question for Trump. Did he want Zelensky to investigate the Bidens? Trump said he wanted Zelensky to "do whatever he can." Whatever the Bidens' involvement in Ukraine, he said, it happened long before Zelensky was in office, so "this was not his fault."

Sounding like a prosecutor giving a closing argument, Trump took a shot at Hunter Biden. "Now, when Biden's son walks away with millions of dollars from Ukraine, and he knows nothing, and they're paying him millions of dollars, that's corruption," Trump said. "When Biden's son walks out of China with $1.5 billion in a fund—and the biggest funds in the world can't get money out of China—and he's there for one quick meeting, and he flies in on Air Force Two, I think that's a horrible thing."

Asked whether it was appropriate for Giuliani, his personal attorney, to get involved in another government's affairs, Trump said, "Well, you'd have to ask Rudy." He said Giuliani was "looking to also find out where the phony witch hunt started, how it started," referring to the Mueller investigation into Russia's election interference. "It was a total hoax. It was a media hoax and a Democrat hoax. Where did it start? . . . Rudy has got every right to go and find out where that started."

Trump railed against Hillary Clinton and her personal emails, former FBI director James Comey and his deputy Andrew McCabe. He belittled Obama, saying his predecessor had provided Ukraine with "pillows and sheets" and now he was sending anti-tank Javelins. But he saved his toughest talk for Nancy Pelosi. "Look, she's lost her way. She's been taken over by the radical left. She may be a radical left herself, but she really has lost her way." He brought up his phone call to Pelosi the day before, saying he wanted to discuss "guns," but "she didn't even know what I was talking about."

He was accelerating now, like a downhill skier, picking up speed as he talked. "I'll tell you what: Nancy Pelosi is not interested in guns and gun protection and gun safety. All she is thinking about is this. She's been taken over by the radical left." His poll numbers had gone up because Americans are "really angry at the Democrat Party," especially at Pelosi.

"And things like, as an example, drug pricing—getting drugs down—things like gun safety, infrastructure, the Democrats can't talk about that because they've been taken over by a radical group of people. And Nancy Pelosi, as far as I'm concerned, unfortunately she's no longer the speaker of the House."

Zelensky looked on, his hands clasped tightly, a silent spectator.

• • •

Two hours later, after a meeting with the president of El Salvador, Trump held a solo news conference. He had a "little announcement" to make. He had spoken to McCarthy and other House Republican leaders and they agreed with him that there needed to be "transparency" about the whistleblower complaint. He didn't pinpoint when it would be released, but he "fully supported" the idea.

It was quite a turnabout. For weeks, Maguire had been keeping it from Congress, indicating that the White House was calling the shots. Now, the complaint would be declassified and made public for the world to see.

The reporters had questions, of course, but the president wasn't ready to take them. He wanted to talk about his three days of meetings with world leaders, about the economy, about the border wall. He also wanted to say a bit more about impeachment, how he was a victim of "viciousness" by the Democrats and the media. The transcript proved the call was "wonderful," "beautiful" and "perfect."

Twenty-four minutes in, he called on a reporter.

Any concerns about the precedent of releasing the call transcript?

"Yeah. I don't like it," Trump said.

"Why did you go ahead and do it?" he was asked.

"Because I was getting such fake news, and I just thought it would be better . . . But I don't like the concept of releasing calls because when a president or prime minister, or a king or a queen, calls the United States, you don't like to say, 'Gee, we're going to release your call to the fake news media, and they're going to make you look like a fool.' What happens is, it's hard to do business that way. You want to have people feel comfortable."

Was he braced for a long impeachment saga?

"I thought it was dead," he said. "It was dead. The Mueller report, no obstruction, no collusion."

He mocked Schiff and Nadler, accusing them of acting "so serious" in public while in private "they must laugh their asses off, but it is so bad for our country."

He said he was under siege from the deep state. "While some partisans and unelected bureaucrats in Washington may choose to fight every day against the interests and beliefs of the American people, my administration is standing up for the American people like no administration has in many, many years. You forgot the American people. You totally forgot the American people."

He would survive this assault, too, he said. "People have said—Rush

Limbaugh—great man—Sean Hannity said it. A lot of people have said it. Mark Levin. They said they don't know of one man anywhere in the world, with all the men they know—or woman—that could handle what I've had to handle."

As Trump was speaking, members of the House and Senate Intelligence committees gathered in their secure hearing rooms to review yet another potentially devastating document: the freshly delivered—but as of now, still classified—whistleblower complaint.

These secure hearing rooms had acquired a nickname. Everyone called it the "SCIF," pronounced "skiff," which came from its unwieldly formal name: Sensitive Compartmented Information Facility. Inside the SCIF, no one had to state the obvious: This was serious business. Classified business. They could read the documents, but no one could make a copy.

Jim Himes of Connecticut, a Democratic member of the House Intel committee, was transfixed by the nine-page complaint. The allegations were so specific, severe and credible. He and other Democrats looked up from the document to glance at their Republican counterparts. Were they floored by what they were reading? Was it denting their faith in Trump's "perfect call"? Himes couldn't tell.

On the Senate side, Republican Ben Sasse of Nebraska read the complaint and told reporters that while Democrats shouldn't have "used words like 'impeach'" before seeing the complaint, Republicans also needed to be careful. "Republicans ought not to be rushing to circle the wagons and say there's no 'there' there when there's obviously a lot that's very troubling there," Sasse said.

Mike Conaway of Texas, a Republican on the House committee, viewed the complaint differently. "I haven't seen anything that bothers me," he said afterward.

Will Hurd was impressed by the complaint's well-written and well-documented presentation. He thought the committee should investigate it thoroughly. His reaction came partly from his CIA training: evaluate the evidence dispassionately, respond accordingly. But he didn't see why an investigation needed to be an impeachment inquiry. He recalled Pelosi's words from March: "Impeachment is so divisive to the country that unless there's something so compelling and overwhelming and bipartisan, I don't think we should go down that path."

Hurd could also see trouble ahead. There was no trust between Republicans and Democrats on the committee. In March, Hurd had joined his GOP colleagues in calling for Schiff to resign as chairman because of partisan statements he had made during the Mueller investigation. The two sides saw the same facts so differently, he thought. That wasn't going to change now.

In the deeper recesses of the conservative echo chamber, release of the call transcript revived a favorite conspiracy theory from the 2016 election: CrowdStrike. Trump had fanned the conspiracy's flames in his conversation with Zelensky: "I would like you to find out what happened with this whole situation with Ukraine, they say CrowdStrike . . . The server, they say Ukraine has it."

"CROWDSTRIKE IS BACK ON THE MENU BOYS," said one thread on the Reddit message board called "r/The_Donald." In another thread, a commenter wrote, "Trump just put 'Ukrainian Crowdstrike' into the consciousness and conversation of every normie that is following this story." Normie was sarcasm, lingo for the average person, someone who needed to be clued in.

CrowdStrike was the Silicon Valley cybersecurity firm hired by the Democratic National Committee to investigate the hack of its computer system in 2016. When the FBI entered the case, agents saw no reason to take custody of the affected servers, as they were able to obtain complete copies of forensic images made by CrowdStrike.

The conspiracy theory went like this: CrowdStrike had taken the server to Ukraine and hidden it there. The company was, the conspiracy alleged, owned by a wealthy Ukrainian. Neither assertion was true. The server was never moved. And CrowdStrike was co-founded by a naturalized U.S. citizen born in Russia—and not Ukrainian.

Post reporters Craig Timberg, Drew Harwell and Ellen Nakashima had been tracking the allegations against CrowdStrike since they first surfaced on conservative media in 2017. They had found no evidence to support the allegations. But now they could see that the president's request to Zelensky had given new fuel to the conspiracy theory's diehard proponents.

Radio host Rush Limbaugh said Trump's reference to CrowdStrike was "momentous." Speaking to his massive audience, estimated at more than 15 million people a week, Limbaugh said, "The Democrats are bent out of shape that Trump even knows about CrowdStrike."

• • •

In the evening, Trump attended a private fundraiser on Manhattan's Upper East Side, on 86th Street between Fifth and Madison, at the home of billionaire hedge fund manager John Paulson. The evening's donations would go to Trump Victory, a political action committee working on behalf of the Trump campaign and the Republican National Committee.

Campaign manager Brad Parscale said the Trump 2020 campaign had raised $5 million since Pelosi's impeachment announcement the day before. The last of Trump's 32 tweets of the day was also his cheeriest: "One of our best fundraising days EVER!"

CHAPTER TWENTY-FIVE

"That's Close to a Spy"

September 26, New York and Washington

Washington's morning rush hour wasn't yet over when the whistleblower complaint, declassified and available for anyone to read, hit the Internet just after 8:30 a.m. on September 26.

Only 15 hours earlier, members of the House and Senate Intelligence committees had to go to their SCIFs to look at the document. Now reporters throughout the capital were studying the seven-page complaint and a heavily redacted two-page appendix, dated August 12 and addressed to the chairmen of the House and Senate Intelligence committees.

The complaint wasn't just about the Trump-Zelensky phone call. It was broader and more explicit in its assertions. "In the course of my official duties," the whistleblower wrote, "I have received information from multiple U.S. Government officials that the President of the United States is using the power of his office to solicit interference from a foreign country in the 2020 U.S. election." The president was not acting alone in this effort, the complaint said. "The President's personal lawyer, Mr. Rudolph Giuliani, is a central figure in this effort. Attorney General Barr appears to be involved as well."

That was paragraph two.

The whistleblower's knowledge, the complaint said, came from conversations with "more than half a dozen U.S. officials" who had "informed me of various facts related to this effort."

That was paragraph three.

The whistleblower stated forthrightly that "I was not a direct witness to most of the events described. However, I found my colleagues' accounts of these events to be credible because, in almost all cases, multiple officials recounted fact patterns that were consistent with one another. In addition, a variety of information consistent with these private accounts has been reported publicly."

That was paragraph four.

The whistleblower had organized the complaint into four categories. First, the July 25 phone call. Then, "Efforts to restrict access to records related to the call." Next, "Ongoing concerns." Finally, "Circumstances leading up to the July 25 presidential call."

The document was thorough, almost like a legal brief. It came with footnotes, including one that offered a primer on Ukrainian politics and players. It contained a series of bullet points that laid out, in chronological order and with references to press accounts, the Giuliani-led campaign to pressure the Ukrainians on matters of interest to Giuliani and President Trump. It described the aid freeze, and how that was a factor in the campaign.

The biggest news, though, was category two: "Efforts to restrict access to records relating to the call." According to the whistleblower, "senior White House officials had intervened to 'lock down' all records of the phone call, especially the official word-for-word transcript of the call that was produced—as is customary—by the White House Situation Room."

Instead of putting an electronic copy of the transcript into the usual computer, accessible to anyone with the appropriate security clearance, White House lawyers had directed that the transcript be stored on a separate network reserved for "classified information of an especially sensitive nature."

For the whistleblower, this unusual handling was evidence that "White House officials understood the gravity of what had transpired in the call." One White House official had described the restricted access as "an abuse" because "the call did not contain anything remotely sensitive from a national security perspective."

At 8:35 a.m., Adam Schiff sent out a tweet with a link to the document. "This complaint should never have been withheld," he wrote. "The public has a right to see the complaint and what it reveals. Read it here."

Schiff and his staff were already feeling energized that morning by Trump's release of the transcript. The president was telling everyone to read it. But for Schiff and his colleagues, the transcript showed that Trump had done exactly what the whistleblower had said.

Emboldened, Schiff gaveled the House Intelligence Committee to order a few minutes after 9 a.m. in hearing room 2154 of the Rayburn House Office Building. Maguire was waiting at the witness table, summoned by subpoena, to answer questions about his handling of the whistleblower's complaint.

It was a moment made for Schiff. He was not only a former federal prosecutor used to presenting cases to a jury—in this instance, the assembled phalanx of journalists and the C-SPAN audience—but he also understood the arc of a good story. When he was a young lawyer in Los Angeles, he had done what nearly everyone dreams of doing when they move to La La Land: He wrote a screenplay.

He spent hours at the Academy of Motion Picture Arts and Sciences library, reading the scripts for then-popular films "Silence of the Lambs" and "Witness." Drawing on his courtroom experience and snippets of dialogue from trials, he typed out a crime thriller. The prosecutor was the hero. Schiff called it "Minotaur." He also wrote a Holocaust-era screenplay. Neither made it to the silver screen.

As he got deeper into the world of intelligence work during his years in Congress, he drafted a spy novel with the working title "A Man Called Seven." Since Trump's election, Schiff, whose district includes Hollywood, had not found the time to keep up his extracurricular writing.

Now as he faced Maguire, sitting ramrod straight after enduring a battalion of clicking cameras at the edge of the witness table, Schiff's prosecutorial and screenwriting sides both made their appearance. The transcript and the whistleblower's complaint had presented him with the material for a compelling narrative. Schiff felt a need to tell the story as vividly and as dramatically as he could, in language that anyone watching on television could easily grasp. He had prepared a nine-minute opening statement.

He began as prosecutor Schiff. "Yesterday, we were presented with the most graphic evidence yet that the president of the United States has betrayed his oath of office, betrayed his oath to defend our national security and betrayed his oath to defend our Constitution," he said. Ukraine "desperately" relied on U.S. military, financial and diplomatic aid to protect itself from Russian aggression. That was why Zelensky was so frantic to get an Oval Office meeting with Trump and to keep the American aid flowing.

"And so what happened on that call?" Schiff said. "Zelensky begins by ingratiating himself, and he tries to enlist the support of the president.

He expresses his interest in meeting with the president and says his country wants to acquire more weapons from us to defend itself."

Then screenwriter Schiff took over. While working on his opening remarks in advance of the hearing, he had remembered former FBI director James Comey saying that Trump reminded him of a mafia don. Then there was Trump himself, calling his former lawyer Michael Cohen a "rat." Seizing on the mob theme, Schiff had crafted a dramatic retelling, in his own words, of Trump's reaction to Zelensky's requests.

"And what is the president's response? Well, it reads like a classic organized crime shakedown," Schiff told the hearing room. "Shorn of its rambling character and in not so many words, this is the essence of what the president communicates."

This sentence was intended as Schiff's signal that he was not going to stick to the document, that he was going to provide "the essence of" what Trump had said. He began with Trump's words, almost as they appeared in the transcript: "We've been very good to your country, very good. No other country has done as much as we have. But you know what, I don't see much reciprocity here."

Then, without stopping to say that he was now leaving the transcript behind, Schiff shifted into his scripted rewrite of Trump's lines: "I hear what you want. I have a favor I want from you, though. And I'm going to say this only seven times so you better listen good. I want you to make up dirt on my political opponent, understand, lots of it, on this and on that. I'm going to put you in touch with people, not just any people. I'm going to put you in touch with the attorney general of the United States, my attorney general, Bill Barr. He's got the whole weight of the American law enforcement behind him. And I'm going to put you in touch with Rudy. You're going to love him, trust me. You know what I'm asking, and so I'm only going to say this a few more times in a few more ways. And by the way, don't call me again, I'll call you when you've done what I asked."

Looking pleased with his dramatic rendition, Schiff said: "This is, in sum and character, what the president was trying to communicate with the president of Ukraine. It would be funny if it wasn't such a graphic betrayal of the president's oath of office. But as it does represent a real betrayal, there is nothing the president says here that is in America's interests, after all. It is, instead, the most consequential form of tragedy, for it forces us to confront the remedy the Founders provided for such a flagrant abuse of office: impeachment."

With the military discipline of 36 years as a Navy Seal and vice admiral, Maguire sat stoically, listening, waiting, as Schiff finished his opening monologue.

While Schiff was doing his caricature of Trump in Washington, President Trump was in New York, at a gathering of staffers and families from the U.S. Mission to the United Nations, airing his grievances and thrashing the Democrats.

The declassified whistleblower's complaint had been released less than an hour earlier, prompting the president to offer his instant analysis. "I just heard while coming up here, they have a whistleblower," he said, drawing sympathetic giggles from the crowd eating breakfast in the InterContinental Hotel ballroom. "He turned out to be a fake, he's a fake, a highly partisan whistleblower."

If not for the "dishonest media," Trump said, no one would be paying attention to this. "The whistleblower came out and said—nothing. Said 'a couple of people told me he' "—Trump was referring to himself—" 'had a conversation with Ukraine.' " He paused, then escalated his attack. "We're at war. These people are sick. They're sick, and nobody is calling it out like I do." As for the whistleblower, "basically that person never saw the report, never saw the call. Never saw the call. Heard something and decided that he or she or whoever the hell it is—sort of like, almost, a spy."

The more Trump talked, the more he sounded like a Wild West sheriff gathering a posse for a "dead or alive" manhunt. "I want to know who's the person who gave the whistleblower—who's the person who gave the whistleblower the information? Because that's close to a spy. You know what we used to do in the old days when we were smart? Right? With spies and treason, right? We used to handle it a little differently than we do now." That last line produced a few laughs and a few hushed murmurs.

Not everyone in the crowd was a committed supporter. This wasn't a political rally or fundraiser. The event was intended as the president's opportunity to thank U.N. ambassador Kelly Craft and her staff for their work during Trump's three-day visit. Someone in the ballroom was recording the event and was alarmed enough at the president's "hang 'em high" language to pass the audio along to reporters at the *Los Angeles Times*.

As Craft looked on, Trump dismissed the news media as "animals" and "scum" and "the worst human beings you'll ever meet." That produced a cry of "Fake news!" from somewhere in the crowd. "And then you have Sleepy Joe Biden, who's dumb as a rock," he said, bringing more laughter and applause from parts of the room. "This guy was dumb on his best day, and he's not having his best day right now," a perfect segue into repeating the allegations about Biden and his son Hunter.

Trump was riffing, having fun. He was in his element.

Inside hearing room 2154 on Capitol Hill, Maguire was delivering his opening statement. His words stood in direct opposition to Trump's. "I want to stress," he said, that the whistleblower had "acted in good faith," had "done everything by the book and followed the law."

Maguire said he took the complaint seriously, but he also felt it was his duty to inform the White House in case the president wanted to claim executive privilege. The situation, he said, was "unprecedented."

Schiff, taking the first turn at questions, picked up a phrase that Trump had been using for nearly a week.

"Director, you don't believe the whistleblower is a political hack, do you?" Schiff asked.

"I don't know who the whistleblower is, Mr. Chairman," Maguire answered, carefully. "I've done my utmost to protect his anonymity."

Schiff bristled. "That doesn't sound like much of a defense of the whistleblower here, someone you found did everything right." He offered Maguire a second shot at the same question. "You don't believe the whistleblower is a political hack, do you?"

"I believe the whistleblower is operating in good faith," Maguire said, his voice rising a bit. "My job is to support and lead the entire intelligence community. That individual works for me. Therefore, it is my job to make sure that I support and defend that person."

"You don't have any reason to accuse them of disloyalty to our country," Schiff said, "do you?"

Maguire, looked down, shaking his head. "Sir," he said, looking up, his gaze steady. "Sir, absolutely not."

The committee's Republican members were ready to pounce as soon as Schiff finished questioning Maguire. Outside the hearing room, Schiff's dramatic reading was already taking flak on the TV networks and the Internet.

"While the chairman was speaking, I actually had someone text me:

Is he just making this up?" said Michael Turner of Ohio. "And, yes, he was, because sometimes fiction is better than the actual words or the text. But luckily the American public are smart and they have the transcript. They have read the conversation. They know when someone's just making it up."

Elise Stefanik of New York, an outspoken Republican on the committee, didn't wait for her turn. She sent out a tweet as the hearing was in progress. "It is disturbing and outrageous," she wrote, "that Chairman of the House Intelligence Committee Adam Schiff opens up a hearing of this importance with improvised fake dialogue."

Schiff wasn't surprised that the Republicans were howling. Too bad. He had said he wasn't quoting Trump's actual words, and he was mocking a man who loves nothing more than mocking people. As soon as Turner was done, Schiff took the microphone again. "My summary of the president's call was meant to be at least part in parody," he said, smiling slightly. If that wasn't clear, he said, "that's a separate problem."

Now Schiff was going to make it abundantly clear. "Of course, the president never said, 'If you don't understand me, I'm going to say it seven more times.' My point is that's the message that the Ukraine president was receiving in not so many words."

But Schiff was too late. He had handed the Republicans an unexpected talking point. Instead of talking about Trump and the whistleblower complaint, the hearing was now focusing on Schiff and his "parody." Next up on the Republican side was Brad Wenstrup, also from Ohio. Before asking Maguire any questions, Wenstrup took direct aim at Schiff.

"You know, I think it's a shame that we started off this hearing with fictional remarks," Wenstrup said, "putting words into it that did not exist, that are not in the transcript. And I will contend that those were intentionally not clear." He paused. "The chairman described it as parody, and I don't believe that this is the time or the place for parody when we are trying to seek facts."

The pummeling was happening simultaneously online, where Republican House members had taken to social media with both thumbs. Ralph Norman of South Carolina: "How stupid does he think the American people are?" Scalise tweeted: "Dems are literally making stuff up now because they have no legitimate reason to impeach @realDonaldTrump."

Ronna Romney McDaniel, chair of the Republican National Committee and Senator Mitt Romney's niece, weighed in, too: "Absolutely disgraceful for Adam Schiff to dismiss his lies about @realDonaldTrump's call with the Ukrainian President as 'parody.' Schiff willfully misled the American people and he should retract immediately!"

The hearing went on, with several more hours of questioning. Schiff's parody kept coming back into play. At about 1 p.m., Air Force One landed at Joint Base Andrews in Maryland after the flight back from New York. Trump told the waiting reporters he had been watching the hearing. "Here we go again," he said. "It's Adam Schiff and his crew making up stories and sitting there like pious whatever you want to call them. It's just a—really, it's a disgrace."

The Republicans were having a field day at Schiff's expense.

By the time Trump was back at the White House, the *Los Angeles Times* had published the president's "spies and treason" comments. A few hours later, the recording itself was posted.

Encouraged by Trump's loose talk about possible punishment for a treasonous mole—"You know what we used to do in the old days"—some of the president's online supporters were already gearing up to find the whistleblower and publish the name. On the pro-Trump Reddit message board "r/The_Donald," a post using a pseudonym said, "This 'whistleblower' needs to be put in the public spotlight, and then f---ing prosecute him/her to the fullest extent of the law."

The quest to identify the whistleblower soon grew into a fixation across the more extreme corners of such platforms as Twitter, Reddit and Gab. It spread to conservative news sites, radio shows and TV broadcasts, but online, it quickly descended into a case study of the Internet at its most disturbing.

On the 4chan message board, a commenter asserted that "the whistleblower is not white," although the complaint gave no hint about race or gender. Many were sure it was a woman. Others insisted on Hispanic or Jewish or Arab. Names flew, without proof, mostly a few of the better-known names from the obvious agencies—the CIA, NSC, the State Department.

It was more than just a guessing game. If the online sleuths were to "out" the whistleblower, the consequences could be serious. Targets of online harassment campaigns had had their addresses, Social Security numbers, names of children or other family members put into the public domain. Major news outlets had decided not to publish the whistleblower's name, partly because of safety concerns, partly because the federal law protected the anonymity of whistleblowers.

Schiff had vowed, in his tweet releasing the complaint, that his committee would do "everything we can to protect this courageous whistleblower." Pelosi had made a similar pledge at a late-morning news conference. "I've been an important part of writing bills to protect whistleblowers from retaliation, and that's what we hope to do in this case as well: Protect the whistleblower."

Doing that wasn't easy. The complaint had been filed under a 1998 law that Pelosi had helped craft during her time on the Intelligence Committee. That legislation, for the first time, set up a legal mechanism for filing a complaint without risking prosecution for leaking classified information. But in 1998, lawmakers couldn't anticipate a world with the reach and anonymity of social media. Whistleblowers knew they were a single tweet away from the public spotlight's harsh glare.

In the *Washington Post* newsroom, the whistleblower's identity presented a different dilemma. Even though the paper did not intend to publish the whistleblower's name, reporters were still interested in finding out as much as they could about the whistleblower's circumstances and intentions in filing the complaint back in August. Now that the complaint had been released, the contents were no longer a mystery. But important questions remained: Did the whistleblower have direct access to documents? Who had talked to the whistleblower? White House insiders? If so, why? Were there more to come?

As *Post* reporters knew all too well from the newspaper's own history, Washington loves a good mystery. During the Watergate investigation that led to Nixon's resignation in 1974, there was "Deep Throat," *Post* reporter Bob Woodward's secret source. Speculation had swirled for decades around Deep Throat's identity before it was finally revealed as former FBI official Mark Felt.

As the rest of the media was absorbing the *Los Angeles Times* story about the audio recording, a *New York Times* report added to the frenzy of the day, describing the whistleblower as a "CIA officer." This was the first such public identification. The story reported that the officer, "through an anonymous process," had first provided information to the CIA's top lawyer, Courtney Simmons Elwood. She had "shared" the officer's concerns with White House officials, "following policy."

The story quoted Bakaj, the whistleblower's lead counsel, as warning the paper not to reveal those details and others. He called the decision to publish "deeply concerning and reckless, as it can place the individual in harm's way." The whistleblower, Bakaj told the *Times*, "has a right to anonymity."

Within an hour, a furious debate was raging on social media. The paper had not named the whistleblower, but had it gone too far by publishing identifying details? Was the paper "doing its job" or "doing Trump's dirty work"? Had it stayed on the right side of a fuzzy ethical line, or smashed through it?

The debate brought a swift explanation from Dean Baquet, the *New York Times* executive editor. He said: "We decided to publish limited information about the whistleblower—including the fact that he works for a nonpolitical agency and that his complaint is based on an intimate knowledge and understanding of the White House—because we wanted to provide information to readers that allows them to make their own judgments about whether or not he is credible. We also understand that the White House already knew he was a CIA officer."

At the White House, officials insisted publicly that there was no "leak hunt" for the whistleblower. Trump was saying, in exchanges with reporters and in his tweets, that he did not know the person's identity. But his aides knew how the president felt about leaks and leakers. Trump was obsessed with them, and often had gone to extraordinary lengths to find out the source of a story he considered unflattering. Now Trump's "spies and treason" talk in New York made plain that the president was in his usual mode, fighting back harder than he was being hit.

One of his biggest supporters, radio talk show host Mark Levin, had a message for the whistleblower's attorney, who had said his client had a "right to anonymity." Levin told Sean Hannity on Fox: "Too bad, pal. Too late. You want to impeach our president, using this BS? We want to know all about your guy."

As evening arrived, Pelosi and her two top lieutenants—Majority Leader Steny Hoyer and Majority Whip Jim Clyburn—met with the "front-liners," the party's nickname for 42 House members facing tough reelection battles, many of them moderate freshmen who had won their seats in pro-Trump territory.

Nearly all the front-liners were now converts to the impeachment movement. But crammed into a small meeting room in the Capitol basement, they pressed two demands. They wanted a focused, efficient and fast inquiry, and they wanted Schiff to lead it. His "parody" hadn't hurt his standing among his colleagues. It might not have been his most shining moment, but at worst, it was a misdemeanor that the Republicans were trying to blow up into a capital offense.

The moderates had come to trust Schiff as an unflappable and reliable leader. They liked his background as a prosecutor. Impeachment was traditionally the jurisdiction of the Judiciary Committee, but the moderates felt that Nadler was overzealous. If impeachment had to be bipartisan and fair to be effective, Schiff seemed like a much better way to go.

For months, Pelosi's balancing act had been to impeach or not to impeach. Now it was a different calculus. How wide a net to cast? Nadler's committee was dominated by Democrats who wanted the inquiry to be as broad as possible, bringing in charges arising from the Mueller report and beyond.

The front-liners argued to Pelosi that they needed to stay tightly focused on Ukraine. The abuse was clear, they said. It would be easier to explain to the public, and it was something that some moderate Republicans might also find impeachable.

Pelosi had no trouble agreeing with them. They had found plenty of common ground.

In choosing Schiff to lead the inquiry, Pelosi was picking someone who was already a villain to Republicans. Schiff had become one of their favorite targets back in the spring, when he was preparing for the release of the Mueller report, making comments about what he and his committee were finding in their parallel investigation.

On Thursday, March 28, Trump took the stage in Grand Rapids, Michigan, for a campaign rally, where he unleashed a new schoolyard nickname: "little pencil-neck Adam Schiff." Trump had already derided Schiff as "sleazy," and "Adam Schitt." Then he thought up "pencil neck," which he tried out at a White House meeting with House Republicans before using it at the rally.

"He's got the smallest, thinnest neck I've ever seen," Trump said at the rally. "He is not a long-ball hitter." The next day, the Trump campaign rolled out a T-shirt with an image of Schiff with a pencil for a neck and a red ball on his nose.

The attacks mounted. McCarthy compared Schiff to Communist

scaremonger Joseph McCarthy. The nine GOP members of the Intelligence panel signed a letter demanding that Schiff step down as chairman, questioning whether he was abusing his position and damaging the panel's integrity. Trump himself called for Schiff to resign his House seat, accusing him of "knowingly and unlawfully lying and leaking."

Schiff was amused by some of Trump's name-calling. He recalled walking through Manhattan with his college-age daughter and people kept recognizing him. Near one restaurant with outdoor seating, a man asked Schiff's daughter to hold his beer while he took a photo with Schiff.

"What am I now, Dad, the beer holder?" his daughter joked as they walked away. Schiff said he was surprised anyone recognized him, a Washington pol from California, that he was now a semi-celebrity in New York City.

"Well you know, Dad, it's the pencil neck," his daughter said.

The assault on Schiff seemed to strengthen his standing within his own caucus and especially with Pelosi. She called the Republicans "scaredy-cats" for attacking Schiff. "What is the president afraid of? Is he afraid of the truth, that he would go after a member . . . a respected chairman of a committee in the Congress?" she had said at the time. "They just don't know what to do, so they have to make an attack."

Now, as she was settling on her strategy and tactics for the impeachment inquiry, she was choosing an ally who seemed fully prepared for what would surely come his way.

The furor arrived before 9 a.m. the next morning.

"Rep. Adam Schiff fraudulently read to Congress, with millions of people watching, a version of my conversation with the President of Ukraine that doesn't exist," Trump wrote on Twitter. "He completely changed the words to make it sound horrible, and me sound guilty. HE WAS DESPERATE AND HE GOT CAUGHT. Adam Schiff therefore lied to Congress and attempted to defraud the American Public. He has been doing this for two years. I am calling for him to immediately resign from Congress based on this fraud!"

Schiff replied online less than half an hour later. "You engaged in a shakedown to get election dirt from a foreign country," he wrote. "And then you tried to cover it up. But you're right about one thing—your words need no mockery. Your own words and deeds mock themselves. But most importantly here, they endanger our country."

Elsewhere online, the campaign to flush out the whistleblower had gone to a new level. Two pro-Trump political activists were offering a $50,000 reward to anyone who could come up with the identity. Decrying the entire episode as a "national disgrace," they said they hoped their reward would succeed in naming the whistleblower and help put "this dark chapter behind us."

National disgrace or not, the impeachment inquiry and the whistleblower complaint were emerging as an impressive boon to the Trump campaign's coffers. Presidential son Eric Trump wrote on Twitter that the campaign had raised $8.5 million from small-dollar donors in two days, on top of the big-ticket donations from the VIP fundraiser in Manhattan the night before. "A BIG thank you to @SpeakerPelosi and the Democrats," he said. "People are sick of your nonsense but please keep it up—you are handing @realDonaldTrump the win in 2020!"

In the battle for the best messaging, it looked like the Republicans were out ahead, once again. Pelosi and Schiff knew the Democrats needed to do better. The hearings would be starting soon, with witnesses in closed-door depositions.

CHAPTER TWENTY-SIX

Welcome to the SCIF

October 3 to 10, Washington

Kurt Volker slipped into his seat at 9:30 a.m. on October 3 in the House Intelligence Committee's SCIF, three floors below ground in the Capitol. As the lead-off witness in this opening phase of impeachment proceedings against President Trump, Volker was the first to enter the "skiff" and its otherworldly environment.

Feeling comfortable in the windowless room was as likely as relaxing in a dentist's chair. The SCIF was essentially a box of steel-reinforced concrete, constructed as part of an expansion and hardening of the Capitol complex after the 9/11 terrorist attacks. Here, the nation's sensitive secrets could be discussed without fear of electronic eavesdropping.

In front of Volker sat eleven members of Congress—five Democrats and six Republicans—plus lawyers and staff members from both parties. Volker was there for a closed-door deposition. That meant no media, no cameras, no one from the public, none of the spectacle-like atmosphere that Maguire had faced a week earlier. But outside the room, *The Washington Post*'s Karoun Demirjian and other reporters were in position, a reminder that impeachment was now Topic A in Washington.

As the majority party in the House, the Democrats controlled the format. Pelosi had put Schiff's Intelligence Committee in charge, "in coordination" with two other committees, Foreign Affairs and Oversight and Reform. Anyone serving on one of the three panels, 109 members in all, about a quarter of the House, could attend and ask questions.

It was a joint inquiry in name, but everyone understood: This was Schiff's show. He gaveled the session into order; he was the only chairman in the room. He and his staff were planning a series of SCIF sessions in the coming weeks, likely to be followed by public hearings featuring major witnesses. Questioning witnesses behind closed doors to gather facts during a high-profile investigation wasn't new. When the Republicans were the majority in 2014 and 2015, they had used a similar approach for their examination of the 2012 attacks on U.S. government facilities in Benghazi, Libya.

"Good morning," Schiff said to Volker, who was waiting at the witness table with his lawyer, Margaret Daum, an expert in congressional investigations. "This will be a staff-led interview," Schiff said, speaking as much to his colleagues as to Volker. "We have tried to keep the room to a reasonable size. We expect the questions to be professional, that you'll be treated civilly." Schiff was putting his Republican colleagues on notice: No grandstanding. He intended to keep this interview on track.

Volker was no longer the special envoy to Ukraine. He had resigned his position on September 27, after the whistleblower complaint had become public with his name mentioned in recounting the events around the phone call. On the day of his resignation, the impeachment panels had sent a letter to Pompeo, saying that the committees had scheduled interviews with Volker and four other State Department employees—Yovanovitch, Kent, Sondland and Pompeo senior adviser Ulrich Brechbuhl. The letter had carried a stiff warning. "Failure of any of these Department employees to appear for their scheduled depositions," the letter said, "shall constitute evidence of obstruction of the House's impeachment inquiry." A subsequent statement was even tougher: "Any effort to intimidate or prevent them from talking to Congress" would also be seen as obstruction.

Pompeo, who had been issued a subpoena for his own testimony, did not explicitly forbid the five officials from going before the committees. But he called the request "an attempt to intimidate, bully and treat improperly the distinguished professionals of the Department of State, including several career Foreign Service Officers. . . . I will not tolerate such tactics."

As requested, Volker had come voluntarily. But Pompeo's pushback was a signal. Schiff could not count on the administration's cooperation. "We very much appreciate your coming here today," Schiff told Volker.

While Volker was being interviewed in the SCIF, Trump was on the White House South Lawn, preparing to leave for a rally in Florida, reporters shouting their questions. One asked: "What exactly did you hope Zelensky would do about the Bidens after your phone call?" The reporter then repeated: "Exactly."

Trump replied: "If they were honest about it, they'd start a major investigation into the Bidens. It's a very simple answer. They should investigate the Bidens."

He did not stop there. He expanded his attack, inviting yet another foreign country to open a separate investigation that could benefit his political campaign. On the opening day of impeachment proceedings, he was truly doubling down. "And, by the way, likewise, China should start an investigation into the Bidens, because what happened in China is just about as bad as what happened with—with Ukraine."

Trump was reviving one of his favorite unproven claims, that Hunter Biden had walked "out of China with $1.5 billion in a fund" and earned "millions" of dollars from a business deal there. That accusation had already earned a "Four Pinocchios" rating from Glenn Kessler, editor and chief writer of the *Washington Post*'s Fact Checker column. That was Kessler's grade for the most egregiously untrue statements.

The final shouted question gave Trump an opportunity for a parting swipe before boarding the presidential helicopter. "Mr. President, why did you recall the U.S. ambassador to Ukraine? Was she a problem?"

"I heard very bad things about her," he said. "I don't know if I recalled her or somebody recalled her. But I heard very, very bad things about her for a long period of time. Not good."

In the SCIF, Volker was explaining why he took the unpaid, volunteer job of special envoy at former secretary of state Rex Tillerson's request in 2017, and how the job had gradually become more complicated. "In May of this year," he said, "I became concerned that a negative narrative about Ukraine, fueled by assertions made by Ukraine's departing prosecutor general, was reaching the president of the United States and impeding our ability to support the new Ukrainian government as robustly as I believed we should."

In a single sentence, he was telling Schiff and the others: The original Lutsenko allegations were false. The Giuliani narrative was wrong. The president was being misled. I was trying to stop the bleeding.

For more than eight hours, Volker described his role as intermediary and participant, his efforts to straddle the line between the regular and irregular channels, his eyes firmly fixed on what he cared most about: keeping the U.S.-Ukraine relationship intact in the face of Russian aggression. The committee counsels were going step-by-step, asking questions in a logical way, but for anyone hearing the details for the first time, it was a dizzying amount of information to absorb.

Volker asserted that he had never been "aware of or took part in an effort to urge Ukraine to investigate former Vice President Biden." He said he had cautioned Ukrainian officials to "distinguish between highlighting their own efforts to fight corruption domestically" and "doing anything that could be seen as impacting U.S. elections." He said he had repeatedly warned various Ukrainian officials that Giuliani "does not represent the United States government."

Before the hearing, he had turned over to the Intelligence Committee about 60 pages of text messages and other communications with Sondland, Taylor, Yermak and other U.S. and Ukrainian officials, many on Trump's freeze of the military aid to Ukraine. Washington being Washington, much of it leaked out quickly. This wasn't part of Schiff's plan for the day.

The three committee chairmen quickly rushed to release more complete excerpts. The leaked portions were "out of context," they said in a letter. They took the opportunity to rebuke Trump for "openly and publicly asking another foreign power—China—to launch its own sham investigation against the Bidens to further his own political aims."

Emerging from the hearing room shortly before 7 p.m., the two sides told different stories about what they had heard. Meadows went to the waiting microphones and said for the Republicans: "What we do know is there was definitely not quid pro quo. Any comments that would indicate that there was some nefarious purpose on behalf of this president was not backed up by the facts today." Meadows added: "Listen, if there was an Academy Award for leading the witness, my Democratic colleagues would have gotten three Oscars today." Spreading that message via Twitter, Jordan wrote that "the facts we learned today from Ambassador Volker undercut the salacious narrative that @RepAdamSchiff is using to sell his impeachment ambitions."

As far as Democrats were concerned, Volker's testimony and texts left no doubt that Trump would not agree to meet with Zelensky unless the Ukrainian president publicly promised to launch the investigations. But they did not make that case as vigorously as the Republicans made theirs.

Eric Swalwell of California, answering a reporter's question about

Giuliani, picked his words carefully, taking it slow on this opening day. "I'll just describe Giuliani as—he's running a shadow shakedown and, you know, what Volker and others knew about it, I think we'll characterize that shortly." If the Ukraine story was clean and simple, easy to explain to the public, the Democrats had yet to find an easy and consistent rhythm for telling it.

On Monday, October 7, a half-dozen top Democratic staffers gathered in room 327 on the House side of the Capitol, a small and unused conference space on the third floor. Few of their colleagues knew what they were doing there. Their mission: Sharpen the Democrats' messaging. Bring it into the big leagues. Come up with a strategy to reach the American public and compete with the Republican narrative.

The Mueller investigation had been a messaging disaster for them. Trump had gotten out front by constantly proclaiming, "No collusion! No obstruction!" He and his team had kept it simple. "I did nothing wrong." "Witch hunt." "Harassment."

Meanwhile, a parade of Democrats had gone on TV for interviews that often wandered off in different directions. Some set sky-high expectations that Mueller had a smoking gun. Others blabbed about every new development: meetings between Russians and the Trump campaign, the Trump Organization's plans to build in Moscow. The details were endless and confusing. In the end, Mueller's 448-page report did not exonerate Trump. But many Trump supporters thought it did because Trump and his messengers, particularly Attorney General Bill Barr, kept saying so. Millions of others had no idea what Mueller's long investigation had turned up.

For the impeachment inquiry, Pelosi was determined that things were going to change. She created a new messaging operation, led by Ashley Etienne, her communications director and an Obama White House veteran. Now in room 327, Etienne was getting started with several of the most experienced communications experts working for House Democrats, including Patrick Boland from Schiff's staff. The out-of-the-way office, which had one window, three TVs and nothing on the walls, was perfect. The group, informally calling itself "327," wanted to fly under the radar. They didn't want their "war room" to become the story. They certainly didn't want anyone calling it a war room.

They decided to gather early each morning to produce a set of talking points and rebuttals to Trump's specific comments. Three main themes guided their thinking: Trump had endangered national security by withholding critical military aid to Ukraine for personal gain; Trump had betrayed his oath to "preserve, protect and defend the Constitution"; Trump had abused his power and no one is above the law. Some members started calling it the ABCs: Abuse, Betrayal, Corruption.

To help maintain "message discipline," Pelosi wanted to designate a select group of members for TV appearances. In addition to Schiff and other House leaders, the TV messengers included Jim Himes, Eric Swalwell, Tom Malinowski of New Jersey and Val Demings of Florida. Debbie Dingell was often slotted for Fox News, a crucial platform for reaching independents. At the most critical moments, up to two dozen members were prepped and TV-ready.

They were instructed to stay focused on what the 327 team was calling the "original sin": Trump's actions and intentions. They were to avoid talking about the other "big characters"—Giuliani, Pompeo, Barr. Giuliani was only to be mentioned in the sense that he was a Trump "henchman." They were not to ask, for example, "What did Pompeo or Barr know and when did they know it?" Talking about them would just divert attention from Trump. They also were told: Don't get pulled into a discussion of the Bidens, because that's exactly what Trump wants. Stay on our message, not theirs.

The impeachment committees wanted to talk with Lev Parnas—about Giuliani, about Ukraine, about anything Parnas knew of importance.

They sent him a letter, asking him to turn over documents by Monday, October 7, and to appear for a deposition on Thursday, October 10. "A growing public record indicates that the President, his agent Rudy Giuliani, and others have pressed the Ukrainian government to pursue two politically-motivated investigations," the letter said. "The Committees have reason to believe that you have information and documents relevant to these matters."

Attached to the letter was a list of 10 requests for Parnas. Did he have records on efforts by him or Giuliani to pressure Ukrainian officials into investigating Burisma? The Bidens? On the recall of ambassador Marie Yovanovitch? Any dealings with President Trump? Or Texas congressman Pete Sessions? Officials at the State Department or the White House? If so, bring them all.

A similar letter went to Igor Fruman. At the same time, a subpoena went to Giuliani. Schiff and his staff were making clear that their inquiry would be wide-ranging.

In the *Washington Post* newsroom, Rosalind Helderman, Paul Sonne and Tom Hamburger were working on a story about Giuliani and his business dealings in Ukraine. Their first call had been to Parnas, in late September.

The conversation had a getting-to-know-you feel. Parnas said he had graduated from Brooklyn's Lincoln High School, and like many immigrants who become U.S. citizens, he described himself as an American patriot. He was helping Giuliani, he said, because he wanted to help Trump, whom he passionately supported. "I think he's going to go down as one of the greatest presidents ever, even with all this negativity," he said.

Parnas had been vague about how he and the former New York mayor had met, saying that people who grow up in the city often "run in the same crowds." He said he had come to know Giuliani while fundraising for Trump's 2016 campaign. "The relationship bonded and built over time. We're just very close," he said.

The reporters believed Parnas was embellishing a bit. Their research showed that Parnas and Giuliani might have met in passing in October 2016, but their substantial interactions began much later, in 2018. That summer, Parnas had pitched Giuliani on becoming a paid spokesman for a company that Parnas owned, Fraud Guarantee. Parnas had not mentioned that in the first interview, so the reporters wanted to follow up.

After the committee's letter on September 30, though, he had stopped returning their calls. Finally on October 2, he had texted Helderman: "I have retained John Dowd as my lawyer please send all questions to him. Thank you." Dowd had represented the president for a year during the Mueller investigation. Parnas had hired one of Trump's former lawyers. The next day, Dowd told the committees that Parnas would not be cooperating with their impeachment inquiry. "Be advised," he wrote, "that Messrs Parnas and Fruman assisted Mr. Giuliani in connection with his representation of President Trump. . . . Thus, certain information you seek in your Sept. 30, 2019 letter is protected by the attorney-client, attorney work product and other privileges."

Additional leaks of Volker's closed-door testimony had infuriated Trump and his team. They were also angry that Marie Yovanovitch and other State Department officials had signaled their intention to testify. On

Tuesday, October 8, White House counsel Pat Cipollone sent a blistering eight-page letter to the Democratic leadership, saying the president had done nothing wrong and characterizing the impeachment inquiry as illegitimate.

"Put simply, you seek to overturn the results of the 2016 election and deprive the American people of the President they have freely chosen," Cipollone wrote. "Many Democrats now apparently view impeachment not only as a means to undo the democratic results of the last election, but as a strategy to influence the next election, which is barely more than a year away. . . . Your highly partisan and unconstitutional effort threatens grave and lasting damage to our democratic institutions, to our system of free elections, and to the American people."

He brought up Schiff's parody of Trump's conversation with Zelensky, a reminder that Trump was not going to let that one go. "The fact that there was nothing wrong with the call was also powerfully confirmed by Chairman Schiff's decision to create a false version of the call and read it to the American people at a congressional hearing, without disclosing that he was simply making it all up."

The Democrats' inquiry had left the president no choice, Cipollone wrote. The president "cannot participate in your partisan and unconstitutional inquiry under these circumstances. . . . The President has a country to lead." No executive branch witnesses. No documents. No cooperation of any kind. A complete shutdown.

Pelosi responded in kind. She accused Trump of trying to "normalize lawlessness." She said in a statement, "The White House should be warned that continued efforts to hide the truth of the President's abuse of power from the American people will be regarded as further evidence of obstruction. Mr. President, you are not above the law. You will be held accountable."

That night, on his Fox Business show, Lou Dobbs cheered Cipollone for his bluntness: "Cipollone's letter lays it straight out: 'You're invalid. Illegitimate. The hell with you.' "

Both sides were dug in deep, and the inquiry had yet to interview its second witness.

On October 9, Parnas and Fruman had lunch with Giuliani at the Trump Hotel in D.C., then drove to Washington Dulles International Airport. They had one-way tickets to Vienna, where they were to meet with Viktor Shokin, the former Ukrainian prosecutor, who was pushed out in 2016, partly under pressure from the United States and other western allies. Shokin had agreed to be interviewed by Sean Hannity and planned to make his allegations against the Bidens on Hannity's Fox TV show. Giuliani was scheduled to fly to Austria the next day to join them and ensure the interview ran smoothly.

Parnas and Fruman relaxed at Lufthansa's first-class lounge, then headed down the corridor to board their flight to Europe. Two government agents stopped them, asked for their passports and escorted them back to the terminal.

There, an FBI team arrested them on federal charges of acting as conduits for large sums of foreign money that had gone to U.S. campaign committees, allegedly concealing the scheme by disguising the source of the donations. Separately, it also alleged that the $325,000 donation to America First Action did not come from their energy company, as stated in federal campaign reports. The indictment said the company, Global Energy Producers, had no revenue or capital investment.

The indictment was unsealed the next morning. Helderman saw the news on her phone at the Nashville airport in Tennessee, where she had been visiting her parents. She immediately emailed her colleagues in the newsroom, who sent her the court documents. The charges against Parnas, Fruman and two others did not mention their dealings with Giuliani. But the indictment suggested to Helderman that the investigators might have a wider probe going on. The indictment was signed by the U.S. attorney in New York's southern district, a job that Giuliani had once held.

Helderman was so floored by what she was reading that she accidentally walked into an airport men's room.

CHAPTER TWENTY-SEVEN

The Disrupter

October 14, Washington

Fiona Hill listened as Adam Schiff read out her bio while she sat in the SCIF, steeling herself for the questions to come. Schiff and his staff were eager to hear from Hill. Her role at the National Security Council had given her a front-row seat on all matters Ukraine—until mid-July, when she had left the job behind, frustrated by the diminished support and respect for what she and other career officials did. She had been one of those "unelected bureaucrats" who the conservative media world was fond of denouncing.

Hill sat quietly, trying to keep her nerves in check, as the Democrats and Republicans took their first swipes of the day at each other—this time over subpoenas. "In light of attempts by the White House administration to direct witnesses not to cooperate with the inquiry," Schiff began, "the committee had no choice but to compel your appearance today. We thank you for complying with the duly authorized congressional subpoena."

Schiff directed his statement to Hill, but his language was formal and legal, intended as much for Republican ears as hers. Devin Nunes, the ranking Republican, wasn't in his usual seat, so Jim Jordan returned Schiff's opening volley. "Dr. Hill, I want to thank you also for appearing today. My understanding is you were coming voluntarily until about an hour ago when the chairman issued to you a subpoena."

Schiff didn't answer. His attention was focused elsewhere. He had spotted Matt Gaetz in the hearing room. What was the young rabble-rouser doing there? Both sides knew the rules: Only members of the three participating committees were authorized to attend.

"Mr. Gaetz, you're not permitted to be in the room," Schiff told him.

"I am on the Judiciary Committee," Gaetz replied.

"Judiciary Committee is not part of this hearing," Schiff said.

"I thought the Judiciary Committee had jurisdiction over impeachment," Gaetz said.

The chairman and the visitor were not on the same page. Schiff was treating Gaetz as an interloper, while Gaetz was telling people it never occurred to him that he couldn't be there. He had decided to come because he and other Republicans were hearing from constituents who wanted a more aggressive defense of the president.

Schiff had a quick decision to make. Enforce the inquiry's rules? Or accommodate?

"Mr. Gaetz, you're not permitted to be in the room. Please leave."

Jordan, in his trademark shirtsleeves and no suit jacket, spoke up.

"Mr. Chairman, really?" Jordan interjected.

"Yes, really," Schiff said.

Schiff and Gaetz exchanged a few more words, until Schiff had heard enough.

"Mr. Gaetz, take your statement to the press. They do you no good here. So, please, absent yourself."

"You're going to have someone remove me from the hearing?"

"You're going to remove yourself, Mr. Gaetz."

Jordan broke in, directly challenging Schiff's authority. "Mr. Gaetz is going to stay and listen to the testimony."

"Mr. Gaetz, you're going to leave the room," Schiff said.

Standoff. Hill hadn't said a word yet. Less than 15 minutes had passed since Schiff had called the session to order.

This was the kind of dramatic moment that Gaetz liked.

He had been a fierce and formidable debater in high school, and he thrived on the bruising give-and-take of partisan skirmishing. Politics was part of his family tree. His grandfather had been a mayor and state senator in North Dakota. His father had been president of the Florida state senate, and from 2010 to 2016, after Gaetz earned a law degree, he joined his father as a state legislator in Tallahassee.

After winning his congressional seat in 2016, at just 34 years old, he had arrived in Washington in a hurry to grab the spotlight and shake up Congress. He didn't worry much about ticking people off with his impatience. He described his approach to *Washington Post* reporter Dan Zak during a 2018 interview. "Well, the first thing is people gotta know who you are," he said. "If you are anonymous, you are a less capable disrupter. So, Step 1: Get known."

A quick way to get known and get ahead in Trump's Washington was to appear on the president's favorite TV shows, especially the ones on Fox. Gaetz's vocal support for Trump put him into a stable of reliable guests who could be called upon as the news demanded. He was fiery and fresh. Trump paid him an old-fashioned New York compliment: "You're a rookie but you're hitting like Mickey Mantle."

Democrats generally regarded Gaetz as a bomb-thrower for the far right, but that underestimated him. He immersed himself in policy fights that interested him, including federal debt, term limits, a balanced budget. He had waded into the climate change debate with a proposal to abolish the Environmental Protection Agency. Above all, Gaetz believed that getting things done in Washington meant getting noticed. Show up, take part, speak up. If he couldn't stay in the SCIF, he could certainly make some noise.

If Gaetz was there to make a point, Jordan's agenda was to keep up the pressure. A champion collegiate wrestler who loved a good fight, Jordan had been added to the committee at Trump's request. The president liked his takedown style.

Now Jordan laid out the Republican objection to the closed-door hearings, the same argument he and his colleagues had been making in public for days: "Mr. Chairman, I think in the 20 hours of testimony we've heard in the two previous interviews, there have been a grand total of 12 members of Congress present. I don't think it's going to hurt to have a 13th member actually hear something that, in my judgment, all 435 members of Congress should be entitled to hear."

This was more than a request to relax the rules for one member of Congress. This was a test. Schiff had to choose: What was the risk of relenting? What was the risk of standing firm? Gaetz seemed almost eager to be ejected, Schiff thought. Then Gaetz could emerge from the SCIF and tell the waiting press, "Hey, I was there to listen, and the Democrats wouldn't let me." Schiff could see the trap being laid.

Schiff fixed his gaze on Gaetz. He had made up his mind. This was not the moment to play Mr. Nice Guy. "Mr. Gaetz, you're not a member of the three designated committees that are participating in this interview. You're not permitted to be here. That is the ruling of the chair, and you are required to leave."

"Do you have a rule that you're able to cite for that?" Gaetz asked.

"I am citing the House rules and the deposition rules. You are not permitted to be here."

"Which rule?"

"Mr. Gaetz, you are simply delaying the procedures in violation of the rules. Please absent yourself."

"Which rule?"

"Mr. Gaetz, why don't you take your spectacle outside? This is not how we conduct ourselves in this committee."

"I've seen how you've conducted yourself in this committee, and I'd like to be here to observe."

Impasse. Ball in Schiff's court. He made his move. Fiona Hill's deposition would be delayed, he announced, so that he could seek a ruling from the House parliamentarian, the House's nonpartisan specialist on rules and traditions. The wasted time, Schiff declared, would be deducted from the Republicans' allotted time for questioning Hill.

The parliamentarian didn't take long. By a quarter to eleven, 45 minutes after the hearing began, everyone was back in the SCIF. The ruling: Gaetz was not entitled to be there. Schiff had prevailed. Gaetz left, while Jordan declared a small victory. "The parliamentarian was also clear that there was no precedent, no basis for docking anyone's time, that this was a legitimate question," he said, in a rebuke of Schiff.

Schiff coldly asked Jordan, "You have an opening statement?"

Jordan used his time to denounce the proceedings. "On September 24, Speaker Pelosi unilaterally announced that the House was beginning a so-called impeachment inquiry. On October 2, Speaker Pelosi promised that the so-called impeachment inquiry would treat the president with fairness. However, Speaker Pelosi, Chairman Schiff and Democrats are not living up to that basic promise. Instead, Democrats are conducting a rushed, closed-door and unprecedented impeachment inquiry. Democrats are ignoring 45 years of bipartisan procedures, procedures that provided elements of fundamental fairness and due process."

With the delayed start, Hill's testimony lasted well into the evening. It was nearly 8 p.m. when she answered the final question. Among other matters, she recounted her June 18 confrontation with Sondland over his Ukraine activities, telling him he was operating with "no guardrails, no GPS," and Sondland's insistence that Trump had put him "in charge" of "the Ukraine portfolio."

She also detailed her serious concerns about the July 10 White House meeting with the Ukrainians, where Bolton had told her that he wanted no part "of whatever drug deal Sondland and Mulvaney are cooking up." Schiff asked her to spell out what Bolton had meant. Hill replied, "He made it clear that he believed they were making, basically, an improper arrangement," offering Zelensky a White House meeting in return for "investigations."

By the time she left the Capitol, it was dark outside. She was done for the day, but she wasn't finished. The committees wanted her back in a few weeks, to tell her story in full, in public, in a hearing room that wasn't underground.

While Hill was still testifying, Gaetz was narrating his SCIF confrontation for *Breitbart News*, calling the proceedings a "clown show." Schiff shouldn't be leading this inquiry at all, he complained. This was Judiciary's territory. Pelosi had heard gripes inside her caucus about Nadler's handling of the first witnesses and switched the inquiry to Intelligence and Schiff. Now Gaetz and others on the Judiciary Committee were "paying the price" for Pelosi's loss of confidence in Nadler.

"Just because you don't like the outcome doesn't mean that the Speaker and the Democrat leadership should be excluding members who want to participate in a process that could ultimately overturn an election," Gaetz fumed. "Not only did Adam Schiff not want the American people to see whatever evidence they're developing, not only do they not want to let the full Congress see their work—they're even barring members of the Judiciary Committee."

Once the parliamentarian had ruled against him, Gaetz told *Breitbart*, he left the room of his own accord. "I wasn't going to make the Capitol Police throw me out by the scruff of my neck."

Gaetz didn't tell the *Breitbart* interviewer what he was planning next. But his tone left no doubt. His disruptions weren't done.

CHAPTER TWENTY-EIGHT

Pointing a Finger

October 16, Washington

Impeachment was now a daily Washington soundtrack. On "Morning Joe," on "Fox & Friends," on NPR's "Morning Edition," the early news was being served with a steady drumbeat of questions, invective and speculation about where the House probe was going.

At the White House, the president was not in a good mood. His frustration was building after three weeks of hearing impeachment, impeachment, impeachment. In a tweet that went out as the sun rose, he accused Democrats of conducting a "totally illegal & absurd Impeachment of one of the most successful Presidents!" Then, he quoted Graham Ledger, a host on the conservative One America News Network: "What is happening to President Trump with Impeachment is a Constitutional Travesty." Only six years old, the OAN cable network was on the president's radar. He was rewarding it with an approving tweet, which almost guaranteed more viewers.

At 7:46 a.m., closing out the morning onslaught, Trump slammed the closed-door proceedings in the House as a violation of his rights. "No lawyers, no questions, no transparency! The good news is the Radical Left Dems have No Case."

His schedule for the day included an afternoon White House meeting with congressional leaders from both parties on the worsening situation in Syria. Pelosi would be there. It would be their first face-to-face encounter since she had set the impeachment inquiry in motion. His turf, 3 p.m.

At the Capitol, C-SPAN was live and streaming. For hours at a time, the camera often showed little more than the foot traffic outside the underground SCIF. Then, the doors would fly open, and a Republican member or two would head for a waiting microphone, sometimes to describe what they were hearing inside, often to amplify Trump's complaints.

Wednesday's witness was Michael McKinley, a 37-year veteran of the State Department. As a one-time Pompeo aide, he was not someone easily dismissed. He testified that he was "disturbed" that "foreign governments were being approached to procure negative information on political opponents." The testimony didn't help Trump's "perfect call" assertion, which was being dented day after day as details of the depositions leaked out.

On C-SPAN, Republicans took turns staying on message. They attacked the Democrats, not McKinley. Inside the room, they said, they had heard nothing that couldn't have been said publicly. Nothing classified. Nothing that justified such hyped secrecy. In the wake of Gaetz's protest inside the SCIF two days earlier, several of his Judiciary Committee colleagues showed up to voice the same objection. "I'm Congresswoman Debbie Lesko from Arizona, and I'm very upset that I'm not able to go in and hear these hearings," she said. "I think it's very unfair."

It was a difficult day for Trump on another front. The House was going to vote on a resolution to oppose his decision to withdraw U.S. troops from northern Syria. His announcement, three days earlier, had created chaos in the region. He was hearing criticism from Republicans as well as Democrats. They were saying that the move had benefited Turkey and Russia, and that he was abandoning the Kurdish fighters who had been Washington's staunchest allies against the Islamic State.

Bipartisan criticism was not something Trump needed with the impeachment inquiry in full swing.

At the White House, the press corps was gathered for the first item on Trump's morning agenda, a public grip-and-grin with Italian president Sergio Mattarella. It was taking place in the Oval Office, prime real estate for a visiting dignitary. This was just the sort of highly visible meeting that Zelensky had wanted, and still hadn't received.

The reporters, aware that Trump and Mattarella would take a few questions, were ready to quiz Trump. Sitting next to Mattarella in matching yellow armchairs, interpreters close by, Trump did not wait for the press Q&A.

The disputed territory in northern Syria, he declared in his opening remarks, was not our fight. Turkey and the Kurds were warring "over land that has nothing to do with us." The Kurds were "no angels," and the U.S. withdrawal was a "strategically brilliant" decision that keeps "our soldiers totally safe."

Mattarella became a bystander as Trump described his willingness to leave the Syrian conflict to others. "Syria may have some help with Russia, and that's fine. It's a lot of sand. They've got a lot of sand over there. So there's a lot of sand that they can play with. But we were supposed to be there for 30 days; we stayed for 10 years. And it's time for us to come home." Leaving Syria behind, Trump went on a geopolitical tour, first Turkey, then Iran, then Saudi Arabia. Italy was barely mentioned. "Thank you for the very interesting remarks you just made," Mattarella said, through his interpreter, when Trump paused and invited him to speak. "I'm sure we will be discussing all of those issues during our talks later."

Mattarella opted for the soft-edged language of diplomacy. "Our bond is fostered by our human relations. And I'm very pleased to be here in this moment in time as we celebrate the Italian-American Heritage Month."

Picking up Mattarella's theme, Trump gave it a personal twist. "I have so many Italian friends. I can't tell you how many Italian friends. And we have a lot also in your government. We have a lot of great friends in your government."

Questions about the impeachment inquiry brought a change in Trump's tone. With Mattarella looking on uncomfortably, Trump's lengthy answer detoured into one of his familiar complaints. "I still ask the FBI: Where is the server?" he said, referring to the CrowdStrike conspiracy theory that the DNC's computer server was somehow in Ukraine.

Fanning out his hands, Trump said: "How come the FBI never got the server from the DNC? Where is the server? I want to see the server. Let's see what's on the server. So, the server, they say, is held by a company whose primary ownership individual is from Ukraine. I'd like to see the server. I think it's very important for this country to see the server. Nobody wants to see it. The media never wants to see it. But I'll tell you, Republicans want to see it."

The interpreter made no effort to tell Mattarella what Trump had said. The Italian leader sat still and silent, his hands clasped tightly on one leg. Trump was asked, "Mr. President, you're going to be seeing House Speaker Nancy Pelosi today. How do you anticipate that conversation?"

He wasn't planning to roll out the red carpet. "I think she's done this country a tremendous disservice. She's created a phony witch hunt—another one. The first one failed. They're all failing." He had an explanation for her side's motives, and it had nothing to do with Ukraine or his actions. "They're desperate to do something, because they know they're going to lose the election."

Just before 3 p.m., the House voted 354 to 60 to oppose the president's Syria troop pullout. The Democrats were joined by 129 Republicans. Following that overwhelmingly bipartisan rebuke of Trump's decision, Pelosi, Schumer, Hoyer and other congressional leaders dashed to the White House for their scheduled meeting. In the Cabinet Room, Pelosi led the charge.

Why, she asked Trump, was he withdrawing the troops, opening the door for Turkish leader Recep Tayyip Erdogan and Russia's Putin to gain a military toehold?

"Why do all roads with you lead to Putin?" she said.

The fireworks began.

Trump said dismissively, "You're just a politician."

"Sometimes I wish you were," Pelosi shot back.

Schumer spoke up. Insults were unnecessary, he told Trump.

Feigning innocence, Trump asked: "Is that a bad name, Chuck?" Then, he returned to Pelosi. "You're a politician," he said. "A third-grade politician." That's what Pelosi heard. Trump's side insisted he had said the more standard "third-rate."

There was no shortage of witnesses to the tense exchange. Nearly two dozen officials sat around the mahogany oval conference table in the Cabinet Room, a nameplate in front of each person except Trump. At least another dozen people sat on wall benches. But with no official transcript, the exact wording of Trump's barb was caught in the crossfire. Pelosi and Trump could argue about their argument.

As the tension rose, so did Pelosi. Trump remained seated. White House photographer Shealah Craighead watched. A moment was developing. She had a clear vantage point. She was ready.

Click.

Craighead's composition made the scene instantly iconic: Pelosi in her royal blue blazer, leaning ever so slightly forward, a finger pointing emphatically at the president of the United States. In every direction, she is flanked by men in dark suits or military uniforms, from the cabinet and Congress. On Trump's left, Mnuchin, McCarthy and Esper. On Trump's right, General Mark Milley, chairman of the Joint Chiefs of Staff; John Sullivan, deputy secretary of state; and Scalise.

Some are watching her, stone-faced. A few have their heads bowed, looking down, as if they would like to be elsewhere. She is the only person standing, and her mouth is open, as if in mid-sentence. Trump's lips are parted, as if he is replying. Their words weren't recorded, but Craighead's photo ensured that the moment would be remembered. It had captured, in arresting clarity, the deteriorating relationship between Trump, on his one thousandth day in office, and the speaker who was trying to remove him from the job.

The meeting was cratering. Hoyer, Pelosi's number two, whispered to her, "This is not useful." Time to go, he said.

They headed for the door. Trump made no effort to stop them.

"We'll see you at the polls," he said as they exited. "See you at the polls."

Pelosi and her lieutenants organized a press conference as soon as they returned to the Capitol. Schumer blamed Trump for Pelosi's walkout. "He was insulting," he said. "This was not a dialogue. It was sort of a diatribe, a nasty diatribe." Hoyer said, "I have served with six presidents. I have been in many, many, many meetings like this. Never have I seen a president treat so disrespectfully a co-equal branch of the government of the United States."

Pelosi's relationship with Trump had gone from bad to worse. She saw no way back. She thought of him as petty and childish. She told reporters the House's bipartisan rejection of his Syria plan had left Trump spinning. "He was shaken up by it, and that is why we couldn't continue in the meeting, because he was just not relating to the reality of it. . . . I think now we have to pray for his health, because this was a very serious meltdown on the part of the president."

At the White House, Trump believed Pelosi was the one who had melted down. Looking at Craighead's photo, he saw a crazed woman caught in the act of disrespecting the office of the presidency. He also saw an opportunity. He would make Pelosi pay for stalking out. He would embarrass her on Twitter. He would send Craighead's shot to his 70 million followers. He had the perfect caption: "Nervous Nancy's unhinged meltdown!"

The photo went up at 5:30 p.m. Ninety minutes later, another Trump tweet went out, stronger than the first. "Nancy Pelosi needs help fast! There is either something wrong with her 'upstairs,' or she just plain doesn't like our great Country. She had a total meltdown in the White House today. It was very sad to watch. Pray for her, she is a very sick person!"

In Pelosi's office, staffers looked at the photo and Trump's tweets in amazement. They thought Trump was totally misreading the image. This was no meltdown. This was a powerful woman speaking her mind, unintimidated by the venue or the men arrayed around the table. Drew Hammill, Pelosi's deputy chief of staff, reckoned that if Trump had consulted others, especially anyone young or female, they would have told him: "She's owning you in that moment."

Hammill showed Pelosi the tweet on his phone. He told her the staff wanted to make it her cover photo on her Facebook and Twitter accounts. Pelosi agreed. They put it up right away. Millions of people saw it. Trump's interpretation was not the one gaining ground.

Hammill thought to himself: I can't believe they gave us this gift.

Within a few hours, the photo and the confrontation were dominating the network shows and social media. Conservative commentators painted Pelosi as a persecutor who had lost control and embarrassed herself. Hannity said on his show: "Of course, the president is right. Her party's deranged, psychotic rage, obsessive 'hate Trump' agenda is all that matters in her world."

Also on Fox, Lou Dobbs told his listeners, "Why in the world should a president of the United States put up with nonsense from the very people who were trying to overthrow his presidency? My god, I have to give him credit for even inviting them."

On the other side of the partisan divide, there was cheering. Chelsea Clinton tweeted: "@SpeakerPelosi looks neither nervous nor unhinged. You, Mr. President, on the other hand . . ." Cecile Richards, the former head of Planned Parenthood, chimed in: "This is my Speaker. More guts than every man in this room rolled together." MSNBC's Lawrence O'Donnell added: "I've been in a lot of presidential meetings in that room and I never saw anyone literally stand up to a president like that because no one ever had to. Only Trump would tweet this perfect picture of his weakness & humiliation."

Jim Himes studied the photo and was impressed. He was from a genteel style of Connecticut politics that valued cooperation over confrontation. But sometimes, he had to admit, a good fight was unavoidable. Pelosi was not afraid to go toe-to-toe with the Brawler from Queens. Her standing among Democrats was now stronger than ever.

That was a good thing, Himes thought, because they were attempting to impeach a president, the riskiest political move most of them had ever made, and Pelosi had led them there.

Risky or not, Mitch McConnell was taking the prospect seriously. Impeachment was starting to take on an air of inevitability. If the House brought charges, the Constitution required the Senate hear them. He told his members at their private weekly lunch that day to prepare for a trial. It might come as soon as they return from the Thanksgiving break, he said. A short six weeks away. He showed them a PowerPoint presentation about the history and process of impeachment. He had also told Jared Kushner to take impeachment seriously, to look at what Clinton's team had done to defend against it, the importance of developing a messaging strategy.

The Kentucky Republican wanted his caucus to be ready. No slipups.

CHAPTER TWENTY-NINE

"Get Over It"

October 17, Washington

Shortly after noon, Mulvaney walked into the White House press briefing room. "Hey guys. How are you all?" he said, as if he were resuming a long-running conversation.

The reporters weren't quite sure what Mulvaney was doing there. Despite his "Hey guys" greeting, this wasn't his usual place. As a former Tea Party congressman from South Carolina and Trump's budget director, he had plenty of experience talking to the press. But he had never taken this stage in his nine months as chief of staff. The White House press secretary, Stephanie Grisham, hadn't done any daily briefings since taking over from Sarah Huckabee Sanders in July, so the press corps was eager to have someone to ask a few of their many questions.

After paying tribute to Elijah Cummings of Maryland, the veteran House Democrat from Baltimore who had died earlier that day, Mulvaney switched to an extended two-step joke. With the Washington Nationals securing a spot in the World Series, Mulvaney said, he had wanted to do the briefing in his Nationals hat. That was nixed, he said, because "it would violate some sort of rule." He had also thought about wearing a Montreal Expos cap—the Nationals had taken over the Canadian franchise when they joined the league—but that, too, was ruled out. "They said," he quipped, delivering the punch line at last, "that it would be foreign interference in the World Series."

A few reporters chuckled, but some in the room were mystified. Did Trump's top aide really want to turn the Ukraine affair and the impeachment inquiry into a comedy routine?

Slapping his hand on the lectern like a starter at a race, Mulvaney kicked off the session with an announcement: The administration was forging ahead with a plan, promoted by President Trump, to host the G7 meeting of world leaders at the Trump National Doral hotel in Florida. "I know you folks will ask some questions about that," Mulvaney said dryly. Every factor was considered, he said, "and it became apparent at the end of the process that Doral was, by far and away" the best choice. Best price, best facility, hands down. He was confident that there was no violation of the "emoluments" clause of the Constitution, which prohibits presidents from profiting from the office.

Skepticism reigned. Several reporters pointed out that it sure looked like a benefit for the president. Mulvaney held his ground. "Listen, I was skeptical," he said, holding up a hand as the reporters' voices rose in unison with new questions. "I get the criticisms; so does he. Face it: He'd be criticized regardless of what he chose to do. But, no, there's no issue here on him profiting from this in any way, shape or form."

Then, unprompted, Mulvaney pivoted unexpectedly to Hunter Biden and his highly paid seat on Burisma's board. Drawing a direct comparison to the Doral issue, he said: "What's the difference between this and what we're talking about the Bidens?" He answered his own question. "Well, first of all, there's no profit here. Clearly, there's profit with the Bidens. And, second of all, I think if there's one difference that you look at between the Trump family and the Biden family: The Trump family made their money before they went into politics."

That's "a big difference," he said, stressing the word "big."

As briefings went, this one was turning out to be more revealing and newsworthy than many. The reporters were making the most of it. Who knew when there would be another one? After five more minutes of back-and-forth about the G7 and Doral, it was time to change the subject. Jon Karl, the chief White House correspondent for ABC News, took the lead.

"So," Karl said, "to the question of Ukraine."

Until now, Mulvaney had been looking directly at his questioners through his round, almost rimless glasses. Not now. Lips pursed, he kept his eyes down as Karl began to talk, shifting papers, waiting, preparing, finally looking up when Karl said: "And you were directly involved in the decision to withhold" the military aid from Ukraine? "Can you explain to us now definitively why?"

Mulvaney was both budget director and chief of staff, two critical vantage points on the aid freeze. "Sure," he said. "It should come as no surprise to anybody" that "President Trump is not a big fan of foreign aid. Never has been. Still isn't." As for Ukraine, Trump had told him many times, "Look, Mick, this is a 'corrupt place.'" The president also was unhappy, Mulvaney said, because the European nations weren't providing much "lethal" military aid—weapons and other hardware. "You've heard the president say this: We give them tanks and other countries give them pillows," Mulvaney said.

After expounding on Ukrainian corruption and European stinginess for several minutes, Mulvaney summed it all up. "And the president did not like that. I know that's a long answer to your question, but I'm still going."

Switching gears, he brought up the twinned conspiracy theories that Trump had been hearing for months from Giuliani: that Ukraine had worked with the Democrats to try to defeat Trump in 2016, and that the DNC's hacked computer server was being hidden in Ukraine. "Did he also mention to me in the past the corruption related to the DNC server? Absolutely. No question about that," Mulvaney said, with a firm shake of his head. "And that's why we held up the money . . . which ultimately, then, flowed."

Mulvaney seemed ready to move on. The reporters weren't.

"But to be clear, what you just described is a quid pro quo," said Karl. Mulvaney knit his eyebrows at the mention of "quid pro quo." Karl explained. "It is: Funding will not flow unless the investigation into the Democratic server happens as well."

Mulvaney didn't deny it. He embraced it. "We do that all the time with foreign policy," he said. He likened the situation to Washington holding up aid to the Northern Triangle countries of Central America—El Salvador, Honduras and Guatemala—until they changed their immigration policies to Trump's liking.

The reporters were astonished. Mulvaney was directly contradicting his boss, who had been insisting for months that there had been no quid pro quo.

Pressing his point, Mulvaney brought up McKinley's closed-door deposition in the impeachment inquiry the day before. McKinley had testified that he quit his job as a top adviser to Pompeo because of the politicization of the department and foreign policy under Trump. "[McKinley] said yesterday that he was really upset with the political influence in foreign policy," Mulvaney said. "I have news for everybody: Get over it. There's going to be political influence in foreign policy."

Mulvaney's blunt words hung in the air. *"Get over it." "There's going to be political influence in foreign policy."* This was new and risky territory.

Among those watching in amazement was Toluse Olorunnipa, a White House reporter for *The Washington Post*. Mulvaney was playing his own version of a Trump card: Make a bold, defiant statement. Give no ground. Dare your adversary to do something about it. At the same time, Mulvaney was openly admitting to several acts that could potentially deepen the president's legal and political predicaments.

The reporters could feel the tension in the room rising. Mulvaney already had made big news—on CNN, one of its "breaking news" headlines said "Trump's chief of staff admits to quid pro quo on Ukraine"—and he wasn't finished. "What you're seeing now, I believe, is a group of mostly career bureaucrats who are saying, 'You know what? I don't like President Trump's politics, so I'm going to participate in this witch hunt that they're undertaking on the Hill.' Elections do have consequences and they should. And your foreign policy is going to change. Obama did it in one way; we're doing it a different way."

Mulvaney drove his point home: "And there's no problem with that."

A hum of noise filtered through the room. Soon Mulvaney and the reporters were fencing, talking over each other. Mulvaney was getting testier by the minute. Ayesha Rascoe, NPR's White House reporter, asked: Wasn't there a difference between changes in foreign policy because of a new administration and using foreign policy for a president's personal political benefit?

Mulvaney's answer was to return to the 2016 election and the DNC server. He pointed out that the Justice Department was already conducting an investigation of those allegations. It was being led by John Durham, the U.S. attorney in Connecticut. Mulvaney had trouble remembering Durham's name, so a reporter helped him out.

"That's an ongoing investigation, right?" Mulvaney said. "So you're saying the president of the United States, the chief law enforcement person, cannot ask somebody to cooperate with an ongoing public investigation into wrongdoing? That's just bizarre to me that you would think that you can't do that."

The briefing had lasted nearly 40 minutes. Its reverberations were just beginning.

Schiff went before the TV cameras two hours later. He seized on Mulvaney's explanation for the aid freeze. Mulvaney had acknowledged, Schiff said, that "military aid to a vital ally . . . was withheld in part out of a desire by the president to have Ukraine investigate the DNC server or Democrats of 2016." Schiff called it a "phenomenal breach of the president's duty to defend our national security" and then offered a sound bite that was immediately incorporated into one of his tweets: "Things have just gone from very, very bad to much, much worse."

Within the Republican ranks, Mulvaney's remarks were treated with a mixture of dismay and disdain. A Republican lawmaker told a *Washington Post* reporter that Mulvaney's comments were "totally inexplicable. He literally said the thing the president and everyone else said did not happen."

President Trump wasn't happy, either. Within a few hours, his personal attorney Jay Sekulow issued a statement distancing his client from Mulvaney's statements: "The President's legal counsel was not involved in acting chief of staff Mick Mulvaney's press briefing."

Mulvaney set about trying to undo the damage. Shortly before 6 p.m., he issued a statement, saying the "media has decided to misconstrue my comments to advance a biased and political witch hunt against President Trump." Engaging in a Washington ritual for political performances gone awry, he sought to spin his briefing in a different direction. "Let me be clear, there was absolutely no quid pro quo between Ukrainian military aid and any investigation into the 2016 election. The president never told me to withhold any money until the Ukrainians did anything related to the server." He said the aid was held up over concerns about corruption in Ukraine and the levels of European Union aid to Ukraine. "There never was any condition on the flow of the aid related to the matter of the DNC server."

Mulvaney's walk-back statement created more confusion. He didn't say he misspoke. He said he didn't say what he clearly had said. Democrats were shaking their fists; Republicans were shaking their heads. Even Sean Hannity, on his radio show, called Mulvaney "dumb" and his comments "idiotic."

It would take a while before the Republicans would "get over" the chief of staff's briefing.

CHAPTER THIRTY

Remember Francis Rooney

October 18, Washington and Florida

Francis Rooney of Florida, a Republican congressman, wasn't at all pleased with what he heard from Mick Mulvaney in his "Get over it" briefing.

The next morning, Rooney said so. Not just with a quick quote for the Capitol Hill reporters, as he had done the day before. But on national TV, on CNN, eight minutes live. Standing alone in a busy House corridor at 10:20 a.m., with the bronze statue of humorist Will Rogers as a backdrop, Rooney waited as CNN's Poppy Harlow displayed one of his quotes onscreen. Harlow said to Rooney, "Mick Mulvaney laid out a quid pro quo. What's your response?"

Rooney plunged deeper into dissent. "Whatever might have been gray and unclear before is certainly quite clear right now, that the actions were related to getting someone in the Ukraine to do these things," he said, his voice firm. "Senator Murkowski said it perfectly. We're not supposed to use government power and prestige for political gain."

Harlow asked, "In your eyes, Congressman, is that an impeachable offense?"

"I want to study it some more," Rooney said. "I want to hear the next set of testimony next week from a couple more ambassadors." He was no expert, he explained, so he was reading about what did or didn't qualify as impeachable. "But it's certainly very, very serious and troubling."

How troubling? Rooney voluntarily invoked Watergate, something the Democrats usually did. "I don't think this is as much as Richard Nixon did," he said. "But I'm very mindful of the fact that back during Watergate, everybody said, oh, it's a witch hunt to get Nixon. Turns out it wasn't a witch hunt. It was absolutely correct."

Harlow pressed, carefully. So, she said, you're not ruling out the possibility that this is an impeachable offense?

"I don't think you can rule anything out until you know all the facts," Rooney replied.

Until now, Rooney had generally respected the unspoken code among Trump's Republican critics: gripe in private, fawn in public. If you can't bring yourself to do that, at least stay quiet. Rooney didn't agree with the president on everything, but for the most part, he had kept his misgivings within party lines. Until now.

On the impeachment inquiry, his voice mattered more than others in his caucus because he wasn't watching from a distance. He was a member of the Foreign Affairs Committee, which meant he had access to the closed-door depositions in the SCIF. He had heard Fiona Hill and Michael McKinley testify, and their accounts had made him uncomfortable. As a former ambassador to the Vatican, he had tremendous respect for the State Department and its diplomats. He hadn't joined the daily parade of Republicans to the microphones outside the SCIF.

Then came Mulvaney's press conference and the acting chief of staff's almost cavalier admission of a quid pro quo, his statement that "we do that all the time in foreign policy." Enough. Now Rooney had emerged as the first Republican directly involved in the proceedings to signal an openness to voting for impeachment.

Still, his plainspokenness was a bit of a surprise. He had always been a team player, and his team had always been the GOP. Now in his second House term, he was 65, silver-haired and safely lodged in a bright-red district. He had endorsed Trump in 2016, with trepidation. But since then, he had been a mostly reliable Trump defender. But he wasn't a shouter. He didn't call attention to himself. He wasn't brash like Gaetz, his fellow Floridian.

Like Gaetz, though, Rooney had benefited from Trump's backing. In 2018, when Rooney was running for reelection, Trump had visited his district, the 19th, which hugs Florida's Gulf Coast, encompassing Fort Myers and the resort towns of Naples and Marco Island. At a rally in Estero, Trump had praised both Rooney and Gaetz for their vocal support. "So great to me on television," Trump had said of Rooney. "I love it when he defends me."

Rooney thought of himself as more businessman than political warrior. He had made his fortune in the family construction firm, and over the years, sizeable chunks of his wealth had gone to Republican candidates and causes. He had given across the GOP ideological spectrum. But most notably to the Bushes. Romney. The Establishment. His loyalty and largesse had led to his ambassadorship, courtesy of George W. Bush. His three years in Rome had whet his appetite for public office. His chance came in 2016, when the Tea Party incumbent in his district had decided not to run. Rooney's nomination was tantamount to victory in the general election. The 19th was a Republican bastion. In the 2012 presidential contest, Mitt Romney had carried it by 22 percentage points. Same margin for Trump in 2016. Rooney won by a landslide, with 65 percent of the vote. His 2018 victory was nearly as large. Barring some catastrophe, the seat was his, for as long as he wanted it.

Now he was rocking that very stable boat. Trump did not take kindly to people he saw as turncoats. Rooney knew it, and he hinted as much to Harlow when she asked about his political future. Was he going to run for a third term?

"I'm not going to decide right away," he said. "I mean, I'm definitely at variance with some of the people in the district who are—would probably follow Donald Trump off the Grand Canyon rim. But I'm going to call it as I see it. We raised our children to do the right thing and I'm going to do the right thing. That's why I took this job."

"Well," Harlow asked, "if you don't run again, will it be because of the president?"

"No," he said. "It will be because I've got other things to do."

As Rooney was wrapping up his CNN interview, *Washington Post* reporter Mike DeBonis was waiting nearby. He had overheard what Rooney was saying in his stand-up with Harlow. DeBonis wanted to ask a few more questions. He had been covering Congress for four years, and politics for a lot longer, and he knew that Rooney's remarks would soon ricochet around the Capitol. Better grab him now, DeBonis thought.

DeBonis knew he had no hope of getting Rooney alone. This was the routine in the Capitol corridors. A member starts talking, and suddenly, there's a media crowd.

The reporters asked Rooney to start over. He did. He had been "shocked" by Mulvaney's comments, he said. "The president has said many times there wasn't a quid pro quo . . . and now Mick Mulvaney goes up and says, 'Yeah, it was all part of the whole plan.'"

He was asked about Mulvaney's attempt to walk back his statements, to say that he had been misunderstood. Rooney didn't accept that. "The only thing I could assume is he meant what he had to say. . . . It's not an Etch A Sketch." The reference to the old toy, with the screen that could be cleared to allow a new picture to be drawn, brought smiles from the crowd.

A reporter pressed him again: Was he calling for Trump's impeachment? Certainly not, he said. But for good measure, he repeated his line about Nixon and Watergate, using almost precisely the same words he had used with Harlow. He made clear that he did not see the allegations against Trump rising to the level of Nixon's wrongdoing. "But I think we need to get all the facts on the table," he said.

There had been grumblings from some Republicans in private about Trump, a reporter said, but none had gone so far as to say they would join with the Democrats and vote to impeach him. Would Rooney?

"I'm a business guy, okay?" he replied. "I'm used to being open to all points of view and making the best decision I can. But there's . . . a lot of water still to flow down under the bridge on this thing."

Rooney was aware he was placing himself in a delicate spot. He knew Trump was thin-skinned and kept score. Mark Sanford of South Carolina had lost his GOP primary in 2018 after Trump had endorsed his opponent. But Rooney told the reporters he was not especially concerned.

"What's he going to do to me? I mean, he can say bad things, but it's just what it is." Rooney said he wasn't worried about another term. "I didn't take this job to keep it. If that means I got to go back to my other job, that's okay, too. I like building buildings and drilling oil wells. . . . I'll be looking at my children a lot longer than I'm looking to anybody in this building."

As word of Rooney's multiple interviews spread on Capitol Hill, Democrats allowed themselves to hope: Maybe, just maybe, if presented with enough compelling evidence, Trump's support would start to fracture.

Griff Witte, a *Washington Post* national correspondent, hopped a plane to Florida's west coast to gauge the reaction in Rooney's district. What were those Grand Canyon rim–jumpers thinking about their congressman? Witte found them as hot as the Florida sand in mid-July. Trump's popularity had only grown in the three years since his romp to victory in the district. Dissent—if that's what Rooney's moderate comments could be called—was not appreciated.

Jonathan Martin, the GOP chair in Lee County, told Witte that his phone was "blowing up" with messages. None was approving. Local Republican Facebook groups were crackling with condemnation. In the tennis clubs, golf clubs and gated communities across the region, a lot of the chatter was about Rooney. Social media was filled with pro-Trump messages calling Rooney a "snake" or a "RINO"—a Republican in Name Only.

On Saturday, Doris Cortese, the Lee County vice chair, got a phone call from Rooney. Cortese was perhaps the most influential person in local GOP politics, famous for her ability to mobilize support or opposition, depending on what was needed. She would be an accurate barometer of the weather ahead. She didn't sugarcoat it. "You've betrayed your country, your president and your constituents," the 80-year-old retired secretary told him. "Get out."

Hours later, he did.

At noon on Saturday, not quite 26 hours after his chat with Poppy Harlow on CNN, Rooney appeared on Fox News. He was in the studio, wearing a dark jacket with no tie, a more casual look than the day before. Host Leland Vittert asked Rooney if he wanted a third term.

"I don't really think I do," Rooney said.

He said he had come to Washington with two major goals: freeing up money that had been designated to protect the Everglades and banning offshore drilling near the Florida coast. "I've done what I came to do and I want to be a model for term limits," he said. Election to Congress should be "public service, not public life," he told Vittert, and he was tired of "intense partisanship" choking Washington's ability to solve problems.

"It's just like we raise our kids and tell our employees," he said. "You have to do the right thing at all times."

The first Republican House member to hint at a break with Trump had been buried under an avalanche of rage. The lesson was clear for all other would-be dissidents: If you care about your political future, remember Francis Rooney.

CHAPTER THIRTY-ONE

"Take the Gloves Off"

October 22 and 23, Washington

Just before 8 a.m. on a gray and dreary Tuesday morning, Trump kicked off his day with a message he knew would light up Twitter: "All Republicans must remember what they are witnessing here—a lynching."

In the previous days, as several members of his State Department and the NSC had descended to the SCIF for closed-door depositions, Trump had railed against the impeachment inquiry as a coup, a witch hunt, illegal and unconstitutional—even "bullshit." But labeling it a lynching, comparing the work of Congress to the most painful, shameful racial violence in American history? Sure, Trump was addicted to partisan warfare. Yes, he seemed willing to say anything, lash out at anyone, go to any lengths to wound any adversary. But "lynching"?

A chorus of condemnations cascaded from Democrats. Republicans were split. Many of his staunchest allies stayed silent, but Mitch McConnell felt compelled to say something. He characterized it as "an unfortunate choice of words." Will Hurd, the only black Republican in the House, called it "crazy" and said it showed "insensitivity to a horrific period in our history." Tim Scott, the only black Republican in the Senate, said he wouldn't have used the word. Ted Cruz of Texas, a vocal critic of candidate Trump in their run for the 2016 Republican nomination, issued an endorsement. "The connotation the president is carrying forward is a political mob seeking an outcome regardless of facts," Cruz said. "And that I think is an objectively true description of what is happening in the House right now."

What was happening in the House right now? Just before 10 a.m., as Trump's tweet was roiling the social media world, a silver-haired diplomat was settling into the witness chair. Schiff's staff had a lot of questions for Bill Taylor, still serving as the acting U.S. ambassador to Ukraine. They did not know what Taylor intended to say.

But they had seen some of Taylor's text messages with Kurt Volker, which had been released to the public. If the texts were any indication of Taylor's knowledge, he could fill in a lot of holes in their understanding of the Ukraine story. The challenge would be to see if Taylor's testimony helped tell that story in a clear, simple and compelling way.

The room hummed with the air of expectation. Only about a dozen members had listened to Fiona Hill's testimony, the day of Gaetz's confrontation with Schiff. The numbers had climbed steadily since then. For Taylor, 55 had checked in. They were almost on top of each other in the crowded room. The combination of the closed-door depositions, 24/7 media coverage and Trump's nonstop tweeting had heightened the already tense mood on Capitol Hill.

Taylor, with his sterling résumé, Eagle Scout demeanor and made-for-radio baritone, did not disappoint. He told the assembled lawmakers under oath that Trump had personally intervened to push Ukraine to announce investigations targeting Democrats to win release of frozen U.S. military aid. Taylor's testimony had included a 15-page opening statement, leaked to *The Washington Post* and published at about 3 p.m., while he was still being questioned. The news spread swiftly through the media landscape, like one of those California wildfires then raging not far from Schiff's district.

Taylor's statement summed up what he had witnessed in Ukraine as astonishing. He said the U.S. relationship with Ukraine was being "fundamentally undermined by an irregular, informal channel of U.S. policy-making and by the withholding of vital security assistance for domestic political reasons." He couldn't believe Trump had demanded domestic political favors from a foreign leader. Democrats felt like Taylor's testimony had blown apart Trump's defense of the July 25 phone call.

At the other end of Pennsylvania Avenue, White House aides privately complained that they were "getting crushed" by the drip, drip, drip of leaks from the SCIF depositions. Trump was losing control of the narrative. Instead of a "perfect call" with Zelensky, it was increasingly starting to be portrayed in the media as a dollars-for-dirt scheme, a shakedown.

Francis Rooney's public rebuke the week before was an open wound for the president. Why were his allies not fighting harder for him? Why did he have to do it all himself? It was time for Republicans to step up. At the Cabinet meeting the day before, with the press there for the opening and the cameras rolling, he had let loose. "Republicans have to get tougher and fight," he had said, as he took the media's questions for more than 30 minutes. "We have some that are great fighters, but they have to get tougher and fight, because the Democrats are trying to hurt the Republican Party for the election, which is coming up."

A reporter asked what he meant. "The Democrats," he said, "have two things" going for them. "They're vicious and they stick together. They don't have Mitt Romney in their midst. They don't have people like that. They stick together. You never see them break off."

Now, as Taylor was still testifying in the Capitol basement, the president was at the White House, huddled with 22 members of the House Freedom Caucus, the most conservative bloc of Republican House members.

"Take the gloves off," he told them.

Mo Brooks of Alabama joined his colleagues in assuring Trump that "we have your back." Trump told them they were waiting too long. "Republicans have to get tougher and fight," he repeated. They got the message.

Gaetz hadn't been at the White House meeting, but he had a plan ready. The next morning, October 23, he led a swarm of Republican lawmakers down the grand spiral staircase in the Capitol complex—mostly men in dark suits and loafers. They arrived at the bottom, just outside the steel-reinforced double doors of the SCIF. They were fired up.

Inside, Laura Cooper, a top Pentagon official, was preparing to testify in yet another closed-door deposition. Schiff wanted to question her about Trump's withholding of the military aid to Ukraine. Lawmakers from both parties were settling in for what promised to be another long day of questioning.

The Democrats' impeachment rules had left Gaetz and other fierce advocates for Trump, like Andy Biggs of Arizona, on the outside looking in. They weren't members of any of the three impeachment inquiry committees, so they couldn't attend the closed-door sessions. Gaetz was on a mission to change that. His first try, a week earlier, had ended in his eviction. He needed a new approach. His first call had been to Scalise, who loved a good fight. Gaetz told him: They might be able to kick me out, but they can't kick out 10, 20 or 30 of us. Let's storm the SCIF. Scalise was in. A few "country club" Republicans opposed the aggressive tactics. But Gaetz told them: This is the Trump era. We're driving now.

At 9:45 a.m., Gaetz and nearly three dozen of Trump's most loyal Republican House members faced a group of slightly startled reporters who were arriving for another tedious day camped outside the guarded doors waiting for dribs and drabs of news. "If behind those doors, they intend to overturn the result of an American presidential election, we want to know what's going on," Gaetz said, his voice sharp.

Gaetz was angry. As he saw it, the Democrats had been interviewing witnesses out of public view, then selectively leaking information favorable to their arguments. Republicans felt like dogs chasing their own tails as they tried to respond. Gaetz wanted all the information out. Make the whole thing public.

Scalise and Biggs, chairman of the Freedom Caucus, followed Gaetz to the microphones and said the proceedings smacked of the Soviet Union, not the United States. Others in the group called them a mockery, a shame, a Star Chamber, unfair, unjust, secretive. Jordan demanded that the whistleblower be named.

After 20 minutes of speeches, Gaetz announced it was time for action.

"We're going to go and see if we can get inside," he said.

"Let's do it. Let's do it," said Mark Walker of North Carolina.

"So let's see if we can get in," Gaetz said. "We're going in."

"We're gonna go!" someone else said.

"Let's do it!"

"Yeah!"

Alex Mooney of West Virginia posted a Twitter video of the group approaching the SCIF's double doors. Mooney narrated: "We're going in. We're gonna try and enter now. Press conference is over. We're gonna go represent West Virginia's second district and other districts in this country and see what's going on. Enough of these secret hearings. I'm going in."

They were met by two security staffers.

"You can't go in here," one warned Gaetz.

"Well, I'm going," Gaetz told her, walking past her and into the SCIF. For a few seconds—to Gaetz it felt like a lot longer—he was alone in the room. Then Gaetz saw Scalise follow, then the rest streamed in, shouting "Let us in! Let us in!"

Louie Gohmert of Texas was screaming about "injustices against the president!" Bradley Byrne of Alabama, who was running for Senate, railed about the closed-door depositions. Gerald Connolly, a Democrat of Virginia, snapped at him: "There are no cameras here, so it won't help your Senate campaign."

Val Demings, the Florida Democrat and former police chief, told the Republicans they should be ashamed of themselves for supporting a president like Trump. She started quoting the Gospel of Mark: "For what shall it profit a man, if he shall gain the whole world, and lose his own soul?" Gohmert shook his head at Demings and kept shouting his objections.

Seated at the far end of the conference room, Schiff watched as the Republican lawmakers entered through three different doors. They surrounded the table, where about two dozen members and staff—and Cooper—were sitting. They were hooting and hollering, saying things like, "Oh, so this is the secret Star Chamber!" Daniel Goldman, sitting next to Schiff, turned to him and said, "What do you want to do?" Schiff decided to leave. He, Cooper and Goldman walked down a corridor to his small office in the SCIF.

Pelosi was in Baltimore attending the funeral of her 90-year-old brother, Thomas D'Alesandro III, the former mayor who had died three days earlier. Schiff phoned the House sergeant at arms, Paul D. Irving, to discuss options. Irving asked if they wanted him to have the intruders removed by force. Schiff said absolutely not.

Seeking a solution to the stalemate, Schiff sent Goldman to invite Jordan, Nunes and Meadows into his office. They were all members of the committees authorized to be at the deposition. They urged Schiff to release transcripts of all the interviews held so far. Schiff had not released any. They wanted to see the full transcripts so they could answer questions from their constituents. They argued that the leaks had been selective and unfair to Trump. Schiff said there had been leaks on both sides. For the moment, he wanted to solve the immediate problem, the invasion of the SCIF. He repeated that the House parliamentarian had already ruled that only members of the three committees could be present. Everyone knew the rules. Jordan, Nunes and Meadows were not going to tell their colleagues to leave. We don't control what they do, they said.

Schiff decided to wait them out, thinking: This can't last long.

• • •

Many of the protesting members had their cellphones, a major security breach in the SCIF, and started using them. Eric Swalwell was furious. He went to the microphones outside the room. "They not only brought in their unauthorized bodies," he said, "they may have brought in the Russians and the Chinese with electronics into a secure space, which will require that the space at some point in time be sanitized." Republicans quickly realized that they had made a mistake. Republican Intelligence Committee member Michael Conaway of Texas collected his colleagues' phones. Jordan acknowledged the error and said it "won't happen again."

Before the phones were rounded up, the protesters had been narrating the occupation on social media. Several tweeted their thoughts, and even photos. Others used secure phones in the hearing room to call staff and have them post on Twitter, Facebook and elsewhere.

At 11:32 a.m., Gaetz tweeted: "BREAKING: I led over 30 of my colleagues into the SCIF where Adam Schiff is holding secret impeachment depositions. Still inside—more details to come."

Four minutes later, Biggs tweeted: "ALL Americans should be outraged at the secrecy by which Adam Schiff and Nancy Pelosi are conducting their unauthorized impeachment inquisition of @POTUS @realDonaldTrump. Everyone should stand for truth, transparency, and due process. That's why I'm storming Schiff's SCIF." He followed up with a series of tweets "reporting from Adam Schiff's secret chamber," which he later said had been "transmitted to staff" for publication.

Byrne tweeted: "Adam Schiff just SHUT DOWN his secret underground impeachment hearing after I led a group of Republicans into the room. Now he's threatening me with an Ethics complaint! I'm on the Armed Services Cmte but being blocked from the Dept. Asst. SecDef's testimony. This is a SHAM!"

Michael Waltz of Florida tweeted that he was a Green Beret and a proud veteran. "This impeachment process does not make me proud. As a sitting member of Congress, I still can't read the transcripts on impeaching our President. I've fought in third-world countries that have fairer processes than what we're seeing today."

Jamie Raskin, Democrat of Maryland, saw the protests as a "total fraud" because dozens of Republicans were authorized to be there. He thought calling the hearings "closed" to Republicans was absurd. He mocked them for "their attempt to act like Freedom Riders," referring to the 1960s civil rights activists fighting racial segregation in the South. Other Democrats howled about hypocrisy. They recalled that Republicans had used the same room, and the same deposition format, for the Benghazi inquiry.

Schiff stayed in his office, away from the fray. As the stalemate wore on, Republicans took turns venturing from the occupied hearing room to the hallway microphones.

"This whole thing is a sham," said Debbie Lesko of Arizona.

"Members have had it," Jordan said.

"We plan to stay there until we have a more open and transparent and fair process," said Meadows.

A reporter asked Meadows if the impeachment format wasn't exactly the same as the Benghazi probe. "From a deposition standpoint," Meadows said, "that's probably correct." But, he argued, "special times would require special accommodations."

While the SCIF takeover was happening, Lev Parnas and Igor Fruman were standing before a federal judge in New York, pleading not guilty to the campaign fraud charges against them. The courtroom had three times as many lawyers as defendants: three for the government, two for Parnas, one for Fruman.

The two sides had agreed on bail arrangements and GPS monitoring, allowing Parnas and Fruman to await their trials at home in Florida and travel to the courthouse in New York. Everything was routine, the usual for an arraignment hearing, until the judge asked: "Is there anything else to be addressed?"

Parnas lawyer Edward MacMahon rose. He wanted to alert the judge to "sensitive" and "complicated" issues that might arise in the case. Names and relationships flew by. Giuliani. The president. Parnas's work for Giuliani, who was working for the president. Parnas's congressional subpoena, which another Parnas lawyer was fighting, saying some documents might be covered by executive privilege.

The judge seemed confused. "You're not suggesting that your client worked for the president, are you?" he asked.

"He did not work for the United States government," MacMahon responded. Parnas worked for Giuliani, he said, and Giuliani "was working for the president of the United States."

Suddenly, Ukraine and impeachment had entered the courtroom, even though the indictment did not mention Giuliani or the president. The judge thanked MacMahon, and said those issues were a matter for another day.

A few minutes later, his wife, Svetlana, at his side, Lev Parnas walked down the courthouse steps to a waiting bank of microphones. He pulled a prepared statement from the inside pocket of his blue suit jacket.

"Good afternoon, everybody," he said. "Many false things have been said about me and my family in the press and media recently. I look forward to defending myself vigorously in court, and I am certain that in time, the truth will be revealed and I will be vindicated. In the end, I put my faith in God. Thank you."

A reporter asked, following up on the exchange in the courtroom, "What was the nature of your work for Mr. Giuliani?" but Parnas had already folded up his statement. His wife put her arm through his, and they kept on walking.

Back in Washington, the occupation of the SCIF was now almost four hours old. About 1:30 p.m., a cart with 15 large pizzas from Domino's mysteriously appeared outside the SCIF. Another 17 pizzas were delivered inside the room. No one said who had ordered them, but Meadows teasingly offered slices to the gathered press.

"There is no quid pro quo," he told them. "You can eat it!"

The reporters declined, saying they could not accept gifts from lawmakers. Goldman had a couple of slices; he joked that the pizza was good, but as a New Yorker, he was used to better.

Some of the Republicans took turns on the secure phone lines, to call their staff and have them update their social media followers including the Follower-in-Chief, President Trump. Finally, his troops were fighting back, and he was happily retweeting their efforts. He picked up Scalise's message: "What are they hiding?? Enough is enough! The American people deserve transparency!" He also shared a video posted by Jody Hice of Georgia, adding approvingly that "some Republicans with some spine and some guts have stormed into the deposition."

Lunch over, the occupiers' numbers started to dwindle. The House had been in session since noon, debating a bill that was designed to protect U.S. elections from foreign interference. Votes were being called, and members needed to be on the floor. By 3 p.m., all the unauthorized members had left. Cooper resumed her seat in the witness chair. Schiff said he would skip his opening statement. Let's get to the questions, he said. Cooper spent the rest of the afternoon describing how the military aid to Ukraine was frozen for two months and then finally released.

To Goldman, the whole thing had felt like a stunt designed to please Trump. It was meant to show the "audience of one" that they were fighting for him, and trying to distract from the evidence emerging from the closed-door hearings.

To Gaetz, it felt like a win and a momentum changer. They hadn't succeeded in getting Schiff to change the rules, but he and his allies had shown the president that they were willing to take off the gloves for him, to do whatever he needed. They had reenergized the GOP echo chamber, a much-needed boost after days of leaked testimony that had set some of Trump's staunchest allies on their heels.

"There's a newfound confidence among House Republicans," Lou Dobbs said on his Fox show that evening. "The Republicans, God bless them for actually doing something. I am so impressed."

His guest was Biggs, fresh from the occupation. "Congressman, I'm doggone proud of you and your colleagues," Dobbs said. "What has gotten ahold of you guys? It's wonderful to see."

Biggs smiled and predicted more to come. "Well, it may have taken us a while to get rolling. But now the stone is rolling and we need to keep it rolling down the hill with a greater velocity." Heads up, Democrats.

CHAPTER THIRTY-TWO

"Lock Him Up!"

October 27, Washington

Four days after leading the charge into the SCIF, Matt Gaetz sat in a luxury suite at Nationals Park, watching Game 5 of the World Series alongside Trump, Melania and Ivanka Trump, and a group of Trump's most enthusiastic supporters. The impeachment inquiry was the focus of political Washington, but for many in the capital, the Nationals were the bigger story. It had been nearly a century since a Washington baseball team, the Senators, had won a championship. Calvin Coolidge, a Republican of a different era, had been in the White House.

The day had already been a memorable one for the president. In a televised speech to the nation, rare for a Sunday morning, he had announced the death of Islamic State leader Abu Bakr al-Baghdadi, killed hours earlier by U.S. Special Forces in Syria. Trump had delivered an 8-minute statement at the White House, proclaiming that al-Baghdadi had "died like a dog," one of his favorite insults. Then, while answering questions from reporters, Trump had channeled his inner reality TV showman and riffed for another 40-plus minutes, narrating the military operation, which he said was like "watching a movie."

Trump's performance had left many astonished at a tone they didn't recognize as presidential. But Trump was in his "modern day presidential" mode, reveling in the moment, describing how al-Baghdadi had died a "crying, whimpering" death. He headed to the ballpark, feeling good.

The Series, between the Nationals and the Houston Astros, was tied at two games apiece. The stadium was packed on a mild October evening, and the amped-up crowd gave a huge ovation to D.C. chef and restaurateur José Andrés when he threw out the ceremonial first pitch. Andrés, honored for his humanitarian work in Puerto Rico and elsewhere, was also a frequent Trump critic.

The presidential limo pulled up into a tunnel below home plate shortly after 8 p.m. The Secret Service whisked the president, first lady and Ivanka Trump into an elevator and up to a luxury box above the third-base line. It was the first baseball game Trump had attended as president, and his first visit to any sporting event in the nation's capital, the place he liked to call "the Swamp."

Gaetz sat near Trump. They were joined in the suite by an all-Republican all-star lineup: Senator David Perdue of Georgia; Senator Lindsey Graham; four House members from Texas, Mac Thornberry, Kevin Brady, Kay Granger and John Ratcliffe; McCarthy; Scalise; Meadows; Biggs and Liz Cheney of Wyoming. It was a congressional Who's Who of Trump World. The Republican National Committee was footing the bill for the box, at $465 a seat.

In the third inning, Trump was introduced on the public address system during a tribute to veterans. A wave of noise rose from the crowd, some cheers, but also boos, which grew louder and lasted longer. Then came a familiar chant, a mocking chant, a chant from Trump's own playbook, slightly modified for the occasion: "Lock him up! Lock him up!" In the right field stands, a large red-and-white banner unfurled from the upper deck, displaying "Impeach Trump!" for the national TV audience.

The president's image was shown on the big screen in center field, which was when many fans in the park first realized he was there. Trump turned to Melania and appeared to say "Whoa," but they and their companions all smiled broadly and kept clapping. The booing wasn't much of a surprise. The region wasn't Trump territory, especially not heavily Democratic Washington, which had voted more than 90 percent for Hillary Clinton in 2016. But it was still a remarkable public trashing of a sitting president.

During the fifth inning, two men held up signs that read "Veterans for Impeachment" from their seats directly behind home plate. The men, Alan Pitts and Naveed Shah, told *Post* reporter Maura Judkis that they were Iraq veterans with Common Defense, an organization for veterans opposed to the Trump administration. "Our oath didn't end when we left active duty," Pitts told Judkis. "We still defend it today, and Congress needs to do the same. They need to step up and hold the president accountable for his illegal and unconstitutional acts." Some fans around Pitts and Shah reacted angrily. A man in a "Make America Great Again" hat told the pair they would "have a big problem" if they got closer to him and his friends.

Fox's Laura Ingraham said, "The left is so caught up in their own seething hatred of the president that they don't even realize that [for] millions of Americans" living outside Washington, "it felt like they were booing them."

Some on the left were also uncomfortable with Americans jeering a president on national TV. "I frankly think the office of the president deserves respect," Democratic senator Chris Coons of Delaware said on CNN, "even when the actions of the president, at times, don't."

The Astros crushed the Nats seven to one. Trump left in the eighth inning. Two games later, in Houston, Washington came from behind to win the seventh game and the championship. The city celebrated with a raucous parade the following Saturday, November 2. It was a moment of pure joy along Pennsylvania Avenue, a respite from partisan outrage.

1

A developing relationship: Russian president Vladimir Putin and President Donald Trump conferred at the G20 summit in Hamburg, Germany, on July 7, 2017. Trump's deference toward Putin and Russia caused consternation among Ukrainian officials, who were counting on continued U.S. support in their long-running war with Russia over Ukrainian territory.

2

Partners: Rudy Giuliani, left, and associate Lev Parnas, in an undated photo from 2018 or 2019, released by the House Judiciary Committee. The two men engaged in an extensive campaign in Ukraine on Trump's behalf, documented in the House impeachment inquiry. Their efforts led to the ouster of U.S ambassador to Ukraine Marie Yovanovitch. They also pressed Ukrainian officials for an investigation of Trump rival Joe Biden and Biden's son Hunter, who had accepted a highly paid seat on the board of a Ukrainian gas company, Burisma.

3 

Posing for history: At the May 20, 2019, inauguration of Ukraine president Volodymyr Zelensky (center left), energy secretary Rick Perry (center) said at a news conference, "The United States will stand with the people of Ukraine." Perry led a U.S. delegation that included (left to right) Lt. Col. Alexander Vindman from the National Security Council in Washington; Joseph Pennington, the U.S. Embassy's acting deputy chief of mission; special envoy to Ukraine Kurt Volker and U.S. ambassador to the European Union Gordon Sondland. Joining the group was Republican Senator Ron Johnson (far right), but not as an official delegation member. Behind Zelensky was Ukraine's deputy foreign minister, Olena Zerkal. Next to Johnson stood Zelensky's wife, Olena Zelenska.

Solemn ceremony: During a visit to Kyiv, national security adviser John Bolton (left) accompanied acting U.S. ambassador William Taylor to lay wreaths at a memorial for soldiers killed in Ukraine's conflict with Russia. The next night, August 28, 2019, Taylor requested a private meeting to tell Bolton that he was "very concerned" about President Trump's freeze on U.S. military aid to Ukraine.

 4

5 

First meeting: Trump and Zelensky on the sidelines of the U.N. General Assembly on September 25, 2019. Trump joked that their July 25 phone call had made them each "more famous." Zelensky asked about his long-promised White House meeting, telling Trump: "I think you forgot to tell me the date."

6

Viral moment: In the White House Cabinet Room on October 16, 2019, House speaker Nancy Pelosi questioned Trump on his decision to withdraw U.S. troops from Syria, a move that benefited Russia. "Why do all roads with you lead to Putin?" she said. Trump called her a "third-rate politician." White House photographer Shealah Craighead's image of Pelosi's finger-pointing went viral after Trump tweeted it. Unlike Bill Clinton's impeachment in 1998–99, social media was a major factor in amplifying the debate.

7

Protest: Amid shouts of "Let us in!," Republican Matt Gaetz of Florida led three dozen GOP House members on a storming of the secure room, known as the SCIF, where closed-door depositions were held. The protest on October 23, 2019, disrupted the questioning for five hours. Gaetz said the impeachment inquiry's first phase should be open to all members, not just the 109 on the three committees overseeing the inquiry.

8 

"Words fail me": Marie Yovanovitch re-enacted her reaction for the House inquiry as she testified on November 15, 2019. She said the color "drained from my face" while reading the transcript of the July 25 Trump-Zelensky phone call. During the conversation, Trump had said Yovanovitch was "bad news" as U.S. ambassador to Ukraine.

 9

Listening in: Alexander Vindman and Jennifer Williams, special adviser to Vice President Mike Pence, at their House hearing, November 19, 2019. Both had been in the White House Situation Room, taking notes as they monitored the July 25 Trump-Zelensky phone conversation. Hours later, Vindman testified, he told an NSC lawyer that he was troubled by the president's statements.

10 

Easy does it: Gordon Sondland engaged with photographers at the start of his November 20, 2019, testimony. He kept smiling through much of the hearing. He dropped a bombshell when he said, yes, of course, the president had created a "quid pro quo" by withholding a White House meeting unless Zelensky announced investigations into the Bidens and alleged Ukrainian interference in the 2016 U.S. presidential election. But Sondland also testified that Trump told him later "no quid pro quo."

11

Gloves off: House Republicans, seeking another tough questioner during the House impeachment hearings, added Jim Jordan of Ohio (left) to the Intelligence Committee team led by Devin Nunes. The two lawmakers held a side conversation during Sondland's November 20 testimony. Later in the day, Jordan subjected Sondland to one of the day's harshest exchanges.

12

Plain talk: Fiona Hill, a National Security Council expert on Russia and Ukraine until July 2019, testified at the impeachment inquiry on November 21, 2019: "I refuse to be part of an effort to legitimize an alternate narrative that the Ukrainian government is a U.S. adversary and that Ukraine, not Russia, attacked us in 2016. These fictions are harmful, even if they're deployed for purely domestic political purposes."

13

Eyes on Hurd: Will Hurd of Texas, a Republican moderate often at odds with Trump, chose to reveal his vote on impeachment during his five-minute slot for questioning Fiona Hill at her November 21 testimony. Democrats were hoping that Hurd, a former CIA officer, might buck his party. Hurd's five-minute speech was one of the House inquiry's most dramatic moments.

Slotkin on the spot: Democratic House member Elissa Slotkin faced a divided and vocal crowd of constituents in Rochester, Michigan, on December 16, 2019. She called the town hall to explain her decision to vote for Trump's impeachment. Slotkin, a former CIA analyst, represented a district that backed Trump in 2016. Some constituents stood by her at the town hall; others called her a "traitor" and a "spy."

14

15

Split screen: Trump's supporters cheered him in Battle Creek, Michigan, on December 18, 2019, as the House voted on the two articles of impeachment in Washington. The president held forth for two hours, in the stream-of-consciousness style he often uses at rallies. He accused Pelosi of waging a "war on American democracy" and pledged to help "vote her the hell out of office."

McConnell's maneuvers: Senate majority leader Mitch McConnell near the Senate floor, January 6, 2020. McConnell drafted rules for Trump's Senate trial designed to bring it to a swift end. But that morning, former national security adviser John Bolton volunteered to testify, complicating McConnell's strategy of calling no witnesses. A key hurdle: keeping centrist GOP senators on his side when the rules came up for a vote. Earlier, McConnell said he was coordinating with Trump's lawyers.

16

17

Walk into history: Crossing from the House's side of the Capitol and into the Senate's, a House delegation formally presented the articles of impeachment on January 15, 2020. Clerk Cheryl Johnson carried the documents, flanked by House sergeant at arms Paul Irving. Seven key Democrats who would present the case against Trump followed in pairs: Adam Schiff and Jerrold Nadler, Zoe Lofgren and Hakeem Jeffries, Val Demings and Jason Crow. Sylvia Garcia was behind them, not visible in this photo.

18

"The court of impeachment": With those words, Chief Justice John Roberts called each trial session to order. On January 28, 2020, White House counsel Pat Cipollone (center, in front of Roberts) concluded the president's defense by telling the senators: "All you need in this case is the Constitution and your common sense."

19

Preparations: The House impeachment managers, led by Adam Schiff (right, conferring with a staff member on January 29, 2020) used a room near the Senate floor as office space during the trial.

20

State of the Union: As Vice President Pence applauded at the end of Trump's annual address to Congress and the nation, delivered on February 4, 2020, Pelosi tore each page of her copy in half, saying later it was her way of protesting "a manifesto of mistruths."

CHAPTER THIRTY-THREE

"KA BOOM!"

November 4 to 7, Washington

Elise Viebeck felt something was odd as soon as she walked into the room.

It was around 9 a.m. on Monday, November 4, and the *Washington Post* reporter was the first to arrive at the small basement office in the Capitol Visitor Center that she was sharing with reporters from CNN and the *New York Times*.

Mondays were usually calm in the Capitol, as lawmakers returned from their districts, but this afternoon promised to be a busy one. Under a new House resolution, passed the week before, Schiff's impeachment inquiry was now authorized to release full transcripts of the closed-door depositions in the SCIF. The first two were expected to be ready around 1 p.m. The reporters were eager to read them.

Viebeck took a close look around the windowless room, studying the dull space, with its small desks and chairs, TVs, water cooler, old newspapers and shelves with a few reference books. Then she spotted it, directly above her desk: On the bulletin board, which on Friday had been empty except for a sheet of workspace rules, someone had pinned a sheet of white paper with a single name printed in a large font.

The name sounded familiar. Then she realized it was the name being bandied about as the identity of the whistleblower, the CIA analyst.

The same name had been circulating for a month on right-wing social media sites, with calls for the mainstream media to publish it. The mainstream media outlets still had not done so, mindful of federal laws protecting whistleblowers and citing concerns for the person's safety. That included *The Post*, where Viebeck had been working as a political and investigative reporter since 2015.

Viebeck found the sign bizarre and a bit threatening. For weeks now, Trump and other Republicans had been demanding to know the whistleblower's identity. The president thought the media ought to be exposing it. Just the day before, in a Sunday afternoon tweet, Trump had said: "The Fake News Media is working hard so that information about the Whistleblower's identity, which may be very bad for them and their Democrat partners, never reaches the Public."

About an hour before Viebeck's discovery at the Capitol, Trump had tweeted: "The Whistleblower gave false information & dealt with corrupt politician Schiff. He must be brought forward to testify. Written answers not acceptable!"

Lauren Fox and Jeremy Herb of CNN had come into the office. "Have you seen this?" Viebeck asked them, pointing to the bulletin board.

The three of them tried to puzzle it out. The anonymous message struck reporters as part of the broader effort to unmask the whistleblower. How had the intruder gotten into the room, which had been locked all weekend? Was the sign placed by a staffer, or a conservative reporter sympathetic to the president? Did the visitor know exactly which media outlets were sharing the space?

They alerted the press gallery staff but didn't file a more formal complaint. The reporters were working long hours during the impeachment inquiry, trying to keep up. Taking time off to file a report would have been a distraction.

Still, it sure felt like part of a coordinated effort. A few hours later, Trump appeared at a rally in Lexington, Kentucky, with Rand Paul, that state's junior U.S. senator. After lavishly praising Trump, Paul turned his attention to the whistleblower, alluding to unverified reports from conservative media outlets that the CIA employee had political motivations to attack Trump.

"We also now know the name of the whistleblower," Paul said, demanding that he come forward to testify and skewering the mainstream media for not publishing his identity.

"Do your job and print his name!" the senator yelled.

A chant arose from the thousands in Rupp Arena, home to the University of Kentucky basketball team: "Do your job! Do your job!"

Two days later, Donald Trump Jr. tweeted the same name and then retweeted a Breitbart story that included the name as well.

Trump Jr.'s use of the name came after a monthlong campaign in the conservative corners of social media to trace and reveal the CIA analyst's identity. The effort had picked up steam in early October, fueled by Jack Posobiec, a Trump supporter and former Navy Reserve officer who had pushed the debunked Pizzagate conspiracy theory that prominent Democratic politicians were involved in a child sex abuse ring. A correspondent for the conservative One America News Network, Posobiec first tweeted the name on October 3, a week after the whistleblower's complaint became public.

Other conservatives, including commentator Dinesh D'Souza, then followed Posobiec with Twitter mentions of the same name. The pace intensified on October 30 after an article appeared on *RealClearInvestigations*, using the name and claiming that he was a partisan who opposed the president. Breitbart followed on November 6, then that piece was shared by conservative radio host Mark Levin.

But it was Trump Jr.'s decision to use the name that gave the online crusaders a sense of victory. The right-wing website *Gateway Pundit* celebrated: "KA BOOM! Donald Trump Jr. Tweets Name Of Whistleblower."

The next day, November 7, Andrew Bakaj decided to act. As the whistleblower's lawyer, he wasn't going to confirm or deny the name. But he could protest on behalf of whistleblowers everywhere.

He wrote a letter to Cipollone, demanding that President Trump stop calling for the publication of the name. "Let me be clear: should any harm befall any suspected named whistleblower or their family, the blame will rest squarely with your client."

As Bakaj was sending his letter, the impeachment committees were releasing the transcripts of two more closed-door depositions. The one with Bill Taylor, from October 22, showed that the campaign to expose the whistleblower had migrated into the SCIF. Stephen Castor, the lead Republican counsel on the Intelligence Committee, was questioning Taylor about the whistleblower's complaint. Castor suddenly mentioned a name and asked if it might "ring a bell." Taylor said it didn't.

Castor tried again. "To your knowledge, you never had any communications with somebody by that name?"

"That's correct," Taylor had said.

The name was the same one that had mysteriously appeared in the basement press room at the Capitol. The mainstream media, in reporting on Taylor's deposition, did not draw attention to Castor's questions. But the conservative media universe jumped on it, and the cycle of stories and tweets began anew, with more calls for the mainstream media to "do its job" and publish the name.

CHAPTER THIRTY-FOUR

Live, from Washington

November 13, Washington

Adam Schiff surveyed the packed hearing room as he approached his seat a few minutes before 10 a.m. It was Day 1 of a major new phase in the impeachment inquiry. The first public witnesses would be testifying.

In the 50 days since Pelosi had taken the House down the risky path of impeachment, the three committees had heard more than a hundred hours of testimony from 15 witnesses. The closed-door sessions weren't quite done, so the inquiry would now be taking place in two contrasting venues: the underground SCIF and the House's grandest hearing room, normally used by the Ways and Means Committee. It was inside the Longworth Office Building, one of the three office buildings used by the House of Representatives and one of Washington's finest examples of the neoclassical revival style.

Ways and Means looked like a congressional venue as Hollywood might imagine it. Graceful circular walls. Soaring white columns. Deep blue curtains with gold trim, the backdrop for two curving banks of counter-style seating, paneled in walnut, with four dozen tan leather chairs. The room was so large that the full House had met there in 1949 and 1950, during renovations to the main chamber.

Schiff and his staff had two witnesses planned, George Kent from the State Department and Taylor, still the acting ambassador for Ukraine. As chairman, Schiff would run the hearing, now the Intelligence Committee's show alone. Next to him would be Devin Nunes. They had once been friends. Neither would say that now.

Nunes hadn't arrived yet. Schiff was already amped up. It had been maybe 25 years since his courtroom days, and he was feeling now what he felt then. For luck, he was carrying a pocket watch from his Lithuanian great-grandfather. He always carried it on election nights, and now it was with him every day of the impeachment inquiry. It grounded him to his roots.

He chatted with his lead counsel, Daniel Goldman, and shook hands with the Republican counsel, Stephen Castor, who took his place two chairs to Schiff's left. The empty seat between them was for Nunes.

A few minutes later, Nunes strode into the room, stopping to say hello to other Republican members as he made his way to his seat. Schiff turned toward Nunes, greeting him. Nunes replied, his gaze straight ahead, no eye contact. Neither smiled. No handshake.

They wore their team colors: Democrat Schiff in a blue tie, Republican Nunes in red. They watched as Kent and Taylor reached the witness table. Photographers swarmed them. Clicks and hums and whirrs took over the room. After a long minute, aides ushered them away.

At the front of the room, sitting inches from each other, not a word had passed between the two stone-faced congressmen. Finally, Schiff tapped his gavel and said, "The committee will come to order."

Outside the hearing room, on several fronts, Republicans were on message.

Earlier that morning, a team of administration heavyweights—Mulvaney, Cipollone and Jared Kushner—had walked to the Old Executive Office Building to work with the White House research staff on email blasts aimed at criticizing the process and undermining the credibility of the witnesses. They were launching the kind of coordinated "shock and awe" online barrage that had worked for them during the Supreme Court confirmation hearings for Brett Kavanaugh.

The night before, at a House caucus meeting, Jordan had put his experience as an Ohio State University assistant wrestling coach to good use, exhorting his colleagues like he was firing up his team. "This process is anything but fair!" Jordan cried. The Democrats were trampling the president's right to defend himself, he said. Go out there and denounce the proceedings as unfair, an abuse, an outrage.

That was Trump's line of attack, too, in his early-morning tweets. The first, just after 7 a.m., quoted Rush Limbaugh, who was on "Fox & Friends": "Millions of Americans will see what a partisan sham this whole thing is." An hour after that, from another "Fox & Friends" guest, Charles Hurt: "Nancy Pelosi cares more about power than she does about principle."

The president finished with a preemptive strike at Kent and Taylor, who had yet to say a word: "NEVER TRUMPERS!" and "READ THE TRANSCRIPT!"

In the hearing room, the spotlight was on Schiff. He welcomed the spectators, who had waited in line for seats in the public gallery, with a familiar warning: "We expect and will insist on decorum."

The room was quiet. "With that," he said, "I now recognize myself to give an opening statement in the impeachment inquiry into Donald J. Trump, the 45th president of the United States."

All the major networks were carrying the hearing live. So were the major newspapers, streaming on their websites. On social media, partisans were poised. If Trump was "modern day presidential," as he had called himself, this was modern day congressional.

Schiff understood that his primary audience—millions of people around the country, many paying attention for the first time—extended far beyond the seats of the grand hearing room. This was a whole new ballgame.

Today there would be no parodies. Schiff was playing it straight. The question at hand, he said, was whether Trump had abused his office by enlisting a foreign government to help in his reelection campaign. "The matter is as simple and as terrible as that," he said.

Like a chef describing a recipe, he marched through the facts, which he said weren't "seriously contested." Step by step, he listed the ingredients of the story to come: the tense relationship between Ukraine and Russia; Zelensky's election and his need to establish a strong relationship with Trump; Giuliani's activities in Ukraine on Trump's behalf; the "smear campaign" against Yovanovitch, leading to her firing; Giuliani's push for "investigations" into the Bidens and Burisma; Giuliani's interest in CrowdStrike and the "conspiracy theory" that Ukraine had meddled in the 2016 U.S. election; the July 10 "drug deal" meeting and Sondland's role in pushing the Ukrainians for the investigations in return for the White House visit that Zelensky was "desperately" seeking; the administration's freeze on $250 million in military aid to Ukraine; Trump's "now-infamous" July 25 "do us a favor" phone call with Zelensky; the whistleblower complaint that followed.

"Although we have learned a great deal about these events in the last several weeks, there are still missing pieces," Schiff said. "The president has instructed the State Department and other agencies to ignore congressional subpoenas for documents. He has instructed witnesses to defy subpoenas and refuse to appear. And he has suggested that those who do expose wrongdoing should be treated like traitors and spies. These actions will force Congress to consider, as it did with President Nixon, whether Trump's obstruction of the constitutional duties of Congress constitute additional grounds for impeachment. If the president can simply refuse all oversight, particularly in the context of an impeachment proceeding, the balance of power between our two branches of government will be irrevocably altered."

Schiff had been talking for more than 12 minutes. He hoped he had hooked the television and digital audiences. He hoped he was breaking through, in simple, clear language. He hoped the witnesses would do the same. "Benjamin Franklin was asked what kind of country America was to become. 'A republic,' he answered, 'if you can keep it.' The fundamental issue raised by the impeachment inquiry into Donald J. Trump is: Can we keep it?"

He then asked Nunes for "any opening remarks he may wish to make." Nunes, still not looking at Schiff, prepared to take the microphone.

For weeks, during the closed-door depositions in the SCIF, Nunes had stayed away from much of the fray. Jordan had often carried the ball. Nunes had attended only half of the interviews and hadn't made a lot of noise when he was there. That was about to change.

As the ranking minority member, Nunes had more standing than power. The Democrats had made the rules for the impeachment inquiry, and they had the votes to enforce them. But the rules guaranteed the Republicans equal time, if not equal say. With a national audience now watching, Nunes had prepared a ferocious broadside against the Democrats, Schiff and their impeachment inquiry. The gloves were off.

He said, his tone pregnant with disgust: "In a July open hearing of this committee following publication of the Mueller report, the Democrats engaged in a last-ditch effort to convince the American people that President Trump is a Russian agent. That hearing was the pitiful finale of a three-year-long operation by the Democrats, the corrupt media and partisan bureaucrats to overturn the results of the 2016 election."

He read his statement slowly and clearly, underscoring "Russian agent" with his voice, trying to convey the absurdity of it.

"After the spectacular implosion of their Russia hoax on July 24, in which they spent years denouncing any Republican who ever shook hands with a Russian, on July 25, they turned on a dime and now claimed the real malfeasance is Republicans dealing with Ukraine."

Accusing the Democrats of "deceptions, large and small," he said they were "the last people on Earth with the credibility to hurl more preposterous accusations at their political opponents."

Their impeachment inquiry, Nunes declared, was "a carefully orchestrated media smear campaign." The Democrats weren't interested in a fair process, he said. They had frozen out the Republicans, he claimed, by refusing to let them call witnesses of their own. "The witnesses deemed suitable for television by the Democrats were put through a closed-door audition process in a cultlike atmosphere in the basement of the Capitol," Nunes said, without mentioning that dozens of Republican lawmakers had attended the SCIF depositions, along with the Republican lawyers, and had questioned the witnesses at length.

Escalating his offensive, Nunes said the Democrats were the ones who should be investigated, not Trump. "The Democrats cooperated in Ukrainian election meddling and they defend Hunter Biden's securing of a lavishly paid position with a corrupt Ukrainian company, all while his father served as vice president," he said, his voice dripping contempt. "Despite this hypocrisy, the Democrats are advancing their impeachment sham."

He said the impeachment should not go forward without an accounting of whether the whistleblower had coordinated with Democrats and whether Hunter Biden's position at Burisma affected "any U.S. government actions under the Obama administration."

"These questions will remain outstanding because Republicans were denied the right to call witnesses that know these answers," he said.

Looking directly at Kent and Taylor, bystanders so far in this duel of opening statements, Nunes said: "Ambassador Taylor and Mr. Kent, I'd like to welcome you here."

Nunes's voice sounded anything but welcoming. "I'd like to congratulate you for passing the Democrats' Star Chamber auditions, held for the last weeks in the basement of the Capitol. It seems you agreed, witting or unwittingly, to participate in a drama. But the main performance, the Russia hoax, has ended and you've been cast in the low-rent Ukrainian sequel."

Nunes wanted to make sure his audience knew how he felt about the "deep state." "I'll conclude by noting the immense damage the politicized bureaucracy has done to Americans' faith in government," he said. "Though executive branch employees are charged with implementing the policies set by our president, who is elected and responsible to the American people. Elements of the civil service have decided that they, not the president, are really in charge."

Taylor and Kent, executive branch employees who implemented the policies set by Trump, looked back impassively.

Schiff was staring straight ahead, trying hard not to show any reaction. He was thinking: These are "Alice in Wonderland" accusations. But he wanted to keep the focus on Kent and Taylor, and not let an eye roll or some other reaction drive the media narrative and distract from their testimony. So he sat expressionless as a stone, as Nunes continued.

"By undermining the president who they are supposed to be serving, the elements of the FBI, the Department of Justice and now the State Department have lost the confidence of millions of Americans who believe that their vote should count for something. It will take years, if not decades, to restore faith in these institutions. This spectacle is doing great damage to our country. It's nothing more than an impeachment process in search of a crime.

"With that, I yield back."

There was a time, as recently as the early months of the Trump administration, when Schiff and Nunes had enjoyed "something of a bromance," as the *San Jose Mercury News* had described it. Both rooted for the Oakland Raiders, and had sometimes traded texts during Raiders games. Schiff once bought Nunes a couple of Raiders mugs.

As a native of California, Nunes had grown up in greater Raider Nation, as the football team likes to call its fan base. Schiff was a transplant from the other coast, born in 1960, in the Boston suburbs, to bipartisan parents, his dad the Democrat, his mom the Republican. He was not quite five months old when Massachusetts senator John F. Kennedy won the White House. The legacy of the Kennedy family, and its Camelot mystique, had been a memorable part of his younger days.

Joining the westward migration in the late 1960s, his family moved to Arizona, then California, settling in Danville, east of Oakland, one of the booming state's wealthier cities. The young Schiff was an early academic star: High school valedictorian. Stanford University degree in political science. Law degree from Harvard, followed by a promising legal career in Los Angeles. Then failure: three losing political races. Finally, in 1996, at the age of 36, his fourth try made him the state senate's youngest member. Even his marriage had a storybook ring to it. Adam had married a woman named Eve.

Schiff served a single term before he was noticed by Democratic power players in Washington. A Kennedy was the one to summon him. Schiff arrived in a snowstorm at the home of Patrick Kennedy, son of Senator Ted Kennedy and the lead recruiter for House Democrats. Kennedy gave him a dry towel, a cold beer and a sales pitch.

Party elders wanted Schiff to run for Congress in what would be one of the highest-profile races in the country. The man who had once defeated him for state assembly in California, James E. Rogan, was now a Republican congressman. Rogan had just voted to impeach President Bill Clinton and had served as one of the House managers who tried the case in the Senate. Democrats wanted his pelt, and they were willing to pour millions into a Schiff campaign. A rising Democratic star from California, Nancy Pelosi, also helped out, providing Schiff with fundraising and campaign advice.

His victory in the 2000 election, by almost 10 percentage points, provided a win on an otherwise dismal night for Democrats, with the Republicans keeping control of Congress and the presidency in limbo, requiring a legal fight in Florida and a Supreme Court ruling to send George W. Bush to the White House.

Schiff, the lawyer, had taken it all in, absorbing the lessons.

Nunes was from a different California, a dairy farm in the rural San Joaquin Valley, about 175 miles north of Los Angeles, in the Central Valley region of the state. His youthful aspirations were close to home. He would be the third generation in his Portuguese American family to earn a living from the land. He was entrepreneurial. When he was 14, he bought seven cows and turned a profit.

For Nunes, education was a chance to immerse himself in the business of agriculture, first at his local community college, then at Cal Poly San Luis Obispo, finishing with a master's degree. Somewhere on his way back to the family farm, he caught the political bug. In 1996, as Schiff was winning his state senate seat, Nunes was elected to his community college's board of trustees. He was 23, one of the state's youngest ever on a community college board.

He was a young man in a hurry. At 25, the minimum age, he ran for Congress. He lost, but his youth brought him some national attention. Three years later, in 2001, George W. Bush appointed him as director of rural development for California, a post in the U.S. Department of Agriculture. The following year, he tried again for the House. Victory. He was 29. "Once I got into politics in 1996, I never thought I couldn't do it," Nunes once said. "I don't worry about what other people think. I do what I think is right. I'm not very shy."

His 2010 book, "Restoring the Republic," was a mix of free-market economics and disdain for big government and "the radical left in Washington." A month after the book's publication, *Time* magazine named Nunes one of its "40 Under 40" rising political stars. Nunes told *Time* he was inspired by George Washington and Ben Franklin, and their reverence for liberty. "The struggle to preserve that liberty grows every time our federal government takes power and rights from the people."

Other interests? If he weren't making laws, Nunes said, he would be "making wine and cheese."

Nunes had been in the chairman's seat first. He had run the House Intelligence Committee from 2015 to 2019, when the Republicans controlled the House. He and Schiff had been serving on the committee together since Obama's first term. They had gotten to know each other better, like each other more.

Ask around about Schiff in the years before Trump, and the word was: Mild-mannered centrist. More likely to compromise than throw partisan bombs. Relentlessly earnest. A vegan who kept almost inedible vegan treats on his desk and spoke in complete and perfectly punctuated paragraphs.

Ask around about Nunes in those years, and the word was: Fierce protector of allies. Partisan lion when necessary, but not showy or loud. Skilled operator, better at politics than policy. Architect of the GOP's 2013–2015 investigation of terrorist attacks on U.S. facilities in Benghazi, Libya, during Hillary Clinton's tenure as secretary of state. The Benghazi probe had boosted his stock among Republicans and lowered his standing among Democrats, who saw the investigation as a political assault on Clinton as she prepared for her presidential run.

Schiff considered their relationship a model for how members of a polarized Congress could work together. They were on either side of the partisan fence, but they were cooperative. Schiff didn't consider Nunes intensely ideological.

Then came Trump.

During the 2016 campaign, Trump visited Nunes's district in the Central Valley. They spent time together, formed a beginning bond. When Trump won, Nunes was named to the transition team. In the early weeks of the administration, Nunes and the Intelligence Committee opened an investigation into Russian interference in the election. Trump was watching closely, already protesting that his campaign had done nothing to merit scrutiny. Tensions were rising, but the working relationship between Nunes and Schiff seemed to be holding steady.

After Trump tweeted an accusation that the Obama administration had wiretapped Trump Tower during the campaign, the two held a joint news conference on March 15, 2017, to announce that the committee had found no support for Trump's allegation. "We don't have any evidence that took place," Nunes said.

Less than a week later, on March 21, Nunes made a late-night visit to the White House, where someone showed him supposed evidence of surveillance on the Trump transition team. The next day, Nunes was back before reporters, this time without Schiff. "What I've read seems to me to be some level of surveillance activity—perhaps legal, but I don't know that it's right," Nunes said.

Schiff, at his own news conference hours later, assailed Nunes's "midnight run," saying it had undermined Nunes's ability to lead the committee's probe. "The chairman will either need to decide if he's leading an investigation into conduct which includes allegations of potential coordination between the Trump campaign and the Russians, or he is going to act as a surrogate of the White House," Schiff said. "Because he cannot do both."

Democrats called for Nunes to step down. He apologized the next day and stepped aside from running the Intelligence Committee's Russia probe.

Nunes had endured searing criticism from Democrats and some Republicans, but on the Fox News talk shows and conservative social media, he was being hailed as a hero.

• • •

In the hearing room, Schiff and Nunes sat side by side, saying nothing to each other as they awaited the opening statements from Kent and Taylor. They were introduced as senior diplomats who had served presidents of both parties with almost 80 years of combined experience. To the Democrats, that was laudable. To some of the Republicans, this was a double dose of the deep state.

Schiff and his staff had debated the best witness lineup for this first day. They had decided on Taylor because, behind the closed doors, he had provided a clear and powerful account of Trump's pressure tactics and why they mattered. But there was risk in asking Taylor to come alone. What if his public performance was a dud? The focus would be all on him. Pairing him with Kent, whose testimony covered less ground but helped bolster key points, would give them a good shot at telling a fuller sweep of the story, they thought.

Together, the witnesses were a one-two punch of military and government service. First came Kent, wearing a yellow, orange and blue patterned bow tie to accompany a gray-check three-piece suit, slightly graying at the temples, but still boyish-looking at 50. He said five great uncles had served in World War II, including one who survived the Bataan Death March. His father, after finishing first in his class at the U.S. Naval Academy in 1965, later took command of a nuclear ballistic missile submarine. Kent had spent 27 years in the State Department's foreign service, including 6 years in Ukraine. All this was in his opening statement.

Calling himself a "fact witness," Kent described why Ukraine occupied such an important role in U.S. policy and then volunteered his view of Hunter Biden's highly paid seat on the Burisma board. In 2015, Kent had called officials on Vice President Biden's staff to warn of the perception of a conflict of interest. "I raised my concern," Kent said. Without mentioning Joe Biden's name, Kent knocked down the allegations that Biden had pressured Ukraine to stop an investigation of Burisma. "I did not witness any effort by any U.S. official to shield Burisma from scrutiny," he said.

Then, describing the Giuliani-led "campaign to smear" ambassador Marie Yovanovitch, Kent said he learned in late 2018 and early 2019 that Giuliani and his associates Parnas and Fruman were working with "some of those same corrupt former prosecutors I had encountered, particularly Yuri Lutsenko and Viktor Shokin." Kent said he had been alarmed. "They were now peddling false information in order to extract revenge against those who had exposed their misconduct, including U.S. diplomats, Ukrainian anticorruption officials and reform-minded civil society groups in Ukraine," he said.

By mid-August, "it became clear to me that Giuliani's efforts to gin up politically motivated investigations were now infecting U.S. engagement with Ukraine, leveraging President Zelensky's desire for a White House meeting," Kent said.

Then it was Taylor's turn. He had aged well into the role of distinguished diplomat: silver hair, rimless glasses and an ability to appear firm, frank and friendly, sometimes all at once. He walked the committee through his 50 years of public service, from his military tours in Vietnam to his State Department postings in Washington, Afghanistan, Iraq, Israel and Ukraine. He described his mounting concerns about the aid freeze: His texts to Sondland, saying "my nightmare" is that the Ukrainians announce the investigations and still "don't get the security assistance." His message to Sondland and Volker, saying "it's crazy to withhold security assistance for help with a political campaign."

Under questioning from Goldman, he recounted how Sondland had told him in early September that although "there was no quid pro quo," if Zelensky did not "clear things up" with a public statement announcing investigations into the 2016 election and the Bidens, "we would be at a stalemate" on the security aid.

Goldman pounced on the contradiction, quoting Sondland's words back to Taylor. "No quid pro quo," Goldman said, "but the security assistance will not come unless these investigations are done." Goldman wanted to make sure he understood. "Is that what you're saying?" he asked.

"That's what was meant by a stalemate," Taylor answered.

Under the rules, Schiff and Goldman had 45 minutes to question the witnesses. Then Nunes and Castor would get an equal shot. Goldman divided his time between Taylor and Kent, trying to braid their accounts in one narrative thread. It wasn't easy.

"Now," he said to Taylor, "we've talked a little bit about the fact that you continually heard that the president was repeatedly saying that there was no quid pro quo, is that right?"

"That's correct," Taylor said.

"And he still says that repeatedly today," Goldman said. "But regardless of what you call it, whether it's a quid pro quo, bribery, extortion, abuse of power of the Office of the Presidency, the fact of the matter, as you understood it, is that security assistance and the White House meeting were not going to be provided unless Ukraine initiated these two investigations that would benefit Donald Trump's reelection. Is that what you understood the facts to be?"

"Mr. Goldman, what I can do here for you today is tell you what I heard from people," Taylor replied. "And in this case it's what I heard from Ambassador Sondland. He described the conditions for the security assistance and the White House meeting in—" Taylor paused, searching for the words, and said, "in those terms."

Taylor had spent a career in an arena where words were chosen carefully. He was choosing his carefully now. Perhaps, from the Democrats' point of view, a little too carefully. Was the story coming through?

Now Nunes and his legal team were on the clock, 45 minutes to quiz Taylor and Kent. Nunes opted to begin with a speech rather than questions. "The Democrats claim," he said, that "the president tried to get the Ukrainians to, quote, manufacture dirt against his political rivals. This is supported by precisely zero evidence. Once again, the Democrats simply made it up."

Trump was justified, Nunes said, in wanting answers about Ukraine's alleged meddling in the 2016 election. "The Democrats downplay, ignore, outright deny the many indications that Ukrainians actually did meddle in the election, a shocking about-face for people who for three years argued that foreign election meddling was an intolerable crime that threatened the heart of our democracy."

Nunes handed the baton to Castor. His first question picked up on Nunes's theme: "President Trump's concerns about Ukraine's role in the 2016 election, you believe he—he genuinely believed they were working against him. Right, Ambassador Taylor?"

"I don't know what President, or candidate, Trump was thinking about the Ukrainians," Taylor said.

Castor persisted. "I mean, didn't he, in his—in his Oval Office meeting on May 23, after the Zelensky inauguration, didn't he—didn't he lament that the Ukrainians were out to get him?"

Neither Taylor nor Kent had been at the meeting, but Taylor agreed that, yes, he had heard of Trump's outburst.

Schiff interrupted. He told Taylor that if he didn't have any firsthand knowledge of an event, he should say so. That brought a chorus of objections from the Republican side, leading to a tense exchange between Nunes and Schiff.

"Does the ranking member seek recognition?" Schiff said, and then twice, "For what purpose does the ranking member seek recognition," with Nunes becoming increasingly exasperated. The two men were locked in. Finally, Schiff cut off the exchange, saying, "We will resume the questioning."

When it came time for individual members to take the stage, they had five minutes each. Demings wanted to hear more about the "irregular channel" and Giuliani's role in it. "Both of you have explained that you grew seriously concerned when you realized that the interest of this irregular channel diverged from official U.S. policy," Demings said. "Was Mr. Giuliani promoting U.S. national interest or policy in Ukraine?"

"I don't think so, ma'am," Taylor replied.

"Mr. Kent?" she asked.

"No, he was not," Kent said.

"What interest do you believe he was promoting, Mr. Kent?"

"I believe he was looking to dig up political dirt against a potential rival in the next election cycle," Kent replied.

"Ambassador Taylor, what interest do you believe he was promoting?" she said.

"I agree with Mr. Kent."

Clear. Direct. Easy to understand.

As the hearing neared its end after five hours, the tension between Schiff and Nunes took center stage. Nunes was pressing for the right to call witnesses. The Republicans wanted to hear from Hunter Biden and the whistleblower, for starters. "You are not allowing those witnesses to appear before the committee, which I think is a problem," Nunes said, referring to Schiff without looking at him.

Schiff took aim at a different Republican talking point. "I can't let it go unanswered: Several of my colleagues made the statement repeatedly that I've met with the whistleblower, that I know who the whistleblower is. It was false the first time they said it, it was false the second through fortieth time they said it, and it will be false the last time they say it." With that, Schiff gaveled the hearing closed. He and Nunes had not looked at each other directly all day.

Across America, the hearing was drawing a huge amount of interest, with an estimated 13.8 million watching on television, according to Nielsen's tracking of viewership on the major network and cable stations. Fox News had the largest audience, averaging about 2.9 million viewers at any given moment, up from its usual daytime average of about 1.5 million. MSNBC was close behind with 2.7 million, up from its usual 1 million. Not counted: people catching video clips on their phones or watching on livestreams at work.

For the millions tuning in to the Ukraine story for the first time, there had been a lot to absorb. The hearing format itself was a challenge: questions that assumed knowledge, answers that weren't always crisp or clear, opening statements that required close listening. Add to that the nature of American life in the digital age, people busy with their lives, catching snatches of testimony from YouTube clips or reading a quoted line or two on Twitter.

Were the facts adding up to a coherent story? Were most people understanding the case that the Democrats were trying to make? Hard to know. Especially hard to know from inside the hearing room, under the bright lights of modern day congressional.

CHAPTER THIRTY-FIVE

"It's Very Intimidating"

November 15, Washington

Marie "Masha" Yovanovitch looked up from the witness table at the gathered House Intelligence Committee members, her glasses glinting in the glare of the lights, and offered them a wide-eyed smile, as a gaggle of photographers recorded the moment with their lenses a few feet from her face.

She removed her opening statement from a brown leather folder. Her lawyer poured ginger ale from a can. She gazed left at the Democrats, the friendlier faces, and right at the Republicans, who, she knew full well, were thinking about her less charitably.

She had come to testify on this Friday morning, under subpoena, about the "smear campaign" that had forced her out of a job she loved and about the president who had called her "bad news" after firing her. Capitol Hill wasn't foreign territory for her. Since 2005, she had testified three times during Senate confirmation hearings for her ambassador posts. But the impeachment inquiry was outside her comfort zone, several levels beyond nerve-racking.

She had turned 61 four days earlier, celebrating her birthday amid the stress of preparing to tell her story and defend herself on live television. Millions would be watching, many taking sides, condemning or cheering. She was accustomed to working in difficult conditions. Over three decades, under four Republican presidents and two Democrats, she had served her country in the diplomatic service, often in dangerous places. But the white-hot spotlight of impeachment? That was a hardship assignment not covered in any State Department training manual.

Yovanovitch had written her opening statement herself. She had gone to her lawyer's office at 7:30 a.m. to go over final details. She had been told she could have four guests in seats behind the witness table. She had chosen them carefully, for their personal meaning to her and their symbolism: Grace Kennan Warnecke, the chairman of the nonpartisan National Committee on American Foreign Policy, and the daughter of one of her diplomatic idols, George F. Kennan; retired diplomat John K. Naland, past president of the American Foreign Service Association; assistant secretary of state Beth Jones, a member of the close-knit group of senior women diplomats who had risen to the highest levels of the service; and her brother, Andre.

Yovanovitch and her guests drove together to Capitol Hill in two cars provided by her lawyers. There was a crowd outside the block-long Longworth Building, standing behind a rope line, tended by police. "You go, girl!" one woman shouted. A congressional aide escorted them to a room, where food and drinks had been laid out. The snacks went untouched as they chatted. Yovanovitch was mostly calm and quiet. The guests were given some guidance: You will be sitting directly behind the ambassador. You will be visible on national television. Keep your faces expressionless.

For the hearing, Yovanovitch had pinned a glittering American flag broach to her black suit jacket. A few moments before they were called to the hearing room, she asked to be left alone to collect her thoughts.

Now, at a few minutes past 9 a.m., she listened intently as Schiff introduced her—immigrant, public servant, anticorruption champion, strong, frank, direct, an "exemplary" diplomat until she became "an obstacle" to the "president's personal and political agenda," and "was smeared and cast aside."

Then she waited as Nunes reviewed Day 1 of the public phase of the hearings, saying "the American people finally got to see this farce for themselves." The testimony from Taylor and Kent on Wednesday, Nunes said with scorn, amounted to nothing more than "second-hand, third-hand and fourth-hand" information—"in other words, rumors."

Nunes did not acknowledge or mention Yovanovitch.

After several minutes of procedural jousting, Yovanovitch pulled the microphone close. "I come before you as an American citizen who has devoted the majority of my life, 33 years, to service to the country that all of us love," she began, glancing down at her statement and then raising her head again, making eye contact with the committee members.

Her voice clear, her nerves mostly in check, she described her personal story, calling her service "an expression of gratitude for all that this country has given to me and to my family." She spoke with evident passion about the importance of Ukraine to U.S. interests. "I worked to advance

U.S. policy, fully embraced by Democrats and Republicans alike, to help Ukraine become a stable and independent democratic state."

She warned of the threat to Ukraine posed by Russia. "The history is not written yet," she said, but "Ukraine is a battleground for great power competition, with a hot war for the control of territory and a hybrid war to control Ukraine's leadership."

Turning to the allegations that Giuliani and his allies had spread as part of a "smear campaign against me," she said each one was false. "I do not understand Mr. Giuliani's motives for attacking me," she said, "nor can I offer an opinion on whether he believed the allegations he spread about me."

She had the committee members' attention, at least for the moment. She had a share of the country's attention, too, on TV and computer screens, mobile phones and tablets.

"Individuals who apparently felt stymied by our efforts to promote stated U.S. policy against corruption—that is, to do our mission—were able to successfully conduct a campaign of disinformation against a sitting ambassador using unofficial back channels," she said. "As various witnesses have recounted, they shared baseless allegations with the president, and convinced him to remove his ambassador despite the fact that the State Department fully understood that the allegations were false and the sources highly suspect."

The successful campaign against her, she said, was a threat to diplomats everywhere. It undermined the U.S. foreign service to which she had devoted her career. It weakened America, she said. She wanted the committee to understand how dangerous that was.

"Perhaps it was not surprising that when our anticorruption efforts got in the way of a desire for profit or power, Ukrainians who preferred to play by the old corrupt rules sought to remove me," she said. "What continues to amaze me is that they found Americans willing to partner with them, and working together, they apparently succeeded in orchestrating the removal of a U.S. ambassador.

"How could our system fail like this? How is it that foreign corrupt interests could manipulate our government? Which country's interests are served when the very corrupt behavior we have been criticizing is allowed to prevail?"

Now she addressed the committee members directly. "These events should concern everyone in this room. Ambassadors are the symbol of the United States abroad," she told them. If one "is kneecapped, it limits our effectiveness to safeguard the vital national security interests of the United States."

Writing her statement, she had decided to close with a defense of public servants, especially those in the State Department. She made a strong plea to protect the department from being "hollowed out." "This is not a time to undercut our diplomats," she told them. "It is the responsibility of the department's leaders to stand up for the institution and the individuals who make that institution, still, today, the most effective diplomatic force in the world."

She had spoken for a little more than 20 minutes.

Goldman had a lot of ground to cover in his opening questions. He was taking Yovanovitch quickly through her ouster: Giuliani's campaign against her, the false allegations showing up in the media, the late-night phone call in April summoning her to Washington, the order to "get on the next plane," the warning that there were concerns "up the street." Yovanovitch kept her answers brief, her sentences short. She was easy to understand.

It was now almost 10 a.m. At the White House, her former boss had heard enough. He grabbed his phone. "Everywhere Marie Yovanovitch went turned bad," he tweeted. "She started off in Somalia, how did that go? Then fast forward to Ukraine, where the new Ukrainian President spoke unfavorably about her in my second phone call with him. It is a U.S. President's absolute right to appoint ambassadors."

Trump's outburst thrilled his supporters online. It sped around large pro-Trump Facebook groups and message boards on 4chan. Donald Trump Jr. pitched in, tweeting about Yovanovitch, Taylor and Kent: "America hired @RealDonaldTrump to fire people like the first three witnesses we've seen. Career government bureaucrats and nothing more."

In the hearing room, Goldman was asking about Trump's July 25 phone call and his comments about Yovanovitch, calling her "bad news." What was her reaction, Goldman wanted to know, to reading the transcript when it was released?

She had known this question was coming. Goldman and others had gone over the same ground in her deposition. But that was behind closed doors. Now millions were watching, observing, judging.

Her reaction?

"I was shocked, absolutely shocked, and—and devastated, frankly," she said.

"What do you mean by devastated?" Goldman asked. His tone was almost gentle.

"I was shocked and devastated that I would feature in a phone call between two heads of state in such a manner, where President Trump said that I was 'bad news' to another world leader and that I would be 'going through some things,'" she replied.

"So I was—" She paused, caught her breath, pursed her lips. "It was—it was a terrible moment. A person who saw me actually reading the transcript said that the color drained from my face." She lifted her hands to her temples, and slowly brought them down, demonstrating the color draining away. "I think I even had a physical reaction. I think—"

She shook her head, her voice soft. "You know, even now, words kind of fail me."

Back in September, reading the transcript for the first time, words had been hard to come by, too. Yovanovitch thought the call was chillingly wrong on every level—Trump's request for the "favor" of investigations; his praise of Lutsenko, the man who had spread false allegations about her; the unexpected and ominous references to her.

She had been confused as well as upset. At the time of the call in July, three months had passed since her firing. She wasn't in Kyiv, she wasn't involved, she had no authority, and yet Trump was still threatening her? "*Well, she's going to go through some things.*" Her mind reeled with questions. What did he mean? Was she under some sort of investigation? Was her pension at risk?

The transcript's release had caused some of her former colleagues to check in. Phil Reeker at the State Department had his deputy call and ask how she was doing. Mike McKinley, then Pompeo's senior adviser, called to ask the same, and to express his outrage that Pompeo still had nothing to say in her defense.

In the hearing room, key staff members of the Intelligence Committee, including general counsel Maher Bitar and deputy director of investigations Rheanne Wirkkala, were sitting behind Schiff, listening to testimony and checking their phones to monitor how the hearing was playing on Twitter.

"This is an insane tweet," Wirkkala texted Bitar and Boland, when she saw Trump's attack on Yovanovitch.

"Should we show it to him?" Bitar responded.

They were all texting each other: Should they alert Schiff now? Wait for a break? Should Schiff bring it up? If he did, how would Yovanovitch react?

They decided to show Schiff what the president had just tweeted. They were not sure what he would do it with it, but they figured it was best to alert him.

Boland, the communications director, was sitting in a small room, just outside the hearing, and he quickly printed an enlarged screengrab of Trump's tweet and handed it to Bitar, who passed it to Schiff. Another staffer also handed a printout to Yovanovitch's lawyer, so she could read it herself.

From the time Trump tweeted, until the printout was in Schiff's hand, about ten minutes had passed. They knew time was of the essence.

Schiff made a quick calculation. As a lawyer and former prosecutor, he knew it was dangerous to ask a witness a question if he didn't already know the answer. But here in his hand was a document showing Trump attacking a witness as she was testifying. Schiff decided that it was too egregious and threatening to ignore. He found a good moment to interrupt Goldman. Yovanovitch looked up at Schiff, curious.

"Ambassador Yovanovitch, as we sit here testifying, the president is attacking you on Twitter, and I'd like to give you a chance to respond." Schiff read aloud the first part of Trump's tweet, "Everywhere Marie Yovanovitch went turned bad. She started off in Somalia, how did that go?"

Yovanovitch attempted an awkward smile.

"Would you like to respond to the president's attack that everywhere you went turned bad?" Schiff asked.

She shrugged slightly as she searched for words.

"Well, I—I mean, I don't—I don't think I have such powers, not in Mogadishu, Somalia, and not in other places. I actually think that where I've served over the years, I and others have demonstrably made things better, you know, for the U.S. as well as for the countries that I've served in."

She spoke of making progress in Ukraine, particularly against corruption, the top U.S. policy priority there. Her composure had returned.

Schiff said, "Ambassador, you've shown the courage to come forward today and testify, notwithstanding the fact you were urged by the White

House or State Department not to; notwithstanding the fact that, as you testified earlier, the president implicitly threatened you in that call record. And now, the president in real time is attacking you. What effect do you think that has on other witnesses' willingness to come forward and expose wrongdoing?"

"Well, it's very intimidating," she said.

"It's designed to intimidate, is it not?" Schiff asked.

She sighed. "I mean, I can't speak to what the president is trying to do, but I think the effect is to be intimidating."

"Well, I want to let you know, Ambassador, that some of us here take witness intimidation very, very seriously," Schiff said.

For Yovanovitch, the moment felt surreal. How many times did she have to endure being insulted by the president of the United States? Yovanovitch was gutted. She fought back tears. When the session broke for lunch, she and her guests retreated to the waiting room. Trump's tweet was all they could talk about.

The Republican side understood the power of Yovanovitch's testimony. Several members made a point of praising her service. Instead of trying to shake her, a different strategy emerged. Nunes declared her testimony irrelevant to the inquiry, pointing out that she had virtually no contact with Trump.

"I'm not exactly sure what the ambassador is doing here today," said Nunes, suggesting that Yovanovitch's complaints added up to little more than a personnel dispute that would be "more appropriate for the subcommittee on human resources."

Nunes was finished with his questions. Time for another test of the rules and Schiff's authority. "I know, Ms. Stefanik, you had a few questions for the ambassador," he said, glancing toward the congresswoman from New York.

From the long, semicircular wooden desks just below Nunes and Schiff, Elise Stefanik leaned into her microphone. She managed a few words before Schiff banged his gavel.

"The gentlewoman will suspend," he ordered, an edge in his voice.

"What is the interruption for this time?" Stefanik asked acidly.

Under the hearing's rules, only Schiff, Nunes and each side's counsel could hold the floor during the initial round of extended questioning. Schiff had wanted to avoid the distraction and tedium of every committee member getting a turn to grandstand. Nunes knew the rules. So did Stefanik, who had tried earlier in the hearing to interject. But many Americans surely didn't. And now they were watching, for the second time, the chairman refusing to let Stefanik have her say—a scene tailor-made to feed Republican grievances.

"You're gagging the young lady from New York?" Nunes asked, incredulity in his voice.

The "young lady" from New York was an unlikely performer in this mini-drama. Elected to Congress in 2014 at the age of 30, she had been the youngest woman to win a seat until Alexandria Ocasio-Cortez came along four years later. For Stefanik, her victory was just the latest success in a short life that had been full of them. She had been raised in upstate New York by parents who had run a small but prosperous plywood business. No one from her family had ever graduated from college, but she had gone from an elite girls-only school in Albany to Harvard, where her friends included future Democratic presidential candidate Pete Buttigieg. Like him, she was studious, thoughtful and entranced by the details of public policy.

From college, it was a straight shot to the George W. Bush White House. She later worked side by side with another Republican policy wonk, Paul Ryan, directing preparations for his debate against Vice President Biden in the 2012 election.

When the Romney/Ryan ticket lost, Stefanik went home to ponder her own political career. The congressional district to the north, where her parents owned a summer cottage, had been largely Republican territory for generations. In 2014, the incumbent Democrat had decided not to run and no prominent Republican was stepping forward to claim the thousands of square miles stretching across the Adirondacks up to the Canadian border. Stefanik had no public identity and no base. Still, she thought: Why not me?

She won easily. On Capitol Hill, her reputation was that of a bipartisan moderate in the tradition of New York Rockefeller Republicans of old. The Tea Party movement was in full swing, but Stefanik steered clear. On issues such as climate change and gay rights, she was determined to try to nudge her party toward more modern and progressive stances, ones that could win over women, millennials and college-educated voters. People like herself.

Then Trump burst onto the scene. Stefanik kept her distance. When asked about him on the 2016 campaign trail, she swallowed hard and said she would support her party's nominee. Her artful dodges earned her a nickname among some local political observers: "the tightrope walker."

When Trump won, she stayed on her thin line. She would back the president when she agreed with him, defy him when she didn't and not make much noise either way. With impeachment now a looming reality, Stefanik knew she could no longer afford to remain Trump-ambivalent. She had seen what happened to Republicans who dared to define themselves as anti-Trump: None of them had their jobs for much longer.

She had heard from many voters in her district. They wore their MAGA hats, they watched Fox News, they loved the president. And now, with Democrats trying to oust him by impeachment, they wanted to know: Was Elise Stefanik going to step up?

In the hearing room, Schiff had ruled Stefanik out of order, requiring her to wait for her five-minute turn like every other rank-and-file member. Now she was on the clock. She started out carefully, even generously. "Before I was interrupted," she began, "I wanted to thank you for your 30 years of public service, from Mogadishu to Ottawa to Moscow to London to Kyiv." She also thanked Yovanovitch for hosting a bipartisan delegation that Stefanik had led to Eastern Europe in February 2018.

Pleasantries over, Stefanik bore down on the Republican themes of the day. "All ambassadors serve at the pleasure of the president," Stefanik said, quoting from George Kent's testimony. "You would agree with that statement, is that correct?"

Of course, Yovanovitch said.

Was it also true, she asked, that stamping out corruption had been a long-standing priority for the U.S. in Ukraine?

Yes, it was, Yovanovitch replied.

Stefanik was heading fast to the real point of her questions: Burisma. She asked if Yovanovitch was aware of Burisma and previous anti-corruption investigations into its activities. Yovanovitch said she was.

"But let's take a first step—a step back," Stefanik said. "The first time you personally became aware of Burisma was actually when you were being prepared by the Obama State Department for your Senate confirmation hearings."

Yovanovitch said that was true. On a hot summer day in 2016, she had sat in a State Department conference room as department experts peppered her with questions lawmakers might ask about Ukraine. The process was called a "murder board," a term that had originated in the U.S. military, referring to tough grilling in preparation for an important exam or presentation.

"What can you tell us about Hunter Biden's being named to the board of Burisma?" one of the experts had asked her. The company, one of many that had been under investigation for corruption, had hired Hunter Biden to serve on its board of directors while his father was leading the Obama administration's anti-corruption efforts in Ukraine. There were concerns within the administration about a possible conflict of interest, but Vice President Biden was particularly sensitive about his family, and those familiar with the situation had an unspoken rule that no one would bring it up with him.

Burisma did not come up at Yovanovitch's confirmation hearing. Now, Stefanik was making sure that Burisma came up loud and clear. Nunes had raised Hunter Biden's position in his opening statement. He said Democrats on the committee were "blind to the blaring signs of corruption surrounding Hunter Biden's well-paid position on the board of a corrupt Ukrainian company while his father served as vice president and point man for Ukraine issues in the Obama administration."

Yovanovitch, anticipating this line of attack, had said in her opening statement: "I have never met Hunter Biden, nor have I had any direct or indirect conversations with him. And although I have met former Vice President Biden several times over the course of our many years in government service, neither he nor the previous administration ever raised the issue of either Burisma or Hunter Biden with me."

But now, listening to Yovanovitch describe how she had been prepped to deal with a potential Hunter Biden question at her confirmation hearings, Stefanik drew a sharp red line under it for the audience outside the hearing room.

"So for the millions of Americans watching," she said, "President Obama's own State Department was so concerned about potential conflicts of interest from Hunter Biden's role at Burisma that they raised it themselves while prepping this wonderful ambassador nominee before her confirmation. And yet, our Democratic colleagues and the chairman of this committee cry foul when we dare ask that same question that the Obama State Department was so concerned about."

Democrats on the committee were rolling their eyes. They thought

Hunter Biden's Burisma job was simply a distraction from the allegations against Trump. There was no evidence Joe Biden had done anything wrong. But his son's high-paid position was a political liability. Now Stefanik was doing her best to highlight it. It was a harbinger of things to come if Biden ended up as the Democratic nominee in the 2020 election.

Before the impeachment process had ramped up, some Democrats had hoped that Stefanik might emerge as a moderate Republican voice. Their hopes were in vain. Stefanik might not be a Trump Republican by natural inclination. But she sure was playing one on TV. Stefanik's crisp performance immediately went viral on conservative social media. Requests to appear on Sean Hannity's program and other leading right-wing shows were pouring into her office.

Soon, she received the ultimate compliment for those in the MAGA crowd, a Trump tweet. "A new Republican Star is born," he proclaimed above a clip of Stefanik's questioning. "Great going @EliseStefanik!"

While Trump's online fans were cheering his Twitter attack on Yovanovitch, the president was having a rare second-guessing moment. He met in the Oval Office with Pence, Cipollone and Kushner. Was the tweet a misfire?

"The fact that he was even asking if it was a mistake tells you he knew it wasn't a good tweet," a White House official told *Washington Post* reporter Josh Dawsey.

Other Republicans were saying publicly that Trump had shot himself in the foot. On Fox, former independent counsel Kenneth Starr, who headed the investigation that led to Clinton's 1998 impeachment, argued that it did not rise to the level of witness intimidation, but showed "extraordinarily poor judgment." "I must say that the president was not advised by counsel in deciding to do this tweet," Starr said. "The president frequently says, 'I follow my instincts.' Sometimes, we have to control our instincts."

Trump's rock-solid supporters weren't troubled. This was Trump being Trump. Nothing new there. "The president's going to defend himself," said Lee Zeldin, Republican of New York. "Don't expect this president of the United States to just to sit back and allow this to go on."

Trump was defiant when he spoke to reporters at the White House later in the day. "I have the right to speak," he said. "I have freedom of speech, just as other people do."

• • •

By asking Yovanovitch directly about Trump's tweet, Schiff had accomplished something unusual: He had knocked the Republicans off message. They were defending Trump, not denouncing the Democrats. Was it a momentum shift?

The Democrats pressed their advantage. This would be the first weekend after the first week of public hearings, and the major shows were booking their guests. The focus was all impeachment, all the time. Himes was scheduled for "Fox News Sunday." Sean Patrick Maloney of New York would appear on ABC's "This Week." Both were paired with Republican House members.

Pelosi had added herself to the Democrats' lineup. She was not going to miss this opportunity. On Friday night, hours after Yovanovitch's testimony, she sat for a taped interview with Margaret Brennan, host of CBS's "Face the Nation." Brennan's first three questions were about Trump's tweet.

"The White House said it was just his opinion," Brennan said. "He wasn't trying to intimidate. What do you think?"

"The president and perhaps some at the White House have to know that the words of the president weigh a ton," Pelosi said. "He should not frivolously throw out insults, but that's what he does. I think part of it is his own insecurity as an imposter. I think he knows full well that he's in that office way over his head. And so he has to diminish everyone else."

Before and after the Pelosi interview aired that Sunday, Trump was on Twitter nearly every hour. He went after Schiff and his "Fake Impeachment." He asked, "Where is the Fake Whistleblower?" Trump posted to his tens of millions of Twitter followers a dozen news clips of Republicans from the Sunday shows, back to bashing the Democrats.

Marie Yovanovitch only came up in his tweet of a video clip from her testimony. Republican Chris Stewart of Utah had asked her: "Do you have any information regarding the president of the United States accepting any bribes?"

"No," she had replied.

Any criminal activity at all? Stewart asked.

She considered a moment. "No," she said.

Yovanovitch, largely because of Trump's tweet, had drawn huge public attention to the hearings.

CHAPTER THIRTY-SIX

"I Will Be Fine for Telling the Truth"

November 19, Washington

Lt. Col. Alexander Vindman strode into the House hearing room shortly after 9 a.m., dressed in his full Army dress uniform. Colorful ribbons and awards were pinned to his lapels, including a Purple Heart and a Combat Infantry Badge, both earned during ground combat in Iraq.

He was not a chiseled-chin officer from central casting. His round face and glasses gave him a bookish look, more librarian than Rambo. As the media cameras circled, he seemed nervous, adjusting his glasses, his head swiveling around the vast hearing room, left, right, up at the chandelier over his head. He looked behind him to where his twin brother was sitting, in a dark suit and red tie.

The witness who would testify along with him, Jennifer Williams, special adviser on Europe and Russia for Vice President Pence, entered the room a few minutes later. As she arrived at the long wooden witness table, Vindman reached over to pull out her chair, an act of kindness and civility. Vindman had every reason to believe that some of the questioning he was about to endure would be neither.

In the three weeks since Vindman had given his closed-door deposition in the SCIF, he had been attacked relentlessly on conservative media by people questioning his patriotism and loyalty to the United States.

The onslaught had begun the night before his deposition, on Laura Ingraham's show on Fox. She pulled out a sentence from a *New York Times* story about Vindman's expected testimony and spun it to suggest Vindman was working for the Ukrainians. "Here we have a U.S. national security official who is advising Ukraine, while working inside the White

House, apparently against the president's interest, and usually, they spoke in English," Ingraham said. "Isn't that kind of an interesting angle on this story?"

The *Times* story did not say Vindman was "advising" the Ukrainians. It said only that the Ukrainians had "sought advice" from him on how to deal with Giuliani.

Ingraham's guest was U.C. Berkeley law professor John Yoo, a Justice Department official in the George W. Bush administration, best known to the public for writing memos after 9/11 that provided the legal justification for interrogation and torture of detainees. Reacting to Ingraham's version of the *Times* account, Yoo said: "You know, some people might call that espionage."

In the morning, before Vindman's deposition began, "Fox & Friends" host Brian Kilmeade said from his studio couch: "We also know he was born in the Soviet Union, emigrated with his family. Young. He tends to feel simpatico with the Ukraine."

On CNN's "New Day," Sean Duffy, a former Republican congressman from Wisconsin, promoted the same theme. "It seems very clear that he is incredibly concerned about Ukrainian defense. I don't know that he's concerned about American policy, but his main mission was to make sure that the Ukraine got those weapons. I understand that. We all have an affinity to our homeland where we came from."

The allegation of dual loyalty, or even that Vindman was acting as a "double agent," quickly circulated in right-wing corners of the Internet. As Vindman was being interviewed in the SCIF, the OAN network's Jack Posobiec was tweeting: "BREAKING: US Army Officer Alex Vindman has reportedly been advising the Ukrainian government . . .—NY Times." Posobiec's tweet was retweeted thousands of times.

The day before Vindman's public testimony, Nunes and Jordan had asked Senator Ron Johnson to provide "any firsthand information you have about President Trump's actions toward Ukraine." They told Johnson they were looking for facts to counter the Democrats' "one-sided, partisan and fundamentally unfair" impeachment inquiry.

Johnson's 11-page letter went into detail about meetings he had attended, including one with Vindman in Kyiv that bothered him. Reading the transcript of Vindman's closed-door deposition had reinforced his concern. A "significant number of bureaucrats," he wrote, have "never accepted Trump as legitimate" and were out to sabotage him. "It is entirely possible that Vindman fits this profile."

Behind Nunes were three homemade signs, strategeticaly placed by the Republicans to show up on television. One said: "99 Days Since Adam Schiff Learned the Identity of the Whistleblower." Introducing the two witnesses, Schiff had stressed that both had listened to the July 25 phone call. "Ms. Williams, we all saw the president's tweet about you on Sunday," Schiff said. "You are here today and the American people are grateful." Trump had belittled her, saying "Jennifer Williams, whoever that is . . ." and suggested that she was a Never Trumper.

"Colonel Vindman," Schiff said, "we have seen far more scurrilous attacks on your character and watched as certain personalities have questioned your loyalty. I note that you have shed blood for America, and we owe you an immense debt of gratitude. I hope no one on this committee will become part of those vicious attacks."

Williams went first with her opening statement. She had joined the State Department at 23, just a year out of Georgetown University. She described the thrill of being sworn in as a foreign service officer by a personal hero, then secretary of state Condoleezza Rice. She had been working for Pence since April, on a temporary assignment from the State Department. She had heard about a dozen presidential phone calls in her career, and she found the July 25 Trump-Zelensky conversation "unusual because, in contrast to other presidential calls I had observed, it involved discussion of what appeared to be a domestic political matter."

Now Vindman's turn. His hands trembled as he said, "I have dedicated my entire professional life to the United States of America." He quickly ran through his central concerns of the past eight months, his nervousness evident in his rushed tone: Lutsenko and Giuliani were "promoting false information that undermined the United States' Ukraine policy," Sondland's "inappropriate" messages to the Ukrainians on their need to deliver "investigations into the 2016 election, the Bidens and Burisma," and Trump's July 25 phone call that so alarmed him he felt a "sense of duty" to report parts of it to the NSC lawyer.

The pages in his hand were fluttering as he said he found it "reprehensible" that previous witnesses—"honorable public servants"—were being personally attacked. "It is natural to disagree and engage in spirited debate, and this has been our custom since the time of our Founding Fathers, but we are better than personal attacks."

Vindman told some of his personal story, of coming to the United States when he was three, 40 years ago, with his father, an older brother and his twin brother. His father, Vindman said, had instilled in his sons a sense of duty and service to their new country. "All three of us have served or are currently serving in the military," he said.

He raised his eyes from his statement and looked directly into the camera. "Dad," he said, "I'm sitting here today in the U.S. Capitol, talking to our elected professionals, is proof that you made the right decision 40 years ago to leave the Soviet Union and come here to United States of America in search of a better life for our family. Do not worry, I will be fine for telling the truth."

Two hours into the hearing, Nunes was questioning Vindman about his discussions "outside the White House" after the July 25 phone call. This was a sensitive area, and Vindman was on edge. He told Nunes that he had talked to two people—George Kent at the State Department and an "individual in the intelligence community," stressing that both had the proper security clearances, both worked on Ukraine policy and he wanted to provide them with "some sort of read-out" so they knew what had happened.

Nunes wanted Vindman to be more specific. "As you know, the intelligence community has 17 different agencies. What agency was this official from?"

Vindman opened his mouth, but before he could reply, Schiff interrupted. "If I could interject here. We don't want to use these proceedings—"

"It's our—it's our time, Mr. Chair," Nunes said, his tone flat, his eyes fixed on some point in front of him.

"I know. But we need to protect the whistleblower," Schiff said. "Please stop. I want to make sure that there's no effort to out the whistleblower through the use of these proceedings. . . . That is not the purpose that we are here for."

During the exchange, neither Schiff nor Nunes looked at the other—as had become the norm.

Nunes didn't miss a beat. "Mr. Vindman, you testified in your deposition that you did not know the whistleblower."

"Ranking Member, it's 'Lieutenant Colonel Vindman,' please," Vindman said.

Nunes did not object to the correction. "Lieutenant Colonel Vindman," he said, "you testified in your deposition that you did not know who the whistleblower was—or is."

"I do not know who the whistleblower is," Vindman said, with a shrug of his shoulders. "That is correct."

"So how is it possible for you to name these people and out the whistleblower?" Nunes asked. He was suggesting that Vindman's way of answering the question—naming Kent but not naming the intelligence community official—meant that Vindman had to know the whistleblower's identity.

"Per the advice of my counsel," Vindman replied, "I've been advised not to answer specific questions about members of the intelligence community."

Shortly after, the White House official account tweeted: "Vindman made it clear that he gave information about President Trump's phone call with President Zelensky to an unnamed individual. Schiff shut down questioning about the unnamed individual to 'protect the whistleblower.' But neither one knows who the whistleblower is?"

Donald Trump Jr. retweeted that, adding: "Schiff has been lying to the American people for three years why would anyone expect that to change now? #FullOfSchiff."

Jordan began his questioning of Vindman politely. "Colonel, I want to thank you for your service and sacrifice to our great country." Then he got down to business. He cited a deposition of Tim Morrison, Vindman's current boss at the NSC, who had taken over from Fiona Hill, saying that he had "concerns" about Vindman's judgment. "Your former boss, Dr. Hill, had concerns about your judgment. Your colleagues had concerns about your judgment. And your colleagues felt that there were times when you leaked information. Any idea why they have those impressions, Colonel Vindman?" With his distinctive look—no jacket, sleeves rolled up, peering intently over his reading glasses—Jordan had become a symbol of the hearings.

Vindman had anticipated the question, which he believed was a misrepresentation of the facts. Hill had actually told Morrison that Vindman was a solid intelligence and military officer but lacked political instincts.

Vindman pulled out a paper and read from Hill's last performance evaluation of him, which was dated July 13, just before Hill left the job on July 19: "Alex is a top one percent military officer and the best Army officer I have worked with in my fifteen years of government service. He is brilliant, unflappable, and exercises excellent judgment."

"So, Mr. Jordan, I would say that I can't say . . . why Mr. Morrison questioned my judgment. We had only recently started working together," Vindman said.

A few minutes later, Jordan took a stab at getting Vindman to name the "intelligence community" official. Vindman's counsel objected, and Schiff again noted that "this committee will not be used to out the whistleblower."

"Mr. Chairman, I don't see how this is outing the whistleblower," Jordan replied. "The witness has testified in his deposition that he doesn't know who the whistleblower is. You have said—even though no one believes you—you have said you don't know who the whistleblower is. So how is this outing the whistleblower, to find out who this individual is?"

Schiff responded by saying: "Mr. Jordan, this is your time for questioning. You can use it any way you like, but your questions should be addressed to the witness—" Jordan tried to interrupt, but Schiff went on. "—and your questions should not be addressed to trying to out the whistleblower."

On Twitter, Trump Jr. was busy tweeting, calling Vindman a "joker" and a "stooge."

The special 327 Democratic messaging group created for the impeachment inquiry had now ballooned to two dozen people. During the hearings, they were monitoring television and Twitter so they could see which points and testimony were breaking through. They also needed to respond rapidly to GOP arguments. The team leader and Pelosi aide, Ashley Etienne, and others were in touch with the entire caucus, asking only those designated by Pelosi to speak about impeachment on TV. Asking an elected official to decline airtime on the biggest issue of the day was not easy. The messaging team told them it would save the member from being embarrassed if he or she sounded uninformed about the fast-moving investigation. No one wanted a repeat of the undisciplined Democratic messaging around the Mueller investigation.

By 9 a.m. each day, 327 had emailed its daily brief to key Democratic members of the House and Senate, as well as political commentators and others who could amplify it. Robert Julien, the bilingual spokesman for Congresswoman Sylvia Garcia of Texas, would quickly translate it into Spanish.

The idea was to make it easier for members of Congress who appear on Univision, Telemundo and other Spanish-language media to stick to the messaging. The translated talking points was given not only to Hispanic members, but also to others fluent in Spanish, including Senators Cory Booker and Tim Kaine, frequent guests on the Spanish-language networks. In their inboxes, they would have the key 327 talking point that "Nobody is above the law, not even the president," written out as "*Nadie está por encima de la ley, ni siquiera el presidente.*" In a memorable moment for many Hispanics, Garcia repeated that message, in Spanish, on the floor of the House.

No one could remember a similar sustained effort to get out the Democratic message in Spanish. More than 40 million people in the United States spoke Spanish as their first language. In Garcia's Houston district, 77 percent of the nearly 800,000 people were Latino. Garcia, a Mexican-American who became a mini-celebrity on Spanish-language news sites as the first Latina to be selected as an impeachment manager, spoke constantly to that audience and knew what resonated, including likening of Trump to Latin American autocrats past and present—Cuba's Fidel Castro and Venezuela's Nicolás Maduro.

Democrats were all too aware that in 2016, a shift of 78,000 votes in three states—less than one-tenth of 1 percent of the 137 million votes cast—would have defeated Trump. They wanted to influence every voter they could reach.

McConnell, a famously fastidious planner, was preparing for Trump's Senate trial, which was looking inevitable.

Now, even as Vindman was testifying, McConnell was convening the first meeting of the "Legal Eagles," a small group of Republican senators with backgrounds in law, including Cruz, Graham, John Cornyn of Texas and Mike Lee of Utah. They met in the majority leader's suite of offices, with high, vaulted ceilings in a space that had housed the original Library of Congress.

Cruz, a Harvard Law graduate, discussed the suddenly hot Latin phrase of "quid pro quo." He started with its meaning, "this for that," a favor granted in return for something else. He argued that an exchange of something of value for something else of value was perfectly common in foreign relations. Telling Venezuelans that Washington would lift sanctions if they would force out strongman leader Maduro was a perfect example. That was an explicit "this for that." For it to be illegal, the exchange would have to rise to the level of bribery, Cruz argued, and Trump's actions came nowhere near that. And, they agreed, it was perfectly reasonable for Trump to demand investigations into corruption in a country with so much of it. Cruz said the GOP needed to make this case to the public. McConnell nodded in agreement.

McConnell began sharpening the talking points he wanted Republicans to stress: Trump was within his rights to block administration officials from testifying, Democrats showed no respect for the president's executive privilege, the House process was shoddy and rushed. Above all, McConnell urged, never waver from the plan. That had gotten him where he was—almost thirteen years as the Senate Republican leader, the longest tenure in history.

He had built a reputation as an effective and unyielding tactician, who cared little about what his critics said of him. He embraced criticism and even posted some of the harshest political cartoons on his office wall. He *reveled* in the scorn of Democrats, who were still steaming over his 2016 stonewalling of Obama's Supreme Court nominee, Merrick Garland, which had altered the court's makeup, perhaps for decades. McConnell had taken the heat then, and he told his team they needed to be steadfast and united now.

Chris Stewart, Republican of Utah and an Air Force veteran, took a thinly veiled shot at Vindman. He noted the wings he was wearing on his lapel belonged to his father, a World War II Air Force pilot and the father of five sons who served in the military. "So as one military family to another, thank you and your brothers for your service, your example here," he said.

He noted that Vindman normally wore a suit to work in the White House but was wearing his dress uniform for his testimony. Stewart called that a "great reminder of your military service," but he also seemed to be suggesting that Vindman was using his uniform to grandstand.

"I'm curious, when Ranking Member Nunes referred to you as Mr. Vindman, you quickly corrected him and wanted to be called Lieutenant Colonel Vindman," Stewart said. "Do you always insist on civilians calling you by your rank?"

"Mr. Stewart, Representative Stewart, I'm in uniform, wearing my military rank. I just thought it was appropriate to stick with that."

Stewart assured Vindman that Nunes had meant no disrespect.

"I don't believe he did," Vindman said, but said he corrected Nunes because he felt that the public attacks on him in the press and on Twitter were "marginalizing me as a military officer."

The media battle was intense. Trump supporters said viewers were not interested in the televised hearings, and not watching. "It is quite staggering to see the drop-off in viewership for these hearings, contrary to what we saw with Bill Clinton, with the Nixon impeachment," Laura Ingraham said on her Fox show. "This is not gathering steam. It's gathering dust."

According to Nielsen, network and cable television viewership had declined from 13.8 million on the first day of televised hearings to 10.9 million for Vindman's testimony. But in the digital age, millions more were watching clips on their phones, or livestreams from news sites. What was the effect of that? Hard to know, harder to measure. Comparing the Trump inquiry to the Clinton and Nixon hearings was pointless. In 1999, no one was watching video on a smartphone and social media didn't exist. In 1974, the personal computer was still a decade away. The Watergate hearings had kept a good portion of the nation glued to their TV screens in the summer of 1973. But there was little glue in today's digital universe, where distraction was a click away.

Vindman was an unlikely TV star, but the Democrats felt like he had been a win for them. In his Army uniform, he had explained his actions, why he felt it was his duty to report what he had heard. Their next witness was from an entirely different strata of American life. The inquiry was about to hear from Gordon Sondland, who had told President Trump on the phone from Kyiv that Zelensky "loves your ass" and would do "anything you ask."

CHAPTER THIRTY-SEVEN

Smiles All Around

November 20, Washington

Gordon Sondland stepped out of a black SUV at the Longworth Building. It was a cool November morning, but he was wearing no coat over his blue suit. He buttoned his jacket around his tall, trim frame, beamed for the waiting cameras and made his way through the metal detectors with a jaunty stride.

He settled into the cocoa-colored chair at the witness table, surveyed the photographers awaiting him and appeared mildly entertained. He looked directly into *Washington Post* photographer Matt McClain's long lens and offered a knowing smile, resulting in a portrait of a man who seemed totally at ease. He leaned over to one of his lawyers and said something, and they both laughed. On the ride over, someone on his legal team had told a dirty joke about a penguin and a seal.

The mood stayed light at the witness table. He fiddled with a gold pen as he waited, his smile never far away from his lips. He was tall and bald, easy for the spectators to spot from the public seats. On his left wrist, slightly covered by the cuff of his crisp white shirt, monogrammed "GDS," he wore a steel Breguet watch that retailed for more than $26,000, a visible reminder of the wealth that set Sondland apart from earlier witnesses on government salaries. Sondland was more executive than executive branch.

He had every reason to worry about the arrows that might be coming his way. Unlike most witnesses, he was not sure which party would be more eager to attack him. He had given 10 hours of closed-door deposition testimony to the committee a month earlier, in which he said he had no reason to believe the White House had linked resumption of frozen security aid to Ukraine with a Zelensky announcement of the investigations Trump wanted. Then on November 4, his lawyer sent a letter to Schiff, revising that testimony.

Sondland said testimony of later witnesses had refreshed his memory. He now remembered, he said, warning top Ukrainian officials that U.S. assistance would probably only flow if Zelensky publicly promised to launch Trump's investigations. Sondland said he "presumed" that was the situation, based on all he was seeing and hearing.

It was an epic reversal. Sondland had seemed solidly pro-Trump at his deposition, but his updated testimony had stamped him as an unpredictable risk. He was undermining Trump's main defense: that the Zelensky call had been "perfect." Lawmakers on both sides were wondering if more surprises awaited them.

Meadows, one of Trump's closest allies on Capitol Hill, told reporters that Sondland's testimony could be pivotal. Meadows argued that only a first-person account of Trump leveraging his office for personal gain could give Democrats grounds to impeach. Would Sondland provide that? "The impeachment effort comes down to one guy, Ambassador Sondland," Meadows predicted.

At the other end of Pennsylvania Avenue, staffers in the West Wing were staying close to their screens. Sondland had refused to share his testimony in advance. President Trump grabbed a pad and a Sharpie, unsure if Sondland would turn out to be his biggest danger or best defense.

Others might have been intimidated or rattled under the circumstances. But at the witness table, Sondland sipped his coffee with the easy demeanor of a man who led a comfortable life and expected to continue doing so. The *Washington Post*'s Robin Givhan was watching on the livestream, scribbling down details for the profile she was writing about his day in the congressional limelight. She was mesmerized. Instead of nervous, Sondland looked strangely delighted to be there.

A phrase came into her head: Resting Happy Face. His look said everything was going to be fine.

Schiff tapped his gavel to open the hearing, highlighted elements of the now familiar Democratic case against Trump, and then turned the floor over to Nunes, who had a few things he wanted to get off his chest.

"Ambassador Sondland, welcome. Glad you're here," Nunes said. "I'm really not glad you're here, but welcome to the fifth day of this circus." Sondland smiled and nodded at the not-quite-a-joke.

Nunes rattled off a thesaurus-ful of words to express his outrage at the proceedings: outlandish, asinine, far-fetched, malfeasance, mania, ludicrous, partisan, extremists, exploiting, crusade, absurdity, frenzy, fanatical, scorched-earth, fake. He said Schiff and the Democrats would probably have wanted to impeach George Washington if they'd had the chance.

Nunes had decided to embrace Sondland. Maybe that would change, but for now, Nunes was treating him as a friendly witness. "Ambassador Sondland, you are here today to be smeared," he warned. Sondland stared back, his grin momentarily gone. "But you'll make it through it, and I appreciate your service to this country, and I am sorry that you've had to go through this."

After swearing an oath to tell the truth, Sondland said the White House and State Department had instructed him not to testify. He had come anyway. "I agreed to testify because I respect the gravity of the moment and I believe I have an obligation to account fully for my role in these events," he said, his demeanor serious as he read from his opening statement.

He was at a disadvantage, though. The White House and State Department had refused to provide him his emails, files, calendars or other records. "In the absence of these materials, my memory admittedly has not been perfect," he said. It sounded like an explanation for earlier inaccurate testimony and a preemptive warning that he might not be able to answer every question.

Sondland jumped right into the fire. He, Perry and Volker—the Three Amigos—had "worked with Mr. Rudy Giuliani on Ukraine matters at the expressed direction of the president of the United States."

Boom.

Sondland said the trio saw no choice. "We did not want to work with Mr. Giuliani. Simply put, we were playing the hand we were dealt. We all understood that if we refused to work with Mr. Giuliani, we would lose a very important opportunity to cement relations between the United States and Ukraine. So we followed the president's orders."

He saw nothing improper with that arrangement, he said. But "if I had known of all of Mr. Giuliani's dealings or his associations with individuals, some of whom are now under criminal indictment, I personally would not have acquiesced to his participation. Still, given what we knew at the time, what we were asked to do did not appear to be wrong."

Sondland said all the relevant decision makers at State and the NSC—including Pompeo and Bolton—were aware of everything the Amigos and Giuliani were doing. "The suggestion that we were engaged in some irregular or rogue diplomacy is absolutely false," he said.

Boom. Everybody was involved, at the highest levels.

"Mr. Giuliani's requests were a quid pro quo for arranging a White House visit for President Zelensky," Sondland said. "Mr. Giuliani demanded that Ukraine make a public statement announcing the investigations of the 2016 election/DNC server and Burisma. Mr. Giuliani was expressing the desires of the president of the United States, and we knew these investigations were important to the president."

Boom. Quid pro quo. Ukraine's this for Trump's that.

He cleared up his views of the aid freeze, in line with his revision to his deposition testimony. He said he had been "adamantly opposed" to any suspension of aid to Ukraine. He had not been able to get a straight answer from anyone in the administration about why the aid had been suspended. He said he came to believe that it was linked to Ukraine announcing Trump's investigations.

"I was acting in good faith," Sondland said. "As a presidential appointee, I followed the directions of the president. We worked with Mr. Giuliani because the president directed us to do so. . . . We had no desire to set any conditions on the Ukrainians."

Sondland continued reading, often with the slightly exasperated voice of a teacher trying to explain something that should be easy to grasp but isn't quite landing.

"I know that members of this committee," he said, looking up at the dais, "frequently frame these complicated issues in the form of a simple question: 'Was there a quid pro quo?' As I testified previously, with regard to the requested White House call and the White House meeting, the answer is yes.

"Mr. Giuliani conveyed to Secretary Perry, Ambassador Volker and others that President Trump wanted a public statement from President Zelensky committing to investigations of Burisma and the 2016 election. Mr. Giuliani expressed those requests directly to the Ukrainians and Mr. Giuliani also expressed those requests directly to us. We all understood that these prerequisites for the White House call and the White House meeting reflected President Trump's desires and requirements."

Boom. Boom. Boom. Trump engaged in a quid pro quo.

Sondland was not some deep state bureaucrat. He was a Trump loyalist, a million-dollar donor and even a bit Trumpy himself: a businessman with a salty vocabulary and an unorthodox approach. Testifying seemed to energize Sondland. Under the witness table, his feet tapped out a steady drumbeat.

"At all times—at all times—our efforts were in good faith and fully transparent to those tasked with overseeing them. Our efforts were reported and approved. And not once do I recall encountering an objection," Sondland said.

Sondland had just laid down a marker. He was not here to defend Trump. Reporters in the room were clacking away furiously on their laptops. The only person not on the edge of a seat was the witness himself. As the questioning got underway, Sondland sometimes sat with his head resting on his right hand as if he were a bit bored. But mainly he looked perfectly happy to be there.

Goldman asked Sondland about his call with Trump, overheard by David Holmes in the restaurant in Kyiv, in which Sondland told the president that Zelensky "loves your ass."

"Yes, it sounds like something I would say," Sondland confessed, prompting a rare burst of laughter in the hearing room. "That's how President Trump and I communicate, a lot of four-letter words. In this case, three-letter."

After Goldman finished, Schiff called a short recess. Nunes turned to Castor with a grim look. In the audience, Lee Zeldin, a Republican congressman from New York, one of Trump's most vocal defenders, stroked his forehead as though trying to ease a migraine.

During the break, Schiff went to the waiting microphones in the hallway outside the hearing room. "We now can see the veneer has been torn away," he said, arguing that Sondland's description of events "goes right to the heart of the issue of bribery, as well as other potential high crimes or misdemeanors."

Moments later on Fox News, Chris Wallace, one of the network's most senior journalists, gave Republicans more reason to worry. "To a certain degree," Wallace said, "he took out the bus and he ran over President Trump, Vice President Pence, Mike Pompeo, John Bolton, Rudy Giuliani, Mick Mulvaney. He implicates all of them." Still, Wallace said, he thought Sondland was trying to "protect himself more than anybody else." Sondland did not testify that Trump specifically told him that aid to Ukraine was being conditioned on investigations, Wallace said. But he said Sondland "added up two and two and got to four."

"I suspect that the Republicans are going to challenge his math skills," he said.

Recess over, Nunes came out swinging. He needed to change the momentum. He ran through the Republican version of events, challenging the Democratic narrative, trying to turn it to his advantage. He asked Sondland about the July 10 meeting with the Ukrainians, now routinely referred to as the "drug deal meeting," because of Bolton's salty comment afterward.

"Were you aware of any 'drug deal' on July 25 when the phone call actually occurred?" Nunes asked, straight-faced.

"I don't know about any drug deal," Sondland said.

Nunes then turned questioning over to Castor, who focused on Sondland's testimony that he "presumed" Trump was holding up aid and a White House meeting in exchange for investigations, but that he had never actually heard Trump say it. Sondland replied it was "abundantly clear to everyone that there was a link."

"Did the president ever tell you personally about any preconditions for anything?" Castor asked.

"No," Sondland said.

Castor zeroed in on Sondland's phone call with Trump in early September, when Sondland had asked the president what he wanted from Ukraine, and he said Trump told him, "I want nothing. I want nothing. I want no quid pro quo. Tell Zelensky to do the right thing."

"And you believed the president, correct?" Castor said.

"You know what, I'm not going to characterize whether I believed or didn't believe. I was just trying to convey what he said on the phone," Sondland replied, refusing to take a side.

Castor questioned Sondland's reliability. "You don't have your notes because you didn't take notes. You don't have a lot of recollections. I mean, this is like the trifecta of unreliability. Isn't that true?"

"Well," Sondland said, "what I'm trying to do today is to use the limited information I have to be as forthcoming as possible with you and the rest of the committee. And as these recollections have been refreshed by subsequent testimony, by some texts and emails that I've now had access to, I think I've filled in a lot of blanks."

"But a lot of it is speculation," Castor said. "A lot of it is your guess, and we're talking about, you know, an impeachment of the president of the United States. So the evidence here ought to be pretty darn good."

Sondland answered GOP questions for 45 minutes, then Schiff suggested a half-hour lunch break. Sondland was not happy. He didn't exactly scowl, but he looked displeased. His lawyer explained that a long delay would mean that he wouldn't be able to make his evening flight back to Brussels. Back to his ambassadorship.

"I appreciate that, Counsel," Schiff said. "We all have a busy schedule these days." He told Sondland he thought they would be done in time for him to make the flight.

Sondland looked happy.

At 11:36 a.m., Trump stood on the White House South Lawn, holding a notepad. He was on his way to an Apple factory in Texas but was running behind schedule because he had been watching Sondland's testimony.

Washington Post photographer Salwan Georges focused his lens on the notepad, which carried the presidential seal and the embossed heading "Aboard Air Force One." Trump had written in thick, black Sharpie the words Sondland had recalled from their phone call in early September: "I want nothing. I want nothing. I want no quid pro quo. Tell Zellinsky to do the right thing." Then, Trump wrote, "This is the final word from the Pres of the U.S."

Trump had tweeted a month earlier that Sondland was "a really good man and great American." Now Trump claimed to barely know him. "I don't know him very well. I have not spoken to him much. This is not a man I know well. Seems like a nice guy, though. But I don't know him well. He was with other candidates. He actually supported other candidates—not me. Came in late."

Trump read from his notepad, quoting himself, saying he wanted "no quid pro quo." He then made his exit. "Thank you, folks. Have a good time. I'm going to Texas."

In the hearing room, Jordan was firing away. The wrestling champ had five minutes, and he was going for a pin.

"Ambassador, when did it happen?" Jordan asked.

"When did what happen?" Sondland said, his face lighting up. Where was Jordan headed?

"The announcement," Jordan said. "When did President Zelensky announce that the investigation was going to happen?" Jordan read back Sondland's testimony that Trump was demanding a public announcement about investigations in return for a White House meeting and security aid.

"You said there needed to be a public announcement from Zelensky," Jordan said, his voice rising even more. "So, I'm asking you a simple question, when did that happen?"

"It never did," Sondland said, looking a little baffled.

"It never did," Jordan repeated back to him. "They got the call July 25. They got the meeting—not in the White House but in New York—on September 25. They got the money on September 11. When did the meeting happen again?"

"It never did," Sondland said again.

"You don't know who was in the meeting?" Jordan said.

"Which meeting are you referring to?" Sondland replied.

"The meeting that never happened! Who was in it?"

Sondland threw his head back and laughed out loud. This was fun. He kept laughing. He tossed Jordan a punch line: "The people that weren't there!"

"You know how Zelensky announced it? Did he tweet it? Did he do a press statement? Did he do a press conference? Do you know how that happened?" Jordan said.

Sondland, still smiling, took a sip from a paper cup.

He said a soft "no," but Jordan wasn't listening. He was shouting now.

The Ukrainians won it all, Jordan said. "They get the call. They get the meeting. They get the money. It's not two plus two, it's zero for three. I mean, I've never seen anything like this. . . . You said to the President of the United States, 'What do you want from Ukraine?' The president: 'I want nothing. I want no quid pro quo. I want Zelensky to do the right thing. I want him to do what he ran on.' "

Jordan asked: "What did he run on, Ambassador Sondland?"

Sondland took another sip from his cup and said, "Transparency."

"And dealing with corruption, right?"

"That's right."

Then Jordan's tone changed, like the arrival of a sudden thunderstorm. Before, Jordan had been pummeling Sondland, and Sondland had been responding as if it were all in good fun, two guys bantering. Now there was no mistaking Jordan's tone. Referring back to Castor's questioning, Jordan bore down hard.

"Mr. Castor raised another important point," Jordan said. "Why didn't you put that statement in your opening statement? I think you said you couldn't fit it in. Is that right? You said we might be here for forty-six minutes instead of forty-five minutes."

Sondland was still trying to be jovial. He laughed again and said: "It wasn't purposeful; trust me."

"It wasn't purposeful?" Jordan said.

"No."

"Couldn't fit it in a twenty-three-page opener? The most important statement about the subject matter at hand, the President of the United States in a direct conversation with you about the issue at hand. And the president says—let me read it one more time—'What do you want from Ukraine Mr. President? I want nothing. I want no quid pro quo.' " Jordan sounded disgusted. He kept pushing.

"Do you know what a quid pro quo is?" he asked Sondland.

"I do."

Jordan had been pounding Sondland for four minutes. His opponent's shoulders were close to the mat, and he was trying to finish the job.

" 'This for that,' right? It looks to me like Ukraine got 'that' three times and there was no 'this.' We didn't do anything. Or, excuse me, they didn't have to do anything." Jordan was spluttering. "Remember what the [whistleblower] complaint said? Remember what the memo said of the whistleblower? This call was frightening, this call was scary, all of those things?"

Sondland looked back at him, impassively, waiting.

Jordan's voice, finally lowered, started trailing off: "None of that materialized. . . . None of that materialized."

"I yield back," Jordan said, switching off his microphone.

Sondland gave his mouth a tiny little stretch. It was impossible to tell if it was a grin or a wince.

On Air Force One, Trump was tweeting.

"Impeachment Witch Hunt is now OVER! Ambassador Sondland asks U.S. President (me): 'What do you want from Ukraine? I keep hearing all these different ideas & theories. What do you want? It was a very abrupt conversation. He was not in a good mood. He (the President) just said,' . . . 'I WANT NOTHING! I WANT NOTHING! I WANT NO QUID PRO QUO! TELL PRESIDENT ZELENSKY TO DO THE RIGHT THING!'"

White House communications specialists sent 14 different sets of talking points to congressional Republicans, a total of more than 3,300 words. "Sondland Could Not Be Clearer, the President Was Not Involved in a Quid Pro Quo," one talking point was headlined, even though Sondland had testified very clearly that there was a quid pro quo. Administration officials emphasized that Sondland was relying on his own presumptions based on conversations with Giuliani—not Trump himself.

Trump was calling Republican House members to argue that Sondland's testimony was good for him. Democrats were confident of exactly the opposite.

In the hearing room, after almost six and a half hours, Sean Patrick Maloney, the New York Democrat, started grilling Sondland. He wasn't much easier on him than the Republicans had been.

"Let me ask you something, who would have benefited from an investigation of the president's political opponents?" Maloney asked.

"I don't want to characterize who would've and who would not have," Sondland replied.

"I know you don't want to, sir. That's my question. Would you—would you answer it for me?" Maloney said.

The two sparred for a couple of minutes. Sondland was evasive. Maloney was increasingly sharp with him, demanding a clear answer.

"Who would benefit from an investigation of the Bidens?" he asked yet again.

"I assume President Trump would benefit," Sondland said.

Maloney straightened up in his chair, a smile as big as one of Sondland's.

"There we have it! See?" he said. The audience in the hearing room broke into laughter and spontaneous applause. Sondland rolled his eyes, shook his head.

"Didn't hurt a bit, did it? Didn't hurt a bit. Let me ask you something," Maloney said.

Sondland cut him short.

"Mr. Maloney, excuse me," Sondland said. "I've been very forthright, and I really resent what you're trying to do."

Maloney darkened.

"Fair enough. You've been very forthright," he said. "This is your third try to do so, sir. Didn't work so well the first time, did it? We had a little declaration come in after you. Remember that? And now we're here a third time, and we've got a doozy of a statement from you this morning. There's a whole bunch of stuff you don't recall. So, all due respect, sir, we appreciate your candor, but let's be really clear on what it took to get it out of you."

Sondland's face was blank.

A few minutes later, Sondland found his Happy Face again as he was questioned by Raja Krishnamoorthi, Democrat of Illinois, who noted that a previous witness had referred to him as "the Gordon problem."

"That's what my wife calls me," Sondland said, and the chamber broke into laughter.

Sondland was still grinning as Krishnamoorthi continued.

"You know," he told Sondland, "on October 8 of this year the president tweeted that you were 'a really good man and a great American.' And of course, on November 8, one month later, he said, 'Let me just tell you I hardly know the gentleman.' "

"Easy come, easy go!" Sondland said, laughing loudly.

Krishnamoorthi had more questions, but he was having trouble. Every time he looked at Sondland's beaming face, he laughed.

In their closing statements, Nunes was from Venus and Schiff was from Mars.

Nunes saw nothing in Sondland's testimony that established that the president had done anything wrong.

Schiff saw a "seminal moment" in the impeachment, and evidence that Trump had conditioned both a meeting and aid on getting his investigations.

Schiff banged his gavel. Hearing over.

Sondland left in a rush. He had a plane to catch.

Would Sondland make his flight? The question had created a small Twitter tornado. Eleven million people had watched parts of his testimony, plus countless more online, and now some of them were trying to help, posting real-time traffic updates and maps on Twitter. "Gordo, you got this!" one tweeted.

Sondland raced out of the Capitol at aboout 4 p.m. The only remaining flight from Washington to Brussels was leaving at 5:50 p.m. from Dulles Airport, 30 miles away, and it was rush hour.

Veteran political analyst Jeff Greenfield joked on Twitter that CNN should have a helicopter following Sondland's car with a countdown clock in the corner of the screen. At 5:39 p.m., CNN's Kaitlan Collins tweeted that, yes, Sondland "had made his fight."

A passenger posted a blurry photo of Sondland hoisting his roller bag into an overhead bin. Apparently, he put the bag in the wrong place and had to move it. He was still in good humor.

"My whole day has been like this," he said, with a big laugh.

After the hearing ended, Fox News host Neil Cavuto was interviewing Congressman Rick Crawford, Republican of Arkansas. Crawford had been removed from the Intelligence Committee to give Jordan a spot.

Cavuto said Sondland's testimony went in both directions. He had declared the existence of a quid pro quo, but he had also quoted Trump saying "no quid pro quo." Naturally, Cavuto said, Democrats were seizing on one and Republicans on the other. He thought many viewers were confused.

"So where do you think this goes?" Cavuto asked Crawford.

"It's tough to say," Crawford said, "because it's really kind of, for a lack of a better term, this is somewhat of a Rorschach test."

CHAPTER THIRTY-EIGHT

"These Fictions Are Harmful"

November 20 to 22, Washington

Fiona Hill was driving her 12-year-old daughter to school on Wednesday morning, something she had not been able to do for most of her two-year White House tenure, when she often left for work before sunrise. They were traveling from their home in Bethesda, Maryland, 20 minutes to Sidwell Friends, an elite private school in northwest Washington.

It struck Hill that their two childhoods could hardly have been more different. She had grown up in northeastern England, with poverty never far from her family's doorstep. Her father had gone to work in the coal mines in County Durham when he was 14; her mother was a midwife. Hill began working in her early teens, washing cars, serving drinks in grubby pubs and cleaning hospital bathrooms. Her daughter attended a school whose alumni included six children of presidents.

As she drove, Hill's mind was racing. She was thinking about the next day, and her scheduled testimony before the House Intelligence Committee's impeachment inquiry. The all-day ordeal would put her on display for millions watching on TV and the Internet.

She tried to put all that aside for the moment. In the car, the more immediate issue was her daughter's exam week at Sidwell.

As Hill posed questions on math and Spanish, her daughter talked about the stress of exams. Hoping to calm her with a bit of perspective, Hill said that at least she didn't have to testify before Congress. Her daughter turned the tables. On her exams, she said, there were right and wrong answers. Get too many wrong, and you fail. Her mother's test was far simpler.

"You just have to tell the truth," she said.

• • •

Before Hill had reached the witness table just before 9 a.m. Thursday, Trump had tweeted 13 times—9 of them about impeachment.

"The Republican Party, and me, had a GREAT day yesterday with respect to the phony Impeachment Hoax, & yet, when I got home to the White House & checked out the news coverage on much of television, you would have no idea they were reporting on the same event. FAKE & CORRUPT NEWS!" he tweeted just after 7:30 a.m.

A few minutes after 8 a.m.: "I never in my wildest dreams thought my name would in any way be associated with the ugly word, Impeachment! The calls (Transcripts) were PERFECT, there was NOTHING said that was wrong. No pressure on Ukraine. Great corruption & dishonesty by Schiff on the other side!"

Then came a rapid series starring Schiff: "Corrupt politician Adam Schiff's lies are growing by the day. Keep fighting tough, Republicans, you are dealing with human scum who have taken Due Process and all of the Republican Party's rights away from us during the most unfair hearings in American History. . . . But we are winning big, and they will soon be on our turf."

"Our turf." The Senate. His trial. He was already looking ahead.

Wearing a somber black jacket and a serious look to match, Hill made the now ritual walk to the witness table as the scrum of photographers clicked away. The day's other witness was David Holmes, from the U.S. embassy in Kyiv. He sat to her left. His crisp haircut and cheerful blue tie gave him the look of a Boy Scout. That's not how many Trump supporters thought of him. In their view, Holmes and Hill were not there as "fact witnesses." Like Vindman and others, they were from the "deep state."

Schiff read their bios aloud, then the microphone went to Holmes for his opening statement. He had a mountain of events to recount. He went through them quickly, citing dates. When he reached Sondland's restaurant phone call to the president, he described the scene in detail: The outdoor terrace, the wine and the president's voice, loud enough for Holmes to hear, saying "So he's going to do the investigations?" and Sondland replying, "he will do anything you ask him to do." Then Sondland saying after the call that the president didn't care about Ukraine, he only cared about "the big stuff," meaning "stuff" that benefited him.

Hill's role was different. Her job put her at the center of Ukraine policy, with a view of the big picture. She could shed light on the events leading up to the Trump-Zelensky phone call on July 25, but she had left her National Security Council job a week before that now-famous conversation.

As she was writing her opening statement, she had thought about how to introduce herself. "I take great pride," she began, "in the fact that I'm a nonpartisan foreign policy expert who had served under three Republican and Democratic presidents. I have no interest in advancing the outcome of your inquiry in any particular direction, except toward the truth."

In her distinctive working-class English accent, she called herself "an American by choice," acquiring her U.S. citizenship in 2002. But she thought of her American roots as going back much further. Her family came from the same region of England as George Washington's ancestors. Her grandfather was a World War I veteran who survived because of U.S. military intervention. Other relatives had fought alongside U.S. troops in World War II.

She held back from the committee some of the harshest details of her upbringing. She had been a gifted student, which gave her a path out of the poverty of her hometown. But it also made her a target of envy and abuse. She understood that those with the greatest animosity toward her were often confronting terrible circumstances at home—alcoholism, teen pregnancy, even incest. She also learned when to stand up for herself, with her fists if necessary, and when to simply ignore the cruelty. When she was 11, a boy set her pigtails on fire while their class was taking a test. Hill smothered her burning hair with her hands and went on with the exam.

She earned an admission interview at Oxford. When she arrived, she found herself surrounded by other female Oxford prospects from fancier schools. As she was ushered in for the interview, one stuck out a leg and tripped her. She tumbled forward, smashing her face on the door. The Oxford admissions official handed her a napkin to help stanch the bleeding from her nose. He told her that her academic record was impressive, but he doubted that Oxford was the best fit for her.

Now, reading from her opening statement, Hill told the committee that she eventually attended St. Andrews in Scotland, where she excelled at Russian studies and won an exchange placement to the Soviet Union. She was in Moscow to witness a summit between Ronald Reagan and Soviet leader Mikhail Gorbachev. She said that was a turning point, as she met an American professor who told her about graduate student scholarships available in the United States. In 1989, she arrived at Harvard to begin her doctoral studies. She told the committee that her background and working-class accent had "never set me back in America."

Alternatively looking at the Democratic and Republican lawmakers, Hill described her role as the intelligence community's senior expert on Russia and Eurasia during the George W. Bush and Obama administrations, then joining the NSC under Trump. She said she thought she could help Trump with his stated goal of improving relations with Russia, while working to deter Russia's threatening conduct, including "the unprecedented and successful Russian operation to interfere in the 2016 presidential election."

Then, without changing the polite, calm tone of her voice, Hill abruptly switched gears. She hadn't come just to answer questions. She had come to engage. "Based on questions and statements I have heard, some of you on this committee appear to believe that Russia and its security services did not conduct a campaign against our country and that perhaps, somehow, for some reason, Ukraine did," she said.

She didn't say "Republicans." She said, "some of you." But she might as well have held up a sign, adding "Trump." Heads swiveled to the front of the room, along with C-SPAN's camera angle. Republican John Ratcliffe of Texas was staring directly at Hill. It wasn't a warm look.

Hill didn't blink. She took a second shot. "This is a fictional narrative that is being perpetrated and propagated by the Russian security services themselves," she continued. "The unfortunate truth is that Russia was the foreign power that systematically attacked our democratic institutions in 2016. This is the public conclusion of our intelligence agencies, confirmed in bipartisan congressional reports. It is beyond dispute, even if some of the underlying details must remain classified."

Republicans on the committee had issued their own report nearly two years earlier, acknowledging that Russia had interfered in 2016 while disputing the intelligence community's conclusion that Russia was trying to help Trump. In his opening statement, Nunes had held up the report. But in public statements since the report, he and other Republicans had picked up Trump's phrase, the "Russia hoax."

In Hill's view, that sort of language played into Russia's hands. The day before her testimony, at an economic forum in Moscow, Putin had made it clear he was enjoying the attention that Ukraine was getting at the impeachment hearings. "Thank God nobody is accusing us anymore of interfering in the U.S. elections. Now they're accusing Ukraine," Putin said.

Hill said Russia's goal was to weaken the United States and undermine U.S. policies in Europe, including support for Ukraine. She listed signs of Moscow's success: "Our nation is being torn apart; truth is questioned; our highly professional expert career Foreign Service is being undermined. U.S. support for Ukraine, which continues to face armed aggression, is being politicized."

As she was testifying, Meadows tweeted his disdain. "A notable theme in these hearings: some career officials seem to act as though their job is to decide America's foreign policy. It's the President who sets policy—not unelected bureaucrats."

Hill said Putin wasn't finished. "Right now, Russia's security services and their proxies have geared up to repeat their interference in the 2020 election. We are running out of time to stop them. In the course of this investigation, I would ask that you please not promote politically derivative falsehoods that so clearly advance Russian interests."

She said Republicans and Democrats have agreed for decades that Ukraine plays an important role in our national security. "I refuse to be part of an effort to legitimize an alternate narrative that the Ukrainian government is a U.S. adversary and that Ukraine, not Russia, attacked us in 2016. These fictions are harmful, even if they're deployed for purely domestic political purposes."

This was an opening statement like none from other witnesses. Hill didn't smile or frown. She looked neither angry nor nervous. She wasn't just talking to the committee. She was talking to the country.

"President Putin and the Russian security services operate like a super PAC," she said. "They deploy millions of dollars to weaponize our own political opposition research and false narratives. When we are consumed by partisan rancor, we cannot combat these external forces as they seek to divide us against each other, degrade our institutions, and destroy the faith of the American people in our democracy."

She promised the lawmakers to "help you to the best of my ability." But, she added, "we must not let domestic politics stop us from defending ourselves against the foreign powers who truly wish us harm."

She looked up at the lawmakers: "I'm ready to answer your questions."

• • •

Schiff was eager to keep Hill talking. He asked Hill why she thought pushing the Ukraine meddling narrative helped Russia.

"The Russians' interest, frankly, is to delegitimize our entire presidency," she said. "One issue that I do want to raise, and I think that this would resonate with our colleagues on the committee from the Republican Party, is that the goal of the Russians was really to put whoever became the president . . . under a cloud." If Hillary Clinton had been elected, Hill said, "she, too, would have had major questions about her legitimacy."

When Nunes's turn came, he had a list of names he wanted to run past Hill and Holmes. The names came from the "alternate narrative" about the 2016 election that Hill had just called fictional. Each had some tie to the Democrats' opposition research on Trump.

Nunes made no attempt to explain the names. He delivered them rapid fire.

Did Hill know Alexandra Chalupa? No, Hill said.

Nellie Ohr? No, Hill said.

Bruce Ohr? They met in official meetings years ago, Hill said, when she worked at the CIA.

Glenn Simpson? No.

Christopher Steele? Yes, she said. Steele was once Hill's counterpart in British intelligence, now retired.

The names had been a part of Hill's deposition a month earlier, too. During questioning by Castor behind closed doors, Hill had lost her patience. "I'm sorry to get testy about this back-and-forth, because I'm really worried about these conspiracy theories. And I'm worried that all of you are going to go down a rabbit hole, you know, looking for things that are not going to be at all helpful to the American people or to our future election in 2020." She said the Senate had just issued a bipartisan report that said Russia posed a threat to the 2020 election. "If we have people running around chasing rabbit holes because Rudy Giuliani or others have been feeding information to *The Hill*, *Politico*, we are not going to be prepared as a country to push back on this again. The Russians thrive on misinformation and disinformation. . . . If we don't get our act together, they will continue to make fools of us internationally."

Nunes stuck to the strategy: Insist that the Democrats are hiding their sins. Tell the folks at home that the 2016 campaign was one dirty mess, and that Donald Trump was a victim, too.

• • •

As Hill and Holmes were testifying, top Republican lawmakers, including members of McConnell's Legal Eagles group, were meeting with top officials at the White House to discuss strategy for a Senate trial. The president was represented at the meeting by Cipollone, Mulvaney, Kushner, Kellyanne Conway and legislative affairs director Eric Ueland, along with advisers Pam Bondi and Tony Sayegh, who had recently been hired to guide the White House's impeachment messaging and strategy.

Trump had been telling people he wanted a quick dismissal. He was miserable about the testimony coming out of the House, and he wanted the Senate to end the trial as fast as possible. The senators in the meeting—Graham, Cruz, Johnson, Mike Lee of Utah, John Neely Kennedy of Louisiana, Tom Cotton of Arkansas—tried to ease Trump off that position, telling him that a majority of the Senate would never go for it.

At the same time, Trump was arguing the opposite to others, saying he wanted a longer trial where Joe Biden, Hunter Biden, Schiff and the whistleblower were called as witnesses. He was spouting his frustration in every direction. Some of his supporters also favored a drawn-out trial with the potential to scramble the schedules of the half-dozen Democratic senators running for president—Bennet, Booker, Harris, Klobuchar, Sanders and Warren—who would be required to stay in Washington as jurors in the impeachment trial.

Cruz believed that calling witnesses would play into the Democrats' hands. They were simply trying to get the Senate to do their investigating for them. He thought they wanted to drag out the trial, hoping the spectacle would be bad for Trump. They had not proven their case, Cruz thought, so now they wanted to go on a fishing expedition.

The consensus in the room was a middle-ground option: a trial of about two weeks, closely coordinated between McConnell's Senate and Trump's White House. Everyone agreed that Trump would have the final say over the approach. The trick was getting him to a place that made the most sense.

At the hearing, Castor was asking Hill about an encounter she had with Sondland just a few days before she left her NSC job on July 19.

In his closed-door testimony, Sondland said he had stopped at her office and found her so angry that she was "sort of shaking." Sondland said she was upset with Trump and "everything having to do the Trump administration."

Castor asked Hill if she would like to "address that." She told Castor, "I was actually, to be honest, angry" at Sondland. She explained why. Sondland "wasn't coordinating with us" and wasn't keeping her informed about his meetings on Ukraine.

Hill said she wasn't surprised that he had come away with the wrong impression. "You know, I hate to say it, but often when women show anger, it's not fully appreciated." She explained. "It's often, you know, pushed onto emotional issues perhaps, or deflected onto other people."

She was telling Castor how Sondland had reacted to her complaint that he wasn't coordinating. He didn't understand, she said, what he was doing wrong. She quoted him as saying: "I'm briefing the president. I'm briefing Chief of Staff Mulvaney. I'm briefing Secretary Pompeo, and I've talked to Ambassador Bolton. Who else do I have to deal with?"

From Sondland's perspective, he was coordinating with everyone, at every level. From her perspective, he was ignoring everyone in the regular Ukraine channel. But then, as she watched Sondland's testimony the day before, she'd had an epiphany. Sondland's actions made sense, "because he was being involved in a domestic political errand, and we were being involved in national security foreign policy, and those two things had just diverged."

Sondland had left the regular channel, and she hadn't understood that. "I realized," she said, "that I wasn't really being fair to Ambassador Sondland because he was carrying out what he thought he had been instructed to carry out. And we were doing something that we thought was just as, or perhaps even more, important. But it wasn't in the same channel."

That didn't mean Hill thought the "political errand" was wise. When she confronted Sondland in her office, she had warned him: "Gordon, I think this is all going to blow up."

She said to Castor: "And here we are."

Hill had become an instant media phenomenon, celebrated or despised, depending on which corners of the media or Internet you visited. Progressive media portrayed her as a truth-telling badass. Conservatives mocked her. Emerald Robinson, the chief White House correspondent for OAN, tweeted: "Fiona Hill with that Prince Andrew accent, and 'Defense Minister' Vindman from the Ukraine. I'm wondering: are any Americans going to testify against Trump?"

Rush Limbaugh mocked Hill on his radio show, imitating her accent. "I'm appearing today as a facts witness, I take with prides," Limbaugh said. "Love the way these Brits speak. Their long T's and D's. 'I'm a facts witness. I takes greats prides.' "

Conservative author Tony Shaffer tweeted to his 95,000 followers: "I've dealt with elitist academic morons just like Fiona Hill my entire career—I was just at the Pentagon w/ an old boss discussing how the bureaucracy is full of these 'book smart' morons—she is an absolute stooge of the deep state & progressive left."

Four hours into the hearing, Schiff recognized Will Hurd to question Hill and Holmes for five minutes.

But Hurd had no questions; he had something to say. He had worked up an 800-word statement the previous day, tweaking it as he listened to Hill and Holmes. They had not said anything that had swayed him on the bottom-line question. None of the witnesses had. So now, with a national television audience watching live and no more "fact witnesses" scheduled, he wanted to explain why.

"Thank you, Dr. Hill, Mr. Holmes, for your years of service to this country and I appreciate y'all being here today," he said in a strong, clear voice, his "y'all" giving away his Texas roots. "Throughout this process, I have said that I want to learn the facts so we can get to the truth."

No one knew where he was heading. Democrats had been hoping for weeks that Hurd, a centrist willing to criticize Trump, might be persuaded by the evidence to support impeachment. They badly wanted at least a couple of Republicans to come over to their side, so that the final vote would not be entirely partisan.

Hurd had read the July 25 phone call transcript closely, and had not seen any evidence of a crime. But he had kept an open mind, waiting to see what the inquiry turned up. He had not liked the closed-door deposition process, especially the questioning by staff counsels. He thought they focused too much on useless detail, instead of getting to the heart of key matters. And he found most of the testimony unenlightening. He expected Volker's October 3 deposition to be powerful because Democrats had built it up so much. But as Volker testified, he found himself thinking, "Where the hell is the stuff the whistleblower was alluding to that was so damning?"

His view was that impeachment required a crime. He had looked for evidence of bribery or extortion. He saw evidence of neither. In October he had gone on "60 Minutes" and said he saw no impeachable offense, and he had criticized the deposition process on "Face the Nation" on CBS. His views were hardly secret, but he was still regularly cited as a bellwether, showing up on some media lists as a possible defector. He was aware that a lot of people were watching him. He adjusted his thick-rimmed black glasses and continued.

"So why are we here?" he said. "Because of two things that occurred during the President's July 25 phone call with Ukrainian President Zelensky—the use of the phrase 'do us a favor, though' in reference of the 2016 presidential election and the mention of the word 'Biden.' "

He was reading, but he was looking up, using his hands and eyes to emphasize certain words. "Biden" was one of them.

"I believe both statements were inappropriate, misguided foreign policy, and it's certainly not how the executive, current or in the future, should handle such a call. Over the course of these hearings, the American people have learned about a series of events that in my view have undermined our national security and undercut Ukraine, a key partner on the front lines against Russian aggression. We've heard of U.S. officials carrying uncoordinated, confusing and conflicting messages that created doubt and uncertainty in Kyiv. . . . I disagree with this sort of bungling foreign policy."

The Democrats couldn't have said it any better. Was Hurd on his way to making the leap?

He was reading quickly now, as if his time were running out. He said many details were still not known. The committee had not heard from Giuliani, Hunter Biden or the whistleblower, all of whom could provide important context, he said. He noted that Ukraine had received all the aid approved by Congress, and that Zelensky was cracking down on corruption.

"So where does this leave us?" Hurd said, slowing down his cadence to deliver his verdict. "An impeachable offense should be compelling, overwhelmingly clear and unambiguous, and it's not something to be rushed or taken lightly. I've not heard evidence proving the president committed bribery or extortion."

He wrapped up: "I hope that we won't let this very partisan process keep us from agreeing on how a free and prosperous Ukraine is important to the security of the Ukrainian people, the United States of America and the rest of the world."

He could have simply asked a few tough questions of Hill and Holmes and moved on. Instead, on this climactic day, he had issued a powerful speech that cleared up any confusion.

Will Hurd was not going to flip.

Five minutes later, Michael Conaway called Holmes, who was sitting next to Hill, indiscreet. As Holmes looked back at him without expression, Conaway told Holmes that the information he had shared about Sondland's call with Trump was embarrassing and unflattering to the president and the ambassador. As a diplomat who attends all sorts of private meetings, would Holmes promise to be more discreet in the future? He asked it as a question, but it sounded more like a scolding.

"Sir, I think it was Gordon Sondland who showed indiscretion," Holmes replied, referring to Sondland's use of an unsecured phone line for a call with the president.

Conaway didn't accept that. He kept pressing his point, but Holmes was having none of it. "Sir, I shared the information I had to share with the right people who needed to know it," he said.

It was the fourth time in 90 minutes that a Republican on the committee had attacked Holmes's judgment or credibility. Jordan had suggested that the call, while memorable to Holmes, was so insignificant that his boss, Taylor, hadn't mentioned it in all his hours of testimony. Taylor had gone over 13 other calls, Jordan said, but "nowhere, nowhere is there a 'Holmes tells Taylor what the president of the United States told Sondland.'"

John Ratcliffe of Texas wondered why Holmes was able to hear Trump's voice some of the time, but not all, clearly suggesting Holmes was not credible.

A visibly angry Mike Turner of Ohio repeated the "loves your ass" and "he'll do anything" comments that Holmes had reported from the phone call. "Mr. Holmes, that information had nothing whatsoever to do with the subject matter of any of these hearings," Turner said icily, making a "zero" gesture with his left hand. "It was anecdotal, it was extraneous."

Holmes raised his eyebrows slightly in disagreement. Turner continued, his voice rising: "Your statements that your interests are protecting Ukraine are very dubious when you embarrass President Zelensky by making those statements you didn't have to make. Who cares that Ambassador Sondland said that?"

The clean-cut young diplomat was taking a beating from the Republicans, who were mostly not taking aim at the facts but shooting at the messenger.

As Hill and Holmes were still testifying, John Solomon, whose reporting for *The Hill* newspaper had played such a key role in Yovanovitch's firing and Giuliani's campaign in Ukraine, took to Twitter.

"How dare Fiona Hill question my patriotism or suggest I was part of a Russian disinformation campaign without a single fact," he wrote. "My sources were all US officials or Ukrainian officials aligned against Russia. Her accusations must have made Joe McCarthy smile up from hell."

Hill had not mentioned Solomon's name in her full day of testimony. She had decried the "fictional narrative" that Ukraine had systematically meddled in the 2016 election, a key element in some of Solomon's columns. But "John Solomon" had not passed her lips all day. She had said the name of his newspaper, "*The Hill*," once, in an unrelated context.

Solomon could be forgiven for feeling a little tender, since *The Hill* had announced to its staff three days earlier that it was conducting a review of his work on Ukraine, which had been criticized during the hearings. Solomon had left *The Hill* in September, saying he would start his own media company.

After *Politico* had reported *The Hill*'s internal review, Solomon defended his work in an email: "I stand by each and every one of the columns that I wrote and that The Hill (both editors and lawyers) carefully vetted. All facts in those stories are substantiated to original source documents and statements."

It was almost 9 p.m. by the time Hill reached home. Her husband and daughter were waiting for her with a warm plate of food. The house was buried in flowers, cards and other gifts from neighbors and admirers. Hill was just happy to be back with her family, done with her testimony. When it was dark and quiet on her neighborhood sidewalks, she stepped outside alone to take her dog for a walk.

• • •

The next morning, November 22, Trump called into "Fox & Friends." He repeated his perfect-call mantra, then went right back to the conspiracy theory that the Democrats and Ukraine had meddled in his election and that the DNC server was in Ukraine. "You know, it's very interesting—it's very interesting. They have the server, right, from the DNC, Democratic National Committee, you know."

"Who has the server?" host Brian Kilmeade said.

"The FBI went in and they told them, get out of here, you're not getting—we're not giving it to you. They gave the server to CrowdStrike, or whatever it's called, which is a country—which is a company owned by a very wealthy Ukrainian. And I still want to see that server. You know, the FBI has never gotten that server. That's a big part of this whole thing. Why did they give it to a Ukrainian company? Why?"

"Are you sure they did that? Are you sure they gave it to Ukraine?" asked host Steve Doocy.

"Well, that's what the word is," Trump said. "That's what I asked actually in my phone call, as you know."

The five days of public testimony had cemented Democratic resolve. Schiff didn't rule out calling more witnesses. But Democrats across the party's ideological spectrum were telling *Washington Post* reporters that they had heard enough. They believed the testimony from Taylor, Sondland, Vindman, Hill and the others had laid out a damning case. They had hoped that a few moderate Republicans like Hurd might join them, but it was obvious now that wouldn't happen.

The House and Senate were about to recess for a 10-day Thanksgiving break. Staffers on Schiff's committee knew they would have no time off. They had already started drafting a final report that would run several hundred pages. They wanted it to be dramatic, exhaustive and persuasive. They would hand it off to the House Judiciary Committee, which would draft the articles of impeachment.

November had been hectic. December would be a zoo.

CHAPTER THIRTY-NINE

"Potomac River Fever"

December 4, Washington

Matt Gaetz was grumpy. He was giving his fourth interview of the day, and it was only 8:30 a.m. "Too many," he told *Washington Post* reporter Ben Terris. The House Judiciary Committee was opening its phase of the impeachment inquiry today, and Gaetz was a committee member. "When the story becomes me rather than the work we are doing, it overtakes the work."

He looked weary, eyes sunken, a victim of his own success. Ever since he and his troops had stormed the SCIF in October, Gaetz had become a subplot in the impeachment drama. He was caustic, angry, the embodiment of the Always Trumpers' fury at Schiff and the Democrats. He was also smart, telegenic and funny. Media catnip.

Now, in his office at the Longworth Building, not far from where the Judiciary Committee would soon question four law professors about the legal basis for impeaching Donald Trump, Gaetz was somewhere between fatigued and fired up. "This is going to be a weird day," he told Terris. "I didn't like getting lectures from law professors when I was in law school."

The earlier interviewers had quizzed him about everything from his law degree to the artwork on his office walls. A three-person film crew from a forthcoming HBO documentary, tentatively called "The Swamp," had their cameras trained on him. "I've forgotten about them, they've been following me around for a year," he explained.

He was sitting on a plush brown couch, beneath a black-and-white poster from his grandfather's 1964 campaign for lieutenant governor. S. J. "Jerry" Gaetz's slogan: "North Dakota's Most Progressive Mayor" and "Unbought! Unbossed! Unbowed!" That year, after speaking at the

Republican state convention, Jerry Gaetz walked offstage, collapsed on the convention floor from a heart attack, and died. He was 49.

His grandson, unbowed at 37, thought the Democrats were making a mistake with their law professor gambit. He told Maria Bartiromo on Fox Business that it was "fool-hearted" to think that public sentiment would be swayed by "the law review coming to life."

The committee's Democrats thought it would be compelling to have three of the nation's top legal minds discussing the constitutional foundations for Trump's impeachment. The idea was to lift the debate above partisanship, to show the public watching on television that there was an irrefutable legal basis for finding Trump's actions impeachable. But the Republicans weren't going along. They weren't going to let Nadler handpick a bunch of "experts," and present them as neutral observers. Professors could be just as partisan as lawmakers. The fourth witness was the Republicans' choice. They were counting on him to bolster their argument that Trump had done nothing that qualified as impeachable.

Gaetz thought the witness lineup would backfire on the Democrats. "They're going to bring what I can only perceive to be as a group of pious, condescending, law professor–academician types to talk to down to the Congress and really talk down to the MAGA movement," he had told former Trump aide Steve Bannon earlier, on Bannon's podcast.

As Gaetz saw it, the Democrats were saying that "what you really need to do is impeach based on this conduct because we the elite, we the permanent Washington, we the smart folks, have decided that according to our norms this is not acceptable conduct." The Republicans needed to avoid getting sucked into a tedious discussion on the most obscure corners of constitutional law. "That plays into the Democrats' hands. We need to talk to the country," he told Bannon. "We can't get Potomac River fever inside the beltway of Washington and follow the Democrats over the cliff here."

Now, with the hearing less than an hour away, Gaetz was facing a different challenge. He said to Terris: "I think anything less than me walking in with a fog machine, pyrotechnics and a WWE belt around my waist is going to be viewed as not meeting expectations."

Nadler was finally getting his chance. Schiff had run the inquiry, but the articles of impeachment had to go through Nadler's Judiciary Committee. He needed to be at the top of his game.

At 10 a.m., Nadler began by citing John Adams, Thomas Jefferson and Alexander Hamilton. "It is important to place President Trump's conduct into historical context," Nadler said. "Today we will begin our conversation where we should, with the text of the Constitution."

Doug Collins, the committee's ranking Republican, was scornful in rebuttal: "America will see why most people don't go to law school. No offense to our professors, but please. Really?" He said the committee "can be theoretical all we want, but the American people are really going to look at this and say, 'Huh? what are we doing?' "

Nadler introduced the witnesses, stressing their credentials. Summoned by the Democrats:

Noah Feldman, Harvard law professor, author of seven books, including a biography of James Madison, Harvard undergrad, Rhodes Scholar at Oxford, law degree from Yale, clerked for Supreme Court justice David Souter.

Pamela Karlan, Stanford law professor, coauthor of several books, undergrad and law degrees from Yale, clerked for Supreme Court justice Harry Blackmun, former Justice Department official focused on voting rights during the Obama administration's second term.

Michael Gerhardt, University of North Carolina law professor, author of a book on impeachment as well as several others, Yale undergrad, master's from the London School of Economics and law degree from the University of Chicago.

Summoned by the Republicans: Jonathan Turley, George Washington University law professor, author of more than three dozen academic articles, University of Chicago undergrad and law degree from Northwestern University.

Feldman, Karlan and Gerhardt each gave statements based on Constitutional law and said they had reached the same verdicts.

"President Trump's conduct as described in the testimony and evidence clearly constitutes impeachable high crimes and misdemeanors under the Constitution," Feldman concluded. He argued that "there's no mystery about the words high crimes and misdemeanors." For the writers of the Constitution, those words would have included "abuse of office for personal gain or advantage."

Karlan focused on Trump's phone call with Zelensky and the request for foreign interference in a U.S. election, which "struck at the very heart of what makes this a republic to which we pledge allegiance." She said:

"If we are to keep faith with our Constitution, President Trump must be held to account."

Gerhardt said he was troubled by Trump's argument that the House inquiry was illegitimate. "If left unchecked, the president will likely continue his pattern of soliciting foreign interference on behalf of the next election and of course his obstruction of Congress," he said. "If Congress fails to impeach here, then the impeachment process has lost all meaning. . . . I stand with the framers who were committed to ensure that no one is above the law."

Turley, aware of his position as the lone expert voice against impeachment, had crafted his statement in a more conversational way. He hadn't voted for Trump, he said. But, he stressed, his political opinions didn't matter. He was concentrating on the factual record. There was, he said, a "paucity of evidence and an abundance of anger."

Emotions had taken charge, he argued. "We are living in the very period described by Alexander Hamilton, a period of agitated passions. I get it. You're mad. The president's mad. My Republican friends are mad. My Democratic friends are mad. My wife is mad. My kids are mad. Even my dog seems mad. And Luna is a goldendoodle and they don't get mad!" That broke the tension momentarily. "Will a slipshod impeachment make us less mad? Will it only invite an invitation for the madness to follow every future administration?"

Turley's verdict: The inquiry was rushed. Missing witnesses, missing evidence. "That is why this is wrong. It's not wrong because President Trump is right. His call was anything but perfect. It's not wrong because the House has no legitimate reason to investigate the Ukrainian controversy. It's not wrong because we're in an election year." There's no good time for an impeachment, he said.

"It's wrong," he said, "because this is not how you impeach an American president."

Republicans and Democrats took five-minute turns asking the professors (or professor) from their team to agree with them on various points. With more than 40 committee members present, it was making for a long afternoon.

A little before 3 p.m., five hours into the hearing, Karlan offered a clumsy pun as Democrat Sheila Jackson Lee of Texas was questioning her. Asked to discuss the difference between a monarch and a president,

Karlan said: "The Constitution says there can be no titles of nobility. So, while the president can name his son Barron, he can't make him a baron."

Gaetz took note. He had a few members in front of him, but he was still thinking about how he wanted to use his five minutes for questions. Before the hearing, Collins had warned everyone on his side to stay away from debating these brilliant legal scholars on the finer points of the Constitution. Gaetz thought that was right.

But he could still go for the jugular. Karlan had handed him an opportunity. Trump supporters in his Florida district wouldn't be laughing at her joke. They would say it was more of the same, another example of the elites laughing at our expense. They would tell him about hiding their political views at work, at their book clubs, at the PTA, from other parents at softball games. As Gaetz described it, they can't "let their MAGA freak flag fly" without being judged, "canceled," written off as "deplorable."

Gaetz was going to "lay down the lumber" on Karlan, he decided. He would build up to it, rather than coming at her with his first question. But he was going to make her regret her joke.

Gaetz had done his homework. This was hardball politics, not a college classroom.

"Professor Gerhardt, you gave money to Barack Obama, right?" he said. His first question.

"My family did, yes," Gerhardt replied.

"Four times?" Gaetz asked.

"I—That sounds about right, yes," Gerhardt said.

Turning to Feldman, Gaetz cited an essay the professor had published in May, which said House Democrats were thinking of impeachment "primarily or even exclusively as a tool to weaken President Trump's chances in 2020." The article was headlined "It's Hard to Take Impeachment Seriously Now."

Gaetz said, "Did you write those words?"

"Until this call on July 25, I was an impeachment skeptic," Feldman replied.

Gaetz hadn't landed the punch he wanted. "Very well," he said.

Before Gaetz could move on, Feldman added: "The call changed my mind, sir, and for good reason."

Gaetz wasn't interested. He had already switched to Karlan, his main target.

He led her through her campaign donations—$1,000 to Elizabeth Warren, $1,200 to Obama, $2,000 to Hillary Clinton. Then, he asked her about a guest appearance that was featured on a podcast called "Versus Trump."

"Do you remember saying the following: 'Liberals tend to cluster more, conservatives, especially very conservative people, tend to spread out more, perhaps because they don't even want to be around themselves.' Did you say that?"

"Yes, I did," Karlan said.

"Do you understand," Gaetz said, "how that reflects contempt on people who are conservative?"

Karlan protested. He wasn't giving the context. She had been talking about the drawing of voting districts, she said. "I don't have contempt for conservatives—"

They were talking over each other now. The exchange had nothing to do with impeachment, but everything to do with Gaetz's plan of attack. He said: "You may not see this from, you know, like the ivory towers of your law school but it makes actual people in this country feel like—"

Karlan tried to head him off. "What the president calls—"

Gaetz cut her off, his voice rising, louder, faster. "Excuse me! You don't get to interrupt me on this time. Now, let me also suggest that when you invoke the president's son's name here, when you try to make a little joke out of referencing Barron Trump, that does not lend credibility to your argument. It makes you look mean. It makes you look like you're attacking someone's family, the minor child of the president of the United States."

Karlan's eyes widened slightly. She hadn't seen this coming. From the Democratic point of view, she was making thoughtful and reasonable contributions that helped their case. She wasn't aware that outside the hearing room, her attempt at humor had become a hot soundbite that was energizing Republicans.

White House spokeswoman Stephanie Grisham fired off a tweet: "Classless move by a Democratic 'witness.' Prof Karlan uses a teenage boy who has nothing to do with this joke of a hearing (and deserves privacy) as a punchline. And what's worse, it's met by laughter in the hearing room. What is being done to this country is no laughing matter."

Trump's presidential campaign issued a statement: "Only in the minds of crazed liberals is it funny to drag a 13-year-old child into the impeachment nonsense. Pamela Karlan thought she was being clever and going for laughs, but she instead reinforced for all Americans that Democrats have no boundaries when it comes to their hatred of everything related to President Trump."

Taking the response to another level, Melania Trump then tweeted: "A minor child deserves privacy and should be kept out of politics. Pamela Karlan, you should be ashamed of your very angry and obviously biased public pandering, and using a child to do it."

Later in the hearing, Karlan tried to repair the damage, while adding a jab at Trump. "I want to apologize for what I said earlier about the president's son," she said as she was answering an unrelated question. "It was wrong of me to do that. I wish the president would apologize, obviously, for the things that he's done that's wrong. But I do regret having said that."

In a day of high-minded discussion of constitutional issues, the main headlines and social media buzz were about the Barron/baron moment. Gaetz hadn't worn a WWE belt, but he had managed to win a round.

That evening, on Martha MacCallum's show on Fox, she quizzed him about his line of questioning. "You didn't try to dismantle their argument that the president abused his power. Why not?" she asked.

He said: "Because I only had five minutes, Martha."

CHAPTER FORTY

"I Don't Hate Anybody"

December 5, Washington

By 8 a.m. the next day, Trump was giving the law professors and the Democrats failing marks. "The Do Nothing Democrats had a historically bad day yesterday in the House," he tweeted. "But nothing matters to them, they have gone crazy. Therefore I say, if you are going to impeach me, do it now, fast, so we can have a fair trial in the Senate, and so that our Country can get back to business. We will have Schiff, the Bidens, Pelosi and many more testify, and will reveal, for the first time, how corrupt our system really is. I was elected to 'Clean the Swamp,' and that's what I am doing!"

An hour later, Pelosi announced that Trump would get his wish of fast action. She was taking the next step, asking for a drafting of the charges. In a formal speech in the Capitol, standing before a backdrop of American flags, Pelosi sought to place a possible Trump impeachment in its historical context, starting with 1776 and a new country's Declaration of Independence from an oppressive monarch, and ending with the law professors' testimony. "

Pelosi said the hearings over the past few weeks had established a clear record: Trump had abused his power for personal political benefit. "The facts are uncontested," she said. "Sadly, but with confidence and humility, with allegiance to our founders and a heart full of love for America, today I am asking our chairmen to proceed with articles of impeachment."

At 11 a.m., at her weekly press briefing, Pelosi was fielding one question after another about her announcement. No, she would not rule out evidence from the Mueller report as a basis for an impeachment article. It was too soon to decide that. Yes, impeachment was the right choice. The hearings had shown Trump to be a "rogue president." If the House didn't act, she said, the message to future presidents would be "you can do whatever you want."

She had left the podium and was nearly out of sight when James Rosen, a reporter for the Sinclair Broadcast Group, shouted a question: "Do you hate the president, Madam Speaker?"

Pelosi stopped cold. She had left many rooms with reporters still asking questions, their voices trailing her.

Not this time. Not with that word—hate—hanging in the air. Rosen was throwing it into the mix, like a stick of dynamite. Pelosi turned, striding toward Rosen, her right arm fully extended, her finger pointing, her face tightening. The roomful of cameras and recorders clicked and whirred, capturing her fury.

"I don't hate anybody. I was raised in a Catholic house. We don't hate anyone, not anybody in the world. So don't—don't you accuse me—"

"I did not accuse you," he said.

"You did. You did."

"I asked a question," Rosen said.

There was already tension between Pelosi and Rosen, a longtime Fox correspondent before he joined Sinclair, a rival media giant with 191 stations and a conservative bent. Pelosi had in the past dismissed Rosen as "Mr. Republican Talking Points."

As Pelosi confronted him, Rosen stood his ground. This wasn't his description, he told her. He was repeating the sentiment of Doug Collins. "Collins suggested yesterday that the Democrats" are pursuing impeachment, Rosen said, "simply because they don't like the guy."

"I have nothing to do with that," Pelosi said.

"I think it's an important point," Rosen said.

Pelosi wasn't reacting to Collins's "don't like the guy." She was reacting to "hate." That was Rosen's characterization, Rosen's word choice. If Pelosi was offended by the word on religious grounds, she also understood its powerful context in American history. Hate was a weapon that had been used against minorities, against women, against immigrants—against any "other." Hate had started wars, and it had torn America in two in the Civil War. It was not an accident that "hate crimes" carried extra penalties. Now hate was rising as a staple of American politics. If someone supports the other party, or a different policy or candidate, they "hate America."

Fox host Tucker Carlson had said a few days before that Vladimir Putin "does not hate America as much as many of these people do," singling out NBC journalist Chuck Todd "and the rest of the dummies." A week earlier, Cheryl Chumley, online opinion editor for the conservative-leaning *Washington Times*, said the list of people who "hate" Trump included Schiff, Maxine Waters of California and the Squad. A few days before that, Jeff Duncan, Republican of South Carolina, sent out a fundraising appeal saying that Democrats "hate us for supporting President Trump."

Pelosi was used to sucker-punch questions at her press conferences, like when a far-right news outlet used to send interns to read cue cards with pre-written questions loaded with horror-film language about abortions. But this one had ignited something inside her. She marched back to the microphones. Pulling up the sleeve of her white blazer, she revealed a bracelet made from bullet casings, the work of a Miami artist moved by the shooting deaths of two small children.

"Let me say this," she said, her tempo quickening. "I think this president is a coward when it comes to helping our—our kids who are afraid of gun violence. I think he is cruel when he doesn't deal with helping our 'dreamers,' of which we are very proud. I think he's in denial about the climate crisis."

She made a motion with her hand, as if sweeping all that away. "However, that's about the election," she said. "Take it up in the election." Impeachment, she went on, "is about the Constitution of the United States and the facts that lead to the president's violation of his oath of office."

Pelosi had been raised in a devoutly Catholic home in Baltimore, where her mother, Annunciata D'Alesandro, had wanted her to become a nun. Her brother Tommy had been groomed to be mayor, she told people, and she was "raised to be holy."

Now looking directly at Rosen again, she said: "I resent your using the word 'hate' in a sentence that addresses me. I don't hate anyone. I was raised in a way that is a heart full of love and always pray for the president. And I still pray for the president. I pray for the president all the time."

She concluded with icy sharpness, "So don't mess with me when it comes to words like that."

After she left, Dana Milbank, a longtime *Washington Post* columnist, heard the reporters exhale in the silence. Milbank and Rosen had chatted earlier. Rosen had been saying that he didn't like the assignment his editors had given him that morning. He had come to the press conference, he told Milbank, to make his own news.

He certainly had, and Milbank was startled by how it played out. Pelosi had been the very definition of deliberate in her public statements that morning. Her reaction to the "hate" question was anything but calm. It was raw, he thought. Powerful. Milbank, one of *The Post*'s most widely read political columnists and a frequent critic of Trump, said he had once doubted that Pelosi was the right leader for Democrats in the time of Trump. He thought she might be too old, too out of step with a caucus defined by its discontent. Many of the new Democratic members were restless, impatient, determined to break with the past. How could Pelosi hope to keep her charges in line?

Now Milbank could see that Pelosi had adapted herself to the moment. Her unique blend of bewilderment, sorrow and scorn got under Trump's skin, infuriating him, provoking him, needling him. She met his mockery with a serene sarcasm. "This is a strain of cat that I don't have the medical credentials to analyze nor the religious credentials to judge," she told David Remnick, editor of the *New Yorker*, in late September, discussing her decision to move forward with an impeachment inquiry centered on the Ukraine affair.

After Pelosi left the room, it took Trump just moments to tweet, portraying Pelosi's angry response to Rosen as proof that she had lost it. "Nancy Pelosi just had a nervous fit," he wrote, adding that she "hates" his judicial appointments and other accomplishments. "She says she 'prays for the President.' I don't believe her, not even close."

Minutes later, Kevin McCarthy sent out a tweet that, like Trump's, echoed Rosen's word choice. "Speaker Pelosi and the Democrats are clearly . . . blinded by their hate for the President."

By evening, Trump was on to other matters. He retweeted an announcement from McConnell's team that McConnell's memoir, "The Long Game," was now available in a new paperback edition, with a foreword written by Trump.

"Get your copy today!" the tweet read.

With impeachment in the House marching toward its inevitable outcome, good relations with the Senate majority leader were now more important than ever.

CHAPTER FORTY-ONE

The Weight of History

December 10 to 12, Washington

Elissa Slotkin needed a few moments of peace.

In her first term as one of Michigan's members of Congress, she had found sustained time to think in short supply. Media appearances. Votes on the floor. Fundraising. Calls with constituents. It never stopped. December was an endless string of holiday parties that had started to blur together like a long march of forced merriment.

Tonight, December 10, had brought her to the National Archives on a rainy Tuesday evening for a holiday celebration with the Problem Solvers Caucus, a bipartisan group of congressional moderates. She made merry for a while, but impeachment was weighing on her. It seemed to be weighing down all of Washington, and much of the country.

She slipped away, into the great building's darkened halls. Now she was alone, after hours, strolling amid the yellowed parchment of America's foundational documents. The scrawls of Washington, Jefferson, Madison. Impassioned words from 18th-century radicals who had overthrown a tyrant. The weight of history bearing down on her. As a former intelligence officer, she had been trained to be careful, rational, analytical. Now she was embroiled in a fight she had tried so hard to avoid. Had she made the right call in September when she signed on to that op-ed? Was impeachment now worth it? Was she up to it?

As she walked silently through the exhibits, she found comfort in the documents. In the great vaulted room where the Constitution is on display, she lingered over Article One, which gave Congress its power. She had a huge decision to make. The House Judiciary Committee was marking up the articles of impeachment. Next week, the full House was likely to vote.

She needed to think, to read, to analyze, to decide. She needed to go to Michigan, to the place where she could think best. She needed to go home.

At the same time Slotkin was balancing her risks and responsibilities among the wisdom of the Founding Fathers, Trump was hosting a rowdy rally in Hershey, Pennsylvania, winding up the crowd about "the impeachment crap."

"Any Democrat that votes for this sham will be voting to sacrifice their House majority, their dignity, and their career. Okay?" he said. "You know, we're dealing with some very bad people. We're dealing with people that don't respect you."

Trump was electrifying the crowd, his people, the way he always did. He railed on Hillary Clinton and the FBI and wind power. It was his usual set of grievances, but this time with its edges sharpened by the grinding wheel of impeachment. "We have to vote these crazy people the hell out of office," Trump said. "And in 2020 I'm going to work like hell that we take over the House. We have to take over the House. We have to. Right?"

Mitch McConnell squinted into the camera lens, eyes blinking, serious. He was in a Fox studio in Washington, about to chat with Hannity on his set in New York, a friendly conversation between Trump's biggest on-air cheerleader and Trump's most powerful ally in Congress. No smile came to the Senate majority leader's face, not even when Hannity introduced him by displaying the cover of "The Long Game," a new edition of McConnell's memoir, with a bright-red sticker saying "new foreword by President Donald J. Trump." This was the kind of mass exposure that authors dream of. For a conservative author, Hannity's show was the mountaintop.

Then came Hannity's first question: What would a Senate impeachment trial look like?

That question was no longer a theoretical one. All day at the Capitol on this Thursday, December 12, the House Judiciary Committee had been arguing over the two proposed articles of impeachment. One accused Trump of abuse of power. The other charged him with obstruction of Congress. Hours of rhetoric had changed no one's position. Twenty-three Democrats poised to impeach. Seventeen Republicans adamant in opposition. A vote loomed before day's end, if chairman Nadler could manage to bring the rancorous debate to a close.

At the White House, the president was setting a new one-day record with 123 tweets, 87 between 7 a.m. and 10 a.m., when the committee was set to resume deliberations it had begun the night before. At 7:22 a.m., he had paused to criticize 16-year-old climate activist Greta Thunberg's selection the day before as *Time*'s Person of the Year: "So ridiculous. Greta must work on her Anger Management problem, then go to a good old fashioned movie with a friend! Chill Greta, Chill!"

In early afternoon, Trump posted a soundbite of Jordan from the hearing room an hour earlier, railing against the abuse of power article: "The elected president sets the policy for unelected bureaucrats. Not the other way around."

Now it was past 9 p.m., the start of Hannity's show, and the committee was still in session, marking up the articles for a vote before sending them to the full House. McConnell, wearing a gray pin-striped suit, told Hannity that the articles under consideration looked like "pretty weak stuff." As McConnell described the process, he sounded almost professorial. "We will listen to the opening arguments by the House prosecutors. We will listen to the president's lawyers respond. And then we'll have to make a decision about the way forward," he said.

Then McConnell made something crystal clear about where he stood. "Everything I do during this I'm coordinating with the White House Counsel," he said. "There will be no difference between the president's position and our position as to how to handle this to the extent that we can."

That caveat—"to the extent that we can"—meant he didn't have the kind of "ball control" that he typically enjoyed with bills from the House. "If I don't like it, we don't take it up," he said. He wasn't exaggerating. There were nearly 400 pieces of legislation passed by Pelosi's House on his desk, awaiting action.

On impeachment, though, the Constitution gave him no leeway, he told Hannity. The Senate had to hold a trial and conduct no other business until it was over. But the impeachment clause was silent on how the trial should proceed. McConnell had almost full control over the rules and the details, as long as he had the votes.

The issue of witnesses had bubbled to the surface once again. Democrats were urging the Senate to hear the testimony of several administration officials whom Trump had blocked from testifying in the House hearings, including Mulvaney. Trump seemed to be on the fence. Part of him hungered for a full-blown, scorched-earth trial, with Republicans calling Joe Biden, Hunter Biden, Schiff and even Pelosi as witnesses. Part of him was listening to more cautious voices, like McConnell's. They were counseling a fast trial, with no witnesses. If the Republicans stayed onside, the outcome was certain. Trump would be acquitted. McConnell's view: Why take the risk that some witness might say something that would complicate Trump's defense?

He had made that very case earlier in the day at the White House, when he met with Cipollone and Ueland. McConnell had been meeting regularly with Trump's lawyers and staff in recent weeks, getting ready, talking over strategy.

Driving his point home to Hannity again, McConnell continued: "We'll be working through this process . . . in total coordination with the White House Counsel's Office" and the lawyers who will be representing the president in the Senate trial, he said. "The president's counsel may or may not decide they want to have witnesses. The case is so darn weak coming over from the House. We all know how it's going to end. There is no chance the president is going to be removed from office."

"Total coordination" wasn't a phrase that played well with some members of his caucus. They thought McConnell had gone too far. One close McConnell ally, a senior Republican senator, said later that some "members thought there could have been a better choice of words. You could easily say, 'It's natural for the Republicans to work with a president of your own party.' "

Republicans were trying to make the case that the House inquiry had been unfair and partisan. Now McConnell's comment made it seem as if Senate Republicans were just as partisan and unfair. Total coordination sounded like the president was running his own trial. Some senators thought it was a rare misstep from a leader whose caucus was solidly behind him and considered him one of the great legislative chess players of all time.

McConnell and Trump couldn't be much different, the taciturn Kentucky process nerd and the volcanic New York developer and reality TV star. Before the impeachment inquiry, McConnell's staff wasn't sure whether he had ever tweeted. Republican senator Lamar Alexander, a McConnell ally from Tennessee, once summed up their differences: "The president is a surprise every minute. Mitch is a surprise about once every century."

Yet McConnell had become a close adviser to Trump, balancing the president's unpredictability and his party's thin Senate majority. The 53 Republicans included several who could stray from the Trump position, depending on the issue. When Trump was angered by the few who publicly said they were troubled by his behavior toward Ukraine, McConnell encouraged him to engage with those members to win their confidence, rather than striking back. He was a brake on Trump's impulsiveness.

As a measure of how far their relationship had come, McConnell had not mentioned Trump in the 2016 hardcover version of his autobiography. Now, in the paperback, Trump's name was on the cover, sharing McConnell's spotlight.

That construction was disturbing to Senator Lisa Murkowski, Republican of Alaska. Famously centrist and willing to buck her party, Murkowski was on everyone's list of Republican senators whose impeachment vote could not be taken for granted. The Democrats also viewed Susan Collins of Maine, Romney and Alexander as potential cracks in Trump's firewall. The Democrats had no hopes of reaching 67, the number required to oust Trump. But if the four moderate Republicans could be persuaded to vote for Trump's removal, the Democrats thought, maybe that would inspire other Republicans who were privately appalled by Trump's conduct. At the very least, the Democrats would avoid a totally partisan outcome.

To Murkowski, senators had a constitutional duty to conduct a fair trial, and that meant not being in "total coordination" with the defendant. She thought McConnell's comments confused the process and were a setback for the Republicans. But with all eyes on her and her fellow moderates, she kept her concerns mainly to herself.

Late in the evening, at 11:15 p.m., a weary-looking Nadler abruptly suspended debate on the articles. He had consulted with Pelosi, and she did not want such a serious vote to be taken so late at night. She didn't want to give Republicans the chance to say that the impeachment happened "in the middle of the night."

"I want the members on both sides of the aisle to think about what has happened over these last two days, and to search their consciences before we cast our final votes," Nadler said. He announced that the committee would recess until 10 a.m. the next day. Republicans jeered loudly. The next day was Friday, and many members had already booked flights and trains back to their home districts, where they wanted to spend the weekend making their case on impeachment to constituents.

Nadler smacked his gavel, hard. The hearing was adjourned.

Doug Collins looked like someone had just slapped him.

"Mr. Chairman, there was no consulting of the ranking member on your schedule for tomorrow, in which you've just blown up schedules for everyone? You chose not to consult the ranking member on a schedule issue of this magnitude?"

Collins was steamed up. So were others.

"So typical," one shouted.

"This is the kangaroo court that we're talking about," Collins said.

"Stalinesque," said Louie Gohmert.

"Unbelievable," said another.

"This is the most ludicrous thing I have seen in my entire life!" Collins said. "To not even consult the ranking member, to not even give us a heads up! . . . This is why people don't like us, this crap!"

Nadler had left the room. The outcome wasn't in doubt. The Judiciary Committee was heading toward approving both articles, with neither party budging. Then impeachment would go to the full House, all 435 members. Most already knew how they were going to vote. But not everyone. In the moderate center, Elissa Slotkin and others were wrestling with the central question: Had the House hearings produced enough evidence to justify impeachment?

On the Republican side, Will Hurd had said no. On the Democratic side, Slotkin had given herself the weekend in Michigan to make up her mind.

CHAPTER FORTY-TWO

"Please Let Her Speak"

December 13 to 16, Washington, New York and Michigan

Before Elissa Slotkin could go home, she had to stop in New York. If she wanted to talk to voters back home in Michigan, there were few more direct ways to do it than by appearing on Fox News. Democratic research showed that independents tended to watch Fox more than other outlets. Hannity, Lou Dobbs, Tucker Carlson and the other fire-breathers appealed to the hardcore Trump crowd. But independents tuned in to see more moderate voices—Bret Baier, Chris Wallace, Shannon Bream. Democrats and the 327 messaging group knew that making their case to the center meant sending out moderates to appear on Fox. So there was Slotkin at 10:30 a.m., in a blue blazer, appearing on the "America's Newsroom" show with Bill Hemmer.

About 20 minutes earlier, the House Judiciary Committee had voted, along straight party lines, to send the two articles of impeachment against Trump to the full House. Slotkin was on the Homeland Security Committee, not Judiciary, so she had watched the historic moment like everyone else. TV networks carried the proceedings live without interruption. The debate on social media was raging. Tens of thousands of Trump supporters had convened in private Facebook groups to watch the proceedings and provide running commentary on what they saw as a sham perpetrated by "scum" Democrats who "should be arrested."

On Fox, Hemmer was posing the questions everyone in Washington was pondering, including Slotkin. "Why are you still, at least publicly, up in the air about how you're going to vote?" Hemmer asked.

"Well, this is probably going to be one of the most serious things I ever vote on," she said. "So, I'm going to take it seriously. I'm going to do what I was trained to do as a CIA officer, which is not to listen to the news, you know, and people yelling and screaming, my colleagues kind of going back and forth. What I'm going to do is take the weekend. I'm going to put the full body of information together, and I'm going to make an objective decision."

Hemmer next asked the tough question. Pointing out that she had won her seat in a Trump district, Hemmer said: "If you vote yes, with your other Democratic colleagues, is your House seat lost in 2020?"

Possibly so, she said. Then, shaking her head slightly and reminding Hemmer of her three tours in Iraq during her years as a CIA analyst, she said: "Sometimes you have to make calls that aren't based on a poll, or on some political consultant. And if this is the end of my political career, at least I'm doing what I think is right, and I'm basing my decisions on integrity. That is the most I can do."

Hemmer leaned in and said, "I'm trying to read your mind, and that last answer sounded like a no," a vote against impeachment. "Is that where you are?"

Slotkin didn't budge. "I literally have not made up my mind."

As they were talking, Nadler stepped to the microphones on Capitol Hill, and Hemmer broke off the conversation to go live to the press conference.

Slotkin headed to the airport, for a trip that would take her away from the noise and the clatter and the relentless news cycle, to a place where she had always done her best thinking.

The Slotkin family farmhouse was set among fields and lakes an hour's drive northwest of Detroit, in Holly, Michigan. All her early childhood memories were forged here, before her parents divorced. The farm, with its red barn and tall tan silo, had been in the family since the early 1950s. It was home.

She lived here with her husband, Dave Moore, a retired U.S. Army colonel who had flown Apache helicopters in the first Gulf War. They had met in Iraq and married at the farm. Now they were living here while Slotkin commuted to her job in Washington.

Her great-grandfather had immigrated to the United States from modern-day Belarus and started off working in a slaughterhouse. He ultimately achieved a prosperous American Dream, founding a meat business that engineered a little piece of Americana: the Ball Park Frank.

She settled down to ponder her choice, spreading papers on an old wooden desk that had once been her great-grandfather's and, before that, had belonged to Woodrow Wilson's secretary of war. Windows looked out onto barren trees and the frigid calm of the Michigan countryside; winter was already here, no matter what the calendar said. She had a lot to read. A bit from the framers: the Federalist Papers. A bit of recent history: the Nixon and Clinton impeachment articles. A bit from now: a dense volume of House procedures and precedents. And, most important, the House Intelligence Committee's 298-page report documenting the case against Donald John Trump.

This was how she worked. Methodically. Reports did not daunt her. Neither did contentious debate. She had spent 18 months in the George W. Bush White House, briefing him on threats and traveling with him overseas as a member of the NSC staff. She had acquired a reputation for being direct, avoiding politics and sticking to the facts. She had done the same for Barack Obama, then transferred to the Pentagon, where she rose to become a top policy maker on some of the nation's thorniest relationships, including Russia.

Now she found herself back home in Holly, making a brutally difficult risk assessment. Her decision could very well determine whether she would have a career in politics or return quickly to private life. At the age of 43, she would prefer not to be shoved to the sidelines.

It also seemed to Slotkin that she was voting on the future role of government. She had been watching the assault on a parade of national security officials who were serving the country, regardless of party. Yovanovitch. Vindman. Hill. Taylor. Kent. Holmes.

Their life was her life. It was her husband's life. It was an ethos shared by her friends, especially the ones who had sworn an oath in the military. Slotkin worried that the assault she was witnessing could turn the government from a world-class source of nonpartisan expertise and counsel into a political lever to be pulled by the president.

She kept thinking, making notes. She went to bed Saturday night, with more reading left to do.

On Sunday, December 15, three days after McConnell announced his "total coordination" with White House lawyers, Senate minority leader Chuck Schumer fired his first salvo in response.

Anticipating a House vote to impeach Trump in the next few days, the New York Democrat sent a letter to McConnell, which he released publicly at the same time. The letter proposed rules for Trump's trial in the

Senate, which Schumer said must "pass the fairness test with the American people."

Schumer knew he had little influence. McConnell had the majority he needed to set rules as he saw fit. Schumer thought it made sense for McConnell to consult with the Democratic side, at least for the appearance of bipartisanship, but McConnell had all the cards, and he had made clear on Hannity's show that he was going to play them for Trump. Schumer's letter was designed to get the Democrats' position out early, and perhaps put some pressure on McConnell.

For Schumer, the coming battle was all about witnesses. The House had heard testimony from 17, in the SCIF and in public, but the White House had blocked testimony from all top White House aides. The House Republicans had repeatedly disparaged most of the 17 witnesses, saying they had no direct knowledge of Trump's actions or his thinking. Well, said the Democrats, we can remedy that. Let's hear from the people who did.

Schumer was proposing subpoenas for four top officials: Mulvaney; Mulvaney's senior adviser, Robert Blair; Bolton; and Michael Duffey, from OMB. The White House had told all four not to appear for House depositions, saying their communications with Trump were protected by executive privilege.

The rules Schumer was proposing were not new, he said. They mirrored those used at the Clinton impeachment trial in 1999. He hoped to reach an agreement with McConnell early. "The issue of witnesses and documents, which are the most important issues facing us, should be decided before we move forward with any part of the trial," Schumer wrote.

McConnell wanted no witnesses at all.

As Sunday afternoon turned to evening in Slotkin's farmhouse, her choice crystallized. Over and over, the framers had warned against the danger of America's leaders soliciting foreign interference in the country's internal affairs. Hadn't this president admitted to doing exactly that? He wanted to be reelected, and he had asked for Ukraine's help to take out a political rival. In the end, it really wasn't that complicated. She stopped reading and started writing. By midnight, she had completed an op-ed, this one for the *Detroit Free Press*, and clicked send on her computer.

She said she would be voting yes on both articles of impeachment and she explained why. The president had "illegally solicited the help of foreigners to influence the American political process." He had obstructed

Congress's inquiry when he "broke with a hundred years of tradition by ignoring the subpoenas."

She concluded: "Over the past few months, I've been told more times than I can count that the vote I'll be casting this week will mark the end of my short political career. That may be. But in the national security world that I come from, we are trained to make hard calls on things, even if they are unpopular, if we believe the security of the country is at stake. There are some decisions in life that have to be made based on what you know in your bones is right. And this is one of those times."

The piece was published online at 7:15 a.m.

Slotkin woke early that Monday morning, December 16, and immediately braced herself. It was going to be a big day.

In a couple of hours, she would face her constituents in a town hall meeting and explain her choice. For weeks, they had been letting her know what *they* thought. More than 1,500 calls to her office, so many that she had to have a third phone line installed. The letter and email count surpassed 6,500.

There had been plenty of messages on both sides. But when tallied up, the weight of opinion in Michigan's 8th Congressional District was clear. The majority did not want her to impeach Trump.

The choice to hold a town hall to explain her vote had been a contentious one within her small staff. Some, recognizing the potential for combustion, urged her not to do it. But she remembered how her predecessor had dodged a reckoning with his voters when he took a tough vote on health care. She had criticized him for it. It would be hypocrisy for her to do the same.

She and her husband set off early, stopping for gas along the way. "Holy crap," he said after a visit to the station's convenience store. The television inside had been tuned to Fox News, where the hosts were counting down the minutes until a major political event: Slotkin's town hall.

When they pulled up outside the student center at Rochester's Oakland University, half an hour's drive from Holly, in Detroit's northern suburbs, the rival camps were already staking out their turf, conferring in quiet corners of the building's chic, gas fireplace–warmed lobby and beneath the cheerfully lit Christmas tree. The homemade signs made the divisions stark.

"Thank you Rep Slotkin for defending the Constitution"

"The Do Nothing Democrats Only Hate and Hurt America"

It was winter break, so the students weren't there. Classrooms were deserted, parking lots were empty. But the student center was full of life. Shortly after ten, less than an hour before start time, the chants began.

"Who's the greatest president in history?" came the call from a man wielding an "Impeach Slotkin" sign. "Trump! Trump! Trump!" was the shouted response from dozens of others outfitted in MAGA hats, shirts and flags in shades of red and camo.

As the minutes until Slotkin's appearance ticked down, an aide circulated among the congresswoman's allies. She was worried the event could get out of hand. If tempers flared, could she count on them to try to de-escalate? "I need you to help keep the peace," she told Bruce Fealk, a retired court reporter who had come to show support for Slotkin with his handmade "Country over Party" placard. He told her he would do what he could.

Just before 11 a.m., 400 people squeezed into a ballroom where 400 chairs had been set out. More filed in and stood at the back. A dozen cameras were trained on the dais, including one from Fox News.

Nearly everyone knew that Slotkin had decided to vote for impeachment. Her *Free Press* op-ed was making the rounds on social media. Other Democratic moderates who had been on the fence were coming down the same way. Elaine Luria of Virginia had declared her support a few days earlier. As Monday morning wore on, Spanberger joined in. So did Ben McAdams of Utah and Joe Cunningham of South Carolina. Jeff Van Drew of New Jersey had announced that he was going in the opposite direction; he planned to switch to the Republican Party to support Trump. As the crowd was filling up the Rochester auditorium, Trump retweeted Ted Cruz: "Hmm. Not sure, when Pelosi began this partisan show trial, that she envisioned it being so bad that it would drive House Dems—from New Jersey, no less—to switch parties."

Slotkin was aware how much depended on her performance. If she faltered under the barrage she knew was coming, even for a moment, the clip would replay endlessly on Fox and other conservative news sites. The headlines and cable chyrons would write themselves: "Democrat defies her district on impeachment, gets pummeled by angry voters."

The event began with a plea. A university official asked everyone to show their disagreements respectfully and, above all, to listen to one another. Then came an honor guard, trooping the colors. Then came the singing of the national anthem. Everyone stood quietly and listened, hand on heart, hat in hand. Slotkin was reassured to have her husband by her side.

Then, as Slotkin was introduced, the boos began: a deep, guttural chorus, along with hurled insults as the congresswoman bounded to the stage.

"Traitor!" a man in a knit cap shouted.

"Deep state!" yelled another.

"Slotkin is a spy!" bellowed a third.

But there was applause, too, and a standing ovation. Smiles and thumbs-up. Before she had said a word, half the room was cheering. Half was jeering. The country in microcosm.

"Please let her speak," said the university official.

"I am glad to see so much enthusiasm for civic engagement," Slotkin deadpanned.

The air crackled with hostility, building with each minute, along with a sense that this chance for citizens to hear from their congresswoman—and vice versa—was one push, one punch, one nasty glance from devolving into a melee.

"I will be voting yes," Slotkin declared, prompting another eruption from both sides. "I can hear that this is a very controversial decision—and I knew that. All I can ask from the people who are listening is that, while we may not agree, I hope you believe me when I tell you that I made this decision out of principle."

Many appeared to be trying to hear their congresswoman out. Up front, senior citizens in red MAGA hats cupped their hands to their ears to try to catch Slotkin's words. That wasn't easy: Not everyone had come to listen. From the back corner, about a dozen Trump supporters heckled her continuously. They kept it up as she talked about impeachment, and as she moved on to other subjects, like veterans, drug prices and trade deals. When she told the story of her mother's death from ovarian cancer, and how that had inspired her to get into politics, they paused for a moment, then quickly resumed shouting.

Some Slotkin supporters in the audience started shouting back. They screamed in each other's faces and ripped signs from each other's hands. Through much of the next hour, Slotkin could barely hear her own voice over the din. Many in the audience struggled to hear her, too. But she kept talking and didn't stumble. There would be no viral clip for Trump's supporters to giddily share.

"I'm just going to keep on rolling, folks," she declared flatly amid the jeers.

Her rationale for supporting Trump's ouster came down to this: The president's behavior was fundamentally different than any she had seen during her years serving commanders in chief of both parties. It was an invitation to adversaries to meddle in American elections. It required a response, or the president would believe he could act against American interests with impunity.

She said her vote was unlikely to end Trump's tenure in office, but it could well end hers. She was prepared to live with that. Supporters roared and detractors hooted. "I will stick to that regardless of what it does to me politically," she said, "because this is bigger than politics."

Most media coverage of the raucous meeting generally stressed that both sides had made their points passionately. The *New York Times* headline was typical: "Slotkin, Backing Impeachment, Draws Instant Protests, and Applause." As Slotkin had anticipated, the far right portrayed it as a smack-down. The *Breitbart* headline was "Revolt in Michigan: Town Hall Turns into Mutiny as Democrat Congresswoman Announces Impeachment Support."

Leaving the campus, Slotkin felt liberated. She had explained her decision as well as she could. What her constituents did with it was up to them.

Slotkin needed to hurry back to Washington. She had an important vote to cast. But first, her husband needed a new coat. On the way to the airport, they bought one at a sporting goods store. It was mid-December, and there was a long winter ahead.

CHAPTER FORTY-THREE

"I Am Not an Impartial Juror"

December 17, Washington

Donald Trump could see impeachment barreling down the train tracks. Nancy Pelosi had the votes in the House. Sure, the Senate would never vote to convict him. But this was about history, too. Pelosi was about to hang a scarlet "I" around his neck. He was going to be just the third president ever impeached, probably tomorrow. That infuriated him. Doubly galling was that "Nervous Nancy," the woman who wouldn't get out of his way, was the one doing it. Aides could see his fury building.

He couldn't stop the inevitable. But he sure could make his thoughts known. This time, Twitter wouldn't do. From his earliest tweeting days, Trump had fancied himself the "Ernest Hemingway of 140 characters." For daily communication with the base, that was plenty, especially after Twitter expanded to 280 characters. What he wanted to say now was going to take more space. He wanted to communicate his grievances about impeachment to the world, but he would do so in a letter to Pelosi, making it a deeply personal and public rebuke of a woman he had come to detest, who was trying to bring him down. He was relishing the opportunity.

He sat in the Oval Office with policy adviser Stephen Miller, crafter of many of his public remarks, and Ueland, working up a draft over the course of a week. They also had help from Michael Williams, an adviser to Mulvaney. They kept their sessions secret from White House lawyers, including Cipollone, who was going to be Trump's lead counsel in the Senate trial. Trump did not want the lawyers reviewing the letter until it was done. He didn't want them dialing back the rhetoric.

By the morning of December 17, they had it: a six-page masterpiece of invective, reflecting his state of mind, a document for historians and scholars to study in the future. The lawyers, once they had their look, warned him away from certain sections. Trump liked his version.

Dear Madam Speaker:

I write to express my strongest and most powerful protest against the partisan impeachment crusade being pursued by the Democrats in the House of Representatives. This impeachment represents an unprecedented and unconstitutional abuse of power by Democrat Lawmakers, unequaled in nearly two and a half centuries of American legislative history.

Right off, he was turning the tables. The first article of impeachment was accusing him of an abuse of power. Now his letter was saying, no, the Democrats were the abusers.

The Articles of Impeachment introduced by the House Judiciary Committee are not recognizable under any standard of Constitutional theory, interpretation, or jurisprudence. They include no crimes, no misdemeanors, and no offenses whatsoever.

Lawyerly. Definitive. No crimes, no recognizable Constitutional standard. His legal team could have written that part. The next sentence was pure Trump, a tweet, same rhythm, same form:

You have cheapened the importance of the very ugly word, impeachment!

Cheapened. Ugly. Words that didn't often appear in a presidential document. Good. Now it was time to get personal, to make this about Pelosi. She had made this happen. She needed to feel the knife edge of his ire.

By proceeding with your invalid impeachment, you are violating your oaths of office, you are breaking your allegiance to the Constitution, and you are declaring open war on American Democracy. You dare to invoke the Founding Fathers in pursuit of this election-nullification scheme—yet your spiteful actions display unfettered contempt for America's founding and your egregious conduct threatens to destroy that which our Founders pledged their very lives to build.

He wasn't going to let anything go. He had heard Pelosi's press conference where she had said, invoking her Catholic faith: "I don't hate anyone."

> *Even worse than offending the Founding Fathers, you are offending Americans of faith by continually saying "I pray for the President," when you know this statement is not true, unless it is meant in a negative sense. It is a terrible thing you are doing, but you will have to live with it, not I!*

The letter flowed on, the adjectives mounting. The impeachment process was: invalid, spiteful, egregious, meritless, disingenuous, baseless, preposterous, dangerous, fake, fantasy and illegal. All because of the congressional Democrats. They were engaging in the very acts for which he was set to be impeached.

> *You are the ones interfering in America's elections. You are the ones subverting America's Democracy. You are the ones Obstructing Justice. You are the ones bringing pain and suffering to our Republic for your own selfish personal, political, and partisan gain. . . . More due process was afforded to those accused in the Salem Witch Trials.*

That summed it up. From witch hunt, one of his favorite phrases for the Mueller investigation, to witch trial.

> *You do not know, nor do you care, the great damage and hurt you have inflicted upon wonderful and loving members of my family.*

He was nowhere near done with Pelosi.

> *This is nothing more than an illegal, partisan attempted coup that will, based on recent sentiment, badly fail at the voting booth. You are not just after me, as President, you are after the entire Republican Party. But because of this colossal injustice, our party is more united than it has ever been before. History will judge you harshly as you proceed with this impeachment charade. Your legacy will be that of turning the House of Representatives from a revered legislative body into a Star Chamber of partisan persecution.*

The letter was hitting many of his favorite notes, using phrases that had become standard fare in the conservative media universe: "attempted coup" and "Star Chamber" and "election-nullification." Now, nearing its end, the letter summoned a few more.

> *Perhaps most insulting of all is your false display of solemnity. You apparently have so little respect for the American People that you expect them to believe that you are approaching this impeachment somberly, reservedly, and reluctantly. No intelligent person believes what you are saying. Since the moment I won the election, the Democrat Party has been possessed by Impeachment Fever. There is no reticence. This is not a somber affair. You are making a mockery of impeachment and you are scarcely concealing your hatred of me, of the Republican Party, and tens of millions of patriotic Americans. The voters are wise, and they are seeing straight through this empty, hollow, and dangerous game you are playing.*

And for the final paragraph, one last burst of frustration and fury:

> *One hundred years from now, when people look back at this affair, I want them to understand it, and learn from it, so that it can never happen to another President again.*

As Trump was preparing to release his letter Tuesday morning, Pelosi met with her caucus in their usual basement room. Pelosi wore a bright red poppy, a memento of her recent trip to Belgium for services marking the 75th anniversary of the Battle of the Bulge, one of the bloodiest clashes of World War II for American soldiers. She told her members of meeting elderly veterans who took her aside and offered encouragement about impeachment. "Keep on going," they told her. "Get this done."

Debbie Dingell could see Pelosi's mind working. The speaker wanted her members to be unified and motivated about tomorrow's scheduled vote, but she also wanted them to be careful. When the roll call was done and the vote announced, no one was to smile, clap, or cheer in any way. It would be a victory for Democrats over a president who was violating his oath, but it was still a sad day, she told them. "We're just doing our job," she said.

Some moderates had still not announced their positions. But when they emerged, several did. They were with Pelosi. "It is with profound sadness I will vote to impeach President Trump," tweeted Anthony Brindisi of New York, widely seen as a Democrat who might break with his party on impeachment. "President Trump is my President too. I've always said I would work with him to get things done, as I have demonstrated. However, I will always put Country first and stand up for what I believe in when I think he is wrong."

Mikie Sherrill of New Jersey, one of seven signers of the September 23 *Washington Post* op-ed, issued a statement saying that she, too, would vote to impeach Trump. Sherrill cited her experience in the military and as a federal prosecutor in explaining her decision. "After reviewing the testimony and the statements of the President himself, it is clear that he used his office for his own personal gain," Sherrill said.

As votes were lining up against him, Trump was tweeting reasons to be grateful for him. "The Stock Market hit another Record High yesterday, number 133 in less than three years as your all time favorite President, and the Radical Left, Do Nothing Democrats, want to impeach me. Don't worry, I have done nothing wrong. Actually, they have!"

A half-hour later, McConnell rose on the Senate floor to respond to Schumer's demand that McConnell allow witnesses at the trial. McConnell was trying out some of the arguments that his Legal Eagles had developed. But first, he rebuked his Democratic counterpart for releasing the letter publicly. By doing that, he said, Schumer had "decided to short-circuit the customary and collegial process for laying basic groundwork in advance of a potential impeachment trial."

He went after the witness issue with gusto. He said Democrats were trying to force the Senate to repair the House's "slapdash work product" that had produced "the most rushed, least thorough, and most unfair impeachment inquiry in modern history." Under the Constitution, McConnell asserted, the House was supposed to hold an impeachment inquiry, then present its evidence to the Senate.

"We don't create impeachments. We judge them," he said.

If the House thought more witnesses were necessary, he argued, they should have called them. For witnesses blocked by the White House, the remedy was to go to court, not to ask the Senate to take over the case.

"The House chose this road," McConnell said. "It is their duty to investigate. It is their duty to meet the very high bar for undoing a national election." He had hit the "attempted coup" note, just as Trump had in his letter to Pelosi. "If they fail, they fail. It is not the Senate's job to leap into the breach and search desperately for ways to 'get to guilty.' That would hardly be impartial justice."

McConnell also disputed Schumer's argument that his proposed rules were identical to those used in the Clinton impeachment. Both selected facts that suited their positions, and both ignored the reality: A Senate trial of a president had happened only twice in more than 200 years. It was foolish to talk about precedent. Senators for each impeachment, more than a century apart, had generated their own rules to fit the circumstances of their times.

McConnell finished with a call for cooperation. "I look forward to meeting with the Democratic leader very soon and getting our important conversation back on the right foot," he said, sounding almost affable.

Schumer stood. If McConnell had really wanted a collegial and cooperative process, he said, he wouldn't have gone on "Hannity" and said he'd be "taking cues from the White House." The House wasn't asking the Senate to do its work, he shot back. The House committees had turned up strong evidence that Trump had abused his power and obstructed Congress, and they would have turned up even more if the White House hadn't blocked those key witnesses from testifying.

To conduct a real trial and judge the charges fairly, Schumer said, the Senate needed to hear from those witnesses. Why not call them? "What is Leader McConnell afraid of? What is President Trump afraid of? The truth? But the American people want the truth, and that's why we have asked for witnesses and documents, to get at the whole truth and nothing but."

Schumer was pushing hard, having his "conversation" with McConnell now, in public. There was almost nothing Schumer could say that would change McConnell's mind. But there was one possible argument that might cause McConnell some anxiety: if the American public saw a no-witness trial as unfair or obstructionist.

Schumer cited a *Washington Post*/ABC News poll, just out that morning, showing that 71 percent of Americans, including 64 percent of Republicans, believed the president should allow his top aides to testify in a Senate trial. The same poll showed that 49 percent of Americans said Trump should be removed from office, while 46 percent thought he should not. Those numbers had been nearly identical in a *Post*-ABC poll in October.

If the Democrats were going to sell impeachment, or at least keep it from backfiring on them in the next election, they needed to keep public sentiment on their side. That was one audience Schumer was trying to reach.

Another was right there in the Senate chamber, the four moderate Republican senators who did not walk in lockstep with McConnell or Trump. Romney had staked out a rare piece of territory that was pro-Republican but not always pro-Trump. Collins and Murkowski had both split from Trump on several issues. Alexander was not running for reelection. None was a firebrand, but they were the best hope for voting for witnesses. One or two or three might even be votes for impeachment.

Securing all four votes for calling witnesses would give Schumer 51, the barest majority, and force McConnell's hand. Winning the battle on witnesses might go a long way toward tilting public opinion more strongly in the Democrats' favor and give them a talking point in the 2020 election. Of course, the Republicans knew that, too, and would be pressing the moderate senators not to cross over to the Democrats' side.

Schumer was making his case, aiming at both audiences, inside and outside the chamber. The American people, he said, understand that "a trial without witnesses is not a trial." They understand that "a trial without relevant documents is not a fair trial." They understand that "if you are trying to conceal evidence and block testimony, it's probably not because that evidence is going to help your case, it's because you're trying to cover something up."

McConnell was having no trouble keeping his side in line. No need to make any decisions yet, he was saying. Let the House vote. McConnell had plenty of patience. He could take Schumer's heat.

A few hours later, McConnell and Senate Republicans met the press to talk about how they viewed their 2019 accomplishments. They talked about defense spending, veterans' health, the unemployment rate. But as soon as they opened it up for questions, reporters wanted to know about only one topic: impeachment.

A reporter asked McConnell to address concerns, based on what he had told Hannity, that he might not be "impartial," as required by the oath he and the other senators would soon have to take.

"I am not an impartial juror," McConnell said. "This is a political process. There is not anything judicial about it. Impeachment is a political decision. The House made a partisan political decision to impeach. I would anticipate we will have a largely partisan outcome in the Senate. I'm not impartial about this at all."

McConnell's blunt statement didn't surprise Democrats as much as it galled them. To them, McConnell's comments were brazen and astonishing. House member Jackie Speier, Democrat of California, said on CNN: "We're going to have to call for a mistrial before it ever gets over to the Senate. . . . I would think Mitch McConnell should recuse himself." There were, of course, no such mechanisms, but her comment reflected the Democrats' exasperation.

Republicans were amused at their indignation. Cruz saw the Democrats "clutching their pearls" and reminded friends that Pelosi and Schiff were already coordinating with Schumer over Senate trial strategy. He could not for the life of him see the difference.

At the White House, Trump's "Dear Madam Speaker" letter was finished and signed. The president had novel plans for how to deliver it. He wasn't going to send a solo copy to Pelosi's office. This was a Trump-sized blockbuster, and it needed an appropriately theatrical release. The White House made copies for every House member and senator. Young White House aides went office to office with the letters, which were packaged with Christmas cards.

Glenn Kessler, of the *Washington Post*'s Fact Checker column, read the letter and saw a compendium of Trump's greatest hits. "It's like a written version of his campaign rallies, replete with false claims we have fact-checked many times before either in individual fact checks or in our database of false or misleading Trump claims," Kessler wrote.

Some Republicans were telling *Washington Post* reporters in background interviews, no names attached, that they thought it was the "normalized crazy" they had come to expect during the Trump era. Trump had his own way of saying things, which people were getting used to even if they didn't always like it. Meadows looked at the letter and thought it would help unify his party. "I think it really was designed to express not only his frustration but the frustration that a lot of Americans are feeling," Meadows said.

On right-wing conservative media, Trump's bare-knuckled letter brought virtual cartwheels of exhilaration. Hannity called it "a powerful, scathing beat down" of Pelosi. Dobbs said it was "beautiful," "terrific," "elegant" and "comprehensive." Talk radio host Hugh Hewitt predicted the letter "will be cited by @POTUS scholars for generations as the defining example of Article II blasting Article I." He said it "will be included in every Con Law casebook in the years ahead."

Media Matters, a liberal group that scrutinized conservative media, wrote: "President Donald Trump sent House Speaker Nancy Pelosi (D-CA) a lie-filled letter attacking his imminent impeachment that some serious journalists described as 'batshit,' 'crazy town' and 'unhinged.' But Trump's allies in the right-wing media, detached from reality, praised the letter as a cogent and historic document worthy of academic study."

The recipient of the letter, Nancy Pelosi, didn't slow down when CNN reporter Manu Raju asked her about it as she walked through the Capitol basement with several caucus members and staff. "I haven't really fully read it," she said. "We've been working. I've seen the essence of it though, and it's really sick."

As the debate raged in Washington, Trump opponents were taking part in more than 600 protests across the country, from Hawaii to Maine. Most of the gatherings were smallish, from a handful of people to a few hundred, but thousands of demonstrators rallied in New York's Times Square.

Tomorrow, the House would finally vote.

CHAPTER FORTY-FOUR

"The President Is Impeached"

December 18, Washington and Battle Creek, Michigan

It was a crisp and cloudless Wednesday in Washington, after days of gloomy winter rain. President Trump was hunkered down in the White House, its windows decorated with red-ribboned wreaths. Trump had nothing on his official schedule except a morning intelligence briefing. The televisions were tuned to the drama at the other end of Pennsylvania Avenue, where the House of Representatives was preparing to vote on his impeachment. The caps lock on the presidential cellphone keypad was also on, and Trump was hard at work, adding to the day's historical record.

At 7:34 a.m., he tweeted: "Can you believe that I will be impeached today by the Radical Left, Do Nothing Democrats, AND I DID NOTHING WRONG! A terrible Thing. Read the Transcripts. This should never happen to another President again. Say a PRAYER!"

On cue, his supporters tweeted and retweeted thousands of times a photo of Trump, with a pair of hands clasped in prayer in front of him, and the message: "I'M PRAYING FOR YOU PRESIDENT TRUMP."

As Trump was firing up his Twitter forces, Nancy Pelosi was getting her hair done, as she did most mornings, at Salon Omer in Georgetown, not far from home. She arrived at the Capitol at 8:45 a.m. and prepped with her staff. Shortly after 9 a.m., she slipped into a seat at the back of the House chamber. She sat by herself in one of the brown leather armchairs, attended by aides passing her papers and notecards. She signed thank-you notes. She sat up straight, watching the House she led come to order.

From her back-row seat, Pelosi could pay attention to every detail. Half the seats were still unoccupied in the grand chamber, where the House has convened since 1857. Huge portraits of George Washington and the Marquis de Lafayette, a Revolutionary War hero and the first foreign dignitary to address Congress, loomed over the room. They flanked the speaker's rostrum where President Franklin Delano Roosevelt spoke on December 7, 1941, hours after Japan's catastrophic attacks on U.S. forces at Pearl Harbor, declaring it "a date which will live in infamy."

A stained-glass bald eagle, illuminated from behind, its wings spread wide in flight, hung in the ceiling, high overhead, with an inscription declaring, "E Pluribus Unum," from many, one. That motto seemed more apt in the aftermath of the Japanese firestorm than on this day, when America's many seemed not a resolutely united one, but an angrily divided two.

The anger appeared in the session's opening tactical maneuver. Biggs addressed Diana DeGette, the Colorado Democrat who had been designated by Pelosi to preside. Biggs said: "Madam Speaker, so we can stop wasting America's time on impeachment, I move that the house do now adjourn."

That little spasm of protest forced a 15-minute vote on his motion. Unsurprisingly, the motion failed 226 to 191. The Republicans could delay the inevitable, but they could not stop the vote. They could, however, score points. Americans would be watching today, including some who had never seen the House in action.

There wasn't much action at the moment. The House often operated with a fraction of the members in the chamber, filling up only for a vote. Today would be different, but not yet. The visitors' gallery, which ringed the chamber from the second floor, was about half full as spectators wandered in and out. People came to see history in the making—only to realize that the making of this history was unfolding at the speed of a clam.

About 20 Republicans sat in their seats, some holding cups of coffee. Across the center aisle, about twice as many Democrats watched as Jim McGovern of Massachusetts spoke first. He invoked Benjamin Franklin and the Constitutional Convention of 1787 and said Trump was acting more like a monarch than a president. Tom Cole, Republican of Oklahoma, replied that Democrats were railroading an innocent man and had "been searching for a reason to impeach President Trump since the day he was elected."

Lawmakers took turns coming to the side-by-side microphones for a minute, two minutes, five minutes—some for as little as 30 seconds. It wasn't so much a debate as a game of verbal ping-pong. The two parties talked past each other, not to each other. No one tried to persuade the other side of anything. Most speakers had a single audience: the television camera pointed at them. They were playing to voters, to their home states, maybe to a video clip for reelection. Party-approved talking points guided both sides.

For the Republicans, impeachment was a charade, a shame, a sham, a total sham, a hoax, a political vendetta, a stain on our Republic, a stain on this Congress, an obsession, a rigged process, flawed, unfair, biased, arbitrary, disgusting, Machiavellian, a circus, motivated by hatred, motivated by bitter rage, based on an intense hatred of Donald Trump, a witch hunt, a coup, wacky, a political weapon, a spectacle, a nightmare, a mockery, a joke, a total joke, illegal, illegitimate, baseless, ridiculous, utterly meaningless, a partisan political stunt, a star chamber, a lasting shame on our House, a debacle, a dangerous precedent, a deep state plot, vindictive, specious, dishonest, Soviet-style, a disastrous political ruse, sinister, a travesty, an embarrassment to our country, an insult to our Constitution, a betrayal of the Constitution, a political drive-by, a slap in the face, raw politics, a Schiff Show, a rush to judgment, a hijacking, a "House of Cards" impeachment, taxpayer-funded oppo research, a display of Constitutional illiteracy, reckless, the fantasy of the radical left wing and radical socialists—and today's vote was "the day the Founding Fathers feared."

Democrats countered with laments and warnings. No one came to Congress to impeach a president. Trump is acting like a monarch or dictator and not a president. His actions were a shakedown. He abused his power. His impeachment was solemn, sad, a duty, heartbreaking, based on indisputable facts. He erodes our decency, degrades our democracy, subverts the Constitution. He is a lawless, amoral president. He cheated. He is promoting a dictatorship (a point made in English and Spanish). He is a clear and present danger. He is engaged in a cover-up. No one is above the law. No president is above the law. He sabotaged national security and obstructed justice. He left us no choice. He's worse than Nixon. Democrats must defend our democracy. Democrats have heavy hearts and feel no joy about impeachment.

Over and over (and over), Republicans argued that trying to oust Trump amounted to spitting on the will of the 63 million Americans who voted for him. One member inflated that to 93 million for good measure. Democrats mainly ignored that argument, except for Hoyer, who shot back that 65 million people had voted for Hillary Clinton. Big applause from the Democrats, a momentary departure from Pelosi's directive: No cheering, be serious.

Pelosi moved among the mostly empty Democratic seats like a queen on a chessboard, protecting and protected by her loyal rooks and bishops. She offered a handshake here, a tap on the shoulder there, sometimes an approving nod or wink. She never stopped fiddling with papers, writing notes with a red pen.

She wore a black sheath that *Washington Post* fashion critic Robin Givhan thought reflected the gravity of the day. Pelosi had allowed herself one flashy adornment: a golden mace brooch, pinned to her dress, below her left shoulder. It depicted an eagle with its wings spread, perched on a pearl mounted on a sheaf of gilded rods. Created by the Washington designer Ann Hand, the brooch was inspired by the mace of the House of Representatives, a symbolic weapon that sits in the House chamber and serves as a symbol of the sergeant at arms's authority.

At the microphones, speakers were citing Ben Franklin, Thomas Jefferson, George Washington, Abraham Lincoln, James Madison, George Mason, Alexander Hamilton, John F. Kennedy, Lyndon B. Johnson, Martin Luther King Jr., Richard Nixon, Bill Clinton and Barack Obama.

Pontius Pilate made an appearance.

"When Jesus was falsely accused of treason, Pontius Pilate gave Jesus the opportunity to face his accusers. During that sham trial, Pontius Pilate afforded more rights to Jesus than the Democrats have afforded this president in this process," said Barry Loudermilk, Republican of Georgia.

Republican prayers were offered, for the other side's sins. "I want Democrats voting for impeachment today to know that I'll be praying for them," said Fred Keller, Republican of Pennsylvania. "From the Gospel of Luke, the 23rd chapter, verse 34. 'And Jesus said, Father, forgive them, for they know not what they do.' "

A series of Republican speeches revealed the depth of bitterness on their side of the aisle. Drew Ferguson of Georgia used his one-minute, 45-second slot to rail against the Democrats and their "corrupt" impeachment. "In 2016, I, along with 63 million American voters representing 304 electoral college votes, went to the polls and we raised our collective political middle finger to D.C. and voted for Donald Trump," he said. "And now you want to remove our voice from office."

Ferguson had a few choice words for his foes. "How dare you, the liberal elites, the condescending bureaucrats and every other kind of swamp critter in this Godforsaken place, tell the American public who the President should be. That's the job of the American voter, not yours. This whole flipping goat rodeo is a sham and a shame and it will not be forgotten."

Kevin Brady of South Dakota said Democrats will "forever be remembered as the Senator Joe McCarthys of our time." In Brady's narrative of events, the Democrats had abused their power, rather than Trump abusing his. "President Trump committed no crime or impeachable offense. None. His legacy won't be stained. Democrats' will. They'll look back at these days in shame because Trump haters in Congress like red haters of the past are willing to plunge America into darkness for raw political gain," he said.

They even attacked themselves. Chip Roy of Texas said: "One might ask if America would be better off taking the first 435 names out of the phone book to represent us in the United States House than what is on display here today."

At 12:08 p.m., Pelosi took to the microphone herself. She had decided to speak earlier in the day, rather than making the Democrats' closing argument. She was anticipating that the Republicans might try to delay the vote until late into the night. She wasn't going to take the risk. No 2 a.m. speech for her.

Speaking early meant she could set the tone, and guaranteed that whatever she said, a clip would make the endless loop of cable television news. She recited the Pledge of Allegiance, with her hand over her heart, to make a point about pledging allegiance not simply to a flag, but to the republic for which it stands.

"Our founders' vision of a republic is under threat from actions from the White House. That is why today, as speaker of the house, I solemnly and sadly open the debate on the impeachment of the president of the United States. If we do not act now, we would be derelict in our duty. It is tragic that the president's reckless actions make impeachment necessary. He gave us no choice."

She called Trump "an ongoing threat to our national security and the integrity of our elections, the basis of our democracy." She said the day was a "national civics lesson," and she used it to rebut the familiar echo chamber language she had been hearing from across the aisle. She defended those who testified against Trump as "decorated war heroes, distinguished diplomats and patriotic career public servants," not deep state subversives.

Pelosi was not known as a soaring orator, but she read her remarks in a firm and commanding voice. She said Trump had abused his power and jeopardized the integrity of U.S. elections by inviting foreign interference, then blocked Congress from investigating. "When the president's wrongdoing was revealed, he launched an unprecedented, indiscriminate and categorical campaign of defiance and obstruction," she said.

She spoke of Elijah Cummings, who had died in October, a pioneering African American legislator, the son of sharecroppers, and one of Pelosi's closest friends. On the day of Cummings's death, Pelosi called him "my brother in Baltimore." Now, on the House floor where they had served together, she called Cummings a "north star," a guiding light. She quoted from one of his final speeches: "When the history books are written about this tumultuous era, I want them to show that I was among those in the House of Representatives who stood up to lawlessness and tyranny. . . . When we are dancing with the angels, the question will be, what did we do to make sure we kept our democracy intact?"

At 12:44, Trump tweeted: "SUCH ATROCIOUS LIES BY THE RADICAL LEFT, DO NOTHING DEMOCRATS. THIS IS AN ASSAULT ON AMERICA, AND AN ASSAULT ON THE REPUBLICAN PARTY!!!!"

When Pelosi finished, Collins swatted at her arguments like so many swarming gnats on a hot Georgia night.

"President Trump did nothing wrong," he said.

Six hundred miles away, in southwestern Michigan, Trump's loyal supporters were filing into Kellogg Arena, an aging Battle Creek venue with 6,200 seats, for what was shaping up to be a visceral protest roar against impeachment. When his campaign was arranging the rally, the date for the impeachment vote had not been set. But aides knew the event would come amid the proceedings, and his hardcore supporters would turn out for him, no matter what. But to be safe, his staff picked a smaller-sized arena they knew the boss could easily pack.

A few supporters had camped out overnight, sleeping on the stone-cold concrete floors of a nearby parking garage. But by 9 a.m., in frigid temperatures, hundreds were already standing in line, 10 hours before the scheduled 7 p.m. start time. Dressed in layers, they shared hand warmers and urged one another not to give up and go home. The temperature never got above 18 degrees all day, and an icy wind blew snow off nearby rooftops. A 66-year-old woman, desperate for warmth, took off her boots and wrapped her cold feet in her coat.

Battle Creek, home to roughly 50,000 people, is best known for cereal. The Kellogg Company, whose name is plastered throughout the city, was founded here. Calhoun County, where Battle Creek is located, was one of more than 200 counties across the country that had voted twice for Barack Obama and then for Trump in 2016.

These counties that flipped, mostly concentrated in the Midwest, especially in industrial and rural areas, were now some of the president's favorite places to go for rallies. Trump barely won Michigan in 2016, a razor-thin margin of 10,000 votes. Calhoun County helped him out. He had ended his campaign in nearby Grand Rapids, just after midnight on Election Day, November 8, before a wildly cheering crowd.

Washington Post political reporter Jenna Johnson arrived in midafternoon, just before officials opened the doors. She had covered Trump's 2016 campaign and his first year in office and, by her count, had now attended more than 200 of his rallies. She knew their rhythms, how the chants of "Lock Her Up" and "Drain the Swamp" would roll through the arenas, how Trump would wind up the crowds, getting them going.

Impeachment would make this one different. Already, there was an undertone of anger as updates from Washington popped up on people's cellphones. A vendor sold pink T-shirts featuring a raised middle finger and "IMPEACH THIS" scrawled in blue. Bright spotlights illuminated the stands, making it difficult for many to look toward the stage without squinting. This was unusual for a Trump rally. It was as if the campaign wanted to light up each and every person there, to shine a literal spotlight on the president's base of support.

The rally-goers were greeted by the blaring soundtrack that played at all of Trump's rallies—a mix of Elton John, the Rolling Stones, Sinatra and Broadway. The arena was decorated with two large Christmas trees topped with red campaign caps.

Johnson wandered through the crowd, getting a feel for the mood. She met people who told her of a local dental clinic that had closed for the afternoon, rescheduling its patients so that employees could attend the rally. The owners of a motorcycle shop said they had shut down for the day so they could "be with our president who thinks of us and is so close to being us."

In Washington, Marine One landed on the South Lawn of the White House at 4:19 p.m., as a frigid twilight descended. The president was in the Oval Office, finishing up a meeting. *Washington Post* reporter Dan Zak, watching from across the Rose Garden, could see Trump through the windows with his adviser Stephen Miller and his daughter Ivanka. A member of Trump's staff carried an armful of posters onto Marine One, tailed by a military aide with the nuclear football. A few minutes later, the helicopter lifted off for Joint Base Andrews in Maryland and the transfer to Air Force One for the trip to Michigan.

In Battle Creek just after 5 p.m., the arena at capacity, the doors closed. Everyone stood to say the Pledge of Allegiance and sing the national anthem. They were exhorted to "sing this loud and proud." That was followed by a chant of "Four more years! Four more years!" One supporter doubled that: "Eight more years! Eight more years!" Then another: "Twenty more years!" A man dressed as Santa Claus shouted: "Impeach Pelosi!"

On Air Force One, Trump was tracking the impeachment vote on TV and the social media buzz from Battle Creek. Just before 6 p.m., he tweeted: "Thank you, Michigan, I am on my way. See everybody soon! #KAG," the acronym for his 2020 campaign slogan: "Keep America Great."

On Capitol Hill, the ping-pong match of indignant speeches was still going strong.

5:51, Ping: "This president has shown himself time and time again to believe that he is above the law," said Maxine Waters.

5:53, Pong: "What is shameful is that Speaker Pelosi has allowed this Democratic witch hunt to move forward," said Ralph Abraham, Republican of Louisiana.

5:54, Ping: "This morning, the president tweeted, 'I DID NOTHING WRONG,' all caps. He believes it, too. He sees nothing wrong with inviting Russian, Ukrainian or Chinese interference into our election," said Jim Himes. "He will wake up tomorrow and do it again if we don't stop him today."

5:56, Pong: "Our president made a campaign promise to drain the swamp, and there are those today relying on swamp creatures' words to preserve the swamp," said Trent Kelly, Republican of Mississippi.

Will Hurd spoke for 90 seconds. "Today we have seen a rushed process divide our country. Today, accusations have been hurled at each other, questioning each other's integrity," he said. "But what happens tomorrow? Can this chamber put down our swords and get back to the work for the American people?"

Elissa Slotkin chose not to speak. She had said what she needed to say.

At 6:35 p.m., Air Force One landed in Battle Creek. At 7 p.m., when Trump was scheduled to take the stage, his campaign manager, Brad Parscale, came out and tossed red campaign hats into the cheering crowd. He said Trump was slightly delayed and then offered a warm-up, accusing the media and Democrats of trying to "erase your vote in 2016 and not give you a chance in 2020."

In Washington at 7:45 p.m., McCarthy was delivering the Republicans' closing argument to the increasingly packed House floor. He spoke from a second set of microphones at the front of the House, looking out at his colleagues rather than up at the speaker's chair. The visitors' gallery was now nearly full, with the debate winding down and the House preparing for the roll call vote. McCarthy spoke for 15 minutes.

"Madam Speaker, I must warn you, I'm about to say something my Democratic colleagues hate to hear," McCarthy said. "Donald J. Trump is president of the United States. He is president today. He'll be president tomorrow. And he will be president when this impeachment is over."

As McCarthy was speaking, Vice President Pence bounded onto the stage in Battle Creek. "I stand with President Donald Trump!" Pence declared. "I stand with President Donald Trump! . . . I stand with President Donald Trump!"

He began listing Trump's accomplishments. "We've taken the fight to radical Islamic terrorists on our terms on their soil," Pence said.

"Fuck Islam!" screamed a man sitting near Johnson.

"Last year the armed forces of the United States captured the last inch of territory beneath the black flag of ISIS," Pence said.

"Fuck ISIS!" another man screamed.

"The American economy is booming," Pence said.

"Boom, boom, boom!" someone yelled.

It was hard to hear Pence amid the chants of "Four more years! Four more years!" and "USA! USA! USA!"

Pence told the crowd that Trump was late because he wanted to "see the strong, unified Republican vote" against impeachment on television. Pence spoke for 14 minutes, touting Trump's record and blasting the "do-nothing Democrats" and the "partisan impeachment."

Pence and McCarthy finished speaking within a minute of each other.

At 8:01 p.m., Schiff strode to his party's podium to give his closing argument against Trump. He carried no notes. Since the days of high school speech contests, he had felt more comfortable speaking without them. He knew the impeachment facts cold. He had a broad outline in his head, but he wasn't sure exactly how he would phrase things.

"Article 1 charges the president of the United States with abusing the power of his office by coercing an ally into cheating in a U.S. election on his behalf," he said.

Republicans booed and the speaker had to gavel them down.

As Schiff was describing the Constitution's "beautiful architecture," the checks and balances designed to keep each branch from abusing its powers, Trump burst into view in Battle Creek to thunderous applause and the country music anthem "God Bless the USA." For the first three minutes, he walked around and waved at his supporters, soaking up their cheers.

Fox News was split-screening Schiff and Trump now. Anchor Bret Baier was struck by the dueling images. "This split screen is quite something, if you look at Michigan, you look at the House floor, who knew that we'd be facing this split screen at this moment." CNN and MSNBC stayed focused on the impeachment vote and never went to sustained live coverage of Trump's rally.

In the House, Schiff finished his seven-minute speech to applause from Democrats, unable to stay quiet at this emotional moment. At 8:08 p.m., voting began on Article 1. Members had 15 minutes to cast their ballots. A green card for "Yes," a red card for "No." Ratcliffe edited his red card to say "Hell No."

As Ratcliffe scrawled, Trump said in Michigan: "It doesn't really feel like we're being impeached. The country is doing better than ever before. We did nothing wrong, we did nothing wrong, and we have tremendous support in the Republican Party like we've never had before—nobody has ever had this kind of support."

On CNN at 8:16, anchor Jake Tapper was saying that Justin Amash, a

Michigan Independent who had recently defected from the Republican Party, had voted to impeach Trump—and that "President Trump is right now in Kellogg Center in Battle Creek, Michigan, having a rally, and that is Justin Amash's congressional district."

At the rally, Trump fans began booing protesters holding signs that said, "Don the con you're fired." Security escorted them out. "That's all right," Trump said. The crowd chanted "USA! USA!"

"Get her out," Trump said, calling one protester a slob. "Get her out of here."

Trump talked about Space Force and funding for historically black colleges and universities. "The radical left in Congress is consumed with hatred and envy and rage. You see what's going on? I'll tell you, these people are crazy."

The Battle Creek crowd chanted: "Four more years!"

At 8:34 p.m., as Trump was calling Elizabeth Warren of Massachusetts "Crazy Pocahontas," Pelosi announced the results on Article 1: "On this vote, the yeas are 230, the nays are 197. Present is 1. Article 1 is adopted." No Republican had voted for Article 1. Two Democrats had voted no. One, Tulsi Gabbard, had voted "present."

Jeers from the Republicans. A few cheers from Democrats. Pelosi shot the Democrats a chastising look, reminding them of her rule: Be solemn. Be serious. And they were not done. Another article awaited.

Republican members chanted, "Four more years! Four more years!"

Pelosi announced consideration of Article 2.

On stage in Battle Creek, Trump showed no sign of being aware that he had just been impeached on Article 1. He was talking about crowd size.

"They never mention the crowds. It's sort of amazing. You know what? I don't think we've ever had an empty seat from the time I came down the escalator," he said, referring to his 2015 announcement for president at Trump Tower in New York. "Is there a better place to be in the world than a Trump rally?"

As Trump was speaking, members of Congress were coming forward with their red and green vote cards for Article 2.

Trump talked about "Crooked" Hillary Clinton and how hard it was to pronounce the last name of Democratic presidential candidate Pete Buttigieg. "Here's what you do, 'boot edge edge,'" he said. He talked about winning Michigan in 2016, then turned to impeachment, as his crowd booed.

"This lawless, partisan impeachment is a political suicide march for the Democrat Party," he said. "Through their depraved actions today, Crazy Nancy Pelosi's House Democrats have branded themselves with an eternal mark of shame."

On MSNBC, the focus was on impeachment. The Battle Creek rally was first mentioned at 8:47 p.m. Nicolle Wallace, a former George W. Bush staffer turned Trump skeptic, was talking about how Trump "thumbs his nose at the rule of law."

Anchor Brian Williams noted that "He's onstage in Battle Creek, Michigan right now."

"I bet he is!" Wallace said.

"No, he is, actually," said *Washington Post* columnist Eugene Robinson.

Wallace: "Where else would he be?"

At that moment on Fox, Carlson was criticizing Hakeem Jeffries, Democrat of New York, for something Jeffries had said earlier. "How do people like that get power in this country? Ridiculous people," Carlson said. Now the Fox screen had three images: The left half of the screen was the House voting, the right half was Carlson fuming, and a box in the lower right showed nonstop coverage of Battle Creek, where Trump had just turned his attention back to Hillary Clinton. He said she didn't have his stamina. The crowd responded: "Lock her up! Lock her up!"

In Washington, Pelosi on Article 2: "On this vote, the yeas are 229, the nays are 198. Present is 1. Article 2 is adopted." Again, no Republican defectors. Three Democrats had voted no. A single "Yaay" brought a scolding hand from Pelosi.

DeGette, back at the speaker's desk, adjourned the House at 8:52 p.m.

Pelosi didn't need or want any fanfare. Three months ago, she had made the decision that impeachment had become worth it. Worth the risk. Worth the battle. Worth the fallout. She had told her caucus that whatever happened in the Senate, Trump had just earned his forever asterisk.

In this rare moment, the House ended its historic session virtually in silence.

In Battle Creek, as Trump was calling Schiff a pathological liar, campaign spokeswoman Kayleigh McEnany stood at the side of the stage and held up a sign showing the impeachment vote results.

"Oh, I think we have a vote coming in," Trump announced. "So, we got every single Republican voted for us. Whoa! Whoa. Wow, wow, almost 200. So we had 198—229, 198. We didn't lose one Republican vote and—and!—three Democrats voted for us."

Referring to Kayleigh McEnany, he continued: "Haley, Haley. Thank you, Haley, great job! Wow. The Republican Party has never been so affronted, but they've never been so united as they are right there ever, never. And I know the senators, and they're great guys—and women, too. We have some great women. We have great guys. They're great people. They love this country."

Trump kept talking for almost another hour. He talked about potholes, how he looked more handsome in the light of old-fashioned lightbulbs than energy-efficient ones, his frustration with low-flow sinks and toilets, firing Comey's "ass," how his hair was real and not a hairpiece. He drifted between ad lib and a traditional campaign speech and back again. He repeatedly repeated himself. It was his second-longest rally ever, at about two hours.

He reminded supporters that anything could happen before the 2020 election, offering a line that Americans had come to recognize as solid truth: "In the life of Trump, ten months is an eternity."

He bashed Hillary Clinton. "I hear she wants to run again—wouldn't that be great?" he said, as his supporters picked up the old favorite chant of "Lock her up!" The crowd's reaction encouraged him. He told the crowd that Bill Clinton couldn't get his wife to listen in 2016. He had told her to come to Michigan more, he said, but she wouldn't.

He narrated how he imagined their conversation, in Trump speak:

"So what happens, so what happens is Bill Clinton said to Crooked Hillary, his very dishonest wife, said, 'Crooked Hillary'—Do you think he calls her Crooked Hillary? He might. Maybe he just calls her 'Crooked.' He said, 'Crooked, I'm telling you, Crooked, I don't like what I'm seeing in Michigan. I don't like what I'm seeing in Wisconsin either.

"And he said, 'You horrible human being, you're going to start listening to me, because you're going to get your ass whooped!' And you know what happened? You know what happened? She didn't listen, fortunately."

He was rolling. At 9:05 p.m., he targeted Debbie Dingell, the Michigan congresswoman who had publicly called for Trump's impeachment.

Dingell's husband, John, the longest serving House member in history, had died in February 2019 after nearly 60 years in office. Trump recounted how he had spoken with Debbie Dingell after her husband's death, saying she thanked him for ordering flags flown at half-staff. Then Trump, mimicking her voice, quoted her saying: "John would be so thrilled. He's looking down."

"I said, 'That's okay. Don't worry about it.' "

Then Trump told the crowd, "Maybe he's looking up, I don't know," suggesting that John Dingell might be in hell.

The crowd seemed unsure how to respond to Trump's insult. Some groaned. Some cheered and clapped.

Trump quickly added, "But let's assume he's looking down."

In Washington, Debbie Dingell had just left the House and was at a holiday dinner at Carmine's Italian Restaurant with the bipartisan Problem Solvers Caucus. As she sat down to eat, a reporter called and asked, "How do you feel about Trump? He said John was in hell."

Dingell, grieving her husband's death, didn't want to "throw a damper" on the party, so she called an Uber and went home. It hurt.

Trump's remarks drew widespread condemnation. Dingell issued a statement calling for civility. "Mr. President, let's set politics aside," she tweeted. "My husband earned all his accolades after a lifetime of service. I'm preparing for the first holiday season without the man I love. You brought me down in a way you can never imagine and your hurtful words just made my healing much harder."

As Trump was holding forth in Battle Creek, Pelosi was at the Capitol, holding a news conference with Schiff, Nadler and other committee chairmen at her side.

Three months shy of her 80th birthday, she had just spent nearly 12 hours on the House floor. She was one of the few members to listen to every speaker.

"December 18, a great day for the Constitution of the United States," she began. She quoted Cummings again: "What did you do to make sure we kept our democracy?" Now she had an answer. "We did all we could, Elijah," Pelosi said. "We passed two articles of impeachment. The President is impeached."

Then Pelosi signaled something no one had seen coming. She said she might not send the articles of impeachment to the Senate immediately. She wanted to know more about the details of the trial McConnell planned to run, especially since the Senate majority leader had already said plainly that he planned to coordinate completely with Trump's lawyers.

"So far we haven't seen anything that looks fair to us," Pelosi said. "We're not sending it tonight because it's difficult to determine who the managers would be until we see the arena in which we will be participating. . . . This is a serious matter, even though the majority leader in the United States Senate says it's okay for the foreman of the jury to be in cahoots with the lawyers of the accused."

Trump was still talking in Battle Creek. He riffed on how modern water-saving dishwashers don't clean dishes properly. He read aloud from his six-page letter to Pelosi the day before, in which he had accused her of waging a "war on American democracy." Trump said Pelosi should focus on the problems of homelessness and poverty in her home state. He pledged to "vote her the hell out of office."

Whenever Trump mentioned Pelosi, a man in the crowd dressed as Santa stood and shouted: "Nancy Pelosi is a ho, ho, ho!"

As the crowd thinned toward the end of his long speech, Trump promised, "The best is yet to come," and departed the stage, to rapturous applause.

At 10:49 p.m., on his flight back to Washington, Trump tweeted a black-and-white photo of himself, with a warning for his followers: "In reality they're not after me, they're after you. I'm just in the way."

After midnight, he was back in Washington, where the story would soon be: Trump on Trial.

Part Four

TRUMP ON TRIAL

CHAPTER FORTY-FIVE

"Trust Me to Run This"

December 20 to January 6, 2020, Washington, Florida and Kyiv

President Trump arrived at Mar-a-Lago on the evening of December 20 for a few days' respite from Washington during the Christmas holidays. His coming trial was very much on his mind. One of his first calls was to McConnell.

Trump and McConnell spoke often, and now the president peppered him with ideas and questions about the best trial strategy. Witnesses or no witnesses? Long trial or short trial? How about an outright dismissal? How to respond to Pelosi withholding the articles? How much to attack Joe Biden?

The president had come to value McConnell as a sounding board. They weren't always on the same page, and their personalities didn't match. Trump favored a brawl, and McConnell preferred chess moves. But their partnership had evolved during Trump's three years in office, bolstered by McConnell's record of legislative victories that had helped Trump fulfill key campaign promises, including a historic maneuver that began nearly a year before Trump's election.

In February 2016, McConnell received news that Justice Antonin Scalia had just died on a hunting trip in Texas. President Obama suddenly had an opening that could tilt the ideological balance of the Supreme Court. McConnell made a tactical decision. He said the seat would remain vacant until after the presidential election—no confirmation hearing, no vote. Obama nominated Merrick Garland, a highly respected and moderate federal appeals judge. McConnell stayed his course. It was a raw, blatant display of power by a Senate leader. Unprecedented.

McConnell's gamble paid off. Hillary Clinton's loss made Garland's nomination into a historical asterisk and cleared the way for Trump to pick from the conservative list. He chose Neil Gorsuch, a federal appeals court judge from Colorado. McConnell steered Gorsuch through the confirmation process all the way to the bench. It was unfair to Garland, and a breathtaking interpretation of the Constitution's requirements for the Senate to provide "Advice and Consent," but politically and procedurally unstoppable. McConnell had gone right up to the line, if not over it.

Following the Gorsuch confirmation, and through McConnell's steadfast support of Supreme Court nominee Brett M. Kavanaugh in the face of furious Democratic opposition prompted by sexual assault allegations, Trump had come to admire McConnell's placid grit. After more than 187 federal court judges had been confirmed by McConnell's Senate majority, Trump boasted: "Generations from now, Americans will know that Mitch McConnell helped save the constitutional rule of law in America. It's true. It's for a long time."

The relationship worked both ways. McConnell had never been a beloved or particularly popular politician in Kentucky. He had earned more respect than affection. Trump, however, was wildly popular in much of the Bluegrass State. McConnell needed Trump, plain and simple, and he needed his constituents to see that he and the president were true partners, each playing a vital role in reshaping America.

That was especially important at the start of 2020, when McConnell had his own reelection to worry about. Unseating McConnell would be a long shot, but Democrats believed McConnell was perhaps more vulnerable than he had ever been. A leading candidate for the Democratic nomination was Amy McGrath, 44, a retired Marine fighter pilot who had narrowly lost a Kentucky race for Congress in 2018. McGrath was one of 10 or so declared Democratic candidates, but she had shown a prodigious ability to raise money and was polling well.

McConnell's every move in the Senate trial would be scrutinized in Kentucky. He needed to be sure that Trump trusted him to handle the impeachment strategy. He didn't want the mercurial president trying to second-guess him from the Oval Office, or on Twitter. Now, on the phone, McConnell eased the conversation in a new direction.

He said: You are getting a lot of advice, Mr. President. I know the Senate better than any of those people you're talking to. And I know how to make my members feel comfortable.

The only thing that matters is the final vote. I'm working on having all 53 Republicans on board. I need to know that you trust me to run this.

Trump was on board.

I agree, the president said. I trust you.

By Sunday morning, December 22, Washington was on holiday pause. Trump was in Florida. Pelosi was at home in San Francisco, preparing for her family's holiday trip to Hawaii. The House was not due back until January 7, and Pelosi was staying the course with her strategy of holding the articles.

The Sunday morning talk shows were chock-full of political guests. NBC's "Meet the Press" featured Senator Cory Booker and Marc Short, Pence's chief of staff. CBS's "Face the Nation" had Republican senator Roy Blunt and Klobuchar. "Fox News Sunday" had Short and Dingell. The topic was impeachment, impeachment, impeachment. Specifically, Pelosi's decision to delay sending the articles to the Senate.

"This thing is kind of bizarre. They had to rush to this impeachment vote and then, all of a sudden, she's sitting on it," Senator Ron Johnson told Martha Raddatz, who was hosting ABC's "This Week" show. Raddatz then turned to a man whose stance on impeachment was being closely watched by political Washington: Senator Doug Jones, who was a little dot of Democrat blue in Alabama's sea of Republican red. He had won a stunning special election victory in 2017 and now faced a difficult reelection campaign in 2020. Voting against Trump would cost him at home. Voting with Trump would cost him with his party.

Jones told Raddatz that he was undecided. He said he hadn't seen proof that the "dots get connected" in the case against Trump. He called on Trump and McConnell to allow top administration officials to testify to provide a fuller account of events. But he said he was keeping an open mind. Republicans hoped they might be able to persuade him to vote to acquit Trump.

As for Pelosi's Washington Hold 'Em strategy? "She's not going to hold these forever," he told Raddatz. "We're going to see these relatively soon, but I don't think it's unfair to ask, 'What are the rules that we're playing by, when we go and we get this over here?' "

Two days after Christmas, in Kyiv, Bill Taylor was finishing his tour as acting ambassador. Pompeo was scheduled to visit the embassy on January 2. The two men had not spoken since their May meeting in Pompeo's office, when Taylor was deciding whether to take the job. A few weeks before Christmas, a senior aide to the secretary had informed Taylor that Pompeo wanted to meet with Zelensky one-on-one, without embassy staff to take notes.

"I'm going to protest," Taylor had replied. "I'm going to become a pain on this."

Taylor worried that such an arrangement would signal that Pompeo did not trust his embassy staff. That might lead the Ukrainians to conclude that they could not trust the embassy, either.

But Taylor soon realized that he—not the embassy—was the problem. Taylor knew his testimony in Congress had upset the president, who had blasted him as a "Never Trumper." So Taylor proposed a compromise: His deputy would accompany the secretary to the meeting. Pompeo's staff agreed. Then they asked Taylor to leave his position six days early so that he would not be in charge when Pompeo arrived.

So now, in the middle of holiday leave for most of the staff, Taylor gathered embassy employees at the embassy's modernist atrium. He knew this would be one of his last acts as a government official. About 500 people—200 Americans and close to 300 Ukrainian staff—had come. The staff cleared out the tables on the ground-floor cafeteria to make room for more people. The remainder filled the staircases to the second level and gathered along the second-floor balcony.

Many of them had returned from their holidays for the farewell, despite Taylor's pleading with them to enjoy their time off and skip his remarks. His first words that day were about Yovanovitch. He remembered well that in Washington the previous spring, as Taylor was weighing whether to take the job, Yovanovitch had become emotional when she told him that her firing was so rushed that she never got a chance to even thank her staff.

Taylor looked out at the room. "I want to remind you all that Masha is not here to say farewell, like I am doing today," he said. The staff broke out in loud and sustained applause for their former boss.

A few days later, Taylor departed Kyiv, his long government career finished. On his office wall, he left behind a framed copy of Pompeo's declaration that the United States would never recognize the illegal Russian annexation of Crimea. He also carried with him a pair of Ukrainian flag cuff links, a gift from Zelensky.

On the morning of Monday, January 6, as Congress was returning from its two-week holiday recess, John Bolton raised the stakes on the question of whether witnesses would testify at Trump's trial. The former national security adviser issued a statement that said: "If the Senate issues a subpoena for my testimony, I am prepared to testify."

Just before he went public, creating a media firestorm, Bolton left McConnell a message explaining his decision. There was no callback. This was a complication for McConnell. His trial plan did not anticipate the spectacle of a former White House official volunteering to be a witness. Schumer and the Democrats had been demanding Bolton's testimony for weeks, along with that of Mulvaney and two other top administration officials. Cipollone had been steadfast: The White House would not cooperate.

Now Bolton's offer threatened to change the dynamic. McConnell could hold off the Democrats by portraying them as opportunists out to get the president at all costs. But what if the centrist Republicans in his caucus began to waver? What if they said, Okay, Bolton wants to testify, let's hear from him, why not?

McConnell needed to recalibrate, come up with a strategy for withstanding the pressure that was sure to build. The Democrats were going to say: What are you afraid of? Don't you want to hear all the relevant facts? McConnell needed to give the moderates a reason not to listen, or at least, not to change their mind on the need for witnesses. Open the door to Bolton, and who else would walk through it? McConnell couldn't let that happen. He had to maintain control.

Bolton knew that his testimony—if he were allowed to deliver it—would be damaging to the president's case. The White House knew that as well. Just one week earlier, on December 30, Bolton had provided the White House with an early draft of a book he was writing. It needed to go through a national security review, standard procedure for former officials in jobs that dealt with classified material.

The submission had given the White House a disturbing sneak preview of what Bolton might say if he testified. The tightly held manuscript had caused an uproar in the West Wing.

Bolton did not see himself as a whistleblower, but he said he had a constitutional obligation not to conceal information relevant to an impeachment proceeding. He was caught between an executive branch barring his testimony and one side of the legislative branch demanding it. Once the House impeachment inquiry had learned of Bolton's colorful characterizations inside the NSC—Giuliani was a "hand grenade," Sondland and Mulvaney were cooking up a "drug deal" on Ukraine—he had graduated to the top of Schiff's witness list.

But the White House had refused, not just for Bolton, but for others around him. In October, House Democrats had issued a subpoena for his deputy, Charles Kupperman. Trump had instructed him not to testify. Trump's lawyers argued that the president's top aides have "absolute immunity" from congressional subpoenas. Neither Kupperman nor Bolton wanted to testify in the House, but they also did not want to face a contempt charge. Both said that they would comply with a court's ruling about whether they must obey the president or honor the subpoena.

In early November, House Democrats withdrew the Kupperman subpoena, saying they would rely instead on the outcome of a similar case that was further along in the courts, involving an earlier subpoena issued to former White House counsel Donald McGahn. Bolton realized the McGahn case would not be settled before he had to make his decision. In his statement on January 6, Bolton said it appeared unlikely that the courts would decide the big constitutional questions at issue before the Senate trial. So, he wrote, "accordingly, since my testimony is once again at issue, I have had to resolve the serious competing issues as best I could, based on careful consideration and study."

Bolton and his lawyer, Charles Cooper, had agreed early on that if he had to testify, they preferred the Senate. Neither had thought it was a good idea to testify before the House, where bitter partisanship was evident at every hearing. More concerning, they agreed, was the idea of a closed-door deposition followed by a public, televised hearing. Testifying twice was inviting trouble. A deposition would create a record that either side could pick apart later, looking for any apparent discrepancy. It was easy to imagine a House member saying at the public hearing, but Mr. Bolton, you said something a little different in your deposition, didn't you? An open hearing in the Senate was a different story, in no small part because the questioning would be overseen by evenhanded Chief Justice John Roberts.

As Bolton had anticipated, Democrats pounced on his offer. Schumer immediately issued a statement saying: "Given that Mr. Bolton's lawyers have stated he has new relevant information to share, if any Senate Republican opposes issuing subpoenas to the four witnesses and documents we have requested, they would make absolutely clear they are participating in a cover-up."

Schiff tweeted: "Bolton is an important witness to misconduct involving Ukraine that he called a 'drug deal.' Bolton refused to testify in the House, following Trump's orders. Now he is willing to come forward. The Senate must allow testimony from him, Mulvaney and others. The cover-up must end."

Democrats were watching to hear what more centrist Senate Republicans would say. They didn't have to wait long. Romney told reporters just hours after Bolton's announcement: "I would like to be able to hear from John Bolton. What the process is to make that happen, I don't have an answer for you. The leaders are trying to negotiate that process right now. . . . What's important is that we hear from him."

Trump had no love or patience for Romney. Obama had drubbed Romney in 2012, earning him a permanent place in Trump's Twitter doghouse. Romney's moderate version of Republicanism was out of step with the party's current leadership. But his independence was also a warning. Senate Republicans intent on protecting Trump were left to wonder if they could count on Romney and the other centrists to stay loyal in the coming weeks.

McConnell had promised Trump 53 senators, no defectors, a wall of support. He wanted to deliver, and Bolton was standing in his way.

CHAPTER FORTY-SIX

"We Need to Get This Thing Going"

January 7 to 12, Washington, Maine and Kentucky

McConnell looked out at the sea of reporters. They were waiting to hear his final plans for the impeachment trial, whether he would bend to the Democrats' insistence on witnesses now that Bolton was offering to testify in defiance of Trump's orders.

"Well, hello everyone. Happy New Year," he said, allowing himself a slight smile. "I think some of you have already written this, but I wanted to make sure you understood that"—he didn't even pause—"we have the votes."

He and his leadership team had just emerged from a closed-door caucus meeting at the Capitol on Tuesday morning, January 7. Now he was telling the press that the Republicans were solidly behind his proposed plan for the trial, which he said would begin as soon as Nancy Pelosi delivered the articles.

For now, he said, no witnesses. That could be decided later, if necessary. His rules of engagement called for opening arguments from the House impeachment managers, then a rebuttal from Trump's defense team, followed by several days of questions from senators, submitted in writing for the two sides to answer. Once that phase of the trial ended, only then would the Senate consider whether to call witnesses.

Precedent had been his guide, McConnell said. The proposed rules mirrored those the Democrats had used in the Clinton impeachment trial. A decision on witnesses did not take place until well after Clinton's trial began, McConnell said, and it would not happen any differently this time. He was sending a message to Schumer and Pelosi when he said, "I want you to understand that we have the votes."

The Democrats weren't giving up. They wanted a single resolution laying out all the rules, including a commitment to call witnesses, before the trial began. Pelosi's strategy of holding back the articles was an attempt to force McConnell's hand. It hadn't worked so far, but Bolton's offer to testify had given Schumer a wedge to reopen the discussions.

Now Schumer was pounding on that wedge, hard. "On the question of witnesses and documents, Republicans may run, but they can't hide," Schumer said on the Senate floor. "There will be votes at the beginning [of the trial] on whether to call the four witnesses we've proposed and subpoena the documents we've identified. America, and the eyes of history, will be watching what my Republican colleagues do."

Schumer kept up the pressure when he talked to reporters later. "The Republican Leader and I have very different visions about what it means to conduct a fair trial," he said. "We say: witnesses and documents: fair trial; no witnesses and no documents: cover-up."

For weeks, Schumer and the Democrats had been pressuring Republican senators to allow four administration witnesses. But none of the pressure seemed to have moved the four Republicans considered most likely to break ranks: Collins, Murkowski, Alexander and Romney.

Murkowski and Romney, in speaking to reporters, sounded fine with McConnell's plan on the witness issue. Romney said: "The Clinton trial process provided a pathway for there to be witnesses."

That night, in a closed-door meeting with her caucus, Pelosi said she still intended to hold the articles until she saw specific trial rules. She believed there was no guarantee, without a resolution in writing, that McConnell would follow through with a vote on witnesses.

Pelosi and Schumer believed that Bolton, Mulvaney and other top officials had firsthand, factual knowledge of Trump's conduct. They could provide relevant evidence, so the senators should want to hear from them, despite Trump's objections. She thought the Republicans were just trying to muddy the waters by threatening to call Joe and Hunter Biden or Schiff. None of them was a witness to Trump's conduct. Agreeing to a Republican demand for testimony from either of the Bidens would be playing into Trump's hands, making Biden the issue on the eve of the first presidential primaries in early February.

But before the day ended, cracks in her delay strategy were starting to show.

"I do think we need to get this thing going," said Senator Angus King, a Maine Independent who caucused with the Democrats.

With the Republicans solidly behind their plan, Senator Chris Murphy said, "She should send the articles over."

Senator Joe Manchin of West Virginia, a Democrat who wasn't a certain vote for removing Trump, agreed: "I think it needs to start."

On Wednesday morning, three days after returning from his Florida Christmas break, the president met with McConnell in the Oval Office. The agenda was to discuss a judicial nominee, but an agitated Trump quickly turned back to impeachment.

Trump had been all over the map for more than a month. One moment, he was demanding that the Bidens, Schiff and the whistleblower testify at an extended trial, telling friends it would be like "the best episode, the grand finale" of a reality show. In the next, he was calling for an immediate dismissal, a declaration that the Democrats had nothing, no evidence worth hearing. Now, in the Oval Office, he was on the quick-dismissal end of the pendulum swing.

McConnell thought they had settled all this in their pre-Christmas phone call, when Trump had agreed to trust McConnell and let him handle the Senate strategy. Apparently not. McConnell knew a quick dismissal was just not going to work. His caucus wouldn't go for it. They had to show that they were taking the process seriously. He gave it to the president straight. A quick vote on a unilateral dismissal was a bad idea. It would fail, and it would split Senate Republicans at the start of Trump's trial.

"Better to be unified than divided," McConnell told him.

Trump trusted his own instincts, but he also was inclined to listen to McConnell, partly because he had twice seen the dangers of ignoring him. In 2017, McConnell had advised him to support Senator Luther Strange of Alabama against his primary challenger, former judge Roy Moore. Trump publicly supported Strange, but he let his former strategist, Steve Bannon, work on Moore's behalf. Moore won the nomination but faced allegations of sexual misconduct with teenage girls in the 1970s, accusations that he denied. McConnell shunned Moore, and the GOP lost the seat to Democrat Doug Jones.

Then in 2018, McConnell had counseled Trump not to shut down the federal government as a tactic in prying loose more money for his U.S.-Mexico border wall. McConnell said it wouldn't succeed, Trump would be blamed, and he would take a hit in the polls. After an extremely unpopular 35-day shutdown, Trump relented. As McConnell had predicted, he got no money for his wall from Congress and his poll numbers dropped.

Trump was also talking about adding some loud voices to his legal team, including emeritus Harvard Law School professor Alan Dershowitz, 81, who had helped represent high-profile clients from O.J. Simpson to disgraced film mogul Harvey Weinstein. Trump also liked the idea of adding some of his favorite brawlers from the House, including Jordan and Gaetz.

McConnell was skeptical. He wanted Trump defended by Cipollone and his other capable lawyers, including Jay Sekulow. But others on McConnell's leadership team were not so quick to dismiss Trump's inclinations. One told *Washington Post* congressional reporter Seung Min Kim that Trump has "the best understanding of television in the country, probably." Trump understood that his jury was much larger than the 100 senators in the chamber, the senator was saying. "He got elected by tweeting," he told Kim. "This guy is a master of media. So when he thinks about that, he's not necessarily wrong."

Senior Republicans were also worried about the witness issue. During the House proceedings, they had argued that Democrats had refused to let them call witnesses who might have made Trump's case. If the Senate now said no to witnesses, would the same criticisms be made against them? Would they be called hypocrites?

Just before noon that Friday, January 11, lawmakers filed out of the House chamber, many heading home to their districts to face questions about what they were doing on impeachment. Pelosi walked toward her office, fending off reporters' questions about her continued delay in sending the articles to the Senate. Beaming, she said her Democrats were "a thousand flowers blossoming beautifully in our caucus."

At that moment, her staff was hitting send on a "Dear Democratic Colleague" letter, announcing an end to the logjam. Pelosi's letter said she had instructed Nadler to prepare a resolution calling for the House to transmit the articles and to appoint managers for the trial.

Pelosi's team spun the delay as a win. As she had said in her letter, important new information had emerged in the 24 days since the impeachment vote, including emails from OMB on the aid freeze and more facts about the role of Mulvaney and White House lawyers in justifying the aid suspension. She was hoping McConnell was feeling a little heat. "Every Senator now faces a choice," Pelosi wrote, "to be loyal to the President or the Constitution."

Republicans practically laughed in her face. Meadows tweeted: "There is no way to spin it: Speaker Pelosi and her Democrat Caucus spent weeks playing games with what is effectively their attempt at overturning an American election. This display was appalling. It is deeply, fundamentally unserious. And it always has been." McConnell, still at the poker table, was not counting his winnings just yet. He kept his glee to himself. His response was a simple "About time."

As Pelosi's letter was being absorbed and dissected, Collins was visiting an elementary school in Bangor, Maine, keeping her options open, as she always had since becoming a senator in 1997.

"We should be completely open to calling witnesses," she told reporters at the school, raising hopes among Democrats, but also raising eyebrows among Mainers who were used to watching Collins walk the line between Maine's Trump-supporting Republican base and a statewide electorate that was far more independent and moderate.

The 67-year-old Collins was part of a long tradition of centrist, consensus-building Maine Republicans, including former senators Margaret Chase Smith, William Cohen and Olympia Snowe. That line had been coming under increasing pressure, including from Maine's last Republican governor, Paul LePage, whose far-right bombast was Trump before Trump.

Twenty years ago, there had been six Republicans among New England's 12 senators. Now there was only Collins, and she was facing a tough reelection challenge, most likely from Sara Gideon, the Democratic speaker of the Maine House of Representatives.

Collins had played a part in all three impeachments of modern times. As a Capitol Hill intern, she had worked for William Cohen while the then-congressman helped lead the Republican revolt against Richard Nixon. As a freshman senator occupying Cohen's former seat in 1999, Collins had spurned her party's leadership and voted to acquit Clinton.

This time around, no one seriously thought she would vote to remove Trump from office. That would be an unforgiveable sin among Maine's rank-and-file Republicans. But her vote on the witness question was unknown. McConnell and his allies were careful not to push her too hard. They understood that she was about as conservative as Maine voters would tolerate in a general election.

In campaigning against Collins, Gideon had been touting Collins's habit of raising moderates' hopes, only to side with McConnell. Memories were still fresh of Collins's role in Kavanaugh's Supreme Court confirmation hearing. Moderates had hoped Collins would break with her party over sexual assault allegations against Kavanaugh, but she ultimately supported him with a dramatic speech on the Senate floor.

Through her four Senate terms, Collins had nurtured a reputation as a bipartisan problem-solver with support from Republicans, Democrats and independents. She had coasted to reelection in 2014. But her Kavanaugh vote had enraged her critics in Maine and helped set the stage for Gideon's run.

Now, as Trump's trial neared, Collins was walking the narrow path again. "I am hopeful that we can reach an agreement on how to proceed with the trial that will allow the opportunity for witnesses," she said. "It is important that both sides be treated fairly."

At 3 p.m. that Friday, excerpts were released from a taped interview that Ingraham had done with President Trump, set to air later in the evening on her Fox show.

"Why not call Bolton? Why not allow him to testify?" she asked.

"No problem other than one thing," Trump said. "You can't be in the White House as president, future, I'm talking about future—any future presidents—and have a security adviser, anybody having to do with security, and legal and other things but especially—" Trump said.

"Are you going to invoke executive privilege?" Ingraham interjected.

"Well, I think you have to for the sake of the office," Trump said.

On Sunday morning, Pelosi looked at the tweet that George Stephanopoulos, host of ABC's "This Week," was displaying on the studio monitor. The tweet was a suggestion from President Trump, posted at 9:58 a.m., two minutes before airtime: "George @GStephanopoulos, ask Crazy Nancy why she allowed Adam 'Shifty' Schiff to totally make up my conversation with the Ukrainian President & read his false words to Congress and the world, as though I said it? He got caught! Ask why hearing was most unfair & biased in history?"

Stephanopoulos then played a clip of Trump from two nights earlier:

"She's obsessed with impeachment. She has done nothing. She's going down as one of the worst speakers in the history of our country."

Pelosi kept her expression neutral as she responded. "Let me just say, it's Sunday morning, I'd like to talk about some more pleasant subjects than the erratic nature of this president of the United States. But he has to know that every knock from him is a boost. He's the president who said I should have impeached George Bush, because of the war in Iraq. And now he's saying I'm obsessed. I held off on this because, frankly, I said Donald Trump is not worth impeachment."

"You did say that," Stephanopoulos said.

"He's not worth it, but when he crossed that line on Ukraine he violated the Constitution in such a way that could not be ignored. So again, I don't like to spend too much time on his crazy tweets, because everything he says is a projection. When he calls someone crazy, he knows that he is." Stephanopoulos started to ask a question, but then stopped, letting Pelosi finish her thought. "But again, it's Sunday morning. Let's be optimistic about the future, a future that will not have Donald Trump in the White House one way or another. Ten months from now we will have an election, if we don't have him removed sooner. But, again, he'll be impeached forever."

In Boone County, in northern Kentucky, just across the muddy Ohio River from Cincinnati, *Washington Post* reporter Griff Witte wandered into PeeWee's Place to ask a few questions about McConnell and impeachment.

Even mentioning the "I-word" raised eyebrows, and a temper or two, in the dimly lit but highly spirited watering hole popular among local Republicans. At the bar, folks told Witte that they were angry about Democrats trying to take down "the best president we've ever had."

In a quiet corner of PeeWee's, Paul Fiser, a 60-year-old lawyer, offered a more nuanced view. He didn't like Pelosi's partisan impeachment, but he also didn't like McConnell saying he would not be an impartial juror. Fiser had backed Trump reluctantly in 2016 and said he would probably do so again in 2020. But he drew a distinction between the president and the Kentuckian who had been in Congress for more than three decades. "McConnell has become the ultimate insider. But people are tired of business as usual. They're looking for unconventional candidates," said

Fiser, who said he was undecided in the Senate race. "He's not a lock like he's been in the past."

Witte's travels through the small cities, affluent suburbs and rolling hill country of northern Kentucky left him with the impression that McConnell was being closely watched by voters who had supported him in the past. "How he handles this impeachment is going to be the big determinant of whether people get behind him," Kevin Gordon, a talk radio host and activist, told Witte. "They should dismiss the charges outright. It's a sham. If McConnell runs the trial the way the Democrats want, people here are not going to be happy."

CHAPTER FORTY-SEVEN

"Today, We Will Make History"

January 15, Washington

Four weeks to the day from the impeachment vote in the House, Nancy Pelosi was ready to send the articles to the Senate. She appeared at a 10 a.m. news conference to announce the seven impeachment managers who would make the House's case in Trump's Senate trial.

Pelosi quoted Lincoln, Henry Wadsworth Longfellow and Thomas Paine, and said the December 18 vote was "an impeachment that will last forever" as she introduced the managers with an emphasis on their comfort level in a courtroom. Led by Schiff and Nadler, all the managers had background in the law.

It was the third impeachment for Zoe Lofgren of California. She had worked as a congressional staffer during the Nixon inquiry and had served on the Judiciary Committee during the Clinton proceedings.

Hakeem Jeffries, a former corporate litigator in New York, had long served on the Judiciary Committee, where he worked closely with Republicans, including Jared Kushner, on a criminal justice reform bill in 2018.

Val Demings was the only non-lawyer among the managers, but she had served as the first female chief of the Orlando Police Department. Sylvia Garcia was a former state senator and longtime municipal judge in Houston.

Jason Crow was the only manager who did not serve on any of the investigating committees, but he had national security credentials as a former Army Ranger officer and member of the House Armed Services Committee. He also had practiced law before his 2018 election to Congress.

It was a diverse group: four men and three women; two African Americans and a Latina; representatives from the Atlantic, Gulf and Pacific coasts. Now their job was to come together and speak with one clear voice.

Just before noon in the East Room of the White House, Trump was celebrating the signing of phase one of a new U.S.-China trade deal. He went around the room and singled out people for praise: Henry Kissinger, now 96 years old, Mnuchin, Commerce Secretary Wilbur Ross, Kushner, business leaders, members of Congress. But nobody got a warmer presidential embrace than Lou Dobbs, one of Trump's most enthusiastic media promoters.

"A man who always liked me—because he's smart, so smart—the great Lou Dobbs. You know, at first, he said, 'He's the best since Reagan.' Then, he got to know me more and more, and he said, 'He's even better than Reagan.' Then, a few weeks ago, somebody told me—and I watch all the time, but somebody has got a very important show, actually. Tremendous audience and very—everybody in this room watches. But Lou Dobbs, he said, 'He's the greatest of them all.' I said, 'Does that include Washington and Lincoln?' And he said yes. Now, I don't know if he was for real, but that's okay. But the great—he is—the great Lou Dobbs. Thank you very much, Lou. Thank you. Great show, Lou."

With Dobbs sitting in the front row next to Kissinger, Trump and Chinese vice premier Liu He signed the formal trade documents, Trump using his signature black Sharpie. Trump then handed out handfuls of ceremonial Sharpies to those in the room to mark the occasion. When the ceremony ended, Trump stepped to the front row. He shook hands with Kissinger first, then Dobbs, who also got a warm pat on the shoulder.

At 5:18 p.m., a ritual being seen for just the third time in U.S. history began in the Capitol. Pelosi, the impeachment managers and House Democratic committee chairs walked into the Rayburn Reception Room for the "Engrossment Ceremony" to sign and send the articles of impeachment.

The two articles sat on a small table, draped in a navy blue cloth, alongside two silver dishes filled with black and gold pens bearing Pelosi's signature. A placard with "#DefendOurDemocracy" hung on the front of the table, which was set up before a huge portrait of George Washington on the wall.

"So sad, so tragic for our country that the actions taken by the president to undermine our national security, to violate his oath of office and to jeopardize the security of our elections, the integrity of our elections, has taken us to this place," Pelosi said. "So today, we will make history."

She finished her brief remarks and moved to the table, with her top lieutenants in a semicircle behind her, watching with solemn expressions. She began the painstaking process of signing a small bit of her signature with one pen, then picking up a new pen to continue. "It makes for a funny signature," she said.

When she finished, she passed out pens as mementos, as Trump had done a few hours earlier in the White House. Gifting pens used to sign official documents is a long-standing Washington tradition. President Lyndon B. Johnson is said to have used more than 75 pens when he signed the 1964 Civil Rights Act. During the Clinton impeachment trial, senators received their own pens to use while signing the oath pledging their impartiality. They discovered, with some amusement, that a typo had left them with pens that read: "*Untied* States Senator." Daniel Patrick Moynihan of New York had his framed for display in his office.

Despite Pelosi's admonishments to avoid any celebration, Maxine Waters, who had been calling for Trump's impeachment since 2017, cried out in joy that Trump was finally impeached, saying, "We're done! We're done! We're done!" before walking out of the room holding her commemorative pen aloft.

At 5:33 p.m., the formal procession to the Senate began, with House clerk Cheryl Johnson carrying the articles, walking side by side with House sergeant at arms Paul Irving. The managers walked two by two behind them: Schiff and Nadler, Lofgren and Jeffries, Demings and Crow, and, finally, Garcia. With news cameras flashing as they passed, they crossed the Rotunda and Statuary Hall to the Senate side of the Capitol.

The procession followed a route first laid out on February 25, 1868, the day after the impeachment of Andrew Johnson, then used again on December 19, 1998, after the Clinton impeachment.

Cheryl Johnson entered the Senate chamber, where Senator Charles Grassley was in the presiding officer's chair, wearing a robin's-egg-blue sweater under his suit jacket.

"The Senate will receive a message from the House of Representatives," Grassley said.

Johnson announced that she bore impeachment articles against the president.

"The message will be received," Grassley said.

McConnell then rose to speak. He said the Senate would receive the managers formally the next day at noon, and then Chief Justice John Roberts would arrive at 2 p.m. to be sworn in himself. Roberts would then swear in all senators as jurors.

"This is a difficult time for our country, but this is precisely the kind of time for which the framers created the Senate," McConnell said. "I'm confident this body can rise above short-termism and factional fever and serve the long-term best interest of our nation. We can do this. And we must."

At 7 p.m., Dobbs was still talking about his big day at the White House. He wanted to make sure nobody missed it. "During today's historic trade deal signing, President Trump graciously gave me a shout-out," Dobbs said. "It was generous. I greatly appreciate his kind words. Here they are." He played the entire video of Trump's remarks, including Trump saying he didn't know if Dobbs "was for real" when he said Trump was a better president than Washington or Lincoln.

"Thank you, Mr. President," Dobbs said when the clip ended. "And yes, I was for real."

Dobbs then moved on to his exclusive interview with Vice President Pence.

Over on MSNBC at 9 p.m., host Rachel Maddow had a big story: the first of a two-part interview with Lev Parnas. Maddow reminded viewers that Parnas was under indictment and awaiting trial in the Southern District of New York. He was a man with something to gain by being helpful to law enforcement and lawmakers. But he was also a man who had been right in the middle of Giuliani's efforts in Ukraine. As Maddow said in introducing the taped segment, people in Parnas's circumstances "don't typically do media interviews." They had talked in New York, and Parnas was accompanied by his lawyer, Joseph Bondy.

"What do you think is the main inaccuracy or main lie that's being told that you feel like you can correct?" asked Maddow, one of the most influential voices on the progressive left.

"That the president didn't know what was going on," said Parnas, with his gravelly Brooklyn accent and his tie loosened just a bit. "President

Trump knew exactly what was going on. He was aware of all my movements. I wouldn't do anything without the consent of Rudy Giuliani or the president."

Maddow asked about the group's campaign against Yovanovitch. Parnas said he wanted to apologize to her for his part in her firing. Maddow asked about the group's motivation, and Parnas said they had feared she would block their efforts to pressure the Ukrainian government to announce an investigation of Joe Biden.

"That was the only motivation?" Maddow asked.

"There was no other motivation," Parnas replied.

Parnas scoffed at the idea that Trump was interested in rooting out corruption in Ukraine: "It was never about corruption. . . . It was strictly about Burisma, which included Hunter Biden and Joe Biden."

Maddow asked if Giuliani had ever spoken to Barr, the attorney general, about his efforts. Parnas said: "Mr. Barr absolutely knew everything. . . . Barr was basically on the team." A Barr spokeswoman immediately called that "100 percent false."

It was Parnas's statements about Bolton, though, that seemed to loom largest over the Senate trial that was about to begin. "I don't know exactly what Mr. Bolton knew, but I know Mr. Bolton was definitely involved in the loop because of the firing of Maria Yovanovitch," Parnas said. "Also, his interactions with Rudy Giuliani. They started butting heads, and he was not agreeing—I mean, from Venezuela to Ukraine, Bolton didn't agree with Giuliani on the way of dealing with it. So, there was tension there. There was—there was definitely tension there."

Maddow asked: "But you believe he knows what the administration was pressuring Ukraine to do?"

"A hundred percent," Parnas said. "He knows what happened there."

Parnas was an imperfect witness with uncertain credibility. But he was telling quite a story. Would the Senate jurors ever have the chance to hear it, or hear from Bolton?

CHAPTER FORTY-EIGHT

"Do You Solemnly Swear?"

January 16, Washington

The trial preliminaries were set to resume at noon, leaving plenty of time for several new story lines. By dawn, CNN had posted excerpts of its own interview with Parnas, in which he told Anderson Cooper he had once "loved" Trump. "I mean, when the FBI came to my house to raid, my wife felt embarrassed because they said I had a shrine to him. I had pictures all over. I idolized him. I thought he was the savior," he said, adding that Congress should call him and Bolton to testify so they could connect "all the dots."

"The truth is out now, thank God," Parnas said. "I thought they were going to shut me out and make me look like the scapegoat and try to blame me for stuff I haven't done," he said.

White House press secretary Stephanie Grisham told Fox News that Trump did not know Parnas. "This is a man who's under indictment and who's actually out on bail . . . we're not too concerned with it." Trump followed up later in the day. "I don't know Parnas other than I guess they had pictures taken which I do with thousands of people," Trump told reporters in the Oval Office. "I don't know him at all, don't know what he's about, don't know where he comes from, know nothing about him."

At 10 a.m., *The Washington Post* reported that the White House had violated federal law when it withheld security aid to Ukraine, according to a decision released by the Government Accountability Office, a nonpartisan agency that reports to Congress.

The GAO said the Trump administration, in withholding $214 million worth of aid, broke a law that governs how the White House disburses money approved by Congress. "Faithful execution of the law does not permit the President to substitute his own policy priorities for those that Congress has enacted into law," the decision said. "OMB withheld funds for a policy reason, which is not permitted." The White House quickly dismissed the finding as an "overreach" and the "media's controversy of the day."

As the GAO report was making news, McConnell was on the Senate floor, slamming the "transparently partisan" House process and calling out Pelosi for her souvenir pens from the day before: "Well, nothing says seriousness and sobriety like handing out souvenirs. As though this were a happy bill-signing instead of the gravest process in our Constitution."

Schumer hit back. "He complains about processes and pens and signing ceremonies, but still does not address the charges against the president and why we shouldn't have witnesses and documents," Schumer said. "God forbid we rush through this trial, and only afterward, the truth comes out."

Moments later, the Senate approved the USMCA, a new trade agreement with Canada and Mexico, delivering on Trump's promise of a new North American trade deal. The vote was 89 to 10. Some bipartisan, non-impeachment business was still happening.

A couple of minutes past noon, the seven impeachment managers, escorted by the Senate's sergeant at arms, Michael C. Stenger, entered the Senate and stood at the front, known as the "well," of the Senate, on the Democratic side. Stenger made an official proclamation, in language from another century.

"Hear ye! Hear ye! Hear ye! All persons are commanded to keep silent, on pain of imprisonment, while the House of Representatives is exhibiting to the Senate of the United States articles of impeachment against President Donald John Trump, President of the United States."

Schiff then stepped to the podium, opened a leather folder containing his remarks and looked out at the senators. A toothache was killing him. The week before, in pain, Schiff had gone to his dentist. The dentist had replaced a filling, but that only made the throbbing worse. He had not slept through the night in several days, waking up every few hours to take more Advil. He kept hoping the pain would go away, and he was too busy preparing for the trial to see the dentist again. Now, as he stood before the Senate, he had a handful of Advil in his pocket, and the pain was radiating.

Ninety-nine senators listened as Schiff read the two articles of impeachment. Only James Inhofe, Republican of Oklahoma, was missing. He was at home with his wife, who had a medical emergency.

The trial meant the four Democratic senators running for president—Sanders, Warren, Klobuchar and Bennet—had to stay in Washington, off the campaign trail. Two other senators, Harris and Booker, had recently dropped out of the race, Booker earlier in the week.

Two nights earlier, Sanders, Warren and Klobuchar had taken part in a debate in Des Moines, Iowa. The Democratic nomination was still up for grabs, with Sanders, Warren and Joe Biden, who had served 36 years in the Senate before becoming vice president, leading the pack. At the Iowa debate, impeachment was hardly mentioned. As with earlier debates, it was always there simmering in the background, but never a main dish.

The Iowa caucuses, the first formal voting in the 2020 election season, were less than three weeks away, and Sanders, Warren and Klobuchar wanted to be in Iowa, trying to keep pace with Biden and Pete Buttigieg, who had every diner and farmhouse to themselves. Their hope of removing Trump through impeachment was directly conflicting with their drive to remove him at the ballot box.

Sanders, Warren and Klobuchar all said they were sending surrogates to Iowa, a state that reveled in drawing the candidates themselves. Buttigieg held five events in a single day in Iowa while his opponents were sitting in the Senate chamber. Biden campaigned in person and introduced a new ad, embracing the impeachment, despite the mud it had splashed on his family. Biden's ad said Trump's alleged efforts to find dirt on the Biden family in Ukraine was an acknowledgment of Trump's fear of Biden's candidacy.

As Schiff spoke, some of the senators took notes, others seemed uninterested. In the White House, Trump chose not to watch, instead working in the Oval Office, which did not have a television.

At 2 p.m., a bipartisan group of four senators—Republicans Roy Blunt and Lindsey Graham, and Democrats Patrick Leahy and Dianne Feinstein—led Chief Justice John Roberts into the chamber to preside over the trial, as required by the Constitution.

Roberts had heard hundreds of oral arguments at the Supreme Court since President George W. Bush appointed him in 2005, but this was his first time as a "trial judge." It was not an assignment he relished.

Roberts was deeply concerned about the court's reputation and credibility. He was widely respected, but also criticized by those on the far right and left. He had always tried to distance himself and the court from partisan politics. Responding to Trump's repeated jabs at "Obama judges," Roberts had taken the unusual step of issuing a statement in 2018. "We do not have Obama judges or Trump judges, Bush judges or Clinton judges," he said. "What we have is an extraordinary group of dedicated judges doing their level best to do equal right to those appearing before them." Trump, stung by Roberts's remarks, called him an "absolute disaster."

For Trump's impeachment trial, Roberts had only one recent model to follow: William Rehnquist's handling of the 1999 Clinton trial. Rehnquist viewed his role as limited and had tried to leave as many decisions as possible to senators. Roberts, who had worked as one of Rehnquist's law clerks, was expected to take a similarly narrow approach.

Now Roberts stood on the dais in the Senate, placed his left hand on a Bible, raised his right hand and listened as Grassley asked: "Do you solemnly swear that in all things appertaining to the trial of the impeachment of Donald John Trump, the President of the United States, now pending, you will do impartial justice according to the Constitution and laws, so help you God?"

"I do," Roberts said.

"God bless you," Grassley replied.

Roberts then turned to the entire Senate, asked all members to raise their right hand and repeat the same oath after him. Each senator, in alphabetical order, walked to the well of the Senate and signed an "oath book."

The televised image of McConnell at the table, signing his name in the oath book, prompted a stream of commentary on social media, pointing out that he had said earlier he wasn't impartial. In McConnell's home state, the *Louisville Courier-Journal* put the contrast into a headline: "Weeks after saying 'I'm not an impartial juror,' McConnell pledges impartiality in oath."

A half-hour later, preliminary rituals done, the Senate adjourned. The trial would get under way the following Tuesday, January 21, at 1 p.m. Both sides now had a long Martin Luther King Jr. weekend to make their final preparations.

CHAPTER FORTY-NINE

Virus

January 17 to 20, Washington

During the holiday weekend, many Republicans and Democrats were heading home to their districts. Others were heading to the airwaves. The messaging battle was going nonstop. On Friday morning, January 17, Dingell appeared on Fox News to keep up the pressure for witnesses at the Senate trial.

The first question from anchor Sandra Smith: "Where do you stand on whether or not witnesses should be allowed to be called?"

Dingell hit the talking points: New evidence had come to light since the House vote. The Senate owed the American people a fair trial. That meant hearing from witnesses with relevant information, like Bolton and Mulvaney. The administration should let them testify. The Senate needed all the facts.

So far, so good. Then Smith asked: "Okay, so if Democrats are allowed to call John Bolton, Mick Mulvaney and/or others, obviously Republicans are going to say, all right, we want Hunter Biden, we want Joe Biden. Where do you stand on that?"

On the screen, a graphic showing Bolton and Mulvaney switched to one with the Bidens, Schiff and "Anonymous Whistleblower."

Dingell made the Democratic case: Bolton and Mulvaney would be fact witnesses, while the Bidens would be theatrical witnesses. "We are not investigating Joe Biden and Hunter Biden," she said. "The charges are against the president and taking funds and using them for his own political purpose. So I'm not going down that rabbit hole. This case is not about the former vice president or his son."

In the early afternoon, Trump welcomed the Louisiana State University Tigers to the East Room of the White House to celebrate their national collegiate football championship. He offered the team an Oval Office tour.

"We'll take pictures behind the Resolute Desk," Trump said. "It's been there a long time. A lot of presidents. Some good, some not so good. But you've got a good one now, even though they're trying to impeach the son of a bitch. Can you believe that? Can you believe that?"

Late on Friday evening, the White House released a list of eight attorneys on Trump's legal team for the trial, led by Cipollone and Sekulow.

The best known was Dershowitz, the Harvard emeritus law professor, who told *The Washington Post* that he was participating on Trump's team to "defend the integrity of the Constitution and to prevent the creation of a dangerous constitutional precedent." Dershowitz said the charges against Trump did not amount to "high crimes and misdemeanors," the standard for impeachment set out in the Constitution. Trump wanted Dershowitz partly because he thought he was good on television. Dershowitz said he was not a full-fledged member of the team; rather, he was simply there to present his views on the Constitution.

Trump had first floated the idea to Dershowitz on Christmas Eve in the dinner buffet line at Mar-a-Lago. Trump asked him to join his impeachment team, but Dershowitz demurred, telling the president that his wife, Carolyn Cohen, a psychologist, would not be pleased. That sent Trump off to find Dershowitz's wife elsewhere in the room. The president persuaded her, and just like that, Trump had added some star power to his defense team.

Adding gravitas to the team—and a dash of irony—were Kenneth W. Starr and Robert Ray, both former independent counsels who had investigated Clinton. The choice of Starr was notable for its echoes of the Clinton impeachment and the poisonous blood between Trump and Hillary Clinton.

Trump had not always been a big fan of Starr, whom he once called a "freak." Footage resurfaced of Trump trashing Starr during an October 1999 interview on NBC's "Today" show: "I think Ken Starr is a lunatic. I really think that Ken Starr is a disaster. . . . I really think that Ken Starr was terrible."

Trump also added former Florida attorney general Pam Bondi, who had been helping with messaging during the impeachment; Jane Raskin, another one of Trump's personal lawyers; and Eric D. Herschmann, a partner at the law firm of Marc Kasowitz, who had represented Trump on other matters. The lawyers had a strong record of fighting for Trump. The new members of Trump's legal team had collectively made at least 365 weekday appearances on Fox News since January 2019, according to Media Matters. The group reported that Starr had appeared 125 times, Dershowitz 110 times, Ray 70 and Bondi 60.

Trump had favored adding some of his most pugilistic supporters from the House to his legal team, including Jordan and Ratcliffe. McConnell counseled against it. In another measure of the trust between them, Trump let the idea go.

On Saturday, Health and Human Services Secretary Alex Azar spoke with Trump for the first time about an emerging new worry: A novel coronavirus was starting to spread internationally after originating in Wuhan, a city of 11 million people in central China.

So far, three people in China had died from the new pathogen and several cases had been reported in Thailand and Japan. The day before, U.S. officials had initiated screening of passengers arriving from Wuhan at San Francisco, Los Angeles and New York airports. But the Centers for Disease Control and Prevention (CDC) judged that the virus's risk to the U.S. population was "low," and few people in the United States were paying it much attention. Azar had been alerted to the virus through discussions the CDC director had with Chinese colleagues on January 3.

Azar had trouble reaching Trump, but when he finally connected with him by phone at Mar-a-Lago, where he was spending the weekend, the president interjected to ask about vaping and when flavored vaping products would be back on the market. Azar had trouble focusing Trump's full attention on the deadly virus spreading in Asia.

At 11 a.m. on Monday, the King birthday holiday, the legal teams for both sides in the impeachment trial conducted their first walk-through of the Senate chamber, which had been fitted out with semicircular tables that had been custom-built for the Clinton impeachment—and presciently stored since then. A new cabinet for senators' phones and other electronic devices had been installed just off the Senate floor. Senate rules for the trial barred all electronics from the Senate floor—including in the press gallery, where reporters were forced to rely on pens and notebooks. Lawyers for both sides also had a workspace set up off the floor: the Democrats in a room near Schumer's office, the Republicans in a corner suite, just off the floor, traditionally used by the vice president.

As the legal teams were walking through the Senate, the political fury was still raging outside. On Fox, Kellyanne Conway warned Democrats to "be careful what you wish for." If they called Bolton, she said, Republicans would definitely call Hunter Biden.

At 6:45 p.m., Trump departed Joint Base Andrews in Maryland for Switzerland, where he was scheduled to attend the annual World Economic Forum in Davos, the elite gathering of some of the world's most powerful figures in business and government.

At 8:15 p.m., the White House announced that eight House Republicans would serve as "part of" the president's team, but not part of his *legal* team. The list included some familiar names from the House hearings: Jordan, Ratcliffe, Collins, Meadows, Stefanik, Zeldin, Lesko and Mike Johnson of Louisiana. President Trump, the White House statement said, was "confident that the Members will help expeditiously end this brazen political vendetta on behalf of the American people."

They would have their chance soon. Three years and one day after his inauguration on a platform outside the Capitol, Trump would go on trial inside the building, accused of abusing the office and the Constitution he had sworn to protect.

CHAPTER FIFTY

"Will Senators Rise to the Occasion?"

January 21, Washington

Mitch McConnell walked into the virtually empty U.S. Senate chamber just before 12:30 p.m., took his place at the majority leader's lectern, bowed his head while the Senate chaplain prayed to God to "keep us from dishonor," recited the Pledge of Allegiance with his hand on his heart and said he wanted to talk about fairness.

In less than an hour, the Senate would reconvene for Trump's trial. The only item on the day's agenda: McConnell's proposed rules. Now, in a preview of the arguments to come, McConnell was accusing the House of an unfair inquiry that had cut the president's legal team out of the process. His rules for the trial would fix that. "Here in the Senate, the President's lawyers will finally receive a level playing field with the House Democrats and will finally be able to present the President's case. Finally, some fairness." McConnell said some variation of "fair" 17 times in his 15-minute statement.

Fairness was not the word that had come to Schumer's mind when he had seen McConnell's final proposal, released the day before. "It was kept secret until the very eve of the trial," said the Democratic leader, with barely controlled anger. "And now that it's public, it's very easy to see why. The McConnell rules seem to be designed by President Trump for President Trump. It asks the Senate to rush through as fast as possible and makes getting evidence as hard as possible."

McConnell's proposal gave Republicans and Democrats 24 hours each to make opening arguments—but required those arguments to be compressed into just two session days for each side, making for long and tiring days that would test the public's patience. That would be followed by

16 hours for each side to submit written questions to the House managers and the president's defenders.

On the witness question, McConnell had stood firm. As he had said earlier, the senators would have the option of voting to call witnesses, but only after hearing from both sides. McConnell's strategy was plain: Let the Democrats have their say, so that no one could accuse the Republicans of not listening, but make the trial as quick as possible.

Now Schumer raged about McConnell's plan. He called it "nothing short of a national disgrace" that would go down as one of the darkest moments in Senate history. The compressed timeline for opening arguments "could force presentations to take place at two or three in the morning so that the American people won't see them," Schumer said. "In short, the McConnell resolution will result in a rushed trial, with little evidence, in the dark of night. Literally, in the dark of night. If the president is so confident in his case, if Leader McConnell is so confident that the president did nothing wrong, why don't they want the case presented in broad daylight?" On Twitter, a new hashtag was circulating: #MidnightMitch.

Schumer vowed to introduce amendments seeking the witnesses and documents blocked by the White House. He couldn't stop McConnell, but he could force the Republicans into a vote that they might have to defend later, including at reelection time. Schumer wanted them on the record as supporting McConnell's "dark of night" plan.

This was Schumer's moment. Throughout 2019, he had deferred to Pelosi, supporting her resistance to impeachment and then backing her conversion. Throughout the House hearings, as the evidence emerged, he had taken to the Senate floor to beseech Republican colleagues to "follow the facts."

His primary focus, however, was on his own caucus, especially those senators running for reelection in states that had gone for Trump in 2016. As the House inquiry was in full swing, his office developed careful messaging guidance for the Democratic senators: Wait for the House to act. Focus on legislation. Avoid saying how you would vote in a trial. Meanwhile, Schumer staffers were creating a digital repository of impeachment material, stockpiling historical information and developments in the House to help members prepare for the inevitable.

Republican senators had been irritated by Schumer's public letter to McConnell in December, which had jumped the gun on the witness question. Why not talk to McConnell first, hash it out? But the letter was a signal of Schumer's overall strategy. He was taking his case relentlessly to the public, rather than saving his arguments for private negotiations that he was powerless to win. A closed-door meeting was McConnell's turf. On camera, it didn't matter that Schumer didn't have the votes. If he could drum up enough public outrage about McConnell's handling of the trial, maybe he could sway moderate Republicans to come over to his side.

Now, on the Senate floor, Schumer was doing double duty, appealing to his colleagues and the TV cameras. He was practically shoulder to shoulder with McConnell, separated by a few feet of blue-carpeted aisle. As McConnell neared the end of his "fairness speech," he had said: "The eyes of the nation are on the Senate. The country is watching to see if we can rise to the occasion."

Schumer finished with the same phrase, as if he were going toe-to-toe with McConnell on his rhetoric as well as his rules. "My colleagues, the eyes of the nation, the eyes of the Founding Fathers are upon us. History will be our final judge: Will senators rise to the occasion?"

At 1:18 p.m., Roberts smacked his gavel and said: "The Senate will convene as a court of impeachment." He swore in Senator Inhofe, who had been absent for the swearing-in ceremony. After Stenger, the sergeant at arms, said his "hear ye's," they were off.

Cipollone had first crack. He said, simply, that his side was fine with McConnell's proposed trial rules. "It is long past time to start this proceeding, and we are here today to do it."

Schiff, his tooth still throbbing, stood to deliver the House managers' arguments against McConnell's plan. Schiff still hadn't found time to go to the dentist. The tooth was extremely sensitive to cold, so Schiff had been drinking his guilty pleasure—regular Coca-Cola, full sugar—at room temperature.

Now he looked out at the Senate floor, dominated by white men in gray and blue suits, the tableau of sameness broken only by a few flourishes, like Grassley's fireball-red grandpa sweater. Many of the 26 female members, the most in Senate history, were dressed in courtroom dark. A few wore bright colors, but no one could compare with Democrat Kyrsten Sinema of Arizona, who arrived in an electric-violet faux-fur coat and bright yellow boots.

Senators sat at wooden desks, stacks of papers before them, some taking notes, some simply watching, as aides moved among them bringing fresh glasses of water. The House impeachment managers and lawyers and the president's legal team sat at tables in the shape of an arc, close to the dais where Roberts was presiding.

Both sides had set out hardened positions in briefs filed in advance. Schiff and the House managers had submitted their 111-page brief on Saturday, arguing their case on both articles. Trump's wrongdoing, they claimed, left the future of the country hanging in the balance, with only the Senate to save it. "The outcome of these proceedings will determine whether generations to come will enjoy a safe and secure democracy in which the President is not a king, and in which no one, particularly the President, is above the law," they wrote.

Trump's lawyers had filed their 171-page rebuttal on Monday. "The only threat to the Constitution that House Democrats have brought to light is their own degradation of the impeachment process and trampling of the separation of powers," they said. "Their fixation on damaging the President has trivialized the momentous act of impeachment, debased the standards of impeachable conduct, and perverted the power of impeachment by turning it into a partisan, election-year political tool."

Now, though, Schiff had to focus on McConnell's rules. He had 45 minutes to give the most powerful argument he could muster about the witnesses and why they were important. He needed to stay out of the weeds. That was Schiff's challenge. How do you make an argument about rules that doesn't sound arcane? At one point, he wandered into a dense discussion of Senate procedures, talking about Rule 6, Rule 7 and Rule 11. "And the list goes on," he said.

Schiff's tone was different from speeches in the House in December, on the day Trump was impeached. Then, no one had tried to persuade anyone else of anything. But now Schiff was giving persuasion a try, aimed mainly at Collins, Romney, Murkowski and Alexander. Maybe, if he hit the right notes, they would vote for witnesses when the time came.

If Schiff allowed himself a flicker of optimism, he could expand the target group to a dozen. Several Republicans had expressed some concern about Trump's actions in Ukraine. Cory Gardner of Colorado was facing a tough reelection campaign in a state that wasn't an automatic win for Republicans. Gardner might want to tell independent-minded Coloradans he had voted to hear witnesses. Two senators were retiring, so they would not face any ballot-box consequences for straying from the party line.

Schiff made eye contact as he spoke. His tone was tough as he laid into Trump, but he was also beseeching. "Let me be blunt. Let me be very blunt. Right now, a great many, perhaps even most, Americans do not believe there will be a fair trial. They don't believe that the Senate will be impartial. They believe that the result is precooked. The president will be acquitted, not because he is innocent—he is not—but because the senators will vote by party, and he has the votes—the votes to prevent the evidence from coming out, the votes to make sure the public never sees it."

He made an impassioned plea. "The American people want a fair trial," he said. "They want to believe their system of governance is still capable of rising to the occasion. They want to believe that we can rise above party and do what is best for the country, but a great many Americans don't believe that will happen. Let's prove them wrong. Let's prove them wrong."

Cipollone was having none of it when he stood to answer Schiff. "It is very difficult to sit there and listen to Mr. Schiff tell the tale he just told," he said. "Talk about the framers' worst nightmare. It is a partisan impeachment they delivered to your doorstep, in an election year. Some of you are upset because you should be in Iowa right now, but, instead, we are here." Bringing the 2020 election into the chamber was a reminder of the Republican argument that the voters, not the Senate, should be the ones to decide Trump's political fate.

"It is outrageous," Cipollone said. "It is outrageous. The American people will not stand for it. . . . I could go on and on, but my point is very simple. It is long past time we start this so we can end this ridiculous charade and go have an election."

He clapped his folder shut, punctuating the moment, and walked back to his seat.

Schumer proposed 11 amendments to McConnell's plan, as he maneuvered to find a way to bring new witnesses, documents or other information before the Senate. All were rejected on party-line votes.

But concerns from Collins, Portman and others had caused McConnell to make one change to his plan. Instead of each side cramming its 24 hours of arguments into two days, McConnell had agreed to make it three. Collins and others had told McConnell in private that "middle of the night" sessions would not appear fair or transparent. But they were too late to undo the mocking trend on Twitter, where #MidnightMitch was going strong.

As the battle over the rules wore on, senators displayed varying degrees of attention span. Some took nonstop notes, some chatted quietly with their neighbors (despite the sergeant at arms's threat of imprisonment), some stood to stretch their legs, some left the chamber. The grind of hour after hour of arguments was rattling nerves. Nadler was at the microphone as the session lurched into the early hours of Wednesday. He was reading from notes, looking up to glance at the president's legal team, when he took the rhetoric to a new level.

The president's lawyers, he said, "will not permit the American people to hear from the witnesses. And they lie, and lie and lie and lie."

Nadler went further. "So far, I'm sad to say, I see a lot of senators voting for a cover-up, voting to deny witnesses—an absolutely indefensible vote, obviously a treacherous vote," he said. "Either you want the truth, and you must permit the witnesses, or you want a shameful cover-up. History will judge and so will the electorate."

Cipollone immediately rose to respond, saying "we don't deserve, what just happened." He accused Nadler of making "false allegations" against the Senate and the White House. "The only one who should be embarrassed, Mr. Nadler, is you, for the way you've addressed this body. This is the United States Senate. You're not in charge here."

Sekulow was practically shouting when he followed Cipollone. "The Senate is not on trial," he said heatedly, returning to his side's table and throwing down his papers in disgust.

That was enough for Roberts. Tempers were flaring, exhaustion was evident after nearly 12 hours of often angry debate, but Roberts was a voice of calm control. "I think it is appropriate at this point for me to admonish both the House managers and president's counsel in equal terms to remember that they are addressing the world's greatest deliberative body," Roberts said.

He recounted a 1905 impeachment trial of a federal judge, when a House manager was admonished for using the phrase "pettifogging," which means bickering over trivialities. "I don't think we need to aspire to that high of a standard, but I do think those addressing the Senate should remember where they are," he said.

It was the first time Roberts had injected himself into the proceedings for anything other than procedural pronouncements. On Day 1, he was living up to expectations of being a hands-off presider. Now he was rebuking both sides. Using the word "pettifogging" was his way of doing it as gently as possible.

It was past 1 a.m. when the Senate voted on McConnell's rules, approving them, 53 to 47, right along party lines. Right where the vote would have been 12 hours earlier. Right where it would have been after another hundred hours. The debate, with all its partisan sound and fury, had changed nothing.

When Roberts gaveled Day 1 to a close at 1:50 a.m., a little smile appeared on McConnell's face. His plan was going fine.

CHAPTER FIFTY-ONE

"Your Head Will Be on a Pike"

January 22 to 24, Switzerland and Washington

Donald Trump's chair was almost too small. He perched on the edge of it, jaw set, eyes locked on CNBC's Joe Kernen. It was late on Wednesday morning in Davos, Switzerland, not quite dawn in Washington. They were in a makeshift interview space, two glasses of water on a tiny round table. The president waited, his hands in steeple formation on his lap.

Kernen's first question was not one the president had been asked before.

"Before we get started," Kernen said, "the CDC has identified a case of coronavirus in Washington State. The Wuhan strain of this. If you remember SARS, that affected GDP. Travel-related effects. Have you been briefed by the CDC? And—"

Trump jumped in. "I have. And—"

Kernen finished his question. "—are there worries about a pandemic at this point?"

"No," Trump said. "Not at all. And we have it totally under control. It's one person coming in from China, and we have it under control. It's going to be just fine."

Everybody found something to dislike about what had happened on Tuesday at the Senate trial. First thing Wednesday morning in Washington, Trump campaign manager Brad Parscale called the proceedings boring. "I can choose 9,000 TV channels, Netflix or Amazon, or I can watch the impeachment. I couldn't even watch it last night, and I'm paid to do it." From Switzerland, Trump spoke on Fox Business and said the

Democrats had gone "totally nuts." At a news conference he called Nadler "a sleazebag" and Giuliani a "high quality person."

Joe Biden, appearing on MSNBC's "Morning Joe" from Iowa, where he was campaigning ahead of the upcoming caucuses, said he was "embarrassed for the institution" where he had represented Delaware for 36 years. Of Trump's Republican defenders in the Senate, Biden said, "I think it's one of those things they're going to regret when their grandchildren read in the history books what they did."

Shortly before 1 p.m., Schiff took a call from Pelosi, who was leading a congressional delegation to Israel to commemorate the 75th anniversary of the liberation of Nazi Germany's Auschwitz death camp. Wednesday was a rare day when all three of the top U.S. leaders were out of the country for part of the time. Trump was on his way home from Davos, Pence was en route to Israel and Pelosi was already there.

Pelosi was calling from her motorcade in Jerusalem, where she was heading to a dinner hosted by Israeli president Reuven Rivlin. Schiff was about to make the managers' opening argument for Trump's removal, and they compared notes. For months, Pelosi had been telling her caucus that they needed to have an impeachment case that could be explained easily to the public. Now one of those explanatory moments—an important one, televised to the nation—had arrived.

As part of his opener, Schiff had chosen Alexander Hamilton for a lead role. Five years earlier, Hamilton might have been a more obscure pick, well known to historians but little more than a name to the average American. But thanks to the wildly popular musical "Hamilton" and its catchy, clever lyrics, Hamilton would resonate with many in the TV impeachment audience. Hamilton was the guy who was "not throwing away my shot." Now Schiff was taking his.

Hamilton had once imagined a scenario in which a future president would put his own interests before the nation's. Quoting Hamilton's view of that future president, Schiff described "a man unprincipled in private life, desperate in his fortune, bold in his temper, possessed of considerable talents, having the advantage of military habits, despotic in his ordinary demeanor, known to have scoffed in private at the principles of liberty."

To protect from that kind of leader, Schiff said, the drafters of the Constitution had created impeachment. Trump, he argued, "has acted precisely as Hamilton and his contemporaries feared."

Most senators were listening, but others were less engrossed. Minutes after Schiff started speaking, Rand Paul, Republican of Kentucky, was busy working on a crossword puzzle. On his desk, he displayed a hand-lettered message with big block letters pleading: "S.O.S." He followed that later with another handwritten message pretending he was an abducted child:

"THESE R NOT MY PARENTS!"

"PLEASE HELP ME!"

Paul wrote "IRONY ALERT" on another scrap of paper.

Schiff laid out the case against Trump for two hours. Nadler would have his turn after a break. During the recess, Schumer said Democrats would not agree to call the Bidens as witnesses in exchange for Bolton and others sought by the Democrats. "That trade is not on the table," he said.

In Iowa, Biden also rejected the idea. "The reason I would not make the deal, the bottom line is, this is a constitutional issue," he said. "We're not going to turn it into a farce or political theater. I want no part of that." He defended his son Hunter. "There's nobody that's indicated there's a single solitary thing he did that was inappropriate or wrong—other than the appearance," Biden said. "It looked bad that he was there."

After the marathon first day of opening arguments, a main Republican complaint on Thursday was monotony and boredom.

"Yesterday was like Groundhog Day, because we heard what we had heard the day before," said Senator John Barrasso of Wyoming on CNN. "And I'm expecting more of the same today, just repeating and repeating and repeating. About every hour and a half, they repeat themselves, they play the same videos, use the same quote."

On the same network, Mazie Hirono, Democrat of Hawaii, brushed off such arguments, saying, "It is hard to listen to things you don't want to hear."

Schiff acknowledged the monotony issue when he resumed his presentation on Thursday. "I must ask you for some forbearance," he told the senators. "There will be some repetition of information from yesterday's chronology, and I want to explain the reason." Schiff said Wednesday's presentation was a detailed narrative of Trump's conduct drawn from hours of depositions and live testimony in House proceedings.

"We will now show you these facts and many others and how they are interwoven," Schiff said. "You will see some of these facts and videos, therefore, in a new context, in a new light, in the light of what else we know and why it compels a finding of guilt and conviction. So there is some method to our madness."

Cruz wasn't convinced. He joked that viewers should play a drinking game—with milk—and take a shot every time the Democrats brought up Bolton's "drug deal" or Mulvaney's "get over it." Marsha Blackburn of Tennessee read a book about "Trump haters" during the testimony. Paul continued doing his crossword puzzle and sketched an image of the U.S. Capitol. Richard Burr of North Carolina passed out fidget spinners to his GOP colleagues to pass the time. A few lawmakers nodded off.

As the second day neared its end, Schiff broke from interweaving facts and testimony to deliver an emotional appeal for doing what's "right." He had finally found time to have a root canal, so he was pain-free and speaking with unusual intensity. "Here," he said, " 'right' is supposed to matter. It's what's made us the greatest nation on earth. No Constitution can protect us if right doesn't matter anymore." His voice was a notch louder now. "And you know you can't trust this president to do what's right for this country. You can trust he will do what's right for Donald Trump. He'll do it now. He's done it before. He'll do it for the next several months. He'll do it in the election if he's allowed to. This is why if you find him guilty, you must find that he should be removed. Because right matters. Because right matters. And the truth matters. Otherwise, we are lost."

Democrats and their supporters were rapturous in their reviews. Chris Coons said Schiff's speech "should have left every senator in the chamber with a lump in their throat thinking about the consequences for the future of our country." *New York Times* columnist Michelle Goldberg tweeted: "If American democracy survives Donald Trump my kids will someday learn in school about the closing Adam Schiff gave tonight." The hashtag #RightMatters trended on Twitter.

Some Republican senators said in private conversations they were impressed with Schiff's speech. But publicly, the official talking point was that Schiff was lousy, and they were offended that Schiff had said Trump could not be trusted. "I don't trust Adam Schiff," Ron Johnson said. A Fox News chyron mocked Schiff: "Amateur Thespian Schiff Tries Out Some New Lines." Carlson called Schiff a "wild-eyed conspiracy nut" on his Fox show.

The loudest conservative voices put one message out to their listeners and followers more than any other: B.O.R.I.N.G. Late Thursday night, Trump tweeted clips of Hannity calling the trial a "SNOOZE-

FEST" and "HOURS AND HOURS OF SCHIFF." "The TV ratings are horrific," Hannity said in one clip. "American people are tuning out loudly."

In China on Thursday, major cities were taking dramatic steps to stop the coronavirus's spread. Beijing and quarantine-blocked Wuhan banned all large gatherings over the coming Lunar New Year festival, the most important holiday on the Chinese calendar. Authorities expanded restrictions imposed on travel from Wuhan to surrounding municipalities, attempting to quarantine about 25 million people—more than the population of Florida. At least 26 deaths had been confirmed in China, and cases had also been detected in Japan, South Korea, Taiwan, Thailand, Singapore, Vietnam and the United States.

In Washington, it was announced that the Senate Health Committee and the Senate Foreign Relations Committee would host for all senators a briefing Friday morning with top administration health officials regarding the coronavirus outbreak. The session was called by Health Committee chairman Lamar Alexander and the committee's ranking Democrat, Patty Murray of Washington. They released a statement that said: "The novel coronavirus is an emerging public health threat. Senators will have the opportunity to hear directly from senior government health officials regarding what we know about the virus so far, and how our country is prepared to respond as the situation develops."

On Friday morning, Robert Redfield, director of the CDC, and Anthony Fauci, head of the infectious disease unit of the National Institutes of Health, led the briefing for the about 14 senators who showed up.

Two coronavirus cases had been confirmed in the United States, and officials were already screening for fever and other symptoms at five major U.S. airports. The State Department and the CDC had also issued a travel advisory, suggesting that U.S. citizens not take unnecessary trips to the affected areas in China.

After the hearing, Fauci told reporters that a travel ban was "not something that I think we're even considering." But he also warned: "I wouldn't be surprised if there are additional cases."

Fauci described how public health authorities had reacted after a case emerged in Illinois. They "identified, isolated and did contact tracing on the people with whom that person came into contact," Fauci said. "That's how you get your handle on an outbreak."

Senator Richard Blumenthal, Democrat of Connecticut, sounded a more cautious note: "We are far from having this potential epidemic under control. We should be worried and concerned about this potential epidemic as a nation."

At 4:18 p.m., Trump tweeted: "China has been working very hard to contain the Coronavirus. The United States greatly appreciates their efforts and transparency. It will all work out well. In particular, on behalf of the American People, I want to thank President Xi!"

Whatever flicker of a good impression Schiff may have made on Republicans on Thursday night, he lost just as quickly on Friday. After his wrap-up of the House managers' case, Republicans zeroed in on his borrowed use of one phrase.

"CBS News reported last night that a Trump confidante said that GOP senators were warned: vote against your president . . . and your head will be on a pike," Schiff said. "I hope it's not true. But I was struck by the irony of the idea, when we're talking about a president who would make himself a monarch, that whoever that was would use the terminology of a penalty that was imposed by a monarch, a head on a pike." Schiff had relayed the quote accurately from a CBS News report from correspondent Nancy Cordes.

Republicans were furious. Collins said out loud in the chamber: "That's not true."

"Not true!" Senator James Lankford of Oklahoma said, telling reporters that Republican senators were "visibly upset" by the comment. "Nothing like going through three days of frustration and then cap it off with an insult on everybody."

Barrasso said Schiff had simply proven that he was "capable of falsehoods. . . . Whatever gains he may have made, he lost all of it, plus some, tonight."

Republicans seemed to have forgotten, Senator Richard Durbin of Illinois said, that Trump's habit of exacting revenge from those who crossed him was "one of the worst-kept secrets in Washington."

Senator Chris Murphy tweeted: "I'm gonna let you in on a secret. Republicans who don't want to defend Trump's corruption on the merits are instead going to complain about how mean the House managers are."

After 21 hours and 18 minutes of opening arguments by Schiff and his colleagues, Trump's lawyers would start making their case the next day. It was Saturday, but McConnell wanted to keep things moving.

The president wouldn't be there, but he would have the floor.

CHAPTER FIFTY-TWO

A Small Earthquake

January 25 and 26, Washington

Donald Trump had been looking forward to this moment for a long time. For four months and one day, since Nancy Pelosi had announced her impeachment inquiry against him, the Democrats had run the show. Their depositions. Their public hearings. Their witnesses. "Shifty Schiff" and his gang laying out their "bullshit" case against him. Today, finally, his lawyers would have a chance to tell his story. His way. With no interruptions.

People watching the trial would get to see him the way Lou Dobbs did: the best president ever, better even than Washington and Lincoln. Trump's first tweet of the morning, at 8:59 a.m., was a quote from "The Great @LouDobbs": "People know, after 3 years of this President, the most historic President in our Country's history, that there is no one who can touch what he's done in 3 years, foreign policy, domestic policy, you name it, it's amazing. Just to have the guts not to be . . . intimidated by this national left wing media, that reduces most politicians and most public figures to whining, crying, puddles of cowardice—it is really something to have a man in the White House who has a courageous heart and does what he says he will do."

The only problem: McConnell's unusual Saturday session. That was eating at Trump. He was a creature of television, so he knew better than most that Saturdays were the worst for ratings. He had tweeted his complaint the day before, saying Saturday "is called Death Valley in T.V."

He wanted as many eyeballs as possible on his show. He wanted ratings. So at 9:37 a.m., he tweeted a programming note to his 71.6 million Twitter followers: "Our case against lyin', cheatin', liddle' Adam "Shifty" Schiff, Cryin' Chuck Schumer, Nervous Nancy Pelosi, their leader, dumb as a rock AOC, & the entire Radical Left, Do Nothing Democrat Party, starts today at 10:00 A.M. on @FoxNews, @OANN or Fake News @CNN or Fake News MSDNC!"

At 10 a.m., Chief Justice Roberts was in his place, the sergeant at arms once again warned everyone to stay quiet on the pain of imprisonment, all 100 senators were in their seats, the press and visitors' galleries were full.

Beneath the desks of McConnell and Schumer were two brass spittoons, well used in the 19th century but now serving as reminders of the Senate's long history. A couple of days earlier, chewing tobacco had made a brief appearance in the chamber, until the sergeant at arms asked Ben Sasse, Republican of Nebraska, to remove his pouch of Red Man from his desk.

The scene was set for Cipollone. Trim at 53, with graying hair and wire-rim glasses, Cipollone had dressed for the day in a smartly fitting dark blue suit and striped red tie. He looked the part of the corporate lawyer he had been for decades, until his friend Laura Ingraham had asked him in 2016 to help prep candidate Trump for a debate against Hillary Clinton.

"Mr. Chief Justice, Senators, Leader McConnell, Democratic Leader Schumer, thank you for your time and thank you for your attention," he said, with a slight, deferential bow of his head in the direction of each person he recognized. He was solicitous and polite. It had been a long week already, he said. He assured his audience that he was going to be "very respectful of your time." No more than two or three hours. Everybody would be out by 1 p.m. at the latest. There was almost palpable relief on the Senate floor.

Then he put the Democrats on trial. "We don't believe that they have come anywhere close to meeting their burden for what they are asking you to do," he said. "They are asking you not only to overturn the results of the last election, but as I have said before, they are asking you to remove President Trump from the ballot in an election that is occurring in approximately nine months. They are asking you to tear up all of the ballots."

Cipollone was an unlikely counselor for Trump. Before he met Trump, his name had never appeared in the pages of his hometown newspaper, *The Washington Post*. That was fine with him. He prized his privacy, and the low profile that came with it. Early in the trial, Roberts mispronounced his name (the correct pronunciation was "sip-uh-LOAN-ee").

While the president was born into privilege, Cipollone was the son of Italian immigrants of modest means. He had attended a conservative institution far from the power centers on the East Coast, Covington Catholic High School in northern Kentucky. His family had moved to the state from the Bronx when his father transferred there for a factory job. He earned a law degree at the University of Chicago and moved immediately into the Chicago-based law firm of Kirkland & Ellis. He left to become the top lawyer at the Knights of Columbus, a Catholic fraternal organization. While there, he filed a brief in a Supreme Court abortion case in support of a Nebraska law that outlawed "partial birth" abortion.

More than anything else, Cipollone was defined by his ultraconservative Catholic faith and his involvement in Opus Dei, one of the most traditionalist and powerful organizations under the Vatican's large umbrella. Several of his 10 children attended the all-boys Heights School in Potomac, Maryland, where Opus Dei was responsible for the school's religious instruction. Until recently, Cipollone had served on the board of another Opus Dei affiliate, the Catholic Information Center, a spiritual and intellectual hub for conservatives on K Street, three blocks from the White House. Two close friends also had done stints on the center's board: Leonard Leo, co-chairman of the influential Federalist Society, a conservative legal group that had provided President Trump with names for Supreme Court nominations, and Bill Barr, Trump's attorney general.

Cipollone and Ingraham had been friends for years. She was a regular guest at the Cipollone home in the Washington suburbs. When she converted to Catholicism, he was her spiritual mentor, eventually becoming her godfather.

Now Cipollone was arguing the president's case, in a clear, deep voice conveying his passion and certainty. He said the Democrats were trying to take away the will of the American voter. "And I don't think they spent one minute of their 24 hours talking to you about the consequences of that for our country—not one minute. They didn't tell you what that would mean for our country—today, this year, and forever into our future. They are asking you to do something that no Senate has ever done, and they are asking you to do it with no evidence. That is wrong, and I ask you to keep that in mind."

Going into the trial, Cipollone had told officials at the White House that he did not want to appear on television news programs and talk shows during the impeachment hearings. Ingraham knew Cipollone never wanted to be a "television lawyer." Cipollone had also argued before the trial that cameras should be banned from the Senate chamber. He thought Trump's case could be damaged by the re-airing of some comments, especially Mulvaney's "get over it" remark. It also would have helped him to maintain his below-the-radar profile.

But now, on television, those watching were getting a full dose of Cipollone and his full-throated attack on the Democrats. "They are here to perpetrate the most massive interference in an election in American history, and we can't allow that to happen," Cipollone said. "It would violate our Constitution; it would violate our history; it would violate our obligations to the future; and, most importantly, it would violate the sacred trust the American people have placed in you and have placed in them. The American people decide elections. They have one coming up in nine months."

As the Senate session started, Steve Bannon, Trump's former chief strategist, was turning his attention to a "pandemic" he saw brewing in China. In October, Bannon had started an hourlong radio show and podcast called "War Room: Impeachment." It aired at 9 a.m. daily and offered an opportunity for conservatives to share news and strategy about the impeachment. But on Saturday morning, Bannon added a second hour, from 10 to 11, for the first episode of "War Room: Pandemic."

"This is a special on this pandemic," Bannon said, to a large conservative audience around the country. "We've ascertained in the last 24, 48 hours, that the biggest story in the world turns out not to be President Trump's impeachment, which has kind of become a farce because of the Democrats, but really, a potential pandemic coming out of China. . . . Over 56 million people are under some form of quarantine, attempted quarantine. That is bigger than Canada. Bigger than the population of the state of California."

Bannon warned that Americans ought to be paying attention. "You may not have an interest in the pandemic, but the pandemic has an interest in you," he said, reminding listeners of the outbreak of SARS, a cousin of this coronavirus, in 2003. "Not just put the fear of God in everybody, it had a dramatic impact on the world's economy, that downturn we had in the early 2000s, part of that was driven by SARS. This is SARS potentially to the 10th power."

• • •

On the Senate floor, Cipollone turned the floor over to two of his assistants and Sekulow. They went down the Democrats' list of alleged wrongdoing, rejecting each one. The president had not applied pressure on Zelensky during their phone call. He had not conditioned aid to Ukraine on any quid pro quo. He had been Ukraine's solid friend, providing military hardware that Obama had refused to send. He had every reason to be suspicious of Ukrainian corruption and skeptical of the European nations for not doing their share. He was not using executive privilege to obstruct Congress; he was well within his rights to refuse to allow administration officials to testify. Later, they said, they would return to provide evidence for each point.

After they spoke, Cipollone returned to the podium to summarize: The Democrats, he said, "basically said: Let's cancel an election over a meeting with Ukraine." He concluded by saying: "Let the people decide for themselves. That is what the Founders wanted. That is what we should all want."

At precisely noon, after just two hours, he abruptly finished.

Roberts adjourned the trial until Monday. McConnell shook hands with Cipollone, gave him a thumbs-up and a smile.

That evening, Saturday, the impeachment wars took a brief pause so political Washington could celebrate one of its annual rituals: the Alfalfa Club Dinner. The black-tie event for about 200 guests was among the most exclusive on the D.C. social calendar. It dated to 1913 and was regularly attended by presidents. At Saturday night's event, the keynote speaker was Mitt Romney, who brought actor Ben Stiller as his guest. Afterward, some adjourned to a traditional after-party at Cafe Milano, the famed Georgetown restaurant.

An even more exclusive after-party was held at the Washington home of Jeff Bezos, the Amazon billionaire and owner of *The Washington Post*, who was breaking in his new $23 million mansion. In addition to Bill Gates and other business titans just back from Davos, the crowd was populated with characters from the impeachment drama: Ivanka Trump and Jared Kushner, Conway, Meadows, Dingell, Esper and transportation secretary Elaine Chao (but not her husband, Mitch McConnell). The guest list had media heavyweights, print and broadcast: *The Post*'s Bob Woodward, and CBS anchor Norah O'Donnell.

Jon Favreau, the former Obama speechwriter and host of "Pod Save

America," tweeted a list of attendees, along with a caustic observation: "I can't imagine why most voters are deeply cynical about politics and think all the fighting is just a game."

On Sunday afternoon, Schumer issued a statement calling on the Department of Health and Human Services to declare the coronavirus a health emergency, which would make tens of millions of dollars available to combat the growing outbreak. "If we have learned anything from the risks that new viruses pose to public health it is that a 'stitch in time saves nine,' and the more we can do to be proactive, the better off the public will be," Schumer said.

He said the emergency declaration would allow the CDC to use $85 million from a fund set aside for such emergencies: "Should the outbreak get worse they will need immediate access to critical federal funds that at present they can't access."

Around 6:30 p.m. Sunday, the *New York Times* sent a small earthquake through the impeachment proceedings. The paper posted a story reporting that Bolton, in a draft of his coming book, claimed that President Trump told him in August that he wanted to continue his freeze on Ukraine's security aid until officials there helped with investigations into the Bidens. The story, by reporters Maggie Haberman and Michael S. Schmidt, was a direct contradiction of one of the key pillars of Trump's defense—no quid pro quo—and it was being made by a man who'd had daily access to Trump at the time.

According to the story, Bolton recounted an August meeting with Trump where Bolton had raised the frozen Ukraine aid, and Trump, citing theories relayed to him by Giuliani, said he "preferred sending no assistance to Ukraine until officials had turned over all materials they had about the Russia investigation that related to Mr. Biden and supporters of Mrs. Clinton in Ukraine." Bolton also wrote that Pompeo had said there was "no basis" for Trump's freeze of the aid.

Bolton's unpublished manuscript of "The Room Where It Happened" had been circulated in recent weeks to close associates and sent to the White House for the required review.

The *Times* reporters called Bolton's lawyer, Charles Cooper, earlier on Sunday, saying they had gained access to portions of the book, or summaries of it. They wanted comment. Cooper immediately called Bolton.

Both were stunned. Cooper was in the midst of a complicated case in Atlanta but broke away repeatedly to confer with his high-profile Washington client. They spoke at length while Cooper paced his room at the Atlanta Grand Hyatt. They were puzzled about the leak, trying to figure out who would have had incentive to pass it to the *Times*. They concluded that the disclosure seemed designed to put pressure on Senate Republicans, force them into calling Bolton to testify. Bolton was willing to abide by a subpoena, but he had not been trying to provoke one.

The House impeachment managers seized on the story, as Cooper and Bolton had assumed they would. "The Senate trial must seek the full truth and Mr. Bolton has vital information to provide," they said in a statement. "There is no defensible reason to wait until his book is published, when the information he has to offer is critical to the most important decision senators must now make—whether to convict the president of impeachable offenses."

Trump had already tried to paint Bolton as a disgruntled former employee. During his trip to Davos a few days earlier, Trump had said at a news conference, "I don't know if we left on the best of terms. I would say probably not, you know. And so, you don't like people testifying when they didn't leave on good terms." He opposed Bolton's testimony, saying it would hurt his ability to do his job. "It's a national security problem," he said. "John, he knows some of my thoughts. He knows what I think about leaders. What happens if he reveals what I think about a certain leader, and it's not very positive, and then I have to deal on behalf of the country?"

Now Trump's response to the Bolton book revelations came in the form of a tweet: "I NEVER told John Bolton that the aid to Ukraine was tied to investigations into Democrats, including the Bidens. In fact, he never complained about this at the time of his very public termination. If John Bolton said this, it was only to sell a book."

Witness or not, Bolton was shaking up the impeachment trial.

CHAPTER FIFTY-THREE

"Every President Believes That"

January 27 to 29, Washington

By Monday morning, the revelations from Bolton's manuscript were roiling the Republican side. Three of the four moderates were making the kinds of noises that McConnell didn't want to hear, and there was media speculation that his no-witness plan was in trouble.

At 10 a.m., Romney told reporters it is "increasingly likely" that more Republican senators will support hearing testimony from Bolton in light of the snippets reported by the *Times*. "It's important to be able to hear from John Bolton for us to be able to make an impartial judgment."

Collins issued a statement saying the report on the Bolton book strengthened the case for calling witnesses. Murkowski said she was "curious as to what John Bolton might have to say." Even Lindsey Graham, one of Trump's fiercest defenders, said he wanted to see the manuscript. "Let's see if it's relevant, and if it is, then I'll make a decision about Bolton." But he warned that if Bolton was called, Trump also should be allowed to call witnesses, including the Bidens. "I promise you this: If we add to the record, we're going to go after Hunter Biden, Joe Biden, all these other people," he said. "We're not going to look at part of it; we're going to look at all of it if we look at any of it."

The White House and Trump's allies were working hard to put even more distance between Trump and Bolton. Giuliani texted *Washington Post* reporter Josh Dawsey, saying he regretted pushing Bolton for the position of national security adviser. Claiming the president had always been skeptical of Bolton, Giuliani said that Bolton "never once raised any objection to what I was doing in defending" the president.

"I put him in the category of John the Backstabber," he told Dawsey.

• • •

McConnell held a closed-door lunch for the Republican senators, where Romney made a strong case to his colleagues for calling witnesses. McConnell urged senators to set aside the witness question until Trump's lawyers finished presenting their case. McConnell was treading carefully. A decision on witnesses would be settled by a simple majority vote, unlike the two-thirds required to remove Trump from office. If McConnell lost the four moderates, that would do it. He'd lose, 49 to 51. He didn't think that would happen, but no reason to find out yet where they stood.

After lunch, on the way to the Senate floor, John Neely Kennedy quipped to *Washington Post* columnist Dana Milbank that Republicans could use an antidepressant: "I think everybody ought to pop a Zoloft. . . . Take their meds." At 12:42 p.m., the newest senator, Republican Kelly Loeffler of Georgia, on the job only a month, went in the opposite direction. She attacked Romney on Twitter. "After 2 weeks, it's clear that Democrats have no case for impeachment. Sadly, my colleague @SenatorRomney wants to appease the left by calling witnesses who will slander the @realDonaldTrump during their 15 minutes of fame. The circus is over. It's time to move on!"

At the White House that afternoon, officials were hearing more on the coronavirus. It did not sound like everything was under control, as the president had said in the CNBC interview from Davos. In the Situation Room, at a packed meeting convened by the NSC, Azar was outlining the challenges that HHS would face if outbreaks were to escalate.

At a meeting in Mulvaney's office, White House aides were pressing senior officials to come up with a plan. Joe Grogan, the head of the White House Domestic Policy Council, argued that the administration needed to take the virus more seriously or it could cost the president his reelection, and that dealing with the virus was likely to dominate life in the United States for many months.

In the Senate, just before 8 p.m., in prime time on national television, Sekulow introduced Dershowitz, the longtime Harvard Law School professor whose list of former students included several of the senators seated before him. Dershowitz, in a black suit, walked from the Trump defense table to the podium, with a stack of papers and three books. His hands in front of him, fingertips pressed together, he told the Senate: "It is a great honor for me to stand before you today to present a constitutional argument against the impeachment and removal not only of this president but of all and any future presidents who may be charged with the unconstitutional grounds of abuse of power and obstruction of Congress."

With the precision and cadence of a man who had honed his lecture-style voice for half a century, Dershowitz said he was laying out constitutional arguments he would have made for Richard Nixon or Bill Clinton, had either one of them been facing the same two articles of impeachment. He was defining his argument as dispassionate, not pro-Trump.

He started, as constitutional scholars often do, with the framers of the document. He walked through the thinking of Hamilton, Madison, Gouverneur Morris and others, and concluded that it was clear that "purely noncriminal conduct, including abuse of power and obstruction of Congress, are outside the range of impeachable offenses." He said impeachment required a crime—bribery, treason, or, as in the case of Clinton, perjury. He said it was not enough for a president to be unpopular or choose the wrong policies, or the president would essentially serve "at the pleasure" of the legislature.

He acknowledged that during the Clinton impeachment, he had stated in an interview that he did not think a crime was required for impeachment, and that abusing trust could be considered. He said he was mistaken because he had not researched the matter deeply enough, as he should have done. He told the House managers they were making the same mistake.

"I am sorry, House managers, you just picked the wrong criteria," he said, looking directly at Schiff and his team. "You picked the most dangerous possible criteria to serve as a precedent for how we supervise and oversee future presidents. . . . The framers understood that if they set the criteria for impeachment too low, few presidents would serve their terms. Instead, their tenure would be at the pleasure of the legislature, as it was and still is in Britain. So they set the standards and the criteria high, requiring not sinful behavior—not dishonesty, distrust or dishonor—but treason, bribery or other high crimes and misdemeanors."

Dershowitz's Senate seminar lasted for just over an hour and included a nod to the current environment of anger and mistrust. "I respectfully urge you not to let your feelings about one man—strong as they may be—establish a precedent that would undo the work of our Founders, injure the constitutional future of our children, and cause irreparable damage to the delicate balance of our system of separation of powers and checks and balances."

As Roberts closed the session, Cruz darted down the aisle toward Dershowitz. Cruz, a Harvard Law graduate furiously shook Dershowitz's hand as other Republican senators arrived, full of praise.

"Professor," called out Romney, who had earned a joint law degree and MBA at Harvard. Romney cracked several loud jokes with Dershowitz, breaking up a group of five senators into laughter.

Moments later Dershowitz felt a thwack on his back—from Norm Eisen, one of the top Democratic counsels for the House Judiciary Committee, who was arguing for Trump's impeachment. Eisen, a Harvard Law graduate, spent several minutes with Dershowitz.

Dershowitz brought some legal star power to the proceedings, but he also had changed the Republicans' mindset and momentum. The day before, they had been struggling to come up with an answer for why they didn't need to hear testimony from Bolton and others. Now Dershowitz had given them an answer: If the allegations against Trump aren't impeachable, why ask to hear more?

Schiff was also a Harvard Law School graduate, and he had audited a Dershowitz course for a while. He went to a few lectures, then gave up on it. Schiff didn't think Dershowitz was teaching the principles of criminal law and procedure. It felt more like "the world according to Dershowitz," mainly the celebrity professor's war stories, told with great dramatic effect.

But Schiff had to admit, as a student of the law, he found it interesting how Dershowitz was building his arguments. Trump's other lawyers were nowhere near as interesting. At least this was captivating. But the more Dershowitz spoke, the more Schiff thought he was going off the deep end. His legal theory seemed to be built out of nothing. Schiff found it absurd. "They fall back on the argument 'Okay, he did it. We all know he did it. But we're going to find a criminal defense lawyer whose expertise is not really constitutional law . . . and make the argument that is, effectively, the Constitution says so what? You cannot impeach a president for abuse of power because it's too nebulous a concept.'"

Among the senators listening was a former Harvard Law professor, Elizabeth Warren. She had been on the faculty with Dershowitz. She thought his presentation was "nonsensical." She told reporters afterward: "His characterization of the law simply is unsupported. I truly could not follow it."

By morning, plenty of legal experts were arguing with Dershowitz's view. His fellow Harvard Law professor Laurence Tribe, called it "an extreme and dangerous" theory in an MSNBC interview. "There is no legal scholar in the country other than Dershowitz who believes it."

Frank O. Bowman, a University of Missouri law professor and author of the book "High Crimes and Misdemeanors," was interviewed for a *Washington Post* story about Dershowitz's presentation. "In making this argument, Alan is essentially alone, and I mean alone," Bowman said. "What Dershowitz did yesterday was stand up and be a guy with Harvard attached to his name and spout complete nonsense that's totally unsupported by any scholarship, anywhere."

The next day, Tuesday, January 28, Cipollone returned to the Senate podium at 2:44 p.m. to close the Trump team's presentation. He promised to be brief. He had prepared something longer, he said, but was discarding most of it because "we have made our case."

"All you need," he said, "is the Constitution and your common sense."

He illustrated his presentation with a highlight reel of comments made by several House managers and current senators who were House members during Clinton's impeachment trial—Nadler, Lofgren and Ed Markey of Massachusetts. Democrats chuckled at their much-younger images. Then Cipollone played a clip of Schumer from December 1998, decrying the Clinton impeachment and saying, "My fear is that when a Republican wins the White House, Democrats will demand payback."

"You were right," Cipollone said, staring at Schumer, who stared back.

Cipollone also took one final shot at Pelosi's favorite phrase of the past year, her often-repeated quote from Benjamin Franklin: "A republic, if you can keep it." Looking toward the Democratic side of the room, Cipollone added his own take: "It's a republic, if they let us keep it." Less than eight minutes after he started, Cipollone closed his binder and announced the defense complete.

After Roberts adjourned the hearing, Cipollone raced over to the table of Democratic lawyers, the ones he had called embarrassments to the law and to the country. They stood and everyone shook hands.

• • •

The Senate reconvened at 1 p.m. the next day, Wednesday, for the first of two sessions of written questions from senators. Cruz passed one to a clerk, who carried it to Roberts, who read it aloud. It was addressed to the president's legal team: "As a matter of law, does it matter if there was a quid pro quo? Is it true that quid pro quos are often used in foreign policy?"

It was a softball for Dershowitz, who stepped up to take a swing at it. "Every public official whom I know believes that his election is in the public interest," he said. "Mostly, you are right. Your election is in the public interest. If a president does something which he believes will get him elected—in the public interest—that cannot be the kind of quid pro quo that results in impeachment."

Ears perked up all over the room. Did Dershowitz really just say that a president can basically justify anything he wants to do, as long as he feels that it helps him get reelected and he believes his reelection is in the public interest?

Dershowitz cited a Civil War example: President Lincoln had told General John Sherman to let his troops go home to Indiana so they could vote for the Republican Party. "Let's assume the president was running at that point and it was in his electoral interests to have these soldiers put at risk the lives of many, many other soldiers who would be left without their company. Would that be an unlawful quid pro quo? No, because the president, A, believed it was in the national interest, but B, he believed that his own election was essential to victory in the Civil War. Every president believes that."

Fifty-three of the one hundred U.S. senators had law degrees. Most had never heard an argument quite like this one. Democrats' heads were popping. Schiff was gobsmacked, thinking how absurd and dangerous it sounded.

Dershowitz argued that a president's decisions can be based on multiple motivations. A clear case of corruption, he said, would be a president saying to the leader of another country, "Unless you build a hotel with my name on it and unless you give me a million-dollar kickback, I will withhold the funds."

Then Dershowitz applied the theory he had just outlined. "But a complex middle case is: 'I want to be elected. I think I am a great president. I think I am the greatest president there ever was, and if I am not elected, the national interest will suffer greatly.' "

Dershowitz sat down. Cruz thought his answer would help frame the argument for a lot of Republican senators. Schiff felt like he was being gaslit.

Late Wednesday evening, just after 11 p.m., Trump announced the formation of a 12-member Coronavirus Task Force, led by Azar. It included Robert Redfield from the CDC, Fauci from NIH and national security adviser Robert O'Brien. The official statement from the White House was muted: "The risk of infection for Americans remains low, and all agencies are working aggressively to monitor this continuously evolving situation and to keep the public informed."

The coronavirus was getting more attention, but the impeachment trial was still dominating the headlines, with what was shaping up as a pivotal day ahead. The witness issue could be put off no longer.

CHAPTER FIFTY-FOUR

"Let the People Decide"

January 30, Washington

On the House side of the Capitol, far from the Senate trial's spotlight, Nancy Pelosi was back to quotidian business, back to her routine.

She had dominated the news for months. But once the impeachment articles were transmitted to the Senate on January 15, she had faded into the background. She stayed in constant contact with Schumer, Schiff, Nadler and the other managers, but did it quietly.

Earlier in the week, she had rallied House Democrats at a caucus meeting. "The moral courage of this caucus is so remarkable," she told them. "History will show that. I do believe that the fate of the nation is riding on what happens." She reminded them to "maintain the dignity, the tone and the focus that our managers have brought to it. Our audience is, of course, the American people. But the challenge is to change the minds of a few senators. That doesn't happen by calling them names."

But now, Pelosi had roads and bridges to build. On Wednesday, she and several committee chairmen had unveiled a $760 billion infrastructure bill. The news conference announcing the bill was one of her most lightly attended since taking over as speaker a year earlier. There were just two TV cameras on hand and not a single network TV correspondent. Every question was about the legislation.

On Thursday at 11 a.m., she was back at the microphones for her weekly news conference. Instead of the somber black and power-red dresses that she had favored for the past few months, she wore a navy jacket with a swirling pattern of pink and violet flowers. It was more than colorful. It was striking.

She had come prepared to talk about the Senate trial. Asked about the witness question, she speculated on the possibility of a 50-50 deadlock if three of the Republican moderates were to join the Democrats. If that happened, she said, she hoped the chief justice would weigh in.

Pelosi praised her House managers and the decision to impeach. "We did our job."

McConnell hosted another lunch for his caucus in the Mansfield Room at the Capitol. As senators made their arguments against calling witnesses, Romney was annoyed. He felt he was being singled out. Romney thought hearing from Bolton was a "no-brainer." If Bolton had spoken to the president about the key issues, why wouldn't the Senate want to hear from him? Yet his colleagues were piling on. If this is meant to persuade me, Romney told them, it's not helpful.

The Republicans discussed the possibility of Roberts casting a vote to break a 50-50 tie. Such a ruling would be historic. Roberts would be within his power to break the tie, but no matter how he explained his vote, it might cast doubt on his impartiality. That was a situation no one wanted, particularly the cautious Roberts. The scenario remained unlikely. Only Romney seemed ready to vote with the Democrats. Alexander, Collins and Murkowski had yet to declare their intentions. But the discussion itself showed that caucus members were thinking about the possibility.

As the trial resumed that afternoon for a second day of questions from the senators, a query went to Roberts that put his impartiality at risk.

"Mr. Chief Justice," said Paul, following the rules for posing a question.

"The senator from Kentucky," Roberts replied.

"I have a question to present to the desk for the House manager Schiff and the president's counsel," Paul said.

Paul's card went to the clerk, who delivered it to Roberts. He read it silently, and cleared his throat.

"The presiding officer declines to read the question as submitted," he said, placing the card on his desk.

Nothing like this had happened the day before. Over 10 hours, Roberts had read out 93 questions. The vast majority were designed to give one side or the other another opportunity to emphasize a point. Softballs. Only a few seemed to be seeking new information, and fewer still were provocative.

Roberts's refusal was mystifying. What was on Paul's card?

It didn't take long for the answer to emerge. Paul stood up, gathered his papers and walked out of the Senate chamber to address journalists. His question had contained the alleged name of the whistleblower, the same name that had been circulating on right-wing media for months. During a rally with Trump in early November, Paul had demanded that major media outlets report the whistleblower's name. Now, during Trump's impeachment trial, Paul had tried to enlist the chief justice of the United States in his campaign to out the whistleblower.

Roberts, with only seconds to think, had said no to Paul's ambush. So did most of the reporters listening to Paul. He mentioned the name that Roberts would not, and as before, most reporters declined to publish it. Much of the media had reported earlier that the whistleblower was a CIA analyst, but not his name. That was still the state of affairs.

"Senator Paul, with all due respect, shouldn't you be in the impeachment hearing right now?" one reporter asked.

"Yeah, I will be shortly," he responded.

Moments later, Paul tweeted his entire question, including the name. He also tweeted separately: "My question today is about whether or not individuals who were holdovers from the Obama National Security Council and Democrat partisans conspired with Schiff staffers to plot impeaching the President before there were formal House impeachment proceedings." Paul's tweet was "liked" by more than 100,000 people.

Trump retweeted several times on the issue, without the supposed name of the whistleblower.

Elizabeth Warren, one of the four sitting senators still in the 2020 presidential race, also tried to drag Roberts into the fray that he was so carefully avoiding. At 5:40 p.m., Warren's question went up to the chief judge.

He looked at it and read it aloud: "At a time when large majorities of Americans have lost faith in government, does the fact that the chief justice is presiding over an impeachment trial in which Republican senators have thus far refused to allow witnesses or evidence contribute to the loss of legitimacy of the chief justice, the Supreme Court, and the Constitution?"

When he finished, he pursed his lips and stared at the Democratic side of the chamber. Schiff made his way to the lectern, just a few feet in front of Roberts, and tried to defuse the awkward moment in his answer to Warren. "Senator, I would not say that it contributes to a loss of confidence in the chief justice. I think the chief justice has presided admirably." Schiff then changed the subject, while Roberts looked like he might rather be anywhere else.

After Warren's question, McConnell wrote a note that he passed to Murkowski: The Democrats are attacking Roberts and the Supreme Court. Her vote to oppose witnesses could help protect them.

McConnell was trying to put an end to this nagging question of calling witnesses. Schiff had floated a compromise, proposing that the Senate take depositions for one week only, hoping to assuage Republican fears of extending the trial for weeks or months. His idea had gone nowhere. At 8:18 p.m., Murkowski sent a question up to Roberts, directed to the president's lawyers. Citing the media reports of new information in Bolton's book, and the need for firsthand information, she pointedly asked: "Why should this body not call Ambassador Bolton?"

The president's lawyers batted the question away, saying the House should have subpoenaed Bolton if his testimony was so important. But the tone of Murkowski's question was intriguing: Was she leaning toward voting to hear from Bolton?

Bolton was in Austin, Texas, giving a paid speech at a lunch sponsored by an investment management firm for wealthy clients. Bolton told the gathering that his unpublished book, which had kicked off the political firestorm, would be off-limits for questions. He said he wouldn't be discussing impeachment, and would focus instead on how Russia, China, North Korea and other global factors might affect the U.S. economy.

"I can't tell you how happy I am to be in Austin," Bolton joked, saying that his next speaking engagement might be in the U.S. Senate.

Bolton gave no indication of what he would say if he were called before the Senate. But he defended government officials who had testified before the House. "All of them acted in the best interest of the country as they saw it and consistent to what they thought our policies were," said Bolton, adding that they should "feel they're able to speak their minds without retribution. . . . The idea that somehow testifying to what you think is true is destructive to the system of government we have—I think, is very nearly the reverse—the exact reverse of the truth."

• • •

That night, as the senators were still asking their questions, Trump was in Des Moines, Iowa, for a campaign rally. "We're having probably the best years that we've ever had in the history of our country, and I just got impeached. Can you believe these people? I got impeached. They impeached Trump," he said, and right on cue the crowd cheered "USA! USA!"

Trump recalled the country's "dark period" during the impeachment proceedings against Johnson, Nixon and Clinton, the exclusive fraternity he had joined when the House had impeached him. "This is a happy period for us. It's a happy period. It's a happy period because we call this impeachment light. This is light," he said.

He was in full campaign mode, ad-libbing from subject to subject, saying whatever came to mind, gauging the reaction, staying with some riffs, dropping others. Right now, he was riffing on the Democrats. They didn't love America, he said, and Pelosi's hometown, San Francisco, was a disgrace. "Needles all over the place, everything else all over the place. I'm not going to get into it, washing down into the ocean, washing down onto their beaches, people living in tents if they're lucky. . . . What's happened? And all she does is work on the hoax."

He shifted to Ocasio-Cortez and her Green New Deal, which brought an immediate "Booooooo" from the crowd. He said the plan would crush our farms and "destroy our wonderful cows. I love cows. They want to kill our cows. You know why, right? You know why?"

"WHY?" the crowd called back.

"They want to kill our cows," the president said. "That means you are next."

From the endangered cows, he rambled through Mexico and "Sleepy Joe" Biden before pivoting back, with fervor and delight from the crowd, almost two hours into his speech, to his impeachment foes. "Shifty Schiff is a very sick person," he said. "He lies awake at night shifting and turning, Shifty. Shifting and turning in his bed, sweating like a dog. 'How am I going to get him? He didn't do anything wrong. How am I going to get him?' Oh, what a sick guy he is."

Trump raised the coronavirus and talked of the U.S. partnership with China to control the outbreak. "Hopefully, everything's going to be great. They have somewhat of a problem, but hopefully, it's all going to be great. But we're working with China, just so you know, and other countries very, very closely. So it doesn't get out of hand."

• • •

As Trump was delighting the crowd in Iowa, McConnell lost one vote on the witness question. Collins had finally chosen a side. She issued a statement saying she supported calling witnesses. That would give both sides a chance to "more fully and fairly make their case" and "resolve any ambiguities." It was a calculation Collins needed to make for her state's delicate conservative-moderate political balance. By voting for witnesses, Collins looked moderate. But no one doubted that she would ultimately vote with her party to acquit Trump.

Senior Republicans were resigned to Collins's decision. "Susan's gonna get a free pass on everything," one senator told *The Washington Post*'s Seung Min Kim. "The whole conference realizes that she is the most conservative person that can get elected in Maine. If it's not her, it's going to be a Democrat." He said Collins was basically told by leadership: "We have enough votes, Susan, you do what you want to do."

With Romney and Collins decided, the Democrats needed two more defectors. What about Alexander and Murkowski?

At about 10 p.m., the two undeclared senators joined in asking a question that sounded to some ears as if they might have made up their minds. Along with Trump supporters Graham, Cruz, Portman and others, they asked: "Assuming, for argument's sake, that Bolton were to testify in the light most favorable to the allegations contained in the articles of impeachment, isn't it true that the allegations still would not rise to the level of an impeachable offense and that therefore, for this and other reasons, his testimony would add nothing to this case?"

Their question was essentially a reframing of Dershowitz's argument. Bolton might have evidence that showed Trump had abused his office, but if his actions were the "wrong criteria" for impeachment in the first place, why bother? No matter what Bolton said, his testimony couldn't change the outcome.

The question had been Cruz's idea. He had thought of it the night before, inspired by a Schiff remark to Trump's lawyers. Schiff had said to them: You're the ones who made Bolton's testimony relevant. You denied any quid pro quo, and Bolton has information that might show one. If you had "stipulated" to the quid pro quo in the first place, we wouldn't be talking about this.

That's it, Cruz had thought. If the Trump legal team were to stipulate to the quid pro quo, wouldn't that remove any need to hear from Bolton?

And if Dershowitz's argument was right, and a quid pro quo by itself wasn't an impeachable offense, what was the risk in the stipulation? The president often said, Sure, I did that, so what?

In the Senate cloakroom, Cruz ran his idea past Graham and asked: "If we could get the White House to stipulate to this, do you think it would help us get the votes of Lisa and Lamar?" Graham was interested. They posed their idea to Murkowski and then Alexander, and both said they were interested. Cruz and Graham ran the idea past Trump's lawyers. They didn't like the idea of admitting a quid pro quo, but they saw the logic of the argument.

The group sent their question up to the desk, saying it was for the president's lawyers. Now they listened as Patrick Philbin, a deputy White House counsel, stood to respond. "Let me start by just making very clear that there was no quid pro quo," Philbin said.

Cruz wanted to jump out of his chair and throttle him.

But Cruz could see that Philbin was getting there, in a roundabout way. Philbin cited Dershowitz, then argued it didn't matter what Bolton said. A quid pro quo was not an impeachable offense. Bolton's testimony was irrelevant.

Cruz was delighted. He hoped it would help win over Murkowski and Alexander. The Republicans could bring the trial to a merciful end, avoiding weeks of testimony that wouldn't change the outcome, but might lead to new disclosures damaging to Trump.

Richard Durbin, the Democrat from Illinois, tried to seize back the momentum. He asked the House managers the same question, giving them a chance to rebut. Schiff stood and said: "We know why they don't want John Bolton to testify. It's not because we don't really know what happened here. They just don't want the American people to hear it and all of its ugly, graphic detail."

The exchange hadn't settled anything, but because the question had come from Alexander and Murkowski, it sent some Democrats into a funk. Bloomberg reporter Laura Litvan tweeted: "When Chief Justice Roberts read the question, my colleague in the chamber said it was like the air went out of the room. 'It's over,' he saw one Democratic senator say."

An hour later, with midnight approaching, Alexander issued a written statement that removed all doubt about where he stood, leaving only the remote possibility of a 50-50 tie on the witness question. "It was inappropriate for the president to ask a foreign leader to investigate his political opponent and to withhold United States aid to encourage that investigation," he said. "But the Constitution does not give the Senate the power to remove the president from office and ban him from this year's ballot simply for actions that are inappropriate."

Inappropriate, but not impeachable. Alexander's version of Dershowitz. It came with a political bonus. It wouldn't work in the reddest of red states. But for Collins in Maine, or Gardner in Colorado, or Joni Ernst in Iowa, "inappropriate but not impeachable" was a soundbite argument that could be taken home to voters.

For Democrats, Alexander's announcement was especially disappointing. The 79-year-old Republican senior statesman, retiring at the end of his current term, had been regarded as a possible conscience vote against Trump. He was put in the same category as Hurd in the House—someone whose manner and record suggested that he might not just reflexively back the president no matter what.

A decorous southerner and a former president of the University of Tennessee, Alexander had made no secret of his distaste for Trump. He had said he was "disgusted" by the 2016 "Access Hollywood" tapes, and he had chided Trump for an "inappropriate choice of words" for calling impeachment a "lynching."

Alexander said he was trusting voters to decide whether Trump should continue in office. The Iowa caucuses were just four days away. The first ballots of the 2020 election were about to be cast. That was underscored by the presence in the chamber of Klobuchar, Sanders, Warren and Bennet, and the constant mentions of Biden. The presidential election was seeping into every aspect of the debate, including Alexander's thinking.

"The question then is not whether the president did it, but whether the United States Senate or the American people should decide what to do about what he did," Alexander wrote in his statement. "I believe that the Constitution provides that the people should make that decision in the presidential election that begins in Iowa on Monday."

Alexander didn't leave it there. He rebuked the House with muscular language and a warning about the country's direction. He sounded as if he had made up his mind long ago, rather than a few hours earlier. "The framers believed that there should never, ever be a partisan impeachment. That is why the Constitution requires a two-thirds vote of the Senate for conviction. Yet not one House Republican voted for these articles. If this shallow, hurried and wholly partisan impeachment were to succeed, it would rip the country apart, pouring gasoline on the fire of cultural divisions that already exist. It would create the weapon of perpetual impeachment to be used against future presidents whenever the House of Representatives is of a different political party.

"Our founding documents provide for duly elected presidents who serve with 'the consent of the governed,' not at the pleasure of the United States Congress. Let the people decide."

Alexander's words had landed like a sledgehammer, a tool that the soft-spoken Tennessee patrician did not often deploy. The next morning, the last day of January, he invited *The Washington Post*'s Paul Kane into his small "hideaway" office on the third floor of the Capitol. Relaxed, but with his tie snugly knotted beneath a sweater, Alexander sat in a chair next to the window, looking out at the East Front of the Capitol and the Supreme Court beyond. The room was a tribute to Alexander's seniority: the window, the sweet view, just one floor from the entrance to the Senate on the second floor. Junior senators have windowless hideaways in the basement, far from the Senate floor.

Those small spaces had become key during the impeachment trial, which had lots of breaks of just 15 or 30 minutes. Rather than schlepping to their main offices across the street in the Russell, Dirksen or Hart Buildings, the lawmakers could get a quick breather, or huddle with staff, and be back on the floor in no time. Throngs of tourists walked down Alexander's third-floor hallway every day and never knew what was behind the nondescript wooden door. Now this was where Alexander chose to escape the furious rattle and roar of the impeachment, sitting with Kane to explain his decision.

Alexander said he had tried to act like an impartial juror. First, he had to drown out the noise. He said he tuned out a geyser of impassioned emails and calls from people who hated Trump or loved him.

He had quietly lobbied McConnell to make sure that there would be no knee-jerk dismissal of the charges, as Trump had demanded, and that the Senate would at least vote to consider witnesses. He said he ultimately decided there was no need for witnesses, because he had already been persuaded by earlier testimony that Trump was guilty. "If you've got nine witnesses who say he left the scene of an accident, you don't need the tenth," he said. Trump asked Zelensky to investigate Biden. He withheld aid as leverage. That was wrong, but not "high crimes and misdemeanors" wrong.

Alexander seemed settled in his mind, at ease with his conclusions. He tried to frame it in historical terms. He had read two books to prepare for the trial: one by Edmund Ross, the senator from Kansas who cast the decisive vote in 1868 against removing President Andrew Johnson from office, and the other "Impeachment: An American History," by Jon Meacham, Timothy Naftali, Peter Baker and Jeffrey A. Engel, published in 2018. Alexander had read the newer book at his desk just hours earlier during the question-and-answer session, focusing on Meacham's chapter on Johnson's trial. He was struck by the importance of bipartisanship in earlier trials. He wasn't sure precisely what constituted a "high crime or misdemeanor," only that part of the definition had to be that both Republicans and Democrats recognized it as impeachable. Bipartisanship was a bedrock requirement, and Alexander didn't see it in this case.

In the soft light of a cloudy morning, Alexander invoked Howard Baker, the legendary Republican senator from Tennessee who had been a hero to Alexander, and for whom Alexander had worked as a staffer in the late 1960s. Baker was the ranking Republican on the special Senate committee convened to investigate the June 17, 1972, break-in at the Democratic National Committee headquarters in the Watergate office building. The burglars left a trail that ultimately led to the Nixon White House.

Baker had been close to Nixon, and the president had been counting on Baker to defend him. But Baker turned out to have a more bipartisan and truth-seeking heart than Nixon realized. Baker's famous line in committee in June 1973, "What did the president know, and when did he know it," was a critical turning point in Nixon's ultimate downfall.

Alexander knew Democrats had hoped he would have a "Howard Baker moment" and turn against Trump. But Alexander said his Baker moment was his decision to prioritize bipartisanship. "I did not want to create a weapon of perpetual impeachment that the House could use to immobilize the Senate and immobilize the executive," he told Kane. "I think that would be bad for the country. And I think that's what this impeachment was."

Kane had one more question. Would Alexander be voting for Trump in the 2020 election? Alexander smiled. "I'm honorary chairman of his Tennessee campaign," he said.

Inappropriate, but not impeachable. With the election less than 10 months away, Alexander and others could live with that.

CHAPTER FIFTY-FIVE

"This Country Is Our Masterpiece"

January 31 to February 4, Kyiv, Florida and Washington

On the last day of January in Kyiv, almost 5,000 miles from the Senate floor, Secretary of State Mike Pompeo stood beside President Zelensky at a press conference. Each wore earpieces to hear the simultaneous translations, and each gave effusive statements about the healthy, strong relationship between their two nations.

"Today I'm here with a clear message: The United States sees that the Ukrainian struggle for freedom, democracy and prosperity is a valiant one," Pompeo said. "Our commitment to support it will not waver."

The tone was upbeat, unequivocal and jarringly dissonant. Five days earlier, after a one-on-one interview with NPR's Mary Louise Kelly at the State Department, he had shouted at her: "Do you think Americans care about Ukraine?"

Pompeo was upset with Kelly for asking if he owed Marie Yovanovitch an apology, and whether he had defended the ambassador when Trump ordered her firing. He claimed the interview was supposed to be limited to questions about Iran. "I have defended every State Department official," he told her.

Then, interview over, Kelly was escorted to his inner office. With her recorder now off, Pompeo dressed her down, F-bombs flying, daring her to find Ukraine on a map, Kelly said on NPR's "All Things Considered." A Pompeo aide produced a map with no writing on it. "I pointed to Ukraine," she reported. "He put the map away."

Now, here he was in Kyiv, with a light snow falling outside on a chilly winter day, offering Ukraine a warm embrace with a big, diplomatic smile. He reminded Zelensky that this was his fourth Ukraine trip. He had come twice as a congressman from Kansas and once as Trump's CIA director, he said.

Zelensky smiled in return. He said the friendship between the countries was strong, and added, "I don't think that these friendly and warm relations have been influenced by [the] impeachment trial."

There was still no date set for a White House meeting. "President Zelensky will be welcome to come to Washington when we have the opportunity to do good things for the American people and the Ukrainian people," Pompeo said. "We'll find the right time."

Zelensky replied: "I would be ready to go tomorrow."

In Washington, a statement by Senator Marco Rubio of Florida set the tone for the day. Even if the allegations against Trump were true, he said, he still would not vote to remove him. The Republicans were digging in; the Dershowitz doctrine was now rock solid. "Can anyone doubt that at least half of the country would view his removal as illegitimate—as nothing short of a coup d'état?" Rubio said. "Just because actions meet a standard of impeachment does not mean it is in the best interest of the country to remove a president from office."

A few minutes later, Murkowski drained the last little bit of drama from the proceedings, announcing that she would vote no on witnesses. "Given the partisan nature of this impeachment from the very beginning and throughout, I have come to the conclusion that there will be no fair trial in the Senate," she wrote. "I don't believe the continuation of this process will change anything. It is sad for me to admit that, as an institution, the Congress has failed."

At 5:30 p.m., the Senate voted, 51 to 49, not to allow witnesses or additional evidence. Only Romney and Collins broke ranks. McConnell's long game had worked out fine. He set a final vote for 4 p.m. on Wednesday, February 5, the day after the president's State of the Union address. Five days to go.

In the afternoon, Trump signed an order declaring the coronavirus a "public health emergency" and dramatically escalating the administration's slow response to the fast-spreading epidemic. Health secretary Azar told reporters that starting that Sunday, most non-U.S. citizens who had recently visited China would be barred from entering the United States. Any Americans who had visited China's Hubei province, where the disease had originated, would be subject to quarantine if the visit had taken place in the previous 14 days.

The government would also require screening and self-quarantine for all other Americans who had recently visited any other parts of China. Major U.S. airlines—American, United and Delta—announced they were suspending their flights to China. The virus's death toll had reached more than 210 people, all in China. Confirmed infections now exceeded 11,000 people in at least 24 countries. Seven cases had been confirmed in the United States.

The Iowa caucuses were held on Monday, February 3. It had been a rough couple of weeks for the Democratic senators in the 2020 race. They were basically on jury duty in Washington, often for 10 or 12 hours a day. They couldn't campaign in Iowa; they didn't even have access to their phones most of the time. They made do with video chats, interviews on radio and TV, and phone calls during breaks in the trial.

Trump had no real Republican competition in Iowa, but his campaign dispatched about 80 surrogates anyway. The list, which included his sons Don Jr. and Eric, read like a who's who from the impeachment inquiry: Mulvaney, Perry, Lewandowski, McCarthy, Meadows, Gaetz, Jordan and Stefanik. Parscale said: "We are putting the Democrats on notice: good luck trying to keep up with this formidable reelection machine."

The following morning, after a long night of trouble in tabulating the Democratic caucus results, Trump was delighted. "The Democrat Caucus is an unmitigated disaster," he tweeted before sunrise. "Nothing works, just like they ran the Country. Remember the 5 Billion Dollar Obamacare Website, that should have cost 2% of that. The only person that can claim a very big victory in Iowa last night is 'Trump.'"

Gallup released a new poll showing Trump with a personal best approval rating of 49 percent. Impeachment had not hurt him among Republicans and independents. But the poll also showed a record 87 percent gap between his approval rating among Republicans, at 94 percent, and Democrats, at 7 percent. The country was more divided than ever.

In the Senate, the floor was back in the hands of the senators after two weeks of impeachment arguments. They were getting their thoughts on the record ahead of Wednesday's final vote. There was more ping-pong oratory. A Republican would praise Trump, then a Democrat would call him unfit.

McConnell stood to say it was hard to believe that Democrats ever thought they would reach 67 votes in the Senate. "Or was success beside the point?" he asked. "Was this all an effort to hijack our institutions for a months-long political rally?"

In response, a slightly weary-sounding Schumer said McConnell was repeating "talking points" that ignored the Republicans' refusal to allow witnesses and documents in the trial. "The administration, its top people and Senate Republicans are all hiding the truth," Schumer said. "They are afraid of the truth."

Collins took the floor to explain how she intended to vote. She had permission to break ranks, if that's what she felt she needed to do to win reelection in Maine, but she took Alexander's route. She said Trump's actions were "wrong" and "improper," but ultimately, not deserving of impeachment. "I do not believe that the House has met its burden of showing that the president's conduct, however flawed, warrants the extreme step of immediate removal from office."

In the afternoon, NPR aired an interview with Giuliani, who said Trump should keep pushing to investigate Biden. "Absolutely, a hundred percent," Giuliani told NPR's Steve Inskeep. "I would have no problem with him doing it. In fact, I'd have a problem with him not doing it. I think he would be saying that Joe Biden can get away with selling out the United States, making us a fool in the Ukraine."

Just after 9 p.m. that night, Trump entered the House chamber for his annual State of the Union address. He walked down the center aisle, shaking hands along the way. He stepped up onto the rostrum, where Pence and Pelosi waited. Pelosi was wearing white, along with dozens of other Democratic women. Their color coordination was a fashion statement in honor of the 100th anniversary of the 19th amendment's final ratification, extending voting rights to women after a long struggle by suffragists.

Following long-standing practice, Trump handed a printed copy of his speech to the vice president and the speaker. Pelosi offered her hand for a shake, but Trump did not take it. It was hard to tell if Trump had seen her gesture, but the frost in the exchange was obvious. Pelosi awkwardly pulled her hand back, with a shrug and a smile. At his State of the Union address the year before, Trump had turned fully toward her and Pence, made eye contact with each and shaken their hands. Not this year. It was the first time he and Pelosi had crossed paths in four months, since Pelosi had walked out of their White House meeting.

Tradition called for Pelosi to say to the chamber: "I have the high privilege and distinct honor of presenting to you the president of the United States." She simply said, "Members of Congress, the president of the United States." The year before, Trump had started speaking without allowing Pelosi to introduce him at all.

Now, in his speech, Trump talked about the economy, the military, education, health care, often in rosy terms that kept the media's fact checkers busy for days. "The years of economic decay are over," he said. "The days of our country being used, taken advantage of, and even scorned by other nations are long behind us." That brought the Republican side to its feet, cheering.

Then came claims of setting records, a hallmark of Trump's speeches and press conferences. "I am thrilled to report to you tonight that our economy is the best it has ever been," he said, adding that he had slashed "a record number of job-killing regulations, enacting historic and record-setting tax cuts." More applause.

"And very incredibly, the average unemployment rate under my administration is lower than any administration in the history of our country." He waited for the cheers to die down. "True," he said.

"African American youth unemployment has reached an all-time low. African American poverty has declined to the lowest rate ever recorded," he said.

"Since my election, U.S. stock markets have soared 70 percent, adding more than $12 trillion to our nation's wealth, transcending anything anyone believed was possible. This is a record," he said.

"All of those millions of people with 401(k)s and pensions are doing far better than they have ever done before with increases of 60, 70, 80, 90 and 100 percent, and even more," he said.

"I am also proud that we achieved record and permanent funding for our nation's historically black colleges and universities," he said.

As Republicans were roaring their approval, Pelosi was tearing a small notch in the page marking each time she believed he had said something false. She thought the speech was a "manifesto of mistruths."

Then, in a move Trump had kept a surprise to heighten its drama on live television, he announced that he was awarding the Presidential Medal of Freedom to conservative radio host Rush Limbaugh, who had recently been diagnosed with lung cancer. Trump said he was bestowing the honor "in recognition of all that you have done for our nation, the millions of people a day that you speak to and that you inspire and all of the incredible work that you have done for charity." Limbaugh stood, visibly moved.

Republicans clapped and cheered as Melania Trump draped the medal around Limbaugh's neck. Some Democrats said they were appalled that the nation's highest civilian honor was going to a man with a long history of outrageous remarks about women, minorities and the LBGT community. Pelosi was offended that Trump was using the House chamber as a backdrop for a reality TV show.

Trump had been speaking for 45 minutes. Half an hour later, after describing America as "a land of heroes" and a place "where legends come to life," he delivered his final homage. "America is the place where anything can happen," he said. "America is the place where anyone can rise. And here, on this land, on this soil, on this continent, the most incredible dreams come true. This nation is our canvas, and this country is our masterpiece."

His final line—"my fellow Americans, the best is yet to come"—brought the House members and senators to their feet, some in exultation, some in relief. Pence stood next to Pelosi, clapping.

In full view of the TV cameras and the nation, Pelosi picked up pages of Trump's speech and ripped them neatly in half. Then she picked up more pages and ripped them. She did it four times, then tossed the torn pages onto the desk, with a dismissive flip of her wrist.

Cruz was disgusted. He thought her defiant display was a sad manifestation of the angry, bitter partisanship he saw from Democrats. All they wanted to do was investigate, attack and impeach Trump. It was corrosive to the country, he thought, and Pelosi's ripped pages said it all.

Himes watched with competing instincts. Normally, he preferred to seek middle ground with his opponents. Sure, Trump often acted like a boor, but why lower yourself to his level in response? But this time, that impulse was being overtaken by something else. Pelosi's little protest was kind of wonderful, he thought. Trump didn't care about the American people, Himes believed. He cared about himself and his portrayal in the media. Pelosi had just stolen his media moment. Her dissent, he decided, was a thing of beauty.

There hadn't been many of those during the impeachment proceedings. It had been a long, difficult haul, and the final act was about to unfold.

CHAPTER FIFTY-SIX

Never Over

February 5, Washington

At 9:30 a.m. on Wednesday, more than four months after Pelosi announced that she was starting impeachment proceedings, Grassley called the Senate to order. The final vote was scheduled for 4 p.m., and senators had the opportunity to speak for 10 minutes each to get their opinion on the record. Jeff Merkley, Democrat of Oregon, was first.

He offered a lament. "Every American should feel the sadness, the darkness, the tragedy of this moment," he said.

Around the same time, members of Trump's Coronavirus Task Force were briefing senators on the U.S. response to the outbreak. Infection totals had reached more than 24,000 people in China, but fewer than 200 in 24 other countries and only a dozen in the United States. The numbers were small, but some senators were not reassured.

Murphy tweeted: "Just left the Administration briefing on Coronavirus. Bottom line: they aren't taking this seriously enough. Notably, no request for ANY emergency funding, which is a big mistake. Local health systems need supplies, training, screening staff etc. And they need it now."

Brian Schatz and Mazie Hirono, both Hawaii Democrats, complained that officials in Honolulu had been given virtually no notice that they would have to begin screening passengers on flights from China. Citing the lack of coordination with state and local officials, Schatz described the administration's handling of the virus as "Keystone Cops." Azar promised to work "seamlessly" with local partners to eliminate any "hiccups."

Task force officials then briefed House members. Pelosi emerged from the hearing and said, "I think we have to be appropriately alert but not fearmongering on this."

At 2 p.m., a subcommittee of the House Foreign Affairs Committee held the first congressional hearing on the coronavirus. Chairman Ami Bera, a California Democrat and a physician, called for cooperation with the Trump administration. "We're on the same team here," Bera said. "This, you know, novel coronavirus doesn't see Republicans or Democrats. It sees human beings. And let's get ahead of this."

At the same time on the Senate floor, Romney stood at the microphone. Just eight years earlier, he had been the Republican nominee for president, celebrated for his moderate conservatism, moderate enough to win in Massachusetts, where he had served a term as governor. He was the son of a GOP legend, former Michigan governor George Romney, and for a time, the beating heart of the party establishment. Today, he was a pariah in a party that had swung far to the right and solidly into the embrace of Donald Trump.

"I swore an oath before God to exercise impartial justice," said Romney, speaking to a Senate chamber with just four senators present. "I am profoundly religious. My faith is at the heart of who I am." Romney, a devout Mormon, appeared to choke up. He paused for 12 seconds before continuing. "I take an oath before God as enormously consequential."

Romney did not need to make a speech. He could stay silent, let his vote speak for itself, whichever way he went. He didn't need to make any more enemies from Trump's side of the party. Trump had already ridiculed him, back in October, when he said that Democrats didn't have a "Mitt Romney in their midst," as if Romney were some sort of turncoat.

Now, recording his thinking for history, Romney laid out his reasons for rejecting the defense's three main arguments. Insisting that a "statutory" crime was required for impeachment "defies reason," he said. As for Joe or Hunter Biden, there was no evidence they had committed any crime; Trump plainly had pursued them for political reasons. "There is no question in my mind that were their names not Biden," Romney said, "the president would never have done what he did."

He rejected the idea that voters should be the only ones to judge Trump's actions. If an impeachable act had taken place, he said, Congress had a Constitutional duty to act. "The grave question the Constitution tasks senators to answer is whether the president committed an act so extreme and egregious that it rises to the level of a high crime and misdemeanor," he said. "Yes, he did."

In his view, Trump had asked a foreign government to investigate his political rival and then withheld vital military aid as leverage. That was extreme and egregious. "The president's purpose was personal and political. Accordingly, the president is guilty of an appalling abuse of public trust," Romney said. "What he did was not 'perfect.' No, it was a flagrant assault on our electoral rights, our national security, and our fundamental values. Corrupting an election to keep one's self in office is perhaps the most abusive and destructive violation of one's oath of office that I can imagine." Romney had generally supported Trump and had voted with him 80 percent of the time. He had been urged repeatedly to "stand with the team" now. But he said voting for Trump's acquittal on purely partisan grounds would, "I fear, expose my character to history's rebuke and the censure of my own conscience."

On the mostly empty Senate floor, Schatz dabbed his eyes with a tissue, moved to tears by Romney's lonely decision to speak out. Senator Roger Wicker, Republican of Mississippi, the only Republican on the floor, walked out of the chamber.

After eight minutes, Romney finished quietly and left quickly.

In an interview earlier, Romney had told *The Washington Post*'s chief correspondent, Dan Balz, one of Washington's most respected political observers, that his "heart sank in dread" when Pelosi announced the impeachment inquiry. He had hoped the defense would present evidence, perhaps Bolton's testimony, that would clear Trump. He said he would not vote for Article 2, obstruction of Congress, because he didn't think Trump's efforts to block witnesses and documents amounted to impeachable conduct. But as a matter of duty and faith, he would vote for Article 1, abuse of power.

Romney knew that his decision would have consequences. There was already a bill in the Utah legislature, aimed at him, that would allow voters to remove a sitting senator. The week before, the Conservative Political Action Conference had disinvited Romney to its annual event.

Shortly after Romney finished speaking, Zeldin tweeted: "Mitt Romney absolutely despises that Donald Trump was elected POTUS & he was not. The sore loser mentality launched this sham impeachment & corruptly rigged & jammed it through the House. It looks like Schiff recruited himself a sore loser buddy on the GOP side to play along." Then Donald Trump Jr. tweeted his view of Romney's dissent. "He was too weak to beat the Democrats then so he's joining them now. He's now officially a member of the resistance & should be expelled from the @GOP."

Criticism even came from his family. RNC chairwoman Ronna Romney McDaniel tweeted about her uncle: "This is not the first time I have disagreed with Mitt, and I imagine it will not be the last. The bottom line is President Trump did nothing wrong, and the Republican Party is more united than ever behind him. I, along with the @GOP, stand with President Trump."

Romney was a minority of one.

At 3:30 p.m., Schumer and McConnell faced off one last time to deliver their closing arguments after almost three weeks of battle.

"The trial of this President—its failure—reflects the central challenge of this presidency and, maybe, the central challenge of this time in our democracy," Schumer said. "You cannot be on the side of this president and be on the side of truth, and if we are to survive as a nation, we must choose truth because, if the truth doesn't matter, if the news you don't like is fake, if cheating in an election is acceptable, if everyone is as wicked as the wickedest among us, then hope for the future is lost."

McConnell responded: "In the last three years, the opposition to this president has come to revolve around a truly dangerous concept. Leaders in the opposite party increasingly argue that, if our institutions don't produce the outcomes they like, our institutions themselves must be broken. . . . The framers built the Senate to keep temporary rage from doing permanent damage to our republic. That is what we will do when we end this precedent-breaking impeachment. I hope we will look back on this vote and say this was the day the fever began to break."

As McConnell finished, Kyrsten Sinema walked over to the desk of Joe Manchin, Democrat of West Virginia, and the two embraced. They had been among the last undecideds from their party, and both had just announced that they would vote to remove Trump.

It meant the Democrats were united in defeat.

At 4:05 p.m., Roberts called the Senate to order. The chamber was now full. Republican senators sat silently at desks mostly free of papers. Pads and pens still lay on the desks of many of their Democratic colleagues, but there was nothing left to write.

Bernie Sanders slouched in his chair, staring straight ahead, speaking to no one. Amy Klobuchar caught Schumer's eye and mouthed, "Good job." Elizabeth Warren sat quietly. If they were going to dislodge Trump, they knew their only chance would come in November. The public galleries were nearly full. The back benches along the chamber's walls, reserved for House members, were occupied by representatives from both parties. History had drawn a crowd. Romney slipped into the chamber at the last minute.

The deputy sergeant at arms called out "Hear ye, hear ye." The clerk read Article 1. At 4:09, according to the digital clock, the clerk began calling the roll, in alphabetical order.

"Mr. Alexander."

Lamar Alexander stood at his desk and said, "Not guilty."

"Mr. Alexander, not guilty."

"Miss Baldwin."

Tammy Baldwin, Democrat of Wisconsin, stood at her desk and said, "Guilty."

"Miss Baldwin, guilty."

The clerk sped through the Bs, and into the Cs.

"Miss Collins."

"Not guilty," said the senator from Maine.

Two minutes later, the clerk said, "Mr. Romney."

Romney, standing at his desk in the back row, said, "Guilty." His colleagues felt the tremor, but no one reacted.

The clerk finally reached Senator Todd Young, Republican of Indiana, the end of the list, at 4:17.

Young stood at his desk and said, "Not guilty."

A clerk handed the tally sheet to Roberts, who read the results: 52 not guilty, 48 guilty. A straight party-line vote, except for Romney. The Senate then voted on Article 2: all 53 Republicans not guilty, all 47 Democrats guilty.

Roberts read the verdict: "The Senate, having tried Donald John Trump, President of the United States, upon two articles of impeachment exhibited against him by the House of Representatives, and two-thirds of the Senators present not having found him guilty of the charges contained therein, it is, therefore, ordered and adjudged that the said Donald John Trump be, and he is hereby, acquitted of the charges in said articles."

The Senate adjourned at 4:40 p.m. One hundred thirty-four days after Pelosi opened the impeachment proceedings, McConnell and the Senate had closed them.

It was over, but it was never over.

Nadler had told reporters earlier in the day the investigations into Trump would continue.

Then, just after the acquittal vote, GOP Senators Grassley and Johnson, on behalf of two Senate committees, sent a letter to the U.S. Secret Service. They wanted records of travel and protective security details for a certain individual and his family during the Obama administration.

Hunter Biden.

EPILOGUE

One Nation, Divisible?

February 6 to early July, Washington

On the morning after his acquittal, Trump appeared at the National Prayer Breakfast in the massive ballroom of the Washington Hilton Hotel. To the strains of "Hail to the Chief" and applause, he advanced toward his place at the head table. The breakfast was already in progress. Before him were more than 3,000 people, including elected officials and foreign dignitaries from more than 100 countries, gathered for the annual celebration of faith and prayer. It was a Washington tradition dating back nearly seven decades, a moment to set aside differences.

He wore a purple striped tie, not his trademark red. He carried nothing, except a plan. Waiting at his seat were print editions of several newspapers. As the applause faded, he reached down, grabbed a copy of *USA Today* and held it aloft for all to see. "ACQUITTED," the headline said.

Cheers from the Trump side of the crowd washed over him. The breakfast cohost, John Moolenaar, a Republican House member from Michigan, grinned broadly and clapped. Trump looked down. Feigning surprise, he picked up another newspaper. The crowd roared again as they saw the *Washington Post* front-page masthead and headline: "Trump Acquitted." Silently, Trump offered the paper to Moolenaar, who smiled and patted the president on his back.

Moolenaar moved to the microphone. "We are thrilled to have you with us today, Mr. President," he said, "and we want to just let you know there are people from all over the world here who have been praying for you, and we want this to be a blessing to you, so thank you, Mr. President." Moolenaar led the applause. The president beamed.

Some in the crowd did not join in the adulation. Moolenaar's co-chair, House member Thomas Suozzi, Democrat of New York, stood by, waiting. Moolenaar then welcomed "our very special guest, Nancy Pelosi, who's going to pray for the poor and persecuted."

Pelosi stayed in her role. "We pray that the moral clarity of faith moves us to demand justice for those who are suffering," she said. "Let us raise our voices in prayer as one in the struggle for freedom." She did not mention the brutal impeachment battle that had just ended.

McCarthy came to the lectern. He alluded to Trump's acquittal in his opening sentence. "The Lord works in amazing ways," he said. "I do not believe he could've picked a better day to bring us all together."

The event's main speaker was Arthur C. Brooks, former president of the conservative American Enterprise Institute and author of "Love Your Enemies," a rallying cry for ending the country's endless political warfare and reflexive hostility. With gentle humor, Brooks challenged the crowd to break away from what he called "the culture of contempt." He recounted a speech he gave to a conservative political crowd about the most effective way to argue with political liberals. "I want you to remember," he had told them, "they are not stupid and they are not evil. They are just Americans who disagree with us on public policy."

Trump was listening, looking at Brooks, his face impassive. Brooks said: "How many of you love somebody with whom you disagree politically?" Brooks raised his hand. So did Moolenaar. Trump did not. Brooks surveyed the crowd's hands and said, "I'm going to round that off to 100 percent." He waited a beat, then said: "The rest of you are on your phones." A wave of laughter came from the crowd. The president did not smile.

Brooks asked, "Are you comfortable hearing someone on your side insult that person you love?" Murmuring in the crowd. "Contempt is ripping our country apart," Brooks said. "Ask God to take political contempt from your heart, and sometimes when it's too hard—" He paused. "Ask God to help you fake it."

Then it was Trump's turn. There was a long standing ovation from the crowd, which included Vice President Pence at the head table and nine Cabinet officers. Pelosi, who was standing with Brooks, clapped, too. Trump said: "Arthur, I don't know if I agree with you." Smiling now, he turned toward Brooks. "I don't know if Arthur is going to like what I'm going to say." A ripple of nervous laughter rose from the crowd. The president grinned.

He read from the teleprompter: "As everybody knows, my family, our great country, and your president, have been put through a terrible ordeal by some very dishonest and corrupt people." His voice was raspy and hoarse; he sounded unusually subdued. "They have done everything possible to destroy us, and by so doing, very badly hurt our nation. They know what they are doing is wrong, but they put themselves far ahead of our great country."

The president's comments quieted the room. He took a shot at Romney, without using his name. The previous day, in explaining his guilty vote on one count, Romney had mentioned his Mormon faith. Now Trump said: "I don't like people who use their faith as justification for doing what they know is wrong."

He then went after Pelosi, sitting only a few seats to his left. "Nor do I like people who say, 'I pray for you,' when they know that that's not so." Pelosi gave a small half smile and said something quietly to herself as Trump continued. "So many people have been hurt, and we can't let that go on. And I'll be discussing that a little bit later at the White House."

Three hours later, two U.S. Marine guards wearing white gloves slid open the tall wooden pocket doors to the East Room, and President Trump entered. The ornate room was jammed with supporters. In the front row: Cipollone, Sekulow, Pence, Pompeo, Barr, McConnell, McCarthy, Ivanka and Melania.

Trump basked in the enthusiastic standing ovation, his second of the day, then said: "Well, thank you very much, everybody. Wow. We've all been through a lot together." He praised his assembled allies as "brilliant" and "popular." He said "everybody wanted to come" to the celebration, but he had to turn some away because of limited space.

Less than a minute into his speech he used the words "witch hunt." And it went from there, a litany of grievances about the "top scum" leaders of the FBI and all his other perceived enemies: evil, corrupt, dirty cops, leakers and liars.

Tuesday night had been the State of the Union. Thursday afternoon was Trump's State of Mind.

"It was all bullshit," he said, in the ornate room where state dinners are often held, and where mourners had come since the 19th century to pay respects around the caskets of Lincoln, FDR, Kennedy and four other presidents.

There was no teleprompter; this was Trump being Trump. He was jumping from topic to topic, foe to foe. Schiff was a corrupt politician, a vicious, horrible person, he said. So was Pelosi. Their aim was "to try and overthrow the government of the United States, a duly elected president." He singled out Alexander Vindman, "Cryin' Chuck" Schumer and Jerry Nadler for special scorn.

"I don't know that other presidents would have been able to take it," he said. He was talking about the strain. Hearing the verdict, he said, he never thought "a word would sound so good: it's called 'total acquittal.' "

The prayer breakfast earlier had been "really good," he said. "I had Nancy Pelosi sitting four seats away, and I'm saying things that a lot of people wouldn't have said—but I meant every—I meant every word of it." The crowd erupted in knowing laughter.

Twenty-one years earlier, Bill Clinton had been impeached by the House and acquitted in the Senate. When it was over, he had stood in the Rose Garden, surrounded by his supporters, to say he was "profoundly sorry" and call for reconciliation.

Trump took a different approach. "We went through hell, unfairly," he said. "Did nothing wrong. Did nothing wrong." He held up *The Washington Post* again, with its huge headline, and handed it to the first lady. "We can take that home, honey. Maybe we'll frame it."

Trump came not just to bury his enemies, but to praise his friends. He called Nunes "the other side's worst nightmare." He gave lavish shout-outs to McConnell, McCarthy, Meadows, Collins, Biggs, Gaetz, Jordan, Lesko, Ratcliffe, Scalise, Stefanik, Zeldin, Gohmert, Turner, Wenstrup, Grassley and Barr. Meadows replied for the room, standing to tell the president, "We've got your back."

After talking for more than an hour, Trump offered an apology, saying, "I want to apologize to my family for having them have to go through a phony, rotten deal by some very evil and sick people."

He called the first lady to the stage. They savored another standing ovation. Then they turned, holding hands, and walked out of the room.

That afternoon, many of those praised by name tweeted out made-for-the-campaign-trail videos of Trump's approval. Two minutes after Trump left the East Room, Elise Stefanik tweeted: "It was an honor to be at the @WhiteHouse for the President's first official remarks since the impeachment charade ended & he was acquitted. I proudly stood up for the Constitution and the truth throughout this process. Thanks for the shout-out @realDonaldTrump." She added a one minute, 13 second clip of Trump praising her. She tweeted twice more in the next couple of hours, including a link to her fundraising account.

Trump's payback started the next day.

He fired Sondland from his ambassadorship in Brussels. He fired Vindman from his NSC job and, for good measure, he fired his twin brother, Yevgeny. They were both escorted from the grounds in the afternoon.

Vindman had figured Trump would fire him and had already taken home photos, books and other personal items. Whenever the day came, he wanted to walk out with his head high and his hands empty. He was not shocked when the NSC's head of human resources came to his desk and said, "I'm sorry but we are letting you go. You need to leave immediately." But he was surprised to learn that Yevgeny was being fired, too. To Vindman, that seemed purely vindictive. The HR director walked them to the door.

Four days after Vindman's dismissal, Trump suggested the Defense Department should consider disciplining him. "That's going to be up to the military, we'll have to see," Trump said when asked by reporters whether Vindman should be punished. "But if you look at what happened, they're certainly, I would imagine, they're going to take a look at that." Trump told the reporters Vindman had done "a lot of bad things."

A lawyer for Vindman, David Pressman, said, "There is no question in the mind of any American why this man's job is over, why this country now has one less soldier serving it at the White House." He said Vindman had lost "his job, his career, and his privacy" for telling the truth.

After Trump's comments, Vindman's legal team sought assurances that the brothers would not face retribution at the Pentagon. Army secretary Ryan McCarthy said Vindman would reenter the Pentagon workforce like any other returning soldier. No retribution.

On February 11, five days after the prayer breakfast, co-chairs Tom Suozzi and John Moolenaar arrived at Pelosi's office with three ministers from the organizing committee, Marty Sherman, David Coe and Tim Coe. They came to apologize.

The prayer breakfast had drawn Republicans and Democrats and presidents and congressional leaders since Dwight Eisenhower was in the White House in the 1950s. Until now, the breakfast had been a celebration of religious freedom, not a place for attacking political rivals. This time, some attendees stood and cheered Trump's divisive words. The group told Pelosi it had been a stain on the event.

Gaston Hall, the ornate theater on the campus of Washington's Georgetown University, was packed on February 12 for an event to honor Marie Yovanovitch. Hundreds of students sat alongside the former ambassador's State Department colleagues, family members and friends. When she walked onstage, they rose, cheering and stomping their feet. She gave them a broad grin and said it was overwhelming.

After Trump had fired her from her post, she had taken a visiting professorship at Georgetown's School of Foreign Service. She had reconnected with her wide circle of Washington and diplomatic friends. She had renovated her house in a Northern Virginia suburb to accommodate her 91-year-old mother, Nadia, who had moved in but died just days before her daughter's congressional testimony.

She had thought she might want another State Department assignment after her year at Georgetown. But in late January, as Trump continued his attacks on the diplomatic corps, she had retired from the foreign service.

Now, as she accepted the university's award for Excellence in the Conduct of Diplomacy, she did not dwell on the ugly end to her 34-year career. Instead, she planted seeds of optimism among the students. "I believe that those of us who choose this life make a difference every day," she said. "For those of you who haven't yet decided that you want to go to work for the American people, I'm hoping that tonight, I can at least convince you to think about it."

She was asked what had given her hope, after the president of the United States had darkly warned that she was "going to go through some things."

She said: "One of the things that has sustained me is the support of all of you. You know, when you 'go through some things,' you have to dig deep a little bit."

On February 19, *The Hill* newspaper released a report on journalist John Solomon's work on Ukraine. *The Hill* said it had undertaken an internal review of 14 of Solomon's columns and videos after State Department witnesses at the House impeachment inquiry had "criticized several of those columns."

The witnesses—Yovanovitch, Kent and Holmes—said they paid attention to Solomon's work because they knew he was getting information from Giuliani, Parnas and Lutsenko. They were concerned, they testified, about what Giuliani was doing in Ukraine, the campaign he was waging.

The review determined that Solomon had failed to disclose that he relied on Ukrainian sources who "had been indicted or were under investigation," and that his sources, in some cases, had included his own attorneys, Victoria Toensing and Joe diGenova, who "had other clients with interest in Ukraine." *The Hill* noted that one of Solomon's most important sources, Lutsenko, the former Ukrainian prosecutor, later recanted allegations reported by Solomon against Yovanovitch.

The Hill's review said, in a list of findings, that it should have made it clearer that Solomon was an opinion columnist, not a news reporter. The paper said it had placed lengthy editor's notes on the stories that remain on its website, pointing out their shortcomings.

The report included Solomon's view of his handling of his sources. "Solomon has denied any coordinated effort with Giuliani, Parnas or others, insisting that he was merely dealing with those individuals in the course of reporting for his columns," the review said. "He has called Parnas a 'facilitator' who helped him in setting up interviews with Ukrainian officials."

The review said Solomon stood by his articles "to this day."

Impeachment fallout continued. On March 2, the White House withdrew a promotion for acting Pentagon comptroller Elaine McCusker, who had raised concerns about the legality of withholding military aid for Ukraine. She had been nominated in November for the permanent job. The White House offered no explanation for pulling her nomination.

Four days later, Trump replaced Mulvaney, whose "get over it" remark had complicated Trump's impeachment defense. He made Mulvaney his special envoy to Northern Ireland, far from the White House action. He named a new chief of staff: Mark Meadows.

Trump also served notice that he was firing Michael Atkinson, the intelligence community inspector general. "It is vital that I have the fullest confidence in the appointees serving as inspectors general," he wrote in an April 3 letter to Congress. "That is no longer the case with regard to this inspector general." The next day he told reporters Atkinson "did a terrible job. Absolutely terrible. That man is a disgrace to IGs."

Atkinson issued his own statement: "It is hard not to think that the president's loss of confidence in me derives from my having faithfully discharged my legal obligations as an independent and impartial inspector general."

When Vindman reported for work at the Pentagon, he did not feel welcome. He was told that his presence made top Pentagon officials uncomfortable. Some feared what would happen if the president or his allies visited and saw him.

His superior officer told Vindman that he would be assigned to an office in an Army building in Northern Virginia, outside the Pentagon complex, to work on plans for a new museum honoring the history of the Army. Vindman was puzzled. What kind of museum? What would it contain? Who would fund it? He was told, "That hasn't been determined."

For Vindman, the reassignment did not pass the laugh test. He decided to use his accumulated leave to take several months off. He worried that his 21-year military career would be forever marked by the impeachment saga. He was considering retiring from the Army in 2021.

Not long after Slotkin had decided to vote to impeach Trump, she was boarding a plane when a passenger in first class looked up. "You're going down, sweetheart," he told her.

Slotkin had known her vote might end her political career after a single term. But much had changed since that December night. Trump's handling of the pandemic had earned him new critics. Millions of Americans had lost their jobs as businesses shut. The stock market was shaky. Now political observers were saying Slotkin would likely hold on to her seat, as she worked diligently to scrounge up masks and gloves for overwhelmed Michigan hospitals. She had nearly $4 million in the bank for reelection, while none of her little-known Republican competitors had raised anything close to that amount.

Stefanik's New York district was looking even safer. After Trump declared her a star for her performance at the impeachment hearings, her fundraising soared. Her campaign committee reported $3.2 million in donations for the fourth quarter of 2019. Trump, meanwhile, continued to reward Stefanik's loyalty. He tapped her to serve on the national task force to "reopen" the economy after the coronavirus shut it down.

• • •

For Kurt Volker, the aftermath of the impeachment controversy was lonelier and costlier than for most. Neither Trump's backers nor the Democrats had claimed him as being on their team. He told friends that was exactly where a professional diplomat should be. But it wasn't easy.

Volker, who had two sons in college, took a financial hit because of the impeachment saga. In the fall, he had resigned from his full-time job as executive director of the McCain Institute, the organization started by John McCain, the late Arizona senator. His widow, Cindy McCain, in an interview on CNN, said she had asked Volker to leave. "Kurt is a good man," she said on "The Axe Files," a show hosted by former Obama adviser David Axelrod. "But this was overshadowing the Institute and it was overshadowing what we do and what we work for."

Volker also had to rebuild his advisory and consulting work, which had been a regular source of income and then disappeared overnight. He was still a senior international adviser at BGR, a D.C.-based consulting firm, and he started his own company to help businesses with strategic advice related to Europe.

He had found that there was an audience interested in his experiences. He gave speeches in Sweden and London. He and Bill Taylor appeared together as part of a panel on Russia and Ukraine sponsored by the Kyiv Security Forum. He was scheduled to speak in Singapore, too, until the pandemic hit. Volker told friends his new life was a major transition, but he was optimistic. He had no regrets.

Bill Taylor was back in the suburban Washington home he and his wife, Deborah, had bought in 1983 as they set about raising a family. Reminders of the last few tumultuous months had joined a lifetime of mementos gathered during overseas postings. On the coffee table, there was a framed picture of Taylor testifying before Congress, a gift from Yovanovitch. Upstairs, on his desk, sat a block of wood with the message "Stand Your Ground," etched in Russian. He had been given it a few days earlier by another impeachment witness.

Taylor had caught snippets of the Senate trial while driving in his car. Deborah, who had watched "every frigging second" of the House hearings, had avoided the Senate proceedings. She felt like she wasn't learning anything new. She had been skeptical from the beginning about her husband working for Trump. The proceedings only reinforced her misgivings. Taylor understood.

People had been asking if he wanted to write a book about his career and the impeachment experience, but he wasn't sure that was for him. Once Trump was acquitted, he had returned to his job at the U.S. Institute of Peace, then the institute had been shuttered, like so much of the country, because of the pandemic. As he worked from home, Deborah sewed and delivered hundreds of homemade face masks to protect against the coronavirus, including one for Yovanovitch.

Bolton's tell-all book was published in late June and rocketed instantly to the number one bestseller spot on Amazon. It contained remarkable details of Bolton's 17 months in the White House, based on notes he kept. The last part of the book focused on Ukraine, and his first-hand interactions with Trump, Giuliani and others. The Justice Department had asked a federal judge to block publication, saying Bolton was revealing classified information. The judge rejected the request, partly because hundreds of thousands of copies had already been shipped to stores. But he also said, in his ruling, that "Bolton has gambled with the national security of the United States." Administration officials said they would try to force Bolton to turn over his $2 million advance.

Republicans criticized Bolton for disclosing his internal dealings in the White House. Democrats were furious that Bolton had not given his account in congressional testimony during the impeachment inquiry and had saved it for a book. Schiff, in a tweet, said Bolton, "may be an author, but he's no patriot."

By June, more than 2 million Americans had contracted Covid-19, the illness caused by the coronavirus, and more than 120,000 had died in four months. More than 42 million U.S. workers had lost their jobs—numbers not seen since the Great Depression.

Then came massive demonstrations, sparked by the May 25 killing of an unarmed black man, George Floyd, by a white police officer in Minneapolis. Hundreds of thousands of people took to the streets, protesting a long history of police abuse and killings of African Americans, and the nation's stubborn, systemic racism. The demonstrations, in multiple cities across the country, gained momentum quickly and swelled as summer approached. Former presidents Barack Obama, Bill Clinton and Jimmy Carter issued statements saying the protesters' grievances were real and should be acknowledged, but condemning violence. Trump called the protesters "THUGS" and demanded massive law enforcement crackdowns. He told governors on a conference call in early June that they would look like "jerks" if they didn't "dominate" the protestors. A wounded nation turned to its president for reassurance and saw only an angry scowl.

On June 1, security forces fired pepper spray, rubber bullets and "flash-bang" stun grenades at peaceful protesters in Lafayette Park, across the street from the White House, so that Trump could walk to St. John's Episcopal Church and hold up a Bible for an awkward photo-op. Days later, an eight-foot-tall black metal fence was erected around the White House. Protesters quickly decorated Trump's security wall with art and signs about racial injustice.

Amid these twin crises—the pandemic that drove Americans indoors and the protests that brought so many into the streets—the investigation and impeachment of Donald Trump seemed to fade quickly from view. Ukraine, the famous phone call, the SCIF storming, the televised hearings, all history now, not news.

But Trump's trial did not end with the Senate verdict. He would soon face a different jury, the American voters. In November, they would decide whether he was worthy of a second term as the nation's president. Republicans, in trying to stave off impeachment, had argued that Democrats were usurping the voters in their zeal to remove Trump from office before his first term had ended. Trump's actions had been political, they said, not illegal. If the voters didn't like what Trump had done, that should be their call.

Now the voters would have their say. They would be free to consider, as they weighed their choice, whether Trump's request to "do us a favor" had meant "do *me* a favor." Broader questions loomed: Had he used his presidency to primarily benefit the country or himself? Was his transactional and confrontational approach a betrayal of his oath, or was it right for the times and the challenges faced by the nation?

Since the republic's founding, and especially after voting rights were extended to every citizen regardless of color or gender, the remedy for dismissing an incumbent president had been at the ballot box. If the president lost popular support, or lost his way, the voters either said "Time for a change," or "We're giving you another chance."

Impeachment was intended for extraordinary moments. Had this been one of them? Or had the Democrats overstepped by bringing charges against Trump? The voters would decide that, too. Across the country, many of the men and women who voted for or against the president would stand for reelection in 2020. Would Elissa Slotkin's constituents throw her out of office? Would Mitch McConnell's?

American democracy confers vast amounts of power and responsibility on those who govern. It also places strategic checks and balances on that power. What our leaders do and say, the risks they take and choices they make, are vitally important to every citizen. Just as important are the tools available to those citizens to hold their leaders accountable, including impeachment. When Nancy Pelosi crossed the line from "he's not worth it" to "we must impeach," when she decided that the risk of doing something was less than the risk of doing nothing, had she made the right choice, for her party, for the nation? The question would be asked for years.

McConnell had warned that what happened to Trump had cheapened impeachment. Every vote in the House and the Senate had broken along almost purely partisan lines. After the country's three Senate impeachment trials—Johnson in 1868, Clinton in 1999, Trump in 2020—it had become clear that impeachment was not the tool the framers might have imagined. What would stop future repeats? A House majority impeaches, a Senate majority acquits. Would every future president dealing with an opposition majority in the House face impeachment? Would every future president with a friendly Senate majority simply ignore Congress's constitutional role in checking the power of the executive branch? Neither political party had held a two-thirds Senate majority in the previous 80 years. It was hard to imagine that changing anytime soon.

Nancy Pelosi knew that the Senate would acquit Trump, yet she chose impeachment anyway. The House vote stained Trump, but he remained in office. That's where impeachment stood, as of 2020. It was not a practical means of removing a president. It had become a censure, an expression of disapproval, a statement to the nation: We the House have chosen to issue the harshest label the Constitution allows us to stamp on a president: impeached. Now We the People must decide what to do about that. The 2020 presidential ballot would include an impeached incumbent for the first time in U.S. history.

The November election would bring challenges never faced before. How would a nation hold an election if the coronavirus remained a pandemic? Was it possible to run a nationwide election largely by mail? Should online voting be considered? Most importantly, at a time of such distrust and dirty tricks, could Americans trust the outcome?

Trump had been put on trial and won. Now it was democracy on trial. America on trial.

Acknowledgments

This book is a product of the immense talent and expertise of the staff of *The Washington Post*. It would not exist without the incredible knowledge and generosity of the finest collection of journalists in the business.

That starts with Marty Baron, who leads the *Post* newsroom with strength, clarity and integrity. We are grateful to him, Cameron Barr, Tracy Grant and Emilio Garcia-Ruiz for guiding the newsroom with calm and wisdom through challenging times, especially when the coronavirus pandemic scattered the entire staff to remote operation. We are also grateful to publisher Fred Ryan for steering the ship with such care and resolve, and to Jeff Bezos for making sure the ship stays afloat. We are also indebted to Steven Ginsberg and Lori Montgomery for their inspiring leadership of the national staff, as well as to editors Donna Cassata, Peter Finn, Matea Gold and Peter Wallsten for sharing their thoughts. They edited *The Post*'s coverage of these events in real time, under extreme deadline and competitive pressure. Their work helped give *Post* readers the first rough draft of this history. They have our awe and gratitude.

We relied on many colleagues to help us with original reporting on this book, above and beyond their incredibly demanding day jobs. Their insights, interviews and knowledge are baked into every chapter. We have written many of them into the narrative to show readers how *Post* journalists do their jobs. Thank you to: Devlin Barrett, Josh Dawsey, Mike DeBonis, Karen DeYoung, Michael Duffy, Anne Gearan, Robin Givhan, Tom Hamburger, Shane Harris, Drew Harwell, Joe Heim, Rosalind Helderman, Greg Jaffe, Jenna Johnson, Seung Min Kim, Carol Leonnig, Greg Miller, Ellen Nakashima, Paul Sonne, Isaac Stanley-Becker, Ben Terris, Elise Viebeck, Dave Weigel, Griff Witte, Dan Zak, Matt Zapotosky, and to *Post* contributors Robert Moore in El Paso and David Stern in Kyiv. A special thank-you to generous friends and colleagues Paul Kane, Dan Balz and Karen Tumulty.

We also relied on the published work of these and many other *Washington Post* journalists. We had the invaluable advantage of hundreds of interviews they had conducted as the events described here unfolded, as well as their insights from interviewing them about their coverage. Thank you to Jacqueline Alemany, Rachael Bade, Aaron Blake, Philip Bump, Robert Costa, Karoun Demirjian, Jackson Diehl, Will Englund, Paul Farhi, John Hudson, Colby Itkowitz, Maura Judkis, Glenn Kessler, Hannah Knowles, Dana Milbank, David Nakamura, Siobhan O'Grady, Toluse Olorunnipa, Ashley Parker, Josh Rogin, Manuel Roig-Franzia, Philip Rucker, Felicia Sonmez, Reis Thebault, Craig Timberg, Anton Troianovski, John Wagner and Erik Wemple.

Thank you to photojournalists Melina Mara and Jabin Botsford, whose beautiful images were priceless documentary evidence that informed our reporting, and to the super-gifted photo editor Bronwen Latimer for making the book come alive visually. Thank you to Julie Tate and Alice Crites for their research, and for just being brilliant. We owe Julie a special shout-out for stepping in, as deadline neared, to help with fact-checking.

We salute the many great journalists who covered the impeachment with such tenacity and skill, including those from the *New York Times*, the *Wall Street Journal*, the *Los Angeles Times*, *Politico*, CNN, the broadcast networks and other outlets. Their work reminded us that the American press is stronger for its competitiveness. We benefited from the breadth and depth of that diverse coverage. We offer a standing ovation to C-SPAN, whose wall-to-wall coverage of the workings of our government was a critical resource for us, and an incredible service to all Americans.

We are grateful to the folks at Scribner, an imprint of Simon & Schuster, for publishing this work and producing so much *Washington Post* journalism in book form. Thanks to Jon Karp, CEO of Simon & Schuster (and Kevin's fellow *Providence Journal* alum!); Nan Graham and Roz Lippel, Scribner's publisher and associate publisher; Brian Belfiglio and Brianna Yamashita for publicizing and promoting the book; Jaya Miceli, Sydney Newman, Erich Hobbing and David Litman for making it look so beautiful; Irene Kheradi, Amanda Mulholland, Jason Chappell, Katie Rizzo, Hilda Koparanian and Elizabeth Hubbard for graceful and uncomplaining production on a breakneck schedule. Thanks to Rick Willett for eagle-eyed copyediting, and to Carolyn Levin for the rigorous legal review.

Special thanks to Colin Harrison, Scribner's editor in chief, who was an exacting, engaged and encouraging editor from start to finish. Colin shared our ambition of bringing this book into the world as quickly as possible, to make it a work of relevance as well as a work of history. He was on our side, always, interested in the story as well as the deadlines. We also thank Sarah Goldberg, Colin's assistant, for her help with all the small details that we never saw. Thanks to Todd Shuster at Aevitas Creative Management, the agent who brought us all together.

We could not have done this project without Isabelle Taft, a truly rare talent. Wise and gifted beyond her years, Isabelle was a full partner on this book. Her research, fact-checking and unflappable good nature are in evidence on every page, and her writing appears in several chapters. We have been amazed at her smarts and her heart. Isabelle is proof that the future of journalism is bright. Thank you, Isabelle.

It has been our greatest pleasure to work with and learn from Steve Luxenberg, the editor of this book. Steve has been part of the *Post* family for 35 years, and every comma in this book has benefited from his immense skill and dedication. He is a master narrative storyteller and ferocious reporter, with a passion for precision and power in language, and a soothing and patient bedside manner. Thank you, Ball'mer. Also, our thanks to his wife, Mary Jo Kirschman, for being a first reader of some of these pages and serving as Steve's sounding board. Her feedback helped make the book better.

Finally, and most importantly, thanks to Kate Sullivan and Tom Sullivan. We wrote the bulk of this book in Covid-19 quarantine, the four of us together at home. In a hard moment, we found endless love and fun in each other's company. We are the luckiest parents ever.

—Kevin Sullivan and Mary Jordan

Notes

Transparency serves us all, as well as future historians, so a guide to these notes might be helpful. We opted for clarity and useful information, avoiding duplication of attribution already in the text.

The voluminous public record of the impeachment and trial, unlike previous ones, includes social media posts. In many cases, public figures provided their first reactions to events on that platform. Where a tweet is quoted extensively and its date cited in the narrative, such as many of President Trump's, we have not provided an endnote. Where a tweet is mentioned without such detail, our notes provide the Twitter name (@realDonaldTrump), date, and time in the U.S. eastern time zone.

Especially important were records and transcripts released by congressional investigators. Seventeen witnesses from government agencies gave testimony in closed-door sessions before the three House committees that conducted the impeachment inquiry. Some were interviews; some were depositions. In the Notes, we have used the inquiry's designations.

Twelve then testified in public hearings. Transcripts were released from both the closed-door and public sessions. The dozen who testified twice, with the dates of their appearances, all in 2019, were: Kurt Volker, October 3/November 19; Marie Yovanovitch, October 11/November 15; Fiona Hill, October 14/November 21; George Kent, October 15/November 13; Gordon Sondland, October 17 (supplemental statement November 5)/November 20; William Taylor, October 22/November 13; Laura Cooper, October 23/November 20; Alexander Vindman, October 29/November 19; Tim Morrison, October 31/November 19; David Hale, November 6/November 20; Jennifer Williams, November 7/November 19; David Holmes, November 15/November 21.

Five others testified only in the closed-door sessions: Michael McKinley, October 16; Philip Reeker, October 26; Christopher Anderson, October 30; Catherine Croft, October 30; Mark Sandy, November 16.

At the end of the House inquiry, in December 2019, the House Intelligence Committee published a final report, "The Trump-Ukraine Impeachment Inquiry Report." We cite the House report for its conclusions, but we generally relied on the witness transcripts in our quest to understand the thoughts and actions of principal figures.

The House inquiry also made public two sets of documents that were helpful in reconstructing the narrative of events surrounding Ukraine: Kurt Volker's text and WhatsApp messages, released October 3 and November 5, 2019, and texts, WhatsApp messages and other documents provided by Lev Parnas, released January 14 and 17, 2020.

Other vital sources came to light as the result of Freedom of Information Act (FOIA) requests by two watchdog groups. American Oversight obtained documents from the State Department, published November 22, 2019; the Office of Management and Budget, published January 22, 2020; and the Department of Energy, published January 28, 2020. The Center for Public Integrity obtained two sets of Department of Defense documents, published December 12 and December 20, 2019.

We drew information from all these records, cited on the following pages.

Prologue

xiii **"Father just came at me with a vengeance"** Nancy Pelosi, interview with Joe Heim, March 6, 2019. This account of the interview is based on the Q&A feature subsequently published in *The Washington Post Magazine*, as well as Heim's observations and parts of his exchange that were not published at the time. The Q&A was posted online on March 11, 2019; it was published in the magazine on March 31, 2019, with the same headline, "Nancy Pelosi on Impeaching Trump: 'He's Just Not Worth It.'"

xv **She had been caught in crossfire** Marie Yovanovitch, public testimony, House impeachment inquiry, November 15, 2019, opening statement [hereafter Yovanovitch public testimony].

xvi **She called for the removal** "Remarks by Ambassador Yovanovitch on the Occasion of the 5th Anniversary of the Ukraine Crisis Media Center's Founding," published online by the U.S. Embassy in Ukraine, March 5, 2019.

xvi **The ambassador's openly calling** Yuri Lutsenko, text to Lev Parnas, March 5, 2019. Lev Parnas documents released by the House Intelligence Committee, PDF file, "WhatsApp messages" [hereafter Parnas WhatsApp messages], pages 89–90. Translation provided by the committee, unless otherwise noted.

xvi **Putin had pushed the idea** On February 2, 2019, Putin said: "As we know, during the election campaign in the U.S., the current Ukrainian authorities took a unilateral position in support of one of the candidates." Putin went on to say "female candidate." Quoted in Shane Harris, Josh Dawsey and Carol D. Leonnig, "Former White House Officials Say They Feared Putin Influenced the President's Views on Ukraine and 2016 Campaign," *Washington Post*, December 19, 2019.

xvii **Giuliani and his team had picked up a new scent** The Trump-Ukraine House Impeachment Inquiry report [hereafter House Impeachment Report] documented the efforts of Giuliani-led efforts in Ukraine. The report said Giuliani had discussions with his Ukrainian contacts about Joe and Hunter Biden in January 2019. House Impeachment Report, page 43.

xvii **"Now the Ambassador points"** Yuri Lutsenko, text to Lev Parnas, March 6, 2019, Parnas WhatsApp messages, page 90.

xviii **"impeach the motherfucker"** Amy B Wang, "Rep. Rashida Tlaib Profanely Promised to Impeach Trump. She's Not Sorry," *Washington Post*, January 4, 2019.

xviii **grinding her teeth** Mary Jordan interview with sources close to Pelosi. Also reported by Molly Ball in "'We've Upped the Ante.' Why Nancy Pelosi Is Going All in Against Trump," *Time*, January 9, 2020.

xviii **"until you have the facts"** Nancy Pelosi, weekly press conference, May 18, 2017. Pelosi's office publishes transcripts of nearly all of her public remarks, as well as statements and "Dear Colleague" letters. All citations of her remarks are based on the transcripts released by her office, unless otherwise noted.

xix **the president "doesn't know right from wrong"** Mike DeBonis, "House Democrats Push GOP to Do More than Talk Tough on Trump," *Washington Post*, August 16, 2017.

xix **"An embarrassment and a grave threat"** "Pelosi Statement on President Trump's Invitation to Putin to Visit Washington," July 20, 2018.

xix **"Not only unconstitutional but immoral"** Nancy Pelosi, "Dear Colleague on President Trump's Muslim Ban and Press Event Tomorrow," January 29, 2017.

xix **"Petulance and obstinance"** Nancy Pelosi, weekly press conference, January 10, 2019.

xix **"Disgusting behavior"** Nancy Pelosi (@TeamPelosi), Twitter post, October 12, 2016, 7:15 p.m.

xx **"Have no choice, sorry, sorry, sorry"** Quoted in Jesse Byrnes, "Trump: Republicans 'Have No Choice' but to Vote for Me," *The Hill*, July 28, 2016.

Part One: Threats

Chapter One: Watch Your Back

3 **On Tuesday, March 19** This account of Uglava's discussion of his conversation with Lutsenko is based on the depositions of George Kent and David Holmes. Kent recalls the U.S. Embassy reporting that Uglava "described his conversation the night before with a completely inebriated, drunk Yuriy Lutsenko, and Lutsenko was angry." Holmes says that an embassy colleague spoke with an unnamed contact who "was drinking with Lutsenko for three hours the night before." Deposition of George Kent, October 15, 2019 [hereafter Kent deposition], page 61; Deposition of David Holmes, November 15, 2019 [hereafter Holmes deposition], pages 15–16, 187.

3 **Yovanovitch "would face serious problems"** Holmes deposition, page 15.

3 **Lutsenko was collecting Ukrainian "mud"** Kent deposition, pages 50–51.

3 **You need to watch your back** Deposition of Marie Yovanovitch, October 11, 2019 [hereafter Yovanovitch deposition], page 41.

4 **Lutsenko had made an alliance** Yovanovitch deposition, October 11, 2019, page 41; House Impeachment Report, pages 40–41.

5 **If Yuri Lutsenko had learned anything** This account of Lutsenko's situation is based on the House Impeachment Report, pages 40–43; House Impeachment Inquiry interview of Kurt Volker, October 3, 2019 [hereafter Volker impeachment interview], page 34; Kent deposition, page 55; and supplemented by reporting from the *Washington Post*'s Paul Sonne.

6 **Yovanovitch had given him a "do-not-prosecute"** John Solomon, "Top Ukrainian Justice Official Says US Ambassador Gave Him a Do Not Prosecute List," *Hill.TV (The Hill)*, March 20, 2019.

6 ***The Hill*'s website had posted two articles** The second article focused on Lutsenko's claims that Ukraine's 2016 investigation of Paul Manafort's political and business activities in the country had been intended to aid Hillary Clinton's campaign. John Solomon, "Senior Ukrainian Official Says He's Opened Probe into US Election Interference," *Hill. TV (The Hill)*, March 20, 2019.

6 **A couple of hours later came a tweet** Sean Hannity deleted this Twitter post. Parnas texted a link to the tweet to Joseph Ahearn on March 20, 2019, and the tweet is included in his documents released by the House Intelligence Committee on January 15, 2020. Lev Parnas, message to Joseph Ahearn, Parnas WhatsApp messages, page 3.

6 **"I just happen to have"** Sean Hannity, "Don't Forget About the Ukraine," "The Sean Hannity Show" (radio), March 20, 2019.

6 **"Tomorrow's the big day"** Lev Parnas, message to Thomas Hicks Jr., March 19, 2019, 8:52 p.m. Parnas WhatsApp messages, page 55.

6 **"Wait Tomorrow good stuff"** Lev Parnas, message to Joseph Ahearn, March 19, 2019, 9:35 p.m. Parnas WhatsApp messages, page 2.

6 **Parnas was pleased** In January 2020, Parnas gave lengthy interviews to MSNBC's Rachel Maddow and CNN's Anderson Cooper. Maddow's interview aired in two parts on "The Rachel Maddow Show," MSNBC, January 15 and 16, 2020. Cooper's interview aired on "Anderson Cooper 360," CNN, January 16, 2020.

6 **The campaign to discredit Yovanovitch** The House Impeachment Report used the words "campaign" and "smear campaign" to describe the efforts of Giuliani and allies in Ukraine. "The attacks against Ambassador Yovanovitch were amplified by prominent, close allies of President Trump, including Mr. Giuliani and his associates," the report concluded. See, in particular, the section titled "Rudy Giuliani, on Behalf of President Trump, Led a Smear Campaign to Oust Ambassador Yovanovitch." House Impeachment Report, pages 15–16, 38–48.

7 **colleagues complained of bias** Jake Pearson, Mike Spies and J. David McSwane, "How a Veteran Reporter Worked with Giuliani's Associates to Launch the Ukraine Conspiracy," *ProPublica*, October 25, 2019.

7 **"Just got word"** Cited in the *ProPublica* article, October 25, 2019.

7 **watched the taping** Described in the same *ProPublica* article, above.

7 **"Have jr. retweet it"** Lev Parnas, message to Joseph Ahearn, March 20, 2019, 12:36 p.m. Parnas WhatsApp messages, page 3.

7 **"You should retweet it"** Lev Parnas, message to Thomas Hicks Jr., March 20, 2019, 12:37 p.m. Parnas WhatsApp messages, page 57.

7 **"an outright fabrication"** John Solomon, "As Russia Collusion Fades, Ukrainian Plot to Help Clinton Emerges," *The Hill*, March 20, 2019.

8 **"Watch Hannity"** Lev Parnas, message to Thomas Hicks Jr., March 20, 2019, 9:02 p.m.; Lev Parnas, message to Joseph Ahearn, March 20, 2019, 9:02 p.m. WhatsApp messages, pages 5 and 57.

8 **"Breaking tonight"** Sean Hannity, "John Solomon: As Russia Collusion Fades, Ukrainian Plot to Help Clinton Emerges," "Hannity," Fox News, March 20, 2019.

8 **"Sounds like our Ambassador"** Laura Ingraham (@IngrahamAngle), Twitter post, March 20, 2019, 9:21 p.m.

9 **"bad mouthing us like crazy"** John Bolton's account of this conversation with Trump from page 454 of his book *The Room Where It Happened: A White House Memoir*, published June 23, 2020. As the book was being shipped, the White House went to court, asking for a restraining order to prevent its distribution. A federal judge rejected the request. The judge, Royce C. Lamberth, did not rule on the White House's contentions that, among other things, Bolton had violated a nondisclosure agreement and executive privilege restrictions. But the judge wrote, after reviewing portions of the book, that Bolton "has exposed himself to civil (and potentially criminal) liability." Lamberth also said Bolton may have failed to wait for the completion of a required prepublication review to ensure that the book did not contain any classified information.

9 **"we gotta get rid of the ambassador"** Rosalind S. Helderman, Tom Hamburger and Josh Dawsey, "Listen: Trump Tells Associates to 'Get Rid of' U.S. Ambassador to Ukraine," *Washington Post*, January 25, 2020.

9 **"concrete evidence from close companions"** Pete Sessions, letter to Secretary of State Mike Pompeo, May 9, 2018. Cited by John Solomon, "As Russia Collusion Fades, Ukrainian Plot to Help Clinton Emerges," *The Hill*, March 20, 2019.

9 **Another $5,400** Indictment in *United States of America v. Lev Parnas, Igor Fruman, David Correia, and Andrey Kukushkin*, United States District Court, Southern District of New York, October 10, 2019, pages 8–9. See also Federal Election Commission campaign reports, Pete Sessions for Congress.

10 **"Obama holdover"** Laura Ingraham, "Analysts Examine Joe Biden And Son Hunter Biden's Ties to Ukrainian Politicians," "Ingraham Angle," Fox News, March 22, 2019.
10 **still not disclosing his complicated relationship** For a description of the various connections between Joe diGenova, Victoria Toensing, their law firm, Parnas, Lutsenko and Solomon, see the extensive footnotes in the House Impeachment Report, pages 155–158.
10 **"pay attention"** Rudy Giuliani (@RudyGiuliani), Twitter post, March 22, 2019, 11:38 a.m.
10 **"the most important piece"** Dan Bongino (@dbongino), Twitter post, March 23, 2019, 10:33 a.m.
11 **"A source close to the White House"** Ryan Saavedra, "Calls Grow to Remove Obama's U.S. Ambassador to Ukraine," *Daily Wire*, March 24, 2019.
11 **extend her tour** Yovanovitch deposition, page 121.
11 **"come out strong"** Yovanovitch deposition, page 62.
12 **Barr was releasing a "summary"** William Barr, letter to Lindsey Graham and Dianne Feinstein, ranking members of the Senate Judiciary Committee; and Jerrold Nadler and Doug Collins, ranking members of the House Judiciary Committee, March 24, 2019.
12 **Yovanovitch wanted a Pompeo statement** Deposition of David Hale, November 6, 2019 [hereafter Hale deposition], pages 22–23.
12 **His assistant messaged "no statement"** Deposition of Philip Reeker, October 26, 2019 [hereafter Reeker deposition], pages 46–47.
12 **the source of Trump's ill feelings** Bolton, *The Room Where It Happened*, pages 454–455.
12 **Yovanovitch called Gordon Sondland** Yovanovitch deposition, pages 267–268.
13 **"Lutsenko used Solomon"** Melinda Haring, "Ukraine Just Showed Us How a Foreign Power Can Play Trump to Its Own Ends," *Washington Post*, op-ed, March 26, 2019.
13 **"Ambassador Yovanovitch represents"** Quoted in John Solomon, "US Embassy Pressed Ukraine to Drop Probe of George Soros Group During 2016 Election," *The Hill*, March 26, 2019.
13 **"Hate to bother you"** JoAnn Zafonte, email exchange with Madeleine Westerhout, March 27, 2019, American Oversight State Department documents, November 22, 2019, page 55. All emails cited in this section, as well as material from the packet Giuliani sent to Pompeo (PDF pages 59–100), are part of that FOIA release [hereafter American Oversight State Department FOIA release].
14 **Hallelujah** Glenn Beck interview, "EXCLUSIVE: Rudy Giuliani Responds to Dems' 'Quid Pro Quo' Claims Amid Impeachment Hearings," "BlazeTV," November 20, 2019, available on YouTube.

Chapter Two: "Ready to Rumble"

15 **"This is the end of my presidency"** Robert S. Mueller III, "Report on the Investigation into Russian Interference in the 2016 Presidential Election," [hereafter Mueller Report], U.S. Department of Justice, March 2019, Volume II, page 89.
16 **Barr had made his claim** William Barr letter to Graham, Nadler, Feinstein and Collins, March 24, 2019, cited earlier.
16 **one tweet included a 54-second** Trump tweet, April 18, 2019, 8:54 a.m.
16 **Trump loved Twitter's immediacy** This account of Trump's Twitter use is based on accumulated *Washington Post* reporting by Josh Dawsey and the White House team.
16 **"modern day presidential"** Trump tweet, July 1, 2017, 6:41 p.m. Trump wrote: "My use of social media is not Presidential - it's MODERN DAY PRESIDENTIAL. Make America Great Again!"
17 **Only about one-fifth** Stefan Wojick and Adam Hughes, "Sizing Up Twitter Users," Pew Research Center, April 24, 2019.
17 **tone it down** During a CNN interview on February 29, 2016, early in Trump's presi-

dential campaign, Melania Trump said that she disagreed with her husband on "many things—some language, of course." Quoted in Mary Jordan, *The Art of Her Deal: The Untold Story of Melania Trump*, page 228. Jordan, based on the extensive reporting she did for her 2020 book, summarized Melania Trump's view this way: "She has not liked everything her husband has said, and definitely has not liked everything he has done," *Art of Her Deal*, page 6.

17 **"Ready to rumble"** Jacqueline Alemany, "Power Up: 'Ready to Rumble': Washington Waits for the Mueller Report," *Washington Post*, April 18, 2019. Other details provided by Alemany, email, April 7, 2020.

18 **Flanked by his two deputies** Barr, "News Conference on Mueller Report Release," April 18, 2019, C-SPAN video.

18 **"The investigation did not establish"** Mueller Report, Volume I, page 2.

19 **"If we had confidence"** Mueller Report, Volume II, page 2.

19 **"total victory"** Press statement by Rudy Giuliani, Jay A. Sekulow, Jane Serene Raskin and Martin R. Raskin, April 18, 2019.

19 **"we're very, very happy"** Bill Hemmer, interviewing Rudy Giuliani on "America's Newsroom," Fox News, April 18, 2019.

20 **"regrettably partisan handling"** "Pelosi, Schumer Call for Special Counsel Mueller to Provide Public Testimony in House and Senate," statement released by the offices of Nancy Pelosi and Chuck Schumer, April 18, 2019.

20 **"disturbing evidence that President Trump"** Nadler news conference on redacted Mueller report release, April 18, 2019, video at C-SPAN.org.

21 **"impeachment is not worthwhile at this point"** Dana Bash, interview with Steny Hoyer, "CNN Newsroom," April 18, 2019.

21 **her 4 million followers** The Internet Archive's WayBack Machine captured a screengrab of Ocasio-Cortez's Twitter account on April 18, 2019, showing she had 3.95 million followers. As of June 2020, that figure had risen to 7.3 million.

22 **"to discuss this grave matter"** Nancy Pelosi, "Dear Colleague on Democratic Response to the Release of Special Counsel Mueller's Report," April 18, 2019.

22 **"I would just say this"** Nancy Pelosi, "Speaker Pelosi Issues Remarks at Press Availability in Northern Ireland," transcript published by Targeted News Service, April 19, 2019.

22 **"I can say as a Ukrainian citizen"** Quoted in Anton Troianovski, "Comedian Volodymyr Zelensky Unseats Incumbent in Ukraine's Presidential Election, Exit Poll Shows," *Washington Post*, April 21, 2019. Other details drawn from a video clip of Zelensky's election celebration created by Reuters and published with the *Post* story online.

23 **"We had you as a great example"** Memorandum of telephone conversation, Donald J. Trump and Volodymyr Zelenskyy [White House spelling], April 21, 2019, released by the White House, November 15, 2019.

23 **Vindman had prepared talking points** Alexander Vindman, public testimony, House Intelligence Committee, November 19, 2019 [hereafter Vindman public testimony].

24 **"look into it"** Trump-Zelensky call memo, April 21, 2019, cited earlier.

Chapter Three: Walking the Fine Line

25 **"While our views range"** Nancy Pelosi, "Dear Colleague: Duty & Democracy," April 22, 2019.

26 **"This isn't about Democrats or Republicans"** Quoted in Rachael Bade, Karoun Demirjian and Jacqueline Alemany, "House Democratic Leaders Say No Immediate Plans to Open Impeachment Proceedings Against Trump," *Washington Post*, April 22, 2019.

26 **There's also a political implication for not acting** Huffman's comment from Nicholas Fandos, "Pelosi Urges Caution on Impeachment as Some Democrats Push to Begin," *New York Times*, April 22, 2019.

27 **"This is not about politics"** This account of the Democratic caucus conference call on April 22 is based on press accounts as well as Mary Jordan's background interviews with Democratic sources.

27 **"the GOP should be ashamed"** Nancy Pelosi, "Dear Colleague: Duty & Democracy," April 22, 2019.

27 **"Well, look, I think"** McConnell quoted in "House Democratic Leaders Say No Immediate Plans to Open Impeachment Proceedings Against Trump," cited above.

28 **Now Delgado stood** This account of Paul Kane's district tour with Antonio Delgado was drawn from work originally published in *The Washington Post*. Paul Kane, "In a Trump District, a Freshman House Democrat Works on Repeating His Success," *Washington Post*, April 27, 2019. Kane provided additional details, not published in his original work.

29 **He wanted it done, now** Bolton, *The Room Where It Happened*, pages 456–457.

Chapter Four: "Courage Is Contagious"

30 **"She refused to be silenced"** Michael Pompeo, remarks at the International Women of Courage (IWOC) Awards Ceremony, March 7, 2019, transcript published by the State Department's Bureau of Global Public Affairs.

30 **"paid the ultimate price"** Marie Yovanovitch, remarks at the Women of Courage Reception in Honor of Kateryna Handziuk, April 24, 2019, transcript published online by the U.S. Embassy in Kyiv.

30 **Some said Pompeo feared** Yovanovitch deposition, pages 63–64.

31 **telling her that was impossible** Yovanovitch deposition, page 130.

31 **Yovanovitch had been cut out** Yovanovitch deposition, pages 65–66.

31 **an urgent call from Washington** Yovanovitch deposition, page 112.

32 **There's "a lot of concern"** Yovanovitch deposition, page 126.

32 **why couldn't she stay** Yovanovitch deposition, page 127.

32 **if Taylor might "hypothetically"** Deposition of William Taylor [hereafter Taylor deposition], October 22, 2019, pages 50–51. In his testimony, and in interviews with *Washington Post* reporter Greg Jaffe, Taylor was uncertain of the date of Kent's call. Kent did not provide the date in his deposition and public testimony. Based on other information, we concluded the call took place Thursday or Friday, April 26–27, but it also could have occurred on Monday, April 29.

32 **Taylor knew that his good friend** Taylor deposition, page 50.

33 **"simply wrong"** Roman Popadiuk, John Herbst, Steven Pifer, William Taylor, Carlos Pascual and John Tefft, letter to David Hale, April 5, 2019, American Oversight State Department FOIA release.

33 **President Trump has "lost confidence"** Hale deposition, pages 43–44.

34 **a unique dilemma for Taylor** This account of Taylor's decision-making, here and later in this chapter, is drawn from Jaffe's multiple interviews with Taylor and Jaffe's previously published work, including "William Taylor Jr., a Key Impeachment Witness, Quietly Returns Home to Trump's Washington," *Washington Post*, February 14, 2020. It is also based on Taylor's deposition and public testimony.

35 **After a long flight** This account of Yovanovitch's dismissal is based on her deposition, pages 128–132, as well as on Karen DeYoung's interviews with State Department officials and others close to Yovanovitch.

35 **"George has asked me to go to Kyiv"** Taylor and Volker, WhatsApp exchange, April 29, 2019, PDF released by the three investigating House committees on November 5, 2019, page 26 [hereafter Volker messages].

36 **"concluding her three-year diplomatic assignment"** Christopher Miller, "U.S. Ambassador to Ukraine, Openly Criticized by Top Ukrainian Prosecutor, Departing Early," *Radio Free Europe*, May 6, 2019. Miller's story was the first to report that Yovanovitch was leaving early.

36 **David Hale wasn't happy** Hale deposition, pages 51–52.
36 **Several press accounts the next day** For example: Robbie Gramer, Amy Mackinnon, "U.S. Ambassador to Ukraine Recalled in 'Political Hit Job,' Lawmakers Say," *Foreign Policy*, May 7, 2019.
36 **after "political attacks"** Josh Rogin, "U.S. Ambassador to Ukraine Is Recalled After Becoming a Political Target," *Washington Post*, May 7, 2019.
36 **two top House Democrats made public** Eliot Engel and Steny Hoyer, "Statement on U.S. Ambassador to Ukraine Masha Yovanovitch," published on the House Committee on Foreign Affairs website, May 7, 2019.
36 **Bolton saw the two matters** Bolton, *The Room Where It Happened*, page 459.
37 **telling the *New York Times* explicitly** Kenneth P. Vogel, "Rudy Giuliani Plans Ukraine Trip to Push for Inquiries That Could Help Trump," *New York Times*, May 9, 2019.
37 **"This is definitely not our war"** Anton Troianovski, Josh Dawsey and Paul Sonne, "Trump's Interest in Stirring Ukraine Investigations Sows Confusion in Kiev," *Washington Post*, May 11, 2019. *The Post* adopted Kyiv as the transliterated spelling for Ukraine's capital city in October 2019.
37 **he was scrapping the trip** Shannon Bream interview with Rudy Giuliani, "Giuliani to Urge Ukraine Officials to Investigate Biden," "Fox News at Night," Fox News, May 10, 2019.
37 **United States had given Ukraine about** "U.S. Foreign Aid by Country," Ukraine, published by USAID.
38 **"What I'm pushing for"** Anton Troianovski, Josh Dawsey and Paul Sonne, "Trump's Interest in Stirring Ukraine Investigations Sows Confusion."
38 **the U.S.-Ukraine relationship "would be sour"** Rachel Maddow interview with Lev Parnas, "The Rachel Maddow Show," MSNBC, January 15, 2020.
38 **Parnas messaged Shaffer** Parnas WhatsApp messages, May 12, 2019.
38 **When Taylor arrived at the Old Executive Office Building** Taylor interviews with Greg Jaffe.
39 **Vindman had drafted the letter** Deposition of Alexander Vindman, October 29, 2019 [hereafter Vindman deposition], pages 270–271.
40 **"I'm still trying to navigate"** Volker-Taylor exchange, Volker messages, also cited in Greg Miller and Greg Jaffe, " 'Alarming Circumstances': A Distressed Diplomat Tells a Tale of Venal Intrigue," *Washington Post*, October 23, 2019.

Chapter Five: High Fives

41 **Volodymyr Zelensky high-fived** David L. Stern and Anton Troianoski, "He Played Ukraine's President on TV. Now He Has Taken Office as the Real One," *Washington Post*, May 20, 2019. A video of the ceremony, created by Sarah Parnass of *The Washington Post* and published with the story, was also used to describe the event.
41 **In his first act as head of state** Volodymyr Zelensky, inaugural address, official website of the President of Ukraine, May 20, 2019.
42 **She was in Kyiv, packing** Yovanovitch deposition, page 308.
42 **At first, Vice President Pence was going** Vindman deposition, page 128.
42 **A White House aide had called** Deposition of Jennifer Williams, November 7, 2019 [hereafter Williams deposition], page 37.
42 **had a theory about Pence's pullout** Holmes deposition, pages 37–38.
43 **cybersecurity adviser** Abby Phillip, "Trump Names Giuliani as Cybersecurity Adviser," *Washington Post*, January 12, 2017; Josh Dawsey, Rosalind S. Helderman, Tom Hamburger and Devlin Barrett, "Inside Giuliani's Two Roles: Power-Broker-for-Hire and Shadow Foreign Policy Adviser," *Washington Post*, December 8, 2019.
43 **help the Ukrainian city of Kharkiv** Rosalind S. Helderman, Tom Hamburger, Paul Sonne and Josh Dawsey, "Impeachment Inquiry Puts New Focus on Giuliani's Work for Prominent Figures in Ukraine," *Washington Post*, October 2, 2019.

43 **When Sondland's name showed up** Vindman deposition, pages 127–128.
43 **Vindman had drafted a congratulatory letter** Vindman deposition, pages 174–178.
44 **the delegation met with U.S. Embassy officials** "DOE [Department of Energy] Records Regarding U.S. Delegation to Ukraine Led by Former Secretary Perry," FOIA release to American Oversight, page 13. Perry's briefing materials for the trip, including the schedule for May 20, 2019, were part of the release.
44 **"Dammit. Rudy," Sondland said** Holmes deposition, page 18.
44 **Putin's spokesman pointedly asserted** "Kremlin Says Won't Congratulate Ukraine's Zelensky on Inauguration," *BBC Monitoring*, May 20, 2019.
44 **"The United States will stand with"** Rick Perry, "Comments to the Press by U.S. Secretary of Energy Rick Perry Following President Zelenskyy's Inauguration," published by the U.S. Embassy in Ukraine, May 20, 2019.
45 **Perry came with a list of people** Desmond Butler, Michael Biesecker, Stephen Braun and Richard Lardner, "After Boost from Perry, Backers Got Huge Gas Deal in Ukraine," Associated Press, November 11, 2019.
45 **Beware of Russia, he said** Vindman deposition, page 131.
45 **Sondland found him articulate** Deposition of Gordon Sondland, October 17, 2019 [hereafter Sondland deposition], page 126.

Chapter Six: The I-Word

46 **a full-court press** Rachael Bade and Mike DeBonis, "Some in Pelosi's Leadership Team Rebel on Impeachment, Press Her to Begin an Inquiry," *Washington Post*, May 20, 2019.
46 **upholding a subpoena** Devlin Barrett, Spencer S. Hsu, Rachael Bade and Josh Dawsey, "Judge Rules Against Trump in Fight over President's Financial Records," *Washington Post*, May 20, 2019.
47 **row after row of 20 seats** Description of room HC5 is drawn from a photograph provided by *The Washington Post*'s Paul Kane and Kane's observations.
47 **Pelosi's message: Keep investigating** Mike DeBonis, Rachael Bade, Josh Dawsey and John Wagner, "Trump Angrily Walks Out of Meeting with Democrats After Pelosi Says He Is 'Engaged in a Coverup,'" *Washington Post*, May 22, 2019.
47 **"It tore the country apart"** Paul Kane, "Democrats Who Stood with Clinton Through Impeachment Urge Caution in Pursuit of Trump," *Washington Post*, May 22, 2019. This account of the May 22 caucus meeting is based on reporting by Kane, Mike DeBonis and their published work. They provided additional details from their notebooks.
48 **"It is just as politicized"** Alexandria Ocasio-Cortez, Twitter post, May 21, 2019, 11:16 a.m.
48 **"only thing" that gave her pause** Quoted in Glenn Thrush, "Pelosi Pushes Go-Slow Strategy on Impeachment as She Goads Trump," *New York Times*, May 22, 2019.
49 **"Are you satisfied"** "Fierce Showdown at the White House Between President Trump and Nancy Pelosi," "NBC Nightly News," NBC News, May 22, 2019.
49 **"It was a very positive meeting"** "Pelosi Remarks Following Meeting on Democrats' Progress in Oversight Efforts to Hold President Trump and Administration Accountable," May 22, 2019.
50 **Today's agenda was to discuss** Mary Jordan background interviews with House Democrats.
50 **"I want to do infrastructure"** "Statement by President Trump," White House transcript, May 22, 2019.
51 **"very, very, very strange"** Nancy Pelosi in conversation with Neera Tanden at the 2019 Center for American Progress Ideas Conference, May 22, 2019, video on YouTube.
51 **A popular version included an image** Rachel Frazin, "George Conway Contrasts Trump Denying 'Cover-ups' with Check to Michael Cohen," *The Hill*, May 23, 2019. Frazin's article included a screengrab of Conway's tweet, with an image of the check.
51 **"threw gas on the fire"** Andy Biggs, interviewed by Neil Cavuto, "President Trump Can-

cels Infrastructure Talks After Pelosi Levels Cover-up Charges," "Your World with Neil Cavuto," Fox News, May 22, 2019.

51 **"The Dimms are no longer borderline evil"** Lou Dobbs, "Radical Dem Leader Pelosi Accuses Trump of Cover-up," "Lou Dobbs Tonight," Fox News, May 22, 2019.

Chapter Seven: "They Tried to Take Me Down!"

53 **sifting through his overnight emails** This account of Harwell's reporting is based on Steve Luxenberg's interview with Drew Harwell, March 12, 2020.

54 **Sarah Sanders had shared a video** Sarah Huckabee Sanders (@PressSec), Twitter post, November 7, 2018, 10:33 p.m.

54 **to make Acosta seem more aggressive** Drew Harwell, "White House Shares Doctored Video to Support Punishment of Journalist Jim Acosta," *Washington Post*, November 8, 2018.

55 **using the word "cover-up" again** Nancy Pelosi, weekly press conference, May 23, 2019.

56 **"a nasty-type statement"** "Remarks by President Trump on Supporting America's Farmers and Ranchers," White House transcript, May 23, 2019.

57 **Sondland could hear White House aides** Sondland deposition, pages 88–89. This account of the May 23 meeting is drawn from three of the four participants (Sondland, Volker and Senator Ron Johnson). Specific citations follow.

57 **they had barely sat down** Sondland deposition, page 75.

57 **"They were out to get me"** Sondland deposition, page 126; Volker impeachment interview, page 305.

57 **Trump doesn't want anything to do** Sondland deposition, page 91.

57 **"Talk to Rudy"** Sondland deposition, page 61.

57 **"Rudy knows"** Sondland deposition, page 70.

58 **"They tried to take me down"** Volker impeachment interview, page 279.

58 **Instead of arguing, he told Trump** Volker impeachment interview, pages 280, 304.

58 **he should expect about 45 seconds** Greg Jaffe and Josh Dawsey, "A Presidential Loathing for Ukraine Is at the Heart of the Impeachment Inquiry," *Washington Post*, November 2, 2019.

59 **"This is a new crowd"** Volker impeachment interview, pages 30, 304.

59 **"That's not what I hear"** Volker impeachment interview, page 305.

59 **Sondland told Trump he was excited** Sondland deposition, page 74.

59 **Senator Johnson felt he was in the strongest position** Johnson, letter to Jim Jordan and Devin Nunes, Republican members of the House Intelligence Committee, November 18, 2019, page 5. Johnson's letter, written in response to a request from Jordan and Nunes for "any firsthand information you have about President Trump's actions toward Ukraine between April and September 2019," gives a detailed account of Johnson's perspective on the May 23 Oval Office meeting.

59 **Sondland resigned himself** Sondland deposition, pages 25–26.

60 **Trump megadonor** Aaron C. Davis, Josh Dawsey, Michelle Ye Hee Lee, Michael Birnbaum, "'Disruptive Diplomat' Gordon Sondland, a Key Figure in Trump Impeachment Furor, Long Coveted Ambassadorship," *Washington Post*, October 14, 2019.

60 **YouTube immediately removed the videos** Drew Harwell, "Facebook Acknowledges Pelosi Video Is Faked but Declines to Delete It," *Washington Post*, May 24, 2019.

61 **The Politics WatchDog page hosted** Harwell, "Facebook Acknowledges Pelosi Video Is Faked but Declines to Delete It." Harwell did not report on the identity of the altered video's creator. Kevin Poulsen, senior national security correspondent for the *Daily Beast*, identified him as Shawn Brooks, a 34-year-old day laborer and "Donald Trump superfan" who ran Politics WatchDog and was trying to drive traffic to his page. Brooks denied altering the video. He blamed another administrator of the page. But he expressed concern at how easily prominent figures like Giuliani were fooled. Giuliani had tweeted a link. "I couldn't believe it," Brooks told Poulsen. "I was reading an article and it said, the

president's lawyer, and I was like, what the hell? If he believed that she was really drunk, and he shared it, that's kind of bad. Somebody that high up."

Chapter Eight: "I Think Your Boss Doesn't Like Ukraine"

62 **On May 28, Bill Taylor** This account of Taylor's meeting with Pompeo is drawn from his deposition and his interview with Greg Jaffe.

63 **He asked about the congratulatory letter** Taylor deposition, page 57.

63 **Pompeo had prevailed on Trump** Taylor deposition, page 57.

63 **The May 29 letter** Donald Trump, letter to Volodymyr Zelensky, May 29, 2019. The letter was first published by the *Daily Beast*: Betsy Swan and Erin Banco, "Exclusive: Trump Letter Promised Zelensky 'Unwavering' Support," November 5, 2019.

64 **For weeks, she had been scouring** This account of Pilipenko's research and memo-writing is based on Mary Jordan and Ellen Nakashima's interviews in March/April 2020 with people directly familiar with the Intelligence Committee's work on Ukraine.

65 **Vogel had published an in-depth story** Kenneth P. Vogel, "Biden Faces Conflict of Interest Questions That Are Being Promoted by Trump and Allies," *New York Times*, May 1, 2019.

65 **He liked working on these puzzles** Mary Jordan's background interviews with people who have worked directly with Schiff.

66 **On June 4, he joined a gala** U.S. Mission to the European Union, "Ambassador Sondland Brings Together U.S. and European Leaders to Advance Transatlantic Relations," published on the mission's website, June 5, 2019.

66 **The food stations featured** This account of the June 4 gala is based in part on photographs posted on Flickr by the U.S. Mission to the European Union: "USEU Independence Day 2019."

66 **The event was underwritten** U.S. Mission, "Ambassador Sondland Brings Together U.S. and European Leaders to Advance Transatlantic Relations," cited earlier. The post includes a video listing the event's sponsors.

66 **Sondland wasn't quite sure why** Sondland deposition, page 86.

67 **"my old friend Jay Leno"** U.S. Mission to the European Union, "Ambassador Gordon Sondland's Opening Remarks at the 2019 Independence Day Celebration," June 4, 2019.

67 **He was the son of immigrants** Davis, Dawsey, Lee and Birnbaum, "'Disruptive Diplomat' Gordon Sondland, a Key Figure in Trump Impeachment Furor, Long Coveted Ambassadorship," cited earlier.

67 **Sondland had put in the "$5 million to $25 million"** Gordon D. Sondland, Executive Branch Personnel Public Financial Disclosure Report, submitted to the U.S. Office of Government Ethics, 2019, page 29.

67 **supporting Jeb Bush** Davis, Dawsey, Lee and Birnbaum, "'Disruptive Diplomat' Gordon Sondland, a Key Figure in Trump Impeachment Furor, Long Coveted Ambassadorship," cited earlier.

67 **Trump's "constantly evolving positions"** Aaron Mesh, "Two Portland Hotel Executives Disavow Donald Trump After Being Listed Among His Event Sponsors," *Willamette Week*, August 7, 2016.

67 **he routed $1 million to the president-elect's inaugural fund** Ashley Balcerzak, "250 Donors Shelled Out $100k or More for Trump's Inauguration, Providing 91% of Funds," OpenSecrets.org/Center for Responsive Politics, April 19, 2017.

68 **He carried a wireless buzzer** Greg Miller, Paul Sonne, Greg Jaffe and Michael Birnbaum, "Holding Ukraine Hostage: How the President and His Allies, Chasing 2020 Ammunition, Fanned a Political Storm," *Washington Post*, October 4, 2019.

68 **"18th century Jefferson-in-Paris behavior"** Davis, Dawsey, Lee and Birnbaum, "'Disruptive Diplomat' Gordon Sondland, a Key Figure in Trump Impeachment Furor, Long Coveted Ambassadorship," cited earlier.

68 **He traveled for meetings to Israel** Miller, Sonne, Jaffe and Birnbaum, "Holding Ukraine

Hostage: How the President and His Allies, Chasing 2020 Ammunition, Fanned a Political Storm," cited earlier.

68 **Some at the NSC thought Sondland exaggerated** Deposition of Fiona Hill, October 14, 2019 [hereafter Hill deposition], pages 66–67.

68 **private dinner for 24** U.S. Mission to the European Union, "Ambassador Sondland Brings Together U.S. and European Leaders to Advance Transatlantic Relations." The description of the seating arrangements is based on another album of photographs online: "Independence Day Dinner," uploaded to Flickr by the U.S. Mission to the E.U.

Chapter Nine: "Who Put You in Charge?"

69 **On June 18, Fiona Hill** This account of Hill's meeting with Sondland and other colleagues is based on her testimony, with additional details from Greg Miller's interviews in early 2020 with a person familiar with the day's events.

69 **Some of the NSC staff had taken to joking** Hill deposition, pages 203–204.

69 **ambassador to the European Union and its 28 members** The United Kingdom formally left the E.U. on January 31, 2020, leaving the E.U. with 27 members. When Sondland and Hill met in June 2019, there were still 28.

69 **Sondland's official role** Sondland deposition, page 20.

69 **He's driving off-road** Hill deposition, pages 62 and 116.

69 **From Hill's perspective, there were now two distinct fronts** Hill deposition, pages 38–43.

70 **Nothing had "officially" changed** Hill deposition, page 59.

70 **The E.U. ambassador was genial** Hill deposition, page 116.

70 **ambassadors in Europe complained** Hill deposition, page 115.

70 **He told her: Steer clear** Hill deposition, page 45.

71 **"Gordon, you're in over your head"** Hill deposition, pages 113–118.

71 **She had taken the NSC job** This account of Hill's experiences at the White House is based on Greg Miller's interviews with a source directly familiar with the events, and also draws from stories originally published in *The Post* by Miller and Greg Jaffe.

72 **At work, she arrived on many days** Greg Miller and Greg Jaffe, "In Aftermath of Ukraine Crisis, a Climate of Mistrust and Threats," *Washington Post*, December 25, 2019.

Chapter Ten: "Where Exactly Is the Line for You?"

74 **A waiter at the St. Regis Hotel** This account of Pelosi's appearance at the Monitor Breakfast is based on C-SPAN's video recording: "Speaker Pelosi at Christian Science Monitor Breakfast Series," June 19, 2019. A transcript of the event was also used: "House Speaker Pelosi Interviewed at Christian Science Monitor Breakfast," *CQ Transcriptions*, June 19, 2019.

75 **James Clyburn, a close ally, had suggested** Jake Tapper, interview with Clyburn, "State of the Union," CNN, June 2, 2019.

75 **Pelosi had deployed her staff** Rachael Bade, "Push to Impeach Trump Stalls amid Democrats' Deference to—and Fear of—Pelosi," *Washington Post*, June 16, 2019.

75 **impeachment gaining ground among Democratic voters** Joshua Jamerson, "Nearly Half of Democrats Back Impeachment Hearings Against Trump," *Wall Street Journal*, June 16, 2019.

75 **even saying Trump should be "in prison"** Rachael Bade and John Wagner, "Pelosi Tells Colleagues She Wants to See Trump 'In Prison,' Not Impeached," *Washington Post*, June 6, 2019.

75 **She was "holding it together"** Rachael Bade, "Push to Impeach Trump Stalls amid Democrats' Deference to—and Fear of—Pelosi," cited above.

75 **Just the day before, Higgins had joined** Jerry Zremski, "Higgins Calls for Trump Impeachment Inquiry," *Buffalo News*, June 19, 2019.

78 ***Washington Examiner* published a short story** Russ Read, "Pentagon to Send $250M in Weapons to Ukraine," *Washington Examiner*, June 19, 2019.

78 **A phone call from Mick Mulvaney's office** Eric Lipton, Maggie Haberman and Mark Mazzetti, "Behind the Ukraine Aid Freeze: 84 Days of Conflict and Confusion," *New York Times*, December 29, 2019.

78 **"Russ—here is a story"** Michael Duffey, email to Russell Vought, June 19, 2019. The email was among those released by OMB in response to American Oversight's FOIA request, published on its website, January 22, 2020; Duffey's email to Vought, page 2 of the PDF.

78 **he emailed Elaine McCusker** Michael Duffey, email to Elaine McCusker, June 19, 2019, Center for Public Integrity DoD FOIA release. The CPI published the emails as a PDF on their website, December 20, 2019; Duffey's email to McCusker, pages 44–45 of the PDF.

79 **McCusker replied, "Copy"** McCusker, email to Duffey, June 19, 2019; Center for Public Integrity's PDF, page 44.

80 **In late June, Volker huddled with Pompeo** This account of Volker's meeting with Pompeo is based on Greg Jaffe's interviews in early 2020 with a source directly familiar with the event.

80 **Volker had scheduled a sit-down** Volker impeachment interview, page 262.

81 **"Please don't publish this letter"** Quoted in Annie Karni, "Kurt Volker, Ukraine and a Turbulent End in the Trump Administration," *New York Times*, October 5, 2019.

Chapter Eleven: Flyover

82 **people streamed to the National Mall** Toluse Olorunnipa and Anne Gearan, "Trump Extols U.S. Military Might in Fourth of July Speech as Jets Fly Over Washington," *Washington Post*, July 4, 2019.

82 **Some wore "Make America Great Again" hats** Peter Jamison, Samantha Schmidt, Hannah Natanson and Steve Hendrix, "Trump's Fourth of July Celebration Thrills Supporters, Angers Opponents," *Washington Post*, July 4, 2019.

82 **banned by federal officials from flying** Marissa J. Lang and Peter Hermann, "'We'll Be Ready for It': Officials on Alert as Activists Plan Two Days of Washington Protests," *Washington Post*, July 2, 2019.

82 **Holding hands with his wife** "President Trump Speaks at 4th of July Celebration," video, C-SPAN, July 4, 2019.

82 **delivered from the teleprompters** Dan Zak, "Evening in America: What It Felt Like on Trump's Fourth of July," *Washington Post*, July 5, 2019.

83 **"Gene, I want you to know"** "President Trump Speaks at 4th of July Celebration," C-SPAN.

83 **"Epic"** Andrew Clark (@AndrewHClark), Twitter post, July 4, 2019, 8:17 p.m.

83 **"#SalutetoAmerica was awesome"** Deron Rossi (@deronrossi), Twitter post, July 4, 2019, 8:17 p.m.

83 **"Biden faces his Waterloo"** Trump retweet of *Washington Examiner* (@dcexaminer) Twitter post, July 4, 2019.

83 **"That's why frankly, we have been spending so much time"** Sean Hannity opening monologue, "Hannity," Fox News, July 4, 2019.

83 **"Reducing our nation to tanks"** Quoted in Olorunnipa and Gearan, "Trump Extols U.S. Military Might in Fourth of July Speech as Jets Fly Over Washington," cited earlier.

84 **Nancy Pelosi was with her family** Maureen Dowd, "It's Nancy Pelosi's Parade," *New York Times*, July 6, 2019.

84 **quitting the Republican party** Justin Amash, "Justin Amash: Our Politics Is in a Partisan Death Spiral. That's Why I'm Leaving the GOP," *Washington Post*, July 4, 2019.

84 **"describes a consistent effort"** Justin Amash (@justinamash), Twitter post, May 23, 2019, 1 p.m.

Chapter Twelve: "Drug Deal"

85 **They had dressed in dark suits** Group photograph tweeted by Rick Perry (@SecretaryPerry), July 10, 2019, 7:15 p.m.

86 **In a political career that started** Karen DeYoung, "John Bolton, Famously Abrasive, Is an Experienced Operator in the 'Swamp,'" *Washington Post*, March 23, 2018.

86 **Bolton's fists-flying tough talk** David Nakamura, "Trump Once Loved John Bolton's Pugnacious Views on Fox News. Now Bolton Is Turning His Sights on the President." *Washington Post*, September 30, 2019.

86 **Bolton opened the discussion** This account of the July 10 meeting is primarily based on the testimony of Hill, Sondland, Volker and Vindman, with additional details from Bolton's book, *The Room Where It Happened*, reporting by *The Washington Post*'s Tom Hamburger and previously published *Post* stories.

86 **Bolton and Perry then talked about** Hill deposition, pages 66–67.

86 **Volker worried that the Ukrainians** Volker impeachment interview, page 66.

87 **Danyliuk had been coached by Sondland** Greg Miller, Greg Jaffe and Paul Sonne, "How a CIA Analyst, Alarmed by Trump's Shadow Foreign Policy, Triggered an Impeachment Inquiry," *Washington Post*, November 16, 2019.

87 **"Giuliani's a hand grenade"** Hill deposition, page 45.

87 **Hill had watched Bolton turn up the volume** Hill deposition, pages 131–132.

87 **"Well," Sondland said, "we have an agreement"** Hill deposition, page 67.

87 **Hill could see Bolton stiffen** Hill deposition, page 145.

87 **NSC team had warned Volker** Hill deposition, pages 54, 113–114.

88 **Bolton, with a glance at the clock** Hill deposition, pages 67–68.

88 **Sondland thought everything** Testimony of Gordon Sondland before the House Intelligence Committee [hereafter Sondland public testimony], November 20, 2019.

88 **He invited Yermak and Danyliuk** Hill deposition, page 68.

88 **Go with them, he told her** Hill deposition, page 68.

88 **Sondland emphasized the importance** Vindman deposition, pages 64–65.

88 **Sondland then explained his view** Vindman deposition, pages 29, 64.

88 **"We can't make any commitments"** Hill deposition, page 69. Hill did not explicitly say in her deposition that this was a direct quote, but she was sufficiently clear and specific about what she said and what Sondland said in response that we determined that the use of quotation marks was justified.

88 **He didn't view the exchange as heated** Sondland deposition, page 112.

88 **Hill said that she didn't want to continue** Hill deposition, pages 69–70.

89 **he and Hill had a quick conversation** Vindman deposition, page 34.

89 **unacceptable as presidential behavior** Bolton, *The Room Where It Happened*, page 464.

89 **"You go and tell Eisenberg"** Hill deposition, page 126.

89 **Perry tweeted the group photo** Rick Perry (@SecretaryPerry), Twitter post, July 10, 2019, 7:15 p.m.

89 **Bolton retweeted it** John Bolton (@AmbJohnBolton), Twitter post, July 10, 2019, 7:39 p.m.

89 **He had sent them a message** Taylor deposition, page 27.

90 **They were "very concerned"** Taylor and Volker message exchange in thread with Sondland on July 10, 2019. Volker messages, page 36.

90 **He briefed Pompeo's chief aide** Taylor deposition, page 27.

90 **he texted Volker, saying he was eager** Taylor and Volker message exchange. Volker messages, page 36.

Chapter Thirteen: "Stray Voltage"

91 **On July 18, Ambassador Bill Taylor sat** Taylor deposition, pages 192–194. This account of the interagency Ukraine policy group is drawn primarily from Taylor's testimony, but also the Kent and Vindman depositions.
91 **he was cautiously optimistic** Taylor deposition, pages 22–23.
91 **he could see no progress** Taylor deposition, page 25.
91 **he didn't want it transcribed** Taylor deposition, page 128.
92 **the call itself had stayed on the talking points** Taylor deposition, page 26.
92 **he had come to believe that all of them** Taylor deposition, pages 23–24.
92 **Taylor was joined by his colleague David Holmes** Holmes deposition, page 20.
92 **Taylor couldn't see who it was, but he heard a woman say** Taylor deposition, page 194. Taylor recalled that the speaker was a woman, but other participants, including George Kent, testified that the OMB representative who announced the aid freeze was a man. Since the OMB representative has not been publicly identified, we chose to defer to Taylor's recollection in writing this scene from his perspective.
92 **Taylor was astonished** Taylor deposition, page 27.
92 **As representatives of every agency** Kent deposition, pages 303–304.
92 **All she knew was that Mick Mulvaney** Taylor deposition, page 28.
93 **"OMB . . . just now said"** Taylor, message in thread with Volker and Sondland, July 18, 2019. Volker messages, page 37.
93 **Vindman left the meeting concerned** Vindman deposition, page 182.
93 **Taylor called Vindman and Fiona Hill** Taylor deposition, pages 28–29.
93 **July 19, Volker met with Giuliani** This account of Volker and Giuliani's July 19 meeting is based on Volker's testimony, with additional details of the conversation from Greg Jaffe's reporting.
94 **His message was that Lutsenko wasn't trustworthy** Volker impeachment interview, page 232.
94 **He bluntly told Giuliani that Biden would never** Volker impeachment interview, page 203.
95 **"I talked to Zelensky just now"** Sondland public testimony, November 20, 2019. Sondland read the email aloud during the hearing.
95 **"I spike directly to Zelensky"** Sondland, message to Volker and Taylor, July 19, 2019. Volker messages, page 37. The misspelling of "spoke" didn't appear to cause any confusion.
95 **"Had breakfast with Rudy"** Volker, message to Sondland and Taylor, July 19, 2019. Volker messages, page 37.
95 **Taylor dialed in to a secure** Taylor deposition, page 195.
95 **One by one, attendees presented their case** Taylor deposition, page 195.
95 **equipment like counter-artillery radar** Sergey Morgunov, Will Englund and Michael Birnbaum, "U.S. Military Aid Bolsters Ukraine's Front Lines, but the Trump Drama Makes Kyiv Nervous," *Washington Post*, November 19, 2019.
96 **Every day, the Ministry of Defense held a half-hour ceremony** Taylor deposition, pages 152–153.
96 **"Glory to the Heroes"** "Representatives of German Delegation Honored Fallen Ukrainian Heroes," the Ministry of Defence of Ukraine website, September 12, 2019.
96 **Taylor believed American money lessened** Taylor deposition, page 153.
96 **all but two representatives from OMB** Deposition of Tim Morrison, October 31, 2019 [hereafter Morrison deposition], pages 162–164.
97 **"We do need to be realistic"** Alisyn Camerota and John Berman, "Rep. Adam Schiff (D-CA) Is Interviewed About Mueller's Testimony, on Impeachment, on Russia's Election Threat," "New Day," CNN, July 25, 2019.
97 **He tweeted a rotating series of slides** Trump tweet, July 24, 2019, 5:52 p.m.
98 **That was followed by a clip** Trump tweet, July 24, 2019, 6:22 p.m.

98 **"Fox News Alert. The Witch Hunt is dead"** Sean Hannity, "Mueller Delivers Disaster for Democrats," "Hannity," Fox News, July 24, 2019.
98 **he had again drafted** Vindman deposition, pages 42–43.
99 **"stray voltage"** Vindman deposition, pages 46–47.

Part Two: Risk

Chapter Fourteen: "Do Us a Favor"

103 **Oleksandr Danyliuk stood** This account of the Ukrainian side's preparation for the call is based on David Stern's reporting, including interviews in March 2020 with Oleksandr Danyliuk and another official with direct knowledge of the events.
103 **"Heard from White House"** Volker, message to Yermak, July 25, 2019. Volker messages, page 19.
104 **Danyliuk had told Bill Taylor a few days earlier** Taylor, message to Volker and Sondland, July 21, 2019. Volker messages, page 37.
104 **Bolton had talked of his fear** Taylor deposition, page 29; Vindman deposition, pages 46–47.
104 **Born in Kyiv** Marc Fisher, "Alexander Vindman: Soviet Emigre and Decorated U.S. Army Officer Wanted to Be as American as Can Be. Now the President Questions His Motives," *Washington Post*, November 8, 2019. This account of Vindman's childhood incorporates portions of Fisher's article.
105 **Vindman's talking points** Vindman deposition, pages 109, 309.
105 ***"Congratulations on a great victory"*** "Memorandum of Telephone Conversation Between President Donald Trump and President Zelenskyy of Ukraine, July 25, 2019," declassified and released by the White House, September 25. As the call was not recorded, the transcript has been called partial or rough. For simplicity's sake in the Notes, it's called the "July 25 call transcript."
109 **Vindman felt the call was getting worse** Vindman deposition, pages 56–57.
109 **he saw concern in Morrison's eyes** Vindman deposition, page 95.
112 **Trump was projecting a different tone** Vindman deposition, page 116.
112 **Zelensky could only interpret it as a demand** Vindman deposition, page 228.
112 **In his view, the call had undermined** Vindman deposition, page 19.
112 **Morrison had a different take** Morrison deposition, pages 60–61.
112 **The call was merely proof** Morrison deposition, page 41.
113 **He was confident that Pompeo** Morrison deposition, pages 16–17.
113 **too busy taking notes** Williams deposition, pages 130–131, 149.
113 **it caught her by surprise** Williams deposition, page 129.
113 **Inappropriate, she thought** Williams deposition, page 149.
113 **If that memo leaked** Morrison deposition, page 43.
113 **Vindman and Morrison turned to the press release** This account of Vindman and Morrison's work on the press release is based on Vindman's deposition and Tom Hamburger's additional reporting.
113 **they crossed out sentence after sentence** Vindman deposition, page 309.
113 **"discussed ways to strengthen"** Statement emailed by deputy press secretary Judd Deere to White House pool reporter Cheryl Bolen, published by White House Public Pool at Kinja.com, July 25, 2019.
114 **Vindman, still upset** This account of Vindman's activities after the call is based on Vindman's deposition, page 96, with additional details from Tom Hamburger's reporting.
115 **Morrison also went to see Eisenberg and Ellis** Morrison deposition, pages 43–44.
115 **"Mike, here's the OGC"** The email was among those released by OMB in response American Oversight's FOIA request [hereafter American Oversight OMB FOIA release]; the July 25 email from Sandy to Duffey is on page 12.

115 **A week earlier, Sandy had returned to work** Deposition of Mark Sandy, November 16, 2019 [hereafter Sandy deposition], page 24.
115 **Duffey had pulled him aside** Sandy deposition, pages 31–32.
115 **Why? Sandy asked** Sandy deposition, page 41.
115 **he had seen Duffey's emails** Sandy deposition, pages 25–26.
115 **Duffey proposed a novel solution** Sandy deposition, page 33.
116 **He had never seen** Sandy deposition, page 87.
116 **He warned Duffey** Sandy deposition, page 34.
116 **They needed to consult** Sandy deposition, pages 40–41.
116 **He also checked in with Elaine McCusker** Sandy deposition, pages 51–52.
116 **the Pentagon could "continue its planning"** Quoted in "Decision, Matter of: Office of Management and Budget—Withholding of Ukraine Security Assistance," U.S. Government Accountability Office, January 16, 2020. The GAO decision, finding that OMB had violated the Impoundment Control Act, included the full text of the July 25 footnote.
116 **the lawyer-approved footnote** Sandy, email to Duffey, July 25, 2019. American Oversight OMB FOIA release, page 12.
116 **"Given the sensitive nature of the request"** Duffey, email to David Norquist, Elaine McCusker, Eric Chewning and redacted recipients, July 25, 2019. Center for Public Integrity, December 20 FOIA release, page 40 [hereafter CPI FOIA release].
116 **She sent Sandy a short message** McCusker, email to Sandy, July 25, 2019. The email was turned over with significant redaction in the CPI FOIA release, page 78. An unredacted version was published later by *Just Security*, an online forum that reports and analyzes national security issues. See Kate Brannen, "Exclusive: Unredacted Ukraine Documents Reveal Extent of Pentagon's Legal Concerns," *Just Security*, January 2, 2020.
116 **"I think we are good"** McCusker, email to Sandy, July 25, 2019, cited earlier.
116 **What's going on with the security assistance?** Laura Cooper, public testimony, November 20, 2019 [hereafter Cooper public testimony]. Cooper testified that members of her Pentagon staff received inquiries from the Ukrainian Embassy on July 25.
116 **State Department officials also received** Cooper public testimony. Cooper also testified that her staff received emails from colleagues at the State Department on July 25, saying that "the Ukrainian embassy and House Foreign Affairs Committee are asking about security assistance."
116 **the Ukrainians' "diplomatic tradecraft"** Deposition of Catherine Croft, October 30, 2019 [hereafter Croft deposition], page 101.
117 **After work that evening** This account of the Vindman brothers' evening is based on Tom Hamburger's reporting.

Chapter Fifteen: The "Big Stuff"

118 **no one in the embassy had** Taylor deposition, page 31; Holmes deposition page 22.
118 **when Holmes arrived at Yermak's office** Holmes deposition, page 23.
119 **Holmes wanted to ask Sondland** Holmes deposition, page 109.
119 **Sondland told the group** This account of the Sondland lunch, and his phone call with Trump, is drawn almost entirely from the Holmes deposition, pages 21–25, and Holmes public testimony. Other details as noted.
119 **"Give A$AP Rocky his FREEDOM"** Trump tweet, July 25, 2019, 5:24 p.m.
120 **Sondland said he meant "big stuff"** During Sondland's public testimony, he was asked about Holmes's account of the lunch. "The only part of Mr. Holmes's recounting that I take exception with is I do not recall mentioning the Bidens," Sondland said. "That did not enter my mind. It was Burisma and 2016 elections." Otherwise, Sondland said, he had no reason to doubt or dispute Holmes's recollection.

120 **"A vote for Mitch McConnell's"** Ilhan Omar (@IlhanMN), Twitter post, June 27, 2019, 3:33 p.m.

120 **"If you see the Senate bill"** Rashida Tlaib (@RashidaTlaib), Twitter post, June 27, 2019, 3:57 p.m.

120 **"All these people have their public whatever"** Maureen Dowd, "It's Nancy Pelosi's Parade," *New York Times*, July 6, 2019.

120 **"That public 'whatever'"** Alexandria Ocasio-Cortez (@AOC), Twitter post, July 6, 2019, 8:49 p.m.

121 **"You got a complaint?"** Mike DeBonis and Rachael Bade, "'Regrets Is Not What I Do': Pelosi Defends Her Comment About Four House Women," *Washington Post*, July 10, 2019.

121 **"When these comments first started"** Rachael Bade and Mike DeBonis, "'Outright Disrespectful': Four House Women Struggle as Pelosi Isolates Them," *Washington Post*, July 10, 2019.

121 **Pelosi tweeted out a smiling photo** Nancy Pelosi (@SpeakerPelosi), Twitter post, July 26, 2019, 10:09 a.m.

121 **"I don't think there ever was any hatchet"** Nancy Pelosi, weekly press conference, July 26, 2019.

122 **it fell to him to review the call's rough transcript** Vindman deposition, page 48.

122 **He noticed that the transcript** Vindman deposition, page 54.

122 **He phoned George Kent** Vindman deposition, pages 140–141.

122 **After his talk with Vindman** This account of the whistleblower's actions after his conversation with Vindman is drawn from previously published *Post* stories and additional reporting by Carol D. Leonnig, including interviews with multiple people with direct knowledge of the events.

123 **"run out the clock. . . . Are you?"** "House Speaker Weekly Briefing," C-SPAN video, July 26, 2019; Nancy Pelosi, weekly press conference transcript, July 26, 2019.

124 **Privately, lawmakers and senior staff members** John Wagner, Kayla Epstein and Rachael Bade, "House Panel Asks Court to Enforce Mueller-Related Subpoenas, a Step Toward Possible Impeachment," *Washington Post*, July 26, 2019.

124 **"We are considering the malfeasances"** "House Judiciary Chair Nadler Speaks to Reporters," C-SPAN video, July 26, 2019.

124 **"Because Department of Justice policies"** "Application of the Committee on the Judiciary, House of Representatives, for an Order Authorizing the Release of Certain Grand Jury Materials," U.S. District Court for the District of Columbia, Judge Beryl A. Howell, July 26, 2019, page 11.

124 **"Democrats want to convince their base"** "Collins Statement on Democrat Petition for Grand Jury Material," July 26, 2019.

125 **Michael Duffey was preparing himself** Sandy deposition, page 54.

125 **This high-level group almost never** Laura Cooper deposition, October 23, 2019 [hereafter Cooper deposition], page 50. This account of the Deputies Small Group meeting on July 26, 2019, is drawn primarily from the testimony of four participants: Cooper, Vindman, David Hale and Tim Morrison,

125 **From David Hale** Hale deposition, page 81.

125 **So did Lt. Gen. Keith Kellogg** Williams deposition, page 117.

125 **participants argued that the stakes were high** Vindman deposition, pages 184–186.

125 **OMB was an outlier** Hale deposition, page 106.

125 **Duffey's stance was seconded** Morrison deposition, page 165.

125 **That brought a chorus of objections** Cooper deposition, page 49.

126 **the same consensus** Morrison deposition, page 164.

126 **Holmes returned to the embassy** Holmes deposition, pages 68–69.

126 **Holmes went to see his supervisor** Holmes deposition, page 159.

126 **He couldn't stop talking about what** Holmes deposition, page 68.

Chapter Sixteen: Plan B

128 **the analyst wanted advice** This account of the whistleblower's search for guidance and the preparation of his complaint is based previously published *Post* stories and Leonnig's interviews with multiple people with direct knowledge.

129 **fuse all the arguments** Vindman deposition, page 186.

129 **Vindman had never met with Trump** Vindman deposition, page 3.

129 **He drafted a background section** Vindman deposition, pages 186–188.

130 **As McCusker understood it, the aid freeze** Brannen, "Exclusive: Unredacted Ukraine Documents Reveal Extent of Pentagon's Legal Concerns," cited earlier.

130 **OMB had extended it with a second footnote** Duffey, email to McCusker, August 6, 2019, from CPI December 20 FOIA release, page 19.

130 **"Amazing teammates have allowed me"** Elaine McCusker opening statement, Senate Committee on Armed Services hearing on her nomination, May 10, 2017.

130 **she objected to saying flatly** McCusker, email to Duffey, Sandy, and redacted recipient, August 9, 2019, from CPI December 20 FOIA release, page 37. The email was almost entirely redacted when released by the Defense Department; *Just Security* reported that the unredacted email showed McCusker saying, "As of 12 AUG I don't think we can agree that the pause 'will not preclude timely execution.'" Brannen, "Exclusive: Unredacted Ukraine Documents Reveal Extent of Pentagon's Legal Concerns."

130 **There were press reports saying** Steve Holland and Jonathan Landay, "Trump Gets Update from Aides on Afghan Peace Plan with Troop Pullout Possible," Reuters, August 16, 2019.

131 **"Any news?"** McCusker, email to Duffey, August 17, 2019, from CPI FOIA release, pages 32–33.

131 **Vindman also was trying to find out** Vindman deposition, pages 187–188.

131 **fielding questions** McCusker, email to Duffey, August 26, 2019, from CPI FOIA release, page 66; McCusker, email to John Rood and Paul Ney, August 21, 2019, from CPI FOIA release, page 17.

131 **Senator Rob Portman of Ohio** Wayne Jones, email to Duffey, August 23, 2019, from American Oversight OMB FOIA release, page 82.

131 **Senator Jim Inhofe of Oklahoma** Virginia Boney, email to Jason Yaworske, August 23, 2019, from American Oversight OMB FOIA release, page 79.

131 **Representative Mac Thornberry of Texas** Josh Martin, email to Jason Yaworske, August 22, 2019, from American Oversight OMB FOIA release, page 80.

131 **Representative Paul Cook of California** Cook, letter to Mick Mulvaney, August 23, 2019, from American Oversight OMB FOIA release, page 81.

131 **"The impact of holding this case"** Tania Hanna, email to Eric Chewning, August 26, 2019, from CPI FOIA release, pages 111–112.

132 **"would be crucial to cementing"** Quoted in Holmes deposition, page 27.

132 **Bolton complained to Morrison and Bill Taylor** Holmes deposition, pages 27–28.

132 **Bolton pressed Zelensky to block** Pavel Polityuk, Vladimir Soldatkin and Tom Balmforth, "Trump Adviser Bolton Tells Ukraine: Beware Chinese Influence," Reuters, August 28, 2019.

133 **"Can I get five minutes with him?"** This account of Taylor's thoughts and actions in late August is based on his testimony, with new details from Jaffe's interviews with him.

133 **Taylor had never written a first-person cable** Taylor, public testimony, House Intelligence Committee, November 13, 2019.

134 **"Can you shed any light"** Caitlin Emma, email to Rachel Semmel, August 28, 2019, from American Oversight OMB FOIA release, pages 96–97.

Chapter Seventeen: Ukraine in a Box

135 **"Need to talk to you"** Yermak, message to Volker, August 29, 2019. Volker messages, page 20.

135 **Taylor thought they sounded desperate** Taylor deposition, page 138.
135 **He shared the draft** Taylor, interviews with Greg Jaffe.
135 **"Meeting on for 2:40"** Taylor exchange with Volker and Sondland, August 29, 2019. Volker messages, page 38.
136 **"President Trump should stop worrying"** "Menendez Demands That the Trump Administration Release Security Assistance Funding for Ukraine," Senate Committee on Foreign Relations statement, August 29, 2019.
136 **"Sensational!"** Quoted by Julia Davis (@JuliaDavisNews), Twitter post, August 29, 2019, 9:45 a.m.
136 **"Terrible news"** Quoted by Julia Davis (@JuliaDavisNews), Twitter post, August 29, 2019, 2:20 p.m.
136 **"No action has been taken by OMB"** Mark Paoletta, email to Edwin Castle and Paul Ney, August 29, 2019, published with redactions in American Oversight OMB FOIA release, page 166. *Just Security* reported the text of the final redacted footnote. Brannen, "Exclusive: Unredacted Ukraine Documents Reveal Extent of Pentagon's Legal Concerns."
136 **"I don't agree to the revised TPs"** McCusker, email to Duffey, August 29, 2019, from American Oversight OMB FOIA release, page 165, and *Just Security*, without redactions.
136 **"Trump not going to Warsaw now"** Volker message to Vadym Prystaiko, August 29, 2019. Volker messages, page 56.
137 **Danyliuk and Taylor were exchanging** Taylor deposition, page 190.
137 **Zelensky opened with a question** Taylor deposition, page 35.
137 **wasn't about the money** Greg Jaffe, Greg Miller and Paul Sonne, "John Bolton Expressed Alarm About Shadow Ukraine Policy, but at Key Moments, It's Unclear What He Did to Stop It," *Washington Post*, November 6, 2019. Additional details, including the Ukrainian side's preparation and comments during the meeting, were reported by Sonne.
137 **Pence was taking notes** Williams deposition, page 83.
138 **Biden did not come up** "Remarks by Vice President Pence and President Duda of Poland in Joint Press Conference, Warsaw, Poland," White House transcript, September 2, 2019.
138 **he had allowed himself to think** Taylor deposition, page 35.
138 **Morrison had watched from across** Morrison deposition, pages 180–181.
138 **Sondland said he had told Yermak** Morrison deposition, page 134.
138 **Morrison was startled** Morrison deposition, page 182.
139 **Taylor shared Morrison's dismay** Taylor deposition, page 36.
139 **"Are we now saying"** Taylor, message to Sondland and Volker, September 1, 2019. Volker messages, page 39.
139 **there had to be a public announcement** Taylor deposition, page 36.
139 **Zelensky had to be the one to make it** Morrison deposition, page 188. There is a slight discrepancy between the depositions of Morrison and Taylor on the question of what Sondland said his "mistake" was during this September 1 phone call. Taylor says that Sondland informed him that "he had made a mistake by earlier telling Ukrainian officials . . . that a White House meeting with President Zelensky was dependent on a public announcement of investigations. In fact, Ambassador Sondland said, everything was dependent on such an announcement, including security assistance." Taylor also said that on this phone call, he and Sondland "discussed the possibility that the Ukrainian prosecutor general, rather than President Zelensky, would make a statement about investigations." Morrison says that Taylor told him the next day that Sondland had said the statement had to come from Zelensky, not the prosecutor general. Since there is no dispute Sondland had told Morrison the statement could come from the prosecutor general, we infer that Sondland had indeed been mistaken about who could deliver the statement, and that his misconception was cleared up before he spoke with Taylor.
139 **Trump wanted him in a box** Taylor deposition, page 36.
139 **Trump should have more respect** Taylor deposition, page 37.

139 **shelling had killed a Ukrainian soldier** "Ukraine Reports One KIA, One WIA amid 21 Enemy Attacks in Donbas on Sept 5," UNIAN, September 6, 2019.
140 **Did they know anything** Chris Murphy, "An Inside Look at My Trip to Germany, Ukraine, Serbia, and Kosovo," Medium, September 16, 2019.
140 **Johnson, who had called Trump to talk** Johnson, letter to Jordan and Nunes, cited earlier.
140 **On September 8, Taylor and Sondland** Taylor deposition, page 39. At his deposition, Sondland initially said he thought his "no quid pro quo" call with Trump took place on September 9. The White House said it couldn't find any record of a September 9 call. At his public testimony, Sondland said he had no reason to challenge Morrison's and Taylor's recollections that it took place earlier. "To the extent that the recollections of various witnesses differ in some respects, we leave to the committee the task of reconciling those differences," his attorney told *The Post* in November. Aaron C. Davis, Elise Viebeck and Josh Dawsey, "Witness Testimony and Records Raise Questions About Account of Trump's 'No Quid Pro Quo' Call," *Washington Post*, November 27, 2019.
140 **What do you want from Ukraine?** Sondland public testimony, cited in House Impeachment Report, page 24.
140 **he had already passed the word** Taylor deposition, page 39.
140 **"When a businessman is about to sign"** Taylor quoting Sondland, Taylor deposition, page 40.
141 **"The nightmare is that they"** Taylor, message exchange with Volker and Sondland, September 9, 2019. Volker messages, page 53.
141 **"no quid pro quo's of any kind"** Sondland to Taylor, same message exchange.
141 **"I suggest we stop the back and forth"** Sondland, same message exchange.

Chapter Eighteen: "Credible Urgent Concern"

142 **Schiff had read the staff's six-page memo** This description of the committee's investigative work, here and later, is based on Mary Jordan and Ellen Nakashima's background interviews in March, April and May 2020.
142 **"just investigate the darn things"** Giuliani quoted in Kenneth P. Vogel and Andrew E. Kramer, "Giuliani Renews Push for Ukraine to Investigate Trump's Political Opponents," *New York Times*, August 21, 2019.
142 **the editorial connected the disparate dots** The Editorial Board, "Trump Tries to Force Ukraine to Meddle in the 2020 election," *Washington Post*, September 5, 2019.
143 **a "read-out" of a July 25 phone call** Adam Schiff, Elliot Engel and Elijah E. Cummings, letters to Michael Pompeo and Pat Cipollone, September 9, 2019. The letters describe the read-out from the Ukrainian government.
143 **the committee released a statement** "Three House Committees Launch Wide-Ranging Investigation into Trump-Giuliani Ukraine Scheme," House Intelligence Committee, September 9, 2019.
143 **"coerce the Ukrainian government into pursuing"** Schiff, Engel and Cummings, letters to Pompeo and Cipollone, September 9, 2019, cited earlier.
144 **Atkinson's office had received a complaint** Described in Michael Atkinson's letter to Schiff and Nunes, September 9, 2019, released by House Intelligence Committee.
144 **Will Hurd's ears perked up** This account of Hurd's reaction from an interview with *Post* contributing reporter Robert Moore, April 1, 2020, and follow-up conversations [hereafter Hurd interview with Moore].
145 **On August 1, he told** Robert Moore, "Texas Rep. Hurd, Lone Black Republican in House, Won't Seek Reelection," *Washington Post*, August 1, 2019.
145 **used Hurd's announcement to warn** Robert Costa and Robert Moore, "'Take Texas Seriously': GOP Anxiety Spikes After Retirements, Democratic Gains," *Washington Post*, August 2, 2019.
146 **Police said the shooter told them** Rachel Hatzipanagos, "Even Before the El Paso Mass

Shooting, Latinos Said Trump's Anti-Immigrant Rhetoric Made Them Feel Unsafe," *Washington Post*, August 16, 2019.

146 **"This is a party that is shrinking"** Hurd quoted in Lou Chibarro Jr., "GOP Congressman Urges: 'Don't Be an Asshole, Don't Be a Homophobe,'" *Washington Blade*, June 26, 2019.

147 **Senator Rob Portman of Ohio was also frustrated** This account of Portman's calls about the aid is based on Isabelle Taft's interview in April 2020 with a Republican staffer familiar with the calls.

148 **McCusker received an unexpected email** Duffey, email to McCusker, Subject: RE: Footnote, September 11, 2019. CPI FOIA release, page 22.

148 **she had shared with Duffey** McCukser, email to Duffey, Subject: USAI Status and Update Plan, September 9, 2019, published with redactions by American Oversight OMB FOIA release, page 120. *Just Security* reported on the text of the redacted line: Brannen, "Exclusive: Unredacted Ukraine Documents Reveal Extent of Pentagon's Legal Concerns."

148 **OMB had drafted its footnote** Duffey, email to McCusker, Subject: RE: USAI Status and Update Plan, September 10, 2019, published with redactions by American Oversight OMB FOIA release, page 124. *Just Security* reported part of the content of the unredacted email.

149 **"You can't be serious"** McCusker, email to Duffey, Subject: RE: USAI Status and Update Plan, September 10, 2019, published with redactions by American Oversight OMB FOIA release, page 124. *Just Security* reported the entirety of the redacted line.

149 **"Copy," she said** McCusker, email to Duffey, Subject: RE: Footnote, September 11, 2019. CPI FOIA release, page 22.

149 **"Not exactly clear but president made the decision"** Duffey, email to McCusker, Subject: RE: Footnote, September 11, 2019, published with redactions in CPI FOIA release, page 22. *Just Security* reported a portion of the redacted text.

149 **"Agree!"** McCusker, email to Duffey, September 11, 2019. CPI FOIA release, page 53.

149 **Vindman learned only the most basic information** Vindman deposition, page 306.

149 **Mark Sandy at OMB got an email** Sandy deposition, page 139.

149 **"Hi—got an email overnight"** Volker, message exchange with Sondland and Taylor, September 12, 2019. Volker messages, page 39.

149 **"I strongly support the president's position"** "Portman Welcomes President Trump Decision on Security Assistance & Urges Other NATO Countries to Do More to Help Ukraine," office of Senator Rob Portman, September 12, 2019.

150 **"It's beyond a coincidence"** Quoted in Caitlin Emma, Jacqueline Feldscher, Wesley Morgan and Connor O'Brien, "Trump Administration Backs Off Hold on Ukraine Military Aid," *Politico*, September 12, 2019.

150 **"So why was it released?"** Lindsey Graham, remarks during Senate Appropriations Committee Markup of Fiscal 2020 Defense and Energy and Water Development Appropriations, *CQ Transcriptions*, September 12, 2019.

150 **"It's a very important decision"** Embassy of Ukraine in the USA, Facebook post, September 12, 2019.

150 **Taylor personally conveyed** Taylor deposition, page 40.

150 **Schiff and his top investigator, Daniel Goldman** This account of Schiff's phone call with Maguire is based on Mary Jordan and Ellen Nakashima's interviews with sources familiar with the call.

151 **"I told Nancy"** "Remarks by President Trump at the 2019 House Republican Conference Member Retreat Dinner, Baltimore, MD," September 12, 2019.

151 **Taylor had a series of discussions with Zelensky** Taylor deposition, page 217.

151 **he expected a Trump-Zelensky meeting** Quoted in "Zelensky, Trump Could Meet in New York Between Sept 23–Sept 26, Date Being Selected—Taylor," *Ukraine General Newswire*, September 12, 2019.

152 **Taylor checked with Danyliuk** Taylor deposition, pages 41 and 217.
152 **"Don't jeopardize it"** Taylor deposition, pages 217–218.
152 **Taylor thought Yermak looked uncomfortable** Taylor deposition, page 41.
152 **"Grateful to the USA"** Volodymyr Zelensky (@ZelenskyyUa), Twitter post, September 13, 2019, 3:17 p.m. Kyiv time.
152 **offering a legal rationale** Jason Klitenic, letter to House Intelligence Committee ranking members, Schiff and Nunes, and Senate Intelligence Committee ranking members, Richard Burr and Mark Warner, September 13, 2019.
153 **"The Committee can only conclude"** Schiff, letter to Maguire, September 13, 2019.
153 **put out a press release** "Chairman Schiff Issues Subpoena for Whistleblower Complaint Being Unlawfully Withheld by Acting DNI from Intelligence Committees," press release, House Intelligence Committee, September 13, 2019.

Chapter Nineteen: "Dig Very Hard, and Very Fast"

154 **The trio had years of experience** This account of Ellen Nakashima, Greg Miller and Shane Harris's reporting on the whistleblower complaint is based on notes, email and text records and recollections of events.
155 **"We have breaking news right now"** Chris Cuomo, "Rep. Jerrold Nadler, D-NY, Interviewed; House Intel Chair: Acting DNI Illegally Withholding Whistleblower Complaint, Possibly to Protect Trump," "Cuomo Prime Time," CNN, September 13, 2019.
158 **He wouldn't discuss specifics** Margaret Brennan, "Interview with Rep. Adam Schiff (D-CA)," "Face the Nation," CBS, September 15, 2019.
158 **adding new detail** Ellen Nakashima, "Trump's Acting Intelligence Chief Told to Turn Over Whistleblower Complaint or Face Public Questioning by Congress," *Washington Post*, September 16, 2019.

Chapter Twenty: Nadler's Audition

160 **"Personally, I think the president"** Nadler quote from "Jerry Nadler Talks Investigations, Impeachment Rules," "The Brian Lehrer Show," WNYC, September 16, 2019.
161 **"was uncomfortable with the task"** For the Mueller Report's description of Trump's directive to Lewandowski, see Volume II, page 5.
161 **He and Trump had a long history** This account about the long-standing bad blood between Trump and Nadler incorporates and relies on Rachael Bade and Josh Dawsey, "Trump's Feud with Jerry Nadler Rooted in Decades-Old New York Real Estate Project," *Washington Post*, April 8, 2019.
163 **He summarized the Mueller report's finding** House Judiciary Committee hearing on Executive Branch Oversight with witness Corey Lewandowski, C-SPAN video and *CQ Transcriptions*, September 17, 2019.

Chapter Twenty-One: "Not Waving You Off"

167 **The whistleblower complaint that has triggered** Greg Miller, Ellen Nakashima and Shane Harris, "Trump's Commgunications with Foreign Leader Are Part of Whistleblower Complaint That Spurred Standoff Between Spy Chief and Congress, Former Officials Say," *Washington Post*, September 18, 2019.
168 **read closely by investigators** Mary Jordan interviews with House Intelligence Committee staffers.
169 **A second source confirmed** Ellen Nakashima, Shane Harris, Greg Miller and Carol Leonnig, "Whistleblower Complaint About President Trump Involves Ukraine, According to Two People Familiar with the Matter," *Washington Post*, September 19, 2019.
169 **the *New York Times* posted its account** Julian E. Barnes, Nicholas Fandos, Michael S.

Schmidt and Matthew Rosenberg, "Whistle-Blower Complaint Is Said to Involve Trump and Ukraine," *New York Times*, September 19, 2019. The time stamps on the *Post* and *Times* stories from Anna Palmer and Jake Sherman, "*Politico* Playbook: How Trump Has Handcuffed Washington," *Politico*, September 20, 2019.

169 **the *Wall Street Journal* added to the emerging mosaic** Alan Cullison, Rebecca Ballhaus and Dustin Volz, "Trump Repeatedly Pressed Ukraine President to Investigate Biden's Son," *Wall Street Journal*, September 20, 2019.

170 **"It's another media disaster"** "Remarks by President Trump and Prime Minister Morrison of Australia Before Bilateral Meeting," White House transcript, September 20, 2019.

170 **Pelosi was taking careful note** This account of Pelosi's thinking in the days leading up to the announcement of the impeachment inquiry is based on Mary Jordan's interviews throughout early 2020 with sources with direct knowledge of the events, and previous *Post* reporting.

Chapter Twenty-Two: "The Women Who Kill"

172 **"'Darlin,' know your power'"** "Pelosi Remarks at Memorial Service of Cokie Roberts," September 21, 2019.

172 **"We need to start thinking about an announcement"** Mary Jordan interview with Drew Hammill, Pelosi's deputy chief of staff, May 2020.

173 **"The conversation I had was largely congratulatory"** "Remarks by President Trump Before Marine One Departure," White House transcript, September 22, 2019.

173 **"I have been very reluctant to go down the path"** Jake Tapper, "Interview with Rep. Adam Schiff (D-CA)," "State of the Union," CNN, September 22, 2019.

174 **"a grave new chapter"** Nancy Pelosi, "Dear Colleague to All Members on Whistleblower Complaint," September 22, 2019.

174 **"Democrats' frustration"** Rachael Bade and Josh Dawsey, "'We've Been Very Weak': House Democrats Decry Their Oversight of Trump, Push Pelosi on Impeachment," *Washington Post*, September 22, 2019.

174 **"No one has seen the complaint"** Jeanine Pirro, "Rep. Kevin McCarthy (R-CA) Weighs In on the Whistleblower Scandal Involving the President and Joe Biden," "Justice with Judge Pirro," Fox News, September 21, 2019.

175 **"I think this is a clear example"** Martha MacCallum, "Trump's Communications with Foreign Leader Part of Whistleblower Complaint," "The Story with Martha MacCallum," Fox News, September 19, 2019.

175 **He picked up the assertion from an op-ed** Trump tweet, September 21, 2019, 5:47 p.m.

175 **"It appears that an American spy"** Greg Jarrett, "The Trump Whistleblower May Not Be a Whistleblower at All," FoxNews.com, September 20, 2019.

175 **"Would you have any availability today"** This account of the writing and editing of the op-ed is based on Michael Duffy's notes and email records, as well as Steve Luxenberg's interview of Duffy in December 2019.

177 **"Is anyone starting to think differently?"** Slotkin, interview with Griff Witte, April 2020.

177 **"Don't get in a knife fight with Elissa"** Quoted in Phoebe Wall Howard, "Why Elissa Slotkin Took Heat from Angry Democrats During Her Campaign," *Detroit Free Press*, November 9, 2018.

179 **"These allegations are stunning"** Gil Cisneros, Jason Crow, Chrissy Houlahan, Elaine Luria, Mikie Sherrill, Elissa Slotkin and Abigail Spanberger, "Seven Freshman Democrats: These Allegations Are a Threat to All We Have Sworn to Protect," *Washington Post*, op-ed, September 23, 2019.

179 **the op-ed writers had one more important call** This account of the phone call is based on Mary Jordan's interviews, as well as Griff Witte's interview with Elissa Slotkin.

Chapter Twenty-Three: "You Don't Really Want to Do This"

181 **Hold for the president** This account of Pelosi's phone call with Trump on the morning of September 24 is based on Mary Jordan's interview with a source familiar with the call.

182 **she flashed the rookie lawmaker** Slotkin, interview with Witte, April 2020.

183 **"People approach me everywhere I go"** John Lewis's speech from House proceedings, C-SPAN video, September 24, 2019.

183 **"I'll be making an announcement"** "Speaker Pelosi Interview at the *Atlantic* Festival," C-SPAN video, September 24, 2019.

184 **announcing that he would "fully declassify"** Trump tweet, September 24, 2019, 2:12 p.m.

184 **Trump had overruled his communications staff** Manuel Roig-Franzia and Josh Dawsey, "Trump Lawyer Pat Cipollone Was a Camera-Shy Washington Everyman—Until Impeachment Made Him a Star," *Washington Post*, January 30, 2020. Also, Ashley Parker, Josh Dawsey and Philip Rucker, "Seven Days: Inside Trump's Frenetic Response to the Whistleblower Complaint and the Battle Over Impeachment," *Washington Post*, September 25, 2019.

184 **Pelosi strode in** This account of the September 24 Democratic caucus meeting is based on Mary Jordan's background interviews.

185 **arm-twisting mission** The Lewis-Tlaib conversation, and Tlaib's quip to Hoyer, from Mary Jordan's background interviews with House Democrats.

185 **"He is a dangerous person to our country"** Griffin Connolly, "Rep. Rashida Tlaib Selling 'Impeach the MF' Shirts for Reelection Campaign," *Roll Call*, September 27, 2019.

185 **They wanted a surgical strike** This account of the Democratic caucus meeting after Pelosi left is based primarily on Griff Witte's reporting, including an interview with Slotkin in April 2020. At the time, the meeting was well covered by many media outlets. One notable account appeared later in the *New York Times Magazine*: Susan Dominus, "Hope and High Drama: A Year with Two New Democratic Congresswomen," November 18, 2019.

186 **Slotkin looked at her phone** Also reported in Dominus's *New York Times Magazine* article. Dominus has other details that Witte confirmed.

186 **instantly turning up on *Politico* reporter** Heather Caygle (@heatherscope), Twitter post, September 24, 2019, 5:04 p.m.

187 **Schiff left the room** Mary Jordan interview with Patrick Boland, House Intelligence Committee communications director, April 2020.

187 **six American flags behind her** "Speaker Pelosi Announcement of Impeachment Inquiry," C-SPAN video, September 24, 2019, and *Post* reporting.

187 **saying Democrats "have been trying"** Rachael Bade, Mike DeBonis and Karoun Demirijian, "Pelosi Announces Impeachment Inquiry, Says Trump's Courting of Foreign Political Help Is a 'Betrayal of National Security,'" *Washington Post*, September 24, 2019.

Part Three: Impeachment

Chapter Twenty-Four: "Isn't It a Perfect Call?"

191 **a pep talk from Trump** This account is drawn from Ashley Parker, Josh Dawsey and Philip Rucker, "Seven Days: Inside Trump's Frenetic Response to the Whistleblower Complaint and the Battle Over Impeachment," *Washington Post*, September 25, 2019.

192 **The document "records the notes and recollections"** July 25 call transcript.

193 **Justice officials told Barrett that the exchange** Matt Zapotsky and Devlin Barrett, "Justice Dept. Rejected Investigation of Trump Phone Call Just Weeks After It Began Examining the Matter," *Washington Post*, September 25, 2019. Zapotsky and Barrett provided us with additional details.

194 **a meeting of her leadership team** Mike DeBonis and Rachael Bade, "Pelosi, Top Demo-

crats Favor Quick, Narrow Trump Impeachment Probe Focused on Ukraine," *Washington Post*, September 25, 2019.

194 **this chest of pure gold** Mary Jordan background interviews.

194 **"That is textbook abuse of power"** "House Democratic News Conference," C-SPAN video and transcript, September 25, 2019.

195 **He had passed out a "Mad Libs impeachment" form** Reported in Philip Rucker, Rachael Bade and Robert Costa, "Trump Deflects and Defies as Democrats Speed Up Impeachment Strategy," *Washington Post*, September 25, 2019.

196 **"Ever since President Trump was elected"** "Minority Leader McCarthy News Conference," C-SPAN video, September 25, 2019.

196 **"Wow. Impeachment over this?"** Lindsey Graham (@LindseyGrahamSC), Twitter post, September 25, 2019, 10:37 a.m.

196 **Schiff and his team gathered** Mary Jordan and Ellen Nakashima's interviews with House Intelligence Committee staffers.

196 **Will Hurd of Texas read the transcript** Hurd interview with Moore, April 2020.

197 **upset enough to write a blistering op-ed** Will Hurd, "Trump Is Being Manipulated by Putin. What Should We Do?" *New York Times*, July 19, 2018.

198 **"What those notes reflect"** Adam Schiff, remarks to reporters, *CQ Transcriptions*, September 25, 2019.

198 **it lit up with bazillions of texts** Greg Miller's interviews with a person familiar with the events.

199 **"It remains troubling in the extreme"** Mitt Romney quoted in Robert Costa, "Cracks Emerge Among Senate Republicans Over Trump Urging Ukrainian Leader to Investigate Biden," *Washington Post*, September 25, 2019.

199 **"There are a number of Republicans"** Parker, Dawsey and Rucker, "Seven Days: Inside Trump's Frenetic Response to the Whistleblower Complaint and the Battle Over Impeachment," cited earlier.

200 **The two men sat in black leather armchairs** "President Trump Meeting with Ukrainian President," C-SPAN video, September 25, 2019. This account is based largely on the video.

204 **"a lot that's very troubling there"** Sasse quoted in Aishvarya Kavin, "Republican Senator on Whistleblower Complaint: 'There's Obviously Some Very Troubling Things Here,'" CNN .com, September 25, 2019.

204 **"I haven't seen anything that bothers me"** Conaway quoted in Richard Cowan and David Morgan, "Intelligence Panel Members, Including One Republican, Say Whistleblower Complaint Disturbing," Reuters, September 25, 2019.

204 **Will Hurd was impressed** Hurd interview with Moore.

205 **"CROWDSTRIKE IS BACK ON THE MENU"** Craig Timberg, Drew Harwell and Ellen Nakashima, "In Call to Ukraine's President, Trump Revived a Favorite Conspiracy Theory About the DNC Hack," *Washington Post*, September 25, 2019.

Chapter Twenty-Five: "That's Close to a Spy"

208 **"This complaint should never"** Adam Schiff (@RepAdamSchiff), Twitter post, September 26, 2019, 8:35 a.m.

208 **Emboldened, Schiff gaveled** "Acting DNI Maguire Testimony on Whistleblower Complaint," C-SPAN, September 26, 2019.

209 **he wrote a screenplay** This mini biography of Schiff is based largely on a profile by Ben Terris: "Adam Schiff Once Wanted to Be a Screenwriter. Can He Give the Trump Presidency a Hollywood Ending?" *Washington Post*, November 1, 2019.

209 **"Yesterday, we were presented"** "House Select Intelligence Committee Holds Hearing on National Intelligence Whistleblower Complaint," *CQ Transcriptions*, September 26, 2019.

210 **he had remembered former FBI director** Adam Schiff interview with Mary Jordan, April 2020. Former FBI director James Comey's 2018 book, *A Higher Loyalty*, described Trump as

a mafia-style leader. When Trump demanded his loyalty over dinner, Comey wrote, he felt like he was at a "Cosa Nostra induction ceremony, with Trump in the role of family boss."

211 **pass the audio along to reporters** Eli Stokols, "Listen: Audio of Trump Discussing Whistleblower at Private Event: 'That's Close to a Spy,' " *Los Angeles Times*, September 26, 2019.

213 **"My summary of the president's call"** House Intelligence Committee, Hearing on Whistleblower Complaint, C-SPAN video and transcript, September 26, 2019.

214 **"Here we go again"** "Remarks by President Trump Upon Air Force One Arrival, Prince George's County, MD," White House transcript, September 26, 2019.

214 **a post using a pseudonym said** Craig Timberg and Drew Harwell, "Amateur Pro-Trump 'Sleuths' Scramble to Unmask Whistleblower: 'Your President Has Asked for Your Help,' " *Washington Post*, September 28, 2019.

215 **"everything we can to protect"** Adam Schiff (@RepAdamSchiff), Twitter post, September 26, 2019, 8:35 a.m.

215 **"I've been an important part of writing bills"** Nancy Pelosi, weekly press conference, September 26, 2019.

215 **describing the whistleblower** Julian E. Barnes, Michael S. Schmidt, Adam Goldman and Katie Benner, "White House Knew of Whistle-Blower's Allegations Soon After Trump's Call with Ukraine Leader," *New York Times*, September 26, 2019.

216 **"We decided to publish limited information"** Dean Baquet, "Why the Times Published Details of the Whistle-Blower's Identity," *New York Times*, September 26, 2019.

216 **there was no "leak hunt"** Josh Dawsey and Carol D. Leonnig, "Effort to Shield Trump's Call with Ukrainian Leader Was Part of Broader Secrecy Effort," *Washington Post*, September 26, 2019.

216 **"Too bad, pal. Too late"** Sean Hannity interview with guest Mark Levin, "Hannity," Fox News, September 26, 2019.

217 **they pressed two demands** Mike DeBonis and Rachael Bade, "Democrats Eye Quick Impeachment Probe of Trump as Freshmen Push for Focus on Ukraine," *Washington Post*, September 26, 2019.

217 **a new schoolyard nickname** Mike DeBonis and Karoun Demirjian, "Trump and GOP Target 'Pencil-Neck' Adam Schiff as Their Post-Mueller Villain," *Washington Post*, September 29, 2019.

218 **walking through Manhattan** Adam Schiff interview with Mary Jordan, April 2020.

218 **"He completely changed the words"** Trump tweet, September 27, 2019, 8:29 a.m.

219 **Two pro-Trump political activists were offering** Paul Bedard, "$50K Reward Offered to Out Trump Whistleblower," *Washington Examiner*, September 26, 2019.

Chapter Twenty-Six: Welcome to the SCIF

221 **the impeachment panels had sent a letter** Eliot L. Engel, Adam Schiff and Elijah Cummings, letter to Secretary of State Michael Pompeo, September 27, 2019.

221 **he called the request "an attempt to intimidate"** Pompeo, letter to Engel, October 1, 2019.

222 **"They should investigate the Bidens"** "Remarks by President Trump Before Marine One Departure," White House transcript, October 3, 2019.

222 **That accusation had already earned** Glenn Kessler, "Trump's False Claims About Hunter Biden's China Dealings," *Washington Post*, September 26, 2019.

222 **"a negative narrative about Ukraine"** Volker impeachment interview, page 18.

223 **Giuliani "does not represent the United States government"** Volker impeachment interview, page 18.

223 **The leaked portions were "out of context"** Engel, Schiff and Cummings, letter to members of the three committees overseeing the impeachment inquiry, October 3, 2019.

223 **"What we do know is there was definitely not"** John Bresnahan, "Trump's Former Ukraine Envoy Reveals Damaging Texts," *Politico*, October 3, 2019.

224 **"he's running a shadow shakedown"** "Representative Eric Swalwell on Kurt Volker Closed-Door Testimony," C-SPAN, October 3, 2019.
225 **room 327** This account of Democratic messaging and communications efforts is based on Mary Jordan's interviews with people with direct knowledge of their work.
226 **turn over documents** Adam Schiff, Eliot Engel and Elijah Cummings, letter to Lev Parnas, September 30, 2019.
226 **Rosalind Helderman, Paul Sonne and Tom Hamburger were working** This account of Helderman's, Sonne's and Hamburger's reporting on Parnas is based on each reporter's records and recollections, as well as some of their previously published stories.
226 **"The relationship bonded and built over time"** Rosalind S. Helderman, Tom Hamburger, Paul Sonne and Josh Dawsey, "Impeachment Inquiry Puts New Focus on Giuliani's Work for Prominent Figures in Ukraine," *Washington Post*, October 2, 2019.
226 **"Messrs Parnas and Fruman assisted Mr. Giuliani"** John M. Dowd, letter to House Intelligence Committee investigation counsel, October 3, 2019.
227 **"Put simply, you seek to overturn the results"** Pat Cipollone, letter to Nancy Pelosi, Adam Schiff, Eliot Engel and Elijah Cummings, October 8, 2019.
227 **She accused Trump of trying to "normalize lawlessness"** "Pelosi Statement on Trump Administration Refusal to Comply with House Subpoenas," October 8, 2019.
227 **Lou Dobbs cheered Cipollone for his bluntness** Manuel Roig-Franzia and Josh Dawsey, "Trump Lawyer Pat Cipollone Was a Camera-Shy Washington Everyman—Until Impeachment Made Him a Star," *Washington Post*, January 30, 2020.
228 **The indictment was unsealed the next morning** *United States of America v. Lev Parnas, Igor Fruman, David Correia and Andrey Kukushkin*, United States District Court, Southern District of New York, October 10, 2019. See next chapter for the first court hearing in the case. Parnas and Fruman pleaded not guilty.

Chapter Twenty-Seven: The Disrupter

229 **"In light of attempts by the White House"** Hill deposition, page 5.
229 **"Mr. Gaetz, you're not permitted"** Hill deposition, page 7.
230 **a more aggressive defense of the president** Matt Gaetz interview with Dave Weigel, April 2020.
230 **a fierce and formidable debater** Dan Zak, "Rep. Matt Gaetz Wants You to Know Who He Is, and His Plan Is Working," *Washington Post*, February 20, 2018.
231 **"Mr. Chairman, I think in the 20 hours"** Hill deposition, page 8.
232 **It was nearly 8 p.m. when** Hill deposition, page 446.
233 **he wanted no part "of whatever drug deal"** Hill deposition, page 71.
233 **"an improper arrangement"** Hill deposition, page 192.
233 **Gaetz was narrating his SCIF confrontation** Kristina Wong, "Exclusive—Matt Gaetz: Democrats Barring Judiciary Committee from Impeachment Inquiry," *Breitbart*, October 14, 2019.

Chapter Twenty-Eight: Pointing a Finger

234 **he quoted Graham Ledger** Trump tweet, October 16, 2019, 7:14 a.m.
235 **he was "disturbed" that "foreign governments"** Deposition of Michael McKinley, October 16, 2019, page 22.
235 **"I'm Congresswoman Debbie Lesko"** "Representative Debbie Lesko in Impeachment Inquiry Testimony," C-SPAN video, October 16, 2019.
236 **"They've got a lot of sand over there"** "Remarks by President Trump and President Mattarella of the Italian Republic Before Bilateral Meeting," White House transcript, October 16, 2019.
237 **"Why do all roads with you lead to Putin?"** Mike DeBonis and Seung Min Kim, "'All

Roads Lead to Putin': Pelosi Questions Trump's Loyalty in White House Clash," *Washington Post*, October 17, 2019.

238 **"He was insulting"** Schumer quoted in Clare Foran, "Democrats Say Trump Had a 'Meltdown' at White House Meeting," CNN.com, October 16, 2019.

238 **"I have served with six presidents"** "Pelosi Remarks at Media Stakeout Following White House Meeting," October 16, 2019.

239 **They thought Trump was totally misreading** Mary Jordan interview with Drew Hammill.

239 **"Of course, the president is right"** Sean Hannity, "Hannity," Fox News, October 16, 2019.

239 **"Why in the world should a president"** Lou Dobbs, "Top Dems Storm Out of Trump Meeting on Syria," "Lou Dobbs Tonight," Fox News, October 16, 2019.

240 **That was a good thing, Himes thought** Mary Jordan interview with Jim Himes, February 2020, and with members of his staff.

Chapter Twenty-Nine: "Get Over It"

241 **"Hey guys. How are you all?"** "Press Briefing by Acting Chief of Staff Mick Mulvaney," White House transcript, October 17, 2019.

244 **"military aid to a vital ally . . . was withheld"** Schiff quoted on "Mulvaney Says There Was a Quid Pro Quo in Trump Withholding Military Aid to Ukraine—Then Tries to Walk It Back," CNBC, October 17, 2019.

245 **"totally inexplicable"** Quoted in Karoun Demirjian and John Wagner, "After Saying Trump Held Back Aid to Pressure Ukraine, Mulvaney Tries to Walk Back Comments," *Washington Post*, October 17, 2019.

245 **"The President's legal counsel was not involved"** Sekluow quoted in Demirjian and Wagner, "After Saying Trump Held Back Aid to Pressure Ukraine, Mulvaney Tries to Walk Back Comments," cited earlier.

245 **the "media has decided to misconstrue"** Mulvaney statement, emailed to White House pool reporter, October 17, 2019. Published by White House Public Pool at Kinja.com.

Chapter Thirty: Remember Francis Rooney

246 **"What's your response?"** Poppy Harlow interview with Francis Rooney, "Newsroom," CNN, October 17, 2019.

247 **"So great to me on television"** "President Trump Eally in Estero, Florida," C-SPAN, October 31, 2018.

248 **"The president has said many times"** Mike DeBonis, "'I Didn't Take This Job to Keep It': GOP Rep. Rooney Hints He's Open to Impeachment," *Washington Post*, October 18, 2019. DeBonis provided unpublished details based on his recollection of his conversation with Rooney.

249 **his phone was "blowing up" with messages** Griff Witte, "Is Trump's Base Breaking Over Impeachment? The Tale of a Congressman's Defiance Suggests Not," *Washington Post*, October 31, 2019.

250 **"I don't really think I do"** Francis Rooney interview with Leland Vitter, "America's News HQ," Fox News, October 19, 2019.

Chapter Thirty-One: "Take the Gloves Off"

251 **"an unfortunate choice of words"** "McConnell: Trump Comparing Impeachment to a Lynching Is an 'Unfortunate Choice of Words,'" NBC News, clip published on YouTube, October 22, 2019.

251 **called it "crazy"** Will Hurd quoted in Quint Forgey, "Trump Provokes Outrage by Calling Impeachment Inquiry 'a Lynching,'" *Politico*, October 22, 2019.

251 **he wouldn't have used the word** Tim Scott quoted in Melanie Zanona, Burgess Ever-

ett and Marianne Levine, "Republicans Quit Trying to Rein In Trump After 'Lynching' Tweet," *Politico*, October 22, 2019.

251 **"an objectively true description"** Cruz also quoted in the *Politico* article.

252 **relationship with Ukraine was being "fundamentally undermined"** Taylor deposition, page 18.

253 **"Republicans have to get tougher"** Jill Colvin and Matthew Daley, "Trump Urges GOP to 'Get Tougher and Fight' Impeachment," Associated Press, October 21, 2019.

253 **"Take the gloves off"** Elise Viebeck, Rachael Bade, Mike DeBonis and Kayla Epstein, "Trump Told Republicans to Fight. They Took the Brawl Underground," *Washington Post*, October 23, 2019.

253 **His first call had been to Scalise** Matt Gaetz interview with Dave Weigel, April 2020.

254 **"If behind those doors, they intend"** Matt Gaetz (@RepMattGaetz), Twitter post, October 23, 2019, 12:22 p.m, video embedded in Tweet.

254 **"We're going to go and see"** Ari Shapiro, "Republican Rep. Michael Waltz Discusses Ongoing Impeachment Inquiry," NPR, October 24, 2019.

254 **Mooney narrated: "We're going in"** Alex Mooney (@RepAlexMooney), Twitter post, October 23, 2019, 12:50 p.m., audio recording embedded in Tweet.

255 **"There are no cameras here"** Viebeck, Bade, DeBonis and Epstein, "Trump Told Republicans to Fight. They Took the Brawl Underground. This account of the SCIF protest relies primarily on *Post* reporting, except where noted, as well as Weigel's interview of Gaetz.

257 **"This whole thing is a sham"** Dana Milbank, "Impeachment Diary: Republicans Fight Impeachment—with Extra Cheese," *Washington Post*, October 23, 2019.

257 **"Is there anything else to be addressed?"** Arraignment in *United States of America v. Lev Parnas and Igor Fruman*, U.S. District Court, Southern District of New York, October 23, 2019.

258 **"Good afternoon, everybody"** "Lev Parnas, Indicted Giuliani Associate Pleads Not Guilty Campaign Finance Crimes 10/23/19," video posted on YouTube by Sandi Bachom, November 24, 2019.

258 **"There is no quid pro quo"** Milbank, "Impeachment Diary: Republicans Fight Impeachment—with Extra Cheese."

258 **as a New Yorker, he was used to better** Dan Goldman, interviewed by Preet Bharara "Stay Tuned with Preet," *CAFE*, podcast, February 13, 2020.

259 **The storming felt like a win** Gaetz, interview with Weigel.

259 **"There's a newfound confidence"** Lou Dobbs, "House Republicans Storm Dems' Impeachment Hearing," "Lou Dobbs Tonight," Fox News, October 23, 2019.

Chapter Thirty-Two: "Lock Him Up!"

260 **al-Baghdadi had "died like a dog"** "Remarks by President Trump on the Death of ISIS Leader Abu Bakr al-Baghdadi," White House transcript, October 27, 2019.

261 **an all-Republican all-star line-up** Josh Dawsey, "RNC Pays Face Value for Trump Party's Luxury Seats at World Series Game," *Washington Post*, November 1, 2019.

261 **"Lock him up!"** Maura Judkis and Josh Dawsey, "Trump Met with Sustained Boos When Introduced at Game 5 of the World Series," *Washington Post*, October 27, 2019.

262 **"The left is so caught up"** Laura Ingraham, "President Trump Booed in Washington D.C. During World Series," "Ingraham Angle," Fox News, October 28, 2019.

262 **"I frankly think the office of the president"** John Berman and Alisyn Camerota, "Sen. Chris Coons (D-DE) on U.S. Raid That Killed Isis Leader Abu Bakr al-Baghdadi," "New Day," CNN, October 28, 2019.

Chapter Thirty-Three: "KA BOOM!"

263 **Elise Viebeck felt something was odd** Viebeck, based on her notes and recollections, provided this account.

264 **"We also now know the name of the whistleblower"** Allyson Chiu, " 'Do Your Job and Print His Name': Rand Paul Demands Media Identify the Whistleblower," *Washington Post*, November 5, 2019.

264 **Donald Trump Jr. tweeted the same name** Donald Trump Jr. (@DonaldTrumpJr), Twitter post, November 6, 2019, 8:58 a.m.

265 **The effort had picked up steam** Isaac Stanley-Becker and Craig Timberg, "Trump's Allies Turned to Online Campaign in Quest to Unmask Ukraine Whistleblower," *Washington Post*, November 7, 2019.

265 **"Let me be clear"** Andrew Bakaj, letter to Pat Cipollone, published on the website of Bakaj's law firm, Compass Rose Legal Group, November 7, 2019.

265 **asked if it might "ring a bell"** Taylor deposition, page 236.

Chapter Thirty-Four: Live, from Washington

267 **Schiff surveyed the packed hearing room** "Diplomats Bill Taylor and George Kent Impeachment Inquiry Testimony," video published by C-SPAN, November 13, 2019.

268 **They were launching the kind of coordinated "shock and awe"** Mary Claire Jalonick and Zeke Miller, "Inside Impeachment: How an 'Urgent' Tip Became 'High Crimes,' " Associated Press, December 23, 2019.

268 **"This process is anything but fair!"** Ben Terris and Rachael Bade, "Jim Jordan Used to Torment GOP Leaders. Now He's Leading Them in Defending Trump." *Washington Post*, November 21, 2019.

272 **He was thinking: These are "Alice in Wonderland"** Schiff interview with Mary Jordan, April 2020.

272 **"something of a bromance"** Patrick May, "California Rep. Devin Nunes: One-Time Rising Star 'in a Hole and Can't Stop Digging,' " *Mercury News* (San Jose), March 28, 2017.

273 **Schiff arrived in a snowstorm at the home of Patrick Kennedy** Paul Kane, "Rep. Adam Schiff Is Well-Versed in the Political Ramifications of Impeaching a President," *Washington Post*, July 20, 2019.

273 **When he was 14, he bought seven cows** Devin Nunes, "California's Gold Rush Has Been Reversed," *Wall Street Journal*, January 10, 2009.

273 **Nunes was elected to his community college's board of trustees** Derek Hawkins and Kyle Swenson, "Adam Schiff and Devin Nunes: From 'Bromance' to Bitter Adversaries," *Washington Post*, February 1, 2018.

274 **"Once I got into politics in 1996"** Charles Case, " 'I Broke So Many Tractors, They Made Me Work with the Cows,' " *The Hill*, September 6, 2005.

274 **"The struggle to preserve that liberty"** "Devin Nunes," 40 Under 40 package, *Time*, October 25, 2010.

275 **"We don't have any evidence that took place"** Hawkins and Swenson, "Adam Schiff and Devin Nunes: From 'Bromance' to Bitter Adversaries," cited earlier.

276 **He said five great uncles had served** Kent and Taylor public testimony; Kent opening statement.

280 **Fox News had the largest audience** Brian Stelter, "Ratings for First Impeachment Hearing Show Healthy Interest and a Serious Partisan Divide," CNN, November 15, 2019.

Chapter Thirty-Five: "It's Very Intimidating"

281 **outside her comfort zone** This account of Yovanovitch's thinking during the hearing and events she discussed is based on Karen DeYoung's conversations with State Department officials and sources close to Yovanovitch.

282 **an "exemplary" diplomat until she became an "obstacle"** Marie Yovanovitch public testi-

mony before the House Intelligence Committee, transcript published by *The Washington Post*, November 15, 2019 [hereafter Yovanovitch public hearing].

284 **"Everywhere Marie Yovanovitch went turned bad"** Trump tweet, November 15, 2019, 10:01 a.m.

286 **"This is an insane tweet"** Mary Jordan interviews with House Intelligence Committee staffers.

288 **Still, she thought: Why not me?** Elise Stefanik, interview with Griff Witte, December 2019. Griff Witte, "A Moderate Congresswoman Went All-in for Trump. Her Constituents Think They Know Why." *Washington Post*, December 13, 2019.

290 **"What can you tell us about Hunter Biden's"** Yovanovitch deposition, page 151.

291 **"The fact that he was even asking"** Quoted in Rachael Bade, Mike DeBonis and Josh Dawsey, "Inside the Decision to Impeach Trump: How Both Parties Wrestled with a Constitutional Crisis," *Washington Post*, December 18, 2019.

291 **"extraordinarily poor judgment"** Kenneth Starr quoted in "'Witness Intimidation Is a Crime': Reaction to Trump Impeachment Hearing," Reuters, November 15, 2019.

291 **"The president's going to defend himself"** Lee Zeldin quoted in Elise Viebeck and Isaac Stanley-Becker, "Attacking Witnesses Is Trump's Core Defense Strategy in Fighting Impeachment," *Washington Post*, November 18, 2019.

291 **"I have the right to speak"** "Remarks by President Trump on Honesty and Transparency in Healthcare Prices," White House transcript, November 15, 2019.

292 **"The White House said it was just his opinion"** Margaret Brennan interview with Nancy Pelosi, "Face the Nation," CBS, November 17, 2019.

292 **"Where is the Fake Whistleblower?"** Trump tweet, November 17, 2019, 3:12 p.m.

Chapter Thirty-Six: "I Will Be Fine for Telling the Truth"

293 **he seemed nervous, adjusting his glasses** "Impeachment Hearing with Lieutenant Colonel Vindman and Jennifer Williams," published by C-SPAN, November 19, 2019.

293 **Vindman reached over to pull out her chair** Robin Givhan, "Lt. Col. Vindman's Uniform Spoke Loud. His Humanity Spoke Louder," *Washington Post*, November 19, 2019.

293 **"Here we have a U.S. national security official"** Laura Ingraham interview with John Yoo, "Ingraham Angle," Fox News, October 28, 2019.

294 **It said only that the Ukrainians had "sought advice"** Danny Hakim, "Army Officer Who Heard Trump's Ukraine Call Reported Concerns," *New York Times*, October 28, 2019.

294 **"We also know he was born in the Soviet Union"** Brian Kilmeade, "House Dems Set Vote on Impeachment Inquiry Process," "Fox & Friends," Fox News, October 29, 2019.

294 **"It seems very clear that he is incredibly concerned"** Alisyn Camerota and John Berman interview with Sean Duffy and Charlie Dent, "New Day," CNN, October 29, 2019.

294 **"Vindman has reportedly been advising the Ukrainian government"** Jack Posobiec (@JackPosobiec), Twitter post, October 29, 2019, 8:41 a.m.

294 **Nunes and Jordan had asked Senator Ron Johnson** Jim Jordan and Devin Nunes, letter to Ron Johnson, published on Johnson's website, November 16, 2019.

294 **A "significant number of bureaucrats"** Johnson, letter to Jordan and Nunes, published on Johnson's website, November 18, 2019, cited earlier.

295 **both had listened to the July 25 phone call** Alexander Vindman and Jennifer Williams, testimony before the House Intelligence Committee, November 19, 2019, transcript published by *The Washington Post* [hereafter Vindman and Williams public hearing].

298 **calling Vindman a "joker" and a "stooge"** Donald Trump, Jr. (@DonaldJTrumpJr), Twitter post, November 19, 2019, 5:07 p.m.

298 **they also needed to respond rapidly** This account of Democratic messaging and communications efforts is based on Mary Jordan's interviews with people with direct knowledge of their work.

299 **the first meeting of the "Legal Eagles"** The meetings of the Legal Eagles were described

to Mary Jordan by Cruz and members of his staff in interviews in March and April 2020, as well as other sources with direct knowledge.

300 **McConnell began sharpening the talking points** Mary Jordan interviews with sources familiar with McConnell's thinking.

301 **"It is quite staggering to see the drop-off"** Laura Ingraham interview with Steve Scalise, "Ingraham Angle," Fox News, November 29, 2019.

301 **According to Nielsen, network and cable television viewership** "Media Advisory: 11.3 Million Viewers Watch Fifth Public Hearing Day of the 2019 Impeachment Inquiry into President Donald Trump," the Nielsen Company, November 25, 2019.

Chapter Thirty-Seven: Smiles All Around

302 **He buttoned his jacket around his tall, trim frame** Robin Givhan, "Gordon Sondland's Most Dazzling Accessory: Resting Happy Face," *Washington Post*, November 20, 2019.

302 **he wore a steel Breguet watch** The *Washington Examiner* reported on Sondland's Breguet watch: Madison Dibble, "Gordon Sondland Wears $55K Watch for Impeachment Testimony," *Washington Examiner*, November 20, 2019. The *Examiner* reported Sondland's watch was a Breguet Marine Chronograph, but representatives of Montres Breguet examined a picture of Sondland at this hearing and confirmed it was a Marine GMT watch, priced at $26,200.

303 **Sondland said he "presumed" that was the situation** Declaration of Gordon Sondland, November 4, 2019, released with Sondland's October 17 deposition, pages 376–379.

303 **"The impeachment effort comes down to one guy"** Mark Meadows quoted in Aaron C. Davis and Rachael Bade, "'Comes Down to One Guy': In Impeachment Probe, All Eyes Turn to Gordon Sondland," *Washington Post*, November 19, 2019.

303 **staffers in the West Wing were staying close to their screens** Aaron C. Davis, Rachael Bade and Josh Dawsey, "'Easy Come, Easy Go': Sondland Embraces His Role in Impeachment History with Nonchalance," *Washington Post*, November 20, 2019.

303 **"Ambassador Sondland, welcome"** Gordon Sondland, testimony before the House Intelligence Committee, November 20, 2019, transcript published by the *Washington Post* [hereafter Sondland public hearing].

306 **Under the witness table, his feet tapped out** Dana Milbank, "In Gordon Sondland, Trump Has Met His Match," *Washington Post*, November 20, 2019.

306 **The only person not on the edge** Givhan, "Gordon Sondland's Most Dazzling Accessory: Resting Happy Face," cited ealier.

306 **stroked his forehead as though trying to ease** Milbank, "In Gordon Sondland, Trump Has Met His Match," cited ealier.

306 **"We now can see the veneer"** "House Intel Chair Schiff on Ambassador Sondland's Testimony," C-SPAN video, November 20, 2019.

306 **"To a certain degree, he took out the bus"** Julia Musto, "Chris Wallace: Gordon Sondland 'Took Out the Bus' and Ran Over Trump, Pence, Others," FoxNews.com, November 20, 2019.

308 **"a really good man and great American."** Trump tweet, October 8, 2019, 8:23 a.m.

308 **"This is not a man I know well"** "Remarks by President Trump Before Marine One Departure," White House transcript, November 20, 2019.

311 **White House communications specialists sent 14** Seung Min Kim, Josh Dawsey and Kayla Epstein, "Sondland's Bombshell Testimony Leaves Trump's Republican Allies Scrambling," *Washington Post*, November 20, 2019.

313 **"Gordo, you got this!"** Doug Landry (@dougblandry), Twitter post, November 20, 2019, 3:52 p.m.

313 **"My whole day has been like this"** "Sondland Put His Luggage in the Wrong Overhead Bin, and Said 'My Whole Day Has Been Like This,'" CNN.com, November 20, 2019.

313 **"So where do you think this goes?"** Neil Cavuto interview with Rick Crawford, "Your World with Neil Cavuto," Fox News, November 20, 2019.

Chapter Thirty-Eight: "These Fictions Are Harmful"

314 **Fiona Hill was driving her 12-year-old daughter** Additional details for this chapter drawn from Greg Miller's interviews.
315 **Schiff read their bios aloud** Testimony of Fiona Hill and David Holmes before the House Intelligence Committee, transcript published by *The Washington Post*, November 21, 2019 [hereafter Hill and Holmes public hearing].
320 **Cruz believed that calling witnesses** Cruz, interview with Mary Jordan, April 2020.
321 **"Fiona Hill with that Prince Andrew accent"** Emerald Robinson (@EmeraldRobinson), Twitter post, November 21, 2019. Robinson later deleted her tweet, but it was captured via screenshot and appeared in an article by James Crowley, "OANN White House Correspondent Implies in Tweet That Hill and Vindman Aren't Americans, Despite the Fact They Are," *Newsweek*, November 21, 2019.
322 **"I'm appearing today as a facts witness"** Rush Limbaugh, "The Rush Limbaugh Show," transcript published on his website, November 21, 2019.
322 **None of the witnesses had** Hurd interview with Robert Moore, April 2020.
325 **"How dare Fiona Hill question"** John Solomon (@jsolomonReports), Twitter post, November 21, 2019, 6:18 p.m.
325 **conducting a review of his work on Ukraine** Michael Calderone, "The Hill Vows to Review Solomon's Ukraine Pieces," *Politico*, November 18, 2019.
326 **"You know, it's very interesting"** Steve Doocy, Ainsley Earhardt and Brian Kilmeade interview with Donald Trump, "Fox & Friends," Fox News, November 22, 2019.

Chapter Thirty-Nine: "Potomac River Fever"

327 **"Too many"** Matt Gaetz interview with Ben Terris, December 2019. Parts of the interview were published in *The Post*. Dan Zak and Ben Terris, "Impeachment Goes to College," *Washington Post*, December 4, 2019.
328 **"a group of pious, condescending, law professor–academician types"** Steve Bannon interview with Matt Gaetz, "War Room: Impeachment," Episode 55, December 2, 2019.
329 **"it is important to place President Trump's conduct into historical context"** "House Judiciary Committee Holds Hearing on Constitutional Grounds for Impeachment," *CQ Transcriptions*, December 4, 2019.
331 **"let their MAGA freak flag fly"** Gaetz, interview with Dave Weigel, April 2020.
333 **"A minor child deserves privacy"** Melania Trump (@FLOTUS), Twitter post, December 4, 2019, 4:50 p.m.
333 **"You didn't try to dismantle their argument"** Martha MacCallum interview with Gaetz, "The Story with Martha MacCallum," Fox News, December 4, 2019.

Chapter Forty: "I Don't Hate Anybody"

334 **"proceed with articles of impeachment"** "Pelosi Remarks Announcing House of Representatives Moving Forward with Articles of Impeachment," December 5, 2019.
335 **She had left the podium and was nearly out of sight** "House Speaker Weekly Briefing," C-SPAN video, December 5, 2019.
335 **"Mr. Republican Talking Points"** Nancy Pelosi, weekly press conference, November 14, 2019.
336 **"does not hate America as much as many of these people"** Tucker Carlson, "Rep. Jim

Jordan: Democrats Didn't Admit They Were Wrong About Russia, Just Moved On to Ukraine," "Tucker Carlson Tonight," Fox News, December 2, 2019.

336 **the list of people who "hate" Trump** Cheryl K. Chumley, "Democrats and Their Tortured Truths Expose Much," *Washington Times*, November 26, 2019.

336 **"hate us for supporting President Trump"** Jim Palmer, "Letter: Rep. Duncan Assumes A Lot About His Constituents," *Greenville News*, November 22, 2019.

337 **"This is a strain of cat"** David Remnick, "Nancy Pelosi: An Extremely Stable Genius," *New Yorker*, September 27, 2019.

337 **"Get your copy today!"** Team Mitch (@Team_Mitch), Twitter post, December 4, 2019, 10:28 a.m., retweeted by Trump, December 5, 2019, 7:33 p.m.

Chapter Forty-One: The Weight of History

338 **Elissa Slotkin needed a few moments of peace** This chapter's description of Slotkin's thinking is based on Witte's conversations with her.

339 **"Any Democrat that votes for this sham"** "Donald Trump Hershey, Pennsylvania Rally Transcript—December 10, 2019," published by Rev.com, December 11, 2019.

340 **looked like "pretty weak stuff"** Hannity interview with McConnell, "Hannity," Fox News, December 12, 2019.

341 **"The president is a surprise every minute"** Sean Sullivan and Seung Min Kim, "Trump and McConnell, Once Adversaries, Have Realized They Need Each Other," *Washington Post*, May 22, 2018.

342 **"I want the members on both sides of the aisle"** "House Judiciary Committee Articles of Impeachment Debate, Day 2 Part 4," C-SPAN video, December 12, 2019.

Chapter Forty-Two: "Please Let Her Speak"

344 **making their case to the center** Mary Jordan interviews with Democratic sources familiar with the work of 327.

344 **"this is probably going to be one of the most serious things"** Bill Hemmer interview with Elissa Slotkin, "America's Newsroom," Fox News, December 13, 2019.

345 **All her early childhood memories were forged here** This account of Slotkin's deliberations is based on Griff Witte's interview with Slotkin in April 2020, as well as earlier interviews conducted for Witte's article "Michigan Democrat in Trump District Will Vote for Impeachment, Says It May Cost Her Reelection," *Washington Post*, December 16, 2019.

347 **"pass the fairness test with the American people"** Chuck Schumer, letter to Mitch McConnell, December 15, 2019, published on the Senate Democrats' website.

347 **The president had "illegally solicited the help of foreigners"** Slotkin, "Rep. Elissa Slotkin: How I Reached My Decision on Impeachment," *Detroit Free Press*, December 16, 2019.

349 **"I need you to help keep the peace"** Griff Witte, "Michigan Democrat in Trump District Will Vote for Impeachment, Says It May Cost Her Reelection." Other details of the event were reported by Witte but not published in the December story. A video was also posted on YouTube by the channel of MLive, "Rep. Elissa Slotkin Defends Trump Impeachment Decision at Town Hall," December 16, 2019.

351 **"Slotkin, Backing Impeachment"** Sheryl Gay Stolberg, "Slotkin, Backing Impeachment, Draws Instant Protests, and Applause," *New York Times*, December 16, 2019.

351 **"Revolt in Michigan"** Sean Moran, "Watch—Revolt in Michigan: Town Hall Turns into Mutiny as Democrat Congresswoman Announces Impeachment Support," *Breitbart*, December 16, 2019.

Chapter Forty-Three: "I Am Not an Impartial Juror"

352 **He sat in the Oval Office with policy adviser Stephen Miller** Philip Rucker, Elise Viebeck and John Wagner, "Trump Rips Democrats for 'Attempted Coup' on Eve of Likely Impeachment," *Washington Post*, December 17, 2019.

353 ***I write to express my strongest and most powerful protest*** Donald Trump, letter to Nancy Pelosi, December 17, 2019, released by the White House.

355 **Pelosi wore a bright red poppy** Heather Caygle, John Bresnahan and Sarah Ferris, "'In a Class by Herself': Pelosi Has Roared Back in the Trump Era," *Politico*, December 18, 2019.

355 **could see Pelosi's mind working** Debbie Dingell, interview with Kevin Sullivan and Mary Jordan, December 2019.

356 **"After reviewing the testimony"** "Representative Sherrill Statement on the Articles of Impeachment," released by her office, December 17, 2019.

356 **repair the House's "slapdash work product"** Mitch McConnell (Kentucky), "Impeachment," *Congressional Record* 165:204 (December 17, 2019), pages S7059–S7060.

357 **"taking cues from the White House"** Chuck Schumer (New York), "Impeachment," Congressional Record 165:204 (December 17, 2019), pages S7062–S7063.

359 **"I am not an impartial juror"** "Senate Republican Agenda," C-SPAN video, December 17, 2019.

359 **"We're going to have to call for a mistrial"** Jake Tapper, "Interview with Rep. Jackie Speier," "The Lead with Jake Tapper," CNN, December 17, 2019.

359 **"clutching their pearls"** Cruz interview with Mary Jordan, April 2020.

359 **a compendium of Trump's greatest hits** Glenn Kessler, "Fact-checking President Trump's Impeachment Letter to Pelosi," *Washington Post*, December 18, 2019.

359 **it was the "normalized crazy"** Josh Dawsey and Ashley Parker, "Impeachment Split Screen: As House Votes in Washington, Trump Rallies in Michigan," *Washington Post*, December 18, 2019.

360 **"a powerful, scathing beat down"** Victor Garcia, "Sean Hannity: Trump Impeachment a 'Corrupt Political Stunt' That Will 'Stain' Democrats Until 2020 'Reckoning,'" FoxNews.com, December 17, 2019.

360 **Dobbs said it was "beautiful"** Zachary Pleat, "Right-Wing Media Praise Trump's Deranged Anti-Impeachment Letter to Pelosi," Media Matters for America, December 18, 2019.

360 **"a lie-filled letter"** Zachary Pleat, "Right-Wing Media Praise Trump's Deranged Anti-Impeachment Letter to Pelosi."

360 **"I haven't really fully read it"** Manu Raju (@mkraju), Twitter post, December 17, 2019, 5:38 p.m.; clip of Pelosi embedded in tweet.

Chapter Forty-Four: "The President Is Impeached"

361 **"Can you believe that I will be impeached today"** Trump tweet, December 18, 2019, 7:34 a.m.

361 **From her back row seat, Pelosi** Kevin Sullivan attended the proceedings on December 18; this account is based on his observations as well as the Congressional Record and C-SPAN footage.

362 **"Madam Speaker, so we can stop wasting America's time on impeachment"** Andy Biggs (Arizona), "Motion to Adjourn," *Congressional Record* 165:205 (December 18, 2019), page H12113. The impeachment proceedings fill nearly the entire *Record* for the day, through page H12207. We have not provided page numbers for each speech because the *Record* is easily searchable online.

364 **pinned to her dress** Robin Givhan, "Nancy Pelosi's Pin at the Impeachment Debate Was a Declaration: The Republic Will Survive This," *Washington Post*, December 18, 2019.

366 **Trump's loyal supporters were filing into Kellogg Arena** This account of the rally is

based on reporting by Jenna Johnson, who attended the event. Johnson and colleague Chad Livengood also published a story in *The Post* at the time, "'We Love You!': After Being Impeached, Trump Embraces the Warm Bubble of a Rally Where He's Listened to and Cheered, No Matter What," *Washington Post*, December 19, 2019.

368 **Marine One landed on the South Lawn of the White House at 4:19 p.m.** Dan Zak, "'THIS IS AN ASSAULT': History Collides with Trump," *Washington Post*, December 19, 2019.

372 **"thumbs his nose at the rule of law"** Brian Williams, Chris Hayes, Nicolle Wallace, Claire McCaskill, Eugene Robinson, Chris Matthews and Neal Katyal, impeachment coverage, "All In with Chris Hayes," MSNBC, December 18, 2019.

372 **"How do people like that get power"** Tucker Carlson, impeachment coverage, "Tucker Carlson Tonight," Fox News, December 18, 2019.

374 **Debbie Dingell had just left the House** Dingell, interview with Sullivan and Jordan, December 2019.

374 **"December 18, a great day for the Constitution"** "Transcript of Speaker Pelosi, Committee Chairs Press Availability Following Passage of Articles of Impeachment," December 18, 2019.

375 **"they're after you"** Trump tweet, December 18, 2019, 10:49 p.m.

Part Four: Trump on Trial

Chapter Forty-Five: "Trust Me to Run This"

379 **One of his first calls was to McConnell** Carl Hulse, Nicholas Fandos and Emily Cochrane, "How Mitch McConnell Delivered Acquittal for Trump," *New York Times*, February 6, 2020.

380 **"Americans will know that Mitch McConnell helped save"** Seung Min Kim and Josh Dawsey, "Trump and McConnell Fall Short in Kentucky—But Remain Steady Allies in Washington," *Washington Post*, November 7, 2019.

380 **You are getting a lot of advice, Mr. President** Mary Jordan background interviews.

382 **"I'm going to protest"** Greg Jaffe, "William Taylor Jr., a Key Impeachment Witness, Quietly Returns Home to Trump's Washington," *Washington Post*, February 14, 2020. Other details drawn from Jaffe's interviews with Taylor.

383 **"If the Senate issues a subpoena"** Rachael Bade, Mike DeBonis, Tom Hamburger and Robert Costa, "Bolton's Willingness to Testify in Trump's Impeachment Trial Ramps Up Pressure on Senate Republicans," *Washington Post*, January 6, 2020.

383 **Bolton left McConnell a message** Seung Min Kim and Rachael Bade, "Inside the Senate Trial: McConnell Stops Rebel Push in GOP for Witnesses," *Washington Post*, February 1, 2020.

384 **Bolton and his lawyer, Charles Cooper, had agreed** Tom Hamburger's reporting, based on interviews with people who had direct knowledge of the events.

384 **"Given that Mr. Bolton's lawyers have stated"** "Schumer Statement on Need to Subpoena Witnesses and Key Documents in Senate Impeachment Trial," released by Senate Democrats, January 6, 2020.

385 **"I would like to be able to hear from John Bolton"** Romney quoted in Seung Min Kim and Rachael Bade, "Inside the Senate trial: McConnell Stops Rebel Push in GOP for Witnesses."

Chapter Forty-Six: "We Need to Get This Thing Going"

386 **"we have the votes"** McConnell news conference, "Senate Republican Agenda," C-SPAN video and transcript, January 7, 2020.

387 **"Republicans may run, but they can't hide"** Schumer, "Impeachment," *Congressional Record* 166:3 (January 7, 2020), page S33.

387 **"The Republican Leader and I have very different visions"** "Schumer Remarks on the Need for a Fair and Honest Impeachment Trial That Includes Key Witnesses and Documents," transcript released by Senate Democrats, January 7, 2020.

387 **"The Clinton trial process provided a pathway"** Seung Min Kim, Mike DeBonis and Rachael Bade, "McConnell Says He's Ready to Begin Trump Impeachment Trial with No Deal on Witnesses," *Washington Post*, January 7, 2020.

388 **"I do think we need to get this thing going"** Kim, DeBonis and Bade, "McConnell Says He's Ready to Begin Trump Impeachment Trial with No Deal on Witnesses," cited earlier.

388 **the president met with McConnell in the Oval Office** Rachael Bade and Seung Min Kim, "When McConnell Speaks, Trump Listens. Impeachment Trial Will Test the Unlikely Bond," *Washington Post*, January 19, 2020.

388 **"the best episode, the grand finale"** Ashley Parker and Josh Dawsey, " 'The Grand Finale': Inside Trump's Push to Rack Up Political Victories as Impeachment Looms," *Washington Post*, December 14, 2019.

388 **"Better to be unified"** Bade and Kim, "When McConnell Speaks, Trump Listens. Impeachment Trial Will Test the Unlikely Bond," cited earlier.

389 **"a thousand flowers blossoming beautifully"** Laurie Kellman, " 'Fail Not': What to Watch Ahead of Trump's Impeachment Trial," Associated Press, January 11, 2020.

389 **announcing an end to the logjam** Nancy Pelosi, "Dear Colleague on Next Steps on Impeachment," January 10, 2020.

390 **"About time"** Amber Phillips, "The Week Democrats Lost the Battle Over the Senate Trial," *Washington Post*, January 10, 2020.

390 **"We should be completely open to calling witnesses"** Michael Shepherd, "Susan Collins Working with 'Small Group' of GOP Senators to Allow Impeachment Witnesses," *Bangor Daily News*, January 10, 2020.

391 **"I am hopeful that we can reach an agreement"** Mike DeBonis and Rachael Bade, "Pelosi Moves to End Trump Impeachment Standoff, Signals She Will Send Articles to Senate," *Washington Post*, January 10, 2020.

391 **"Why not call Bolton?"** Laura Ingraham, "Exclusive Interview with President Trump," "Ingraham Angle," Fox News, January 10, 2020.

392 **"I'd like to talk about some more pleasant subjects"** George Stephanopoulos, "Nancy Pelosi; One-on-One with the Speaker of the House," "This Week," ABC News, January 12, 2020.

392 **Griff Witte wandered into PeeWee's Place** Griff Witte, "A Pact with Trump on Impeachment? McConnell's Kentucky Backers Demand It," *Washington Post*, January 12, 2020.

Chapter Forty-Seven: "Today, We Will Make History"

394 **"an impeachment that will last forever"** "Transcript of House Impeachment Managers Announcement," Pelosi office, January 15, 2020.

395 **"A man who always liked me"** "Remarks by President Trump at Signing of the U.S.-China Phase One Trade Agreement," White House transcript, January 15, 2020.

395 **a ritual being seen for just the third time in U.S. history** Avi Selk and Maura Judkis, "The Rare and Bizarre Ritual of Marching the Impeachment Articles from the House to the Senate," *Washington Post*, January 16, 2020.

395 **The two articles sat on a small table** "House Delivers Articles of Impeachment to Senate," C-SPAN video, January 15, 2020.

396 **"So sad, so tragic for our country"** "Pelosi Remarks at Engrossment Ceremony Photo Opportunity for Articles of Impeachment and Procession of Impeachment Managers," January 15, 2020.

396 **a typo had left them with pens that read "*Untied* States Senator"** M. Dion Thompson, "OUT OF ORDER; Odd Misspelling on Senators' Impeachment Pens Is Just the Lat-

est Stroke in Parker's Legacy. The Company Has Been Writing History Ever Since the Spanish-American War." *Baltimore Sun*, January 16, 1999.

396 **"We're done! We're done!"** Selk and Judkis, "The Rare and Bizarre Ritual of Marching the Impeachment Articles from the House to the Senate," cited earlier.

397 **"During today's historic trade deal signing"** Lou Dobbs, "President Trump and China Vice Premier Sign Historic Phase 1 Trade Deal," "Lou Dobbs Tonight," Fox News, January 15, 2020.

397 **"President Trump knew exactly what was going on"** Rachel Maddow interview with Lev Parnas, "The Rachel Maddow Show," MSNBC, January 15, 2020.

Chapter Forty-Eight: "Do You Solemnly Swear?"

399 **"they said I had a shrine to him"** Anderson Cooper, "Parnas: President Trump Knew Exactly What Was Going On," "Anderson Cooper 360," CNN, January 16, 2020.

399 **"This is a man who's under indictment"** Steve Doocy, Ainsley Earhardt and Brian Kilmeade, "White House: It's a Great Week for the Country Despite Democrats' Impeachment 'Noise,'" "Fox & Friends," clip published on FoxNews.com, January 16, 2020.

399 **the White House had violated federal law** Jeff Stein, Ellen Nakashima and Erica Werner, "White House Hold on Ukraine Aid Violated Federal Law, Congressional Watchdog Says," *Washington Post*, January 16, 2020.

399 **"Faithful execution of the law does not permit the President"** Thomas H. Armstrong, "Decision, Matter of: Office of Management and Budget—Witholding of Ukraine Security Assistance," U.S. Government Accountability Office, January 16, 2020.

400 **dismissed the finding as an "overreach"** Jeff Stein, Ellen Nakashima and Erica Werner, "White House Hold on Ukraine Aid Violated Federal Law, Congressional Watchdog Says."

400 **"Hear ye! Hear ye!"** "Exhibition of Articles of Impeachment Against Donald John Trump, President of the United States," *Congressional Record* 166:10 (January 16, 2020), page S266.

400 **A toothache was killing him** Adam Schiff interview with Mary Jordan, April 2020.

402 **"We do not have Obama judges or Trump judges"** Mark Sherman, "Roberts, Trump Spar in Extraordinary Scrap over Judges," Associated Press, November 21, 2018.

Chapter Forty-Nine: Virus

403 **"Where do you stand on whether or not witnesses should be allowed"** Sandra Smith, "Rep. Dingell: What's Important Is That the American People Are Able to Witness a Fair Trial," "America's Newsroom," clip published on FoxNews.com, January 17, 2020.

404 **"We'll take pictures behind the Resolute Desk"** Jacob Bogage, "Trump Drags LSU Football Team into Impeachment Fervor During White House Visit," *Washington Post*, January 17, 2020.

404 **"defend the integrity of the Constitution"** Elise Viebeck, Josh Dawsey and Manuel Roig-Franzia, "Trump Expands Legal Team to Include Kenneth Starr, Alan Dershowitz for Impeachment Trial," *Washington Post*, January 17, 2020.

404 **Trump had first floated the idea to Dershowitz** Roig-Franzia and Dawsey, "Trump Lawyer Pat Cipollone Was a Camera-Shy Washington Everyman—Until Impeachment Made Him a Star," *Washington Post*, January 30, 2020.

404 **"I think Ken Starr is a lunatic"** Viebeck, Dawsey and Roig-Franzia, "Trump Expands Legal Team to Include Kenneth Starr, Alan Dershowitz for Impeachment Trial," cited earlier.

405 **collectively made at least 365 weekday appearances on Fox News** Bobby Lewis, "Trump's New Impeachment Defense Team Has Been on Fox News over 350 Times in the Past Year," Media Matters for America, January 17, 2020.

405 **Azar spoke with Trump for the first time about an emerging new worry** Shane Harris, Greg Miller, Josh Dawsey and Ellen Nakashima, "U.S. Intelligence Reports from January and February Warned About a Likely Pandemic," *Washington Post*, March 20, 2020.

405 **So far, three people in China had died** Caroline Kantis, Samantha Kiernan and Jason Socrates Bardi, "UPDATED: Timeline of the Coronavirus," *Think Global Health*, April 22, 2020.

405 **semicircular tables that had been custom-built** Michael D. Shear, "Dust Off the Impeachment Tables, a Senate Trial Is Underway," *New York Times*, January 17, 2020.

406 **"be careful what you wish for"** Sandra Smith, "Kellyanne Conway Warns Democrats: Be Careful What You Wish For," "America's Newsroom," Fox, clip published on Fox's YouTube channel (Fox News), January 20, 2020.

406 **"end this brazen political vendetta"** "Statement from the Press Secretary Announcing Congressional Members of the President's Impeachment Team," White House transcript, January 20, 2020.

Chapter Fifty: "Will Senators Rise to the Occasion?"

407 **"keep us from dishonor"** Barry C. Black, "Prayer," *Congressional Record* 166:12 (January 21, 2020), page S287. All speeches in the Senate cited in this chapter are from the January 21, 2020, edition of the *Congressional Record*, unless otherwise noted. We have not included page numbers for each speech because the *Record* can be easily searched online for a particular quote.

410 **"whether generations to come will enjoy a safe and secure democracy"** Adam B. Schiff, Jerrold Nadler, Zoe Lofgren, Hakeem S. Jeffries, Val Butler Demings, Jason Crow and Sylvia R. Garcia, "Trial Memorandum of the United States House of Representatives in the Impeachment Trial of President Donald J. Trump," presented to the Senate, January 18, 2020, page 8.

410 **"their own degradation of the impeachment process"** Jay Alan Sekulow, Stuart Roth, Andrew Ekonomou, Jordan Sekulow, Mark Goldfeder, Benjamin Sisney, Pat A. Cipollone, Patrick F. Philbin, Michael M. Purpura, Devin A. DeBacker, Trent J. Benishek and Eric J. Hamilton, "Trial Memorandum of President Donald J. Trump," presented to the Senate, January 20, 2020, page 12.

411 **caused McConnell to make one change** Seung Min Kim and Elise Viebeck, "Resolution Changed to Relax Timetable, Ease Admission of Evidence," *Washington Post*, daily impeachment live blog, January 21, 2020.

Chapter Fifty-One: "Your Head Will Be on a Pike"

414 **Donald Trump's chair was almost too small** Joe Kernan, "Watch the Full CNBC Interview with US President Donald Trump from Davos," "Squawk Box," clip posted on CNBC.com, January 22, 2020.

414 **"I can choose 9,000 TV channels"** Paul Farhi, "First Day of Senate Impeachment Trial Becomes a Modest TV Hit with 7.5 Million Watching During Prime Time," *Washington Post*, January 22, 2020.

415 **Democrats had gone "totally nuts"** Maria Bartiromo interview with Donald Trump, "Mornings with Maria," Fox News, January 22, 2020.

415 **he called Nadler "a sleazebag"** "Remarks by President Trump in Press Conference, Davos, Switzerland," White House transcript, January 22, 2020.

415 **"I think it's one of those things they're going to regret"** Bill Barrow, "Biden and Sanders' Rift Could Define Closing Days in Iowa," Associated Press, January 22, 2020.

415 **Pelosi was calling from her motorcade in Jerusalem** Nicholas Fandos, "Even from Half a World Away, Pelosi Keeps a Tight Grip on Impeachment," *New York Times*, January 23, 2020.

416 **"THESE R NOT MY PARENTS!"** Dana Milbank, "'S.O.S.! PLEASE HELP ME!' The World's Greatest Deliberative Body Falls to Pettifoggery," *Washington Post*, January 22, 2020.
416 **"We're not going to turn it into a farce"** Matt Viser, "Biden Says He Refuses to Be Part of Impeachment Witness Deal," *Washington Post*, January 22, 2020.
416 **"Yesterday was like Groundhog Day"** Dana Bash, "Interview with Sen. John Barrasso (R-WY)," live impeachment coverage, CNN, January 23, 2020.
416 **"It is hard to listen to things"** Poppy Harlow and Jim Sciutto, "Sen. Mazie Hirono (D-HI)," "CNN Newsroom," CNN, January 23, 2020.
417 **He joked that viewers should play a drinking game** Ted Cruz (@TedCruz), Twitter post, January 23, 2020, 11:53 a.m.
417 **read a book about "Trump haters"** Mariah Timms, "'Marsha' Trends as Nation Notices Sen. Blackburn Reading a Book, Tweeting During Impeachment Arguments," *Tennesseean*, January 23, 2020.
417 **Paul continued doing his crossword puzzle** Sarah Ladd, "Sen. Rand Paul Works on Crossword Puzzle, Paper Airplane During Impeachment Trial," *Louisville Courier-Journal*, January 23, 2020.
417 **Richard Burr of North Carolina passed out fidget spinners** Niels Lesniewski, "Burr Is Giving Senators Fidget Spinners to Stay Busy During Trial," *Roll Call*, January 23, 2020.
417 **"should have left every senator in the chamber with a lump in their throat"** Brian Williams interview with Chris Coons, "The 11th Hour with Brian Williams," MSNBC, January 23, 2020.
417 **"I don't trust Adam Schiff'** Sheryl Gay Stolberg, "Emotional Schiff Speech Goes Viral, Delighting the Left and Enraging the Right," *New York Times*, January 24, 2020.
417 **"SNOOZEFEST"** Trump tweet, clip of Sean Hannity's show, January 23, 2020, 10:48 p.m.
418 **"HOURS AND HOURS OF SCHIFF"** Trump tweet, clip of Sean Hannity's show, January 23, 2020, 10:44 p.m.
418 **"not something that I think we're even considering"** Quoted in Nathaniel Weixel and Peter Sullivan, "Top Health Officials Brief Senators on Coronavirus as Infections Spread," *The Hill*, January 24, 2020.
418 **"I wouldn't be surprised if there are additional cases"** Mike DeBonis and Siobhán O'Grady, "Senators Attend Health Briefing, Call on China to Remain Transparent," *Washington Post*, coronavirus liveblog, January 24, 2020.
419 **"We are far from having this potential epidemic under control"** Weixel and Sullivan, "Top Health Officials Brief Senators on Coronavirus as Infections Spread," cited earlier.
419 **"vote against your president . . . and your head will be on a pike"** Adam Schiff, presentation of impeachment case, *Congressional Record* 166:15 (January 24, 2020), page S565.
419 **"That's not true"** Mike DeBonis, "Adam Schiff Delivered a Detailed, Hour-Long Summary of the Democrats' Impeachment Case. Some Republicans Dismissed It Because of One Line." *Washington Post*, January 24, 2020.

Chapter Fifty-Two: A Small Earthquake

421 **"is called Death Valley in T.V."** Trump tweet, January 24, 2020, 7:37 a.m.
422 **chewing tobacco had made a brief appearance** Lindsay Wise and Natalie Andrews, "Impeachment Trial's Marathon Days Make Many Senators Restless," *Wall Street Journal*, January 23, 2020.
422 **"thank you for your time and thank you for your attention"** Pat Cipollone, "Opening Statement," *Congressional Record* 115:16 (January 25, 2020), page S568.
423 **Cipollone was the son of Italian immigrants of modest means** Roig-Franzia and Dawsey, "Trump Lawyer Pat Cipollone Was a Camera-Shy Washington Everyman—Until Impeachment Made Him a Star," cited earlier.
424 **"This is a special on this pandemic"** Steve Bannon, "SPECIAL Ep 1: War Room: Pan-

demic, Why the China Coronavirus Is So Important," *War Room* podcast, January 25, 2020.

425 **An even more exclusive after-party** Marlene Lenthang, "EXCLUSIVE: Jeff Bezos Throws Lavish Party at His New $23 million, 11-Bedroom Washington DC Mansion Attended by Ivanka Trump, Bill Gates and Ben Stiller," *Daily Mail*, January 26, 2020.

426 **"I can't imagine why most voters are deeply cynical"** Jon Favreau (@jonfavs), Twitter post, January 26, 2020, 11:47 a.m.

426 **said he "preferred sending no assistance to Ukraine"** Maggie Haberman and Michael S. Schmidt, "Trump Tied Ukraine Aid to Inquiries He Sought, Bolton Book Says," *New York Times*, January 26, 2020.

427 **Bolton was willing to abide by a subpoena** This account of Bolton's reaction to the leak is based on Tom Hamburger's interview in May 2020 with a source familiar with Bolton's thinking.

427 **"The Senate trial must seek the full truth"** "House Managers Statement on New York Times Report on John Bolton," published by the House Intelligence Committee, January 26, 2020.

427 **"I don't know if we left on the best of terms"** "Remarks by President Trump in Press Conference, Davos, Switzerland," White House transcript, January 22, 2020.

Chapter Fifty-Three: "Every President Believes That"

428 **"It's important to be able to hear from John Bolton"** Romney quoted in Erica Werner, Paul Kane and Seung Min Kim, "Leaked Bolton Book Threatens to Upend Senate Impeachment Trial," *Washington Post*, January 27, 2020.

428 **"curious as to what John Bolton might have to say"** Lisa Murkowski (@lisamurkowski), Twitter post, January 27, 2020, 12:46 p.m.

428 **"Let's see if it's relevant"** Rachael Bade and Karoun Demirjian, "Graham Says He Wants to See Bolton's Manuscript," *Washington Post*, impeachment live blog, January 27, 2020.

428 **Giuliani said that Bolton "never once raised any objection"** Ashley Parker, Josh Dawsey and Matt Zapotosky, "White House Works to Contain Damage from Allegations in Forthcoming Bolton Book," *Washington Post*, January 27, 2020.

429 **Romney made a strong case to his colleagues** Seung Min Kim, "Newest GOP Senator Accuses Romney of Trying to 'Appease the Left' in Favoring Witnesses in Trump Impeachment Trial," *Washington Post*, January 27, 2020.

429 **"I think everybody ought to pop a Zoloft"** Dana Milbank, "Trump's Lawyers Suffer from Bolton-Induced Amnesia," *Washington Post*, January 27, 2020.

429 **In the Situation Room, at a packed meeting** Eric Lipton, David E. Sanger, Maggie Haberman, Michael D. Shear, Mark Mazzetti and Julian E. Barnes, "He Could Have Seen What Was Coming: Behind Trump's Failure on the Virus," *New York Times*, April 11, 2020.

429 **White House aides were pressing senior officials** Shane Harris, Greg Miller, Josh Dawsey and Ellen Nakashima, "U.S. Intelligence Reports from January and February Warned About a Likely Pandemic," *Washington Post*, March 20, 2020.

429 **"It is a great honor for me to stand before you today"** Alan Dershowitz, presentation of impeachment defense, *Congressional Record* 166:17 (January 27, 2020), page S609.

431 **furiously shook Dershowitz's hand** Paul Kane, "Warm Greetings for Dershowitz from Republicans, Democratic Counsel," *Washington Post*, impeachment live blog, January 27, 2020.

431 **It felt more like "the world according to Dershowitz"** Schiff interview with Mary Jordan, April 2020.

431 **"They fall back on the argument"** Rachael Bade, Karoun Demirjian, Mike DeBonis and Ann E. Marimow, "Senate Republicans Seize on Dershowitz Argument, Say Trump's Actions Aren't Impeachable," *Washington Post*, January 27, 2020.

432 **"I truly could not follow it"** Nik DeCosta-Klipa, "Elizabeth Warren Clashes with For-

mer Harvard Colleague Alan Dershowitz over His Impeachment Trial Argument," *Boston Globe*, January 28, 2020.

432 **"an extreme and dangerous" theory** Lawrence O'Donnell, "Laurence Tribe: Dershowitz Defense of Trump 'Extreme' and 'Dangerous,'" "The Last Word," MSNBC, January 28, 2020.

432 **"Alan is essentially alone"** Bade, Demirjian, DeBonis and Marimow, "Senate Republicans Seize on Dershowitz Argument, Say Trump's Actions Aren't Impeachable," cited earlier.

433 **Fifty-three of the one hundred U.S. Senators had law degrees** Jennifer E. Manning, "Membership of the 116th Congress: A Profile," Congressional Research Service, June 1, 2020, page 5.

434 **"The risk of infection for Americans remains low"** "Statement from the Press Secretary Regarding the President's Coronavirus Task Force," White House transcript, January 29, 2020.

Chapter Fifty-Four: "Let the People Decide"

436 **hearing from Bolton was a "no-brainer"** Seung Min Kim and Rachael Bade, "Inside the Senate trial: McConnell Stops Rebel Push in GOP for Witnesses," *Washington Post*, February 1, 2020.

436 **"The presiding officer declines to read the question"** John Roberts, presiding in Trump impeachment trial, *Congressional Record* 166:20 (January 30, 2020), page S694.

437 **"shouldn't you be in the impeachment hearing right now?"** "Senator Rand Paul News Conference," C-SPAN, January 30, 2020.

437 **"Democrat partisans conspired with Schiff staffers to plot"** Rand Paul (@RandPaul), Twitter post, January 30, 2020, 1:19 p.m.

437 **"does the fact that the chief justice is presiding"** Elizabeth Warren, question during Trump impeachment trial, *Congressional Record* 166:20 (January 30, 2020), page S717. All other questions and responses from the trial in this chapter are also drawn from this edition of the *Congressional Record*, unless otherwise noted.

438 **"I can't tell you how happy I am to be in Austin"** Jeremy Wallace and Taylor Goldenstein, "John Bolton Happy to Be in Texas on Thursday—1,500 Miles from D.C.," *Houston Chronicle*, January 30, 2020.

438 **"All of them acted in the best interest of the country"** Bolton quoted by Austin TV station KXAN, cited by Veronica Stracqualarsi and Kevin Liptak, "John Bolton Defends Trump Administration Officials Who Testified in House Impeachment Inquiry," CNN, January 31, 2020.

439 **"the best years that we've ever had in the history of our country"** "Donald Trump Iowa Rally Transcript: Trump Holds Rally in Des Moines, Iowa," Rev.com, January 30, 2020.

440 **a chance to "more fully and fairly make their case"** "Senator Collins' Statement on Vote on Witnesses and Documents," released by Susan Collins's office, January 30, 2020.

440 **"Susan's gonna get a free pass on everything"** These quotes are from a senior Republican senator interviewed by Seung Min Kim in January 2020.

440 **That's it, Cruz had thought** Cruz, interview with Mary Jordan, April 2020.

441 **"it was like the air went out of the room"** Laura Litvan (@LauraLitvan), Twitter post, January 30, 2020, 10:26 p.m.

442 **"the Constitution does not give the Senate the power to remove the president"** "Alexander Statement on Impeachment Witness Vote," statement released by his office, January 30, 2020.

443 **"If you've got nine witnesses who say he left the scene of an accident, you don't need the tenth"** Paul Kane interview with Lamar Alexander, January 31, 2020.

444 **He had read two books to prepare for the trial** Paul Kane, "Sen. Alexander's Rejection of

Witnesses in Trump Trial Leaves Democrats Disappointed but Hardly Surprised," *Washington Post*, January 31, 2020.

Chapter Fifty-Five: "This Country Is Our Masterpiece"

446 **"Today I'm here with a clear message"** John Hudson, "Pompeo Visits Zelensky in Kyiv, Vows U.S. Support for Ukraine 'Will Not Waver,'" *Washington Post*, January 31, 2020.

446 **Kelly was escorted** After airing her Pompeo interview, Kelly described the aftermath with "All Things Considered" co-host Ari Shapiro. "Pompeo Won't Say Whether He Owes Yovanovitch An Apology. 'I've Done What's Right,'" NPR, January 24, 2020.

447 **"nothing short of a coup d'état"** Marco Rubio, "My Statement on the President's Impeachment Trial," *Medium*, January 31, 2020.

447 **"there will be no fair trial in the Senate"** "Murkowski's Statement on Senate Impeachment Process Vote," statement released by Murkowski's office, January 31, 2020.

447 **Trump signed an order declaring the coronavirus a "public health emergency"** Allison Aubrey, "Trump Declares Coronavirus a Public Health Emergency and Restricts Travel from China," NPR, January 31, 2020.

448 **"We are putting the Democrats on notice"** Quoted in Annie Karni and Maggie Haberman, "On the Day Democrats Vote in Iowa, Trump Plans to Flood the Zone," *New York Times*, January 28, 2020.

448 **a personal best approval rating** Jeffrey M. Jones, "Trump Job Approval at Personal Best 49%," Gallup, February 4, 2020.

449 **"Or was success beside the point?"** Mitch McConnell, "Impeachment," *Congressional Record* 166:23 (February 4, 2020), page S814.

449 **"Absolutely, a hundred percent"** Steve Inskeep, "Giuliani Says Trump Should '100%' Investigate Biden After Expected Senate Acquittal," "All Things Considered," NPR, February 4, 2020.

450 **She simply said** Sheryl Gay Stolberg, "Trump and Pelosi Exchange Snubs at the State of the Union Address," *New York Times*, February 4, 2020.

450 **"The years of economic decay"** "Remarks by President Trump in State of the Union Address," White House transcript, February 4, 2020.

451 **Cruz was disgusted** Cruz interview with Mary Jordan, April 2020.

451 **Himes watched with competing instincts** Himes interview with Mary Jordan, February 2020.

Chapter Fifty-Six: "Never Over"

453 **they aren't taking this seriously enough** Chris Murphy (@ChrisMurphyCT), Twitter post, February 5, 2020, 10:09.

453 **administration's handling of the virus as "Keystone Cops"** Erica Werner and Yasmeen Abutaleb, "Some Lawmakers Confront Trump Administration over Coronavirus Response," *Washington Post*, February 5, 2020.

454 **"We're on the same team here"** "House Foreign Affairs Subcommittee on Asia, the Pacific and Nonproliferation Holds Hearing on Coronavirus," *CQ Transcriptions*, February 5, 2020.

455 **his "heart sank in dread"** Dan Balz and Robert Costa, "Romney Votes to Convict Trump on Charge of Abuse of Power, Becoming the Lone Republican to Break Ranks," *Washington Post*, February 5, 2020.

456 **the two embraced** Paul Kane, "Inside the Senate Chamber for Wednesday's Acquittal Vote," *Washington Post*, February 5, 2020.

458 **They wanted records of travel** Charles Grassley and Ron Johnson, letter to James Murray, published on Grassley's website, February 5, 2020.

Epilogue: One Nation, Divisible?

459 **held it aloft** National Prayer Breakfast, February 6, 2020, C-SPAN video and transcript.

461 **"It was all bullshit"** "Remarks by President Trump to the Nation," White House transcript, February 6, 2020.

463 **He fired Sondland** Toluse Olorunnipa, Tom Hamburger, Josh Dawsey and Greg Miller, "Trump Ousts Vindman and Sondland, Punishing Key Impeachment Witnesses in Post-Acquittal Campaign of Retribution," *Washington Post*, February 7, 2020.

463 **"That's going to be up to the military, we'll have to see"** "Remarks by President Trump at Signing Ceremony for S.153, the Supporting Veterans in STEM Careers Act," transcript released by the White House, February 12, 2020.

463 **Vindman had lost "his job, his career, and his privacy"** Paul Sonne, "U.S. Military Isn't Investigating Vindman, Top Army Official Says," *Washington Post*, February 14, 2020.

464 **"make a difference every day"** Marie Yovanovitch, "Transcript: Marie Yovanovitch Speaks at Georgetown, Gives Warning About State Department," published by Rev.com, February 12, 2020. Other details drawn from Karen DeYoung's interviews with sources familiar with Yovanovitch's thinking.

464 **Solomon's work on Ukraine** "The Hill's Review of John Solomon's Columns on Ukraine," *The Hill*, February 19, 2020.

465 **"That is no longer the case"** Ellen Nakashima, Josh Dawsey and Shane Harris, "Trump Says He Will Fire Intelligence Watchdog at Center of Ukraine Allegations That Led to Impeachment," *Washington Post*, April 3, 2020.

465 **"That man is a disgrace to IGs"** "Remarks by President Trump, Vice President Pence, and Members of the Coronavirus Task Force in Press Briefing," White House transcript, April 5, 2020.

466 **"my having faithfully discharged my legal obligations"** Ellen Nakashima, "Inspector General Who Handled Ukraine Whistleblower Complaint Says 'It Is Hard Not to Think' Trump Fired Him for Doing His Job," *Washington Post*, April 6, 2020.

466 **"You're going down, sweetheart"** Slotkin, interview with Griff Witte, April 2020.

466 **She had nearly $4 million in the bank** Ally Mutnick, "Cash-Rich Democrats Tighten Grip on House Majority," *Politico*, April 19, 2020.

466 **Her campaign committee reported $3.2 milion** Michael Goot, "Cobb Raises $2.05 Million, Stefanik More Than $3.2 Million in Fourth-Quarter Campaign Fundraising," *Post-Star* (Glen Falls, N.Y.), January 8, 2020.

467 **"Stand Your Ground," etched in Russian** Taylor, interviews with Greg Jaffe in early 2020. Parts of this section were previously published in Jaffe's article, "William Taylor Jr., A Key Impeachment Witness, Quietly Returns Home to Trump's Washington," *Washington Post*, February 14, 2020.

468 **Trump called the protesters "THUGS"** Trump tweet, May 29, 2020, 12:53 a.m. Twitter labeled this tweet with a note that it "violated Twitter Rules about glorifying violence," but left the post up because it may "be in the public's interest." Earlier in the week, it had added a note to a Trump tweet about mail-in ballots leading to fraud that said, "Get the facts about mail-in ballots."

469 **they would look like "jerks" if they didn't "dominate"** Robert Costa, Seung Min Kim and Josh Dawsey, "Trump Calls Governors 'Weak,' Urges Them to Use Force Against Unruly Protests," *Washington Post*, June 1, 2020.

Index

A$AP Rocky (rapper), 119–20, 126
ABC, 97, 168, 242, 292, 381, 391
Abraham, Ralph (House member), 368
"Access Hollywood" tape, xix, 145, 442
Acosta, Jim, 54
Adams, John, 329
Affordable Care Act (Obamacare; 2010), xvii, 448
Afghanistan, 34, 130, 131, 145, 277
Ahearn, Joseph, 6, 7, 8
Alemany, Jacqueline, 17
Alexander, Lamar (senator), xxiv, 341–43, 358, 387, 410, 418, 436, 440, 441–45, 449, 457
"All Things Considered" (radio show), 446
Amash, Justin (House member), 84, 370–71
Amazon (company), 414, 425, 468
America First Action (super PAC), 6, 9, 228
American Enterprise Institute, 78, 460
American Foreign Service Association, 282
"America's Newsroom" (TV show), 344–45
Andrés, José, 260–61
Atkinson, Michael (inspector general, intelligence community), xxvi, 128–29, 144, 147, 465–66
Atlantic (magazine), 183
Atlantic Council, 10
Auschwitz death camp, 415
Avakov, Arsen (Ukrainian official), 3
"Axe Files, The" (TV show), 467
Axelrod, David, 467
Azar, Alex (secretary, Health and Human Services), 405, 429, 434, 447

Bade, Rachael, 75, 121, 174
Baghdadi, Abu Bakr al-, 260
Baier, Bret, 344, 370
Bakaj, Andrew, 128–29, 215–16, 265
Baker, Howard, 444
Baker, Peter, 444
Baldwin, Tammy (senator), 457
Balz, Dan, 455
Bangor, Maine, 390
Bannon, Steve, 328, 388, 424
Baquet, Dean, 216
Barr, William (U.S. attorney general), xxiii, 12, 16, 18, 19, 20, 26, 108, 109, 110, 184, 193, 207, 210, 224, 225, 398, 423, 461, 462
Barrasso, John (senator), 416, 419
Barrett, Devlin, 193
Bartiromo, Maria, 328
Bash, Dana, 21
Battle Creek, Mich., Trump rally in, 366–67, 368, 369, 370, 371, 372–73, 374, 375
Behar, Joy, 168
Benghazi attacks (2012), congressional investigation of, 221, 257, 274
Bennet, Michael (senator), 320, 401, 442
Bera, Amerish "Ami"(House member), 454
Berger, Rick, 78
Bezos, Jeff, 425
BGR Group, 40, 467
Biden, Hunter, xvii, xxvi, 3, 29, 36, 38, 42, 65, 87, 88, 94, 109, 111, 113, 126, 131, 132, 169, 171, 173, 184, 193, 194, 198, 201, 202, 212, 222, 225, 228, 242, 269, 271, 276, 289–90, 295, 311, 320, 323, 334, 341, 387–88, 398, 403, 406, 416, 426, 427, 428, 454, 458
Biden, Joe, xvii, xxvi, 6, 10, 14, 38, 42, 79, 80, 83, 87, 88, 94, 109, 111, 113, 120, 126, 131, 132, 137, 138, 142, 170–71, 173, 184, 193, 194, 195, 196, 198, 201, 212, 222, 223, 225, 228, 242, 269, 271, 276, 277, 288, 289–90, 295, 311, 320, 323, 334, 341, 379, 387, 388, 398, 401, 403, 415, 416, 426, 427, 428, 439, 444, 449, 454
Biggs, Andy (House member), 51, 253, 254, 256, 259, 261, 362, 462
Bitar, Maher, 285–86
Blackburn, Marsha (senator), 417
Blackmun, Harry, 329
Blair, Robert (Mulvaney aide), 105, 125, 347
Blakeman, Brad, 175
Blumenthal, Richard (senator), 419
Blunt, Roy (senator), 381, 401

Boggs, Lindy Claiborne, 172
Bohdan, Andriy (Ukrainian official), xxvi, 89–90, 151
Boland, Patrick, 153, 224
Bolton, John (national security adviser), xxv, 23, 24, 29, 37, 39, 63, 70, 85–88, 89, 90, 98, 99, 104, 113, 126, 129, 130, 131, 132–34, 146–47, 167, 233, 306, 307, 321, 347, 382–85, 386, 387, 391, 398, 399, 403, 406, 416, 417, 426–27, 428, 431, 436, 438, 440, 441, 455, 468
Bondi, Pam, 320, 404, 405
Bondy, Joseph, 397
Bongino, Dan, 10
Booker, Cory (senator), 299, 320, 381, 401
Bork, Robert, 86
Bowman, Frank O., 432
Brady, Kevin (House member), 261, 365
Bream, Shannon, 37, 344
Brechbuhl, Ulrich (Pompeo aide), xxv, 12, 33, 35, 62, 63, 68, 221
Breitbart News, 233, 265, 351
Brennan, Margaret, 292
Brindisi, Anthony (House member), 356
Brooks, Arthur C., 460
Brooks, Mo (House member), 253
Buffalo News, 75
Burisma (Ukrainian gas company), xvii, xxvi, 3, 12, 65, 87, 88, 94, 111, 122, 138, 139, 169, 171, 225, 242, 269, 271, 276, 289–90, 295, 305, 398
Burns, Ken, 104
Burr, Richard (senator), 417
Bush, George W., xv, 39, 48, 86, 177, 248, 273, 274, 288, 372, 392, 401
Bush, Jeb, 67
Bush (G.W.) administration, 32, 34, 71, 125, 175, 294, 317, 346
Buttigieg, Pete, 79, 83, 288, 371, 401
Byrne, Bradley (House member), 255, 256

Capito, Shelley Moore (senator), 191, 199
Carlson, Tucker, 335–36, 344, 372, 417
Carter, Jimmy, 468
Castor, Stephen (Republican counsel, impeachment inquiry), xxiv, 265–66, 268, 277, 278, 306, 307–8, 310, 319, 320–21
Cavuto, Neil, 313
Caygle, Heather, 186
CBS, 158, 160, 292, 323, 381, 419, 425
Center for American Progress, 51, 53, 55, 65
Centers for Disease Control and Prevention (CDC), 405, 414, 418, 426, 434
Chao, Elaine (secretary, Transportation), 425
Cheney, Liz (House member), 196, 261
China, 132–33, 202, 222, 223, 256, 368, 395, 405, 414, 418, 419, 424, 438, 439, 447–48, 453
Christian Science Monitor breakfast, 74–77, 187
Chumley, Cheryl, 336
CIA, 60, 71, 113, 122–23, 127, 128, 144, 145, 168, 176, 177, 186, 196, 204, 214, 215, 216, 263, 264, 265, 319, 344, 345, 437, 447
Cicilline, David (House member), 48–49, 164–65
Cipollone, Pat (White House counsel), xxiii, 36, 143, 184, 227, 265, 268, 291, 320, 341, 352, 383, 389, 404, 409, 411, 412, 422–24, 425, 432, 461
Cisneros, Gil (House member), 176
Civil Rights Act (1964), 396
Civil War, U.S., 335, 433
Clark, Katherine (House member), 194
Cleaver, Emanuel, 185
Clinton, Bill, xx, 9, 47, 80, 240, 273, 291, 301, 346, 347, 357, 364, 373, 386, 387, 390, 394, 396, 402, 404, 405, 430, 432, 439, 462, 468, 470
Clinton, Chelsea, 239
Clinton, Hillary, xvi, xvii, 7, 8, 10, 14, 17, 20, 29, 36, 56, 60, 65, 72, 80, 131, 202, 261, 274, 319, 332, 339, 363, 371, 372, 373, 379, 404, 422, 426
Clyburn, Emily, 173
Clyburn, James (House, majority whip), xxiii, 46, 75, 173, 174, 216
CNBC, 414, 429
CNN, xiv, 17, 21, 54, 75, 97, 123, 140, 151, 152, 155–56, 160, 173, 244, 246, 248, 250, 262, 263, 264, 294, 313, 359, 360, 370, 399, 416, 467
Coe, David, 463
Coe, Tim, 463
Cohen, Carolyn, 404
Cohen, Eliot A., 81
Cohen, Michael, 51, 210
Cohen, Steve (House member), 174
Cohen, William, 390
Cole, Tom (House member), 362
Collins, Doug (House Judiciary Committee, ranking minority member), xxiv, 98, 124, 163, 165, 195, 329, 331, 335, 343, 366, 406
Collins, Kaitlan, 313
Collins, Susan (senator), xxiv, 342, 358, 387, 390–91, 410, 411, 419, 428, 436, 440, 442, 447, 449, 457, 462
Comey, James (former FBI director), xviii, 202, 210, 373
Common Defense, 261–62

Conaway, Michael (House member), 204, 256, 324
Connolly, Gerald (House member), 75, 255
Conroy, Patrick, xiii
Conservative Political Action Conference, 455
Constitution, U.S., impeachment clause in, xx, 19, 48, 240, 329–31, 338, 340, 353, 356, 370, 400, 402, 404, 410, 415, 417, 430–33, 437, 442–44, 454–55, 469–70
Constitutional Convention (1787), 362
Conway, Kellyanne (counselor to the president), 320, 406, 425
Cook, Paul (House member), 131
Coons, Chris (senator), 262, 417
Cooper, Anderson, 399
Cooper, Charles, 384, 426–27
Cooper, Laura (Defense Department; impeachment witness), 95, 253, 255, 258–59
Cordes, Nancy, 419
Cornyn, John (senator), 299
coronavirus, *see* Covid-19
Coronavirus Task Force, 434, 453
Cortese, Doris, 250
Costa, Robert, 199
Cotton, Tom (senator), 320
Covid-19, 405, 414, 418–19, 424, 426, 429, 434, 439, 447–48, 453–54, 466, 468, 470–71
Craft, Kelly (U.N. ambassador), 211
Craighead, Shealah (White House photographer), 237–38
Crawford, Rick (House member), 313
Crimea, 22, 44, 382
Croft, Catherine (State Department; impeachment witness), 92, 116
Crow, Jason (House member), 176–77, 179, 394, 396
CrowdStrike, 107, 111, 113, 196, 205, 236, 269, 326
Crowley, Joe, 48
Cruz, Ted (senator), xxiv, 145, 251, 299–300, 320, 349, 359, 417, 431, 433, 434, 440–41, 451
C-SPAN, 54, 55, 150, 200, 209, 234–35, 317
Cummings, Elijah (House Oversight and Reform Committee, chairman), 46, 143, 241, 366, 374
Cunningham, Joe (House member), 349
Cuomo, Chris, 155–56

Daily Wire, The (website), 11
D'Alesandro, Annunciata, 336
D'Alesandro, Thomas, III, 255, 336
Daniels, Stormy, xix, 51
Danyliuk, Oleksandr (Ukrainian official), xxvi, 85–89, 103–4, 110, 111, 137, 140, 152
Daum, Margaret, 221
Davis, Julia, 136
Dawsey, Josh, 38, 174, 192, 193, 199, 291, 428
DeBonis, Mike, 248
Defense Department, U.S., xxv, 78, 92, 95, 96, 105, 115, 116, 122, 125, 130, 131–32, 136, 148, 149, 150, 186, 322, 346, 463, 465, 466
DeGette, Diana (House member), 362, 372
Delgado, Antonio (House member), 28–29
Demings, Val (House member), xxiv, 26, 225, 255, 279, 394, 396
Demirjian, Karoun, 220
Dershowitz, Alan, 389, 404, 405, 429–32, 433–34, 440, 441, 442, 447
Des Moines, Iowa, Trump rally in, 439–40
DeStefano, Johnny, 9
Detroit Free Press, 347, 349
Deutsche Bank, 51
Diehl, Jackson, 143
diGenova, Joe, 8, 10, 465
Dingell, Debbie (House member), 172, 180, 194, 225, 355, 373–74, 381, 403, 425
Dingell, John, 373–74
Dobbs, Lou, 51, 227, 239, 259, 344, 360, 395, 397, 421
Doocy, Steve, 326
Dowd, John, 226
Dowd, Maureen, 120
D'Souza, Dinesh, 265
Duda, Andrzej, 137
Duffey, Michael (OMB), xxvi, 78–79, 115–16, 125, 130–31, 136, 148–49, 347
Duffy, Michael, 175–76, 178, 179
Duffy, Sean, 294
Duncan, Jeff (House member), 336
Durbin, Richard (senator), 150, 419, 441
Durham, John, 244

Edelman, Eric, 81
Eisen, Norm, 431
Eisenberg, John (NSC, deputy White House counsel), xxv, 89, 114–15, 127, 128
Eisenhower, Dwight, 463
elections, U.S.:
of 1964, 86
of 2000, 86, 273
of 2012, 29, 248, 288, 385
of 2014, 288
of 2016, xvi, xvii, xviii, xix, 8, 10, 15, 16, 18, 27, 28, 36, 37, 43, 60, 65, 67, 87, 88, 94, 104, 107, 111, 113, 132, 139, 140, 145, 160, 162, 163, 177, 184, 187, 196,

elections, U.S. (*cont.*)
197, 205, 226, 227, 243, 244, 245, 247, 248, 251, 261, 269, 270, 275, 277, 278, 288, 299, 305, 317, 318, 319, 323, 325, 364, 367, 369, 371, 373, 392, 408, 422
of 2018, 21, 28, 29, 48, 76, 145, 178, 247, 248, 249, 394
of 2020, xvii, xviii, xxi, 97, 142, 145, 194, 206, 207, 219, 290, 318, 319, 339, 358, 368, 369, 373, 380, 381, 392, 401, 411, 437, 442, 445, 448, 470
"11th Hour, The" (TV show), 151
Ellis, Michael (NSC), 114–15
El Paso Times, 145
El Paso Walmart shooting (2019), 145–46
Elwood, Courtney Simmons (CIA general counsel), 123, 127, 215
Emma, Caitlin, 134
Engel, Eliot (House Foreign Affairs Committee, chairman), 37, 46, 143, 185
Engel, Jeffrey A., 444
"Engrossment Ceremony," articles of impeachment for, 395–97
Erdogan, Recep Tayyip, 237
Ernst, Joni (senator), 199, 442
Eshoo, Anna G. (House member), 47
Esper, Mark (secretary, Defense), xxiii, 113, 126, 130, 131, 148, 149, 238, 425
Etienne, Ashley, 224, 298
European Union, xxv, 12, 38, 43, 66, 67, 69, 106–7, 119, 132, 194, 245

Facebook, 10, 54, 60–61, 150, 239, 250, 256, 284, 344
"Face the Nation" (TV show), 158, 168, 292, 323, 381
Fauci, Anthony (NIH), 418–19, 434
Favreau, Jon, 425–26
FBI, xvii, 59, 65, 83, 202, 205, 210, 215, 228, 236, 272, 326, 339, 399, 461
Fealk, Bruce, 349
Federalist Papers, 346
Federalist Society, 423
Feinstein, Dianne (senator), 401
Feldman, Noah, 329, 331
Felt, Mark, 215
Ferguson, Drew (House member), 364–65
Fiser, Paul, 392–93
Fitton, Tom, 174
Floyd, George, 468
4chan, 10, 214, 284
Fox, Lauren, 264
"Fox & Friends" (TV show), 11, 27, 234, 268, 294, 326
Fox Business Network, 60, 227, 328, 414–15
Fox News, xiv, xix, 6, 8, 10, 17, 19–20, 37, 51, 65, 83, 87, 98, 146, 160, 166, 174–75, 216, 225, 228, 231, 239, 250, 259, 262, 275, 280, 289, 291, 293–94, 301, 306, 313, 333, 335, 339, 344, 348, 349, 370, 372, 391, 399, 403, 405, 406, 417
"Fox News at Night" (TV show), 175
"Fox News Sunday" (TV show), 291, 381
Franklin, Benjamin, 270, 274, 362, 364, 432
Freedom Caucus (House), 253, 254
Freedom Riders (civil rights), 183, 256–57
Fruman, Igor, xvi, xxvi, 4, 6, 9, 14, 225–26, 227–28, 257, 276

Gabbard, Tulsi (House member), 371
Gaetz, Matt (House member), xxiv, 163, 166, 229–32, 233, 235, 247, 252, 253–54, 256, 259, 260, 261, 327–28, 331–32, 333, 389, 448, 462
Gaetz, S. J. "Jerry," 327–28
Garcia, Sylvia (House member), 299, 394, 396
Gardner, Cory (senator), 410, 442
Garland, Merrick, 300, 379–80
Gates, Bill, 425
Gateway Pundit (website), 265
Georges, Salwan, 308
Gerhardt, Michael, 329, 330, 331
Gideon, Sara, 391
Giuliani, Rudolph, xvi–xvii, xxi, xxvi, 3, 4, 5, 6, 10, 13–14, 17, 19–20, 24, 29, 30–31, 32, 35, 37–38, 42–43, 44, 57–58, 59, 60, 63, 64–65, 67, 68, 70, 73, 80, 81, 85, 87, 89–90, 93–94, 95, 98, 107, 108–9, 110, 111, 112, 120, 131, 132, 138, 142, 143, 146, 151, 168, 169, 193, 194–95, 199, 200, 202, 207, 208, 210, 222, 223, 224, 225–26, 227, 228, 243, 257, 258, 269, 276–77, 279, 283, 284, 294, 295, 304–5, 306, 311, 319, 323, 325, 384, 397, 398, 415, 426, 428, 449, 465, 468
Givhan, Robin, 303, 364
Global Energy Producers, 9, 228
Gohmert, Louie (House member), 254–55, 343, 462
Goldberg, Jeffrey, 183, 184
Goldberg, Michelle, 417
Golden, Jared (House member), 178
Goldman, Daniel (Democratic counsel, impeachment inquiry), xxiv, 150, 151, 255, 258, 259, 268, 277–78, 284–85, 286, 306
Goldwater, Barry, 86
Google, 54, 107, 177
Gorbachev, Mikhail, 316
Gordon, Kevin, 393
Gorsuch, Neil (Supreme Court justice), 379–80
Government Accountability Office (GAO), 399–400

Graham, Lindsey (Senate Judiciary Committee, chairman), xxiv, 18, 150, 196, 261, 299, 320, 401, 428, 440, 441
Granger, Kay (House member), 261
Grassley, Charles (senator), 396–97, 402, 409, 453, 458, 462
Greenfield, Jeff, 313
Grisham, Stephanie (White House press secretary), 44, 241, 332, 399
Grogan, Joe (White House Domestic Policy Council), 429
Group of 7 (G7), 131, 241–42
Group of 20 (G20), 79

Haberman, Maggie, 426–27
Hadley, Stephen, 39–40
Hale, David (State Department, undersecretary), xxv, 11–12, 33, 36, 125
Hamburger, Tom, 226
Hamilton, Alexander, 82–83, 329, 330, 364, 415, 430
Hammill, Drew (Pelosi aide), 172–73, 180, 239
Hand, Ann, 364
Handziuk, Kateryna, 30, 31
Handziuk, Victor, 30
Hannity, Sean, 6, 7, 8, 10, 13, 83, 98, 166, 204, 216, 228, 239, 245, 291, 339, 340, 344, 347, 357, 359, 360, 417–18
Haring, Melinda, 10, 13
Harlow, Poppy, 246, 248, 249, 250
Harris, Kamala (senator), 79, 83, 320, 401
Harris, Shane, 154–55, 156, 157, 159, 167, 168, 169, 171
Harwell, Drew, 53–55, 60–61, 205
Haspel, Gina (CIA, director), 113
Health and Human Services Department, U.S., 405, 426, 429
Heim, Joe, xiii, xiv–xv, xvii, xxi
Helderman, Rosalind, 226, 228
Hemmer, Bill, 19–20, 344–45
Herb, Jeremy, 264
Herschmann, Eric D., 404–5
Hewitt, Hugh, 360
Hiatt, Fred, 179
Hice, Jody (House member), 258
Hicks, Thomas, Jr., 6, 7, 8
Higgins, Brian (House member), 75
High Crimes and Misdemeanors (Bowman), 432
Hill, Fiona (NSC; impeachment witness), xxv, 38–39, 69–73, 86, 87, 88–89, 93, 95, 99, 105, 112, 122, 198–99, 229, 230, 232–33, 247, 252, 297–98, 314–22, 324, 325, 326, 346
Hill, The, 5–6, 7, 8, 10, 65, 90, 319, 325, 464–65
Hill.TV, 5–6
Himes, Jim (House member), xxiv, 26–27, 204, 225, 239–40, 291, 368, 451–52
Hirono, Mazie (senator), 416, 453
Holly, Mich., Elissa Slotkin's home in, 345, 346
Holmes, David (U.S. embassy, Kyiv; impeachment witness), xxv, 42, 43, 44, 92, 118–19, 120, 126, 132, 135, 306, 315, 319, 320, 322, 324–25, 346, 465
Houlahan, Chrissy (House member), 176, 178, 179
House of Representatives, U.S.:
  Appropriations Committee, 131
  Armed Services Committee, 256, 394
  Foreign Affairs Committee, 36, 143, 220, 221, 223, 225, 226, 229, 231, 233, 247, 253, 255, 265, 267, 454
  impeachment managers, 410, 412, 419, 420, 427, 430, 432, 435, 436, 441
  Intelligence Committee, xxiv, 64, 65, 97, 128, 142, 143, 144–45, 150–51, 153, 154–55, 162, 196, 204, 207, 208–11, 212–14, 215, 218, 220–21, 222–23, 225, 226, 229, 231–33, 234–35, 251–52, 253, 255, 256, 265, 267–68, 269–72, 274, 275–80, 281–85, 286–87, 289–90, 293, 295–98, 300–301, 302–13, 314, 315–19, 320–26, 346, 357
  Judiciary Committee, xxiv, 16, 18, 26, 46, 48, 97, 123, 124, 155, 156, 160–61, 162, 163–66, 186, 187, 195, 217, 229–30, 233, 235, 326, 327, 328–33, 338, 339, 342–43, 344, 353, 357, 394, 431
  Oversight and Reform Committee, 46, 143, 220, 221, 223, 225, 226, 229, 231, 233, 253, 255, 265, 267
  Ways and Means Committee, 267
Hoyer, Steny (House, majority leader), xxiii, 21, 37, 46, 185, 216, 237, 238, 363
Huffman, Jared (House member), 26
Hunt, Kasie, 49
Hurd, Will (House member), xxiv, 144–46, 196–98, 204–5, 251, 322–24, 326, 343, 369, 442
Hurt, Charles, 268

"Impeachment: An American History" (Meacham, Naftali, Baker, and Engel), 444
Impoundment Control Act (1974), 96, 116
Indiana University, 103
InfoWars (website), 72
Ingraham, Laura, 8, 10, 11, 262, 293–94, 301, 391, 422, 423–24
Inhofe, James (senator), 131, 401, 409
Inskeep, Steve, 449
Iowa caucuses, 401, 442, 448

Iran, 80, 86, 133, 146, 236, 446
Iraq, 34, 104, 277, 345
Iraq War, 48, 177, 261, 293, 345, 392
Irving, Paul D. (House sergeant at arms), 255, 396
ISIS, Islamic State, 235, 369

Jarrett, Gregg, 166, 175
Javelin anti-tank missiles, 11, 107, 108, 148, 202
Jayapal, Pramila (House member), 166
Jefferson, Thomas, 82, 329, 338, 364
Jefferson, William, 147
Jeffries, Hakeem (House member), 194–95, 372, 394, 396
John, Elton, 367
Johnson, Andrew, 396, 439, 444, 470
Johnson, Cheryl (House clerk), 396–97
Johnson, Jenna, 367–68, 369
Johnson, Lyndon B., 364, 396
Johnson, Mike (House member), 406
Johnson, Ron (senator), xxiv, 43, 57, 59, 60, 139–40, 294–95, 320, 381, 417, 458
Jones, Beth, 282
Jones, Doug (senator), 381, 388
Jordan, Jim (House member), xxiv, 98, 191, 223, 229, 230, 231, 232, 254, 255, 256, 257, 268, 270, 294, 297–98, 309–10, 313, 324, 340, 389, 405, 406, 448, 462
Joseph, Connor, 175, 176, 178, 179
Judicial Watch, 174
Judkis, Maura, 261
Julien, Robert, 299
Justice Department, U.S., 15, 16, 18, 19, 20, 59, 83, 124, 127, 147, 193, 194, 244, 272, 294, 329, 468
"Justice with Jeanine Pirro" (TV show), 174

Kaepernick, Colin, 83
Kaine, Tim (senator), 299
Kane, Paul, 28, 29, 443, 444–45
Kardashian, Kim, 119, 120
Karl, Jon, 242, 243
Karlan, Pamela, 329–31, 332–33
Kasowitz, Marc, 405
Kavanaugh, Brett M. (Supreme Court justice), 158, 268, 380, 391
Keller, Fred (House member), 364
Kellogg, Keith (Pence aide), 105, 125
Kelly, Mary Louise, 446
Kelly, Trent (House member), 368–69
Kenna, Lisa, 13–14, 141
Kennan, George F., 4, 282
Kennedy, John F., xiv, 172, 272, 364, 461
Kennedy, John Neely (senator), 320, 429
Kennedy, Patrick, 273
Kennedy, Ted, 273
Kent, George (State Department; impeachment witness), xxv, 3, 5, 32–33, 34, 35, 90, 92, 122, 128, 221, 267, 268, 271, 272, 276–77, 278, 279, 282, 284, 289, 296, 297, 346, 465
Kernen, Joe, 414
Kessler, Glenn, 222, 359
Kilmeade, Brian, 294, 326
Kim, Seung Min, 389, 440
Kim Jong Un, 168
King, Angus (senator), 388
King, Martin Luther, Jr., 82, 183, 364
King, Peter (House member), 192, 199–200
Kissinger, Henry, 395
Klitenic, Jason (DNI, general counsel), 150, 152
Klobuchar, Amy (senator), 320, 381, 401, 442, 457
Kopan, Tal, 76
Kranz, Gene, 83
Krishnamoorthi, Raja (House member), 312
Kupperman, Charles (deputy national security adviser), 105, 125, 384
Kushner, Jared, 66, 68, 200, 240, 268, 291, 320, 394, 395, 425
Kvien, Kristina (U.S. embassy, Kyiv), 126
Kyiv, Ukraine, daily life and political events in, xv, 30, 31, 32, 103–4, 111, 118–20, 126, 132, 135, 138, 381–82, 446–47
  U.S. Embassy in, xxv, 3, 5, 33, 42, 44, 60, 62, 91, 126, 315, 381–82
Kyiv Security Forum, 467

L3Harris Technologies, 131–32
Lafayette, Marquis de, 361–62
Lafayette Park (Washington, D.C.), 469
Lankford, James (senator), 419
Lawfare (blog), 157
Leahy, Patrick (senator), 401
Ledger, Graham, 234
Lee, Mike (senator), 299, 320
Lee, Sheila Jackson (House member), 166, 330
"Legal Eagles" (McConnell's advisory group), 299–300, 320, 356–57
Lehrer, Brian, 160
Leno, Jay, 66, 67, 68
Leo, Leonard, 423
Leonnig, Carol D., 169
LePage, Paul, 390
Lesko, Debbie (House member), 235, 257, 406, 462
Levin, Mark, 204, 216, 265
Lewandowski, Corey, 160–61, 162–66, 186, 448
Lewis and Clark, 83

Limbaugh, Rush, 11, 203–4, 205, 268, 322, 451
Lincoln, Abraham, 184, 364, 394, 395, 397, 421, 433, 461
Lincoln Memorial, 83, 84
Litvan, Laura, 441
Liu He, 395
Loeffler, Kelly (senator), 429
Lofgren, Zoe (House member), 394, 396, 432
"Long Game, The" (McConnell), 337, 339, 342
Los Angeles Times, 211, 214, 215
Loudermilk, Barry (House member), 364
Louisville Courier-Journal, 402
Love Your Enemies (Brooks), 460
Luria, Elaine (House member), 77, 176, 178, 349
Lutsenko, Yuri (Ukrainian official), xvi, xvii, 3–6, 7, 8, 12, 13, 14, 32, 65, 89, 90, 94, 222, 276, 285, 295, 465

MacCallum, Martha, 174–75, 333
MacMahon, Edward, 257, 258
Macron, Emmanuel, 106
Maddow, Rachel, 10, 166, 397–98
Madison, James, 329, 338, 364, 430
Maduro, Nicolás, 299, 300
Maguire, Joseph (director of national intelligence), xxvi, 144, 147, 150–51, 152, 153, 154, 155, 156, 157–59, 169, 173, 182, 203, 209, 211, 212, 213, 220
Malinowski, Tom (House member), 225
Maloney, Sean Patrick (House member), 291–92, 311–12
Manchin, Joe (senator), 388, 456
Markey, Ed, 432
Marshall, George, 4
Martin, Jonathan, 249–50
Mason, George, 364
Mason, Jeff, 201
Mattarella, Sergio, 235, 236
McAdams, Ben (House member), 349
McCabe, Andrew, 202
McCain, Cindy, 467
McCain, John, 467
McCain Institute for International Leadership, 40, 467
McCarthy, Joseph, 218, 325, 365
McCarthy, Kevin (House, minority leader), xxiii, 98, 174, 187, 191, 195, 203, 217–18, 238, 261, 337, 369, 448, 460, 461, 462
McCarthy, Ryan (secretary, Army), 463
McClain, Matt, 302
McConnell, Mitch (Senate, majority leader), xviii, xxiv, 27, 120, 187, 240, 251, 299, 300, 320, 337, 339, 340–42, 346–47, 356–57, 358–59, 374–75, 379–81, 383, 385, 386–87, 388–89, 390, 391, 392–93, 397, 400, 402, 405, 407–9, 410, 411–12, 413, 420, 421, 422, 425, 428, 429, 436, 438, 440, 443, 447, 449, 456, 458, 461, 462, 470
McCusker, Elaine (Defense Department), xxv, 78–79, 116, 130–31, 136, 148–49, 465
McDaniel, Ronna Romney, 213–14, 456
McEnany, Kayleigh, 372–73
McFaul, Michael, 136
McGahn, Donald (former White House counsel), 26, 48, 384
McGovern, Jim (House member), 362
McGrath, Amy, 380
McKinley, Michael (State Department; impeachment witness), 235, 243, 247, 285
McMaster, H. R., 72
Meacham, Jon, 444
Meadows, Mark (House member), 174, 191, 223, 255, 257, 258, 261, 303, 318, 359–60, 390, 406, 425, 448, 462, 465
Media Matters, 360, 405
"Meet the Press" (TV show), 381
Menendez, Bob (senator), 136
Merkel, Angela, 106
Merkley, Jeff (senator), 453
Midland-Odessa shooting (2019), 146
Milbank, Dana, 336–37, 429
Miller, Greg, 154–55, 156–57, 159, 167, 168, 169
Miller, Richard W., 65
Miller, Stephen (White House policy adviser), 352, 368
Milley, Mark (Joint Chiefs of Staff, chairman), 238
Mnuchin, Steven (secretary, Treasury), 146, 184, 200, 238, 395
Moolenaar, John (House member), 459–60, 463
Mooney, Alex (House member), 254
Moore, Dave, 345
Moore, Robert, 145
Moore, Roy, 388
"Morning Edition" (radio show), 234
"Morning Joe" (TV show), 234, 415
Morrison, Tim (NSC; impeachment witness), 95, 105, 109, 112–13, 115, 126, 132, 138–39, 297–98
Mosbacher, Georgette, 68
Moynihan, Daniel Patrick, 396
MSNBC, xiv, 10, 151, 160, 166, 239, 280, 360, 370, 372, 397–98, 415, 432
Mueller, Robert S., III, xvi, 12, 14, 15, 16, 18, 20, 25, 26, 79, 97, 98, 107, 123, 124, 155, 224

Mueller investigation, xvi, xix, 8, 14, 15–16, 19, 21, 26, 64, 65, 98, 114, 123, 160, 161, 163, 169, 187, 202, 205, 224, 226, 298, 354
Mueller report, 12, 15, 16, 17, 18–22, 25, 27, 46, 47, 48, 49, 84, 97, 124, 151, 156, 161, 163, 164, 165, 170, 177, 183, 203, 217, 224, 270, 334
Mulvaney, Mick (acting chief of staff, White House), xxiii, 29, 36, 43, 68, 71, 78, 87, 88, 89, 92, 93, 95, 105, 125, 131, 146, 148, 200, 233, 241–45, 246, 247, 248–49, 268, 306, 320, 321, 340, 347, 352, 383, 384, 385, 387, 389, 403, 417, 424, 429, 448, 465
Murkowski, Lisa (senator), xxiv, 246, 342, 358, 387, 410, 428, 436, 438, 440, 441, 447
Murphy, Chris (senator), 139–40, 388, 419–20, 453
Murray, Patty (senator), 418

Nadler, Jerrold (House Judiciary Committee, chairman), xxiv, 18, 20–21, 26, 46, 51, 75, 97, 123–24, 155–56, 160–66, 185, 186, 203, 217, 233, 328–29, 339, 342–43, 345, 374, 389, 394, 396, 412, 415, 416, 432, 435, 458, 462
Naftali, Timothy, 444
Nakashima, Ellen, 154–55, 156, 158–59, 167, 168–69, 205
Naland, John K., 282
National Committee on American Foreign Policy, 282
National Institutes of Health (NIH), 418, 434
National Prayer Breakfast, 459–61, 462, 464–65
National Security Council (NSC), xxv, 23, 24, 38, 39, 42, 60, 63, 68, 69, 70, 71, 73, 87, 89, 92, 93, 95, 98, 99, 105, 109, 114, 122, 125, 126, 127, 129, 130, 132, 149, 192, 198, 214, 229, 251, 295, 297, 304, 316, 317, 320, 346, 384, 429, 437, 463
NATO, 60, 68, 149
NBC, 49, 79, 336, 381, 404
NBC News-*Wall Street Journal* survey, 75
"New Day" (TV show), 294
New Democrat Coalition, 26
New Yorker, 337
New York Times, 37, 64–65, 120, 142, 158, 159, 169, 173, 197, 215–16, 263, 293, 294, 351, 417, 426–27, 428
Nielsen ratings, 280, 301
Nixon, Richard, xx, 51, 55, 76, 96, 105, 157, 215, 246, 249, 270, 301, 346, 364, 390, 394, 430, 439, 444
Norman, Ralph (House member), 213
North Korea, 79, 80, 86, 168, 438
NPR (National Public Radio), 172, 234, 244, 446, 449
Nunes, Devin (House Intelligence Committee, ranking minority member), xxiv, 98, 144, 229, 255, 267, 268, 270–72, 273–75, 276, 277, 278–80, 282, 287, 290, 294–95, 296–97, 300–301, 303–4, 307, 312, 317, 319, 462

Obama, Barack, xv, xvii, 29, 71, 133, 177, 197, 201, 202, 244, 274, 290, 300, 331, 332, 346, 364, 367, 379, 385, 402, 425, 468
Obama administration, xvii, 10, 11, 16, 107, 224, 271, 275, 289–90, 317, 329, 437, 458
O'Brien, Connor, 134
O'Brien, Robert (national security adviser), 167, 200, 434
Ocasio-Cortez, Alexandria (House member), 21, 48, 49, 120–21, 178, 288, 421, 439
O'Donnell, Lawrence, 10, 166, 239
O'Donnell, Norah, 425
Office of Management and Budget (OMB), xxvi, 78–79, 92, 93, 96, 115, 116, 125, 130, 131, 133, 134, 136, 148, 149, 347, 389, 399–400
Ohr, Bruce, 319
Ohr, Nellie, 319
Olorunnipa, Toluse, 244
Omar, Ilhan (House member), 120
One America News Network (OAN), 234, 265, 294, 321
Orban, Viktor, 38–39
Oregonian, 55

Paine, Thomas, 77, 187, 394
Parnas, Lev, xvi, xvii, xxvi, 4, 6, 7–8, 9, 14, 38, 93, 94, 225, 226, 227–28, 257–58, 276, 397–98, 399, 465
Parnas, Svetlana, 258, 399
Parscale, Brad (Trump campaign), 206, 369, 414, 448
Paul, Rand (senator), 264, 416, 417, 436–37
Paulson, John, 206
Pelosi, Nancy (House, speaker), xiii–xv, xvii–xix, xx–xxi, xxiii, 18, 20, 21–22, 25–26, 27, 46, 47–48, 49–52, 53–57, 60–61, 74–78, 80, 84, 97, 120–21, 123–24, 143, 151, 153, 156, 161, 162, 170, 172–74, 176, 177, 178–80, 181–82, 183–85, 187, 191, 194, 195, 198, 202, 204, 206, 215, 216, 217, 218, 219, 220, 224, 225, 227, 232, 233, 234, 236–40, 255, 256, 267, 268, 273, 292, 298,

334–37, 340, 342, 352–56, 357, 359–60, 361–62, 364, 365–66, 368, 371, 372, 374–75, 379, 381, 386, 387, 389–90, 392, 394, 395–96, 400, 408, 415, 421, 432, 435–36, 439, 449–52, 453, 455, 458, 460, 461, 462, 463–64, 470
Pence, Mike, xxiii, 38, 42, 43, 85, 105, 125, 136, 137–38, 146, 148, 291, 293, 295, 306, 369–70, 415, 449, 451, 460, 461
Pennington, Joseph (U.S. embassy, Kyiv), 42
Perdue, David (senator), 261
Perez, Carol, 31–32, 33
Perry, Rick (secretary, Energy), xxiii, 41–42, 43, 44, 45, 57, 59–60, 68, 86, 88, 89, 91, 92, 95, 106, 200, 304–5, 448
Philbin, Patrick, 441
Pilipenko, Diana, 64, 65
Pirro, Jeanine, 174
Pitts, Alan, 261–62
Pod Save America (podcast), 425–26
Politico, 134, 135, 136, 142, 150, 186, 319, 325
Politics WatchDog (website), 54, 61
PolitiFact, 61
Pompeo, Mike (secretary, State Department), xxiii, xxv, 7, 9, 11, 12, 13–14, 29, 30–31, 32, 33, 35, 36–37, 40, 60, 62–63, 80, 81, 90, 93, 95, 113, 126, 130, 131, 133, 135, 141, 143, 144, 146, 184, 200, 221, 225, 235, 243, 285, 306, 321, 381–82, 426, 446–47, 461
Poroshenko, Petro, 5, 22, 23, 37, 42, 58
Portman, Rob (senator), 131, 147–48, 149, 411, 440
Posobiec, Jack, 265, 294
Pressman, David, 463
Problem Solvers Caucus, 338, 374
Prystaiko, Vadym (Ukrainian official), xxvi, 89–90, 136, 150
Putin, Vladimir, xvi, xix, 22, 23, 34, 38, 39, 43, 44, 58, 62, 63, 72, 85, 103, 132, 136, 137, 168, 169, 197, 237, 317–18, 335–36

Raddatz, Martha, 381
Raju, Manu, 123, 360
Rascoe, Ayesha, 244
Raskin, Jamie (House member), 256–57
Raskin, Jane Serene, 19, 20, 404
Raskin, Martin, 19, 20
Ratcliffe, John (House member), 261, 317, 324, 370, 405, 406, 462
Ray, Robert, 404, 405
Read, Russ, 78
Reagan, Ronald, 42, 316, 395
RealClearInvestigations, 265
RealClearPolitics, 76
Redfield, Robert (CDC, director), 418, 434
Reeker, Philip (State Department; impeachment witness), xxv, 31, 34–35, 68, 285
Rehnquist, William, 402
Remnick, David, 337
Restoring the Republic (Nunes), 274
Rice, Condoleezza, 295
Richards, Cecile, 239
Rivlin, Reuven, 415
Roberts, Cokie, 172
Roberts, John (chief justice of the United States), 384, 397, 401–2, 409, 410, 412–13, 422, 425, 431, 432, 433, 436–38, 441, 456–58
Robinson, Emerald, 321–22
Robinson, Eugene, 372
Rogan, James E., 273
Rogers, Will, 246
Rogin, Josh, 36
Rolling Stones, 367
Romney, Mitt (senator), xxiv, 199, 213, 248, 253, 288, 342, 358, 385, 387, 410, 425, 428, 429, 431, 436, 440, 447, 454–56, 457, 461
Rood, John, 125
"Room Where It Happened, The" (Bolton), 426–27, 428, 438
Rooney, Francis (House member), 246–50, 252
Roosevelt, Franklin Delano, xiii, 362, 461
Rose, Max (House member), 178
Rosen, James, 335, 336–37
Ross, Edmund, 444
Ross, Wilbur (secretary, Commerce), 200, 395
Roy, Chip (House member), 365
Rubio, Marco (senator), 447
Russia, xv, xvi, xix, 7, 8, 11, 12, 14, 15, 18, 19, 22, 23, 24, 28, 34, 35, 37, 39, 40, 43, 44, 45, 58, 63, 64, 65, 69, 71, 72, 78, 84, 86, 91, 92, 96, 97, 98, 105, 106, 107, 112, 119, 120, 125, 129, 132, 133, 134, 136, 137, 138, 139, 141, 143, 150, 151, 169, 171, 197, 202, 205, 209, 224, 235, 236, 237, 256, 269, 270–71, 275, 283, 293, 316–17, 318, 319, 323, 325, 346, 368, 382, 426, 438, 467
see also Soviet Union
Ryan, Paul, 288

Salute to America, 82, 83
Samuels, Elyse, 54
Sanders, Bernie (senator), 56, 79, 320, 401, 442, 457
Sanders, Sarah Huckabee (White House press secretary), 27, 54, 241
Sandy, Mark (OMB; impeachment witness), xxvi, 115–16, 125, 149

Sanford, Mark, 249
San Francisco Chronicle, 76
San Jose Mercury News, 272
SARS virus, 414, 424
Sasse, Ben (senator), 204, 422
Sayegh, Tony, 320
Scalia, Antonin, 86, 379
Scalise, Steve (House, minority whip), xxiii, 191, 195, 200, 213, 238, 253–54, 258, 261, 462
Schatz, Brian (senator), 453, 455
Schiff, Adam (House Intelligence Committee, chairman), xxiv, 51, 64, 65–66, 97, 128, 142, 143, 144–45, 146, 147, 150–51, 152–53, 154–56, 157, 158, 162, 166, 168, 169, 173, 186, 187, 196, 198, 203, 205, 208–11, 212–14, 215, 217–18, 219, 220–21, 222, 223, 224, 225, 226, 227, 229–30, 231–32, 233, 244–45, 251–52, 253, 255, 256–57, 258–59, 263, 264, 267–68, 269–70, 272–73, 274–76, 277, 279–80, 282, 286–87, 289, 291, 292, 295, 296, 297, 298, 302, 303–4, 306, 308, 312, 315, 319, 320, 322, 326, 327, 328, 334, 336, 341, 363, 370, 374, 384, 385, 388, 391, 394, 396, 400–401, 403, 409, 410–11, 415–17, 419, 420, 421, 430, 431, 433, 434, 435, 436, 437–38, 439, 440, 455–56, 461–62, 468
Schiff, Eve, 273
Schmidt, Michael S., 426–27
Schumer, Chuck (Senate, minority leader), xxv, 20, 49–50, 56, 237, 238, 346–47, 356, 357–58, 383, 384–85, 386, 387, 400, 406, 407, 408–9, 411, 416, 421, 422, 426, 432, 435, 449, 456, 457, 462
Schwartz, Lacey, 29
SCIF (Sensitive Compartmented Information Facility), descriptions of, 204, 220
  House depositions in, 220–21, 222–23, 229–30, 231–33, 235, 247, 251–57, 258–59, 260, 263, 265, 267, 270, 271, 293, 294, 319, 327, 347, 469
Scott, Rick (senator), 199
Scott, Tim (senator), 251
Secret Service, U.S., 10, 261, 458
Sekulow, Jay, 19, 20, 98, 245, 389, 404, 412, 425, 429, 461
Senate, U.S.:
  Appropriations Committee, 150
  Armed Services Committee, 131
  Budget Committee, 78
  Foreign Relations Committee, 78, 418
  Health Committee, 418
  Intelligence Committee, 144, 204–5, 207
  Judiciary Committee, 16, 18
"Servant of the People" (Ukrainian TV show), 22
Sessions, Jeff, 160, 161, 163
Sessions, Pete (House member), 7, 9, 225
Shaffer, Sergey, 38
Shaffer, Tony, 322
Shah, Naveed, 261–62
Sherman, Marty, 463
Sherrill, Mikie (House member), 77, 176, 178, 356
Shokin, Viktor (former Ukrainian official), 14, 171, 227–28, 276
Short, Marc (Pence chief of staff), 381
Simpson, Glenn, 319
Simpson, O. J., 389
Sinatra, Frank, 367
Sinclair Broadcast Group, 335
Sinema, Kyrsten (senator), 409, 456
"60 Minutes" (TV show), 323
Slotkin, Elissa (House member), xxiv, 77, 176–78, 179, 182, 186, 338–39, 343, 344–46, 347–51, 369, 466, 470
Smith, Margaret Chase, 390
Smith, Sandra, 403
Snowe, Olympia, 390
Solomon, John, 6–7, 8, 9, 10, 11, 13, 14, 33, 65, 90, 325, 464–65
Sondland, Gordon (U.S. ambassador, European Union; impeachment witness), xxv, 12–13, 43, 44, 45, 57–58, 59, 60, 66, 67–68, 69, 70–71, 73, 86, 87, 88–89, 91–92, 93, 94–95, 98–99, 106, 112, 118–20, 126, 132, 135–36, 138, 139, 140–41, 149, 151–52, 199, 221, 223, 232–33, 269, 277, 278, 295, 301–13, 315, 320–21, 324–326, 384, 463
Sonne, Paul, 226
Soros, George, 72
Souter, David (Supreme Court justice), 329
Soviet Union, 4, 65, 104, 132, 254, 294, 296, 316
  see also Russia
Spanberger, Abigail (House member), xxiv, 77, 175–77, 178, 179, 185–86, 349
Speier, Jackie (House member), 359
Starr, Kenneth W., 291, 404, 405
State Department, U.S., xiv, xv, xxv, 3, 4, 7, 13–14, 30, 31, 33, 34, 35, 36, 39, 43, 59, 60, 62, 64, 68, 70, 71, 80, 90, 92, 96, 109, 116, 122, 128, 133, 135, 143, 149, 214, 221, 225, 226, 235, 247, 251, 267, 270, 272, 276, 277, 281, 283–84, 285, 286, 289, 290, 295, 296, 304, 418, 446, 464
  Bureau of European and Eurasian Affairs at, xxv, 12, 31, 32
State of the Union address (2020), 447, 449–52, 461
Statue of Liberty (documentary), 104

Steele, Christopher, 319
Stefanik, Elise (House member), xxiv, 213, 287–91, 448, 462–63, 466
Stenger, Michael C. (Senate sergeant at arms), 400, 409
Stephanopoulos, George, 391–92
Stewart, Chris (House member), 292, 300–301
Stiller, Ben, 425
Stoddard, A. B., 76–77
Stone, Roger, 72–73
Strange, Luther, 388
Sullivan, John (deputy secretary, State Department), 12, 33, 35, 238
"CNN Sunday Morning" (TV show), 173
Suozzi, Thomas (House member), 459–60, 463
Supreme Court, U.S., xix, xx, 86, 157, 158, 268, 273, 300, 329, 379–80, 391, 401, 423, 437, 438, 443
Swalwell, Eric (House member), 124, 166, 223–24, 225, 256
Syria, 72, 234, 235, 236, 237, 238, 260

Tanden, Neera, 51
Tapper, Jake, 75, 370–71
Tate, Julie, 168
Taylor, Deborah, 39, 63, 91, 135, 467, 468
Taylor, William B., Jr. (acting ambassador to Ukraine; impeachment witness), xxv, 32–34, 35, 38, 39–40, 60, 62–64, 85, 89–90, 91–93, 95–96, 104, 117, 118, 119, 132–34, 135–36, 137, 138, 139–41, 149, 150, 151–52, 252, 253, 265–66, 267, 268, 271, 272, 276, 277–79, 282, 284, 324–25, 326, 346, 381–82, 467–68
Tea Party, 241, 248, 288
Terris, Ben, 327, 328
"This Week" (TV show), 292, 381, 391–92
Thornberry, Mac (House member), 131, 261
Thunberg, Greta, 340
Tillerson, Rex, 58, 222
Timberg, Craig, 205
Time, 175, 274, 340
Tlaib, Rashida (House member), xviii, 21, 120, 185
"Today" (TV show), 404
Todd, Chuck, 336
Toensing, Victoria, 8, 465
Tribe, Laurence, 432
Troianovski, Anton, 37
Truman, Harry, xiii
Trump, Barron, 331, 332, 333
Trump, Donald, Jr., 7, 11, 36, 264–65, 284, 297, 298, 448, 456
Trump, Eric, 219, 448
Trump, Ivanka, 260, 261, 368, 425, 461
Trump, Melania, 17, 21, 30, 82, 146, 260, 261, 333, 451, 461, 462
Trump Organization, 224
Trump Victory (PAC), 206
Turley, Jonathan, 329, 330
Turner, Michael (House member), 212–13, 324, 462

Ueland, Eric (White House, legislative director), 320, 341, 352
Uglava, Gizo, 3, 5
Ukraine, xv–xvi, xvii, xxv, xxvi, 3, 5, 6, 7, 9, 10, 11, 12, 14, 19–20, 22–24, 30, 31, 32, 33, 34, 35, 36, 37–38, 40, 41, 42, 44, 45, 57–60, 62, 63, 64–66, 69–70, 71, 78, 80, 81, 85–87, 88–90, 91–93, 94, 95–96, 98–99, 104, 106, 107–8, 109, 110–11, 112, 113, 114, 115, 116, 118, 119, 120, 122, 125–26, 129–30, 131–32, 133, 134, 135, 136–38, 139–41, 142, 143, 146, 147, 148, 149, 150, 151–52, 168, 169, 170–71, 173, 174, 177, 184, 185, 186, 193, 194, 197, 198, 200, 201, 202, 205, 208, 209–10, 211, 217, 221, 222, 223, 225, 226, 229, 232–33, 236, 237, 241, 242–43, 245, 246, 252, 253, 257, 259, 269, 271, 276, 277, 278, 279, 280, 282–83, 284, 289, 290, 293–94, 295, 296, 302–3, 304, 305, 306–7, 309, 310, 315–16, 317–18, 319, 321, 323–24, 325, 326, 337, 342, 347, 368, 382, 384, 385, 392, 397, 398, 399, 401, 410, 425, 426, 427, 446–47, 449, 464, 465, 467, 468, 469
  see also various entries for named Ukrainian officials
UkraineAlert (newsletter), 10, 13
Ukraine Crisis Media Center, xvi
United Nations, 184, 200, 211
  General Assembly of, 58, 151, 175, 179, 181, 191
  U.S. Mission to, 68, 69, 211
USA Today, 459
U.S. Institute of Peace, 33–34, 468

Van Drew, Jeff (House member), 349
Viebeck, Elise, 263–64
Vietnam War, 34, 277
"View, The" (TV show), 168
Vindman, Alexander (NSC; impeachment witness) , xxv, 23, 24, 38, 39, 43–44, 45, 70, 86, 87, 88, 89, 92, 93, 95, 98–99, 104–5, 107, 109, 112, 113, 114–15, 117, 122–23, 125, 128, 129–30, 131, 132, 134, 149, 293–98, 299, 300–301, 315, 321–22, 326, 346, 462, 463, 466
Vindman, Yevgeny (NSC lawyer), 104, 105, 114–15, 117, 293, 463
Vittert, Leland, 250

Vogel, Kenneth P., 64, 65
Volker, Kurt (special envoy, Ukraine; impeachment witness), xxv, 35, 40, 43, 45, 57–60, 62, 78, 80–81, 85, 86–87, 88, 90, 91, 92, 93–94, 95, 103–4, 106, 118, 119, 135–37, 139, 140, 149, 220, 221, 222–23, 224, 226, 252, 277, 304–5, 322–23, 467
Vought, Russell (OMB), 78

Walker, Mark (House member), 254
Wallace, Chris, 306–7, 344
Wallace, Nicolle, 372
Wall Street Journal, 75, 169, 173
Waltz, Michael (House member), 256
Wang, Joe, 198
Warnecke, Grace Kennan, 282
Warren, Elizabeth (senator), 79, 320, 332, 371, 401, 431–32, 437–38, 442, 457
"War Room: Impeachment" (radio show and podcast), 424
Washington, George, 82, 274, 304, 316, 338, 361, 364, 395, 397, 421
Washington Examiner, 78, 79, 83
Washington Post, xiii, 7, 13, 17, 28, 36, 37, 38, 53, 54, 75, 84, 121, 123, 124, 142–43, 145, 154, 158–59, 160, 162, 167, 168, 169, 173, 174, 175–76, 178, 179, 180, 192, 193, 199, 205, 215, 222, 226, 230, 244, 245, 248, 249, 252, 261, 263, 291, 302, 303, 308, 326, 327, 336, 337, 356, 359, 364, 367, 368, 372, 389, 392, 399, 404, 422, 425, 428, 429, 432, 440, 443, 455, 459, 462
Washington Post/ABC News poll, 357–58
Washington Times, 7, 336
Watergate scandal, 55, 157, 215, 246, 249, 301, 444
Waters, Maxine (House member), 336, 368, 396
Weinstein, Harvey, 389
Weiss, Andrew, 36
Wenstrup, Brad (House member), 213, 462
Westerhout, Madeleine, 13
WhatsApp, xvi, 7, 8, 38, 95
whistleblower, 122–23, 127, 128–29, 143, 144, 147, 158, 174–75, 207–9, 211, 212, 214–16, 219, 254, 263–70, 271, 279, 292, 295, 296–97, 298, 310, 320, 323, 388, 403, 437
  complaint of, 150–51, 152–53, 154, 155, 157–58, 159, 167–70, 173, 174, 177–78, 179, 182, 198, 199, 203, 204–5, 207–9, 221
Whitaker, Matthew, 174–75
Wicker, Roger (senator), 455
Williams, Brian, 151, 372
Williams, Jennifer (Pence aide; impeachment witness), 42, 105, 113, 293, 295
Williams, Michael, 352
Wilson, Woodrow, 346
Wirkkala, Rheanne, 285–86
Witte, Griff, 249–50, 392
WNYC, 160
Woodward, Bob, 215, 425
World Economic Forum, 406
World War I, 316
World War II, 4, 132, 133, 276, 300, 316, 355
Wuhan, China, 405, 414, 418

Xi Jinping, 419

Yermak, Andriy (Ukrainian official), xxvi, 85–89, 94, 95, 103, 118, 119, 135, 138, 142, 152, 223
Yoo, John, 294
Young, Todd (senator), 457
YouTube, 54, 60–61, 64, 280
Yovanovitch, Andre, 4, 282
Yovanovitch, Marie "Masha" (ambassador to Ukraine; impeachment witness), xv–xvi, xvii, xxv, 3–5, 6, 7, 8–13, 14, 24, 29, 30–31, 33, 34–37, 39, 42, 63, 65, 70, 85, 91, 108, 109–10, 193, 221, 222, 225, 226, 269, 276, 281–87, 289–92, 325, 346, 381, 398, 446, 464, 465, 467, 468
Yovanovitch, Nadia, 31, 32, 42, 464

Zafonte, Jo Ann, 13
Zak, Dan, 230, 368
Zapotosky, Matt, 193–94
Zeldin, Lee (House member), 291, 306, 406, 455–56, 462
Zelenska, Olena, 66
Zelensky, Volodymyr, xxvi, 22–24, 31, 33, 34, 36–38, 39, 41–45, 57, 58, 59, 63, 64, 66–67, 68, 73, 80, 81, 85, 86, 88, 89, 90, 91, 93, 94, 95, 98, 103–4, 105–14, 115, 118, 119, 122, 125, 126, 128, 132, 135, 137, 138, 139–40, 141, 142, 143, 149, 150, 151–52, 168, 169, 173, 181, 184, 191, 193, 194, 195, 197, 198, 200–202, 205, 207, 209–10, 214, 218, 221–22, 223, 227, 233, 252, 269, 277, 278, 284, 295, 297, 302, 303, 305, 307, 308, 309, 316, 323, 325, 329, 382, 391, 425, 444, 446–47
Zremski, Jerry, 75

About the Authors

Kevin Sullivan and **Mary Jordan** are Pulitzer Prize–winning journalists for *The Washington Post*. A married couple, they were based abroad for 14 years as *The Post*'s co–bureau chiefs in Tokyo, Mexico City and London. Sullivan writes about national and international issues. Jordan is a national political correspondent. They are the coauthors of the #1 *New York Times* bestseller *Hope: A Memoir of Survival in Cleveland* and *The Prison Angel: Mother Antonia's Journey from Beverly Hills to a Life of Service in a Mexican Jail*. Jordan is also the author of *The Art of Her Deal: The Untold Story of Melania Trump*.